Looking Within

The Music of John Palmer

Dialogues and Essays

Edited by Sunny Knable

Vision Edition

Vision Edition
www.visionedition.com

Vision Edition 0013-MC

ISBN 978-0-9931761-7-3

Photo and Cover Design by Grace Palmer

CONTENTS

FOREWORD

To thoroughly understand a composer's music, one must go beyond listening and towards the written word: words either written by composers or those written about them. Texts include encyclopedia entries, biographies, autobiographies, manifestos, articles, programme notes and even in contemporary times, blog posts. These resources are incalculably useful for performers, analysts, scholars and listeners searching for ways to deepen their understanding and connection to the music. Rarely does one text have it all. But this book on John Palmer is neither a biography or autobiography, nor a treatise or manifesto, and it is certainly not a casual piece. Instead, it comprises elements of all through elaborate dialogues with the composer interspersed with essays by guest writers that clarify compelling aspects of Palmer's works. Through the conversations, we get the life-lived details and personal voice of an autobiographical account but with the objectivity of a biography thanks to the probing questions offered by the interviewers. It contains the deeper philosophical musings common to texts like John Cage's *Silence: Lectures on Writings*.[1] It has the ideals and political positioning within the art form reminiscent of Milton Babbitt's controversial essay titled *The Composer as Specialist*.[2] And there are deep dives into the technical details of his music that might only be encountered in a scholarly text. The 30 dialogues and six essays in the book become an unusually intimate way to understand a composer like Palmer, whose ideas on music are as expansive as his output: upwards of 230 musical works since the 1970s that range from contemporary 'classical' music, including electroacoustic music, to songs, experimental music and works that defy categorisation.

With academic positions at the universities of Oxford and Hertfordshire, as well as the University of Music and Performing Arts of Stuttgart since 2000, it would be easy to put Palmer in a category of privileged, ultra-intellectual composers sitting in the ivory tower composing in isolation. Palmer, rather, had an unconventional path towards composition. He felt a mystical pull as a young boy and left home without family support to pursue a musical life at the age of 18. Palmer's professional trajectory was not straightforward, working several jobs and across several countries, sometimes questioning whether a career composing music was viable. It took time for him to garner notice. His long path and commitment to art are reflected in his musical output, where intuition and a spiritual mindset based in Eastern philosophies guide his musical creativity. Studying Cage's alchemy of music and philosophy opened sound potentials in Palmer's mind, but he brought these ideas together with controlled facility over technical aspects of music composition. A background in improvisation and jazz still percolates within his works even as he leaves behind traditional musical language and continues explorations in sound, propelled by an interest in the works of Jonathan Harvey, that extend into electroacoustic music composition including acousmatic works. In total, it is a path that led to a particularly diverse output of music.

Throughout the book, Palmer emphasises the dialectical nature of his compositions: the synthesis of seemingly antithetical elements, such as darkness and light, loudness and quietness, dense pitch construction and static timbres, and more. Bringing these elements together in ways where they seem to naturally articulate a whole is Palmer's expertise. But, in these dialogues, readers will uncover that Palmer's dialectics run even deeper into his own life and

---

[1] Cage (1961).

[2] For publication, the editor at *High Fidelity* changed Babbitt's original name of his 1958 article into the more controversial and better-known title *Who Cares if You Listen* which poorly summarises Babbitt's argument. Similarly to Babbitt, Palmer promotes knowledge and education as helpful, if not necessary, to understanding complex music. Both composers also make the argument that complex music has a necessary place in society, one shielded from market constraints. See Babbitt (1958:38-40).

beliefs. For example, he started as a pop musician and songwriter, a lover of popular music, and speaks of how this informed his music. But he simultaneously mirrors Theodor Adorno's famous critiques of popular music as a frivolous standardisation of art that creates blind consumers rather than critical listeners. Even as he innovates his own solutions to sonic opposites, he is wary of a contemporary classical music industry that promotes innovation as a trend. He consistently experiments with sound but doesn't consider himself an experimental composer. These interviews uncover Palmer in all his paradoxes, revealing a human complexity that articulates his whole being and brings humanity to these pages.

Musicologist David Metzer identifies a strain of modernism continuing into the twenty-first century that he calls the 'mode of enquiry', an investigation driven by curiosity where *"points of interest explored by the pieces include aesthetic ideals, compositional material, and facets of expression."* [3] These dialogues and essays reveal Palmer carrying forth a modernist tradition in this sense, an enquiry into sound and the spiritual in music, infusing it not only with his own aesthetic ideals but with personal expressivity and an intense search for transcendence. As he conveys, *"Expression, articulation and eloquence are intrinsic in the texture I am composing."*[4] This expression, articulation and eloquence is felt throughout the book. Reading through the interviews, one feels face to face with the composer in deep conversation. Despite the breadth and variation of Palmer's musical works, this book makes clear how all could originate from the same man. In a time when few composers are willing to go on record about their thoughts and positions in the field in fear of being pigeonholed, this book will become an important document for current and future listeners and performers of Palmer's music.

Anna Reguero
Musicologist and Arts Journalist

Stony Brook, New York, 31st, August, 2021

---

[3] Metzer (2009:6).
[4] From Palmer's conversation with Peter Wiegold, page 80.

INTRODUCTION

36 VIEWS OF JOHN PALMER

Is it possible to sum up the whole of a man? That is the question that lingers in my mind after editing this sizeable collection of interviews and articles on John Palmer's life and work. Composer, performer, musicologist, professor, improviser and writer; these are a few of the roles we associate with him outside of his personal life, but in which order should we put those labels? Does each of the individual words really represent those aspects of his musical life so completely? John Palmer is primarily the composer of contemporary classical music: opera, orchestral, chamber, solo, keyboard, electroacoustic music and more. He is an excellent performer: a pianist with a talent for performing his own and other composers' works. Yet, he is also an improviser with a background in jazz, popular music and the avant-garde. Each of these sub-categories, too, seem to be an insufficient distinction. We could continue to assign more and more nouns and parse the meanings down to a finer and finer place until we arrive at an atomic level, but that is not the goal here. It is the comprehension of the whole man we're after, or at least as much as this book will allow.

In the arts, we are accustomed to the idea that a musician is capable of having more than one focus, but John Palmer takes this to the extreme. As he admits in these interviews, he has been working constantly in the last 40 years and to an extent that is almost mad by comparison to the typical composer. A search through his archives will reveal many albums of his own music, a plethora of published pieces on Composers Edition, a wealth of recorded improvisations and performances, and writings in the form of essays, a book on Harveys' *Bhakti* and the 2013 book *Conversations*. More tellingly, his musical work is not all there is to him. As you will get a sense from this collection, Palmer is a deep thinker, a teacher, an analyst and an excellent writer who is interested in many subjects outside of music. Look through the list of subjects of each article and the reader will find that some of those include codes, language (etymology, semiotics), philosophy, psychology, Eastern inspirations, poetry, theatre and spiritual practices. Though he may be reluctant to promote his own accomplishments, his editor will happily do so if for no other reason than because he is a truly remarkable person.

As for this project, the idea was germinated in 2020 and completed over the course of eight months in 2021. The original intent was to have a number of artists, musicians and writers from various facets of his life perform interviews and then write articles based on those interviews. The enthusiastic participants include those from four continents and 13 countries![1] Due to the COVID-19 pandemic, its physical limitations and its way of clearing the schedule of nearly every interviewer, the concept progressed into a series of written, not spoken interviews. Why not? Nearly every serious interviewer in any publication comes prepared with a series of carefully sculpted questions that are written out and then read, leaving the interviewee to potentially fumble through something that they might have recollected or said better if they had the time. This makes for an important distinction between a book of recorded interviews which will, perhaps, show more in the way of mannerisms, personality and spontaneous thought, versus this collection, in which Palmer had the time to flesh out his explanations, demonstrate his points and sculpt the substance of his ruminations. This is why you will find many interviews having charts, graphs, notes, musical examples and footnotes. While this might not reflect natural parlance, the reader will find that the result is eloquently

---

[1] Europe (UK, France, Germany, Spain, Switzerland, Italy, Russia); North America (USA, Canada); South America (Brazil); Asia (Japan, India); Oceania (Australia).

written, well-researched and enlightening as to the inner and outer workings of our protagonist.

This book comprises 36 pieces of writing (30 interviews and 6 articles) which offer unique views on John Palmer, the musician and the man. They are organized into 10 chapters which are grouped by subject from the general to the specific. It was important to keep a sense of chronological flow in the arrangement of these subjects because, as the reader will note, a kind of narrative emerges from the succession of interviews that is revealing of John Palmer's thought process. These narrative responses can range from practical ("as I already stated in a previous interview…"), to musical ("as you have noticed in the analysis of…"), to emotional ("I've been asked before and I don't want this to be misconstrued…"), as if peering into a type of journal about Palmer's musical activities, compositional constructions and artistic inspirations. The only time that this chronology of events is interrupted is when articles are placed next to the appropriate subject. One should also note that each interviewer comes to the table with their own personality, preoccupations and artistic tastes, and the composer responds to each of them differently. These together with the articles make for a kaleidoscopic view of our main subject.

For those who have but a cursory knowledge of Japanese artwork, they will notice that the title of this Preface is a nod to the collection of woodblock prints by Katsushika Hokusai, "36 Views of Mount Fuji". This is done purposefully for as the reader may already know, some of Palmer's musical inspirations come from the Japanese culture; those include the use of Japanese instruments (shakuhachi and koto), the Japanese language, Japanese poetry and Zen Buddhist teachings. While Palmer would hesitate to put these out front if only because some readers might misconstrue his connection to Japan or to Spirituality, this title is also chosen to emphasise that the book offers different views of a central character. Further, as a composer, performer and teacher, this editor shares many of Palmer's inspirations, including improvisation, eclecticism, the use of instruments outside of the typical Western tradition (accordion), and elements of the Japanese culture.

Each reader will, of course, receive something different in the way of new information from this book. Composers will recognise themselves in many of these pages, but they will perhaps be challenged to expand their own knowledge outside the realm of music. Performers will learn about the inner world of a composer and glean ways of interpreting Palmer's music; they might even be inspired to search out and learn his works. Musicologists will note Palmer's place in music history as a kind of bridge from the 20th century's preoccupation with austerity to the 21st century's willingness to embrace the personal; they will make connections between John Cage, Jonathan Harvey and John Palmer, but they might also revaluate their conceptions of these figures. The non-musician might know more about the terms outside the realm of music which are discussed here, from acoustics, literature or philosophy, but they might have to search out the meanings for some of the specialised musical terms referenced. In the writing of this book, there was not an explicit effort to educate the reader, but to simply reflect the true cogitations of the composer.

That brings us back to the initial question: is it possible to summarise a man? In about 400 pages and with 36 viewpoints, we can try. As the adage goes, there are as many personalities of a person as there are other people. As in, each person brings out another aspect of someone else. You might also extend this idea to outlets: for each activity a person engages in, they express another side of themselves. In this respect, by representing so many viewpoints of the same person, we might get closer to knowing him, and reveal something about ourselves in the process. Ultimately, it is our relationship to John Palmer, our similarities and differences, and what we bring to this book as an audience that will determine what resonates within us.

That is why it was so difficult to decide on a title for this book, because John Palmer is so many things to so many people. One title that was considered was written by one of our interviewers, Anne LeBaron. Her phrase, 'Luminous Imagination', as well as her superbly written article, sums up the bigger picture of John Palmer; he is all of those labels we assigned to him (composer, performer and musicologist), but behind all of those there is one word that facilitates their existence: imagination. It is in the following pages where Palmer's imagination shines a light so that we might better comprehend his music, himself and our fascination. As the title of this book states, this is what we are asking of the readers: to look within the music, to look within the composer and to look within themselves. Having read through these pages many times, this editor can assure the reader that to know John Palmer and to know yourself if only a little bit better, it is worth looking within.

Sunny Knable

New York, 11th August, 2021

CHAPTER ONE

BROAD TOPICS

IN THE BEGINNING…AND ALL THAT JAZZ
Daniel Biro

DB. You have had a very unconventional musical path. What were your early influences as a listener, and how and when did you become aware of the importance of music in your life?

JP. The earliest memories of music I can recollect are linked to American swing and Bebop, singers of the likes of Frank Sinatra and Ella Fitzgerald. I grew up with the sound of Bossa Nova, and the Anglo-American, Brazilian, French and Italian pop music of the 1960s and 1970s. Another early memory I have is the sound of the Gregorian Chants I heard in the Latin Mass before it was abolished by the Holy See in 1967 and a broadcast of Charles Ives's *The Unanswered Question* which impressed me deeply. At the age of six, I took my first classical piano lessons. By the age of 12, I would play the traditional classical repertoire of J.S. Bach, Mozart, Chopin at an intermediate level, but what kept my musical attention alive was jazz, folk and pop music. I would spend hours listening to the radio and the records I would find in the house, as well as watching the TV shows of those years. Always interested in any form of music that would come across my life, I remember listening to old 78' vinyls of European operettas and American big-bands. My early piano teachers were very strict and dry. They certainly did not convey any love for the music I was supposed to play. What I still remember very vividly is a sense of anxiety about not making mistakes during piano lessons. The music model they taught me was very rigid and I did not enjoy those lessons at all. I remember coming back home and instead of practising scales, arpeggios and Mozart's sonatas, I would improvise on the preludes and nocturnes by Chopin. Improvising was true fun for me, but I could not play my improvisations to my teachers as they wouldn't allow me to do so. At the age of 13, I got frustrated with this kind of classical music teaching; I took up a guitar and within 10 minutes I learnt a few chords and wrote my first song. By that time, I was improvising on the piano and the electric organ on a daily basis and enjoyed playing by ear the songs I would hear on the radio, TV or on the records collections of my parents. In the 1970s, I already knew I wanted to be a musician and played keyboards in a few amateur bands with my friends. These were the years of progressive rock. In retrospect, I feel somewhat sad that the rigid classic music education I grew up with induced me to dislike that tradition. On the other hand, I experienced a liberating joy in listening to and playing jazz, pop and rock. The fact that I would be able to play anything I heard on the piano or the organ gave me great satisfaction and self-confidence. I loved reproducing and improvising on anything I would hear on the radio and TV as well as playing my own versions of Chopin's nocturnes and preludes. As a young pianist, I loved playing the solos of Erroll Garner, Eumir Deodato and Oscar Peterson to mention a few names.

When progressive rock bands exploded in the 1970s, I discovered King Crimson and Jethro Tull, Yes, Genesis, Area, PFM and many others. The virtuosity of Emerson, Lake and Palmer, in particular, was a major source of inspiration in those days: I loved the solos of Keith Emerson, the virtuosity of Carl Palmer, the large forms of their pieces, the iconoclastic lyrics of Peter Sinfield and the versatility of Greg Lake as a singer, bass player and guitarist I would improvise for hours on my father's Hammond L-100 organ or on the piano. I didn't have a clue about contemporary 'classical' music at the time, but I knew that I was not much interested in the music of the past.

DB. Before becoming a composer of contemporary 'classical' music, you wrote music in mainstream genres. What did each genre offer you as a composer? Starting with jazz.

JP. By the early 1980s, I had a good knowledge of contemporary jazz. I perceived all these very different musicians as very inspiring. In 1980, I discovered a higher level of quality and virtuosity in piano music. When I first heard Thelonious Monk, I was impressed by his very simple and yet angular use of harmony, melody and rhythm. The contrasting lyricism of Bill Evans was soon surpassed by the early Chick Corea and then especially Keith Jarrett, Cecil Taylor and Anthony Braxton. This was a moment in music history when jazz reached another level, standing above any form of music labelling. It was through these musicians that I began to appreciate the chamber music setting, especially trios, quartets and quintets. I suppose my perception of chamber music as a dialectic condition must be rooted in those early listening experiences related to small jazz groups. What I learnt from all kinds of jazz and Bossa Nova was a complex level of harmony and refined perception of melody which felt very advanced to me at that time. Whereas from the pop scene of those days, it was rhythm, virtuosity and large forms that really excited me. I adored Carl Palmer's virtuoso drumming. For example, this was the first time I experienced what I would call an emancipation of rhythm from a merely supportive function to an independent, almost polyphonic-contrapuntal voice within the trio. Sadly, the ELP's reunion in the 1990s reduced Palmer's drumming to a mere accompaniment function, much to my disappointment. Keith Emerson impressed me not only for the virtuosity of his solos but also for his large control of form that in those days was matched by Robert Fripp's King Crimson, Ian Anderson's Jethro Tull, John McLaughlin and Frank Zappa.

The guitar virtuosity of John McLaughlin offered a sensitive approach to improvisation where, for example, rests would play a major role in the breathing of the phrases. The stylistic versatility of this musician, whether alone, with the Mahavishnu Orchestra or the Shakti group, is something I still love discovering. To my mind, Jeff Beck's and Frank Zappa's vigorous virtuosity resembles a Beethoven-like kind of structural solidity. From Baden Powell, João Gilberto and Antonio Jobim, I was intrigued by the-sophisticated use of harmony and melody and the way these would relate to syncopated rhythms and the warm lyricism of the texts. I am also very fond of Arab and African jazz. You can hear unique melodies in the songs of Tunisian Dhafer Youssef, for example.

Looking back, I think the first seeds of my career as a composer are linked with two important events: a performance of Edgar Varèse's *Ionisation* in London, in 1976, and a solo concert of Keith Tippett in Florence, in 1977. Both events introduced me to a radically different and much more daring approach to sound, gesture and form. This major breakthrough would later lead me to contemporary 'classical' music.

In 1981, I started studying the classical piano again. I was earning a living playing with my trio in restaurants and nightclubs in the evening. During the day, I was taking private piano and music theory lessons, and practising the piano as much as I could. I went back to piano lessons because I felt the need to get a good piano technique: I simply wanted to be a professional pianist. At the same time, I wanted to learn how to compose music for larger instrumental forces. I was very keen to learn everything there is to know in the musical world beyond genres and categorisations. Up to that point I had written about 100 songs and many progressive rock pieces for my bands. From 1981 to 1983, I wrote piano pieces somewhat influenced by Bill Evans, Chick Corea and Keith Jarrett. From about 1984 onwards, I began to write piano pieces in an increasingly 'classical' fashion. I would use a bitonal fusion of jazz harmony and neo-romanticism, often enriched by impressionistic colours. I think you can hear these influences in early piano pieces like *Missing Rhymes* (1984), *Hieroglyphs* (1986) and *Three Preludes* (1986-1987). There is a lot of hidden jazz in my music. You can hear this in pieces like *Manhattan* (1989) for solo piano, *Renge-Kyo* (1992) for piano and electronics, or in a more recent piece like *Crossing Dialogues* (2013) for violin, cello, vibraphone and piano, where improvisation is also a crucial part of the performance.

But I somewhat hesitate to speak about jazz as an umbrella definition because nowadays there are so many facets to it. In the past 40 years, jazz has taken so many different directions that it is really difficult to pin it down to a single genre or even a few styles. There are so many forms and understandings of jazz now that, in my opinion, it is impossible to define jazz as one genre. The jazz played by Swedish or Dutch musicians is so different from the jazz played by American, French or Arab musicians. I have many piano recordings of my improvised compositions, as I call them, that I would love to release at some point. This is a lifetime desire that I still want to accomplish. What I enjoy most as a pianist is the fact that I can abandon any form of preconceived idea and let my intuition lead the way to what will flow naturally. But then I ask myself: is this jazz? How do we define jazz in 2021?

DB. How do you perceive songwriting in pop and rock idioms?

JP. Throughout the years I have continued to listen to songs of all sorts, especially Brazilian, Italian, French, British and American. I still perceive songs as the most immediate expression of vocal music. I say this because I have always loved poetry, and the combination of words and notes is something I still love listening to. I grew up with the music of American songwriters of the likes of Richard Rodgers, Lorenz Hart, Irving Berlin, Cole Porter, George and Ira Gershwin. I adored Antonio Jobim, Vinicius de Moraes, João Gilberto and still like to listen to Toquinho, Chico Barques and Caetano Veloso. From the swing and Bossa Nova traditions, I appreciated not only the rhythmic drive that distinguished them from mainstream pop songs, but more importantly, the way that words would match a refined quality of melody and harmony. In the young American songwriter scene of the 1970s, I was drawn to the highly individual styles of Joni Mitchell, James Taylor, Paul Simon and the gripping idioms of Stephen Stills and David Crosby; in the UK the lyricism of Paul McCartney, George Harrison and Gilbert O'Sullivan.

I am equally attracted by the inquisitive lyricism of French singers like Barbara, Georges Moustaki and the daring social and human introspection of Charles Aznavour, Léo Ferré and the Belgian Jacques Brel; the authenticity of Nina Simone, Robert Wyatt, Cat Stevens, Pino Daniele and Graham Nash; the social and psychological reflections of Italians like Giorgio Gaber, and the emotional power of Claudio Baglioni. To these names, I must add the passionate and colourful Balkan, Neapolitan folk music, the Portuguese Fado and the gentle simplicity of Celtic traditions (do you remember Alan Stivell?). To me, songwriting remains the most direct and powerful form of musical poetry. I perceive it as the most candid expression of feelings, thoughts and emotions, as well as social and political concerns. A song may not change the world, but it has changed me for the better on many occasions.

DB. Do those experiences still influence or inform your compositional work today?

JP. I have been asked this question many times and I confess that the older I grow, the more unsure I feel about the answer. How far does the music we listen to influence the music we write? Although virtually any music we listen to may make an impact of some kind in our mind, I am not sure if this really influences or informs my compositional work. In any case, I think this may vary significantly from composer to composer. I recently gave a masterclass in Wales. The session began with a discussion about the music I heard when I was a boy and at some point, I mentioned the Beatles and some of the things I liked about them. Later in the session, after listening to my piece *Thereafter*, for organ and electronics, one of the students said that he didn't hear any similarity between that piece and the music of the Beatles! I couldn't believe my ears! This rather naïve statement made me think about the way we tend to think of influence in music. I suspect there is a superficial understanding of this issue that derives from the commercial thinking of the pop music industry including many pop musicians. Helmut Lachenmann likes the Beatles: do we hear Beatles influences in his music? This would be ridiculous of course! The student didn't understand two things: firstly, that when we listen to music, it doesn't necessarily mean that we will end up writing in the style of that music, and secondly that composers endeavour to find their own voice. History of music teaches us that the early works of a composer may well show an influence of previous composers, but this influence gradually disappears as the composer establishes his own idiom. The young 'Classical' Beethoven sounds so different to the late 'Romantic' Beethoven. And look at the Beatles! If you compare their first album *Please, Please me* (1963) to *Abbey Road* (1969), you can hear a huge stylistic difference between the beginning and end of their songwriting. As I hinted earlier, I experienced jazz, pop and rock as liberating practices. I enjoyed the variety of idioms and styles, and they certainly gave me an open-mindedness about musical diversity. I am sure each of these genres and styles must have left an imprint in my musical world, but I can't say that I use these early idioms in my music today, unless you are implying my songwriting, which to this day, apart from some public concerts in the 1970s, has remained a private, part-time activity.

It is ultimately a matter of cultural openness; I say 'cultural' because music is an expression of culture. The rhythms of South African folk music can be so intriguing and yet so different to those of Indian music, for example. I love the rhythmic and polyphonic complexity in Albanian folk music. Albania is probably the only country in the world with such a refined tradition of polyphonic singing. You find polyphonic singing in South Albania and monophonic styles in the North. The resulting harmonies are often quite remarkable. Two-part songs are sung by women. Three-part songs may be sung by men and women. Four-part songs flourish in the South West region around Labëria and they are one of the most complex forms of polyphonic singing in the world. I also find the asymmetric metres and forms of these songs most inspiring. It is often mind-blowing what complexity these folk musicians manage to achieve in their songs and instrumental pieces while still retaining an amazing level of emotional density. Music of this quality is a continuous inspiration. I used fragments of Balkan folk songs in *Transfiguration* (2006) for trombone and electronics, where I juxtapose these fragments to the dramatic virtuosity of Vinko Globokar's trombone. Similarly, I have used Georgian folk melodies in *Undying Borders* (2015) for violin and electronics.

DB. How does improvisation fit into your work today? Is giving the interpreter space to improvise within a given composition a problem because some players may not be up to it? Or is it about the repeatability of one's work? Would you, for instance, consider creating your own ensemble with musicians whose improvisational skills you could trust?

JP. My first approach to music was through improvisation and I still love improvising on my grand piano. In the past 35 years, I have reduced the number of improvisation sections in my works rather dramatically. The reason for this is that the majority of classical performers cannot improvise, and the majority of those who can improvise have a tendency to follow a rather intellectual idea of improvisation that I find both very limited and limiting. I remember in the 1980s being regularly frustrated by the 'constipated' approach to improvisation of the young classical musicians who played my music. And I remember going back home after the first performance of a piece and writing out all those improvised sections myself in order to fix the improvisation on paper once and for all.

In those days, this was a major issue because I was playing and listening to a lot of jazz and it felt normal to include improvisation in my chamber, ensemble pieces and piano music. But I soon realised that when I improvise on the piano, it is I who does the improvising. What I mean is that by including improvisation in a score, I had to come to terms with the fact that other performers would improvise in their styles and *their* understanding of the music. At this point, it became inevitable that I had to either accept whatever the 'classical' musicians would play in their improvisations or cut off the improvisatory moments altogether in order to protect the quality of the music. I decided to go for the latter because it became clear that the improvisatory skills of those classical musicians were not good enough! I kept improvisations in several piano pieces, but that is because I was playing them myself at the beginning of my career. When other pianists would play my music, their improvisations would not meet my expectations and would effectively destroy the piece. This led me to write out my own improvisations in the score in order to make sure that my piece would retain a formal and stylistic coherence.

Having said that, as the levels of the classical musicians I worked with rose enormously from the 1990s onwards, I have continued to include improvisatory sections in some of my pieces. Working with instrumentalists of the calibre of Vinko Globokar, Neil Heyde, Yoshikazu Iwamoto, Klaus Schöpp, to mention a few, has given me continuous inspiration and I love using individual virtuosity as additional emotional power to the music I write. These are controlled situations in which I know that an aleatoric passage at that particular time in the score will not go wrong. You find this in some ensemble and chamber pieces where I often delineate a specific pitch material and a well-defined texture within a clear time constraint that will guarantee an effective use of the improvisation. I am thinking of ensemble pieces like *You*, *Legend*, *Transparence* or in *Crossing Dialogues*. The improvisatory moments in these pieces are often nothing but cadenzas given to a soloist. The other stratagem is supplying the performer with a specific selection of notes to be used for the improvisation.

I have considered creating my own ensemble with improvisers many times in my life. In the 1980s, the results were so unsatisfactory that I didn't pursue the idea further. I played a few improvisation sessions in various duos in the 1990s, but these projects didn't last long. I have always liked the idea of having my own trio or quartet, but again, lack of time has always been an obstacle in my life as I have other activities that are equally or more important. I still cherish this idea though, and perhaps one day I may find the right musicians whose improvisational skills I could trust, as you say. This would be wonderful!

DB. At some point in your work as a composer, you made a conscious effort not to resort to traditional, i.e. classical tonality. Why?

JP. I remember you made a similar remark when you heard the recording of the *Musica Reservata* CD. The truth is that I have never made a conscious effort not to use classical tonality in my life. My musical idiom has never been an intellectual choice, but an instinctive one. Only in one or two of my early piano pieces, I have used a tinge of traditional tonality. And when I say 'traditional tonality' it is in relation to functional classical tonality. But even then, I always make sure to create a tonal ambiguity that would keep the texture interesting and varied, rather than too obvious. I am not interested in repeating the past. Why should my music sound exactly like a Baroque, Romantic or Impressionistic or jazz piece? You can hear a strong diatonic idiom in some of my recent piano pieces, but the way I deal with diatonicism is not 'classical' in terms of functional tonality. When I use diatonic textures, I never think in classical terms: the syntax is completely different.

DB. How do you reconcile the use of pure acousmatic methods with instrumental composition? (Usually, composers are either doing one or the other. Rarely both).

JP. The discovery of acousmatic music in the early 1990s was one of the most important moments in my life. The major difference between acousmatic and instrumental composition is that in the acousmatic work everything is fixed forever, while an instrumental part will always sound different according to the interpretation of the performer. When I perform an acousmatic piece, I use the mixing console as a musical instrument, meaning that I create spatial motions manually, from left to right or front to back during the execution of the piece. Sometimes, I use the equaliser knobs as quasi-filters in order to alter the timbral qualities of the sound during the diffusion of the piece. We are talking about subtle nuances of course. This is one reason why I like using analogue mixing consoles, by the way. But these are indeed minor changes and not comparable to what instrumentalists can achieve in their interpretations.

One of the reasons why I love writing for acoustic instruments combined with electronics is that when I use fixed electronics, these are often brought to a new light by the interpretation of the acoustic instrument. In other words, although the electronic sounds are fixed, the interpretation of the instrumentalist will influence our perception of the loudness and timbral qualities of the electronics. This is a very interesting experience. So rather than 'reconciliation', it is a matter of partial interaction, fusion, a facet of unity through duality. This dichotomy is very much in my mind when I compose the fixed electronic part because I always compose the electronics in relation to the instrumental part. In this way, I ensure that both parts belong to a coherent musical discourse.

DB. Do you have secret desires, compositionally speaking, that you haven't fulfilled so far in any genre or cultural environment?

JP. Yes! Following my recent opera *Re di Donne*, I would like to write a work encompassing music and theatre using more daring musical idioms and scenic fashions. I would be in charge of all the theatrical aspects of the performance. I can very clearly envisage a form of meta-art encompassing sound, word, colour and theatre articulating beyond the current limitations imposed by each genre. Another secret desire of mine is to be able to use pianos that are tuned microtonally as I did in my *Piano Concerto*. I say this because many artistic directors are still showing a conservative approach to concert planning which is not helping the development of new music idioms. I would like to see pianos tuned microtonally and being used regularly on stage. By the same token, I would like to shake the pop music industry and their consumeristic approach to the musical art which I believe is damaging the mind of too many people who have grown accustomed to 'muzak'. These people still remain immune to artistic standards. In my opinion, we need a deeper and ethical approach to music as an expression of human values rather than a commercial product.

DB. Is the act of composing a spiritual goal in itself or is it a means to an end? Is music inherently spiritual or not? If not, can it be used to reach higher spiritual goals? Or is music just like any other human endeavour, limited by our intellect? In other words, is music the reflection of your pre-existing spiritual ideas or does music bring you to discover new levels of awareness?

JP. I think there are many answers to your questions, and these will vary depending on the composer. I can only talk about my perception of music and life. As you know, I cannot detach musical expression from its ontological nature: I do think that any form of artistic expression springs from an inner energy and desire to communicate. And yes, I feel this energy to be essentially spiritual. My experience has shown me that higher spiritual goals may be reached if the listeners are prepared to open their minds to the music. Then again, it also depends on the music. I don't think rock music would trigger a deeper awareness of who we are, but perhaps I am wrong. Repetition may evoke a primeval awareness of ritualistic transcendence through the use of recurrent rhythmic or melodic patterns. Yet, when I use simple musical patterns in my music, I prefer to bring in recurrent elements of surprise, such as a change of metre, melody, rhythm, harmony, that may enrich the transcending experience.

One of the things I love about music is that it can be anything, really. Ultimately, music reflects the personality of the composer. There is a lot of intellectual music in the contemporary 'classical' scene. You can hear it in the sound itself! And when I talk to composers, I can *hear* their music reflecting their personality in a striking way. I don't think that intellect is a limiting factor in making music. On the contrary, it is a matter of how intellectual one can be. The intellect can indeed be limiting but can also be unlimited and un-limiting! I really think it depends on how the music is felt in the first place. This topic is more complex than we may think because the perception of simplicity and complexity is not only related to the density of a musical texture. Psychoacoustics is teaching me a lot in this sense. The brain is a very complex organism and I can choose out of many listening modalities. To me, music reflects psychological experiences that are reshaped through sound and allow me to dig into new levels of consciousness. This is the most gratifying experience in my life.

THE CONVERGENCE OF TWO DIRECTIONS
Nick Storring

NS. I'm fascinated by the importance of allusion in your output. Where some composers prefer pure abstraction or to simply downplay a given piece's subject matter, your works often appear to spring from clear impetuses, often textual ones. The notes that accompany *some* of your pieces appear to come from a place of trusting music's capacity to carry a clear intention forward, whereas a number of others (such as the *Trans* series) seem to actively probe at perception itself. For you, how does sound (setting aside text) function symbolically? And how much do you trust it to convey concepts to listeners?

JP. The listeners' issue is beyond my work as a composer. It is a topic we simply cannot relate to scientifically because each listener hears music differently, also depending on the knowledge of the subject. In other interviews, I have spoken about the importance of education and the relativity of the whole issue (writing 'accessible' music, writing for an audience, and so on). How does sound function symbolically for me? This is a difficult and very interesting question. The Swiss psychologist C.G. Jung wrote,

"The artist translates archetypal motifs into the language of the present, and so makes it possible for us to find our way back to the deepest springs of life. Therein lies the social significance of art: it is constantly at work educating the spirit of the age, conjuring up the forms in which the age is most lacking." [2]

It seems clear that the archetypal motifs mentioned by Jung are symbols that reside in those 'uncharted territories' of the mind. The history of the human race, as well as our contemporary world, are full of symbols of all sorts: from very ancient to very new ones. Most people don't realise that everything we do in our daily life symbolises something: the colours we choose, the food we eat, the way we speak, the choices we make, the way we dress, and so forth. It is therefore natural that whatever an artist creates must come with a set of personal and collective symbols. As a global society, we are still using symbolic systems that have evolved over thousands of years and have become our cultural DNA, whether we are aware of them or not.

---

[2] Jung (1984:82).

An instrumental sound per se doesn't 'function symbolically'. It is *music* that elicits meaning and represents symbols in my mind. And it is my mind that 'functions' by recognising or assigning symbols to melodic, harmonic and rhythmic configurations. For a composer, this is the crucial difference between writing sounds and composing music.

If we take an alphabet, for example, every single letter is meaningless when taken in isolation. Letters acquire meaning when they begin to form words. In the same manner, it is not a single note that contains a meaning or represents a symbol, but the union of different notes that will prompt meanings or symbols in the mind. Let me give you an example about the making of a motif: I decided to compose a short phrase based on eight different notes. I set the notes in a certain order 'a', thus creating a musical statement functioning as an axiom for my discourse. By re-arranging the same pitches, that is changing the intervals within the phrase, I will come up with a different phrase where the notes are now arranged in a different order 'b'. This is how I create new phrases, by re-arranging the same eight notes in the remaining six orders. Although the pitch material has remained the same (the same eight notes), I have created eight different melodies, and by manipulating the intervals I have prompted different symbols and mental images in my mind. In pitch-based music, it is not a single note that triggers symbolic reminiscence, but the intervals between two or more notes that make a melody. The same happens in the perception of colours where, for instance, the gloomy and dark symbolism associated with the colour black is traditionally contrasted by the perception of lightness we associate with white. Black needs white in order to be perceived as black, and vice versa. Black itself, without the contrasting lightness of white, is less effective, or not effective at all because in this case, it is a non-referential object. Darkness cannot be perceived as such unless it is opposed to the symbol of lightness that will emphasise its nature by contrast.

The sense of 'blackness' in sound is perceived by our brain as 'fullness'. Psychoacoustics reveal that our perception of pitch is related to the rate of oscillation of the wavelength (the frequency) and that the invisible body (spectrum) of the sound in combination with the intensity of the acoustic signal will also be perceived as the colour (timbre) of the sound. By studying and working with sound, I have become increasingly aware of the symbolism that sound can have, and its effect on the listening mind. When focusing on a prolonged sound, for example, a drone, its timbre represents a self-contained universe that, due to its spectral nature, is static and non-static at the same time. It is static because the main bulk of the sound remains the same; it is non-static because on a micro level many partial tones are actually changing throughout the prolongation of the sound. The symbol I hear out of this musical event is twofold as it embraces stasis and mobility at the same time. Due to its abstract nature, music is the most hermetic of all arts. Melodies, rhythms, harmonies, durations and timbres don't represent themselves, but mirror symbols and notions of the composer's inner universe of values, emotions, preoccupations and beliefs. I became increasingly aware of this issue by composing and *listening* carefully to what I had written, and by studying the subject throughout many years.

NS. I've seen Cage cited as a major influence on your work, and yet I wouldn't likely call your work Cagean, partially on account of what I addressed in the previous question. How did you initially meet him? How has the Cagean listening philosophy informed your compositional outlook and practice? To what degree is the indeterminate a part of your work?

JP. I am glad and grateful to you for having pointed out the difference between Cage's music and mine so clearly. I keep reading the word 'influence' in writings about composers, and I must say I find that quite irritating. Let's be frank: anything we listen to is potential 'influence' on our music, isn't it? Having studied with this or that composer or having been a friend of another composer doesn't mean that one has been influenced by this composer. But people seem to love to label these circumstances as 'influences' in my or your music. How reductive! The same happens if you have studied or analysed the music of another composer for a while: the readers will immediately speak of the 'influence' that this composer must have had on your own music. I find this attitude really unimaginative and even insulting, I must say.

I studied Cage's music rather intensively in the late 1980s. At that time, listening to his music and reading about his artistic mind was a very revealing experience. I also met John on a couple of occasions and had the privilege to discuss many interesting topics by letter and personally. I loved the man, and he certainly was an important mind for me at that time of my life: I admired his involvement with Zen philosophy (which was very close to me) and the way he would combine art and philosophy in his music and daily life. There was also a beautiful sense of Oneness about his person which fascinated me. I equally admired his courage and controversial attitudes about music and art, and I learnt a lot from his compositional procedures before he embraced chance operations. I had known and used the I Ching before I came across John Cage, but the way he used it in his artistic work was an important mind-opener for me philosophically and musically. I was fascinated by the way he would combine Zen attitudes and the implicit Taoism of the I Ching with his aesthetics of sound, and how he would deal with choice (or lack of) in his compositional procedures. As a pianist, I also played his music regularly in the late 1980s and early 1990s.

Cage was also important to me because in the late 1980s I was zealously searching for my individual voice which I wanted to be rooted in an ideal equilibrium of determinate and indeterminate procedures. Studying his concept and application of indeterminacy in his works was very interesting and beneficial to my compositional mind of that time. I studied the core of his music aesthetics and musical works very meticulously. John's controversial views were important also because they challenged my traditional way to listen to, and think of, music. I certainly felt closer to his compositional mind (pre- and post-change operations) than to the serial/post-serial European avant-garde. Incidentally, one of the things I enjoyed in *some* American composers was the fresh approach to music which I found rather liberating and, in any case, closer to me than the 'Bolshevik' attitude of some European serialists.

I first met John Cage after a concert he gave in Wetzikon, Switzerland in May 1990. On that occasion, he performed a very long piece for water and shells and at the end of the concert, I went to talk to him. Two days later, I attended his second concert in Zurich where his piano concerto *Fourteen* had just been premiered. After the concert, we spoke again, and he invited me to see him in New York. Three months later, on 28th August, we spent the afternoon in his Manhattan loft and discussed several musical, aesthetic and cultural issues. A small part of these discussions is included in a book of interviews called *Conversations* which was published in 2013.[3] At that time, John was revising the *Freeman Etudes* for violinist Paul Zukofsky. He told me the story about the piece and how he stopped writing it at some point. A performance by Irvine Arditti persuaded him to complete the cycle, and he took me through the procedures he was using at that time. John showed me every single element of the sonic material (pitch, articulation, loudness, duration, register and bowing techniques) he had selected through chance operations, and explained the way he catalogued and classified each element (it was all in paper format). His table was full of an 'orderly disorder' that caught my attention. He told me he was working on Book Four of the *Etudes* and discussed with me the content of an approaching lecture on his mesostics. He was always interested in listening to other people's opinions. At the end of the visit, John presented me with the manually edited introduction to the mesostics writing he was going to read in his forthcoming lecture.

In those days, I was certainly more inspired by Cage's organisation of sound than by the

---

[3] Palmer (2013:22-28)

serial matrixes of Stockhausen and Boulez, or by the post-serial European avant-garde. I guess the reason for this was that John's procedures appeared to me as being flexible, unpredictable and less static than those based on a fixed 12-tone system. Also, there was something refreshing and appealing in Cage's cosmic and philosophical approach to sound as opposed to the technical and rigid attitude of the post-serialists. One could hear it clearly in his music. For example, I was fascinated by, and still love, the unpredictable texture and the refreshing immediacy of the *Music of Changes* cycle for piano. I think my way of working with permutations is much more linked to Cage's procedures than to the matrixes of Integral Serialism used by Boulez, for instance. In that sense, Cage certainly made an impact on my architectural mind, especially on the way I would organise the spine of my musical works, integrate free insertions and uncontrolled elements in the framework of the music. Cage helped me to think beyond and *bigger* than 12 notes.

The Cagean listening philosophy was really important for me in those days. A few years earlier, I had been struck by Messiaen's studies of bird songs which had a strong impact on me and opened up a new and more attentive type of listening in my life. I remember studying Messian's recordings and writings very attentively and undertaking some small research on bird songs myself. If Messiaen was the initiator of attentive listening in my life, Cage's aesthetics turned out to be the consequent revolution about the way I would listen to natural and musical sounds. Cage was the one who opened the door to a deeper awareness of sound. The encounter with Pierre Schaeffer's musique concrète in 1991 was the next step that led me into a professional cognition of sound as an acoustic and psychoacoustic phenomenon. I then studied electroacoustic composition and created my first electronic studio in London in 1991.

In some of my acoustic works of that time, I experimented with structural procedures informed by Cage's early works. My piano piece *Déjà vu* is a case in point. Perhaps I should mention that, as a pianist, I used indeterminacy many times in my performances, and would find many affinities between my improvisational practice of those years and some of John's ideas about aleatory music. It is also worth mentioning that performing his piano pieces gave me the opportunity to experience his most aleatory works from the perspective of a performer, something which initially I found very exciting, but after a couple of years frustrated me increasingly. In those years, I was going through a major change about the way I included improvisation and aleatory elements in my music, and I surely learnt a lot from playing and analysing the latter works I have mentioned. In the end, if there is an end, the search for a balance between determinacy and indeterminacy in my own works ended up with the triumph of determinacy at the expense of indeterminacy. This was a time when I began to withdraw many aleatory (acoustic) works following the poor performance of other performers who didn't have the skills to improvise convincingly. I only kept a few of these pieces, and in a very revised form in which the aleatory elements and improvisations would be reduced to a minimum. The ability of classical performers to play indeterminate music, or to improvise, is a discussion that deserves a separate chapter.

Like with a few other composers, the importance that Cage had at that particular time of my life doesn't mean that my music would sound like his, or that I was interested to adopt his systems in my music or become an epigone. On the contrary, the more I studied his music the more I became aware of substantial contradictions that, at the end, left me very puzzled about his artistic and philosophical integrity, and, I am afraid to say, his music competence as well. At some point, I even began to feel allergic to the Cage-myth that has conquered the contemporary music scene ever since; this is a different aspect of course, but I thought I should mention it as well. Today, I find the Cage mystification I experience in the new music circuits rather decadent, to be honest: a form of commercialism *à la mode*. What I find deplorable in the Cage legacy is the embarrassing confusion between the notion of sound and music. John really never studied acoustics, electronic music and, most importantly, the basic notions of psychoacoustics. In any case, throughout the 1990s, I gradually departed from Cage's aesthetics because I felt that he didn't understand the psychology of music listening and that he was using his attacks to tradition without a serious examination of his arguments. In his philosophy of music, he ignored cognition completely, and that is a major flaw. To claim that I hear the traffic of Manhattan's Sixth Avenue the same way I hear a Beethoven symphony and that the traffic's noise *is* music, is not only a sign of great musical ignorance but also a philosophically ridiculous statement that cannot be taken seriously. Every music student knows that sound and music are two different things.

NS. As an artist with quite an eclectic output, to what extent do your own listening habits impact your aesthetic choices?

JP. I guess to a great extent, although I suspect it would be arduous to measure the impact exactly. Since I was a little child, I have listened to literally anything that would come across my ears, from Gregorian Chants to the folk music of the Middle East, from Blues to Rimsky-Korsakov, from French chansons to Bebop, and I have learnt to love music of many genres, idioms and styles. I know many classical musicians who only listen to classical music, but for me, this would be unthinkable. I am often told that one can hear avant-garde jazz in some of my piano music, for example. Well, that doesn't surprise me at all because I have been a jazz pianist.

There is a moment in *Beyond the Bridge* (for cello and electronics) where I hear a motif consisting of four ascending notes that are exactly the same notes you find in a phrase of the song *The Autumn Leaves*. Now, I can swear to you that when I wrote *Beyond the Bridge*, I surely wasn't thinking of *The Autumn Leaves,* a song I love but that was miles away from my mind when I was composing this piece. It was only many years later that, by re-listening to the piece, I suddenly went, *"Oh, but that's the tune of The Autumn Leaves!"*. I confess I was rather surprised to notice this evident resemblance and, at first, I wasn't sure how to take it. I remember thinking, *"should I feel ashamed?", "will the audience recognise the tune and ridicule my piece now?", "will someone accuse me of plagiarism?".* At some point, I decided to let go of all of this questioning and accept the 'hidden motif' for what it means within the context of *Beyond the Bridge.* Was it deliberate? Certainly not! Was it a coincidence? Well, I don't believe in coincidence. If there are archetypal truths, then my compositional mind must be absorbed by my subconscious to such an extent that it is not surprising if occasionally the subconscious pops up and becomes an active force in what I am composing. This is a force that has the power of decision in the most unexpected circumstances.

NS. Returning to the subject 'seeking' I observe in many of your works, where do you situate yourself in relation to the ethos of experimentalism? How and to what extent is a piece of music a hypothesis or proposition to you?

JP. After so many years of composing, I no longer think in terms of writing experimental music, or writing a microtonal, tonal, or atonal piece. These labels have long become meaningless to me. Back in the 1980s, I composed and played a lot of so-called experimental music; I tried all the things I wanted to try out and it felt good to do so. When I write music, I concentrate on what I want to write regardless of idioms and styles. It is the idea of the music, the artistic and philosophical drive in relation to the topic I am dealing with, that I am interested in exploring. The means I use for this exploration will be shown by the music itself as it unfolds. New Zealand composer and musicologist Robin Maconie once said that a musical composition is but a document of the composer's perception of the world. I am well aware that any musical work I write is a reflection of, and a proposition to, the world! Sometimes I need to articulate a debate where I want to explore a hypothesis about an existential topic in a dialectic way, by using a confrontational discourse maintained by a polyphonic texture. Other times, I prefer to give voice to an intimate space that needs to be articulated with more subtlety and less formalism. I am not, and don't want to be, a monolithic composer. One reason why as a pianist I have always felt more attracted to a Ricercare rather than a Fugue, for instance, is that I felt at ease with the lightness and unpredictability deriving from asymmetric or not overly controlled forms as opposed to the rigid formalism of a strictly defined texture. Traditionally, this conceptual strictness about order, form and structure is a very Germanic feature. At its best, it has produced stunning works which I admire and respect, of course, but I am often left with a sense of rigidity that is foreign to me. This could be a reason why as a young pianist I would enjoy playing Scarlatti rather than J.S. Bach, Chopin rather than Beethoven, and Cage rather than Stockhausen.

As a composer, I need to express my propositions with diversity and a varied palette of techniques that allow me to change and evolve throughout my life. Perhaps this is the reason why I am not attracted by monolithic composers such as professed ultra-modernists or minimalists whose compositional idiom never evolves. That kind of music always sounds the same to me and speaks neither to my intellect nor to my heart.

NS. One might characterise the mainstream, 20th century, European compositional milieu as an 'arms race' of sorts; a clash of ideologies all striving for the nebulous concept of innovation. As someone who is based in Europe and whose career has straddled the 20th and 21st centuries, how would you characterise the present state of music?

JP. Europe is not one country, and there are significant differences between anglosaxon/ northern countries, central and Eastern countries. All in all, the present state of music could be described as pseudo-pluralistic. I write 'pseudo' because the obsession with ideologies (old ones and new ones) is still very much alive, especially in central Europe. Germany is the country that still exemplifies this attitude.

NS. To what extent is your musical practice oriented towards a historical future?

JP. Well, it would be arrogant of me to claim anything of this kind. I remember after the world premiere of *Musica Reservata*, a well-known pianist and senior professor at the University of Music and Performing Arts of Stuttgart approached me and said enthusiastically, *"this is the music of the future!"*. I could clearly see in his eyes that he really meant what he said, and I have been thinking a lot about that statement ever since. At first, I was flattered by his words, then I asked myself: *"how is the music of the future going to sound like?"* What I find interesting is that *Musica Reservata* is not at all an avant-garde, modernist piece. It is not minimalist either, so I kept wondering what kind of quality he meant. The only thing I can say about *Musica Reservata* is that it is intense music; it is music that comes from the heart and soul, where each note, each rest and each rhythm has been selected very carefully in a state of profound meditation. If that is what the pianist meant, the future of music would sound like a celebration of introspection. This would be wonderful, and the dreamer in me loves the idea. On the other hand, I think there will always be many kinds of music, each reflecting different attitudes, philosophies, beliefs, and so on, and this should be so. My own musical practice is oriented towards the now. When I compose, I am not concerned with the past because yesterday is a memory and not a living reality. In this sense, it doesn't exist. The future is ahead of us. The only reality is the present, the 'now'. And I feel this 'now' as the most beautiful *present* (in both senses!) I have in this life, both as a musician and man.

NS. To what extent is transgression (especially aesthetically) important to you?

JP. If by 'transgression' you do mean an act that goes against a rule, a law, a conventional society, I could imagine that the content of my music may sound uncomfortably transgressive in these days of enormous superficiality. Whatever I do and compose comes from the heart and I wouldn't feel comfortable with the idea of offending anyone. Surely, I want to make some points about our existence on this planet and contemporary society, but isn't that something that all artists do? Is it not the role of art to reflect on the human condition? I do think it is important to challenge a social/human/political status-quo if we feel the necessity to do so. I certainly do. Every time I have written a piece as a result of a social or political situation that has horrified me (for example, the Balkan wars), I have been very aware of the position I was going to take by writing that music. Art should denounce injustice, hypocrisy and the atrocities committed by the human beast. I think there is aesthetic transgression in my music, but it is not apparent: one has to really listen carefully and enter the music in a state of total immersion in order to *feel* the content. An eloquent example is my quartet *Formal Transgressions* (2013).

Art is not a mere exhibition of one's own talent: art calls for critique. This is the ability to discuss and evaluate important issues; to observe ourselves and society critically and reflect on who we are and what we experience. Today more than ever, art should invite us to deflect those mechanisms of thought that have been atrophied by consumerism and the frivolity of the entertainment industry, by the ruthless laws of marketing and commercialism, by corrupted politics and journalism, and by the abusive use of social media. We are becoming machines, people without brains, serial products that are born to die as soon as possible. Today the majority of people die at 30 and are buried at 80. The decadence of the arts in our society has become a major tragedy at the beginning of the 21st century. The main ingredients of cultural discourse, such as critical reflection, debate and denunciation, are losing their meaning while being crushed by the vulgarity of a new entertainment sub-culture that is dominating all the communication channels that keep a society together. Today, too many people engaged in social, political and cultural activities are ignorant, uncritical, dull and rude. Much of 'artistic' creation is numbing the population rather than edifying it, and the majority of people are still not understanding that this is a method of psychological and social control. This situation is gradually destroying our humanity and it is no wonder that many people have become tired of critical thinking. We live in a society that does no longer tolerate forms of individual creativity and thinking. Günther Anders's notion of 'Industrial Religion' has been now replaced by the 'Social Media Religion'. It seems that the fascination of the Evocative is being replaced by loud and aggressive sounds and a stream of cheap creativity that are flattening our intelligence.

The value of respect, friendship and love has been superseded by self-interest, social indifference, apathy, hatred and the lust for urgent sexuality that are destroying the human race from within. Our worst enemy has become our neighbour, the state, our politicians, but also our manipulated self; a living zombie that is wandering in and around us out of control. Imagine what would happen if art regained its original power of intellectual and social urgency, reinstating the dignity, depth and elegance of its language with the clarity of a dissent that will not adhere to what we are gradually becoming. Imagine what the world would be like if once a week people would spend two hours listening to a musical work by J.S. Bach, watching a Shakespeare play, reading a poem, tasting the philosophical content of a piece of art, let it sink into their mind and heart, and finally ask themselves what they could do to become better and more fulfilled, and make this world a happier place?

NS. Are you more concerned with innovating or effectively synthesising different aspects of what is around you or came before you?

JP. I don't think in terms of wanting to innovate or synthesise. When I compose, I am focused on what I am writing without thinking of innovating or synthesising anything. There was a time, at the beginning of my musical career, when I wanted to be original for the sake of being original, but those days are long gone. My concern is to write music that is honest and authentic, and therefore true to myself. The music establishment as I keep experiencing it, is just an industry like another. Most of these people think in terms of selling a product to the market, and I am talking from experience. I am disillusioned by the idea of the classical music industry as a guarantor of cultural and critical reflection. It seems to me that the main concern of festivals, orchestras and record companies nowadays is to sell 'products' in line with the prevailing dictates of fashion. I want to remain true to myself, and I don't care if my music is not being perceived as innovative, really. Being innovative is not an artistic criterion.

NS. Your own journey has been fairly idiosyncratic and I'm curious about that. Your shift from the fringes of popular music from the mid 1970s-80s into 'composerdom' is of particular interest to me as someone whose own work hovers between 'concert music' and exploratory music of a different nature. What prompted this change in direction? What features of your earlier work have you integrated into your compositional output? What is your current relationship to music outside of contemporary composition?

JP. The reason for my change of direction was to pursue quality. As a teenager, I wrote pop songs and played the keyboards in a couple of bands (we are talking about the 1970s). At some point, I exhausted all the possibilities that pop music offered me. Although I still enjoy writing a good song, I became aware of the musical limitations of this genre, so I went back into jazz with a mature approach. By this time, I was in my 20s. As a pianist, jazz offered me a much wider range of harmonic, melodic and rhythmic combinations. And a jazz pianist had a technique that was superior to the technique of a keyboard or piano player in a pop band. But technique was not only about technique in itself, really. The music that came with that genre was of a superior level. So, in the early 1980s, I started playing jazz anew and discovered pianists like Bill Evans, Chick Corea, Keith Jarrett and Cecil Taylor to mention a few. I was now navigating in a refined musical world. But even this world soon became limited (this does not apply to Keith Jarrett and Cecil Taylor, though) and I soon wanted to discover more. I joined the Conservatoire of Lucerne, improved my pianistic skills and studied the developments of music composition in the 20th century as much as I could. From the progressive jazz/cross-over/new tonality scene, I ventured into Schönberg and Webern up to the Serialism of the 1950s and all the musical directions that followed that generation. I undertook postgraduate studies in Composition at Trinity College of Music and did a PhD in Composition at City University in London. I also broke through the wall of electronic music, which had been the last taboo to deal with. It was the constant search for quality in music as in life, and the desire to learn, know and understand that kept me going and discovering unknown musical horizons.

Firstly, I wanted to achieve the best possible quality in the way I was playing the piano and composing. Secondly, I wanted to understand the developments of music, learn from them as much as possible because I wanted to be a professional musician. A sense of professionalism has always been very important to me. If I want to build a house, I know I must study architecture otherwise the house I am going to build will fall apart. Each art has its rules, laws, styles and so on. By the same token, a professional musician is someone who has studied the musical art. As a pianist I can play a simple melody in so many different ways: 'staccato', 'legato', 'non legato', grouping the notes a certain way instead of another, play 'piano', 'forte', 'fortissimo' and so forth. Listen to the majority of pop pianists and you will find that apart from some very rare exceptions, they don't have a clue about how to play a melody, they don't have the technique, and you can hear it in the way they bang on the piano. It is true that some of them may be talented individuals, but in my opinion, they are not professional musicians. What prompted the change in direction was the search for quality and competence, both as a pianist and composer.

It's difficult to define what features of my earlier work I have integrated into my compositional output, really. I think all the works I have written are linked to each other. What I don't have time to finish today, I will finish tomorrow. I listen to any kind of music, and I have a substantial CD collection. My relationship with music is a daily activity even when I don't compose. I listen to a variety of styles, I love singing for pleasure, I improvise at the piano, I teach, I also play the guitar, and, although less frequently, I play the koto and percussion instruments. As a musicologist, I am interested in the aesthetics of music and analysis of musical works of the past 100 years. I have an electronic and recording studio where, time permitting, I research sound and do all sorts of recordings.

NS. Where does the pluralism of approach and style come from in your work?

JP. I guess from the diverse background and interest I have in any kind of music. I literally listen to anything I come across because I love music, as I love sound per se.

NS. In our conversations, you alluded to spectralist techniques and mentioned that they held a spiritual significance to you. First of all, how do you make use of spectralist tactics/spectral thinking in your compositions? The temptation is to regard spectralism as a very scientific way to do things. How do you square the micro-, earthbound focus and technical features of this approach with the vastness of spirituality?

JP. It was the work of Jonathan Harvey that opened this world to me more than any other composer. I was already heading that way on my own but coming across Jonathan's music was a revelation. In 1991 works like *Bhakti*, *Mortuos Plango Vivos Voco*, *From Silence* and *Madonna of Winter and Spring* impressed me very strongly. This was the time when my first electronic studio in London became a many-sided laboratory where I experimented with all sorts of sound transformations and laid the foundation of my own electroacoustic techniques. The second half of the 1990s was another crucial time for me because as a Senior Lecturer in Composition at the University of Hatfield, I 'discovered' Psychoacoustics, an area of research and teaching I have pursued ever since in my Professorship at the University of Music and Performing Arts of Stuttgart from October 2000 onwards. The reason why I mentioned this is that, in my opinion, spectral thinking and 'techniques' can be really understood only in conjunction with psychoacoustics.

As a composer, I don't tend to intellectualise spectral techniques as some composers seem to be inclined to do. My approach is immediate and, perhaps, simpler. Psychoacoustics has taught me what cognitive listening is about. Working in the electronic studio (analysing spectra of all sorts, modifying the sound with filters etcetera) has been an experience that has enhanced my sensitivity about sound as both a micro and macro-universe. I can experience the vastness of spirituality in one single sound every time I access its spectrum. It is like entering an underworld of unexpected sounds and vibrations interrelated to each other: a wonderful network of secret connections that I love exploring as a composer and listener. There is a very spiritual feeling when working with a spectrum. Again, this is not an intellectual speculation: I just feel the sacredness of a sound very directly in my soul and under my skin. I have a natural inclination for sounds of all sorts; it is a very sensual attraction. This is probably linked to the fact that I am synaesthetic: an experience that is really impossible to verbalise. For example, when I analyse a spectrum, I perceive colours that are changing in time. I experience a variety of simultaneous sensations, perceptions, and a sense of motion in an inner and outer space simultaneously. Sometimes I even experience a sense of taste associated with sound.

NS. Your personal interests appear to orbit spiritual matters, healing, and pertinent, longstanding philosophical questions. Many of these things are a part of your music, appearing in titles, programme notes and sometimes more explicitly in your electroacoustic works. On a broader level, what sort of state do you hope to bring about in listeners through your work? Can one look at your catalogue from an aerial view and ascertain an overarching goal there, separate from the individual concerns of each piece? Do you consciously work to manifest this in your pieces? If so, how (from a sonic point of view)?

JP. I fear that by replying to your questions I may destroy that sense of mystery that should pervade all works of art. Should we verbalise mystery? Should not the music say it all? Is it not the listener that should feel the music from a neutral position? My goal is to share my life experience with the world through music and I like to exploit all the musical possibilities at my disposal in order to share my thoughts and reflections, my stories, an emotion I may feel strongly, and so forth. What the listeners make out of it is no longer in my hands. I would hope to convey a sense of ethical values, human dignity, the courage of debating and confronting ourselves with the world and our own shadows in order to enhance the awareness of who we are. I am conscious about my values, of course, as I am aware of wanting to share them through music.

I have said on other occasions that my music is autobiographical, and I feel absolutely at peace with that! Each piece I write is a story, a sonic poem, a moment of my life that I wish to celebrate with music and share with a future listener. I am not afraid of showing feelings and emotions through sound. I remember my first composition lessons were all about 'don't fall in love with the sounds', 'stick to the rules' and all that. Edison Denisov used to repeat this mantra insistently. Then came the hard-liner modernists, who are still dominating the music scene in many parts of Europe. They spoke about the 'moral integrity' of the composer and the 'responsibility of this and that'. You know, I have become very allergic to this kind of music Bolshevism. Music should continue to speak from the heart as well as the mind. Ideologies have always destroyed art and I like to stand for the sincerity of my vision. Once, composer Tod Machover said,

"Art that is merely self-referential, that speaks only of its own materials and forms, is sterile and superficial. The elements of artistic language must be carefully adapted by the artist to represent a particular human vision. It is precisely this delicate marriage of deep, original vision with a fitting, concise and expressive form that ultimately determines the value of a work of art. Art can and must represent human reality, but needs to objectify and elevate this reality by giving it form".[4]

Depending on the circumstance, my musical debates may imply a confrontational discussion requiring a 'tough' idiom (this is where the chromaticism of atonality and the power of virtuosity can play a major role), or I will explore the lucidity and austerity of diatonicism and the world of 'quasi-silence'. These two directions often converge in the same piece.

---

[4] Emmerson (1986:194).

GENESIS, CONSISTENCY AND FORMAL DESIGN
Jeffrey Holmes

JH. What is the meaning of your music? Are there extra-musical associations such as drama, programme, transcendence? Is your music more concerned with formalism? If both, how do these opposing elements interact or coexist?

JP. The question of what music means is enormous and complex at the same time, especially if addressed to oneself and the music we write. Music is a form of revelation to composers in their solitude, and to the listeners. I could ask myself: why do I write music in the first place? Why do I dream? Why do I live? The music I write exists as a natural manifestation of my being: but what is the meaning I have assigned to my artistic life, one could ask? The following, provisional, answers result from long and attentive observation: search, communication, discovery, evolution, yearning, celebration, individuation, declamation, reunion and vision; to explore a process of self-knowledge through sound. Music is too big an art for me to be divided into formalism and expressionism. I write music where meaning lies in the perception of the musical relationships between sounds, untouched by non-musical references. And I do write music where structural relationships indicate or stem from a search for debate, transcendence and confrontation. I don't think these two elements are opposite, but if they were, they coexist in the perceptual interaction of structure/symbol, construction/metaphor and sonic configuration/mental representation.

JH. What do you use to create consistency? Do you have recurring theoretical structures, such as harmonies or developmental techniques that you build your music from? How much of your music is intuitive in design?

JP. Consistency, as a general and specific attribute, is very important to my music. The first idea that comes to my mind, however, is consistency throughout my oeuvre, I mean having created music *consistently* in the past 47 years. In this case, the key has been faith in what I believe in and have been doing all these years, and an enormous amount of incessant work. I have gone through several crises in my life, mainly due to a serious lack of recognition I have had to cope with, perhaps due to the fact that I moved from one country to another frequently, and this may have not put me in a position to take root in a specific national context. As a consequence, I have lacked all the regular connections that will ensure a composer to be heard and promoted accordingly. Another reason may have been the fact that I have been a 'late arriver', as Bill Evans would put it, since I had to rebuild my life from scratch at the age of 18. This delay has been fatal to the eyes of many promoters of contemporary music: I was always considered too old everywhere I lived, and therefore no longer interesting enough to be performed as a 'new upcoming voice'. The new music scene can be a 'ruthless' machine and I have paid a big price for not being 'young enough' to deserve attention. I could tell stories of incredible discrimination and humiliation I have gone through up to these days. Twice in my life, I have seriously lost faith in my work and have been on the edge of giving up composition due to an increasing sense of frustration about what I have just said. The first time was in Switzerland in the 1980s, and it was a dream I had where Athena appeared to me whispering words of encouragement and support in such a determinate fashion that I felt impelled to persevere on my chosen path (this episode is somewhat 'portrayed' in my piano piece *Athena*). The second, and similar, occasion occurred in London in the 1990s, and it was Jonathan Harvey's faith in my music that persuaded me not to give up.

Apart from these moments of deep darkness, or perhaps *because* of them, the secret for my consistency has been a profound love for music in all its manifestations and an almost maniacal working schedule exceeding any normal and 'reasonable' lifestyle. I knew I had to catch up for the time I had lost in my youth. I often remembered Frank Zappa saying something similar in an interview where he continued to stress that only by working constantly and on a daily basis, did he manage to get through many difficult moments in his career. This kind of general consistency throughout my life has been a result of my grit, perseverance and love for music.

A second aspect of consistency you may refer to is most probably linked to the architecture and procedures employed in my works. The answer to this aspect is: ensuring a solidity of form, which is something I am very meticulous about. I use a variety of formal and structural methods. The most evident are corresponding formal relationships within what I call 'outer-form' and 'inner-form' (to use Felix Salzer's terminology) and the establishment of precise pitch-fields (sometimes based on the harmonic series of one or more notes). I am very interested in asymmetric forms, often converting the structure of a poem, for example, into an equivalent musical form. I also use fractal-like proportions and multiplication of simple elements such as a harmonic series or a specific pitch-field. As I love harmony, I frequently set up an entire edifice of form on a single chord or melodic unit revisited as a harmonic agglomerate. This is a formalistic approach to composition which I enjoy using as well. In such cases, a chord turns into a universe of inner intervallic relationships that are unfolded by simple yet precise constructs and patterns that I multiply, juxtapose and shift in time.

Intuition is very important to me too, also when working with pre-established and fixed procedures. From that point of view, even the strictest procedure is enriched by the intuitive unfolding of material. In addition, there are several works of mine whose design and unfolding of pitch, rhythm and so forth is totally intuitive. Works of this kind spring from an extra-musical topic such as an image, a thought, a feeling or a sensation. In such cases, I plunge into imaginary worlds and let my fantasy unfold freely. Many of these works are linked to symbols, mythology, personal questions, social, psychological or spiritual themes.

JH. What is the genesis of a particular piece? Is it conceptual, or are your initial ideas improvised? How much time do you spend composing at an instrument vs. on paper or into a computer notation program?

JP. The genesis varies from work to work. Sometimes it is conceptual and formalistic, other times it springs from a sensation or a strong urge to communicate something that is important to me (a feeling about a social or interpersonal issue, for example). At other times, the genesis may be 'localised' to an instrument on which I may improvise first. Frequently, it is a meditation that triggers a musical idea or an entire work. I don't have a fixed system. I used to compose at an instrument 40 or 30 years ago, but this has decreased throughout the years, although, as a pianist, I often end up playing at the piano what I am composing for this instrument. I am not a string player, but I have often composed a string piece on the instrument as well, especially when I use extended techniques. The cello is an instrument I have used many times in such a fashion. Paper remains my favourite medium on which to compose, with the occasional check at the piano. In recent years, I have used computer notation programs about which I have mixed feelings. Although I do appreciate the quick typesetting procedures and all the score and parts production technicalities that come with it, I can't take such programs (like Sibelius) as a serious aural reference regarding what I am writing. It's not much about the control of pitch structures, but more about the inadequacy to reproduce a decent aural image of timbre, loudness, resonance, agogics and other subtle components.

JH. How does hierarchy operate in your formal design? Are your musical materials cyclic?

JP. Hierarchy is an important aspect of formal design, whether it is pre-determined according to a set of defining principles, or not. I have written electroacoustic works where timbral transformation and resonance are the top priority of the musical discourse. On other occasions, rhythmic structures are as important as pitch. The latter, in all its possible forms of organisation, remains a main musical element in most of my works. So far, the only cyclic material I have deliberately used as such can be heard in the *Trans* cycle (written from 2000 to 2014) including two chamber works, one work for ensemble and seven solos: *Transitions* (for clarinet, violin, cello and piano), *Transference* (for flute, clarinet, violin, cello and piano), *Transparence* (for solo viola, flute, clarinet, violin, cello, piano and electronics), *Trans-solo 1* through to *Trans solo 6* (respectively for piano, clarinet, violin, cello, flute and viola) and *Over* (for solo violin).

Sometimes the formal design used for one work has been used for another work. The most notable example is the asymmetrical star matrices I used in *Epitaph* (for cello and electronics) and *Transfiguration* (for trombone and electronics). Although the generating idea was the same (wanting to find a graphic symbol of hope and light against the themes of pain and despair), the form of the two 'generating' stars is different.

JH. What is the role of metre: agogic, or purely synchronous?

JP. Both. It depends on the context of the composition.

JH. Do you have preferred genres: chamber, vocal, orchestral, etc.?

JP. 30 years ago, I would have replied with a 'yes' (instrumental, chamber, orchestra and electroacoustic). Meanwhile, I have grown to appreciate any musical genre.

CHAPTER TWO

OPERA *RE DI DONNE*

A CONVERSATION ON *RE DI DONNE*
Anna Cepollaro

AC. Your opera *Re di Donne*, which premiered at the Teatro Lirico Sperimentale in Spoleto, is freely inspired by news stories that have aroused great interest in the Italian public opinion. What prompted you to choose the tragic case of the murder of a young girl in a small town in the south of Italy as the theme of your new work?

JP. There are two reasons that led me to make this choice. First of all, I was asked by the Artistic Director of the Teatro Lirico Sperimentale, Michelangelo Zurletti, to choose a theme for the opera that was related to daily news; it had to be a topic linked to social or political events from everyday life and, if possible, to Italian news. I decided to choose femicide because this is a very serious problem internationally. Personally, this choice is a consequence of a sensitivity that I have always had towards social injustice, especially with regard to the weakest, including children and women. In today's society, this issue is still so burning that it needs to be treated with determination and courage. My aim was to help raise a stronger awareness about this form of crime.

AC. In the opera, you outline the characters of three women. How did you translate their different characteristics into music?

JP. Although they have several common traits, the three women are quite dissimilar: on the one hand, we have the two young cousins, Ivana and Martina, who are being manipulated by Rocco; on the other hand, there is Frida, Martina's mother, who is a problematic middle-aged woman who conceives and executes the murder of her young niece, Ivana. In reality, however, the female characters total four, because the character of Ivana is explored from two different perspectives: a living Ivana who is part of the story, and another Ivana who is already dead. The latter begins and ends the opera, reflecting with anguish and pain on the events that have led to her death. During the course of the opera, the dead Ivana is not part of the story, but in Scene Two, in the middle of the quarrel taking place between Martina and Rocco, she appears in the scene wondering how her naivety could ever have caused this tragedy. Finally, at the end of the last scene, she appears again on stage expressing her still unresolved regret at having caused this tragedy. Her final words are wrapped by a sense of disbelief and an irreparable awareness of her misery. The presence of this dead character at the beginning and end of the opera is significant because it invites us to ponder over the consequences of vanity, fragility and our own weaknesses. Musically, the dead Ivana is characterised by slow, short, diatonic melodies that are meant to highlight the doubts of someone who is reflecting on the tragedy after the tragedy from another, timeless dimension.

 The electronic sounds reinforce a sense of afterlife that is still alive and somehow very much present in the unfolding of the story. You hear sounds that resemble breathing and fragments of speech as if wanting to emphasise a surreal condition of the soul where the personal tragedy of Ivana, as a victim of her own naivety, is still unresolved. Conversely, at the beginning of the story, the musical character of the living Ivana is joyful as she is still unaware of what is yet to come. She remains light, lively and naive for most of the opera. Her phrases are articulated within a direct dialogue taking place with each of the other three characters. Martina's phrases are based on chromatic and angular intervals in order to highlight a vain and more complex psychology. Frida's own vanity is mixed with perfidy and wickedness. It is this combination that will eventually lead her to kill Ivana. Frida's phrases are equally angular and similar to those of her daughter Martina, if more varied and contrasting. What is important to add is that the characters each have their own melody that distinguishes them from each other, as an individual leitmotiv that sometimes is obscured by the speed of the tempo. The extroverted characters of Frida and Martina are juxtaposed by the double introversion of Ivana, alive and dead.

AC. With an ensemble of nine instruments, in addition to electronics, *Re di Donne* is a chamber opera in which each character has his double in an instrument. In this way, each protagonist is always present, even when he is not singing. Is it a symbolic game of mirrors?

JP. Yes. During the conception of the opera, it was immediately clear to me that a chamber opera must reflect a kind of music texture that has to be essentially chamber music. This is the reason why I chose instrumental writing that is typically polyphonic, and that provides instrumental alter-egos to the five characters. I say five because the character of Ivana is treated within two different situations, before and after her death. This twofold condition implied two different tools. Your notion of a game of mirrors reflects exactly my idea of creating a musical texture that was as unitary and integrative as possible. In this sense, each character retains its own instrumental counterpart as an idiosyncratic feature of the personal drama.

The instrumental alter-ego of Rocco, the macho and arrogant manipulator of the two girls, is the trombone; Martina's alter-ego is the clarinet; Frida's instrumental counterpart is the cello. The living Ivana is by far the most fragile character of all, and her instrument is the flute. Finally, the vocal part of dead Ivana, singing from a metaphysical dimension, is reinforced by the abstract sounds of the electronics. These sounds derive from breaths and sobs; you can hear sung, spoken and sighed vowels. They also include recordings of water some of which are transformed and blurred with the vocal sounds. This system of voice-instrument assignments ensures that the five characters effectively are continuing a dialogue that is symbolised by the instruments. I did this because I wanted to explore the psychological contrasts of each character from an instrumental perspective, that is detached from the actual vocal dimension. I like to think of chamber music as a perfect platform for dialectics. From this perspective, *Re di Donne* offers a meta-semantic dimension that integrates vocal and instrumental sounds.

AC. Do the narrative developments condition the orchestration or is it always the music that leads the game?

JP. For me, Opera (with capital 'O') must remain primarily a musical work. If not, it is not an opera, but theatre accompanied by music as a decorative background. Certainly, the narrative must have the main role, without which there cannot be a story, but in my conception of Opera, music should not be a form of accompaniment to the story, but an artistic expression having the same importance of the theatrical aspects, a sonic manifestation that cannot be less important than the word. Undoubtedly, during the unfolding of the story, there will be moments where the vocal narration is leading the game, while at other times it is the music that takes everything into her hands. In this dualism of narration and music, visual as opposed to auditory perception, the more you listen, the more you see, and the more you see, the more you listen.

AC. The story you have dealt with is rather tragic, but your writing does not seem to follow

this raw and realistic aspect solely. In some places, it also seems to cloak itself in symbolism and hidden codes…

JP. Very often, my music is full of codes, references and symbols that may be cryptic for those who do not know them. I think this is part of a composer's personal language and style. I think it is fair to say that the raw and tragic writing of *Re di Donne* is often interspersed with lighter moments that aim at highlighting the banality and superficiality of the characters. These moments were necessary for two reasons. First of all, in order to create a balance of musical styles that would avoid the pitfall of using one monolithic language that may have burdened the perception of the tragedy with unnecessary monotony. The second reason is linked to the very idea of theatre that translates to psychological introspection. I wanted to portray the vanity, perfidy and superficiality of the characters from an ironic perspective, aiming particularly at ridiculing the characters of Rocco and Frida. As often happens in Shakespearean theatre, for example, jokes, irony and satire are used as contrasting elements that are needed to highlight the drama. In *Re di Donne*, irony and the ridiculing of Rocco and Frida should emphasise the squalor and cultural rot of the characters. In this sense, all the arias of Rocco and Frida suggest a double meaning: the obvious tragedy implicit in the dialogues and events, and the comic aspect implicit in the way their moral and ethical emptiness is articulated.

AC. And what role does musical language play in the narration of events and the social context in which they occur?

JP. Undoubtedly a very important role. Before writing the work, I listened carefully to the Italian language spoken by young people today. I studied the most characteristic accents and linguistic inflexions of today's youthful language with a particular reference to the Tuscan accent. I say Tuscan because, in my mind, the events narrated take place in a Tuscan city on the river Arno. So I listened to many recordings of casual conversations between groups of young people gathered in Italian canteens and bars and I transcribed many inflexions used in daily speech in musical intervals.

The kind of conversations I focused on were deliberately not educated. It was essential to use a popular language including slang expressions as spoken by young people. This type of transcription took me a long time because it is the kind of work that requires a lot of attention. For example, the first dialogue of the opera begins with Frida asking Martina *"are you getting ready?"* (it. *"Ti stai preparando?"*). In composing the melody for this phrase, I first spoke it with a Tuscan accent and then, based on the characteristics of the accent, I converted it into a vocal phrase based on the musical intervals implicit in the spoken phrase. In this case, there is a slight melodic rise necessary to reinforce the fact that it is a question with an accent in the last syllable *"do"*, as opposed to a Southern accent where the accent would fall on the penultimate syllable, a little elongated, *"ran"*. The melody corresponding to *"are you getting ready?"* is this: F4, G♯4, F♯4, C4, G4, B♭4 (see Fig.2.1). After the initial note F, the following three notes descend to low C (G♯4, F♯4, C4) and then rise from C4 to G4 and B♭4, with the ascending interval of the minor seventh passing through the interval of a fifth (the G). If I had used a Southern accent, just to mention another possibility, I would have lowered the penultimate G to an E♭ and then finished the downward phrase on the same low C. Consequently, the psychological and dramatic effect would have been different.

The same can be said about the rhythms. They too reflect spoken language and must be fast and pressing. These features are prolonged and developed by the instruments of the ensemble. At the same time, the tempi arise from the speed of the spoken conversations of Italian youngsters. These rapid and often quasi-obsessive sequences of dialogues can be heard clearly in the first three acts of the opera, as they convey both a sense of agitation and superficiality that is typical of an informal kind of spoken language. The instrumental texture reinforces these phrases by multiplying them polyphonically among the instruments: this reflects the kind of chamber music I was referring to earlier.

Fig. 2.1: *Re di Donne*, Scena Prima, bb. 24-27.

AC. The world premiere of *Re di Donne* was very successful. The music critic Enrico Girardi of Corriere della Sera defined your ability to deal with the voice as "incisive". What is the importance of the voice in your works?

JP. I think the incisiveness Enrico Girardi is referring to may be related to what I said earlier about the genesis of the vocal phrases. Nowadays, there is an intrinsic incisiveness in the way young people tend to speak to each other, and I have tried to transfer this feature onto the vocal phrases in the most realistic way. The accents and sonic inflexions of the spoken language are simulated by corresponding rhythms, intervals and accents that mould the melodies of each singer. Furthermore, they are repeated, varied and developed in a sophisticated way by the instruments of the ensemble.

My relationship with the voice is a long story that goes back to when I was two years old. Recently I was told that when I was that little, I was insistently trying to sing the songs I heard on the radio and television; we are talking about the sixties. Since my early childhood I have always been naturally attracted to vocal music: from Gregorian Chants, folk, pop to jazz and classical music. Still today, I love humming and singing for fun; it is an emotional expression that is very much part of me; I couldn't live without it. I think that this emotional relationship with singing is very much reflected in the music I write, and I mean in my instrumental music as well. I am reminded of a very evocative account that describes musical creation this way: firstly, composition is born from silence, in a second phase silence becomes song (implying that the composer begins to sing!); in the third and final phase the song is played by the musical instruments. I think there is a grain of truth in this statement, even when paradoxically it's about music that is unsingable. In this case, I would speak of an abstract or metaphorical song, perhaps an imaginary or hidden song. Surely, a very important aspect of the voice in my music is its 'instrumental' nature. I really like to use the voice not only as an expression of emotions, meanings, concepts and thoughts, but also as an acoustic instrument detached from linguistic and semantic connotations. In many orchestral or chamber pieces, I often use the voice as an instrumental sound, that is without a text, merging with the other instruments. The voice has a uniquely expressive and emotional characteristic that in many ways makes it superior to other instruments.

AC. And what relationship is there between the voice and the instruments?

JP. In *Re di Donne* the connection between vocal and instrumental parts remains constant from start to finish. Often, a vocal part is part of the polyphony of the ensemble as, for example, at the beginning of Act One in the dialogue taking place between Frida and Martina and then between Martina and Ivana. On other occasions, the instruments reinforce the vocal parts by playing in unison. But often the unison is broken by an instrumental line dropping by a semitone from the vocal part, thus creating a dissonance in the hybrid melody. This technique is used as a stratagem for obtaining tension in vocal phrases, as if wanting to transfigure the voice itself. In my mind, this is a symbol of the social distortion or diversification implied in the behaviour of the protagonists.

AC. How did the public receive your work?

JP. From what I was able to notice and by what was confirmed to me by members of the audience, at the beginning of the opera many listeners seemed to be nervous. They obviously knew that the topic was linked to real tragedies that have shaken the country for many years. This awareness aroused a sense of curiosity and apprehension. The attention of the audience grew focused with the unfolding of the narrative. What struck me most was that at the end of the event, the female audience strongly endorsed the need to deal with such a disturbing topic publicly. And from what I read later on in the newspapers, the same opinion was unanimously expressed by those critics and journalists who attended the premiere.

AC. What do you feel when one of your works goes on stage and the curtain closes: a sense of emptiness or completion?

JP. If you are referring to musical works in general, this depends on some important factors, for example, whether the relationship between the mental representation and the acoustic experience of the music was successful, or whether the quality of the performance was good or not. If the mental representation corresponded to the acoustic experience and the execution was good, I experience a sense of completeness because I am finally listening to the music I have been working on for a long time *and* in my mind. Although, it is often possible to feel a sense of emptiness, as you say, which derives from the fact that once the music is over, one can feel a sense of finality that can lead to contrasting feelings of any kind. On other occasions, I feel the critical need to refine this or that detail, and the sensation that the work is not yet completely finished.

RE DI DONNE: THE EMBODIED COMPOSER
Paul Alan Barker

We are perhaps inured to the idea of music as disembodied. Recordings and sound systems are inescapable in every aspect of our lives, particularly in cities, even beyond the specific activities such as dance and concerts which they may serve. The pandemic that was current while I wrote this has exaggerated or monopolised this practice and clarified our need for liveness. I was unfortunately unable to be in Italy to see John Palmer's opera live although I have seen a video and the score. This may indicate a contradiction given the title of this essay, but it also enables me to articulate the loss felt through the absence of operatic performance. These performances have played a core role throughout my life and doubtless in conjunction with the pandemic propelled me to imagine *Re di Donne* from this perspective. But even without that context, John Palmer's words clearly articulate and witness the composer's complicity:

"I gradually began to feel each character with my own skin: I felt the horror, the selfishness, the malice they carry inside, but also their moral poverty and inner misery. The music I was writing would flow out of these strong emotional states. I could sense with my own skin the poverty of their human condition and their heart-breaking personal tragedy."[5]

Palmer's experience relates to the visceral nature of the composer's work: instrumentalists and singers perform viscerally, through their bodies, whereas classical composition in the West is often associated with cerebral activity. Of course, the cerebellum is just as much a part of our body as our nervous system, so it is no surprise to discover that composers involve their whole body in composing as he describes. Opera, of all artistic forms, is best equipped to reflect the wholeness of humanity rather than its separation or division. Whether this occurs consciously for composers or not is moot, but this depends upon the facility of the individual's words in relation to musical thought. Musical thought is non-verbal. When music combines with words, as in opera, the narrative which drives character and plot encourages a verbal corollary. Some composers like Palmer are drawn to words. He describes the push and pull that creates dramatic tension on stage between the meanings of the words and the music; here he illustrates how their dominant position fluctuates:

"… in an operatic context, the leading discourse is set by words, so there is a clear supremacy of the word. Having said that, I decided to involve the instruments as musical characters as well and to write melodies that would characterise the behaviour of the characters even before using the words. In many circumstances, I wanted the music to be leading the way. But … I do tend to ascribe meaning to sound in a non-vocal context."

The question of the ascendency of music or words is not necessarily a simple binary choice. The composer describes the subtle, fluctuating and synergetic relationship between sound and meaning, words and music, which his characters have to embody. It is notable that he reflects that certain aspects of the process remain unconscious:

"In Re di Donne, *I wanted to create two discourses for each of the four characters; one being more apparent (the text supported by a specific melody) the other being more hidden (the melody unsupported by the text). Notice that I am hinting at a text that is supporting a melody and not the other, more obvious, way around. By plunging into the mind of each character, I came up*

---

[5] This and all subsequent quotations come from an interview with John Palmer conducted in February 2021.

with musical phrases that would express a particular statement even before I would deal with the word. Of course, many times the word would come first while other times both word and melody would emerge at the same time. But the power of a melodic line would often come first. Perhaps, this is due to the fact that the earliest forms of music I came across were songs, and that I grew up with a sense of semantic expressivity inherent in a tonal melody. This is something I have never explored consciously."

Palmer introduces what he calls *correspondences* to amplify or enlarge the embodiment of the character on stage. The representation of characters onstage is not necessarily limited to one person 'pretending' to be another, and theatre often produces more telling structures: Kurt Weill's *Seven Deadly Sins* was written for two Anna's, one a singer, the other a dancer; from Mozart's *The Magic Flute* to the Wagner Tubas Valhalla motif in *Das Rheingold*, the association of characters with instruments throughout much opera is not unusual. Similar techniques are echoed in *Re di Donne* where correspondence serves as this form of extended embodiment:

"...words will never really manage to explain music. In any case, to me, opera as a genre remains an essentially musical work and, contrary to more established views on the subject, music must come first! So, each character of the story will generate not only the vocalisation of the text but also the instrumental lines that may or may not support the vocal parts. Furthermore, at some point, the melodies will depart from these initial settings and begin to have a life of their own. Ivana (alive) is corresponded by the flute, Ivana (dead) by the electronics. Martina's instrumental alter-ego is the clarinet. Frida's counterpart is the cello, and Rocco's instrument is the trombone. I set such correspondences at the very conception of the opera."

However, in relation to opera, words may help articulate psychological, emotional, physical and intellectual perspectives of musical thought. He extends this to morality and ethics and his introduction of artistic social responsibility is telling:

"I think it was Luciano Berio who once said that at the beginning of his career, he was convinced he could change the world with his music, but then very soon he had to come to terms with the fact that this was impossible. Although I agree that our music may not 'change the world', I am still convinced that if we all learned how to listen to music with a good combination of heart and mental openness, music would make us more sensitive and refined people, thus better persons. By each of us becoming a better person would we not automatically create a better world? I would still hope that by writing an opera on femicide I may contribute to create a stronger awareness of this burning problem. I know this is not pop music and that our audience is small, but this is what I can do best being who I am. What compelled me to make it a sung story is a perhaps naïve desire to want to help eliminate the problem of femicide by inviting people to reflect on those moral, psychological and social conditions that lead to this kind of crime."

The relationship between words and music may be an understandable obsession for any opera composer. That relationship functions on many levels: the written word, the spoken word and the sung word all work in different registers, in different modes, almost as different languages. Written music and performed music either carries or reflects on text with a similar diversity. But for Palmer, there are specific considerations that reflect on the relationship of opera to theatre and novels and suggest the composer's skill necessarily extends in that direction:

"...[when] writing for an opera [one] must take into consideration the theatrical component, the dramaturgy of the opera and the personality of the characters involved in the story. The music has to be linked to their psychology and the behaviour unfolding throughout the narrative. The *opera requires a more specific psychological writing where each melody and harmony that we write must reinforce the meaning of the dialogues that are taking place on stage. Writing for opera is perhaps more similar to writing a novel or directing a theatrical piece. In each case, the word remains the leading force of the artistic discourse."*

The composer echoes Edward Cone's view[6] that the composer's role is not mere word-setting but offers a reading, a view which performers must embody for audiences to share. This is not merely the responsibility of the performer, but the process begins in the body of the composer. McGilchrist refers to Rudolph Laban around the following passage to support this: *"Even if language no longer seems to us in the West to 'body forth' meaning in this way, it may be that at least our understanding of music still shares this inhabiting of the movements of the other - the performer, the singer, perhaps even the composer."*[7]

    Re di Donne 'bodies forth' meaning in the same way that Laban (referred to above by McGilchrist) describes how the *"reception of these drums or tom-tom rhythms is accompanied by a vision of the drummer's movement, and it is this movement, a kind of dance, which is visualised and understood."* [8] Palmer embodies the characters as a natural response to the narrative, as part of the process of composing. He has produced music that potentially affects a listener with a similarly visceral effect. As to whether opera and concert music share this characteristic, he ascribes different approaches:

"...in Re di Donne, I have written phrases and entire passages that I would never write in a concert piece, simply because operatic music must support the meaning of the words within the development of the story. In the arias 'Io non mi tingo' or 'Le donne', for example, the kind of classical tonal language I have used would be senseless and out of place in my concert music. In an opera, therefore, a composer is facing a more restricted scenario of musical choices. This restriction forces you to think in a certain way that is specifically linked to the dialogues of the characters and the content of the story."

If there is a division around embodiment between theatrical and concert music, some would argue against it. For instance, Charles Rosen urges for a perception of his piano performances to bypass the aural directly to the muscular, bringing together both mind and body: *"I think it is time to enlarge our conception of music and recognize that it brings at least two pleasures, one muscular and the other intellectual; neither is directly linked to hearing!"*[9] It is the body that composes music, the body which of course contains heart, brain, soul, muscle and blood, as well as the intellect, so I have never understood why music may be taught only as an intellectual exercise. Palmer points to the source of that particular problem:

"...is this not a general problem stemming from classical music education? Disembodied music at its very best may sound interesting, but not more than that. It is certainly not transcending because it lacks those psychological and physical elements... I still remember how I felt when I began to cohabit in each of the four characters of Re di Donne and I recall the very moment I realised that they were now living in me! This experience has been rather dark and upsetting. I felt like going through their personal hell and squalor, feeling what they were feeling, thinking what they were thinking. There were moments I felt I was going insane. Certainly, the musical

---

[6] Cone (1974)
[7] McGilchrist (2009: 122).
[8] Laban (1960: 86).
[9] Rosen, (2020: 97-8).

dramaturgy springs from this experience at the edge of madness. Ultimately, though, I must say that I reached a point where I felt a strong sense of compassion for each of them."

For Palmer, the composer's role is evidently parallel to that of an actor: without a sense of identity of the character, there can be no understanding or empathy and the 'truth' of any moment cannot be captured. The formation of a theatre actor in the United Kingdom builds safety into the explorations of character that might be otherwise overwhelming. balancing technique with that emotional freedom. He implies that classical music education pulls back from such exploration in order to avoid the emotional risks of embodiment which he described. Embodiment for an actor, a singer, an instrumentalist and a composer may differ, but it would be more interesting to pursue their commonality. If their isolation as disciplines is to be questioned, it might be achieved through education. In opera, there is a potential for a musical-dramatic unity articulated through the synergetic relationship of the disciplines to which Palmer alludes:

"Re di Donne is based on a rather disturbed relationship between man and woman, but also between woman and woman, and you are right to point out that the sociological issue that comes with it is a complex one. The three female characters and the only male character are each associated with an instrument that functions as the alter-ego that is expressed only by instrumental sound. The reason behind this choice is essentially semantic because for me a musical phrase has an inherent meaning that is comparable to a spoken (vocal) phrase."

In this work, there is little evidence of separation of such meanings; words and music are often as indissoluble in sound as in meaning, just as the voices emanate from the bodies but seep beyond them into the instruments and the fabric of the theatre, engulfing the audiences' senses as well. If all opera is a potential embodiment of music, *Re di Donne* makes embodiment both its subject and object. The women's bodies are evidently the centre of Rocco's attention, but are separate from them as people. He is the cause of Ivana's death, but her voice nevertheless returns, disembodied but empowered to deliver the final sung words, where sound and sense combine: the 'Re' of the ironic title becomes entwined with 'misere' (Fig. 2.2).

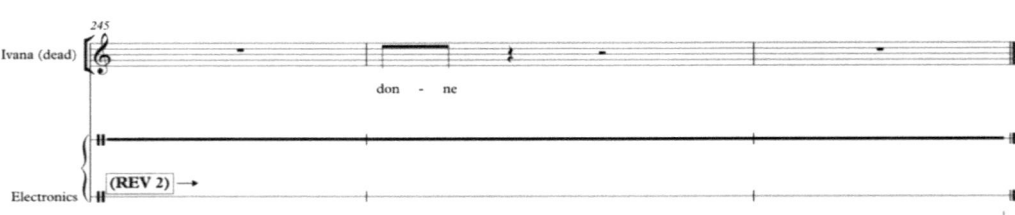

Fig. 2.2 End of *Re di Donne*.

"...*EXPERIENCING THE POWER OF THEATRE MUSICALLY*":
JOHN PALMER'S CHAMBER OPERA *RE DI DONNE*
Egbert Hiller

"*Hell is other people*" (Jean-Paul Sartre, *Huis clos*)

Re di Donne: 'King of Women'. The pithily apt title of John Palmer's chamber opera for four singers, ensemble and electronics is already indicative of the incendiary nature of its subject matter. First performed in September 2019, the British composer's work deals with the topic referred to as 'femicide': the murder of women solely on the grounds of their gender. The history of humanity is riddled with crimes of this sort and, even today, it still occurs to a horrifying extent all over the world, even in supposedly 'civilised' countries, as deeds recently perpetrated in Austria, the United Kingdom and France have underscored.

First performed at the Teatro Carlo Melisso in the Italian city of Spoleto, *Re di Donne* was commissioned (with funding from the Ernst von Siemens Music Institute) for the Teatro Lirico Sperimentale. John Palmer was responsible for the idea and conception of a story based on a brutal atrocity that highlights the issue of gender-related murder. He is also the co-author of the libretto whose plot is based on an actual event that occurred some years ago in Puglia, southern Italy. The libretto vividly depicts the many-layered psychological dimensions of this story, which revolves around the power struggles between two women and one man in a triangular relationship. The lives of the women are destroyed by ruthless sexism and machismo, jealousy and the urge to control, whereas, in the end, the man comes out of the affair unharmed and unprosecuted by the law. In this context, the opera does more than merely assume a critical point of view. While it certainly makes accusations, it expands its scope far beyond individual destinies by using its textual and documentary elements as graphic symbols and sometimes exaggerating them to produce grotesque, expressionistic distortions, without however descending to the level of poster art. Although the characters become archetypes, their behaviour and actions are not determined by immutable divine beings, but by human beings themselves. 'Hell is other people', that key phrase from Jean-Paul Sartre's *Huis clos*, might also be the motto of *Re di Donne*.

The opera is conceived as a one-acter and divided into five scenes that closely correspond to one another in terms of time and space. The plot unfolds in a 'room' (not further specified) as its primary location, with a beach, bar and prison as subsidiary locations. While the course of events preserves the chronology of the story, Palmer has incorporated an additional, metaphysical level into this 'realistic' or 'physical' level by contrasting the 'living' characters Ivana, Martina, Rocco and Frida with the 'dead' Ivana, who reflects retrospectively on the events leading to her death. She appears at three points in the opera without, however, seriously interrupting its narrative flow: rather, both points of view are inextricably intertwined with one another. The dead Ivana represents a kind of external viewpoint, as though she has been momentarily elevated to a higher state of perception and awareness. In the beginning, explains Palmer, "*the dead Ivana questions her behaviour during her lifetime and regrets her weak position in the relationship with Rocco*".[10] She reappears to observe herself during a quarrel between Martina and Rocco right at the end of the opera; according to Palmer, "*the seamless integration of the metaphysical sequences into the story remains crucially important because this is my way of inviting the audience to reflect on this crime from a critical psychological perspective*".

Moreover, there is no contradiction between this psychological perspective and the

---

[10] This and all subsequent quotations come from an interview with John Palmer conducted by the composer Violeta Dinescu.

build-up of tension. On the contrary: our experience and understanding of these events, circumstances and human depths are made even more acute by them, casting a spell over us all right from the start. As early as the Prologue, it becomes unmistakeably evident that *Re di Donne* is not presenting some kind of abstract sign language, but rather placing flesh-and-blood people under the microscope of artistic observation, with both emotional emphasis and analytic perceptiveness at the same time. *"Tension"*, the composer observes,

"is an element I deliberately wanted to use both in the dramaturgy of the events and in the music. Tension is drama. The Ancient Greek δρᾶμα (drama) corresponds to what we call 'action' in English. That means that the action itself, the plot, is already 'dramatic'. In the case of Re di Donne, *there is a precise sequence of actions based on the true story of a woman's murder. The subject is already highly dramatic and tragic per se."*

To achieve and sustain internal unity and rigorous connections between vocal and instrumental parts, Palmer derived the instrumental melodies from those of the singers.

"Each vocal part correlates with an instrument, which plays the same melody, varies it and develops it independently. This results in an interactive network of motifs and melodies that become intricately interwoven with one another over the course of the opera. The technique encompasses all types of musical texture from monody to polyphony by way of heterophony, creating an intensity that abolishes any dividing line between theatre and music. There is no discrepancy between words and notes, and every musical phrase is reflected in what is sung and what is played to an equal extent."

Rocco, the sole male character, is assigned a trombone as his 'alter ego', which symbolises the characteristics of a macho patriarch in abstract instrumental terms. The trombone and Rocco portray the same kind of human behaviour, with a reciprocal relationship underlying the interplay between the two sound worlds, human and instrumental: a human can become an 'instrument' and an instrument, 'human'. However, the trombone does not enjoy sole rights of representation with regard to Rocco, since other instruments can also appropriate his 'voice', and vice versa. This becomes clearly apparent, for example, in the case of the trombone and double bass: despite their sharp contrasts of melody and rhythm, both can still fuse with Rocco's voice.

This procedure is not an isolated example: similarities of the contour between voices are a constant in *Re di Donne*, though, at the same time, such analogies and relationships may equally quickly be dissolved again in the interests of heightening dramatic tension. At times, even the handling of polyphonic structures in the voices and instruments exudes a 'free jazz feeling', something with which Palmer feels a particular musical affinity. The term 'free' in the sense of 'ad libitum' might also be applied to Rocco's repeated outbursts of dirty laughter (e.g. Scene 1, bars 178–184, Fig. 2.3, or Scene 2, bar 64) which, while clearly integrated into the musical polyphony to a certain extent, at the same time, break free from it, underpins the theatrical element. According to Palmer, from a theatrical viewpoint, the laughter emphasises *"Rocco's arrogance and conceitedness. I tend to identify mentally with the characters in my opera in order to better understand them psychologically and dramatically, and my encounter with this appalling, manipulative character was a highly unsettling experience for me."*

Not the least of the reasons for the 'unsettling' aspect of Palmer's 'encounter' with Rocco's persona was the fact that, although Rocco had been adapted for the music theatre, in essence, the drama involved a person who actually existed. Palmer was similarly motivated by the real story when it came to the configuration of the vocal parts in *Re di Donne*. *"I needed two young sopranos for the two young cousins Ivana and Martina, an alto voice for Martina's mother*

Frida, and a low voice for Rocco. Since Rocco is still a young man, I decided on a baritone rather than a bass." By contrast, the choice of instruments was influenced by the commission's specifications and the resulting pragmatic considerations.

"I only had a very limited number of instruments to play with (eight) and therefore, knew I would have to make compromises. I identified Ivana with the flute, her cousin Martina with the clarinet, Frida with the cello and Rocco with the trombone. These four instruments, therefore, became essential, and I determined the remainder according to the functional requirements of the music. To obtain a wide harmonic spectrum, a piano was indispensable; I needed percussion to articulate rhythm and pulse in the dramatic development; and the high and low string sounds of the violin and double bass complemented the cello. In addition, there were the electronics, which are just as important as the conventional instruments."

For the composer, electronic sounds are a standalone instrument that can be more versatile than an orchestra. In *Re di Donne,* they enrich and influence the sound world to a crucial extent, without merely decorating it. Palmer explored the possibilities of electronic music in depth, in particular the relationship between its timbres and acoustically produced sounds. In *Re di Donne,* he used three different electronic music techniques. First, he engaged with musique concrète to provide a 'cinema for the ears'. Recordings of concrete sounds, processed and transformed, support the opera's narrative and dramatic aspects. Secondly, Palmer manipulated and transformed the vocal and instrumental parts by electronic means in order to bring out the dramatic elements of specific situations and heighten their expressive power. And thirdly, he used the electronics to modify and expand the acoustic space so that it could also become a screen on which to project the dead Ivana's recollections as part of a dialectic between 'near' and 'far'.

For John Palmer, opera is a special genre because of its interplay of diverse (and sometimes also heterogenous) forces and demands a specific kind of musical thought that must differ from work to work. He regards every musical work and every combination of forces as a new challenge that is directly connected with moments or phases of his life, which might leave their traces in the relevant work as in a mirror. Here, Palmer also makes use of his abilities as a practising musician who is proficient on several instruments and also appears as a performer. *"The distinction between composers and instrumentalists or performers in so-called classical music is a relatively recent phenomenon,"* says Palmer.

"This distinction does not exist in jazz and popular music. For me personally, it would be unthinkable because both areas fertilise each other in my work. I regard the tendency towards specialisation in classical music as something of an error. On the other hand, in the end, it is, of course, the quality of the music that counts."

In addition, John Palmer is also a musicologist, which he likewise regards as a useful expansion of his available creative possibilities, because *"the richer a composer's life is, the richer their music will be. In this way, I can experience music on several levels, and that gives me a better understanding and deeper interior view of my work."* Above all, it is his inner sensibility that plays a crucial role in his compositional work. Considerations of style, let alone national styles, or cultural influences dependent on geographical origin, are alien to his way of thinking. Nevertheless, his opera *Re di Donne* is an impressive demonstration that external events can set his inner artistic world ablaze, and with explosive results. By condemning violence against women, the work thereby transcends the individual concrete case and the use of physical force and indirectly makes a stand against the murder threats and tirades of hate and contempt that are now omnipresent in social media in particular, and which, coupled with (threats of) sexual violence, are in many cases directed particularly against women.

Topical as its subject matter is, John Palmer's music eschews any kind of pathos or demonstrative gestures. *Re di Donne* is modern music theatre in the best sense of the word, and Palmer means 'music theatre' literally because he links the opera *"above all with the revelation that comes from experiencing the power of theatre musically"*. In *Re di Donne*, therefore, traditional and avant-garde effortlessly interpenetrate one another: jazz and folk music elements are equally at home as strident cascades and signals for the wind instruments. The sonorities are tightly bound up with the characters, but, at the same time, open up metalevels, islands of abstraction and 'spaces between', that are illuminated with searing intensity and vast expressive range.

Fig. 2.3 *Re di Donne*, Scena Prima, bb. 178-184.

38

CHAPTER THREE

SPIRIT AND POETRY

BREATHING SPIRIT
Suzanne Josek

SJ. In your work, I find many references to breath. Could you tell me about the role of breathing as an inspiration for your work? Which one would you choose: inbreath, outbreath, or the pause in-between? And why?

JP. I love the meaning of words and their etymology: in Latin the verb 'respirare' (to breathe) derives from 're-spirare', and 'spirare' means 'to blow'. The verb 'spirare' derives from 'spiritus' (spirit). In the oldest written documents of the planet, breath is portrayed as an invisible force that symbolises the origin of life. It is a perfect metaphor for the divine. Breath is also the first manifestation of life on the physical plane, the motor of earthly life. It is the succession of inhaling (inspiring) and exhaling (expiring) that allows us to live. Thus, the act and sound of breathing symbolise life in its most physical and spiritual significance. In addition, the notion of breathing suggests *inspiration* (in-spiration) to accomplish something creative. I have written several musical works related to the physical and emotional power of breathing, as well as its metaphysical significance. I attach a very sacred meaning to both the notion and the sound, the physicality of which suggests an implied sensuality that is equally sacred. By inhaling, I tend to listen, open up and receive; by exhaling, I tend to create, articulate and celebrate. The pause in between suggests a very mysterious and elusive moment: a condition of life and non-life occurring at the same time.

SJ. Many titles of your pieces refer to specific spiritual concepts. I am thinking of the *Trans* cycle, *I am, Renge-Kyo, Transfiguration, Inwards*, amongst others. Which spiritual notions are the most important to you?

JP. The most important notions are self-realisation (including self-empowerment), transcendence, life after life, emptiness, non-duality and unity. Clearly, they are all interrelated. The first three (self-realisation, transcendence and life after life) imply a process of motion, the desire to achieve a goal in and beyond earthly life. The other group (emptiness, non-duality, unity) is related to a contemplative state of mind (emptiness) and the awareness of our true nature (unity in non-duality): motion and stasis embrace action and stillness.

SJ. The world around us is constantly talking, commenting and judging; it is a busy world in which everything sounds loud and seems to be so reduced. What is the role of silence, shadow and subtlety in your work?

JP. Silence, together with love, is the greatest victim of contemporary society. It is one of the most powerful and sacred experiences of life: the ultimate spiritual experience. Silence is the best friend of the soul because, in silence, we remember who we are. In silence, we listen unconditionally to our inner voice. This is why silence and listening are sisters. I would go even further and claim that listening is the most generous form of silence because when we listen, we open up our souls to the world around us. My experience of silence within a musical context is illuminated by the Japanese notion of 'ma', the perception of an energy that is alive between two sounds, in other words, the perception of silence as a musical force. What I mean is that a rest between sounds is heard as an important facet of the sound itself; one is complementary to the other. Therefore, the presence and absence of sound are two sides of the same musical reality. With this in mind, the role of silence in my work is a crucial component of the musical discourse. This may sound contradictory at first, but it is an important aspect of the perception of the Yin and Yang principle in music.

The most pronounced use of silence in my works occurs in *Satori*, for solo harpsichord, where the fugitive resonance of the short harpsichord phrases is consistently swallowed by silence, as if silence was the leading motif of the music and the short phrases of the harpsichord a decorative contour. The same musical logic can be heard in *Without*, for solo violin, where the passionate nature of the short violin phrases reinforces this contrast in a dramatic manner. Listening to *Satori* and *Without* from this perspective can change the perception of the music quite dramatically. *Still*, for bass flute, viola and guitar, is another piece where I explore silence in a similar fashion, albeit within the dense and colourful texture of the three instruments and a sophisticated use of resonance. *Alba* (for violin, viola, cello and piano) plays with silence in terms of fluctuating performative experience: each sound produced by the four instruments comes out of stillness in order to re-enter it through subtle sonic transformations taking place on the border of the imperceptible.

I use the notion of 'shadow' (or 'ghost') quite literally in musical terms, primarily, but not only, through the use of electronics as a sonic contour, a related silhouette, of the acoustic instrument. In *Woanders*, for piano and electronics, the narrative of the piece consists of the interplay of several pianos intertwined in such a way that at times it is impossible to distinguish the piano on stage from the shadow-pianos of the electronic part. A similar situation can be heard in *Beyond the Bridge*, where the two dislocated celli in the electronic parts comment on the main cello on stage, this time from different spatial and temporal dimensions. However, in *Woanders,* this technique is more interwoven and perhaps refined. In *Towards the Soul,* for trombone quartet, 'shadow notes' (extremely soft trombone sounds) constitute the only sonic material of the piece; the result being a subtle aura of sound that invites the listener to enter a range of delicate notes perceived on the edge of silence. *Of Shadows Unveiled*, for flute, bass clarinet and piano, explores a similar texture enriched by the contrasting gestures of the wind instruments contradicted by the harmonic responsibility of the piano. Generally, the role of shadow sounds is to supply an alter ego to the instrumental phrases in order to create sonic ambiguity and a sense of space through dynamic separation, distinction and sometimes contrast. Subtlety is very important as an expedient of ambivalence, uncertainty, and a suggestion of the ineffable.

SJ. What does it mean to you to be on a spiritual path both as a human being and composer, especially in our time?

JP. Being on a spiritual path means to become aware of the sacredness of life and take responsibility for my existence on this planet. It means to practise the art of self-transformation and self-empowerment in order to achieve the ultimate realisation of my true nature, as suggested, for instance, by Buddhism. A mystical path does not mean that you are always nice and smiling and that all problems in your life have suddenly gone. Such a journey implies hard work on the ego. It is a *real* experience that requires constant vigilance and full awareness of what I am doing, how I am doing it, and what I am thinking of. As a composer, I am searching for a connection with my sacredness by including, rather than excluding, what are usually perceived as the dark sides of one's personality while celebrating the journey to light as honestly as possible. Sometimes, I strongly feel that the notes I write reflect not only a search, but also a condition of 'knowing', and that composition reflects a process of self-knowledge; a form of prayer, evocation and celebration. You mention our time: I think we live in a very confusing and contradictory historical phase. I do see major plagues such as superficiality, materialism, egotism, separation and a profound misunderstanding of love spreading everywhere at an alarming rate. I also see the dictates of commercial interests emphasising a consensus of 'normality' in the average person that obfuscates a sense of ethical direction, especially in the younger generations. Comfort and selfishness seem to have become the mindset of the majority, yet I still believe in the positive resources of humanity. I do think that the intelligence of the human race is full of creativity and positive thinking. This makes me feel confident about the future. It is indeed possible to come out of this challenging historical phase if ethical values are nurtured by each of us on a daily basis.

SJ. How would you describe your spiritual path? When did your quest begin? Has it been an evolution in stages or did it unfold seamlessly? Have there been specific encounters and experiences (people, art, nature) that have triggered your journey?

JP. I may describe my journey as a desire to explore my connection with the 'source' (where I come from) and to live and work according to this desire. Like everybody else, I am the result of key choices I have made on the threshold of situations that I may have forgotten. I have had an inclination for the mystical since I was a child. I have always searched for meaning in my life: a meaning that would give me a sense of what I am doing and feeling. Due to the conditioning of external forces such as the negative thinking of parents, family, friends and society at large, as soon as we are born, we begin to depart from our spiritual nature and enter the world of negative thinking and suffering.

There have been many specific situations, events and encounters that have inspired my journey. As a young boy, I felt I had to take my destiny into my own hands. I remember many instances when I would clearly observe the moral mediocrity of contemporary society and the superficiality of materialism, and I would ask myself where I could find a more interesting meaning to my life. My heart knew where I needed to be. This was also a time where I was reading a lot about history, archaeology, philosophy, literature, mysticism and parapsychology. I wanted to understand where the human race comes from and where we are supposed to go after death. I searched for spiritual intimacy on the threshold of joy and pain, life and death, the visible and the invisible, the tangible and the intellectual. I have followed my instinct in many painful situations and difficult decisions I have had to make.

Somehow, I have always felt that intuition, unspoiled by external conditioning, knows more than the intellect and that it is much smarter than reason. I think my conscious quest began more or less at the age of 12 when I first realised that my needs were of a different nature than those of my schoolmates. This is a time when I was very much inspired by the life of Jesus Christ, John the Baptist and Francis of Assisi. I embraced this kind of courageous vision with great fervour and passion. By the age of 15, I remember feeling a very strong vocation for priesthood. I was determined to make this choice at 18. I should mention that this was in the 1970s, a time marked by a strong generational urge to want to improve the world. In those days, spiritual values went hand in hand with social concerns and the desire to live in a more just world implied active social and charitable work. I loved this kind of active spirituality. During this time, I encountered many wonderful people with whom I would share spiritual practices and social work. Music also played an important role. The songs we sang added a touch of encouragement and poetry to our ideals and reinforced a sense of community. My first songs were all born in an environment where love was the ideal that we shared. My first conscious experience of love took place within a Christian environment that strongly inspired my human and spiritual needs. If from the Christian tradition I have learnt the meaning of love, it is from

Eastern philosophies and practices, especially Yoga, Taoism and Buddhism, that I have learnt the importance of silence, the power of meditation and the art of taking responsibility for my own destiny. In nature, it is the sea that conveys the sensation of the eternal while feeding me with inspiration and the power of imagination.

SJ. In an earlier interview, you said, *"I have always felt that music should not be detached from [...] a spiritual search."* **Where do you see the link between spirituality and art in general and in music in particular? What is the role of spirituality in music? And what is music then?**

JP. In my experience, music can access the condition of knowing. I don't mean that the composer speaks from a position of knowledge, although this may be possible (I am reminded of the life of Japanese artists in traditional Japan). What I am saying is that the composer is *potentially* writing in a condition of knowing, which is different. There is a clear distinction between the two states. I don't think that composers have to have or show any special knowledge, but I think the inherent potentiality of reflection and individuation implied in the creative act can enable them to access a condition of knowing. This reminds me of what some people call the 'redemptive' significance of art. I see the link between music and the spirit first of all in the very fact that the invisible becomes audible. Think of a fantasy game where the Invisible is seeking to express itself through the creative action of the artist. By 'Invisible', I mean not only a thought, an idea or a feeling, but also the voice of the subconscious: a jungle of 'subterranean' interconnections, associations and impulses. Music is certainly a reflection of the human condition, and, in the context I have just delineated, can become a powerful channel leading to the awareness of a pristine condition of the spirit. Our intelligence may often be limited by logic, but the power of art is unlimited and visionary.

SJ. What is a spiritual work? Are there non-spiritual works? Or is all music spiritual?

JP. I don't think that all music has a spiritual connotation. I also don't think that in order to sound 'spiritual', music must relate to titles or words that may have a spiritual meaning. It is the musical syntax itself (the choice of timbres, harmonies, melodies, in other words, the *texture*) that can evoke a sense of the spiritual. It is the nature of the sonic content and the power of the idiom and style of the music that may or may not trigger a spiritual, emotional, or, by opposition, even a mundane sensation to the listener. I think there is still a big misunderstanding about this point in the musical tradition of the West. Asian traditions have understood this in an exemplary manner.

SJ. How do you actually include the metaphysical in your music? How do you translate the spiritual into your music? How does the metaphysical relate to the physical or to the body?

JP. I never *think* of including the metaphysical in the music I write; it is not about making a rational choice. When I compose, everything flows in the most natural way. I don't try to deliberately translate what could be a 'spiritual' quality into the music. The piece *Spirits* is the most striking example of what I am saying because it is music that I heard in my dreams; therefore music I have not composed, at least not consciously. When I write music, I open my mind to my inner voice: I listen to a surge within me, an instinct that tells me what to write, where, when and how to write it. It is not only an intellectual process, but a most natural impulse. The physical and the metaphysical are interlocked. Mind, spirit and body are interconnected, and the spiritual can be experienced as sensual.

SJ. You often mention your connection to Buddhist thought, and some works of yours refer to it in a more explicit way. Buddha's first statement is about the evidence and acceptance of suffering (duḥkha). How do you refer to suffering (fear, despair, death) in your artistic work?

JP. Our experience on this planet is determined by how we choose to perceive reality. To me, pain and suffering are the doorways leading to profound states of consciousness. Tragedy itself may be nature's great purifier, as it can burn away the arrogance and vanity of the ego and take us back to the essential nature of the soul. Psychologically, pain is the difference between *what is* and what we *want it to be*. Experiencing painful situations is an inevitable part of life. I always try to learn from them rather than choose to distract myself with something superficial that does not lead anywhere. In a world full of apathy, selfishness and disconnection from our humanity, any form of suffering is an opportunity to advance ourselves. As with any other form of adversity, when pain and suffering occur, I take this circumstance as a challenge to my ego; what I mean is that I see an opportunity to better understand my human nature and hopefully become a better human being, for myself and in relation to the others. I know that beyond any form of suffering and adversity, there is a bridge leading to self-knowledge, that is, a profound perception of human values: a bridge leading to the conquest of new mental horizons. It was the experience of suffering that led Buddha, Christ, Gandhi and Mandela to do what they did. If you read the biographies of the most inspiring people in the world, you can clearly see that these people had one thing in common: intense suffering. It is because of suffering that they managed to surpass themselves and create great things. I believe that everything we experience happens for a reason. Every end will inevitably mark a new beginning, and the darkest time of night comes immediately before dawn.

My artistic work is biographical and, consequently, emotional. I cannot detach music from real life, and vice versa. There are many references to suffering (despair, death) in my music; I have no fear whatsoever of dealing with such topics. On the contrary, I often feel a moral obligation to do so. In my world, art should not be detached from life. In my music, as in my literary writings, I refer to suffering as a condition of reflection, confrontation, growth and purification. Fear is not a topic I am particularly interested in. Despair and death are the counterpart of love and life. For example, in *Epitaph*, for cello and electronics, the love for a friend who has committed suicide must come to terms with the feelings of pain and despair in the absence of hope. The dark side of love holds the flux of the musical discourse in a terminal attempt to defy the blind force of pain through agony and to flow to the final acceptance of death, symbolised by three final 'pizzicati' of the cello on the lowest note C.

In a recent work entitled *I, Medusa*, for mezzo-soprano, double bass and electronics, Medusa's fate is portrayed in two opposing conditions: the young priestess exalting her love for Athena and the monster trapped in rage and despair. Love is opposed by hate as a result of despair. By juxtaposing these two contrasting aspects, I wanted to explore some archetypal forms of love and pain in relation to a moral authority (Athena) beyond their dualistic appearance. The suffering of the Medusa monster explores the elemental assumption of hate as a negation of love and the inability of the monster to protect her natural state of love symbolised by the young priestess before she is raped by Poseidon. I wish to delve into the dualistic framework (the dilemma) that segregates human beings from their natural condition through socially accepted forms of deceit, corruption and punishment at the expense of the weakest.

Death is indeed a recurrent theme. The *First String Quartet* is a meditation upon a feeling of earthly love in conjunction with the loss of a very close person. Here, the experience of death is explored as a subtle game of painful separation and the perspective of eternal love. This is why the subtitle of the quartet is *Jeu de Mort* ('Game of Death' or 'Death Play'). In *Transient* (for soprano, prepared piano and electronics), inspired by a poem I wrote in 1988 in memory of a friend who passed away, death is questioned as a *"transient breath of whispered existence"* and a living state of reunion with the primordial essence of life: *"for now, I remember the original name"*. The text is whispered, spoken, sung, and transfigured by the electronics, while breathing is proposed as a metaphor for life after life.

SJ. Many people read religious or spiritual texts and tend to deal with philosophy in an intellectual or academic way, but only a few people practise spirituality. Is there a spiritual practice that you observe regularly? If so, what is the meaning of spiritual practice for your artistic work?

JP. My understanding of a spiritual tradition is that in order to be so, it has to be connected to real-life experience rather than a mental construct to be discussed intellectually. Of course, we have an intellect and we should use it as much as possible in order to understand all aspects of life, but a truly spiritual path is something that needs to be practised. To *know* the path is not to *walk* the path. Up to the age of 18, my understanding of the spiritual was moulded by the Christian tradition. The discovery of Yoga and Hinduism in 1978 opened up a new door to Eastern traditions, especially Taoism and Buddhism. I have followed several disciplines throughout my life, although I must say that regularity has always been an issue for the irregular schedule of a musician. In recent years, I tend to identify myself with an all-encompassing practice that includes meditation, study and, more importantly, living in the awareness of the 'now' throughout the day. I find that self-transformation or self-empowerment practices, informed by modern science, and quantum physics in particular, have injected an enormous vitality and freshness into my life as they offer a modern understanding of spiritual science that is unifying and transcending all the traditions of the past rather powerfully. When I write music, I enter a state of awareness that I believe is spiritual by nature. Mystical realism is very connected to my music because my artistic work is a very important part of my life. Everything I do in my private life is reflected in my work, and the music I write is a reflection of my personal evolution. For me, the act of composing is essentially a spiritual practice. Listening to my inner voice implies a still environment and a willingness to live and work in solitude. Thomas Edison once said that the best thinking is always done in solitude, and I suspect that when he said that, he may have well implied a sense of spiritual consciousness in the work we undertake.

SJ. The well-known mystic Rumi said that we should keep *"breaking our hearts until they open"*. How does love relate to your music? What is love for you personally?

JP. Love is a frequency rather than a feeling: an ocean of high positive energy. When I swim in this ocean, I am 'in love'. When I love and allow myself to be loved, I dwell in a timeless state of happiness where pain is replaced by joy, scarcity changes into abundance, anxiety turns into peace, and separation becomes union. Love is the light of life, a unique condition that makes me see each thing in its original beauty. There are several references to the different aspects of love in my musical works. The trombone and ensemble piece *You*, for example, stems from a collection of texts of mine entitled *Fragments of You*, where I give voice to a search for the divine. In this context, the 'you' evokes a Christian idea of God as a counterpart of my 'I', the dialectics of the piece being based on searching for a condition of unity between 'you' (my divinity represented by an external deity) and 'I' (my earthly nature). The solo trombone symbolises the 'I'. The search for the 'you' evolves through all sorts of challenges symbolised by the different textures of the music. A similar dichotomy takes place in *There*, for string orchestra and string quartet, where the string quartet's passionate gestures are trying to establish points of contact with a larger, immanent, dimension (the string orchestra). The 'you-I' dichotomy of *You* is proposed anew in the 'here-there' dimension of *There*.

My *Piano Concerto* was inspired by a text I wrote about earthly love, and pain when dealing with grief and agony. The choir gives voice to fragmented speech and shouts that emphasise, by contrast, the condensed microtonal phrases of the solo piano echoed by the orchestral piano in a search for love that seems to end nowhere. The piano piece *Se Potessi* is based on a poem by Leopoldo Verona, where love for the divine is expressed in a few verses of stirring lyrical beauty. The form of the music is based on the same metres of the original verses. Therefore, the piano phrases follow the same metric declamation of the poem. *A-mors,* for piano, is based on the melodic and harmonic material I used in a love song I wrote in 2011. In Latin, 'A-mors' means 'no-death' and I refer to the idea of love as an emotional force that is essentially eternal. There are other, subtler, and less explicit ways in which the notion and experience of love relate to my music, usually within a larger scenario of content, including emotional or social topics.

YEARNING FOR THE UNSPEAKABLE
Charlotte Leport

CL. *"Yearning for the unspeakable"* is a line from your poem *Fragments of You*. All art could be seen as the translation from the ineffable into a work that can be perceived by our senses and ultimately by our soul. In your works *Waka* and *Still*, you 'translate' the Japanese literary forms of haiku and waka into music. These poetic forms are strict, and your scores are extremely precise and detailed, resembling celestial maps and webbed structures of the finest filigree. The experience of hearing the translation of these forms is paradoxically one of trance and suspended space. What is the relationship for you between form and space, and between structure and freedom?

JP. In the past 35 years, I have endeavoured to acquire a sense of unity in composition resulting from both freedom and discipline, inspiration and rigour. Both aspects are very important to me as being integrative activities of the same ethos. I am using the word 'ethos' in its Greek etymology, as a moral sense, describing the creative power of music and the ability to give shape to thoughts, percepts, emotions and behaviour. My experience has been that there is an element of transcendence in structure and an element of order in intuition. I strive to give voice to a kind of music that may convey both aspects. The music of J.S. Bach is the most remarkable example of what I am trying to say. When I listen to Bach's music, I experience a unique sensation of wholeness and spiritual fulfilment that transcends the structure of pitch relationships. When I analyse the music, I am always stunned by the mathematical precision of the pitch structures. I have always found this fascinating and inspiring! Clear structures are necessary in order to create a discernible platform for the discourse to articulate itself. I should add that, very often in my work, these structures spring from intuition. Logical thinking provides clarity to the form, which is necessary of course, but it can limit our intuitive intelligence. Throughout the years, I have come to realise that instinct knows more than the intellect, that intuition is wiser than my logical mind because it is visionary and limitless.

CL. You have written *"I see no distinction between the abyss of despair and the eternal"*. This awareness seems to be deeply woven into creative consciousness. We are only in the sixth chapter of Genesis when we read *"and it grieved God in his heart that he had created man"*, followed by the purification of the flood. King David in his psalms sings from the abyss *"from the depths I cry unto thee"* and the first Greek Dramatists lead us through a trial by fire in their tragedies. The root of the word 'tragedy' is 'goat song', reminiscent of sacrifices and of the ineluctable forces of nature. Sacrifice is also an offering up of something of

ourselves. Do you perceive suffering and sacrifice as an essential 'rite de passage' in the creative process and if so, how is music a vehicle for its expression?

JP. You mention grief, tragedy, sacrifice and suffering. To these, I would like to add the notion of adversity. Generally speaking, I think that we don't need to suffer in order to be creative. Surely, I can be creative out of joy, love and excitement, so I don't think that suffering and sacrifice are essential for the creative process to take place. Also, our experience on this planet is determined by how we choose to perceive reality. This is a crucial point for understanding how we in the West have been brought up to perceive the concept of grief and suffering in dualistic terms. What if we changed some of these parameters and state, for example, that grief is the difference between *what is* and what we *want it to be*? That sacrifice is a crime towards the sacredness of life? That suffering takes us into a condition of mental darkness because we are allowing a negative force to retain its power over us?

I am not trying to sound like an iconoclast for the sake of it, but I am questioning up to which point alternative views could have an enlightening effect on the way we think, feel and work. My phrase *"no distinction between the abyss of despair and the eternal"* suggests that the experience of grief may imply a doorway into a deeper awareness of who we are, that tragedy may be nature's purifier as it burns away the arrogance of the ego, and may indeed lead us to a state of original authenticity. I know from my own experience that painful situations can be triggers for a deeper understanding of my humanity. Suffering may have an enormous influence on the creative process, too. But this doesn't mean that we must suffer in order to be wonderful people or write good music! Composing is a creative activity that offers a process of individuation (in the Jungian sense of the word) to those composers who are willing to confront themselves with their 'vulnerability'.

From the point of view of a listener, music brings us into contact with archetypal information that transcends the concerns of the individual by revealing a collective awareness. The 'concern' voiced by the composer is not only the message of an individual, but the concern of an entire community. This is what I mean when I say that music binds human beings together, that music *transcends*, that music has a healing power on us. We can experience this power very strongly, especially during critical times such as wars or personal and social crises because suffering makes us more sensitive to our existence. Many composers in the past, from Monteverdi and Beethoven to Wagner and Harvey have emphasised this point in one way or another. Do you remember the story of the Sarajevo cellist Vedran Smailović? During the siege of the city in 1992, he played Albinoni's *Adagio in G Minor* in destroyed buildings and under the threat of Serbian bombs and shooting soldiers. The impact of music on devastated survivors was enormous. I have read the most touching testimonies on a story that has helped so many people in those moments of absolute despair. Like Wagner, Jung insisted that art gives voice not much to the concerns of an individual or a specific situation, but it conveys eternal ideals that are *beyond* the individual and a specific situation. Adversities like grief, tragedy, sacrifice and suffering pose a challenge to become better human beings by facing the obstacles that are in front of us and within us. In a world full of apathy and selfishness, an obstacle may turn out to be a blessing and a unique opportunity to advance ourselves. Beyond any kind of adversity, I see a bridge leading to a clearer and nobler dimension: the conquest of new mental horizons! How can music be a vehicle for its expression? The vehicle is *not* sound itself, but the consciousness of the composer.

CL. Heinrich Heine wrote, *"Where words leave off music begins"*. The word and its poetic potential are clearly a motivating force for you. The scores of *Still* and *Waka* are based on the Japanese poetic forms of waka and haiku, yet we do not hear the words as much as their rhythms, syllabic structures and, importantly, breathing emphasised in your scores.

The link between breathing and the soul is well established. In moments of divine visitation, biblically, voices, rather than words, were perceived. Must words leave off their conventional context in order for the voice of music to be heard?

JP. Perhaps. Poetry is a dimension in which language is most beautifully articulated. Poetry speaks on the threshold of silence. It is born from silence; it is articulated on the edge of silence: it returns to silence. This is one reason why I love it, particularly very short literary forms such as wakas (tankas) and haikus, or any other form based on paucity. I find it very inspiring that in the Celtic world, as well as traditional Japan, a poet lived in contact with nature. To be a poet was a vocation similar to that of a monk. Poets were symbols of the power of nature and were given a special status by the local community: they were granted access to the inexplicable, the mysterious. I have always loved that image and asked myself: could, or should, composers be the same?

The sacredness of poetry is very precious to me; I myself have been writing poems since I was a child. The more abstract the word, the more elusive is the message; the more elusive the message, the stronger the evocation of ephemeral images and visions. Words and music can go hand-in-hand. At the end of the Renaissance Vincenzo Galilei, the father of Galileo, predicted the development of a new understanding of words and music based on new premises: the first Monteverdi opera was to follow soon. Words and music became strongly allied in a joint pursuit to explore the psyche in a way that would have been unthinkable until then. A new musical era began and the new marriage has ever since produced one of the most sublime musical genres, the opera. But the 'voice' of music, as you put it, goes deeper, because music is a form of poetry *in* sound, poetry *of* sound, the *sound* of poetry.

By its nature, the realm of sound is more abstract than the realm of a word. The abstractedness of sound, detached from verbal symbolism, conveys waves of sensations and perceptions that affect the world of the subconscious without deviation. By words leaving the scene, the voice of music is heard in its most pristine nature because sound is detached from the semantics of language and will refer more intensely to things other than itself. Therefore, music without words is more intimate and enigmatic than music accompanied by words. Instrumental music doesn't suggest the representational realm of an external world but offers the exposed expression of the artist's mind and soul. It articulates an unfathomable space urged unequivocally by the unspoken language of imagination, intuition and introspection: a space where visions, ideals and dreams are articulated by untouched knowledge.

By choosing poetic forms for my instrumental music, I am intentionally exploring the poetic flavour of music. Jonathan Harvey once described my work *Waka* as 'mysterious'. What I think he meant was exactly this sense of elusiveness resulting from the combination of a structure rigorously grounded in metrical verses and the gestalt of the instrumental phrases, as if they were words. The declamatory nature of 'unsung words' can indeed be perceived as a form of sutble eloquence evoking a sense of concealed recitation.

CL. Roger Scruton wrote, *"When we hear music, we do not hear sound only, we hear something in the sound, something that moves with a force of its own."* [11] As a composer, is this mysterious force something that possesses you before you compose, motivating you to transmit its essence, or is it something that manifests itself after the work is completed?

JP. Both, and in two different ways. During the process of composition, this force is inside me, in my mind, spirit and body. I am 'pregnant'; and a pregnancy is painful and often exhausting. This 'otherness' that is seizing me is unfamiliar and daunting at the same time: it takes all my

---

[11] Scruton (1999:19-20).

energy. It is a very physical and mental experience, and I know I must plunge into the abyss of creation. As a listener, after the work is completed, I am physically and mentally detached from the creative process, and the impact of the music is more objective. I now find myself in a more neutral position. It's like seeing my image in front of a mirror. Now I listen to the complete work in the most minute structural detail while allowing this force to enter my mind indiscriminately and from another direction.

CL. Are extra-musical ideas essential for the listener to know before engaging with your music?

JP. I don't think so. Music should speak for itself. On the other hand, the more we know about the extra-musical information linked to a musical work, the better we can appreciate and perceive the music. Another important factor is the listener's experience and competence as a listener. The less experienced the listener, the more helpful any information about the music may be.

CL. In *Transient*, we do hear specific words, and each word is wedded to a precise pitch. In these nine minutes of timelessness, your mystical poem is woven between soprano, prepared piano and electronics. Your use of echo, whisper, decay time, resonance and reverberation gives the impression that our world of speech and sound is the audible mirror of a parallel world of silence born of a transcendent trance. Was the poem of a meditative trance? Takemitsu said that music is a form of prayer. Was this music conceived from a sustained state of prayer?

JP. I agree with Takemitsu's idea in a wide-ranging sense, but the word 'music' is too general for me simply because it can signify so many things. What is he referring to exactly when he uses the word 'music'? Does he mean: *Performing* music? *Listening* to music? *Composing* music? My own version would be this: *composition* is a form of prayer; *performance* is the realisation of prayer; *listening* is participation in prayer. Who is 'praying' is the composer, while the performer is giving voice to that prayer. The condition of prayer reflects a focus on a specific intention reinforced by belief and devotion which complement the centre of attention. In that sense, the music of *Transient* was indeed conceived from, or in, a state of prayer grounded on a sense of emptiness and grief. Yet, it was the feeling of love that incited me to write what is nothing but a message from the heart to my departed friend. I would not say that the poem was of a meditative trance, but, thinking back, perhaps it was. It depends on what we mean exactly by 'meditative' and by 'trance'. There is certainly a sense of meditation intrinsic in the words of the poem. The meditation I am referring to is a state of profound reflection about the loss of a dear person and about death in universal terms. A state of meditative trance is similar to being close to death. When a person is close to death, the veil between the physical and metaphysical is very thin. A similar mental state can be experienced during the process of composition.

CL. The mystical and meditative states of Eastern faiths are clearly important to you. You state that the path of a mystic has an ethical dimension. In a conversation we had, you said: *"spirituality is an ethical challenge rather than a complacent state of mind."* We should not imagine the mystic to be an escapist. Just as the mystic Hallaj would pray so loudly he woke all his neighbours, so composers have stirred up collective consciousness with their music, for example, Schoenberg and Shostakovich…

JP. Meditative states and collective consciousness are two different conditions, but, yes, sometimes they may be present in the same phenomenon. I have always been drawn to any form of mysticism or meditative state, and I must stress, not only in conjunction with Eastern traditions. In fact, I am rooted in Western forms of mysticism, which came first in my life. Also, the notion of mysticism changes from tradition to tradition, especially between West and East, and these differences are sometimes dramatic. In my case, this has never been an intellectual choice, but a natural need to connect with something higher than myself which embraces and transcends me at the same time. From my understanding, I believe that a truly mystical experience goes beyond tradition or categorisation. Names and approaches may change, but the experience is the same. A true mystic is not an escapist. On the contrary, he is grounded in earthly life, and his living testimony is effectual to society. Sometimes, I call it 'mystical realism', bearing no direct link to the work of Nikolai Berdyaev, although I subscribe to many of the points he made, such as the notion of 'Apokatastasis'. I experience mystical realism as a contemporary, independent, form of experiencing the mystical in everyday life which includes personal ethics and social integrity. In recent years, I have become interested in the secularisation of mysticism, also in conjunction with the discoveries of modern science.

CL. How is the ethical role of an artist and mystic expressed in your works?

JP. I am not really sure if I understand what you want me to say, but my most immediate answer would be: by the music itself! Ideally, I would like the listener to find the answer to this question by listening to the music, and, if possible, without verbal elucidation. Music provides the most natural answer to this question. Nothing has any value other than the value we place on it. At the technical level, perhaps I should mention that I tend to use symbols that have a cryptic nature, but speaking about them would deprive the listener of their individual dignity in the journey to discovery. A decipherment can only be done by the listener who decides to undertake this path. Similar to alchemy, music is the sensual and divine art of individuation and transcendence.

CL. Your unique and mysterious approach to poetic forms and music reminds me of Rimbaud's mention of engendering a 'rational derangement of the senses'. I am curious to know about the relationship between the artist and tradition, and our ways of changing the past through artistic engagement with it: let us say, transforming the past. But maybe your immersion in Eastern tradition means that you are able to conceive of yourself utterly free from tradition and influence? There is a Buddhist phrase about being born new in a lotus flower every morning. Maybe it's like that for you, rather than Samson tearing down the pillars?

JP. You keep stressing Buddhism, but this is only one part of me. As I said earlier, I am not only immersed in Eastern traditions. They reflect only one aspect of my life; surely an important one, but not the only one. I embrace any practice that is genuine and resonating with me. For example, I feel a strong affinity to the mysticism of ancient Egypt, Celtic paganism, the sacred traditions of ancient Greece and Asia Minor, as well as early Christianity. The word 'transformation' can mean so much, and I prefer to emphasise the ability to change oneself from within. In that sense, my music reflects a desire for continuous transformation and the enhancement of human values. Being born anew every day is indeed what I tell myself every morning. Music is the most oracular of all arts because it points us to a sense of connection with ourselves that is independent from external influences, ideologies and religious dogmas. This connection is essentially a mystery. Since I was a little child, I felt the richness of an invisible world living inside me and a strong desire to connect with it. And I still feel a place in myself that is essentially eternal. Composing music is the most stimulating and demanding process that allows me to undertake this journey of self-discovery. Where does the light go when the candle is blown out?

CL. Pierre Boulez likens the art of composing to the work of an archaeologist digging deeper beneath civilisation until he finds himself. When I examine your scores for *Waka* and *Still*, I imagine you digging deep within the Japanese culture. Is it yourself that you seek? Or something else?

JP. These pieces are not about Japan, but about my spirit, my journey of self-knowledge or gnosis. These values are universal. As a matter of fact, within me there is *also* something else. This 'something else' is the 'unknown', and the *Unknown* is the only place I can create from.

CL. In the realms of visual and literary arts, the mystical artist is often tormented by the Promethean curse, which is the threat of punishment for creating fire. In particular, mystical artists have asked themselves whether they are mirroring the divine creative force or vying with it, revelling in their own power rather than celebrating the transcendent gift. Many visual and literary artists have destroyed their creations for fear of vanity or idolatry. Is the invisible realm of musical creation free from the torments I mentioned above?

JP. Many activities in contemporary society are consciously or subconsciously designed to suppress our inner voice. Composing offers me an insight into the self by taking me on a journey into the puzzling realms of memory, passion, yearning, contemplation, desire and awareness. Every time I create, I find myself in a kind of sacred ground because I am trying to chart the geographies of the Invisible: I explore visions and dreams. I must reflect on the degree of my decency by questioning the contradictions of human existence, exploring my own shadows, and trying to reconcile them. This journey into the realm of existence is full of torments of all sorts. I often must border despair and anguish in order to find another dream to dream. As Eugene Ionesco once said, *"Ideologies separate us. Dreams and anguish bring us together"*.

CHAPTER FOUR

CHAMBER MUSIC, CURIOSITIES, ENSEMBLE

THE *TRANS* CYCLE
Klaus Schöpp

KS. Just like all other pieces (*Transference*, the six *Trans Solos*, *Over* and *Transparence*) in the *Trans* cycle, *Transitions* is an extremely virtuoso and demanding composition. When you sent us the score, you didn't know about Modern Art Ensemble. When you compose, do you have specific musicians in mind? Do you envisage their performance skills and individual expressivity before you compose the music, or do you write for an ideal instrumentalist and then send the score out there, as if sending a message in a bottle, knowing that the musician who will find it will be the right one for the music? And is the fact that the bottle must be found a part of the message you are trying to convey?

JP. First of all, I should say that I have always loved working with performers. This is a privilege that may occur when writing for a single musician or a very small group of musicians such as your ensemble, for example. When I know the performers personally, I am already aware of their strengths and bear them in mind during the process of composition. If I happen to know the performers' name before I begin to write the score, I listen to their interpretations in order to get an idea of their musical qualities. This is very important because I like the performer's skill to inspire my musical imagination. The more I know about the performer's qualities, the more I am in the position to emphasise this or that aspect in the music I am writing. What I am saying doesn't mean that I am neglecting the primary importance of the musical idea; on the contrary, it is the conception of the music that comes first, and this is usually not related to the performer's skills.

There have been cases when the virtuosity of a performer has inspired me so much that I have been driven to write a new piece immediately: a real 'Sturm und Drang' situation that is impossible to prevent. A most notorious case is my piece *Koan*, written in 1999 for solo shakuhachi and ensemble when I came across a recording of extended techniques by shakuhachi master Yoshikazu Iwamoto. I was so inspired by these amazing sounds that I knew I had to write a piece based on this wonderful instrument immediately. I remember writing *Koan* in seven days and nights: it was a massive impulse triggered by Iwamoto's virtuosity and the idiosyncratic sound of the shakuhachi.

The opposite case is illustrated by the genesis of *Epitaph*, written in 1997 for cello and electronics. This extremely virtuoso piece was triggered by an uncompromising urge to express my pain at the loss of a dear friend. This strongly emotional music had to be written for its own sake, as it were. At the time I didn't care much if I would find a cellist brave enough to play the piece; I only knew the piece had to be written down, being aware that it would be extremely difficult to find a cellist prepared to play it. In fact, a few years later I came across cellist Neil Heyde who courageously decided to record the piece. Neil's amazing virtuosity and admirable dedication to detail made the CD recording possible. Today, I am still aware that there are very few cellists in the world who will ever want to play this fierce piece.

I like your image of the message in the bottle: this is often (but not always) the case, and you and your ensemble reacted to the score of *Transitions* enthusiastically. I didn't know Modern Art Ensemble personally when I wrote this piece, but I had a feeling that the music would resonate with you, which happened to be the case. You found the bottle, or better, the bottle was sent to you who then cared to open it, read the message and decided to bring it to life. Your musical curiosity, adventurousness and love for discovery led you to respond to the message. I do think that all these interrelated actions will ultimately lead to the realisation of an idea.

KS. Following on from that, I would be interested to know whether there is a specific audience in your mind that you are writing for? After all, this music is not only demanding for the players but also extremely demanding for the listener.

JP. No, I never write for a specific audience, and I never think of writing or wanting to write for an exclusive audience. When I compose, I write the music as it needs to be written. Listeners who are willing to listen will listen. Those who are unwilling to listen won't listen. It is as simple as that. The notion of a 'demanding' music is always relative. Music that is demanding to me, may not be demanding to you, and vice versa. I sense there will never be a consensus on this topic because people have different perceptions, opinions, musical training, and different degrees of willingness to expand their mental horizons.

KS. The first time I read the score of *Transitions,* I remember being so enthusiastic about the neat and precise handwriting, the clear structure and the clearly crafted sections of the piece. Of course, I immediately noticed the solos and their resemblance to the golden ratio as well as the highly diversified and contrasting varieties of the musical texture. My question is this: do you fix the form of your works right at the beginning of the composition or does the form evolve gradually during the writing process? Do you begin with a single sound, a gesture or a colour as trigger for the music?

JP. In most cases, I work like an architect in that I establish an outline of the form before I begin to write down the notes. Depending on the situation, the form may be adjusted to a specific musical need in order to evolve hand in hand with the flow of my intuition. In that sense, a pre-established form may incur changes and refinements during the writing process. The way I begin to write a new piece depends on many factors as I am not interested in using the same compositional procedure for all my works. When I establish a form, I also set detailed music information such as the choice of pitch-fields, metric relationships and so on. Sometimes, the beginning of a piece is triggered by the content of a pre-established pitch field that I have chosen a-priori. Some other times the content of the initial phrase stems from an intuition, an improvisation on a selected pitch material or an improvisation without any pre-determined pitch content. In the latter case, after choosing an improvised material, I create a framework that allows me to control how I want to expand the original idea in a coherent way.

There are pieces where I have created a one-to-one relation between pitches and words: for example, the pitch content of *Renge-Kyo*, written in 1993 for piano and electronics, derives from the letters of the title being ordered alphabetically and opposed to a set of corresponding pitches where, for example, the letter R corresponds to the note F♯, the letter E to the note B and so forth. On other occasions, I meditate on something like an extra-musical idea and open my mind to something of an abstract nature. There are also pieces that are born out of a strong urge to want to convey a strong emotion triggered by a social or political situation. In this case, the pitch content is strongly related to a feeling I am experiencing about that situation: it can be a feeling of anger, love, shock or urgency. When I begin with a single sound or gesture, I often allow my intuitive response to that sound or gesture to unfold either as freely as possible or within a framework based on precise proportions of form and pitch material. Generally speaking, I tend to merge intuition with structure, syntax with perception, and order with imagination. In fact, many of these procedures and modalities are often interacting in the same musical work.

KS. The three ensemble pieces, *Transitions, Transference* **and** *Transparence,* **can be interpreted as a kind of concertante music while the six** *Trans-Solos* **as cadenzas. Is the concerto the main topic of your musical work, or is it just one out of the many others?**

JP. I wouldn't claim that the concerto form is my main preoccupation, but it is certainly a very recurrent feature in many works I have written, especially for ensemble and orchestra. I am attracted by the confrontation or interaction taking place between musical instruments as a representation of discourse, dialogue, interchange of opinions and emotions. Composition involves a dialectic process. Each piece of the *Trans* cycle is a segment of a whole, a large tale as it were, whose complete narrative is articulated by smaller yet interconnected accounts.

KS. We premiered your big ensemble piece *Transparence* **together with the six** *Trans-Soli* **at the Konzerthaus in Berlin in 2014. I still remember the pre-concert talk and how you would answer my questions with the same sentence 'it's about dialectics' which made me somewhat sweat and sort of forced me to describe my very personal experience of the pieces. Your music lives from contrasts of all sorts: extremely polyphonic and chromatic virtuoso passages, sometimes sharpened microtonally, the use of instrumental blocks cutting into dramatic events and being followed by passages of a calmer and more reflective nature, oscillating harmonics that slowly move forwards and unfold onto islands of poetic rapture. Your notion of dialectics comes to my mind again: are the harsh dissonances necessary in order to emphasise the idyllic beauty of the sound as the ultimate cause of the music? Are we dealing with two sides of the same coin?**

JP. From a holistic perspective, two opposite qualities, such as ugliness and beauty, for instance, are complementary rather than exclusive. In my music, there is a lot of room for dialectic dynamism, that is a search for a sense of completion where conflict and opposition are vigorous originators of unity. I am not interested in a monistic interpretation of life based on a separate physical or metaphysical notion of orderliness. My music reflects a desire to confront apparently inseparable differences wherein everything exists with everything else, and where opposite elements participate in a unified organism represented by the musical work per se. Like any other form of art, music is a reflection of the human condition. I am searching for creative connections between opposite forces, contradictory elements, the logical and the illogical, the physical and the metaphysical. Dualism is a reductive condition of the mind and a concept of static parametric equality of values which I am suspicious of. When I talk about *dialectics* in music, I mean the exploration of a network of connections and interrelations between phrases, harmonies, colours, gestures, rhythms, metres, dynamics as syntactic diversities of the same unifying reality. In other words, the diversity of single musical elements is explored as a set of interwoven entities constituting an all-encompassing unity *because* of their dissimilar and contrasting idiosyncrasies. It is the same concept of 'Complexio Oppositorum' and 'Coincidentia Oppositorum' that Nicholas of Cusa and Giordano Bruno advocated in the Renaissance. Opposite forces interact in order to create a unifying principle intrinsic to their individual nature. To use a neurological analogy, this all-encompassing unity can be compared to the human brain and its formation in two distinct but interconnected hemispheres, the rational and the intuitive, where the interaction of the two modus operandi is essential for the cognitive process to exist as a complete and unifying activity.

KS. Apart from *Over,* **in all the titles of this cycle (***Transitions, Transference, Transparence* **and** *Trans-Soli***) the Latin prefix 'trans' is very emblematic of a passage to something.**

Despite the recurrent use of timbral transitions in the traditional sense of the word, the use of timbre is not necessarily the main theme of these works. What I mean is that it does not have the same importance as in a work like Schönberg's *Farben* or the music of Debussy and Grisey, for example. In *Transference* the notion of 'transfer' is exemplified by quotations from *Transitions* suggesting a process of conversion and evolution occurring from one piece to another. Instead, the transparency suggested in *Transparence* seems to be evoked by the use of the electronics that includes the same ensemble sounds emerging from behind the real ensemble at different moments in time. Then there are the *Trans-Soli* offering more 'tangible' virtuoso pieces, rich in highly contrasting textures, extreme timbres, but also moments of stasis and reflection. They, too, seem to refer closely to the meaning implied in the titles, and their transitional function within the cycle is most ostensibly related to the timbral alternation of the different instruments. Do these appropriate, yet weirdly displaced titles also refer to something else? Something aside or beyond the music?

JP. Yes, they do. It is about daring and questioning conventions. It is the notion of 'going beyond' something, a passage to something else, the condition of transferring an idea from one mental space to another. Chamber music epitomizes a theatre of transitive gestures and actions delineated by intrinsic *trans*-formations of melody, harmony, duration, timbre and dynamics. By 'transitive', I mean when something affects something else. For example, a melody affecting another melody, a chord affecting another chord, or a fragment of a piece affecting the music of another piece.

In *Transitions* (for clarinet, violin, cello and piano), these transformations are explored through compression and expansion of melodies and harmonies. In *Transference* (a quintet including flute, clarinet, violin, cello and piano), I was interested in both the notion of transferring and the state of being transferred. I transferred seven fragments of *Transitions* to the new piece and set a new emphasis on the process of compression and expansion that characterised both works. In *Transparence* (the final septet for solo viola, flute, clarinet, violin, cello, piano and electronics), I transferred fragments of *Trans-Solo 6*, for solo viola, to the new piece. These fragments affect the music of *Transparence* by adding new rhythmic impulses and melodic qualities to the polyphony of the piece, by supporting the leading role of the viola now reinforced by the addition of the electronics, and by providing extended forms of timbre and spatial attributes to the whole ensemble. In *Transparence*, the content of *Transitions* and *Transference* is finally extended and *trans*cended onto a comprehensive polyphonic morphology, reaching a paradoxical peak in the gradual dissolution of the pitch content that characterises the whole cycle. The gleaming, almost glassy timbre of the closing texture is a reminder of a return to a state of pristine purity at the border of silence.

KS. Is your music a mirror? A mirror of our time, our society, our existence?

JP. Music gives voice to our perception and experience of the world, and any form of art is a mirror of the time it has been created. But mirrors reflect an incredible amount of details: they reveal unseen realities and lateral arguments, subtle accidents, the existence of illusions and coincidences. Like in a cosmology that includes traditional notions of the universe, the existence of parallel universes and the presence of a multiverse simultaneously, mirrors are gateways to paradoxes, uncharted regions of the mind, deception, fantasy and apparitions of unexpected conditions.

KS. Has the *Trans* cycle been stimulated by personal encounters, experiences, or by a special event in your life?

JP. The *Trans* cycle was triggered by personal experience.

KS. Can you expand on that?

JP. The music I write stems from my experience of life. Like all of us, I have experienced ups and downs of all sorts, conscious and subconscious choices, and I have gone through processes of renewal, transformation, evolution and change. Each of these circumstances has induced me to become aware of the importance of reflection, confrontation and communication. What I call dialectics defines the desire to contextualise confrontation and communication as a musical discourse. You may well say at this stage that my music is biographical, and you would certainly be right because I cannot detach music from life. When I am facing a problem or a new situation in my life I will react in a certain way as a result of a critical approach, an analytical thought and my intellectual honesty. I make an effort to understand the problem, to challenge possible repetitive patterns of my behaviour, and to learn how to know myself better in order to transform myself into a more considerate, compassionate and hopefully loving human being. This dialectic thinking must include the courage to see myself 'naked' in front of a mirror and face my own shadows. There is a sense of danger and fear that comes with it because I am being confronted with my own vulnerability in front of the potential tyranny of my ego. With this in mind, any personal and social experience is a potential source of reflection and a trigger of intellectual and emotional responses that can lead to a path of personal evolution.

The *Trans* cycle is an attempt amongst others to depict this psychological scenario, and illuminate, with critical concern and uncompromising intensity, a desire to understand who we are in relation to other people, and, at the same time, understand other people's behaviour in relation to us. This is why the awareness of conflict and interaction between two forces, two or more musical instruments, is so critical in a chamber music context of this kind. Understanding this means also to understand my view of virtuosity not as a mere exhibition of craftsmanship, but as a vehicle to self-discovery through a process of confrontation.

KS. When we premiered *Transparence,* you performed the electronics with us. Our soloist, Jean-Claude Velin, recorded a few passages of the solo viola part in advance, and you used these recordings in the electronic part of the piece. In a composition of this kind, what is the role of your work in the recording or electronic studio? How does your composing relate to the recording studio?

JP. I recorded these extracts and processed them in order to transfigure the solo passages of the viola and provide additional sonic material for the viola cadenza. It is not only a matter of playback since the recordings have also been transformed electronically. For example, I altered the timbre of the original phrases by adding subtle ring modulation and varying degrees of filtering. Some phrases were transposed above and below the original pitch, and a wider virtual space was added by using different types and sizes of reverberation and delay, and so forth. The newly processed phrases add new layers of pitch content, loudness, timbral and spatial diversity to both the full texture of the acoustic sextet and the solo sections of the viola. The role of the electronic studio has a primary importance to my work simply because it is an integrative part of the compositional process. I compose the electronics as I compose the rest of the music. The only difference is that composing with electronics allows me to hear the sounds I am working on straight away, and this is a big advantage that helps my imagination when dealing with the instrumental parts.

KS. And two more trite questions: do you work with sound engineers? Do you have all the equipment you need?

JP. I have my own studio with almost all the equipment I need, so I am not depending on another studio, although this may vary from project to project. This does, of course, facilitate my work. The only time I collaborate with sound engineers is when I am involved in recordings of large pieces or specific projects produced by a Radio or a similar studio like the ZKM in Karlsruhe and the Electronic Studio of the Technical University in Berlin.

KS. The COVID crisis has forced musicians to give up concert life. Do you think we can live only with recordings? Do we need the concert hall? After the pandemic, will things simply continue as they did before? What do you think it's next?

JP. I enjoy recordings very much, but I can't envisage a society without live music. Technology has made virtual performances possible, but those are not concerts and can't replace live music. So yes, we *can* live only with recordings, but this would be a tragedy for our global society. The concert hall, as well as theatres and any kind of venue, remain indispensable and irreplaceable. My general impression of the current situation is that society won't be the same after the COVID crisis and some things are already changing drastically. I mean this both on a mental level as individuals, and on an infrastructural and political level as a society. I do think that we are at a crossroads and that many things won't be the same in the future. Personally, I am concerned about an increasing split between two opposite tendencies: the multiplication of egocentric, dishonest and nationalist attitudes, and the evolution of a respectful and compassionate attitude towards nature and between people. I am for the latter.

THE LIGHTENING OF A FIRE
Eva Böcker

EB. Your way of writing for the cello in *Epitaph* is unusual and does not make use of any clichés connected to the instrument. Can you explain how you came to choose the cello for this very personal and emotional piece?

JP. I love the cello in a very special way. It is an instrument with amazing expressivity, extensive range and a unique variety of timbre. In order to bring out the emotional power of this fierce piece, I needed a powerful instrument that would allow me to use as many contrasting colours and dynamics as possible. The cello simply was the most suitable acoustic instrument for the dramatic music of *Epitaph*.

EB. It seems that we share a fondness for the harpsichord. Can you describe your attraction to this instrument?

JP. The harpsichord is such an idiosyncratic instrument! I 'discovered' it while studying piano at the Conservatoire of Lucerne and chose it straightaway as the second instrument for my academic training. I was lucky enough to study with Peter Solomon who was a very open-minded and excellent musician. In retrospect, I think that from the very beginning, I did not make the mistake that many pianists do, namely, to think that a harpsichord is a surrogate of the piano, or a second-class kind of keyboard instrument without sustain and dynamics. Sometimes I hear pianists and organists playing the harpsichord as if it were a cheaper version of the piano or the organ, which is preposterous. The harpsichord is an instrument in its own right. There is an aura around the harpsichord sound that I find captivating and unique, especially when used in a chamber music context. It is that glittering, sparkling sound quality combined with the attack of plucked strings producing notes of short duration that makes the instrument so exclusive and inimitable at the same time.

Since the strings are plucked by a jack triggered by a keyboard mechanism, the harpsichord cannot produce dynamics and the duration of the notes is inevitably very short. Although it is technically impossible to play dynamics and sustain a sound on the instrument, as a pianist, I was very captivated by the tricks used by harpsichordists to create what effectively are auditory illusions of dynamics and duration. For example, you can create a sense of dynamics depending on how long you hold a note, how fast you arpeggiate a chord, how quickly you attack a key, or on the detailed finger work that is needed for a certain kind of articulation that will help to create these effects. Articulation is rather difficult to achieve because, unlike the piano where there is a hammer striking the strings, in a harpsichord the strings are plucked. Although the plucking of a string may appear as an easy mechanism (even banal to some pianists), in reality, this is very difficult to control because I need a variable amount of force to make all the keys sound in a musically coherent way. The plucking itself reminds me of both the guitar and the harp. In that sense, the harpsichord evokes a strange combination of the piano and the guitar.

EB. Intervals and the spaces between the sounds play a significant role in your meditative piece *Satori*, for solo harpsichord. The piece demands very concentrated listening, and I was astonished to feel that the length of each of the silences, or spaces, felt to me absolutely compelling, almost as if I had generated each new sound myself. Can you outline your use of intervals and spaces in this piece and their relationship to each other?

JP. We only hear what we're ready or capable to hear. Ultimately, listening is awareness. I love to compose and respond to music that *invites* rather than *demands* listening. *Satori* may be described as a meditation in silence and sound. The use of intervals and spaces in this piece stems from an experience of deep stillness, and the relationship between intervals and spaces results from my intuitive approach to the music. I sat down at the harpsichord and went into silence for a few minutes. Then, at some point, when I felt ready, I began to play without any pre-conceived plan. The first note that came out of this state of profound peace was an E5 played on the first manual with a buff stop. I listened to the decay of the note very carefully and responded intuitively by repeating the same note in what is now bar 2. The following gesture begins with E and E♭ in the same register and is played each on a different manual. At this point, the narrative of the piece begins.

In my mind, the semitone can be a 'one-sound' unity that includes the complementarity of two adjacent frequencies: a unity composed by duality. This may sound as deriving from theoretical speculation, but it is not. When I play a semitone, I experience a sense of unity that is formed by two contrasting elements which I perceive as being part of the same pitch construct: like two sides of the same coin. To be specific, I perceive the friction of the oscillations of the two intervals of a semitone played simultaneously as a sparkling sense of 'living' peace, a sensorial experience of unity having an open character. If you begin to hear a dyad this way, at some point, you begin to feel this sense of vibrating identity that I am trying to describe. By the same token, a dyad consisting of a major seventh will trigger an intriguing sense of 'false octave', and suddenly the perception of pitch structure in your mind seems to change: two notes like E and E♭ played together will arise a sensation of a kind of unity that is 'alive' as a result of the frequencies friction. Perhaps this could be described as a 'false-unison'. Hence, a semitone evokes the perception of a dualistic unity: a vibration resulting from two different frequencies played at the same time, whereas the frequency friction of the semitone will produce a shiny and fizzy sound. But one sound only! I often use this 'dual-unity' sound in my piano pieces, as it is a sound that I experience as peaceful and, at the same time, 'living'.

Traditionally, we define a semitone as a dissonance and therefore we learn to perceive it as an unstable, harsh and jarring interval, but the semitone can also be perceived as a very captivating stable sound whose definition goes beyond the classic consonance-dissonance dichotomy. The third gesture of *Satori* is based on the perception of a semitone I have just described. As I said earlier, when I meditated at the harpsichord and began to play, I didn't have any time or interest to enter into intellectual speculation about what I was playing; on the contrary, I just let my mind freely react to the short resonance and silence that followed the short phrases.

The third bar begins with Eb5 and E5 on two different manuals, one of them being muted by the buff stop in order to add a subtle ambiguity of timbre. When I listen to the music now, and from a detached and analytical perspective, I can see how in bar 3 the E-Eb semitone defines the content of the music throughout the end; the quaver triplet is based on the same idea. In bar 4, the semitone of bar 3 is expanded into the whole-tone E-D (see Fig. 9.1, page 334). Again, this happened very spontaneously when I wrote the piece, as I felt the need to expand the intervals further. I remember how I let each gesture vibrate in space while reacting to each resonance before I would begin with the next phrase.

EB. Your music is very varied. Do you like using a particular concept for several pieces, in order to go as far as possible with an idea, or do you prefer to look for a new approach for each piece?

JP. Although I do sometimes use an explicit concept and procedural background for interrelated pieces such as in the case of the *Trans* cycle, I usually deal with a new piece as a new challenge coming with a new set of musical choices. In this sense, my music represents different moments of a personal journey that are interrelated but remain unique in their individual and exclusive nature. I write music where sounds, form and meaning come together at a particular point in time, as a mirror of a specific situation that I am experiencing in my life. My music is essentially evolutive, and this evolution relies on my ability to change and progress. I am not interested in dogmatic or monolithic approaches to procedures and techniques. My attitude towards composition is diversified, manifold, thus polylithic.

EB. For how long can an idea for a new work linger in your mind, before you actually begin writing anything down?

JP. Very long or very short; it depends. There are no rules for this. And when there is a deadline, I have to work effectively in a very short time. I do have ideas that linger in my mind for some months or even years until I find an opportunity to put them on paper. I have experienced the need to write down an idea very quickly as a result of a very strong motivation to do so. This has been the case for *Koan,* the *Piano Concerto* and the *Second String Quartet* to mention a few.

EB. Is it important to you that a musically unschooled listener can appreciate, or even understand your music?

JP. Absolutely. One of the most gratifying experiences in my life is when musically untrained members of the audience approach me at the end of a concert and tell me how touched they have been by the music. To be true, I don't think it is a matter of 'understanding' the music, but much more importantly, to feel it and let it resonate in our mind, soul and body.

EB. Is it easy for you to accept that every listener will perceive and understand your music differently? Do you wish the interpreter's perception to be as close as possible to yours?

JP. When in one of my previous answers I mentioned that I am interested in music that *invites* rather than *demands* listening, I meant what I said also as a listener. As a composer, I want to *invite* the listeners to listen to my music without expectations of any sort. I am aware that each listener will perceive it differently anyway. This is inevitable, and I don't have a problem with that. I certainly feel that I don't have the right to impose a point of view or a fixed recipe on how to listen to music. On the other hand, knowledge does help to appreciate art. Like for the music of other composers, the more the listeners know about my music, the more they will be in the position to appreciate it. Ultimately, it will be up to them to decide what they want to do with it. I am often told that some works of mine are more accessible than others, but then I wonder how these people measure the level of accessibility. Are they saying that diatonicism is more accessible than chromaticism by default? Are they implying that a sparse texture is more accessible to music containing a lot of notes? Who sets the psychological criteria for the evaluation of an alleged degree of accessibility? Is it about establishing criteria for emotional or perceptual values? In reality, I shall never know how my music will be perceived by others: the only thing I know for sure is that it will certainly be perceived differently from the way I perceive it. Often, I experience listeners telling me how touched they have been by my music. I have even heard of a case in Tokyo where a Japanese member of the audience was literally in tears when she heard the world premiere of *From the Lake,* for oboe and piano. This is a situation I particularly treasure because it simply gives me great joy to see that what I am trying to convey through my music may touch other people to such an extent. I just feel very grateful when I see I can reach the hearts and minds of other people in such a strong way.

When I work with performers, I experience all sorts of situations and behaviour. Each interpreter is a unique and very different person. What I have noticed throughout the years is that those interpreters who are closer or more similar to me as a person will be better attentive to the details entailed in the music. They will usually ask more, they will want to know more not only about technical issues but also about the idea behind the music. They can feel the music resonating with them and this is a very special experience for me. Naturally, I wish the interpreter's perception to be close to mine. It's like with actors: they must be able to feel and understand a certain playwright well if they want to perform their part well. The same applies to music where an interpreter is an actor obliged to know *and* feel as much as possible about the music in order to *interpret* it accordingly.

EB. Do you sometimes wish that listeners can delete their memory of music of the past in order to avoid any recognition of previously heard patterns or tonalities? And do you hope for listeners of contemporary music to achieve that level of openness?

JP. I would like to reply to these questions as a listener. Why would I need to delete my memory of the music of the past in order to appreciate a piece of new music? Why cannot the two coexist? Why would my passion for the music of John Dowland, Josquin des Prez, Claudio Monteverdi and Carlo Gesualdo be an obstacle for my appreciation of the music of Boulez, Birtwistle, Stockhausen and Berio? Each listener carries a background of knowledge, information, emotion and curiosity. Anyone who is really willing to appreciate something new will always find a way to discover the novelty. Rather than 'deleting' the past, I would rather advocate to 'integrate' the past, unless you are referring to a more specific, non-comparative approach to how to listen to the music of today without referring to the music of the past. In that case, the question is about the modality of listening to different kinds of music and I think this can be acquired through knowledge. The more I know what to listen to in the music of J.S. Bach, the more I appreciate it. The more I know what to listen to in the music of Globokar, the more I will appreciate it. I often say to my students that a fundamental mistake that many, even classically educated, listeners make when they listen to music from Schönberg and Varése to today, is that they listen to this music with the same aural and psychological expectations they listen to the music of Mozart and Brahms. This will never work. It's like listening to Brahms with the same modalities I need for listening to the music of Xenakis. Education is the key here, and people should not think that it is that difficult to achieve. I know from experience that each time I explain the difference between tonal and atonal music, for example, people do begin to hear atonal music with another ear because they begin to understand where, why and how to shift their attention to the texture. And when, additionally to the different approach to pitch, I explain to them the modernists' need for asymmetrical forms, new sonorities and advanced use of rhythm and metre, they do begin to listen to the music of the past 100 years with a different and more open mind. This always works! I have experienced it again and again in my life. All this is to say that those who are keen to listen to contemporary music can achieve this level of openness through inquisitiveness and the acquisition of basic information conveyed by someone who can instil a dose of passion in the process of explanation. Prejudice and ignorance are the worst enemies to an unconditional experience of new music. In my experience, both can be eliminated very easily with education.

EB. Are any of your earliest childhood memories linked to music, and was there a precise moment when you realised that music would play an important role in your life?

JP. Most of my childhood memories are linked to music because I was always very reactive to it. I was recently told I was already singing back the songs from the radio at the age of two or three. I began to study the classical piano at the age of six, and it must have been two or three years later that the music of Chopin gave me the clear signal that I wanted to be a musician. This realisation became stronger when I got involved with jazz and popular music, and more so a couple of years later when I heard the music of Debussy and, especially, Edgar Varèse for the first time. By the age of 10 or so, I knew that music was very important to me. As a teenager, this awareness was crystal clear, and music became my measure of time rather literally. The most important 'curiosities' of my life are linked to specific pieces of music in all genres.

EB. How and when did you decide to compose your first piece? Did it evolve out of a desire to experience and to hear something you imagined but had never heard, or to create something similar to music that had inspired you?

JP. My earliest pieces were improvisations on piano pieces by Chopin. Sometimes I would write them down, but very seldom. Then I began to write songs and instrumental pieces for the piano and the electric organ. I also composed music for a few bands I was involved with, and later on, I went back to piano music being strongly inspired by Chopin, Debussy, followed by Schönberg and Webern. The desire to write my own music was first linked to the music that inspired me in those days. Listening to the music of such disparate composers as Edgar Varèse and Keith Tippett live took me immediately to another level of musical awareness. From that moment on, I became aware of wanting to achieve my own voice as a composer and I entered the next level of music thinking and making. Initially, the impact with Varèse and Schönberg was decisive.

EB. Do you think music can influence our behaviour as human beings? Can it resolve the problems of the world we live in?

JP. Yes, I think music can influence our behaviour in a positive and negative way. Music that is aggressive and always loud has a harmful effect on the psyche. The opposite applies to music that is soft and gentle. The new science called Music Therapy is showing amazing results about the power of sound and music on our lives. I don't think music can resolve the problems of the world directly but can surely educate and refine our personality and make us better and more sensitive people. And better and more sensitive people can certainly resolve the problems of the world.

EB. Do you sometimes 'see' music in graphic shapes, lines, or colours?

JP. I can associate music shapes with graphic shapes, and I am a synesthete. Synaesthesia is a complex science and, in my case, I perceive colours in conjunction with sounds, numbers, words, vocal sounds, names and sometimes even accents and taste. Any stimulus can raise a synaesthetic perception in my mind. It is well known that synaesthetic perceptions are not subject to voluntary control but can be repressed by conscious control of attention. I tend not to suppress them. These sensations are similar to normal perceptions and sometimes the triggering stimulus can be a thought or a concept. For example, to me the notion of 'existence' triggers the colour blue or white, depending on the context. The reading of a poetic verse or musical phrase (without hearing them) can trigger a specific colour or taste. Sometimes I dream of a place where I have been in the past and, while I am dreaming, I am smelling a specific odour that is linked to that place. I also hear sounds in association with certain places or memories. The strongest synaesthetic experience occurs with colours, words and sounds.

EB. Do you consider all sounds, when you listen to them actively and consciously, as music?

JP. Sound and music are not the same thing. Technically and artistic speaking, music is not sound, but the art of composing with sounds. It is the results of a combination of sounds put together according to a certain logic and organisation. The latter may range from being strictly controlled to very intuitive, but in each case it is arranged by the intelligence of the composer. Such intelligence may be systematic and rational or intuitive and perceptual. Hence the question for me is not whether I listen to sound actively and consciously, because I do this anyway, but how these sounds are put together. I certainly don't perceive a single sound as music whether I listen to it very consciously or not.

EB. Does some music annoy you, or even make you angry?

JP. Yes, cheap music. It's the music itself that annoys me, but also what people make of it and how they often sanctify it.

EB. Would you agree that the political and worldwide economic system leads to a reduction in diversity in music and in the arts in general? Some countries make an effort to subsidise (contemporary) classical music. How would you attempt to explain or defend this before a person who is indifferent to classical music and against subsidising the 'elitist' arts; someone who believes that it should be left to the market to decide which genre of music should survive?

JP. Music, like any other form of art, is a necessity of the human race. It educates us and it is a basic need of our existence. Everybody and any form of government should understand this. By cutting funds allocated to education and the arts, governments are destroying the future of society. A market is a commercial system based on competition where buyers and sellers interact in order to sell and buy a product. The criteria behind this environment are based on profit and therefore cannot tie in with the nature of culture as an existential necessity. The market establishes the prices for a product according to supply and demand. In order to function well, supply is depending on the demand generated by the buyers. This means that suppliers respond only to the demand of a specific product, not to extra-commercial issues. They don't care about culture. If the demand for cheap music is strong, suppliers will supply that very product regardless of its quality. Leaving cultural decisions to the market means that music in the future will essentially be reduced to a product dictated by commercial interests. If this situation continues to grow in this direction, it seems that music as an art form will disappear. Regarding your point about subsidising the 'elitist' arts, I must say that I have never believed in contemporary 'classical' music as being an elitist form of art. If I want to become an architect, I will study architecture before I can call myself an architect, won't I? If I want to become a doctor, I will go to university and study medicine first before I can exercise my profession. Why should not the same apply to music?

EB. Would you like to see changes in the way classical music (old or new) is generally presented? Are changes needed in order to solve the problem of fading audiences?

JP. In my opinion, the key to the problem is education. The problem of fading audiences reflects the lack of a certain kind of culture combined with intimidating marketing strategies that are taking over the daily life of our societies at an increasing pace. I believe we need more *idealistically* pragmatic thinking, and more *pragmatically* idealistic approaches to how music can be first of all taught and then presented to the audiences. It seems that, as a result of post-modernism, we are gradually losing the meaning of quality and the importance of culture. I believe education to be the ultimate road to freedom. As W.B. Yeats once said, *"education is not the filling of a pail, but the lighting of a fire."* This is where in my opinion the root of the problem lies.

There are two other aspects that I would like to mention. One is the attitude of classical music performers that much too often does not help to promote new music. When you look at jazz musicians playing on stage, you clearly see that they are enjoying what they are doing. Their playing, their faces, their bodies convey a clear sense of pleasure, amusement and delight that I rarely see in classical musicians. I often discuss this issue with my students who are trained to become professional classical music performers and only some of them will admit this is a grey area of music education. Most instrumental teachers I know don't care about this problem. Much of our music-making training is far too strict, 'unmusical' and at times even brutal. Our musicianship is severely judged by the terrifying measure of not making mistakes, for example. The other day I watched a video of a performance of *Dérive* by Pierre Boulez conducted by himself and I was struck by the horrified eyes of the musicians who were playing this piece under his baton. Let's be frank about this: isn't it just ridiculous? What impression are these terrified musicians conveying to the audience? Where has the joy of playing music gone? How will such musicians ever win new audiences?

The other aspect I want to briefly touch upon is a certain presumptuousness that can be detected by many composers who seem to only want to emphasise their intellectual and artistic distance from contemporary society. This attitude is certainly damaging the image of new music as it reinforces a sense of stiffness and self-referential image that is still keeping a divide between a few obsessed pseudo-intellectuals and the rest of society.

EB. What do you think about the established concert format: several pieces being played in a row on a stage of a concert hall? Can the alteration of concert settings change the way classical music is perceived or will music offered to a passer-by in a train station or an airport only encourage it as a consumer product?

JP. Music should never become a consumer's product and I don't think it is the format of a concert that can change this situation. Surely, it is important to make a concert as appealing as possible and constantly offer new ways of presenting music to the audience in a world that seems to be progressively inundated by a myriad of distractions. Maybe too many!

ENSEMBLE WORKS: *YOU, KOAN, BLURRING DEFINITIONS, LEGEND*
Peter Wiegold

You (trombone and ensemble)

PW. To what extent is the discourse in *You* pitch-led? Please comment also on the function of other parameters in the working out of the discourse.

JP. The discourse is based on pitch as an imaginary counterpart of word, the piece having been inspired by a text I wrote in 1988. Unlike in other works of mine, there is no pitch-word structural equivalence in the organisation of sound. The words of the text were used merely as an impulse for reflection and meditation from which I created an autonomous unfolding of pitch. However, there are three moments in the first movement (bb. 21-24, bb. 32-35 and bb. 43-45) where a concealed text is spoken in a fragmented way by the wind instrumentalists into their instruments as a sort of ambiguous and distorted prayer that is not meant to be perceived as such. Apart from these short episodes, the link between pitch and word remains at the 'poietic level'[12] of the musical work.

The fabric of the piece springs from the harmonic series of the lowest B♭ of the trombone (see Fig. 4.1). The main motif of the first movement is based on the 16th, 17th, 21st, 23rd, 24th and 25th partials of the harmonic series corresponding to B♭5, B5, D quarter-sharp6, E6, F6, G6 and transposed three octaves lower in tempered tuning. The resulting row is re-arranged on E3 (E, F, G, B♭, B, E♭) and B♭2 (B♭, B, E♭, E, F, G). The central note of the row, B♭, stands in a sort of conflict with the note E. The B♭/E axis is a recurrent feature during the piece (Fig. 4.2).

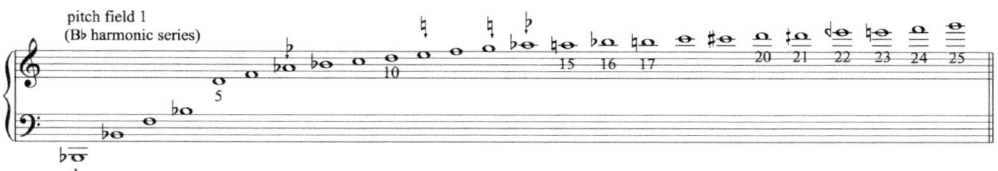

Fig. 4.1: *You*, harmonic series of B♭.

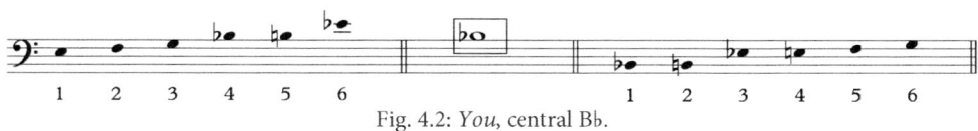

Fig. 4.2: *You*, central B♭.

Essentially, *You* is based on the interconnection between the row and the harmonic series of B♭1, as well as the remaining notes of the row: B, E♭, E, F and G. The piece is divided into three movements. The first movement is based on the semitone intervals 1-4-2-1-1 (with a quarter-

---

[12] As described by Molino and Nattiez.

tone deviation deriving from the 21st partial). This relation constitutes the matrix for the movement:

Prime = 1-4-2-1-1 original matrix (harmonics: 16-17-21–23–24–25).
Retrograde = 1-1-2-4-1 reversed matrix (harmonics: 16–17–18–20–24–25).

During the unfolding of the music, both rows are shifted along the harmonic series as melodic material:

1-4-2-1-1 up   (original matrix upwards)
1-4-2-1-1 down   (original matrix downwards)
1-1-2-4-1 up   (reversed matrix upwards)
1-1-2-4-1 down   (reversed matrix downwards)

From which I fixed the original matrix this way:

16-17-21–23–24–25   (original matrix upwards)
16-15-11–9–8–7   (original matrix downwards)
16–17–18–20–24–25   (reversed matrix upwards)
16–15–14–12–9–8   (reversed matrix downwards)

and so on, downwards (15, 14, etc.) to be transposed to all 24 partials. In the figure below the same procedure is applied to the other notes of the row: B, E♭, E, F and G (Fig. 4.3).

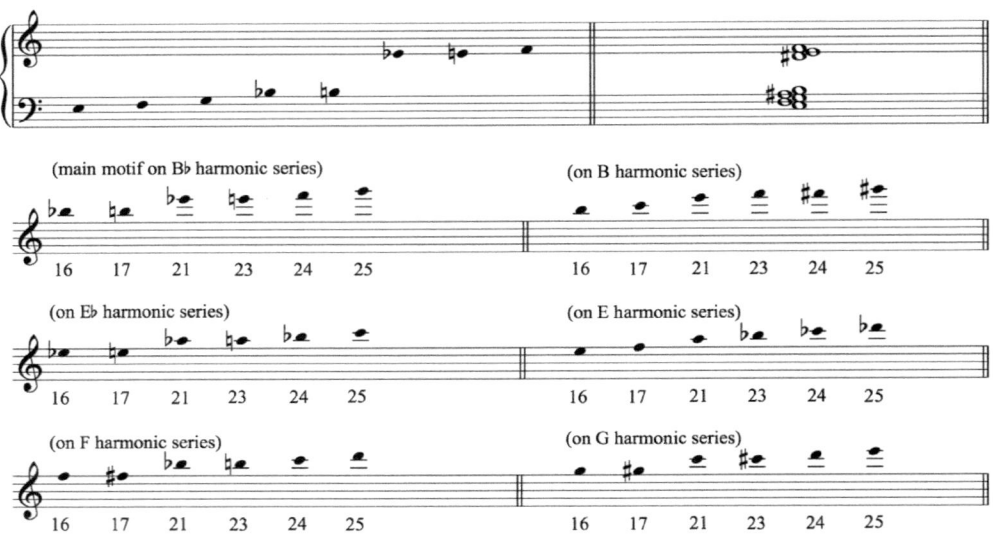

Fig. 4.3: *You*, procedure application to B, E♭, E, F and G.

The second movement is constituted by 13 units (phrases) set in ascending order. The pitch material is based on the pitch chart of matrixes of the six main pitches. Below you can see the matrixes of B♭ (Fig. 4.4). The third movement is based on the re- and de-construction of the harmonic series of the trombone enriched by 13 spectral radiations descending to and ascending from the fundamental, including variations. The harmonic series of the prime notes will ultimately converge in B♭.

You - pitch chart 3

Fig. 4.4: *You*, matrix unfolding on B♭.

The extract from the score below (bb. 46-49) shows unit 5a (section 9 descending) based on G♭, where the trombone is leading the discourse, coloured in by the piano and the harp. The flute, trumpet and horn are timbrally reinforcing the B played by the trombone using the same technique of playing and singing simultaneously (Fig. 4.5).

Fig. 4.5: *You*, bb. 46-49.

Regarding the function of the other parameters, a set of durational values is linked to the partials of the harmonic series. The chart below (Fig. 4.6) shows the longest value of a brevis corresponding to the fundamental note of the harmonic series and the gradual decrease of duration up to the 25th partial. At times, this framework for rhythmic structures is used precisely, however, it is mainly used as a trigger for intuitive rhythmic gestures. In the second movement, the pitch and rhythm matrixes gradually merge and unfold increasingly freer towards the end of the movement. It is worth mentioning that the climax leading to the 'tutti cadenza' at the end of the second movement is built upon a radiation of spectral content emanating from the harmonic series of E1 initiated by the B4, the eighth partial of the series (see Fig. 4.7).

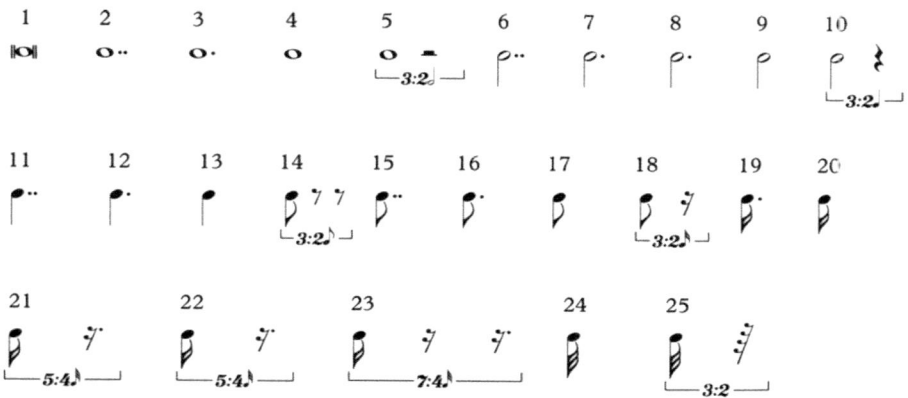

Fig. 4.6: *You*, list of durational values.

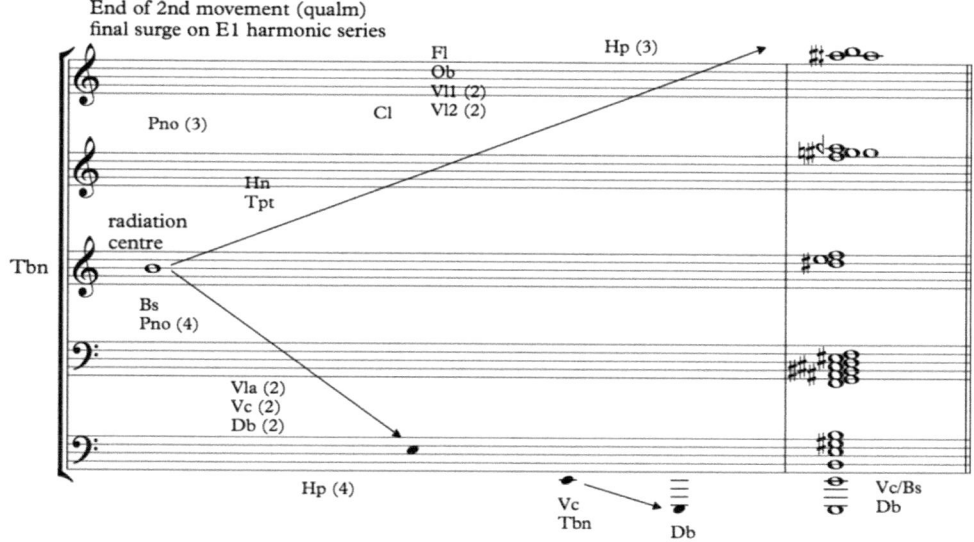

Fig. 4.7: *You*, radiation of spectral content (end of second movement).

Further below, bars 249-251 show the accrual of pitch and rhythm merging leading to the group cadenza (see Fig. 4.8). The remaining parameters are used intuitively according to the logic affected by the unfolding of the music.

Fig. 4.8: *You*, bb. 249-251.

PW. The trombone has a crucial role in this piece. What is its motivation? Is it passive, suggestive, demanding or rhetorical? Is it leading a journey *away* from something? Does the trombone have a dialectical relationship with the other instruments?

JP. The trombone is the protagonist of the story. The motivation is linked to the first text of my poem *Fragments of you* (1988) that inspired me to write the music:

searching paths for unspeakable skies	*find me flooded*	*time's charm I cannot recall*	*where was I when they cried your dreams*	*timeless time you becoming in me*
beauty forgotten in darkness	*secret remembrance*	*the night you knew I died*	*for implausible lies*	*I becoming in you*
	yearning	*in darkness*	*unfinished*	*returning*

Both Martin Buber and Søren Kierkegaard argued that it is not possible to say 'You' if one has not first been able to say 'I'. Even if one is alone, the process of becoming a person implies a relationship to something beyond the person. Thus, the 'I' category is recognised as a reality not aimed at itself but related to something else. The trombone is the alter-ego in search of a reunion with an indefinite presence that is perceived as inner peace and spiritual fulfilment. It is drawing a journey towards a goal that needs to go through dissimilar and contrasting circumstances. The trombone's presence within the ensemble is rhetorical and must be powerful and influential in addition to being soft and concealed. The journey is both a solitary and communal search whereas the trombone dictates the pace of the discourse from the front, as it were, and from within the ensemble. In the example below, bars 173-175 (Fig. 4.9), the trombone phrase (commenced in bar 172) is 'coloured' in by the clarinet and gradually reinforced by the polyphonic interventions of the other instruments. While leading to a collective texture, the trombone gradually becomes a homogeneous part of the ensemble by accentuating short notes that will later return to a linear unfolding.

The piece is characterised by the frequent change of function of the trombone part. For instance, long phrases (the leading voice that triggers the events of the other instruments) played in a polyphonic context are frequently followed by a communal texture where the soloist loses its individuality in order to become part of the group as if gaining a new perspective to its nature through the group (especially in the third movement). The search for a sense of the divine within human nature (the 'you' entity) seems to be paradoxically bound to a journey that must go through the confrontation with society (the ensemble). In this sense, the trombone's dialectical relationship to the other instruments is a recurring tenet of the piece. Similar to Pirandello's novel *One, No One and One Hundred Thousand*,[13] 'You' is the awareness that a person is one and not one at the same time, and that reality is both subjective and objective. The protagonist of the novel is unique (One) but, at the same time, he is not so to the others (No One), and he must be aware that as a member of a crowd he is 'One Hundred Thousand' to someone else. In other words, one self that implies different selves and nobody at the same time. But unlike in Pirandello, in *You* reality doesn't crumble into the infinite vortex of relativism, as the inner state of unity with oneself is attained at the end of the journey, in the third movement. This journey is ultimately leading to unity.

---

[13] Pirandello: *Uno, Nessuno e Centomila* (see Bibliography).

Fig. 4.9: *You*, bb. 173-175.

Koan (shakuhachi and ensemble)

PW. It is, by its nature, difficult to pin down precisely what a koan is. Enigmatic, illogical, perhaps ambivalent, paradoxical.

JP. I tend to agree with you! D.T. Suzuki once wrote that *"Zen naturally finds its readiest expression in poetry rather than in philosophy because it has more affinity with feeling than with intellect; its poetic predilection is inevitable."*[14] As I read this sentence back in the 1980s, I asked myself: why not music? Is music more distant in eliciting feeling than poetry? I don't think so. I have read so many different views about the topic that I have come to terms with the fact that the nature of a koan remains truly undefinable. One of the postulates Suzuki kept stressing throughout his life was that the aim of the koan is to force the student to assume an inquiring attitude.[15] Perhaps the most all-encompassing definition of a koan has been provided by a Westerner, John Snelling, who wrote that koans are *"profound or enigmatic questions which serve as a focus, concentrating the mind on the central issue: the question of essential nature - of what is sitting here now, searching for itself".*[16] The koan has also been defined as a riddle, and the list could go on and on, but I would like to give you a personal account of my own experience which is ultimately the reason that prompted me to write the piece.

    When I meditate on a koan it feels as if the habitual chains of thought have been suddenly cut off from my reasoning. I experience doubt, hesitation and distress in front of an insurmountable wall that is standing in front of me, not allowing me to go further through the usual channels of rational understanding. Consequently, I begin to feel helpless and lost, up to the point that I feel like wanting to bang my head on the wall in despair. On many occasions, I have given up at exactly this point of despair. On other occasions, I have kept trusting my determination of wanting to break through the wall. Zazen, and meditation in general, have taught me to exercise a strong will of the mind as a psychological device that would allow me to emancipate my mental and spiritual powers and ultimately expand my self-knowledge. I then want to trust again! I decide to feel that what I am going through is necessary in order to transcend the boundaries of logical dualism and awake into different perspectives of reality. I continue fearlessly this unbearable confrontation with the wall. I keep going and going, this time beyond my usual limits until I reach a point where I suddenly notice I am entering a hitherto unacquainted realm of the mind. The illogical words of the koan have unlocked an insight that is now clearly distinct and luminous to me. I now know I am experiencing an altered perception of myself and I begin to perceive my nature for what it is beyond the dualism of my old rational thinking. I begin to *see* what I see, to *listen* to what I hear, and to *recognise* what I feel. The same concept that was once irrational is now the gateway to a new understanding of the world in me and around me. It is this very personal experience coupled with the enlightening shakuhachi playing of Yoshikazu Iwamoto that prompted me to write my 'public document'[17] within a few days.

    Sometimes I wonder if it is possible to consciously transform the practice of music into a genuine revaluation of the sacred that is inherent in each of us. This is probably my main preoccupation in composition. When I deliberately try to pursue this goal, I realise a tendency to employ highly economical forms and procedures. I should mention that I wrote *Koan* at a time when I was reading the haikus of Matsuo Basho,[18] a poet who consciously transformed the perception of poetry into an authentic spiritual path. The succinctness of the 17-syllable haiku

---

[14] Suzuki D.T. (1969:117).
[15] Suzuki D.T. (1969:105).
[16] Snelling (1987:237).
[17] Another meaning of the word 'koan'.
[18] 1644-1694.

form was so present in my mind that I intuitively decided to create a meta-haiku form for *Koan* based on 17 phrases, each made of 17 syllables corresponding to phrases of unequal duration. In the piece, there are also concealed figures composed of 17 pitches or pitch-units that suggest an enigmatic layer that is, I think, impossible to hear.

PW. Can you trace key moments of contradiction or ambivalence on both gestural and structural levels?

JP. Although I draw my inspiration from anything that has a direct connection with life, including a precise musical idea, when I write music, there is a point where the piece flows by itself, beyond any predeterminate idea, techniques or methodology. The entire set of polyphonic lines in *Koan* are a source of continuous fluctuation throughout the piece. This is both controlled and 'non-controlled'. One key moment of both gestural and structural ambivalence is the shakuhachi-flute duet beginning in bar 61, which is followed by a shakuhachi-oboe dialogue. The timbral affinity of the two instruments evokes a sense of ambiguous identity. The underlying principle of these quasi-double cadenzas is the stark contrast of two rhythmic phrases interlocked in one. It is less their respective rhythmic surface that comprises their significance, but rather the asymmetric manner in which the continuous alternation of register in the two instruments determine a chain of 'contradictory' motions combined with the ambiguity of timbre that is, in turn, contrasted by constant dynamic fluctuation. The interchanging articulation of phrases underlines the varying degrees of intensity of two forces at work in persistent confrontation. The identity of this and other similar passages remains ambivalent throughout the piece (Fig. 4.10).

Fig. 4.10: *Koan*, shakuhachi-flute duet, bb. 61-81.

Another key moment occurs from bar 120 to 131 where the shakuhachi's impulses are disputed by the timbral variations of the clarinet, viola and cor anglais, the prolongation of which will lead to a 7-part polyphonic texture based on interlocked gestures of the strings and woodwinds.

The collective flow of energy is based on single individual actions accentuated by metric changes. This kind of polyphonic writing reflects the psychological situation I described earlier when discussing my own experience with koans (Fig. 4.11).

Fig. 4.11: *Koan*, bb. 120-131.

Another indicative moment occurs from bar 167 to 183 where the shakuhachi's cries (the multiphonics) are responded by short and loud phrases of the ensemble (bb. 167-169 below) followed by a timbral 'pianissimo' reaction of the ensemble to the second shakuhachi multiphonics (bb. 170-172), defining a moment of intensity through a spacious, albeit short, shakuhachi-ensemble polyphonic diversity announcing the focused pitch-rhythm compression of the piano percussion duet beginning in bar 173 (Fig. 4.12).

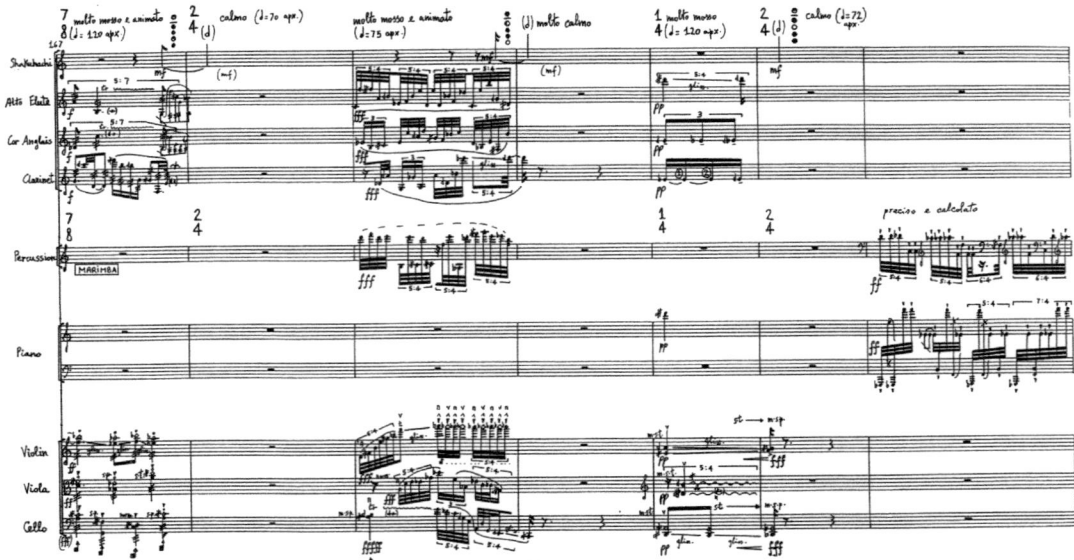

Fig. 4.12: *Koan*, bb. 167-173.

The sense of renewed urgency that follows from the piano-percussion duet gradually matures into a new polyphonic line leading to the piano solo in bar 190 where the inequality of rhythmic figures will indicate another idiomatic geometry of unequal gestures (Fig. 4.13). There are other similar points in the piece where the interaction between two or more instruments, or between the shakuhachi and the ensemble, occurs as a form of simultaneous interpenetration and conjoint integration that is kept together by the ambivalence of gesturality. In such cases, the simplicity and complexity of the texture are but two sides of the same coin. The apparent contradiction of gestural separation and distinction is, in reality, a pseudo-opposition implied in the cognitive process that is operating when meditating on a koan. Throughout the piece, the texture of the music relies on these inner micro-contradictions (the confusion of the mind) interlocked with the all-embracing flow of the music. The two layers remain inseparable.

Koan conveys a stream of linear diversity in which contradiction and contention are a necessary exaggeration of diversity (textural details) established by the inner conflicts arising from irrational reasoning. The fluid nature of the piece is characterised by recurrent gestures, sudden alterations of colour and register, unpredicted changes of metric, rhythmic and harmonic structures that increase or decrease the illogicality of 'contrasting affinity'. Single gestures and large units of phrases, especially those contrasted by instrumental blocks, assume cumulative accountability in the ductus of the discourse. A gesture is not only a single entity, and it can be perceived as a plurality of smaller components constituting the same motion and comprising the same pursuit. From this perspective, gestures are ambivalent shapes of micro-organisms that characterise the energetic flow of the music on a micro-level. Perhaps there is also a sense of deceptive illustration inherent in the design of every single musical phrase, but this may reflect an overly-personal interpretation. When meditating on a koan, the inner turmoil caused by all sorts of diverging reflections may in the end leave no permanent trace after the process is through. This condition is paradoxically addressed at the outset of the piece by the sustained sounds introduced by the first shakuhachi gesture as a signal of an anticipated end of the journey that is about to commence. In a Zen vision of the world, contradiction and unity are convertible ideas: ultimately it is mind alone that understands mind. For our purposes, however, the authority remains the music discourse itself.

Fig. 4.13: *Koan*, bb. 188-193.

PW. One could argue that there is a resolution at the end of the piece on the note D. Perhaps you can discuss the concept of arrival, resolution, stability or whatever this moment represents in the context of a koan. Is the final shakuhachi D to F a hint of ambivalence? If so, can you trace this moment back in pitch or other terms?

JP. The resolution stems from the shakuhachi's quest for meaning and self-assessment in order to invigorate a critical stance despite the obstacles encountered in the journey. Arrival, resolution and stability are the result of a form of activity that implies a processual evolution of ideas, gestures and phrases unfolded throughout the piece. Ultimately, a piece creates itself. The discourse of *Koan* is centred on a dialectic of individual-group energy maintained by articulation categories such as 'glissando', 'pizzicato', repetition of a note, harmonic sound, 'staccatissimo' and 'legato'.

Given the variety of ways in which a sense of stability may be achieved, I decided to begin the journey on a simple postulate rooted on a D2 note played by the bowed piano and ending on the D4 note of the shakuhachi, immediately followed by the unexpected F4 as a sign of a pseudo-resolution that hints at a new beginning (an hypothetical forthcoming koan). Achieving a goal requires effort, and effort requires enthusiasm and impetus. The sense of final stability provided by the last two shakuhachi notes is implied in the sonority at the beginning of the piece I have just mentioned. The note D is a point of arrival that is, at the same time, the beginning and, more importantly, *the* beginning of another imaginary koan, as if to stress the necessity of a mental process that needs to be repeated again and again until the final goal has been reached. This is the reason behind the unexpected appearance of the note F in the final bars of the piece. Like in Homer's *Odyssey*, where there's still another adventure waiting for Odysseus after he has returned to Ithaca and taken back his kingdom, the final note F reopens the curtain on a new koan yet to come. The solution at the end of the koan is but a new departure for the next journey.

Blurring Definitions (ensemble)

PW. Here we find the archetypal form of Western dialectics (hypothesis, antithesis and synthesis) reaching its final discourse. Could you trace the reasoning in musical and philosophical terms in this final work of the series? A conventional approach to such a form would suggest resolution, and if so, where is this foregrounded in the piece?

JP. In a dialectic discourse, known as Hegelian dialectic (although it was developed by J.G. Fichte), the logical arguments are set in the order you mention: the initial proposition (thesis), the negation of that proposition by a contrasting idea (antithesis), and the synthesis. This kind of reasoning is a typical example of classical Western rationalism which I decided to embrace in order to debate how, with purity of intent, contradictions can co-exist and establish a model of personal and social advancement. Indeed, the key word of the triptych was the idea of progress through the union of the initial contradiction.

The interesting thing about the kind of synthesis I had in mind was not much the fact that it provides a conclusion to the dispute, but that it offers new propositions based on the reconciliation of the initial opposition. The idea of finding new horizons and aims is always crucial for me, as I believe that two contrasting issues can always co-exist in another, transcending, paradigm. This is essentially the idea of the triptych comprising *Hypothesis* (for solo percussion), *Antithesis* (for string trio) and *Blurring Definitions* (for ensemble). In musical terms, the exceptionally dense pitch and rhythm-based texture of *Hypothesis*, with its inner conflict between the vibraphone part and the unpitched percussion, is starkly contrasted by the 'static' timbre-based texture of *Antithesis* consisting of sparse and elusive sounds of a string trio. Loudness is contrasted with quietness, extroversion by introversion.

Blurring Definitions is an attempt to define a symbolic synthesis articulated by the main elements of the previous works, namely pitch and rhythm (*Hypothesis*) and timbre (*Antithesis*). Between the Prologue and the Epilogue of this conclusive address, the three central statements (*Afterimage*, *Mirage* and *Aurae*) are generated respectively by the first violin, the flute and the cello, and interconnected by two short interludes played by percussion instruments. The resolution hints at achieving two goals: firstly, the co-existence of diversity within the same reality, that is the integration of the textural elements of the previous two pieces; secondly, the emancipation of the two previous realities into a new proposition projected onto three wider perspectives. In order to maintain a relation to the physical reality, I decided to use three natural phenomena of visual illusions: the afterimage (a phenomenon that occurs when the eye continue to see an object after the object itself has been physically removed); the mirage (where out of an initial visual reality, another image appears to the eyes, as the fata morgana illusion); and the aura or halo (the energy field that can be seen around a person, place or object under specific atmospheric conditions). Metaphorically, these three phenomena suggest the same idea of transcendence (looking beyond something) that is the resolution to the debate.

Perhaps I should mention that in order to reinforce a sense of formal unity between the pieces of the triptych, I used the same metric model constructed on the first seven prime numbers: 2, 3, 5, 7, 11, 13, 17. The percussion instruments of *Hypothesis* provide the links (named *reflections 1* and *2*) between *Afterimage* and *Mirage*, and between *Mirage* and *Aurae*. The three main movements each have a leading instrument. The violin leads all the phrases and delivers the rhythmic and gestural impetus of *Afterimage*. The bass clarinet, aided by the elusive presence and ambiguous role of the flute, leads the timbral discourse of *Mirage*. Thirdly, the cello steers the enlightenment process implied by *Aurae*.

PW. I note the powerful idea that the arrival before the epilogue is at a point of *Aurae*. What is this 'distinctive atmosphere or quality' resonant of?

JP. This movement refers to the quality of an aura as a reflection of light from an object; a shining radiation that is also an energy field. The 'object' in question is the cello, the leading instrument, whose phrases, motives and single pitches are contoured by the ensemble in a manner similar to a halo where a sphere of 'luminous' sounds encircle the cello sounds, thus providing a sonic layer of gleaming quality as in an audible refraction of the cello phrases. The 26 melodic fragments of the cello are therefore transcended by the instruments of the ensemble by reinforcement of the cello line (unison doubling), transposition (based on the order of the harmonic series), prolongation of phrases and motifs, 'illumination' effects created by 'crescendi' and resonance, counterpoint to the cello fragments, echo-like effects (based on repetition) and reinforcement of the cello texture by doubling of the cello phrases in 'piano' and 'pianissimo'. I added three other criteria linked to time: real-time (the instruments play the same rhythmic values of the cello fragments), time-stretched (the instruments play longer durational values of the notes played by the cello) and time-compressed (the instruments play shorter durational values of the notes played by the cello).

On the whole, the entire movement is characterised by a constantly moving halo-like effect around the cello phrases. In the first example below (Fig. 4.14, bb. 202-206), the halo to the cello fragments 8 (marked in red) occurs respectively by transposition of a fifth (Vl II), an octave (Vl) and by prolongation (Vl I), marked in blue. The first phrase of the cello fragment 11 is transposed an octave higher by the viola, the second phrase by the wind instruments and the first violin.

Fig. 4.14: *Blurring Definitions*, bb. 202-206.

In the following example (Fig. 4.15), one can see the echo prolongation of the end of cello fragment 11 by the wind instruments, the first violin and the double bass. The cello fragment

12 is echoed by transposition by the second violin. Fragment 13 is transposed by the viola a major third higher and counterpointed by the other instruments.

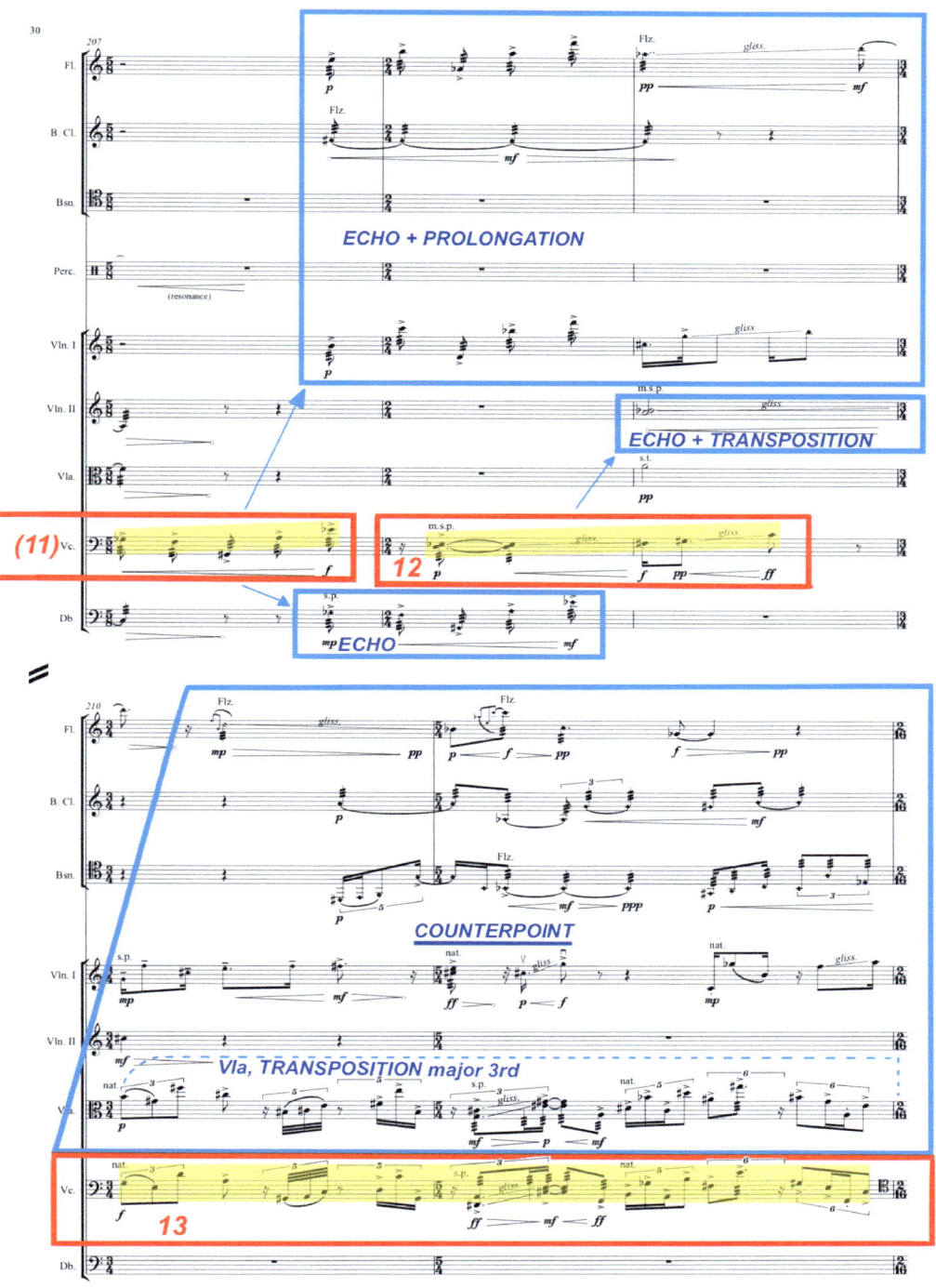

Fig. 4.15: *Blurring Definitions*, bb. 207-211.

PW. What is the significance of the rhythmic unisons in this section?

JP. In the context I have just explained, rhythmic unison is a part of the halo effect. Apart from the counterpointed auras, rhythmic unison is necessary in order to set a clearly audible connection between the cello phrases and the transformations being carried out by the other instruments of the ensemble.

PW. Why is the eloquence concealed? Where in the piece can we find the 'shadows' of it?

What I meant by 'concealed eloquence' was essentially about meaning. The choice of texture in my work is very important because it reflects symbols and psychological implications. When I compose, I have a natural tendency to be particularly alert about these implications (codes, emotions, associations and references) and I am meticulous about the utmost detail of a musical phrase because the act of composing is as if I am telling a story or thinking aloud. Therefore, the music I write is similar to a language with its own syntax and, to a certain degree, grammar. The shaping of a phrase, for instance, is something that can take me a great deal of time to finalise. When I listen to instrumental music, my mind is usually filled with images; I naturally tend to detect units, structures and phrases that make sense to me. Listening is a search for meaning through the recognition of syntactic elements that hold the piece together. It's the same way I would listen to someone speaking English, French or German. When I compose, this awareness of musical syntax evokes references and symbols. I am not deliberately trying to force them on what I am writing; they are just there, in my mind. Ogden and Richards have suggested that the elusive and subjective nature of this experience may be interpreted as a reference to signs based on states of mind operating in an organised and articulate condition:

"If images of any sort are involved in these states of beginning to think of things, it is certain that they are not always involved qua images, i.e., as copying or representing the things to which the reference points, but in a looser capacity as mere signs and not in their capacity as mimetic or simulative signs." [19]

Expression, articulation and eloquence are intrinsic in the texture I am composing. Leonard Meyer was explicit when he wrote that, *"Texture has to do with the ways in which the mind groups concurrent musical stimuli into simultaneous figures, a figure and accompaniment (ground), and so forth. Like other musical processes textural organization, or the lack of it, may give rise to expectation."* [20] Umberto Eco and Jean-Jacques Nattiez have shed more light on the interrelation between the realm of signals and meaning illuminated by information theory. To me, music exists as a symbolic form. A pitch-based texture has an inherent (concealed) eloquence linked to references and symbols elicited by the syntax and by the 'grammatical' relationships established by the intervals I am using, supported by rhythm, articulation, phrasing and gestures. To quote Nattiez,[21] structuralism is only explaining musical works *"on the level of their immanent configurations"*. This limited approach to music doesn't tell us anything about music as a consciously experienced phenomenon, and consequently about the phenomenological significance of the musical discourse.

The 'shadows' of the concealed eloquence I was referring to are to be found in each section of *Blurring Definitions* as a result of the syntactic allusions to the two preceding pieces *Hypothesis* and *Antithesis*. Phrases, or sounds shaped in a certain way rather than another, may

---

[19] Ogden and Richards (1985:60-61).
[20] Meyer (1956:185).
[21] Nattiez (1990:28).

elicit specific meaning and symbols which reside in the self-governing domain of the mind: my introspections remain very personal. Consequently, I don't expect a listener to share the same experience or the same view.

Legend (harp and ensemble)

PW. Each of these pieces contains instruments that lead. In this case, the harp as 'storyteller'. Can you tell me about the piece and its architecture?

JP. 'Storyteller' indeed. While writing *Legend*, my imagination was focused on the intersection of metaphorical narrative elements sparked by the harp, the narrator of the tale. The piece is based on continuous unfoldings of phrases and gestures evolving in a process of timbral/metric modulation and melodic transformation. Actually, I can describe many of my pieces as stories and chronicles of a journey, but this piece is a particular one. Legends are expressions of the collective unconscious as they articulate central ideas that have been indispensable in the history of humanity. The imaginary world they elicit has fascinated me since early childhood. Legends trigger a state of consciousness that detaches itself from the immediate flow of temporal events and inhabit a spatial dimension beyond chronological time; they exist as living allegories that are pertinent to contemporary life. They are timeless allegories.

     The music of *Legend* stems from the note A. According to a numerical proportion of 1:3, implying an intermediary value of 2, the note A generates the intervals of a prime, a second and a third (major and minor, interchangeably). The result of this basic procedure produces the material displayed below (1, 2, 3). By swapping the F♯ in the second group with the F♮ of the second group, the resulting formula will unfold three main motifs (or 'themes') and the subsequent harmonic regions (Fig. 4.16).

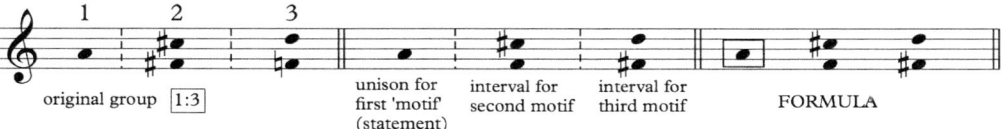

Fig. 4.16: *Legend*, generative pitch material.

In the following step of the unfolding process (TEXTURE 1), the original pitch material is divided into three statements defined as A1, B1 and C1. They will delineate resulting areas of development in the general form of the piece. In the chart below one can see the first unfolding of pitch for A1 and C1 (Fig. 4.17).

     The following chart (Fig. 4.18) shows the three statements superimposed and the points in time where they occur in the piece. I used the same relational-temporal principles of form and pitch unfolding I used in *Beyond the Bridge*: statement (abbreviated as '**St**'), variation ('**Va**'), development ('**De**'), contrast ('**Co**'). The first statement (theme 1, the A) is played by the flute, theme 2 by the harp and theme 3 by the vibraphone. The chart shows the Outer Form (in the sense delineated by Felix Salzer). The distribution of the regions is asymmetrical and was made intuitively. On the top of the background model, additional phrases are inserted in the texture freely, such as the tumultuous beginning of the harp right at the onset of the piece. In the Inner Form, the distribution of material is equally asymmetrical, and I set some reference points in both pitch structures and spatial movement of sound. The horn, trombone and trumpet are located as far as possible at the back of the ensemble, creating a kind of spatial background layer; the string quartet is placed in the middle as the spatial middle ground; the piano flute, clarinet and percussion occupy the foreground layer; finally, the harp is located on the left side of the conductor. Altogether, four lines of instruments are on stage. Another principle is that of 'Time' divided into 'past', 'present' and 'future', with a predominance of 'past' which must keep the principle of 'Development' to a minimum (there are only three 'Developments', namely, A2, B2 and C1.)

Fig. 4.17: *Legend*, pitch material and first unfolding.

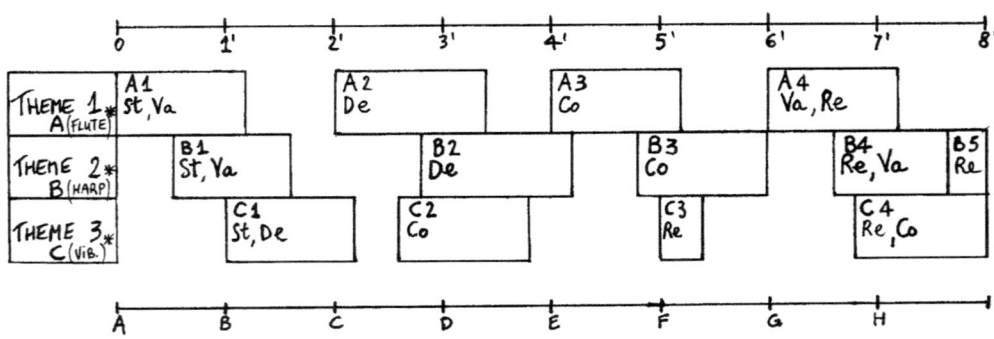

Fig. 4.18: *Legend*, large form.

The main textural preoccupations are based on 'Modulation' and 'Transformation'. For 'Modulation', I implemented a 'signal' (a timbre with a specific loudness and duration) to a pitch in order to allow more 'signals' (pitches) to be unfolded without interference. 'Transformation' was in the form of mutation of one element (timbre, pitch, etc.) into another.

The melodic unfolding of each theme is carried out by changing instruments throughout the work. The remaining textural spaces are areas of reinforcement of timbre (the addition of sonorities or 'effects') to the four melodic lines. Timbral variations and combinations are the result of a mainly linear polyphonic thinking as 'treatment of parts', and some areas are characterised by a specific instrumental group and spatial location, for example, the string quartet occupying the second farthest line on stage. The chart below should give an idea of the instrumental assignment of themes and sections (Fig. 4.19).

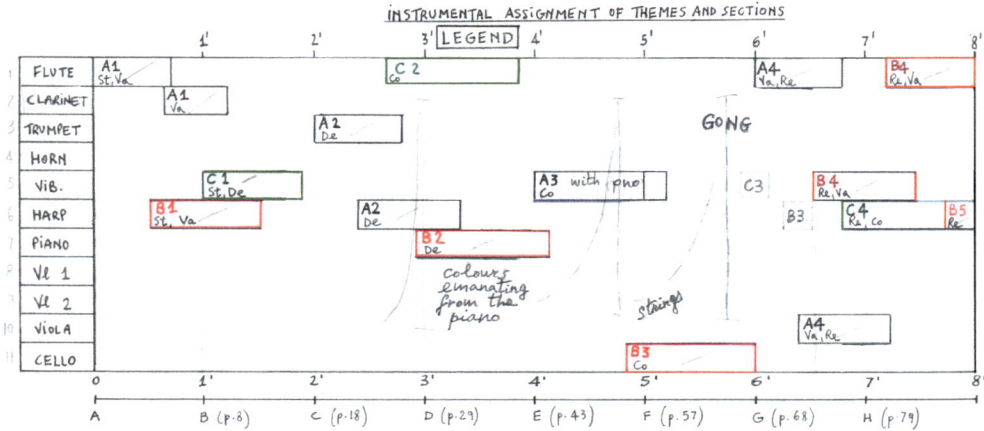

Fig. 4.19: *Legend*, instrumental assignment.

Notice that I mention names of electroacoustic practices such as the words 'effect' and 'treatment'. Indeed, I applied the idea of these sound transformations to the acoustic context of the piece. In the general plan of the piece, I designed a specific category including the following: Reverb, Pitch-shift, Reverse, Delay and 'Nebulae' (meaning a note surrounded by a 'cloud' of microtones and additional overtones in order to create foggy areas of indistinct pitch). I was interested in implementing the basic ideas of these electronic techniques with acoustic means and within a purely acoustic texture.

The organisation of metres is another important aspect of the architecture of the piece. I used five basic tempi referring to the crotchet at 54, 72, 80, 92, 114 and 124. The following chart shows how I subdivided them by metre and speed in groupings that I named 1&8, 2&7, 3&6 and 4&5, based on a palindromic direction converging to the centre 4&5. The succession of the metres can be seen in the lower part of the chart. Pulse modulations have been labelled as 'p.m.' (see Fig. 4.20).

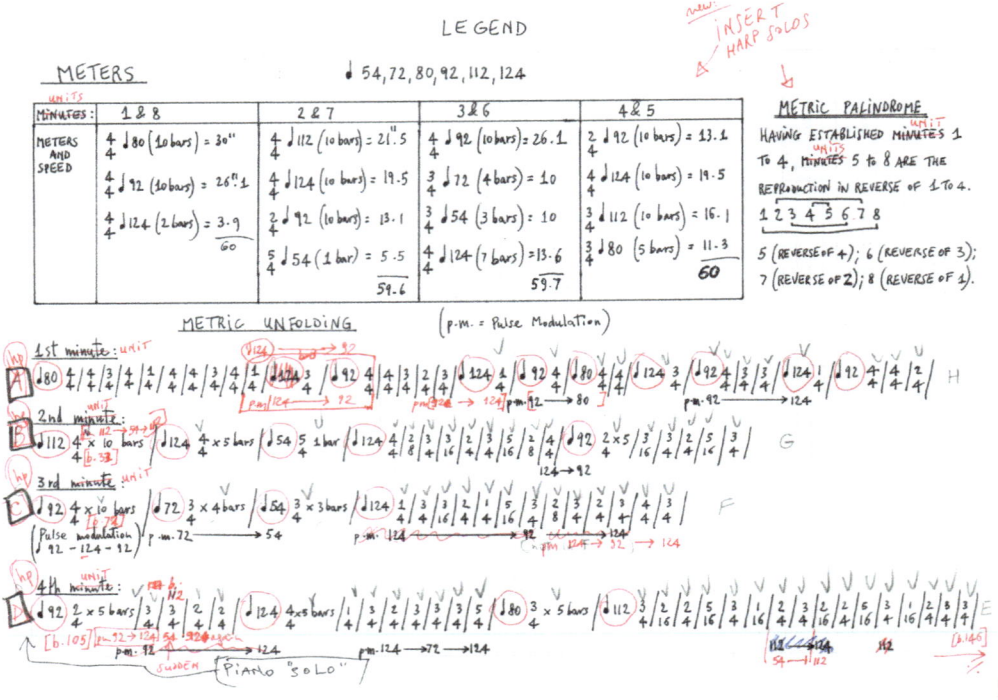

Fig. 4.20: *Legend*, chart of metric unfolding.

It is crucial to mention that the harp is tuned microtonally. The tuning is shown in the chart below (Fig. 4.21).

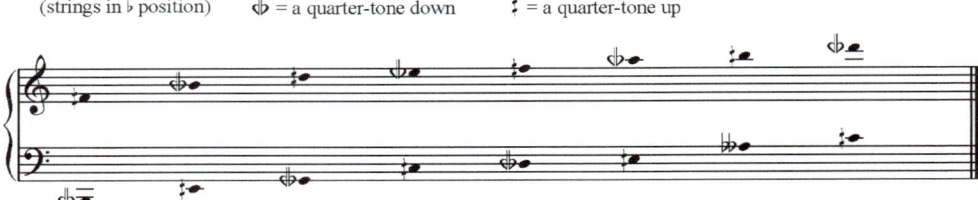

Fig. 4.21: *Legend*, tuning of the harp.

I have selected four fragments of the score that should give an idea of the textures of *Legend* and some of the techniques I have mentioned so far (Figs. 4.22-4.25). The first extract is about the beginning of the piece, bars 1-2. The decisive statement of the harp marks the beginning of the narration. In terms of form, it is the first important injection of free interventions that characterise the harp part throughout the piece. The polarity of the account is already emphasised here: the first phrase is marked with a 'molto deciso e impetuoso' and the second phrase with a 'calmo e molto rubato'. Notice also the change of tempi (Fig. 4.22).

The second extract shows an application of the 'pitch-shift' (transposition) idea between the harp, the piano and the cimbalon in bars 144-148. We shouldn't forget that the microtonal tuning of the harp is 'clashing' with the tempered tuning of the piano and cimbalon (Fig. 4.23).

Legend

Fig. 4.22: *Legend*, bb. 1-2.

Fig. 4.23: *Legend*, bb. 144-148.

The next example includes the 'accelerando' beginning in bar 210 leading to one of the peaks of the piece. The harp line is supported by three dissimilar textures grouped by instrumental families: the strings' demisemiquavers, supported by 'crescendo', are reinforced by the temple blocks, ranging from 'pianissimo' to 'fortissimo', leading to 'pizzicato' and 'tremolo' chords complementing the increasing sense of urgency with irregular rhythmic figures. The brass group holds together by 'distorting' the harp's rhythms with 'heterophonic' rhythmic figures while the rhythmic unison of the woodwinds provides an 'independent' counterpoint leading to the flutter-tongue and multiphonic 'crescendo' notes synchronous with the brass (see Fig. 4.24).

Fig. 4.24: *Legend*, bb. 210-211.

The fourth extract below (Fig. 4.25) shows an application of the 'nebulae' effect mentioned earlier. The bass octave motion of the harp, triggered by the harsh (twangy) timbre in 'sforzatissimo', continues on the sustained fluctuating sounds of the woodwinds. The timbral modifications of the wah-wah mute by the trumpet and trombone, and the circular bowing of the two violins, produce strident harmonic sounds at irregular pace and add further timbral ambiguity to the steady pace of the harp.

Fig. 4.25: *Legend*, bb. 241-243.

PW. Such instrumental use throughout the piece is close to the responsibility of a concerto. But there is generally not a great 'drama' in their interaction with the other instruments. Is this a 'quiet' dialectical relationship? What would 'quiet' mean?

JP. Although the traditional concerto is still well alive today, the general perception of the word 'concerto' has gone through so many radical changes in the past 70 years that definitions vary from composer to composer; I am thinking of John Cage's *Concerto for Piano and Orchestra* as an extreme case in point. Since the 1950s, there is a tendency, especially in works for a solo instrument and ensemble, to stress the dichotomy of the 'individuum-collective'. This image is still dialectic, and the word 'concerto' still implies anything that juxtaposes these two forces.

    The vigorous sense of drama that has tinged the orchestral concerto tradition in the past three centuries has certainly created a perception of interaction in music that is still genre-related to this day, and I suspect my own orchestral concertos reflect that tradition to an extent. However, the ensemble, as a modern cultural entity, facilitates a subconscious detachment from the orchestral tradition, enabling composers to follow a more relaxed and personal approach to the basic idea of the 'concertante'. Although the notions of dialogue, confrontation and interaction remain crucial in my works, I am equally drawn to the ideas of communication as *integration*. The quietness you are referring to suggests a newly-defined relationship between an individuum and the world. This view may explain your perception of a lack of traditional drama in these ensemble works.

    The world we live in is a world of relations, and the idea of the concerto form as embodiment of a social circumstance that is essentially relational is very pertinent to our time. In fact, being *mutual* by definition and *relational* in character, the concerto, as a metaphor, is an accurate mirror of modern life. The ensemble confronts the soloist as the soloist confronts the ensemble. The consciousness of the 'I' is such because of the 'You' (the others). In essence, the concerto form remains a primal effort to establish a relation with the world. Moreover, the idea of the concerto embodies a desire for communication that may take place on multiple levels. For example: soloist-to-audience (regardless of the ensemble); soloist-to-ensemble ('internal' communication, so to speak); and soloist-and-ensemble (together) to the audience. The latter may be divided according to the function of ensemble. For example: ensemble as a recipient and reservoir that amplifies the soloist; ensemble in direct confrontation to the soloist; ensemble expanding the soloist's discourse; ensemble as the subconscious (as a reflection of the soloist) and the soloist expanding the ensemble's discourse; the soloist as the subconscious (as a reflection of the ensemble). All these different roles (and I am sure a few more can be found) make the concerto a very rich and versatile form of contemporary composition. As Martin Buber once said: *"In the beginning is relation"*.

PW. What is the mythic temporal space?

JP. The inner universe of self-knowledge.

PW. Given your philosophical and spiritual outlook, are elements of cycle, or the cyclical, significant in the works?

JP. As with other composers, cycles are significant in my work because they denote something of particular significance that deserves to be dealt with in different temporal, instrumental, or genre-related contexts. The classic definition of 'cycle', at least in the West, denotes a sequence of actions or happenings that occur in a particular order and that may be repeated. In art, it is about a group of works connected to each other through the same issue. Every time I hear the word 'cycle', the first notions that come to my mind are: time, process, reincarnation, unity and collection. In my mind, a musical work is the acoustic document of an idea that manifests itself at a specific point in time. It is the indication of something of a non-physical nature that is limitless and does not have one form only. If this idea is alive on a metaphysical plane, it resides permanently there, and at some point, in chronological time, it may re-take shape in another musical work because it needs to be scrutinised again. The nature and the circumstance of such rebirth will depend on how exhaustively the composer may have fulfilled his task in the first work at that point in time. If for some reason the task remained incomplete or needs to be resurrected under another shape or context, the idea itself will call for a new 'evaluation'.

There are few cycles in my output, and each of them reflects what I have just said. Cyclical forms may involve a cathartic experience, fulfilling and illuminating, yet at times troubled and unsettling. I perceive a musical cycle as an attempt to define an awareness of something of a particular importance over a large portion of time and in a pseudo-circular mode. The urge will be strong: it must come, go and come back in one's lifetime. My life story is made by changes, developments and some questions that may need to be answered at different times. Cycles can also be manifestations of both a meta-work and single works unified in one larger unit. In my experience, the two notions are complementary.

PW. What in your work is the balance between a search for self-discovery, self-awareness ('you') and the desire to present a rational or enlightened view to an audience?

JP. A process of self-discovery always goes hand in hand with a sense of self-awareness. In my experience, the interrelating conditions of self-awareness and self-discovery are instinctively (subconsciously) reflected in the desire to present a personal view to a listener, regardless of whether such a view may be rational or enlightened. It is the musical work as existential phenomenology rather than causal perspective (the explanation of internal structural/physical mechanisms of the piece) that will reveal that balance. The choice of topics (musical and non-musical), the sonic material, the techniques of sound organisation, the instruments and so on are contributors to a greater, all-encompassing reality that rise above sound. Thus, a provisional answer could be: the balance is the work itself in its totality and as a phenomenological experience.

PW. How important is the audience to you?

JP. Heidegger said that a subject (I) cannot be who he is without the world (you, they, an audience). If I exist, it is because I am in this world and in relation with it. The meaning of my existence is therefore not only about being in the world but also about being with others. Existence implies openness to the world and to others. If I exist, it is because I am in the world, therefore I exist in a 'co-being' with others. The fact that co-being with others is an integral part of my existence means that my perception of existence is what it is in view of others. Simply put, we are all connected and important to each other. Every psychological event arises from a relationship with the world, and to speak of an individual is to speak of a constituent part of the collective. By the same token, to speak of the collective is also to speak of an individual who is a part of it. If I need 'you' to understand who I am, you need 'me' to understand who you are.

PW. What do you fear most about composing?

JP. Nothing.

CHAPTER FIVE

ORCHESTRAL MUSIC

THERE
Johannes Klumpp

JK. When you go back to a piece you wrote more than 25 years earlier, how quickly do your old thoughts come back to your mind? Do you feel strange about this kind of situation? And do you feel the urge to make radical changes in the piece? How does your present 'you' come to terms with the older 'you'?

JP. First of all, I need to mention that I didn't have to revise the music of *There* for the premiere that you conducted in 2019. I only refined some indications in the score. Nevertheless, the fact that I heard the piece for the first time in 25 years has been a rather emotional experience because I could finally hear the music that had been living in my imagination all these years. I must admit that it's been quite pleasing to find out that the music sounded exactly as I had imagined it so many years ago. Your points seem to be related to the problem of revising an old work, though.

Undoubtedly, re-visiting an old piece 20 or 30 years later poses many questions. It means going back to the person I was all those years ago, therefore, having to deal with someone I no longer am. With this in mind, my issues are: how can I remain loyal to the old 'me' now? Should I revisit the piece with the same mind of the old 'me' (which won't be entirely the same anyway) or should I allow the present 'me' to take over? How can I ensure that the musical thoughts of yesterday are appropriate to my perception of today? And how relevant is this second point actually? My answer is that I tend to be very pragmatic when faced with these kinds of questions: my present 'I' must come to terms with the older 'I' according to the situation, and each situation is different. Radical changes can be draining work, but then why would I have to change the piece *that* radically in the first place? If the need for such radicality was so strong, would it not make more sense to re-write the piece from scratch? And if I decided to do so, to what extent is it really the same piece? I think this is a personal matter of 'historical' authenticity in that I have to decide to what effect the revision process has ethical implications about the re-examination of the original idea including the implementation of a new opinion on the old one. If I felt the urge to make radical changes in the piece, I would do so.

On a practical level, is a re-interpretation of the old 'me' through the eyes of the new 'me' worth the pain of revision? The correct answer may depend on whether the piece has been performed or not. I have been in situations of this kind a couple of times: if the old piece had not been performed, I realised that, if necessary, the piece could 'die' in order to allow a new piece to be born out of it. But such a fatal sentence would not make sense if the old piece had been performed and my new viewpoint was 'ethically' entitled to prevail. If the piece to be revised had been performed, the 'historical' authenticity is an issue to be tackled most basically and according to a clear analysis of the situation.

JK. In *There,* it seems evident that an 'I' factor (the passionate playing of the string quartet) is contrasting with a more cosmic component (the string orchestra). Is this 'I' your alter ego?

JP. The dichotomy you are depicting is the raison d'être of the piece. My direct answer to your question is: yes, it is a part of me. On a subtle level, however, the larger dimension represented by the string orchestra is another simultaneous indication of my existence that is as crucial as the more passionate one represented by the string quartet. One needs the other in order to achieve a sense of unity resulting from two complementary opposites: the physical (passion, suffering, yearning) and the metaphysical (acceptance, integration, peace). The first is calling for the second. The latter is responding. I am saying this because existence cannot be defined only in dualistic terms. Life is not only a finite temporal experience between antithetical events such as birth and death. To separate the physical from the metaphysical, the emotional from the spiritual would be absurd. The alter ego you detect in the music played by the quartet is also latent, by contrast, in the music of the orchestra. We need art to celebrate our tumultuous existence on this planet in a holistic way. Music takes us beyond ourselves and has the power to project the search for existential meaning onto the experience of a life that, at some point, is no longer our own. It expands our knowledge of ourselves while widening our mental boundaries beyond ourselves.

When I compose, I am aware that sounds, form and meaning are expressions of the same truth; this is the truth of my daily story which is similar to yours, and yet remains an individual experience. Like yours, my life isn't fiction, but a story that is factual. My 'I' and many other 'I's are *living* together, side by side, because everything I write stems from a necessity to communicate something real that is pertinent to life. What I write reveals a part of me and, at the same time, that part of you that is similar to me. This 'I' that we all share may not always be shining and nice because darkness and light are two aspects of the same reality. Music reveals paths and clues that are often uncomfortable, challenging or terrifying while conveying our secrets and emotions, visions and desires. It is an account of someone's life performed by someone else, like in the theatre where the actor's job is to portray a character of a story that has been set by the author. The narrative of my life and yours may be similar or even the same, yet each of our stories has something personal that is sacred and mysterious at the same time, and that is asking to be discovered through the music. Perhaps this is what Virginia Woolf meant when she wrote, *"There are some stories which have to be retold by each generation"*.[22]

JK. In some parts of the score, where the 'I' prevails, you write instructions such as *con disperata tensione, molto teso e violento* that suggest a very subjective approach to the music. In the world of contemporary music, however, we are more used to the idea that music-making should be objective rather than subjective. Are you consciously opposing objectivity? Can one suffer objectively?

JP. Art is subjective. Complete objectivity is impossible to achieve: any form of art has something subjective in it. Even the most serial or aleatory composition has an element of subjectivity that is inherent in the choice that induced the composer to use that very technique or procedure rather than another. John Cage's indeterminacy was a choice resulting from his lifestyle and philosophical ideas. Brian Ferneyhough's complexity and Arvo Pärt's simplicity reflect philosophical choices that are strictly personal, therefore highly subjective. The sound of any kind of music is the result of a choice, and a choice implies a decision that remains essentially subjective. One of the continuous problems of Modernism, especially in Continental Europe, is a silent conspiracy that has managed to split art from the heart, and more specifically, music from real (subjective) life. Objective music, if it exists, is, by nature, cold. Subjective music speaks to the heart because it is *real*. It's as simple as that. And this is why the music I write needs to be performed and conducted from the heart.

---

[22] Lee (1999:11).

JK. The score is notated very precisely and all the extended techniques you used work very well. To what extent does experimenting with instrumental techniques, trying it out for yourself as it were, belong to the way you work?

JP. Whenever possible, when I use extended techniques, I try out what I write on the instrument because I like to double-check the timbre of the sounds I am working on. If I don't have the instrument, I'll borrow one. When I composed the two most demanding pieces for strings I have ever written, namely *Epitaph* (for cello and electronics) and *Over* (for solo violin), I tried out each technique by myself (bow position on the string, bow pressure, bow angle, finger pressure, and so on) and note by note. Today I have reached a point where I can say that I feel confident about using extended techniques for string instruments. I no longer need to try out each technique I use because I have a good idea of what to expect. Mind you, there is always something to discover and I remain open-minded and willing to extend my knowledge of any musical instrument. Wind and brass instruments are trickier because I don't have the basic technique of sound production, and that doesn't put me in the position to experiment with these instruments the way I would with a string, keyboard or percussion instrument. In any case, what I enjoy very much is working together with instrumentalists as much as possible. This usually works well with soloists, chamber groups and ensembles. As you know, it is a more difficult situation with orchestras, but then this is where the conductor comes in...

JK. The original draft of *There* was based on turbulent political realities. Which were they? To what extent are these still audible today in the final version?

JP. The 1990s were the years of the Balkan conflict and I was terrified not only by the atrocities committed in those wars, but also by the cruelty and perversity of the human mind in general. The polarity between the physical and the metaphysical that we discussed earlier has also another facet: I composed the string quartet's intense polyphony as a sign of social and personal turmoil resulting from the horror of war and hostility. I was feeling anger, pain, disbelief and protest against any kind of disrespect for civil rights. On the other hand, the sustained chords of the string orchestra mirror an ethically superior reality, a vision for a humane condition that I associated with the colour blue and the sky.

JK. And this fits perfectly with what I was about to ask you: in what way was Kandinsky's work *Towards the Blue* an inspiration for *There*? And what about the notion of inspiration? How do you manage to translate inspiration into music without composing 'illustratively'?

JP. Kandinsky's picture, *Towards the Blue* (1939), suggests an interesting mixture of pure abstraction and naïve art. The initial title of *There* had been the same title of the picture, the blue of the sky symbolising the larger metaphysical dimension opposing the physical plane proposed by the string quartet. When I decided to write *There*, Kandisky's picture was in my mind as another representation of a similar idea. I remember being struck by the two lateral objects in the picture vaguely resembling two string instruments such as a violin with an extended fingerboard or a bouzouki-like instrument. On the top of the picture, the two hypothetical instruments cross each other inside the blue. Also, the four curved lines on the left end side of the picture, aligned with the 'fingerboard' of the black instrument, suggested a musical staff, and the three pencil-like objects seemed to invite me to write notes on the staff. These music references, and the blue stain as a region of connection, contributed to the inspiration of the music.

Composers draw incentives from different sources. Mahler stressed the autobiographical aspect, Berlioz and Schönberg were affected by poetry, Rimsky-Korsakov was captivated by the folkloristic traditions of Russia, Hindemith was obsessed with technique, Benjamin Britten and Mozart would emphasise the concern of the audience, paintings are an unlimited source of inspiration for Harrison Birtwistle, and so forth. In his book *Music and Inspiration*, Jonathan Harvey speaks of an 'intriguing sense' that occurs when feeling *"the air of another planet"*,[23] as he puts it. In my case, I don't necessarily need a visual reference in order to get inspired. This may be just one source amongst others. Inspiration is a fascinating topic that, in my opinion, is strictly linked to the individual's power of imagination. The two go hand in hand. You can't get inspired if you are unable to send your imagination into turmoil and then turn that turmoil into reality.

When I refer to life experience, it is not about translating biographical events and wanting to convey my emotions to the audience. This would be far too simplistic and reductive. The issue is deeper than that. What are life experiences if not a trigger, let alone a mirror, of something of a deeper significance? Is the artistic experience not a gate to broader states of awareness? What is my intuition actually revealing to me when I am composing? Is it a mirror of the subconscious? Let's think of an intuition, an idea, a landscape, a poem, and even a mystical experience: are these sources of inspiration not the perception of something bigger than ourselves? When I wrote *There*, notions like *Towards the Blue* and *Music for the World* (another initial title) echoed in my mind throughout the compositional process. They were already there before I wrote the score. I felt a strong desire to share with the world the idea of a better life. We know how Beethoven felt when he wrote his ninth symphony. He exemplified his vision of a united world with the *Ode of Joy*. It was about composing music for the world that would fulfil an ideal of agreement, peace, unification and perhaps identity. The music of *There* was born out of the same impetus.

JK. During our conversations, you made a point about the employment of quarter tones in your music. You said that they imply a significant sensuality. What are microtones for you? Can you describe what exactly microtonality evokes in your mind?

JP. When we listen to music of the Middle East, just to mention one tradition, we can feel a natural sensuality in the melodies of the songs that is congenital in the music. In many non-Western music traditions, microtonality belongs to the vernacular and is not perceived as an extra musical ingredient. In the 20th Century, some pioneer composers such as Alois Hába, Juliá Carrillo and Harry Partch have produced microtonal works of pristine beauty where the approach to pitch is 'uncontaminated' by the rigid restrictions of equal temperament. Like in Arabic music, I have always perceived this as a very liberating musical experience. The European avant-garde has integrated microtonality in all sorts of genres and individual styles; I describe microtonality as a re-integration of an all-encompassing emancipation of pitch perception.

The sensuality I was referring to in our conversation may be compared to blurred colours in paintings. If we look carefully at a blurred background or image, the first thing we notice is a sense of abstraction as a result of the lack of sharpness. I experience something similar when I look at ancient ruins, for example, the pigments decay we see on ancient Greek or Roman wall paintings. The images are perceived as vague and unfocused. In music, the succession and superimposition of intervals create horizontal and vertical spaces (melody and harmony) that are full of tension and intensity. If we listen carefully to a minor third and a minor sixth interval successively, for instance, we can hear there is a quality (something 'psychological') that is differentiating these (acoustic) frequencies in our mind. Similarly, when two or more notes sound together, we react to the vertical space created by these frequencies.

---

[23] Harvey (1999:161).

The historical division of intervals in terms of dissonances and consonances has created specific cognitive responses to what we call melody and harmony. Now, the harmonic series, which is nothing else than the 'genetic code' of a sound, is based on micro-intervals that are microtonal by nature. By superimposing two pitches, the interval we hear contains a natural pulsation that is inherent in the nature of the harmonic series, but the tuning of equal temperament 'rectifies' the interval by eliminating the pulsations, that means by changing the tuning until these pulsations disappear.

This adjustment turned out to be so practical that has characterised our Western music tradition of the past 250 years or so. It is not only a matter of practicality, though. As always, any technical and sociological change taking place during the course of history reflects a general transformation of the Zeitgeist of a specific era. It is not a coincidence that equal temperament in Europe established itself at the rising of the Age of Enlightenment; a time marked by a new surge of intellectual clarity: the importance of reason, the ideas of progress and liberty. This growing sense of clarity and social order matched perfectly the urgency for a new aesthetic of sound based on the same need of clarity that equal temperament could provide. In terms of pitch cognition, the first volume of J.S. Bach's *The Well-Tempered Clavier*, written in 1722, is a compelling example of a kind of order and clarity that is self-transcending. The music of Beethoven is very similar in that sense.

If equal temperament suggests clarity, microtonality hints at blurring, indistinctness and ambiguity. If equal temperament suggests realism, microtonality depicts hyperrealism. If equal temperament suggests the known, microtonality insinuates the unknown. The mysterious and undefinable sounds of quarter-tone or eighth-tone intervals have an exotic quality that I perceive as sensual, liberating and captivating at the same time. For example, the enigmatic charm of an Arab folk song or a work like Alois Hába's *Suite in quarter-tones for 4 trombones*, opus 72 (written in 1950) would lose their beauty if performed in equal temperament. The qualities I have described, however, are most clearly definable in music that is played at slow motion, such as the Hába's piece or much of ancient Greek music. In this context, sensuality is a synonym for something 'strange', exotic, alien: a *curious* quality that adds that extra touch of ineffability to a musical discourse.

JK. In *There*, you are also using an untypical spatial arrangement of the orchestra in relation to the soloists. I guess this was essential for the realisation of the music. What is the significance of such an unusual arrangement of the instruments?

JP. In order to stress the near-far and physical-metaphysical dichotomy, I decided to split the string orchestra into two interacting groups: the main (orchestral) group to be positioned in a big semicircle around the string quartet, and the quartet to be located in the centre of the stage and circumscribed by the orchestra. In the diagram reproduced below (Fig. 5.1), you can see the large semicircle of the orchestra enclosing the small semicircle of the quartet. With this arrangement, I wanted to stress two things: firstly, the segregation of the earthly (the quartet) from the otherwordly (the orchestra); secondly, the connection between these two distinctions as if belonging to the same unifying reality. The significance being that segregation and integration are parts of the same truth.

The arrangement of the orchestral instruments is based on their frequency range, from the lowest to the highest. The lowest instruments (the double bass and the cello) are located in the middle, further back on the stage. Two viola groups occupy an intermediary position on each side of the semicircle, while the two violin groups are located at the front end of the line, closer to the audience. The red double-arrows in the diagram show the to-and-fro motion of sound taking place on both edges of the large semicircle: the bass-treble-bass registral motion begins in the centre, reaches both ends of the semicircle and returns to the centre.

The motion on the right side of the stage begins from the double basses and reaches the second violins through the violas; on the left end side, the motion begins from the celli and reaches the first violins through the violas. The far-near-far movement of sound in space, therefore, corresponds to the low-high-low change of register taking place around the string quartet. Within the large semicircle, I have set a second spatial trajectory taking place between the quartet and the orchestra (see the blue arrows on the diagram) whereas the fiery phrases of the quartet are addressed to the orchestra (the recipient) and dissolved into distant prolonged sounds.

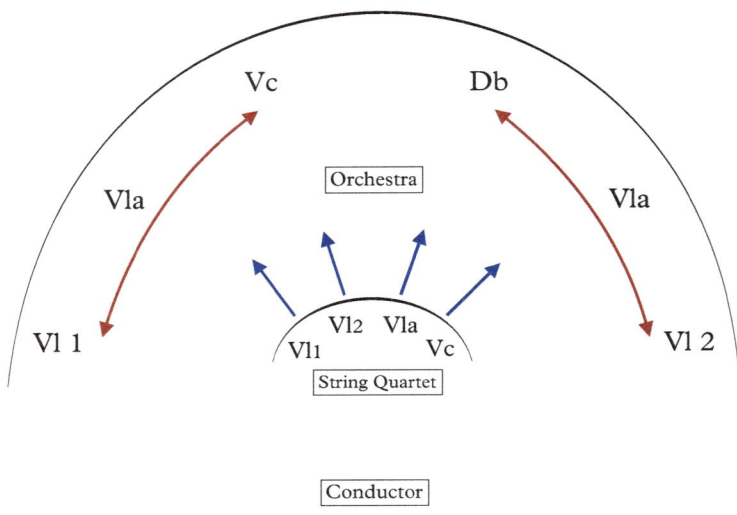

Fig. 5.1: *There*, spatial arrangement of instruments.

JK. Throughout the piece, two different worlds are constantly influencing each other: the realm of the 'individual' and the dimension of the celestial. The borders between the two poles remain permeable or perhaps become permeable. To what extent is a political thought such as 'everyone lives in a bubble' related to this music?

JP. I think there are several ways to look at these two interacting worlds, and 'living in a bubble' may imply different meanings. In any case, permeability is a crucial point I have tried to make by having the string quartet forcefully searching for points of contact with the string orchestra. The latter is responding by receiving and embracing the message while absorbing and projecting it onto a larger, symbolically timeless, dimension. The orchestra acts as both the redeeming counterpart and the filter of the quartet. Permeability must remain imperative in order to establish communication, create movement and, ultimately, in order to accomplish synthesis. There is also a social significance to it, in that the life of an individual is inextricably linked to the life of the collective, and the concerns of the collective are echoed by individual experience. Back to the point I was making earlier, using personal experience isn't necessarily self-referential because it reflects the existential questions of the collective. This is why private concerns are tangible signs of a universal preoccupation, and the personal bubble you are referring to may be interpreted as a result of different social conditions.

JK. I can remember the premiere well. What does the composer feel and learn when his piece is born?

JP. A premiere is always something special and unique. I think a learning process is already implicit in the process of composition, but a premiere provides you with the first acoustic experience, thus with the music itself, rather than your ideas about the music. Listening to the realisation of my musical ideas is something I cannot adequately describe verbally. What I can say, though, is that it implies an element of fulfilment, and, at the same time, confrontation with myself. The music brings with it its own life, and while my conscious mind stands empty and filled with wonder before the music, I am overwhelmed by a flood of thoughts, emotions and images. I feel like having to admit that it is my own inner nature revealing itself and uttering things I could not have entrusted to my tongue. I realise that I have executed the drive of an apparently alien impulse in me and followed a trajectory that has led me somewhere else; that I am part of a primordial process of creation and subordinate to a higher force. Perhaps the greatest learning is the sensation that my work, the music I am now listening to, is greater than myself and exerts a power that is above me.

JK. What did you hear in the piece that you didn't know before?

JP. From a technical point of view, in the case of *There*, I heard nothing that I didn't know before, as all the sounds corresponded exactly to what I had written and imagined in my mind. Personally, listening to my music for the first time is like discovering sides of me I never knew existed, at least not consciously. Knowing something can be a very challenging experience, as I may recognise uncomfortable aspects of myself and contrasting definitions of whom I am supposed to be. Sometimes, I am facing emotions and images I never intended to trigger and which I am now confronted with for the first time. This means assimilating subconscious information into consciousness. At this point, I may realise that I have acted as a channel for elemental images to be evoked by music.

HYPOTHETICAL QUESTIONS, PIANO CONCERTO, THERE, DOUBLE CONCERTO, NOT TWO
Vittorio Parisi

Hypothetical Questions (orchestra)

VP. I find it extremely interesting that you decided to revise an early work. Generally speaking, I must say that, from a conductor's point of view, the serial pieces of the 1950s are a real nightmare. This is because the possibilities of interpretation are reduced more or less to zero and the role of the conductor is confined to that of a machine. A new kind of specialized conducting technique was born in order to conduct that music; Pierre Boulez's technique was just an example, and I'm not sure it was such a good thing. Looking at the score of your *Hypothetical Questions* one can clearly see your compositional preoccupations at the time you wrote it. I can certainly understand the predicaments you had about serialism in those days. When I was a very young composer myself, before definitively leaving composing for conducting, I wrote a concerto for orchestra based on serial principles, but I felt the necessity to interrupt the two sections of the concert by introducing a trumpet and double bass free jazz cadenza. Total serialism was fascinating at the time, but it soon became very boring to me. Did you actually consider *Hypothetical Questions* as a true performance piece or a statement of denial of a serial approach to composition? And how do you relate to serial techniques and fixed systems in composition?

JP. The answer to your first question is: both. I should say right at the beginning that I have never written a truly serial piece in my entire life. On a couple of occasions in my early output, I have used what I call quasi-serial techniques based on one-to-one procedures that, once unfolded, I would subsequently negate by disputing their rules and eventually undermining them from within the same system that created them. I actually think that, *if* well-engineered (and I must stress the 'if'), especially at the beginning of a piece, a one-to-one compositional procedure may be revealing at times. But, apart from very few works, I share your views about the boredom conveyed by a kind of music that remains essentially mechanical.

Like many other fellow composers, as a young man, I studied Integral Serialism and learnt from it as much as I could in terms of discovering new techniques of sound organisation. After all, the need for systems and procedures has characterised Western composition since Gregorian chants. However, I soon viewed serialism as essentially a historical necessity that contributed to the creation of new idioms and new types of texture. I looked at the failure of serial systems as a stimulus leading to the establishment of new musical directions and further diversifications of compositional practices. Perhaps I should add that in those days, I was much more inspired by John Cage's procedures in his works of the 1940s (before he embraced chance operations) than the total serialism of the European avant-garde. My piano piece *Déjà vu* (1988) epitomises that phase of my life. Techniques are only the means that enable us to create music, and it is the musical result, not the technique, that I am ultimately interested in. Ludwig Wittgenstein once said that *"philosophy is not a body of doctrine, but an activity."*[24] Similarly, composition is not a body of doctrine, but an activity. If composition was to be reduced to a mere set of rules and procedures, it would lose its evocative power. I have never been interested in writing a serial piece. I use my own 'home-made' systems and techniques that enable me to create both a solid structural foundation upon which the music can flow in a formally and aesthetically coherent way and the inclusion of intuitive decisions.

When I compose, I have a general direction in mind. A path is defined by the organisation of form, pitch, metre, timbre and so forth. Rules and procedures are important as they indicate the general route and the initial goal of the journey. But once the journey begins, I defer to my gut feeling where and when to turn left or right, so the goal itself may change as a result of the diversions that have occurred during the creative process. This contradiction is a fundamental part of the creative game: a sign of action, rather than theorisation. Wittgenstein would define it as a meaningful and necessary undertaking for the unfolding of a discourse. Rational rules may be made necessary by methodical convention, but it is the experience of *experience* that is the ultimate factor of artistic creativity.

In the late 1980s and early 1990s, I was very much in search of equilibrium between pre-determinate procedures and intuition in my musical works. I had become aware that I didn't want to write music resulting from fixed rules and pre-established systems without giving voice to my intuitive creativity. Having already explored this preoccupation in my early orchestral pieces, *Omen* and *Concertino*, I found myself questioning a wider palette of approaches to structure and technique that would allow me to consolidate a vivid texture and a stronger declamatory style within a pre-delineated form.

In 2010, I began to revise an orchestral work called *Counterparts* that I had written in 1991-1992. This piece had been inspired by a poem called *A Dialogue of Self and Soul* written by the Irish poet William Butler Yeats. While re-reading the poem nine years later, I decided to change the title of my piece into *Hypothetical Questions*. During the revision, I focused on strengthening the existing framework of the piece while, at the same time, quenching my desire to give voice to my intuition, as inspired by the poem. I dedicated a great deal of time to a substantial re-organisation of the original material, and created free interventions in the course

---

[24] Wittgenstein (1961:49).

of the new compositional process. The revision became so rigorous that I soon found myself shaping new musical gestures out of the old ones: this is when I fully realised that I was writing a new work from the relics of the old one. While giving increasing space to intuitive interventions (the new *hypothetical* questions), I kept all the pre-established unfolding of pitch, loudness and time as the spine of the work, whereas towards the end of the composition, the original formulas would only function as mere parametrical suggestions at the disposal of my intuition. On a technical level, I can say that *Hypothetical Questions* was born out of these new questions based on the vestiges of *Counterparts*.

In *A Dialogue of Self and Soul,* an energetic approach to dialectics is portrayed most authentically in an imaginary dialogue where the Soul is lamenting about the actions of the Self (the body). With the typical directness that characterises Yeats's emotional imagery, the questions raised by both the Soul and the Self manage to retain a cryptic connotation throughout the dialogue. For example, the Soul would ask, "*Who can distinguish darkness from the soul?*" while the Self would ask, "*What matter if the ditches are impure? What matter if I live it all once more?*" The conflict between traditional morality and human desire is resolved by paradoxically choosing the body (the Self) rather than the Soul. The poet chooses the Self as a symbol of the joy of life with all its failures, as opposed to the strict morality of the Soul. By reversing the Christian doctrine, Yeats declares the victory of the Self over the Soul. *A Dialogue of Self and Soul* echoes a debate culture that is typical of Anglo-Saxon Christianity which moulded the environment Yeats grew up in. A tradition of this kind is often articulated in dramatic tones that are used as necessary devices to enhance an ontological investigation about the meaning of existence. This form of dialectics is still very much alive in English-speaking academic circles and tends to transcend even the established norms of ideological conventions that characterise a specific tradition: a debate exists as a platform for critical discussion. This form of dialectics as an impulse to musical discourse is very much present in many of my works.

Similar to Yeats's poem, when I compose music, I choose notes and assemble them in such a way that they allude to semantic significance and extra-musical reflections, often interwoven with symbols and imagery of a timeless connotation. In the construction of form, I am attracted to allusive reflections, as well as the use of symbolic structures, sometimes aided by numerology. On the basis of such reversion, in *Hypothetical Questions*, I continued the debate by adding more questions while trying to transcend the polarity of soul and body and the limitation of rational thinking (the serial procedures). I decided to keep the gestures (questions) of *Counterparts* derived from the original quasi-serial rules and to extend the texture of the piece by adding imaginary, intuitive questions that would transcend the strict 'morality' inherent in the pre-determined procedures. A new layer of intuitive, irrational phrases would now circumscribe the original phrases established by the initial framework; these newly established 'dialectics of the mind' would merge the rigour of the past (the morality of bygone serialism) with the uninhibited sensuality of the present (the power of intuition and imagination). In this way, the ontological debate I was after would hopefully become arguable, argumentative and contentious, while proposing daring and questionable hypotheses. I also documented the revision by producing three scores, each reflecting an intermediary phase leading to the final version of the score.

VP. How can the strict techniques you used for *Hypothetical Questions* coexist with such an evocative poem in your mind?

JP. As I said, I transcended strict formalism by adding new gestures based on intuition. However, I don't view compositional systems and procedures as rigid technicalities, but rather as hidden 'organisms' of the music, without which the musical form of the artistic conception cannot be tangible to the ear. Luigi Nono defined sound organisation as "*...the very existence* *of spiritual order, creative discipline and clarity of thought*.[25]   Nono's insight is important because it hints at the intricate relationship between the revelation inherent in the creative process, the necessity of structure, and the musical artefact as such. For me, the organisation of sound lays between these two poles: it provides a route that allows the abstraction of the conception to become music.

By merging system and inspiration, the rational and the irrational, I consciously embrace the aesthetic and intellectual conflict that may result from such an experience. In *Hypothetical Questions*, strict techniques appear at the beginning of the piece, but they dissolve in time. In my mind, the techniques I used coexist rather well with the evocative qualities of Yeats's poem as their in-built flexibility allowed me to create a variety of conflictual gestures based on different shapes and articulations that would emphasise the diversity of the allegories implied in a musical phrase, and the autonomous qualities of the in-between areas characterised by sustained sounds.

I mentioned the word 'conflictual' because conflict is intrinsic in both works (*A Dialogue of Self and Soul* and *Hypothetical Questions*). In Yeats's poem, conflicts are depicted by subtle insinuations about correlated aspects of human existence: the psychological, spiritual, rational and the physical. The Soul's incongruent attitude towards the experience of love and war, death and birth is a case in point. This struggle is the stimulus needed in order to keep the tension of the poem alive. *Hypothetical Questions* exploits a similar conflict by introducing dissimilar elements and rhythmic configurations that result from, and contrast with, the gestures generated by the quasi-serial impulses.

An example of such divergent actions can be heard in bars 17-23 (Figs. 5.2 & 5.3) where the serial gesture played by the percussion and keyboards in bar 17 is opposed by the rhythmic linearity of the woodwinds in bars 17-18 which, in turn, is contradicted by an intuitive 'crescendo' of the strings with contrabassoon, bassoon and bass clarinet in bar 18. This 'crescendo' leads to an interspersed texture, resembling a 'Klangfarben*harmonie*'[26] in bars 19-20 resulting from an intuitive unfolding of pre-determined pitch material stretched over two bars and ornamented by a quasi-pointillistic gesture extended to the end of bar 20.

The following divergence in bars 21-23 is delineated by an unexpected block of sounds dominated by the multiphonics of the woodwinds and the strings 'tremoli' triggered by the 'pizzicato' of the double basses. The 'crescendo' of the muted trumpets in bar 23 is the spark of the next rhythmic gesture. The latter results from the contrasting combination of the stretched quasi-serial phrase led by the marimba, vibraphone and piano and the intuitive homophonic line of the flutes doubled by the oboes.

Pre-determined form is questioned by spontaneous interventions of intuitive actions. Another example occurs in bars 185-188 (Figs. 5.4). This time four conflicting elements are being superimposed. The music may be heard in three simultaneous timbral layers: the backbone provided by the quasi-linearity of the piano, marimba, roto-toms and timpani phrases is disputed by the 'staccato' chords of the wind section dramatized by the 'crescendo' of the contrabassoons, trumpets, trombones and tubas, while the strings, harps and celesta provide a pointillistic layer of rhythmic vigour played loudly.

As T.S. Eliot suggests, "forms have to be broken and remade".[27] The end of a language calls for the beginning of a new language based on the re-evaluation of a former idiom informed by critical assessment of its artistic value. Each musical work we compose is not only writing itself but also re-writing the past and inventing the future.

---

[25] Nono (1959:4).
[26] My definition (related to Schönberg's and Webern's 'Klangfarbenmelodie').
[27] Eliot (1969:37).

Fig. 5.2: *Hypothetical Questions*, bb. 17-20.

Fig. 5.3: *Hypothetical Questions*, bb. 21-24.

Fig. 5.4: *Hypothetical Questions*, bb. 185-188.

Piano Concerto (microtonal piano, orchestra and choir)

VP. Your microtonal *Piano Concerto* is very interesting. The score reminded me of Salvatore Sciarrino's concerto *Una immagine di Arpocrate*, surely not for the writing style, but because in Sciarrino's piece the celesta follows the solo piano writing by playing more or less the same part. Similarly, in your *Piano Concerto* the orchestral piano looks like a shadow that follows more or less precisely the solo piano part. Does this 'double' represent something very important for you?

JP. Yes. The orchestral piano is the mirror and indeed the shadow of the solo piano: it is its alter ego. The different microtonal tuning, however, releases a transfigured echo effect that produces an enigmatic reflection of the sounds played by the solo piano.

VP. Definitely the microtonal setting gives the piece a special sound. In your programme note, you talk about a sort of cry. The audio (demo) recording of the microtonal piano is impressive, at times even frightening in its compelling intensity. Was your choice of microtonality a result of a specific, even isolated, compositional preoccupation in your life? Do you think microtonal music will have a dominant part in the future?

JP. I conceived the *Piano Concerto* as a fully microtonal work where the microtonal piano is the protagonist of the story. I use microtonality quite often in my works, but this is the only large piece that is entirely based on microtones. I think the use of microtonal music in today's music scene is very widespread already, and I hear many composers today working with a sort of 'pan-tonality' that includes every kind of tonal systems. Personally, gone are the days when I thought in terms of tonal, atonal and microtonal.

VP. Although the use of microtonality in Western classical music has emerged strongly in the past century, its origin is rooted in much folk music of the world, including the music of the Far East. I know you have spent part of your life in Rome and, although I cannot see any evidence that would speak for it, I must ask you if there is any link between your music and the music of Giacinto Scelsi. If not, how far is the use of microtonality in your music linked with the philosophy of the Far East?

JP. I share with Scelsi a strong interest in Eastern philosophies and arguably the narrative device known as 'stream of consciousness', but I don't think there is any plausible link between my music and his. At least, this is how I see it today, and from my very subjective perspective. However, I must say that I know little of his music, perhaps a dozen pieces or so. Although I have listened to, and enjoyed, much music of the Far East, I don't think my use of microtonality is particularly linked to those musical traditions either, at least not directly or consciously.

VP. In your music, I do not find a big use of multiphonic sounds for woodwinds. Having had the honour to conduct your opera *Re di Donne*, I noticed how parsimoniously you use multiphonics techniques. Considering that many contemporary composers seem to be fascinated by these techniques, I'd like to ask your opinion on this issue. Multiphonic sounds play a big role in spectral works, for example. What do you think about this musical movement that played such a big part at the end of the century? Has this influenced your way of composing?

JP. Similar to what I said about microtonality, multiphonics belong to extended instrumental techniques and I use them whenever I feel they have to be used. I don't have a 'compartmental' or academic approach to sound, and I don't compose in terms of musical movements or ideologies. When I choose multiphonics to be employed at a specific point in the composition, I do so naturally and according to my musical instinct. I never think that I have to use techniques and styles in line with this or that idiom or 'school'. I feel that a musical work can be either good or bad regardless of its idiom, and that any approach to sound and technique must relate to the poietic content of the piece. That's what ensures artistic evolution.

There (string quartet with string orchestra)

VP. In regard to *There*, I only know one piece in the repertoire that has been written for string quartet and string orchestra: that is *Introduction et Allegro* by Elgar. Your British heritage may imply a link between your *There* and Elgar's piece, although I tend to doubt it. Is my assumption correct? Or is this piece somehow connected to or inspired by Sylvano Bussotti's symphonic poem for string quartet and orchestra *I semi di Gramsci* written in 1973? I would like to know how the orchestral setting of this work came about and why, for example, you decided not to use woodwinds as a reinforcement of an effect of distance which seems to be so important in this work.

JP. You are correct about Elgar's piece. I do know it, but there is no relation to it whatsoever and I certainly did not have it in mind when I wrote *There*. I am afraid, I don't know *I semi di Gramsci* by Bussotti at all. The idea of the orchestral setting of *There* was very simple. Initially, I thought of a string orchestra and a string quartet to be extracted from the same orchestral players in order to create two opposing instrumental groups on stage. The idea remained the same. However, later on I realised that it would make more sense to employ an independent string quartet in order to emphasise the difference of interpretation and the definition of two dissimilar instrumental groups. For this reason, the score is written for an autonomous string quartet (as the soloist) and a string orchestra, as two separate musical entities.

VP. Your writing clearly indicates the dichotomy of the string quartet and the string orchestra; on the other hand, the two different groups (the chamber and the orchestral) are strongly intertwined. How does this interconnectedness affect the meaning of the piece? In the programme note, you mention the 1991 Balkan war and the search for points of contact.

JP. The Balkan war was a pretext, the trigger that would give voice to my feelings against any kind of war. I felt impelled to indicate a proposition that may help to resolve social crises by uniting, rather than stressing, opposition. The piece is a search for points of contact between two different realities: the individual (the string quartet) and an ideal society (the string orchestra). A second, perhaps more cryptic, meaning symbolises the search for unity with a universal force, an allegorical place ('there') symbolised by the orchestra. The suffocating sense of despair, intrinsic in the phrases played by the string quartet, is projected onto a larger spatial dimension characterised by sustained chords acting as a distant reservoir in which the passion of the phrases played by the quartet dissolves in the idea of reunion. My question was: is it conceivable to find unity in apparent division?

The process of segregating 'here' (the quartet) from 'there' (the orchestra) suggests a paradoxical precondition for an experience of reunion; a return of the individual to its social and universal dimension. In this sense, what we experience as 'here' (on this planet) may be interpreted as a necessary condition for personal emancipation leading to a deliberately unspecified and freely interpreted notion of 'there'. I perceive many aspects of 'there-ness'; one of them can be attained by going through what has often been called the 'dark night of the soul', where a sense of, perhaps, karmic clarification may follow out of a confrontation with our personal shadows and through the experience of separation. In any case, *There* illustrates a search for reunion with the cosmos, a desire for 'participation mystique'. Musically, the interconnection of 'here' and 'there' in the piece is emphasised not only by the different shaping of pitch structures and the juxtaposition of polyphony and homophony in the quartet and the orchestra, but also by two kinds of sound motion in space.

The first motion is direct: quartet-to-orchestra and vice versa; the second motion is circular and takes place on the edge of the string orchestra (refer to Fig. 5.1 on page 96). In the first motion, the orchestra acts as a resonance body of the quartet, and as an extension of the quartet's phrases on a larger space. The second motion occurs within the orchestra being located around the quartet: harmonic blocks are being shifted on both sides of the orchestra and within two routes beginning and ending in the centre, at the back of the stage and in the middle of the large semicircle. The bass string instruments (double basses and celli) are located in the centre of the semicircle. The two external points on both sides of the semicircle are occupied by the first violins (to the left) and the second violins (to the right). Thus, the sound of the orchestra is constantly moving back and forward, left and right on stage, in opposition to the 'static' sounds of the string quartet coming from the centre of the stage and the middle of the orchestra.

VP. At the beginning of the piece, there is a sort of pedal that brings up a hint of tonality. I also found some tonal references in your opera *Re di Donne*. If I add the use of musical quotation in *Not Two*, I must ask you if the relics of tonality have a specific meaning for you or whether, just like in *Re di Donne*, they are meant to provide a mere reference to a significant, albeit short, moment of the plot?

JP. When I compose, I don't think about the music I write in connection with tonal genders. What I mean is that I don't think in terms of tonality, microtonality, atonality, styles and idioms unless I need to provide a clear cultural or historical reference in the piece, as I did in both *Re di Donne* and *Not Two*. In such cases, the relics of tonality function as a reminder or an indicator of something that is already known, something that is familiar to the audience. The meaning of tonal references remains specific, and related to the narrative of the music. The tonality that is usually in my mind when I compose comprises all 12 or 24 intervals (including quarter tones) of the chromatic scale. I seldom use smaller micro-intervals.

Double Concerto (Violin, Cello and Orchestra)

VP. Your reference to the ancient Chinese philosophy of Yin and Yang in your *Double Concerto* is intriguing. Knowing you, I guess there may well be several implications of this concept in this concerto. For instance, I can think of the location of the two soloists on the left and right sides of the conductor…

JP. Yes. One implication is that the two soloists should be located one to the left, the other to the right side of the conductor in order to visually stress this opposition on stage. Throughout the pieces, there are several references to the Yin and Yang principle. It is the interconnectedness of opposite forces that I was interested to explore: the notion of Oneness that stands above its apparent duality. This is why in the programme note, I mention the 'Yin-Yang' principle without the 'and', as a unitive and connective principle that encompasses and transcends duality. Symbolically, this unity is a reminder of a primordial union with the divine that is described by many ancient texts around the world: the Scandinavian Asgard, the Hindu Shambhala, the Greek Arcadia, just to mention a few.

This mythological reference is symbolised by the note C which is the first note played by both soloists at the beginning of the piece in bars 5-6 on two different registers C4 (violin) and C2 (cello) while bringing out as many harmonics as possible including a microtonal glissando in the violin part. The nebulous timbre resulting from the harmonics is symbolically very important because it provides an aura of micro sounds coexisting with the fundamental C note: the resulting timbral ambiguity is integrated as a complementary attribute of the main pitch.

As a reminder of a primordial state of unity, the same note is played on different registers by the two soloists. This is a recurrent feature, especially at the beginning of the piece. The first double cadenza (bars 86-111) is nothing more than a timbral and pitch expansion of the original note C (in Fig 5.5 you can see bars 86-101). I should add that there are no single cadenzas in the piece. All the cadenzas are played by the solo cello and violin together. This is a very important feature indicating that the two solo instruments are interlocked in a state of interdependence throughout the piece. The two instruments must also swap their role within the unfolding of the concerto, thus rendering their function interchangeable, and asserting a sense of timbral ambiguity in their simultaneous playing. They are two instruments and one instrument at the same time.

Fig. 5.5: *Double Concerto*, bb. 86-101, excerpt from the first cadenza.

107

VP. Do you think that the coalition of two opposing forces can represent unity, or more specifically, that unity as the sum of two different forces may exemplify a sort of perfect triangle?

JP. A oneness that encompasses duality may be interpreted as a triangle, yes. I am reminded, amongst others, of the Trinity in Christianity comprising the Father, the Son and the Holy Spirit, and the equivalent sacred triangle of Osiris, Isis and Horus in ancient Egyptian religion. From this perspective, the third pole of the triangle would be the orchestra, as the container and amplifier of the two solo instruments. When I wrote this piece, I defined the orchestra (the third element) as 'life', implying a stage where the scenes of the music are taking place.

VP. The idea of duality seems to be so evident by the frequent use of duos you are making: two soloists, instrumental couplings, and the blocks of different and interchanging instrumental groups. Are there specific instances in the work where an axiom represented by the number 3 (as a result of 2+1) is clearly outlined? Or is the whole music of the concerto supposed to illustrate this principle?

JP. The double cadenzas I was referring to earlier is certainly the most evident manifestation of the 1=2 or 2=1 principle. But the concerto as a whole is based on this very principle. I designed a sequence of contrasting symbols that follow each other in chronological order until the end of the concerto. These are: 1) body/spirit; 2) matter/energy and water/fire; 3) dark/light; 4) earth/sky and hell/heaven; 5) night/day; 6) soft/hard; 7) moon/sun; 8) space/time; 9) death/life; 10) reaction/action. I also determined four types of main musical actions, which I named 1, 2, 4, 5. Notice that I did *not* use the number 3! The reason for this is that I wanted a hypothetical number 3 to be the orchestra as the container of the two soloists. The chart below (Fig. 5.6) shows the chronological events of the above dualities.

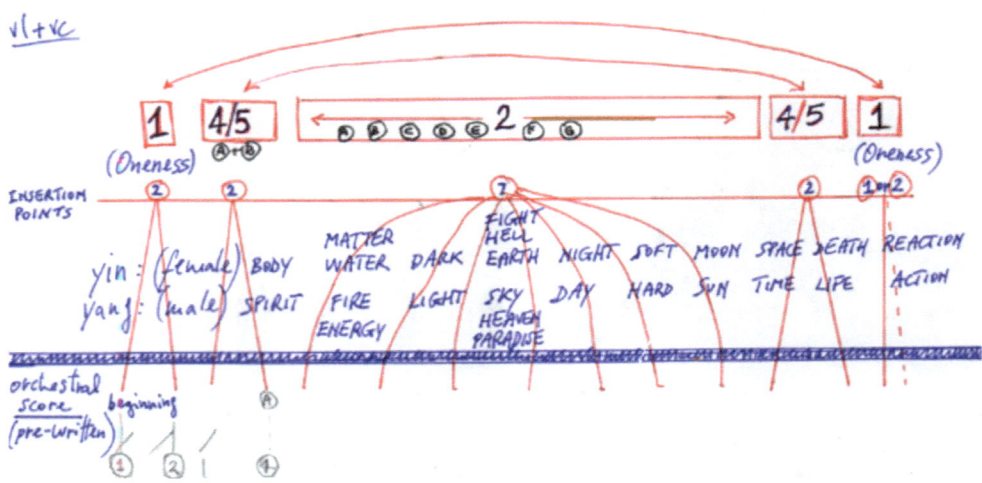

Fig. 5.6: *Double Concerto*, chart of dualities.

The four elements, or principles, set the main musical 'scenes' of the two soloists. These are four:

1) *Oneness* (one note emerging from a nebula).

2) *Dialectics* (the two soloists chase one another in a linear and alternating form). We can hear this texture at the end of another double cadenza from bar 164 to 170;

4) *Highest* (together high);

5) *Lowest* (together low).

Examples of 4 and 5 can be heard in the solos parts of bars 33-35 and 325-329. Fig. 5.7 below shows an example of '*Highest* (together high)' where both musicians are playing on the highest range of their instruments (bars 325-329).

Fig. 5.7: *Double Concerto*, bb. 325-329.

A fusion of 2, 4 and 5 can be heard in the central cadenza in bars 206-222 where the two solo instruments chase each other over a wide range of six octaves emphasising an interplay taking place through all the registers of the instruments (Fig. 5.8).

Fig. 5.8: *Double Concerto*, bb. 214-222.

Not Two (orchestra)

VP. I think that *Not Two* represents a significant step forward in the art of orchestration. Also, in this work, the use of multiphonics is rather limited. Is this limited use of multiphonics in any way linked to the way you are prolonging the orchestral sounds by using reverberation?

JP. I don't think so. Each piece I write is different and the texture I had in mind for *Not Two* did not require regular use of multiphonics. They occur mainly towards the end of the piece. Other than that, they can be heard a couple of times in the 'tremoli' of the bass clarinet, occasionally in the bassoon (bar 28) and in the oboe part in bars 58-60 (see Fig. 5.9) or bars 148-149. On these occasions, their strident timbre is reinforcing the shouting of the wind players in order to highlight the dramatic character of this particular moment in the piece. The contrast with the strings writing is rather evident. The function of electronics is to diffuse some orchestral sounds on wider spaces as a symbol of another dimension that, although being distant, is an important part of the musical discourse. Again, I am playing with the spatial idea of 'here' and 'there'.

VP. Does the use of electronics applied to acoustic sounds represent your need to find something that goes far beyond the normal sound of a large orchestra or is it a structural element of the composition?

JP. Both, depending on what kind of electronics we are talking about. The term 'electronics' consists of a huge world of sound manipulation that it is impossible to generalise with one meaning only. With all respect for the traditional orchestra, which I love, the electronics comprise a body of instruments that are much bigger and more powerful than any orchestra. In the case of *Not Two*, the use of electronics is 'confined' to the motion of sound in space. But in order to clarify this, I must mention the use of space I make in this piece. Two types of space characterise the music of *Not Two*. Firstly, I use a 'horizontal' space where the orchestral sounds are shifted from one side to the other of the stage (space 1). This kind of spatialisation is inherent in the orchestral writing; therefore it is 'acoustic'. Secondly, I use a 'diffused' space (space 2) where the orchestral sounds are projected onto a larger spatial dimension through amplification and reverberation (electronics).

In Space 1 (the 'acoustic' space) the *local* dimension of the orchestra is typified by the string group divided into two opposite halves, thus creating an antiphonal effect within the strings section as opposed to the 'immobile' space of the rest of the orchestra. For example, percussion 1 is located on the right side, and percussion 2 plays on the left side. The violins, violas and cellos are split into two corresponding and opposing halves in a semicircle. Thus, the sounds move from left to right and vice versa whereas the double basses are located in the centre of the semicircle (positioned in front of the conductor). The location of strings in the semicircle is very important: as I said, the double basses are located in the middle of the semicircle; from the centre to the left side, anti-clockwise we find two cellos (1-2), two violas (1-2), and the first violins (1-6); from the centre to the right side, clockwise we find two cellos (3-4), two violas (3-4), and the second violins (1-6).

Space 2 (diffused) is the space extended electronically by amplification (space 2a) and reverberation (space 2b). At least four loudspeakers are located in the rear of the hall (for amplification and reverberation) and four loudspeakers in the front of the audience, behind the orchestra (for reverberation only). These spatial strategies constitute an important structural element of the composition. The diagram in the figure below gives an idea of the spatial distribution of sound (Fig. 5.10). (The number of loudspeakers 1-2 is meant as stereo groups).

Fig. 5.9: *Not Two*, bb. 58-61.

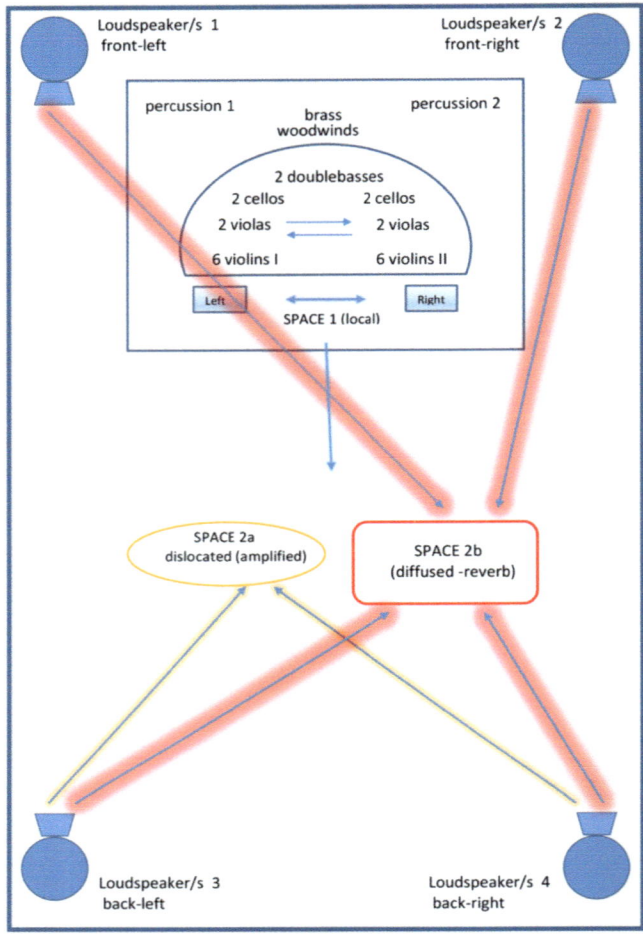

Fig. 5.10: *Not Two*, Diagram of spatial distribution of sound.

VP. Finally, when speaking about your music, you often refer to the reality of our world. In *Re di Donne*, this reference was clearly perceived by the stunning way you managed to handle the dramatic topic of femicide (the audience, the players and myself on the podium were all unanimous about it). Yet, in a non-operatic context, how do you think this implication, or even message, can reach an audience without the aid of a text, and using a musical language that only well-educated or knowledgeable people can understand?

JP. Obviously, in a non-operatic context, this is difficult to achieve unless you are writing a song, a piece for music theatre, or an oratorio. I think the answer to your question can be very complex and, at the same time, very easy. Let me start with what I think is the most important point: education! There are, of course, listeners who *feel* contemporary 'classical' music without knowing the arcana of its language. These are many sensitive people who can capture the essence of what is being played to them rather intuitively and with great mind-openness. Music is both an art and a science, and I think there is a very basic argument to consider when discussing this issue: in order to 'understand' (actually, I prefer the word 'appreciate') music, the listener should gain some knowledge about how the musical art works, or, at least, have a natural inclination for sound and artistic communication. It's the same thing I would have to do if I wanted to appreciate a piece of engineering, a painting, or learn a new language. I am afraid there is not much to negotiate on this point because the reality speaks for itself: I won't be able to understand a Japanese person who is speaking Japanese to me unless I study Japanese. If I don't make an effort to learn Japanese, my understanding of the Japanese language will be nought. By the same token, if people don't make an effort to know at least some basic information or features about new music, and if they are not keen to learn new ways to listen to music, they will never enter this dimension. A learning process requires interest, curiosity, passion, an open mind and a willingness to take up new challenges. In 40 years of teaching, I have seen that uneducated people can acquire the necessary skills to educate themselves and appreciate the music of the past 100 years. Where there is a will and a genuine interest to learn something different, there is always a way. The more we know the 'metier', the more we will be able to enter that realm of appreciation and emotional response that we call 'understanding'. And this works for everybody.

The second point I want to make is that, as a composer, my job is to write music. I *love* music, and as a result of this love I took up any challenge that I was faced with in my life in order to learn to know and 'understand' all kinds of music. I have learnt as much as possible about the musical art as a compositional craft. If this attitude may sound too radical to the ears of musically uneducated people, there is really not much I can do about it. It is my reality. I certainly won't write music in order to please someone who wants to listen only to Mozart or the Beatles. Even when writing a simple song, I never think of writing in order to please an audience: I just write the music the way it must be written. Art is art, and cannot, and should not, be concerned about the level of knowledge of this rather vague notion that we refer to as the 'audience'. As a composer, I must be loyal to my aesthetics of music and artistic aims. In order to write music, I have to listen to a musical percept and unfold the music I imagine by 'listening out' and bringing it to shape through my creativity. 'Listening out' actually means listening to myself, a situation that can turn out to be full of surprises. I believe this is all I should feel responsible for. The music I write reflects questions about the daily life I experience as an individual and member of society: the daily life I am referring to is a mirror of the 'reality of our world' as you have put it. Exploring emotions, perceptions, and some fundamental questions of existence may be a form of personal realism that I believe can reach any person who is willing to listen.

TRANSPARENCE, PIANO CONCERTO, NOT TWO
Dan Weymouth

DW. I am very aware of falling into the trap of making statements and then saying, essentially, 'so, what do *you* have to say about this?' In a live interview setting, I would avoid this annoying practice, and ask more general, and leading, questions. However, in the absence of a verbal dialogue, through which you and I could both guide each other and discover a mutual pathway through the issues, it seems necessary to put the questions in context from the outset. Thus, I hope that you will feel completely free to 'interrupt' me at any time to respond, even before I get to the actual questions. I only investigated three works (*Transparence*, the *Piano Concerto*, and *Not Two*) so my questions are based on a very small sample, and I have no pretence of knowing your full (and extensive) catalogue. Please bring in other examples as either support or refutation.

When I do get to the questions, you will notice that they frequently combine aspects of the music itself with considerations of the process of making and presenting the music.

(This reflects my own approach to the art of composition as well as my understanding of your approach.) For argument, we might term these aspects (and this is not in any way an exhaustive list) as:

1. **Craft-internal**: the genesis of the musical material, 'composerly' things such as sketches, generative ideas, and so forth.
2. **Craft-external**: what you intend to be perceived by the listener; form and narrative.
3. **Artist-internal**: your thoughts behind the creation of a particular piece, and being an artist in general; how specific pieces fit into your overall oeuvre.
4. **Artist-external**: what you would like the audience to receive; considerations of the social function(s) of a particular piece and of music in general.

While I am separating them out in this list, they are of course inextricably related. This is one of the reasons we value and need music: it can operate on multiple levels at once. Question zero: what are your thoughts regarding the above bullet list? I hope that these questions, and the inference out to your larger body of work and life as an artist, generate a stimulating, although temporally displaced, dialogue.

JP. I will be utterly candid about my response. My initial thoughts tend to be of an ontological nature and direct me straight to the question of whether a comprehensive description of music can remain essentially related to psychoacoustic experience, with all the phenomenology that comes with it, or to the representation of an intellectual decision, a simulacrum of theoretical speculation. In both cases, my view of music composition and artistic creativity in general echoes C.G. Jung's notion of works of art being manifestations of the collective unconscious channelled by the artist. I often speak of music as a vehicle that brings about a stream of consciousness evoking what I define a 'living mythology' of our times.

In my experience as a composer, the creation of music is identical to an act of incantation where each structural aspect of music (a melody, a chord, a timbre, and so on) conjures up mental images and references that are analogous with those we find in mythology. These images hold meanings of various degrees. The establishment of a hierarchy of structural components is a case in point: why is it that we find ourselves stressing a chord or a timbre and not another? Or repeating a motif, rather than proposing a new one? Why did Franz Joseph Haydn, for example, decide to exploit unexpected modulations in his late symphonies that were scandalous to the audience of his time? This must imply that we are perceiving some musical elements as being more crucial than others, a sonic configuration more important than another. In other words, a depiction or 'description' of something being more significant than another. The use of hierarchy of musical elements in the process of composition stands as a reminder of scales of sensations, perceptions and intuitions that we try to distinguish and discern through the choice of explicit components.

Choosing a specific intervallic structure for a melody or a chord rather than another, for instance, is not a mere feature that may please my fancy, but a sign of something of deeper significance. Like in the archetypes illustrated by ancient Egyptian, Indian, Greek and Mexican myths, these patterns of behaviour are still alive today and continually revived by the work of contemporary artists. These epitomes can be found everywhere and at all times. They are with us in dreams, images, visions and intuitions that transpire as channels of feelings, emotions and events of the subconscious on a regular basis. Music is a manifestation of the magical and the mysterious that still keeps enchanting and exciting me. For the rationale of my answers, I would like to regroup the four aspects you mention in two categories named 'internal' and 'external'.

In the renowned tripartition of Jean Molino, the *craft-internal* activity in composition includes what Jean-Jacques Nattiez has reiterated as the 'poietic' and 'neutral' level of music. I need to mention this because analytical criteria are very important in terms of the identification of structural clarity in the interrelation of events that will eventually manifest the *external* (the 'aesthesic' level) that embraces the audience's perception of a musical work. For the sake of clarity, I also need to differentiate the genesis of the musical material from the production of sketches, generative ideas, and similar procedures. The origin of the musical material resides in dimensions that are largely obscure to us. By 'obscure', I don't mean a negative, dark or unintelligible region of the mind, but rather an unfamiliar, unknown or subconscious domain of shrouded knowledge that is explored by the composer.

In line with Molino's tripartition, I distinguish three interrelated events that define the compositional process: the 'obscure' level of inspiration; the production of rules and procedures; the finalization of the musical thought in the score. These three phases are linked by a gradual process of transition evolving from one psychological and artistic concern to another. In the first transition, the obscure level of the archetypal produces the generative ideas and compositional procedures. This is often a 'painful' part of the making of a musical work because the subconscious is just beginning to transform itself into 'conscious shape'. In this sense, the systematization of pitch arrangement and charts of rules and proportions indicate not only structural devices, but also transformative manifestations of the source of inspiration and 'interfaces to consciousness' located between the original idea and the final shape of the music. Their purpose is to give final shape to the quest for individuation by converting subconscious conditions into consciousness. In the second transition, such generative procedures (extended to the definition of structural relationships, choice of metre and rhythm, design of form and so on) provide the structural foundation of the music discourse that is eventually defined by the completion of the score. By this time, the agitated and often conflictual life of the subconscious is transformed into a 'document of consciousness' that is the music itself. I experience each phase and transition of this process as an experience of gradual acquaintance and familiarization with fluctuating aspects of the Self. I say 'fluctuating' because such manifestations are varying, unpredictable, diverging and changing. Jung would call this a process of 'individuation'. Perhaps I should add that I also compose out of intuition, and in such cases the transition between the 'obscure' nature of the poietic phase and the realisation of the score is apparently direct, as the intermediary phase is not documented, therefore remaining a clandestine activity of the creative process.

During the course of action that I have just outlined, the unfamiliar takes gradual shape into a newly created scenario: the Unfamiliar becomes Familiar, the Unknown Known. This situation reminds me of Hegel's words, *"Das Bekannte überhaupt ist darum, weil es bekannt ist, nicht erkannt"*, meaning that the known (the familiar) is such because it is *known* (bekannt), rather than *perceived* (erkannt). The difference is subtle but crucial. In other words, we know something because this *something* is somehow already *known* by us in some remote areas of the mind. In view of this, composing music becomes an act of revelation of such subterranean realities of the psyche. The genesis of the musical material is already known by the subconscious and it is perceived consciously, while the thoughts behind the creation of a particular piece are inextricably linked to the way I will organise the structural elements of the music that I am bringing to life. Being an artist means to become familiar with these dimensions of the mind and bring out archetypal phenomena through the art of sounds that we call music. By remaining aware that I will never really know myself, the music I write will retain a sense of mystery, and the experience of my existence, alive.

Critically, I want to allow myself a slight digression. I sometimes wonder how the unfamiliar-familiar paradigm may affect my perception of music in general and the cognitive experience of my own music in particular. Let me be specific: alongside the disguise of the familiar, unexpected things await us. For example, we have often experienced when people close to us become so familiar that, one day, we lose the meaning of their presence in our life. This happens because these people have become routine to us; thus, as time goes by, the acquired familiarity may decrease the perception of that initial gleam that made these people so distinctive and unique to us. By the same token, I wonder if the mental process of familiarisation with music may lead to a gradual sense of diminution or disorientation in the way we perceive a musical work. Becoming gradually acquainted with pitch and rhythmic structures of a composition does not necessarily mean that I, the composer, may fully comprehend the music I am writing. From the perspective of a listener though, this question opens up a set of cognitive parameters that may deserve a larger context for discussion. The reason why I am mentioning this is that I question whether the sparkle we experience during the first aural experience of a musical work may effectively lose its original meaning and sense of excitement due to the routine of repetition. If that was the case, the perception of the 'familiar' in music could actually lead a listener to a gradual neglect of the primary thrill caused by the art. Could the acquaintance with music become a damaging factor in the perception of the archetype in music? And what could ensure an enduring freshness about the way we perceive music in general?

Regarding the 'craft-external' and 'artist-external' question, I have to say that I have never really adhered to, nor comprehended, the relevance of such issues. It is interesting to mention that I am asked this kind of question only by British and American colleagues, and to a lesser extent, other English-speaking musicians. This doesn't happen in Continental (Western) Europe, but I have noticed a similar inclination to such preoccupations in Eastern Europe. Obviously, a strong cultural issue must be at stake here! I have to say that my answer has not changed throughout my life. I honestly don't understand the reason for such a concern. When I am composing, I am certainly not thinking whether what I am writing may please someone else. Why should I? Why should I be concerned about what an undefinable audience may want to receive? And in any case, what kind of audience are we talking about? Art is not about pleasing the needs of the audience, and I am surely not inclined to create a product for mass consumption. In my view, an approach of this kind is alien to the nature of creativity and condemns the artistic integrity of any musical work written with such a purpose. It would imply a submission of art to the requirement of the masses or to non-artistic goals that remind me of political agendas or profit-making interests, the result being a consumption product of no artistic relevance.

Education is what comes to my mind. If I wanted to appreciate the art of paintings, I would certainly be interested to know something about that art; I would naturally make an effort to gain at least a minimal knowledge on the subject which would allow me to appreciate those paintings. If I wanted to become a lawyer, the first thing I would do is enrol in a university where I could study Law. If I wanted to appreciate the disciplines of architecture or literature, I would want to get at least a minimal knowledge on these subjects. Thus, I would like to ask the 'audiences': why is the same criterion not applicable to music? For the sake of clarity, I need to point out that what I am saying does not refer to you personally at all. You know well how much I appreciate the high quality of your music and aesthetic standards.

In order to avoid potential confusion, I should assert that I am not advocating a Babbittian 'Who Cares if You Listen' attitude which somehow has always sounded dubious to me. I *do* care if people listen to my music, if they perceive and appreciate the form and narrative of my artistic discourse. But that doesn't mean that I have to write what people want to hear! This would be utterly impersonal and absurd, even to any pop and jazz musician I have met and worked with. In fact, I have never come across a musician in any genre who would write a piece in order to please the audience. Songwriters write the songs they need to write out of a surge to communicate something important to them and that needs to be spoken out. I am thinking of Cat Stevens's *Father and Son*, the Beatles' *She's Leaving Home*, Charles Aznavour's *Comme Ils Disent*.

In jazz, the same urge is expressed in intrinsic musical parameters reflected by the adoption of specific harmonic, melodic and rhythmic patterns. This technical preoccupation is even stronger in the world of Western classical music and can be enhanced by an extra-musical idea providing a higher sense of inherent integrity to the musical work: let's take Beethoven's third symphony, Scriabin's *Prometheus: The Poem of Fire*, or Luigi Nono's *Il Canto Sospeso*, just to mention a few examples. Of course, a song will be understood by everybody, while a piece of 'classical' music will require an adventurous attitude for the untrained listener. But what I have said earlier about other professions applies to music as well. If the audience is truly interested in music, they will surely make an effort to learn, explore, and find out how to listen to any genre of music accordingly. Unfortunately, the majority of people these days do not really bother about wanting to explore music as a form of art that may require some kind of knowledge or effort. The devastating success of popular music since the 1950s has created an attitude of complacency in the majority of people that has been 'sanctified' by commercial interests. The result of this situation is that we are losing a sense of appreciation of musical quality. Again, English-speaking countries seem to epitomise this attitude.

Transparence (viola and ensemble with electronics)

DW. One of the things I notice about *Transparence* is that, while it is indicated as being for viola and ensemble, the viola doesn't occupy the 'heroic' role one would find in a standard Classical/Romantic concerto. (The *Piano Concerto* is a little more complicated in this regard.) At the beginning of *Transparence*, the soloist is mostly providing colour and harmonic fill, sometimes in opposition to the rest of the ensemble. Even later, when the solo viola has a more active role, it appears more as a leader than as a soloist per se; it almost always occurs with at least one other instrument. It does have cadenzas, but they are very understated, and very much melded with the electronics or ensemble background. Not until bar 260, after the third and final cadenza(ish), about 4/5 of the way through the piece (counting either bars or minutes), do we get an unambiguous declarative passage, and it is quite short, and soon overwhelmed by the ensemble (refer to Fig. 5.11, bb. 259-264). The viola does 'speak' one last time (marked 'furioso') but now it is paired with the piano, which tends to take the aural lead. How do you see this treatment of the soloist in light of tradition? Is this a purely musical decision, perhaps inspired by the generally unassuming 'voice' of the instrument? Or might it reflect your attitudes towards social structures in musical organisations, and in general? I know that this is part of a large cycle of pieces: does the use of the viola reflect an idea carried over from earlier pieces in the cycle?

JP. The role of the soloist in *Transparence* is not comparable with that of the classical tradition. I wanted the viola part to play from within the ensemble in order to be a leader *in* the ensemble rather than a traditional 'stand-alone' soloist. The viola is the inner voice of the ensemble and therefore, it is fully integrated into the texture of the other instruments. It is part of it. As you have rightly pointed out, it is also providing colour and harmonic fill to the rest of the ensemble. Tradition is also defined by our current practices of composition and I think the role of the soloist in this piece has an integrative and inclusive, rather than exclusive, position between the acoustic and electroacoustic ('real' and 'surreal') sounds. It is also a decision linked to the task I assigned to the viola as the signifier of a process of inner transformation that must begin from within a given situation. Metaphorically speaking, I consider life on this planet as a theatre of dissimilar experiences that, if interpreted correctly, can permit us to evolve ethically and spiritually. How can we change the world for the better if we are unable to change ourselves in the first place?

Transparence is the conclusive piece of the *Trans*-cycle, a group of chamber and solo pieces where I deal with virtuosity as transcendental means rather than 'heroic' show-off. The dialectical debate initiated with *Transitions* (for clarinet, violin, cello and piano) evolves through a series of solo and chamber pieces leading to the dissolution of dialectics into silence. As the final piece of the cycle, the role of *Transparence* is to bring this long debate to an end. The piece begins with excerpts from the previous chamber and solo pieces that are now sublimated by a ghost ensemble (the ensemble processed by the electronics), the viola being the trigger of a final process of sonic transparence (the dissolution of pitch into timbre) that is taking place in the ensemble.

Fig. 5.11: *Transparence*, bb. 259-264.

Also, the viola leads both ensembles (the visible and the invisible) to the final transformation of short virtuoso phrases into sparse sound; a sonic dissolution of pitch leading to the edge of silence. The material of the viola part derives from the solo viola piece *Trans-solo 6*, and, together with the transfigured excerpts of the previous chamber pieces (*Transitions* and *Transference*) and a few segments from the other *Trans-solo* pieces, provides the backbone to this final work.

The *Trans*-project may be defined as the design of an evolutionary process starting from dialectic confrontation and leading to the realm of quasi-silence. It evokes a journey to the invisible, a world that is increasingly becoming more translucent as the piece goes by. The allusion to my views of life should be clear enough by now. This final process of dissolution is underlined by the instrumental sounds of the ensemble gradually losing their sonic identity and merging with water and wind sounds in the quasi-cadenza passage leading to what I called the 'aethereal dimension of memory' in the final bars of the piece.

This process of sonic transformation is articulated in gradual steps: the instrumental sounds of the ensemble turn first into water-like timbres and finally into wind-like vibrations. Similar to what I did in *Beyond the Bridge*, for cello and electronics, in *Transparence*, I am also dealing with the notion of memory as a symbol of connection between past and present leading to something else: a kind of all-encompassing sense of the future that is awaiting us on another, non-physical, dimension. The 'sound of memory' is evoked by the use of space extended by the electronics through reverberation and the transfiguration of phrases through pitch-shift and ring-modulation. There are five 'space/memory' moments in the piece that may be compared to a kind of hidden Leitmotiv. These reminiscences are based on three fundamental principles of electroacoustic interaction:

1. Electronics as extension of acoustic instrumental timbre. A 'ghost' (electronic) instrument 'colours in' a live (acoustic) instrument. An example of this can be heard from bar 94 to 101, where an excerpt from the recording of the viola piece *Trans-solo 6*, projected by the electronics, doubles a phrase played by the viola on stage in a sort of fake (distorted) unison effect (Fig. 5.12 shows bars 95-97).

2. Electronics as extension of acoustic space. Instrumental sounds of the ensemble are projected onto wider acoustic spaces through reverberation or by playback of the 'ghost' ensemble. An example of this occurs from bar 102 to 108 where sparse viola sounds (mainly dyads) are processed onto large spaces using a decay time of 5 seconds. At other times, a phrase played by an acoustic instrument elicits distant sounds played the 'ghost' ensemble. A notable example occurs from bar 111 to 113 when the 'tremoli' of the acoustic instruments are taken over by 'tremoli' of 'ghost' clarinets in the electronic part (refer to Fig. 5.13). A similar instance occurs later, from bar 182 to 184, where a short piano phrase triggers the distant sounds of the 'ghost' ensemble.

3. Acoustic sounds as extension of electronic sounds. In such a case, an acoustic instrument 'colours in' a 'ghost' instrument. An example of this occurs from bar 163 to 170 where the instruments of the ensemble are imitating and improvising on the 'tremoli' played by the 'ghost' clarinets (electronics).

The 'senza misura' viola and electronics 'calmissimo' passage resembles a 'cadenza'-like context instigated by the ghost viola in the electronics while the live-viola is responding to it by means of sparse pitch-shifted and delayed sounds extended by reverberation. This is the central point of the piece and, at the same time, the prelude to the forthcoming dissolution of pitch into quasi-silence.

119

Fig. 5.12: *Transparence*, bb. 95-97.

Fig. 5.13: *Transparence*, bb. 111-113.

DW. Is a live performance more real?

JP. Everything we hear is *existent*. Electronics (playback, amplification and live signal processing) provide a nimbus which complicates the issue of what is played live and what is recorded: the real and the surreal. I love this ambiguity! Live processing is a part of it.

DW. There is even one place where the soundfile playback directly 'echoes' instrumental material played earlier.

JP. This must be one of the 'space/memory' passages I mentioned earlier or a similar situation. In performance, this would be nuanced by sound reinforcement for the acoustic instruments. I have used excerpts from the chamber pieces *Transitions* and *Transference*, from some *Trans-solo* pieces and mainly from the solo viola piece *Trans-solo 6*. These excerpts are processed with ring-modulation, filter, delay, pitch-shift and reverberation. Towards the end of the piece, I have used additional water and wind sounds in order to enhance the process of sonic disintegration of the instrumental sounds and their dissolution into quasi-silence as to elicit a sense of timbral translucence and candidness (the 'transparence' referred to in the title).

DW. As indicated in the score, they are to be miked, and you make specific reference to performed spatialisation of the instruments by a sound projectionist. (Such live 'diffusion' of sound into multiple speakers is a performance practice more common in Europe than in the United States.)

JP. All the acoustic instruments need to be amplified in order to enhance a sense of sonic ambiguity with the 'ghost' (pre-recorded and processed) instruments displaced in time and space via the amplification. The electronic part is quadraphonic.

DW. You have also gone to great lengths to make the instrumental sounds themselves diffuse and in some cases unrecognizable. Even so, hearing this music live will be significantly different from hearing it recorded. The cues of being able to see the instruments, and the related ability to focus on them aurally, make issues of parsing the instrumental sounds themselves from the electronics quite different in a live context than from a recording. Not to mention the aural effect of quadraphonic placement of sounds.

JP. Yes, as in all works with electronics, no recording can substitute the experience of a performance. This is particularly the case when there is a quadraphonic (or bigger) system at stake.

DW. One notices a similar aspect of *Not Two*, wherein amplification is used to allow certain soft extended techniques (unusual ways of playing the instruments) to be audible in an ensemble setting. In a studio setting, this amplification could be done as part of the mixing process. There are instructions regarding quadraphonic sound diffusion for this piece as well.

JP. The mobility of sound in space is very important for me. In *Not Two* the amplification is also used as a means of accentuation of specific melodic lines.

DW. Is it your intention to 'play' with the recognizability of instrumental sounds, or is this part of a larger project to make all sounds a continuum?

JP. Rather than a continuum, I am interested in creating timbral ambiguity as a sonic domain conveying multiple images of sounds that are transforming themselves while moving in space, as if the conscious and subconscious were chasing each other in a symbolic crossing between the personal and the collective. In a scenario of this kind, modifications of pitch, timbre, duration and instruments location should evoke multiple perceptions of space and time.

DW. Given all of the above, is live performance, for you, still the 'reference standard', as opposed to recordings? (Recordings would then be, I suppose, documentation of the standard.)

JP. I don't think I have a reference standard, although as a pianist myself I enjoy performances with acoustic instruments as ritualistic celebrations of music on stage. As a composer, too, I am intrigued by the dialectics of interaction taking place between acoustic and electronic instruments. It is not a coincidence that all my early electroacoustic pieces were written for acoustic instruments and a considerable amount of live electronics. But it really depends on the nature of the project. I also compose acousmatic music, and I find this genre as the perfect vehicle for a listening experience of pure imagination due to the visual detachment from acoustic instruments.

DW. How do you feel about this with regard to your numerous works for electronic playback (no acoustic instruments) alone? In this regard, you might mention the special case of a piece such as your *Phonai*, for synthesizer and 'tape', but which you indicate could be presented as fixed media without the involvement of live performance. Would this be essentially the 'same piece'?

JP. This is a question I have asked myself several times. Is Brahms's *Fourth Symphony* played live the same symphony heard on a CD? Am I the same person you are talking to during a Zoom session? My answer is that it depends on the approach and meaning we are assigning to a musical performance. On a 'documentary' level, *Phonai* is certainly the same composition whether it is played as an acousmatic piece or live with the synthesizer. But when I play it on the synthesizer on stage, each performance is different because my interpretation is never going to be the same. The sensuality of live gestures is lost in the fixed media. Having said that, when I perform my acousmatic music from the mixing desk, I always bring in tiny modifications of timbre (through the equaliser knobs) or motions of sound in space (through the output faders of the mixing console) that will be different from concert to concert. It is my instinctive way to 'adjust' the fixed electroacoustic sounds to the acoustic characteristics of the concert hall. You may remember that when I performed my quadraphonic tape piece *"…as it flies…"* on your stereo sound system at Stony Brooks in 2001 (you were sitting next to me), I *performed* the piece on the mixing desk as I have just described. Having to face the limitation of the stereo system that was available at that time, I tried to emulate manually the original quadraphonic spatialisation from the stereo file. For example, I used subgroups 1-2 (front) and 3-4 (back) of the mixer to project the sounds to-and-fro and front-back. By so doing, I created a sense of fake quadraphonic mobility of sound that added a sense of spatial liveliness to the stereo file. Was it the same piece? I think it was, but in a more limited version.

DW. How does the increasing prominence of recorded performances as a way of disseminating music colour your view of these matters? Do we lose something when we listen to a piece (even a piece intended for electronic playback) in our own quarantined space? How does this reflect your view of the social function of music and performance?

122

JP. Music is music, regardless of where it is heard. I do surely enjoy music in my private space, whether quarantined or not. I can analyse a piece and repeat a recording as long as I want, for example. But this is one reality only. From an acoustical point of view, my grand piano sounds very different when placed in a concert hall. In my studio, the same instrument is another instrument, and an electronic piece will lose its brilliance when heard in a small room or on an average home Hi-Fi system. Space is so crucial for the perception of sound.

From a social perspective, however, concert life is essential. I think that we do lose something very important by only listening to music in our limited private space. Performances remain unreplaceable, both as artistic and social events, because the shared enjoyment of music has a crucial meaning and impact on the individual and even more so on the community. Concerts are vehicles of culture, sociality, communication and civil progress.

Piano Concerto (microtonal piano, orchestra and choir)

DW. Your *Piano Concerto* makes extensive use of quarter tones. Not only do they occur in the line instruments, but both the featured piano and the orchestral piano, as well as both harps, are detuned, or, given the intention of the music, one should probably say 're-tuned'. In the case of the piano(s), individual strings on the same note are tuned differently. (For the non-musician: each key on a grand piano plays, except for the very lowest notes, two or three strings simultaneously. These are usually tuned in unison for each key.)

For much of the middle register, where one would traditionally see much of the melodic material, string tunings for each key tend to be close, producing a blurring of the sound. However, for some keys, especially those in the extreme registers, the related groups of strings are tuned to produce audible chords when a single key is played. This has a dual sonic effect. The piano's reach is broadened, in a sense, while, at the same time, the piano is decentring: making it less the heroic soloist and more a part of the orchestral timbral landscape. In addition, while some composers use alternate tunings to make a point about the purity (or lack thereof) of some intervals, this does not seem to be your aim, here. I'd be curious to hear your thoughts on this.

JP. I am glad you used the verb 're-tune' instead of 'de-tune'. I believe there is a significant difference between the two concepts. The Latin prefix 'de' means 'away from', 'off', 'down from', and implies a sense of deviation from a universal convention, thus it suggests a pejorative connotation, as if digressing from the 'right' thing that is our standard tempered system. 'Re-tune' means 'tune again' which is exactly what I did. Indeed, the microtonal universe of the *Piano Concerto* stems from the re-tuning of the piano, as being the central instrument of the piece.

Following the desire to create a sonic world that would be as intricate and dense as possible, I re-tuned my own grand piano in order to work first-hand with the sounds I wanted to produce. As I shall expound later, the piece is about the complexity of relationships. The idea behind the microtonal piano and microtonality, in general, was the desire to create a sonic universe full of condensed, minute and almost impenetrable relationships between the solo piano, mirrored by an orchestral piano and the rest of the orchestra, including a choir. The density I had in mind had to make full use of microtonality. In order to reach this goal, I made the decision to re-tune my own piano by using a tuning that would be as impenetrable, complex and 'compressed' as possible. For this reason, I decided not to use any of the established tuning systems and to create a unique tuning (a 'non-system') based on my instinctive and emotional response to sound, rather than a fixed tuning method. By contrast, at that time, I perceived microtonality as a 'meta-tonal' meeting point that would allow microtonal motifs and chords to be controlled within a precise framework of pitch content. By 'meta-tonal', I mean a pitch micro-space that would allow me to control a notation system based on quarter tones with utmost precision, as I did in *Epitaph* (for cello and electronics) and *Transfiguration* (for trombone and electronics).

The tuning of the piano has been a major concern of mine since my childhood. I began to bang on the piano at the age of three, I took my first piano lessons at the age of six and besides my piano playing, I trained as a piano tuner from the age of 16 to 19. While I was tuning the pianos of my customers, I remember wondering why the piano could not be tuned in different ways other than the temperate system. I recall wanting to hear a piano without tuning limitations of any kind; an instrument unrestricted by the musical conventions implied by the tempered system. I also remember experimenting with unusual tunings during my training. I have ever since searched for microtonal pianos and alternative solutions that would allow pianos to use different tunings. As a former piano-tuner, I know very well that this is a very easy thing to do, and I continue to struggle with the idea that the music establishment is still ignoring this reality.

Prompted by a text called *Within* that I wrote in 2001, I sat at my grand piano and began to experiment with different tuning possibilities on each string of the instrument, literally one by one. I spent several months trying to find a tuning that would be realistic and safe to achieve within the mechanical laws that regulate the tension of the strings, and effective enough from a timbral perspective and for artistic expressivity. Simply put, I decided to create a daring microtonal soundscape by taking into account all the technical limitations of the strings without damaging the piano. My tuning would be challenging, yet entirely created within the realistic possibilities of the task. I merged the technician (the piano-tuner) with the artist (the pianist and composer).

In the *Piano Concerto*, each of the 88 strings of the solo piano has its unique re-tuning that originates an individual piano sound. The same thing applies to the orchestral piano, although this tuning varies slightly from the tuning of the solo piano. For example, the three strings of the central C key (C4) of the solo piano are tuned (from left to right): C quarter-flat, C quarter-flat and B quarter-flat. The three strings of the same C4 key of the orchestral piano are tuned (from left to right): C natural, C natural and B quarter-sharp. By comparing the two sounds we can see that the first and second strings produce a friction of a quarter tone (C natural against C quarter-flat) while the third strings will produce a friction of a semitone (B quarter-flat against B quarter-sharp), the result being a very dense cloud of micro-oscillations 'fighting' each other and producing the most remarkable sound. Thus, the orchestral piano acts as the distorted mirror of the solo piano. In the chart below, you can compare the tuning of both pianos covering the range from key Ab3 to Db4, thus including the C4 key. On the left side you see the tuning of the solo piano and on the right side you see the tuning of the orchestral piano (Fig. 5.14).

The idea of the music stems from the title of the poem *Within* (you can read the text on page 134) which, in turn, was born out of a bursting impulse to challenge self-complacency and dysfunctional entanglements that we often experience in our behaviour, while inviting us to look *within* ourselves in order to find a meaningful life and a sense of self-realisation. In musical terms, the notion of *Within* is symbolically explored *within* a micro-dimension of sound contained *within* a single key of the piano through a re-definition of pitch based on microtonal intervals. Thus, each key of the piano becomes a micro-universe of complex and irregular micro-relationships of intervals. The attentive listener will notice an intended contradiction inherent in the piano part, in that the passionate gestures are clashing with their own 'entangled', i.e. microtonal, sounds, as if the purity of intent of the piano phrases is constantly denied by the inner anarchy of every single sound. The example below, bar 303, might give you an idea of the interweaving microtonal universe of the two pianos (Fig. 5.15).

Piano Key	String	Tuning	Piano Key	String	Tuning
Ab	2	G♩3	Ab	2	G♯3
	3	G♮3		3	G♯3
A3	1	A♮3	A3	1	Ab 3
	2	A♩3		2	A♮3
	3	Ab 3		3	A♭b3
Bb3	1	A♮3	Bb3	1	A♯3
	2	B♩3		2	B♮3
	3	B♩3		3	B♯3
B3	1	B♩3	B3	1	B♮3
	2	B♩3		2	B♯3
	3	B♯3		3	Bb 3
C4	1	C♩4	C4	1	C♮4
	2	C♩4		2	C♮4
	3	B♩3		3	B♯3
Db4	1	Bb 3	Db4	1	Bb 3
	2	C♯4		2	C♩4
	3	Bb 3		3	Bb 3
Piano 1 - soloist			Piano 2 - orchestral		

Fig. 5.14: *Piano Concerto*, comparative example of piano tuning.

Fig. 5.15: *Piano Concerto*, b.303.

In a larger musical context, another aim was to create a sonic scenario of complex and ambiguous relationships, not only between the two pianos, but also between the two pianos and the two (also microtonally tuned) harps, and between the solo piano, the choir, and the remaining instruments of the orchestra. This network of micro-relationships has been designed rather painstakingly over several months of experimentation. From an orchestral perspective, the sounds of the solo piano are both broadening and de-centring, to use your words: expanding and retracting at the same time. The following excerpt should speak for itself. In bars 298-300 a radiation of undulating microtonal harmony, initiated by the core group of the microtonal pianos and harps, with vibraphone and marimba (Fig. 5.16) flows into an ocean of waving 'tremolandi tutti' including the choir in bar 301 (Fig. 5.17).

DW. In some places where the soloist is most exposed, chords ring for a long time, so we are obviously directed to the sound of the chords.

JP. Yes, to the micro-universe of the piano sounds I have just referred to. These microtonal chords and resonances are often prolonged or commented on by the voices of the choir or the instruments of the orchestra.

DW. One notices, in these places, the different rates of the 'beating' [an internal pulsation caused by notes slightly out of tune] from chord to chord. How intentional is this?

JP. It is very intentional. These internal pulsations (the oscillations I meant earlier) create a high degree of tension and a sense of anxiety and apprehension which is echoed by the choir.

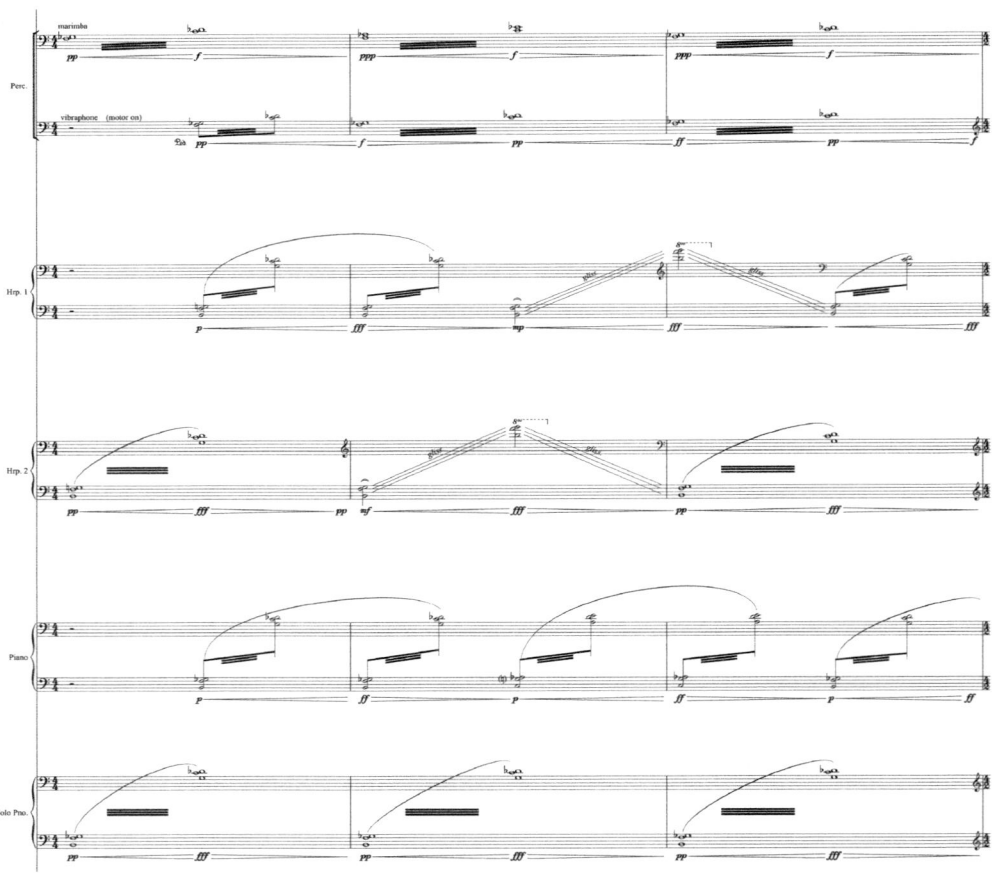

Fig. 5.16: *Piano Concerto*, bb. 298-300.

126

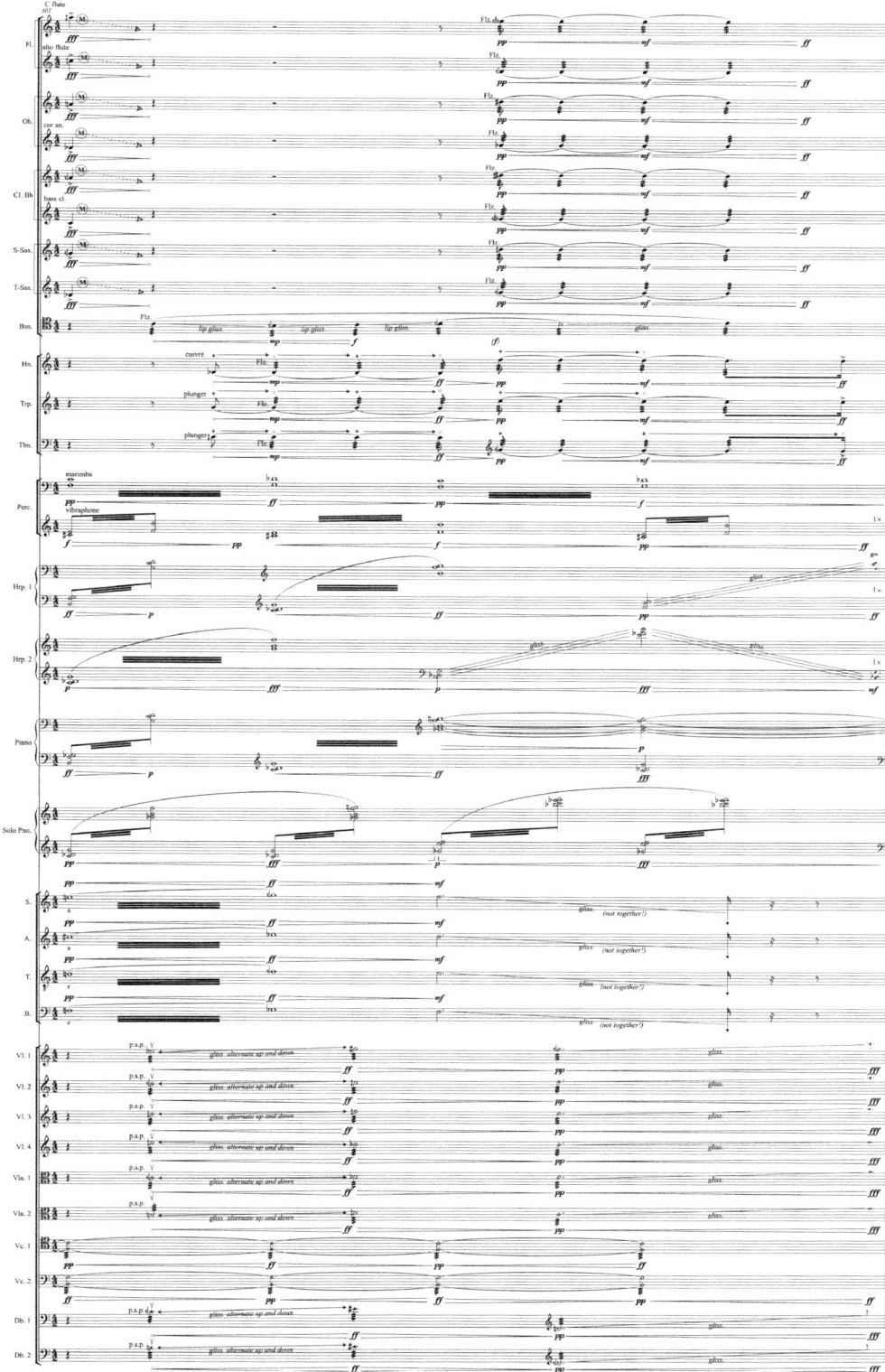

Fig. 5.17: *Piano Concerto*, b. 301.

127

DW. Did you use a mechanism or rubric for controlling the various rates?

JP. I didn't want to have one. As I said earlier, there is no unifying tuning system in the *Piano Concerto* simply because I wanted to avoid a sense of uniformity. The sound I was after should provide an unpredictable and varying sense of apprehensiveness and indecision, at times even nervousness and fear. Each tuning has its own rate of beatings.

DW. In a more general sense, is it your intention to recast the instrument itself?

JP. This was another important aspect I hinted at earlier. As a pianist myself, I wanted to redefine the piano as an instrument that can sound equally beautiful, but intriguing and inspiring beyond the tempered tuning system.

DW. Does this tuning make it less 'Western', with all that implies?

JP. There is an element to it as well. It is not a coincidence that when I began to write the *Piano Concerto,* I had just come back from Japan where I had been struck by the idiosyncratic use of microtonality in Gagaku and other Japanese traditional music. The research I undertook allowed me to establish the two tunings I selected for the two pianos in a way that would suggest a breakaway from a Western typology of piano sound. Also, the tuning of the solo piano was created in such a way that it would allow me to 'bridge' the different thematic materials used in the three instrumental groups. This is how I tried to unify cultural diversities (the three melodic materials) and, at the same time, transcend traditional Western conventions (the tempered tuning of the piano) by deliberately working *within* the organic forces of a traditional orchestra, both musically and metaphorically, and yet by choosing the piano as the protagonist of this unusual concerto.

DW. In spite of the 'de-centring' of the solo instrument, this is definitely a concerto. The solo piano serves as a principal generator of the musical rhetoric, is present almost all of the time, and often serves as a formal marker. However, even though there are some 'grande canto' moments for the soloist, many times a large orchestral build-up is followed by a very quiet and understated solo piano statement. For instance, the longest and most active soliloquy (bar 272, M, Fig. 5.18) starts around 'mezzo forte' and becomes gradually quiet. It then builds, but then fades away again (on the form chart, you indicate this as 'cadenza').

JP. The understated passages of the piano are equally important because they mean that the soul (the piano itself) is playing from *within* the orchestra.

DW. The other cadenza (bar 358, Fig. 5.19), identified as such in your pitch sketches (which I call the 'secondary cadenza'), does have the fairly standard orchestral buildup as an entry point, and does start out with the piano at a 'forte', although qualified with a 'poco'. But this passage is marked 'molto calmo', and features long, held notes and chords, with chordal orchestra commentary. Given the space around these sounds, the effect is certainly more colouristic, or perhaps even ritualistic, than kinetic. Similarly, the solo piano at the very end of the piece end has 'forte' chords, but they are very far apart and become a last resonant shout.

JP. This cadenza has an inwards-looking nature. I wanted to emphasise a sense of reflection leading to the final chord in the penultimate bar, where this last shout is echoed by the orchestral piano and reinforced by the two harps and the percussion.

Fig. 5.18: *Piano Concerto*, bb. 272-292.

Fig. 5.19: *Piano Concerto*, bb. 358-363.

DW. We have already discussed the denatured aspect of the piano tuning, which in addition to other things, makes the piano in some ways more diffuse. Finally, in the performance notes, you specify that the solo piano (as well as the orchestral piano) is to have the lid (top) removed. This has the aural effect of making the piano more a part of the ensemble: the sound goes everywhere, as opposed to being directed at the audience (which is one of the functions of the piano lid.) By removing the lid, one also removes one of the telltale visual markers of this gigantic instrument, which both identifies its operator as a VIP in the orchestral setting, but also can actually obscure other members of the ensemble.

JP. Yes, the detachment of the lid is a statement in both senses: acoustic and visual, because I wanted the piano sounds to be an integrative part of the orchestra and to be diffused everywhere in the concert hall; symbolically, because the piano sounds are supposed to come from *within* the orchestra, rather than be imposed on the instruments.

DW. So, one returns again to the question of the role of the soloist. I'd be curious to have you talk about this, in terms of the form, the sonorities, and the intent of this particular piece. Also, what are your thoughts about the social relationships implied, between the soloist and the ensemble, between the soloist/ensemble and the audience, and between this particular concerto and the history of the (Western) concerto?

JP. I considered the soloist mainly as a member of the orchestra rather than a 'notable' addition to it. The *Piano Concerto* is not about the celebration of a star (the traditional virtuoso-image in its supreme role of leadership). The solo piano symbolises a normal individual like you and me; a real person who is struggling with real life situations of doubt, grief, despair and, at the same time, searching for an answer that may transcend these circumstances. The sonorities of all the instruments and voices should converge in a unifying cloud of sound, that is a common reality including a collective question about the meaning of social coexistence. I have also tried to establish inner bridges between the instrumental groups *within* and beyond the concerto tradition by creating recurring gestural links between autonomous layers: the two microtonal pianos (the solo piano and the mirroring piano of the orchestra), the two harps, the choir and the chamber orchestra. I decided to use such instrumental forces as complementary factors questioning their coexistence as established by Western music tradition.

DW. One of the many striking things about the *Piano Concerto* is your inclusion of a 16-voice amplified choir, frequently written in eight parts. Other composers who have done this have used voices as a 'soloists' of sorts (often delivering text) or as colouration of the ensemble. In your *Piano Concerto*, you go beyond this. For one thing, the chamber choir serves as a 'second diapason'.[28] Speaking very generally, in most orchestra pieces, the string section acts as this default, the 'diapason'; they carry the main musical narrative, while the brass, winds, and percussion add colour and accent. In much of the *Piano Concerto*, the groups of instruments are presented in blocks, much as one might see in (jazz) Big Band arranging, with the strings still having their role as a diapason. However, the chamber choir seems to have this role as well: in fact, they are present on 80 of the 98 pages of the score. More than that, especially towards the beginning of the piece, the chamber choir tends to alternate with the strings, that is, voices and strings seldom occur at the same time. How does the presence of the voices affect our sense of the form of the piece?

---

[28] A word of explanation for the musician or non-musician without special knowledge of the organ: 'diapason' is the term used in organ music to refer to the set of pipes that are most used: the default, in essence.

JP. I can see where your insights are coming from, of course, yet the *Piano Concerto* does not follow the sound organisation of the orchestra. As you said, at the beginning of the concerto, the choir tends to alternate with the strings; the two groups seldom merge. My intention was to find a hybrid form lying between an instrumental concerto and a 'distorted' song, whereas the voices are also employed as purely instrumental parts reinforcing the overall timbre of the orchestra. Adding voices to an orchestra is akin to adding colour *and* emotional power to the texture, so I wanted this human element to be represented very clearly throughout the piece, as if injecting a continuous emotional intensity to the music. After all, it was a text about a human condition that instigated me to write the concerto.

For most of the piece, the choir sings mainly single vowels and muted sounds as remnants of disintegrated words sustained or sung in slow motion and emphasised by timbral changes as a suppressed emotional anticipation of bar 342, when the first word of the text, *"who"*, marks the beginning of the end of the concerto (Fig. 5.20). The emotional charge provided by the vocal sounds up to that point (bar 342) is often presented in harmonic blocks much alternating with the strings and providing a sense of anxiety emphasised by the recurrent swelling resulting from crossing 'crescendi' and 'diminuendi'. At other times the vocal blending with the orchestral instruments is more subtle and undulating as in the 'Avanti' and 'Più mosso' sections from bar 169 to bar 182. I perceive the voices as a strong emotional presence rather than an accentuation of formal proportions in the piece.

DW. The voice is, of course, the most intimate of 'instruments', being most directly related to the body. I would argue that you 'denature' the voice(s), analogous to how you denature the piano, in a couple of ways.

JP. Yes, this was the idea.

DW. The amplification you ask for encourages a style of singing that is much gentler (less 'pointed') than one would hear from singers accompanied by a standard orchestra. Do you have in mind vocalists trained in using the microphone?

JP. Not particularly, to be true, but of course, the vocalists have to be aware of how to sing with a microphone.

DW. Are you perhaps thinking of a less operatic, and a lighter more 'pop' (or in fact Baroque), sound?

JP. Surely not operatic. The voices should sound as 'normal' as possible in order to stress the unspoiled sensuality of a natural voice.

DW. For much of the piece, the singers use phonemes (individual particles of sound), even using breath sounds and fricatives ('fffffffff-sh!' is one very striking crescendo gesture). This also renders the vocalists more as 'instrumentalists'. Can you speak about your sense of this?

JP. As I mentioned earlier, I consider the voice primarily as a musical instrument. This is a recurrent feature in my music. The voice offers an immense resource of timbral qualities and considerable dexterity which makes it a most unique instrument. Back in the late 1980s, the first movement of Luciano Berio's *Sinfonia* had impressed me about the way the composer would merge vocal and instrumental sounds in one cohesive texture whose timbral and

Fig. 5.20: *Piano Concerto*, bb. 342-343.

133

harmonic plasticity fascinated me. Although quite different, Stockhausen's *Stimmung* was another work that had caught my imagination in those years. In *Omen* (1991), for orchestra and choir, I went further than Berio by using single vowels as colours having both harmonic and rhythmic function. I used stronger chromatic intervals between the voices and in relation to the orchestral instruments, added inhaling and exhaling sounds, more consonants and interspersed vocal interventions of a more contrapuntal nature within the general texture. I think that in the *Piano Concerto* all these elements are more emphasised and elaborated. The voice can convey strong emotional power without semantics. This is something that has always fascinated me.

DW. Just slightly over three-quarters of the way through the piece (bar 342), the singers do finally present the poem identified in the notes at the beginning of the score. This comes as a natural outgrowth of the presentation of vocal sounds (vowels, then humming, then consonants) and the text is presented pointillistically, with individual singers exclaiming (in some cases, shouting) the individual words, or even portions of words ('el' as part of 'else'). Given the nature of the text itself, could you comment on this manner of presentation of the text?

JP. The art of reading is not as easy as it may seem because each written text is governed by its own rules: usually, a narrative structure, or a system of recurrent ideas. Without going into literary theory, when I read an extremely condensed text, I must be able to decipher every single word and analyse its content by a syntax that may not be apparent. A condensed text forces me to engage with concepts in a critical way because the words are speaking for themselves, without the support of syntactic structures. In short, my intuition is forced to explore an underworld of myriad denotations buried in the words themselves and their position within the text. The meaning of 'we' followed by 'you' will be different to the same 'we' followed by 'she'. The emotional effectiveness of a reduced text goes hand in hand with the willingness of the reader to enter a chasm of meanings and sub-meanings that are waiting to be interpreted in relation to the other words of the text. Reduction calls for focus and condensed signification. Different connotations may surface as a result of multiple choices. From this perspective, the raw nature of condensed texts poses a powerful challenge to the reader. The text of *Within* comprises 19 words disposed in a vertical alignment. Visually speaking, each word corresponds to a line of the poem. For the sake of spacing, I am displaying the text on two horizontal lines:

who / else? / you / I / they / we / she / he / it / us / me / them /
why? / where? / when? / suspended / in / between / within

The restriction posed by a text of such sparsity obliges the reader to concentrate on the meaning of every single word as a condensed (allegedly bleak?) expression of a concealed universe of emotions squeezed into a constrained outburst of hidden desire and passion, hope and affliction, action and reaction. Such can be the intensity of restrained meaning.

DW. Referring again to the classical Western model of the concerto, the soloist might be considered as the protagonist. This 'actor' in some cases inspires the orchestra, and in some cases struggles against it, but there is a definite sense of the soloist as an individual, set against (contrasted with) the collective of the orchestra.

JP. Yes, but the role of the protagonist is also emerging from *within* the orchestra, while the orchestra 'exists' as its halo. The pianist may seem to be playing against the collective, but, in reality, is a part of it.

DW. This relates to the earlier question about social function(s) implicit in your *Piano Concerto*. But all of the above factors (the tuning of the solo instrument, the role of the soloist, and the use of the voices) also raise interesting questions about the 'location' of the protagonist. One notices, in this regard, that the solo piano is not present in the fourteen bars (bar 342 ff) where the choir makes the first and longest presentation of the obvious text. In fact, the piano's 'secondary cadenza' comes right after these fourteen bars. (One is tempted by thoughts that a super-hero and their secret identity avatar never appear together). The choir does return eight bars into this secondary cadenza, but only with non-vowel sounds (hisses and hums, essentially). Vowels do not return until after the solo piano stops playing. Are you thinking, then, of some sort of 'distributed' protagonist, where the solo piano and the chamber choir take on different aspects of a central actor? Or does the piece exist with no central actor apart from the collective? In this regard, could you speak of the ending allargando of the piece, which features a long fade of highly spaced (and reverberant) piano chords, with the final word of the poem, in a 'forte' whisper (again, the advantages of amplification!), 'within'?

JP. I would like to quote a phrase by C.G. Jung: *"One does not become enlightened by imagining figures of light, but by making the darkness conscious."* This is a piece about entangled relationships that are dark and complex at the same time. One partaker (the solo piano) is questioning this state of affairs from *within* a cobweb of interchanging relationships. Your suggestion of a 'distributed' protagonist makes a lot of sense in that each participant represents a different aspect of the piano that is included in the collective. The final 'allargando' represents a symbolic invitation to find the answer to these personal and social entanglements *within* us.

Not Two (orchestra)

DW. The three pieces I considered are obviously from the same composer. The pieces all evidence your desire to expand the traditional 'voice' of instruments with extended playing techniques, quarter tones, and electronics. There is an obvious interest in, along with a very refined facility with, timbre (tone colour) and textures as a central narrative and formal device. The pieces also share a philosophical underpinning that allows a large, one could say kaleidoscopic, variety of material to coexist within a form, without using stylistic modulation. However, of the three, *Not Two* is significantly more direct, having both a more overt narrative, and a more extroverted surface. All three pieces are, as I say, kaleidoscopic, but the sounds in the first two arrive more in overlapping layers of waves, especially in the *Piano Concerto*, while *Not Two* seems more intentionally (obviously) sectional.

In addition to the formal rhythm being more marked, the surface rhythm (i.e. the rhythms we hear) is also more overt in *Not Two*. There are many more passages with 'organized rhythm' (i.e. an obvious pulse), although they are not very long, and are frequently subverted. But even when there is not an overarching beat, there are more places where multiple instruments share the same rhythm. A very direct example of this is the timpani quavers that start *Not Two*. This rhythmic gesture is gradually expanded and revealed to be motivic, recurring as an accent or interruption, and eventually dominates the narrative (at least as a framing device) for significant portions of the second half of the piece. One could argue that even your use of long reverb tail in *Not Two* is a more 'direct' implementation of the sort of long orchestrated resonance that is such a central feature of the *Piano Concerto*. In the *Piano Concerto*, in part, because these passages are *drawn* down, rather than decaying naturally (that is, the 'decay' is extended, and is not unidirectional, but rather occurs in waves), the overall affect, at least to me, seems very much like an expression of pain or distress, while the effect in *Not Two*, with its natural decay, seems much more the result of a celebratory shout.

What I am getting at can be stated simply: (many of) the foundational ideas are the same, but the approach is significantly different. Do you see this as evidence of a different era (in your own composition) or different streams? In other words, given that the completion of the concerto and *Transparence* are not close (2001 and 2014 respectively), while *Not One* is from 2017, are these pieces in different 'generations' during which time your compositional aims and interests changed? Or is this simply a matter of each piece being about what it is about, reflecting different interests which coexist in time (although not in pieces)?

JP. I think your assumptions are factual and connected to each other. It is often claimed that a composer's output is a continuous revisiting of the same central preoccupation and I think there is an element of truth in that because composition is a process, not an event. If compositional aims and interests change the same way I change as an individual, it is equally accurate to claim that there is a common thread that binds all these pieces together. The seemingly different approaches or directions that may appear in single works will inevitably converge in a mainstream of enduring thoughts and preoccupations during a lifetime. Each personal and social event has an effect on us, whether consciously or subconsciously, hence a musical work may be compared to a stand-alone document of such events. The composer is a sort of photographer of the inner-life who brings out thoughts, emotions and perceptions related to specific life experiences at specific points in time. Yet each experience is a part of a whole as each musical work is a part of an evolutionary path that encompasses a unifying chronicle of life. Therefore, each piece I write is a part of a larger narrative that is my life story composed of smaller stories. When I finish composing a piece, I close a chapter of my life in order to begin a new one afresh. Every end marks a new beginning. What we call an 'Opus' of works is but a network of interconnected snapshots of life fragments that can be heard in their individual quality and vigour.

DW. Even the sketches for the three pieces are very different. Those for the first two pieces include very precise numerical tabulations of timing, event density, etc., while those of *Not Two* are much more graphic and verbal. Now, it is possible that the same sort of pre-compositional work went into *Not Two* but, as I have said, this latter piece seems like it has a different compositional genetic structure. Could you talk about the relationship of pre-compositional work to your streams (or eras, as the case may be)? (We will return to the consideration of sketches later as well.)

JP. I think experience teaches a great deal. There is a time when a composer needs to write down every structural design as precisely as possible before the writing of the notes in the score begins. Then we experience the acoustic result of all those procedures in the music we hear when the piece is performed. With time, this repeated experience allows us to feel confident about the relationship between structural design and the musical result. This is the point when we begin to integrate technical strategies in the music intuitively. Having said that, the charts of *Not Two* are rather precise in their portrayal of the organisation of form, metre, space, quotes and orchestration.

DW. Finally, an overarching question for this section. In our correspondences, you have made numerous references to the holy, the transcendent, meditation, Zen and Buddhism. I know that discussion of spirituality seems to be somewhat taboo in intellectual exchanges, perhaps partly as a consequence of the drive towards scientific rationality in the 20th century, and most certainly as a result of the co-option of religion by demagogues to use as a cudgel against reason. Yet the basic attraction to the numinous remains strong in the human mind, and to me seems an important component in understanding your work. Thus, I would be interested to have you talk about how you think your approach to life (philosophies, spiritual insight and practices) influences your music (either in eras or streams). Are there central metaphors that persist throughout your work? Do philosophical/spiritual considerations percolate down to the level of use of material and techniques?

JP. The answer to both questions is: yes. First of all, my approach to life has indeed a direct influence on the music I write. I cannot, and would not want to, separate the two, because music is the most intimate and visceral experience of my life and as such, it is directly linked to everything I feel, experience and think. Philosophies, spiritual insight and practices are an essential part of my life and I cannot live without them. Earlier on, you spoke about streams in my life and I mentioned how they all converge to one all-encompassing stream.

An attempt to describe a persistent metaphor in my compositional work would sound like this: I am reflecting on the mystery of our existence as critically and honestly as possible. I am trying to discover some forgotten landscapes of our presence on this planet by exploring the experience of suffering and joy, passion and enlightenment, the visible and the invisible, while longing for a vision that may celebrate a fulfilled humanity. Philosophical or spiritual considerations do very much permeate the choice of material and techniques, and I could speak a great deal about this important aspect of my creativity. What I would mention in this context is that this poietic level is crucial for my compositional work because it supplies the intellectual and emotional impulse to the writing of the music. I could give you many examples, but they would be too many for our purposes, but let me just give you one example related to the music of *Not Two*. The idea of this piece was born out of an urge to celebrate a vision of light as a symbol of eternity encompassing and transcending the notion of duality as a manifestation of unity. In Hindu philosophy, the Sanskrit word 'Advaita' (not-two, or non-duality) implies the non-existence of duality. A simple explanation of this is that the ultimate spiritual reality (Brahman) encompasses the phenomenal transient world of dualism, and that all divisions are illusory appearances of the same unifying reality. The somewhat raw programme note of this piece is a kind of koan I wrote that is posing a puzzle to the readers. I wrote it following the death of Jonathan Harvey:

Prophets of Light / Gone into silence / Or is there music / On the other side? / Not Two.

If we look at the charts of *Not Two*, we can see several references to the notion of duality and unity as the structural genesis of the work. I decided to base the main structural proportions of the music on the formula 2=1, meaning that duality (2) is actually a manifestation of unity (1). The numbers 2 and 1 lay the foundation of all structural decisions regarding form, pitch, orchestration, space and so on. In the main chart underneath the title *Not Two*, there is a kind of subtitle that reads: "*An attempt to establish contact points with another reality*". We can see the first implication of the 2=1 ratio still at a conceptual level. Below in the same chart, I wrote six short phrases:

1) *Two worlds co-existing: here-there / saint-devil – Two in One!*
2) *Intense discomfort of the imagination! A process of dismemberment*
3) *I must conquer my sacrifice to a purgatory myth / a ceremony of self-inflicted violence?*
4) *The powerful voice of sacrifice!!!*
5) *My unproclaimed faith in the subconscious*

6) Unpredictable collision of two realities – irregular energy

On another chart the above thoughts begin to take shape into structural decisions:

1) *strings speak phonemes* (as an indication of two functions of the string players)
2) *bells+brass (two opposing instruments)*
3) *overworld-underworld* (what I meant was the inclusion of quotation as the underworld)
4) DUALITY: *contact points between 2 worlds*
5) DUALITY: *journey to another world – Odysseus? Prometheus? (Mahler/Wagner/Scriabin)*
6) DUALITY: *strings: normal pitch and pitch resulting from harmonic finger pressure = 2 worlds sounds*
7) CONTRAST: *vocal sounds – instrumental sounds*
8) CONTRAST: *timpani ff – strings (using harmonic finger pressure) in ppp (collision)*
9) CONTRAST: *also simultaneously: strings play and sing*

Another important aspect of the music of *Not Two* is the motion of sound in space. This, too, is based on two sides of the stage: left and right, whereas the circular motion of sound within the orchestra symbolises unity, which is a unifying spatial gesture that encompasses the instruments located on each side of the stage. More importantly, the left side of the orchestra is associated with the overworld, the right side with the underworld.

A general effect of space is characterised throughout the piece by the starkly contrasting 'lontanissimo' and 'vicinissimo' indications.[29] These are rendered not only acoustically by the use of dynamics values in the instrumental writing, but also by the use of amplification and reverberation reinforcing an illusion of a moving space taking place within the general sound of the orchestra. These indications speak for themselves and I could continue with further details in the score pointing out where, at a local level, the 1-2 ratio is used as a driving principle of gestures, dynamics, interconnections of melodic lines and movements of sound.

DW. You also use voices extensively in *Not Two*, by asking instrumentalists to sing. Given the voice's relationship to the quotes (about which more, later) their use doesn't seem to be purely colouristic. That is, there also seems to be a narrative, or philosophical, meaning beyond the strictly musical use of the voice (this is supported by some of your remarks in the score). Could you comment on this? Do you think the use of the voice in *Not Two* has the same narrative significance as it does in the *Piano Concerto*?

JP. There are two categories of vocal sounds I request from the instrumentalists: on the one hand, the short and rather percussive consonants of the brass and woodwind instrumentalists; on the other hand, the long-sustained pitches sung by the string players. The dismantled language of the wind instruments resembles the vocal sounds of the choir in the *Piano Concerto*, their role being one of creating a sense of anxiety similar to the one of the *Piano Concerto*. However, in *Not Two* anxiety is strongly opposed by the linear writing of the strings. There is, I think, a rather striking moment at the beginning of the piece, in the 'Mosso e frenetico' section in bars 53-61 (Fig. 5.21, bb. 53-57), where the violent vocal sounds of the wind instruments contrast in a tough manner with the lyrical Mahler quotation of the string players played in 'pianissimo'. Such contrasting moments are very recurring in the piece as a continuous reminder of the dualism I mentioned earlier.

The vocal sounds of the string players are opposite to the vocal sounds of the wind instruments. They appear for the first time in the middle of the piece and rather unexpectedly

---

[29] Lontanissimo (it.) = very far. Vicinissimo (it.) = very near.

Fig. 5.21: *Not Two*: bb. 53-57.

in bar 164 (Fig. 5.22), their sound being amplified while the rest of the orchestra is not playing. The instrumentalists have to sing in unison with the note they are playing. The indication in the score speaks for itself: *"String players sing and play simultaneously. The singing should resemble a dramatic yearning and the voices should <u>not</u> sound lyrical as in the opera tradition. Hence do not use vibrato! Women may sing an octave higher, yet not falsetto! Gradual timbral transformation may be used, but only between the "i" and the "u" (the "i-o" transition should occur suddenly)."*

A similar gesture occurs a few bars later, where again only the strings are playing, but this time the voices are processed by an extremely long reverberation (35 seconds!) which suddenly infuses a massive sense of space in the music. The end of the 'crescendo' is accentuated by a tam-tam stroke played 'fortissimo' and let resonate. Perhaps in all its simplicity, this is the most dramatic gesture in the piece because the sense of yearning is most clearly emphasised. There are a few other passages of this kind also played in 'pianissimo'. Apart from bar 341 at the very end of the piece, where the string players are holding a vocal sound unsupported by their instruments, the singing of the string players is always sustained with the sound of the instrument. *Not Two* and the *Piano Concerto* are two very different musical works, and I wouldn't really say that the use of the voice in both pieces has the same narrative significance, but there are similarities, as the voices are used as intensifiers of emotion, commotion and, of course, timbre.

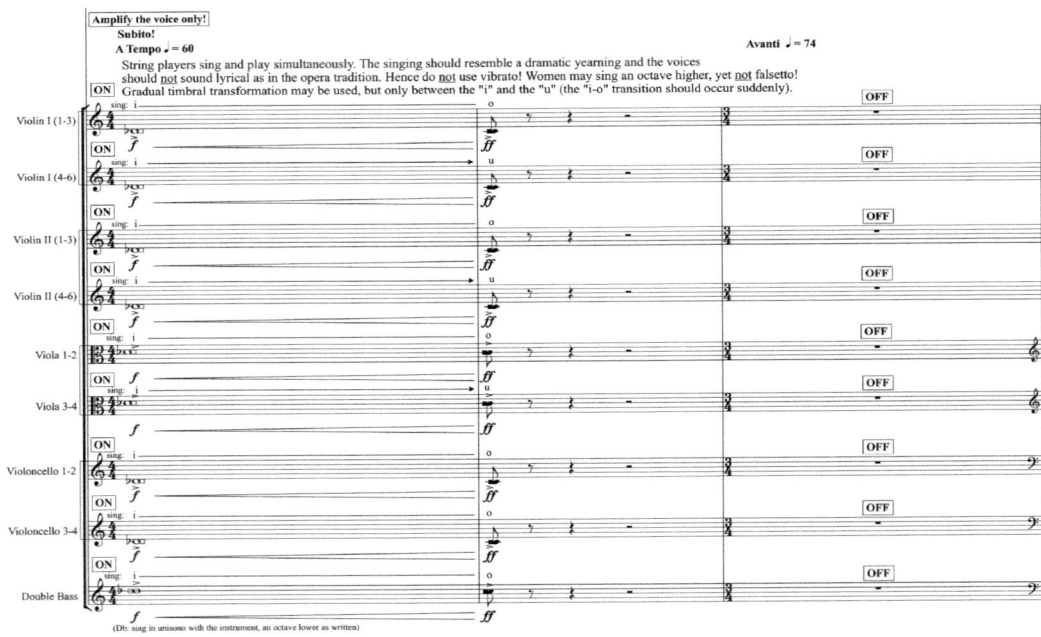

Fig. 5.22: *Not Two*: bb. 164-166.

DW. *Not Two* is notable in its use of musical quotes from Mahler, Wagner, and Scriabin. Composers sometimes use quotes as an homage (cf. Charles Wuorinen *A Reliquary for Stravinsky*, or my own *in [all] the time we have left*), as artistic/social/cultural commentary (arguably Berio's *Sinfonia*), in the service of 'stylistic modulation' (cf. John Zorn and Oded Zahavi), or as nostalgia (many recent compositions). It doesn't seem to me that you are taking any of these approaches. Most of the overtly melodic passages are, in fact, these quotes. Even a place which is quasi-melodic, with the strings bowing 'molto sul ponticello'

(very close to the bridge, which produces a 'glassy' sound) and playing 'tremolo', is marked 'quasi Scriabin', and so on. There are melodic fragments elsewhere, but they seem to be less lyrical and more textural. These melodic quotes, however, are often obscured (if not completely 'opaqued') with pitch and temporal offsets and the application of very heavy reverberation. Given this, what function do these quotes serve? Do you think that a listener would perceive them directly, or simply perceive that 'something' is going on? [In this regard, Schoenberg's *"I feel (the) air from another planet"* comes to mind.] Does the placement of the quotes have formal significance? (It would seem they do, given that the afore-mentioned rhythmic motive leads into and breaks apart at the longest section of quotes.)

JP. Your Schönberg reference says it all. I am usually reluctant to use musical quotations, but in *Not Two*, I decided it was important to create a Late-Romantic sound that would exemplify yearning as a signifier of memory emphasised by a historical condition of our culture. Rather than writing in that style myself, I decided that original excerpts would work much better as they can create a sense of direct reminiscence, a kind of 'I have heard that tune already' effect which is what I was after. For me, it was important to elicit a sense of something familiar that is 'in the air', even if not consciously recognised.

I selected three excerpts from Scriabin's *Le Poème de l'extase*, several fragments from Mahler's *7th Symphony* (the Andante amoroso) and from the *9th Symphony* (the Adagio of the 4th movement), and five excerpts from the First Act of Wagner's *Tristan and Isolde*. In order to highlight the full romantic character of the quotations, the string players are required to use the same bowing techniques and expressivity they would use when playing these historical works. This different interpretation style should be heard as clearly as possible as a sign of stylistic contrast to the contemporary techniques used for the sounds of the main texture. The late-romantic tonal idiom of the quotations versus the atonal idiom of the main texture is a disparity that must be highlighted throughout the performance (a further sign of duality in search of unity).

The placement of the quotes does have formal significance, too. The **first** quotation (Mahler) occurs at the beginning of the piece, in bars 55-61 (the beginning of the phrase can be seen in Fig. 5.21, page 139), and may not be discernible by the audience as is masked by the rest of the orchestra. It includes four simultaneous segments from Mahler played in 'pianissimo'. The 'nascosto' (hidden) indication is self-explanatory: the gentle lyricism of the four melodies supplies a veiled quintessence contrasting to the vague sonorities of the other strings produced by playing 'behind the bridge' (b.t.b.), to the violence of fragmented vocal sounds spoken by the wind instruments, and to the obsessive rhythm of the timpani.

The **second** quotation occurs in the middle of the piece, in bars 167-172 (the beginning of the phrase can be seen in Fig. 5.23). The strings are reinforced by the bassoon, contrabassoon and tuba. The Wagner excerpts are distributed in eight distinct parts played by the strings and begin with a 'mezzo forte' with a crescendo leading to a 'fortissimo' and remaining on a 'forte'. The additional bassoon, contrabassoon and tuba parts enhance the complexity of the polyphonic writing. The duality implied in the two conflicting idioms (the tonal language of the Wagner and the atonal idiom of the rest of the orchestra) is highlighted by the contrasting instrumental writing, that is the linearity of the Wagner melodies and the waving motion of the motifs played by the woodwinds. The polyphonic density proclaims an assertion of conflicting passion that must be immediately contrasted by an unexpected harmonic block played and sung by the string players followed by a tam-tam stroke and the resonance of the string reverberation coupled with that of the tam-tam. The central placement of this harshly contrasting action is significant enough to justify its importance. There is also an important dichotomy between the first and second quotation, namely a further sign of a subtle form of

Fig. 5.23: *Not Two*, bb. 167-169.

duality displaced in time and therefore more difficult to perceive. The first Mahler quotation represents the introverted Yin (the passive, negative, female principle in nature played very softly, in 'pianissimo'), while the second Wagner quotation represents the extroverted Yang (the positive/active/male principle in nature, played loudly, from 'mezzo forte' to 'fortissimo') in its erupting energy increased by rhythmic intensification.

The **third** quotation occurs from bar 217 to 232 (Fig. 5.24 shows bars 218-220) and includes three simultaneous segments timbrally reinforced by the singing of the string players. At the beginning, the Mahler and Scriabin excerpts are superimposed as I wanted to create a sort of sub-texture to the texture that would produce an ambiguous sensation of late-romantic flair disrupted by short polyrhythmic staccato gestures articulated by the woodwinds. A short Wagner motif is superimposed to the other segments at the end of this insertion. The slow-motion and long notes played in 'pianissimo' are a reminder of the Yin principle symbolised in the first Mahler quotation. However, the sustained lyrical quality of these long melodies is highlighted by a long reverberation with a decay time of 15 seconds, which projects them onto a very distant space as a reminiscence of an everlasting yearning of the human race to reunite with a timeless force of nature.

The **fourth** and final Mahler-Wagner-Scriabin quotation in bars 306-322 (Fig. 5.25 shows bars 308-311) begins with one extract by Mahler played simultaneously with two extracts by Wagner. This three-part polyphony is enriched by a fragment from Scriabin four bars later. What makes this four-part polyphony unique is that I ask the string players to use harmonic finger pressure in order to bring out a distorted sound of the original melodies. In my mind, this is one of the most evocative moments in the piece and a reminder that the yearning must disperse in order for the original desire of unity to become a living reality. In the temporally dislocated Yin and Yang symbolism mentioned earlier, the implicit masculine element must now transfigure the lyricism of the previous quotations from within the timbre of the melodies. The fierce sounds produced by the use of harmonic finger pressure played 'molto sul ponticello' (m.s.p.) must distort the purity of the strings sound suggesting that a strained metamorphosis of thought should be embraced by the poetry of life (the 'romantic' lyricism).

DW. As I have mentioned, the sketches for both the *Piano Concerto* and *Transparence* include quite detailed charts working out numerical matrices for a number of musical/formal parameters. These seem more rigidly applied in the *Piano Concerto*; there are places in *Transparence* where the score seems to not strictly 'stick to the plan'. I hasten to add that the resulting music is not at all rigid, but rather remarkably flowing and organic. The *Piano Concerto*, as I have suggested, is especially fluid; the predominate effect is of long meta-phrases which continually shy away from fruition, either by being interrupted (usually, not abruptly, but by another wave), by reaching a peak which turns out to be an anti-peak, or by dwindling before a full crest is reached. The result is a very haunting and haunted narrative. In any case, I'd be curious to hear your comments on how the 'plan' (the details) relates to the result. How do you think about the relationship between what you want the piece to say and the means by how you get there? Do you find that you need to make adjustments (as suggested by what I observe in *Transparence*), and what is the nature of those adjustments? How important do you feel such detailed pre-composition is to a piece of music, i.e. what might be lost without it?

JP. The plans I design are very important in order to lay the foundation of the music in its proportions and structural interrelationships of form, pitch, duration and timbre. Once I begin to write down the notes, however, I allow the music to lead me, as it were. This means that I prefer to follow the direction suggested by the music at a particular point in time, rather than carry out a mechanic execution of what was suggested by the plan. Each time I have to choose between music and structure, I choose music, in other words, my intuition. I always *need* to make adjustments triggered by an intuitive response to what the music is 'telling' me. If I didn't do that, what I write would result in a mere conversion of mathematical proportions and interrelationships in sound. I think the art of music is more, much more than that.

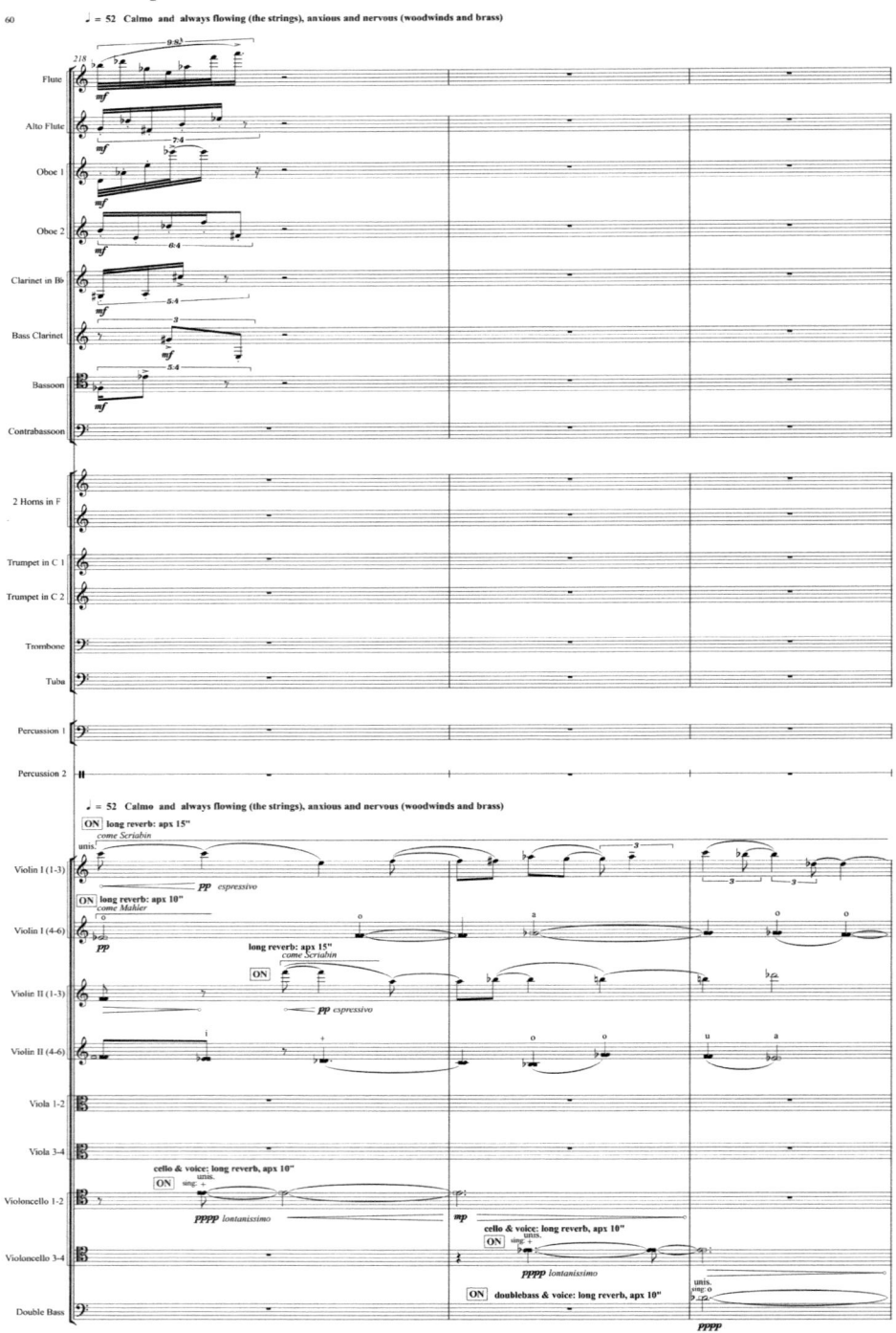

Fig. 5.24: *Not Two*, bb. 218-220.

Fig. 5.25: *Not Two*, bb. 308-311.

DW. How important do you feel such detailed pre-composition is to a piece of music, i.e. what might be lost without it?

JP. I think it is as important as laying out the necessary measurements for the foundation and proportions of external and internal walls, rooms and roof in an architectural plan when you build a house. It's about creating a unifying form that will hold the musical edifice together. What might be lost is a cohesive sense of form in the piece.

DW. I don't want to leave this topic without considering the golden mean, which as you know is a ratio in considerable evidence in nature, and which has and has had appeal to certain artists with Classical inclinations. Identifying locations in pieces that correspond to the golden mean can be a bit of a mug's game, after all, in most complex pieces there are a lot of things going on. So, I hesitate to make too much out of this, but …

The 'primary cadenza' in the *Piano Concerto* starts at bar 272; the golden mean of the 439 bars of that piece would be in bar 271. In *Transparence*, lengths of bars are more variable, but in terms of performance time, the golden mean of the 19 minutes of the piece is around 11:45, which turns out to be four seconds off from being smack in the middle of the combined viola and tape cadenza (so identified in the score) which is the longest formal articulation of the piece. *Not Two* may be, as I have suggested, a little looser, but one notes that the golden mean of the 347 bars of the piece is bar 214, which is just three bars shy of the start of the longest (by far) section of musical quotes in the piece. Coming, as it does, during a lacuna of the rhythmic motive (as I mentioned before), this is also a major formal articulation in the piece. I wonder, therefore, whether this is intentional on your part? Intentional or not, I wonder how you would feel about my suggestion that this reveals a rather Classical approach to form: not in the sense of having 'neo-Classical' forms (i.e. modern fugues or sonata forms), but rather a somewhat bar approach to large-scale formal balance.

JP. I am impressed and delighted by your analytical insights. They inspire me. When I sketch out the architectural plan of the music, I am aware of the conscious and subconscious effects of my albeit limited knowledge of golden ratios, as well as philosophical and esoteric systems including numerology and divination practices of different cultural traditions. Very often I use well-defined systems that I apply to the form of my pieces and unfold them without compromises on a rational (mathematical) level. This is a case when a number takes on a transcending, and therefore divine, significance (I am thinking of the Kabbalah as a case in point). Other times I leave it to my intuition to feel and unfold such proportions on a 'skin level'. I think there is a magic in all this that is impossible to verbalise and perhaps should be left unspoken, as a silent tribute to nature. Nonetheless, I am always intrigued by analyses that will help elucidate these proportions. I tend to feel the experience of life (as an all-encompassing phenomenology of existence) and music as a parallel *living* reality. To be precise, I can state that there is no difference between my (general) perception of life and my (specific) perception of music. The earlier includes the latter, so I am never surprised to read insights such as those you have just voiced out.

Your suggestion of a classical bar approach to large-scale formal balance resonates with me in terms of architectural design and philosophical approach to form. The other, more concealed, world of the subconscious is a parallel reality that is more complex and demanding in the context of a rational discussion. I ultimately experience music as the voice of both the individual hidden in the collective, and the collective spirit intrinsic in the individual: as such, music is a thermometre of society. That is what the old Chinese emperors knew well when they undertook long travels in order to listen to the local music of disparate regions of the empire.

They knew that the music played in those far-reaching districts would mirror the socio-political and ethical conditions of the people inhabiting those regions and would then take action accordingly.

DW. You are obviously an artist for whom words are important. You have written considerably on a variety of topics, and a free-verse poem is an integral aspect of the *Piano Concerto*. I also know from my conversations with you, that you are a person who feels things deeply, and has a wide and dare I say spiritual approach to the world. One can certainly hear this in your music. For instance, in a private conversation, you describe the *Piano Concerto* as essentially a 'cri de cœur'; this is borne out in the music, as I have mentioned previously. However, the programme note in the score of the *Piano Concerto* talks about the interaction of intervals (tuning) and of the soloist with the ensemble, not the intended emotional effect of the piece. Even the poem *Within* that we eventually hear is itself somewhat abstract, although the manner of its delivery, shouted by the soloists against agitated textures, is not.

Even in the case of *Not Two*, which has a programme note that is quite poetic and certainly suggests the transcendent impulse within the music, there is a very telling remark in the sketches which does not appear anywhere in the score (including that programme note). As you mentioned earlier, this remark is "*An attempt to establish contact points with another reality*" (Fig. 5.26 shows your general plan). Is this, then, another sort of pre-compositional planning, where there is a programme that you use to guide the piece, but which remains in the background?

JP. Yes, very much so!

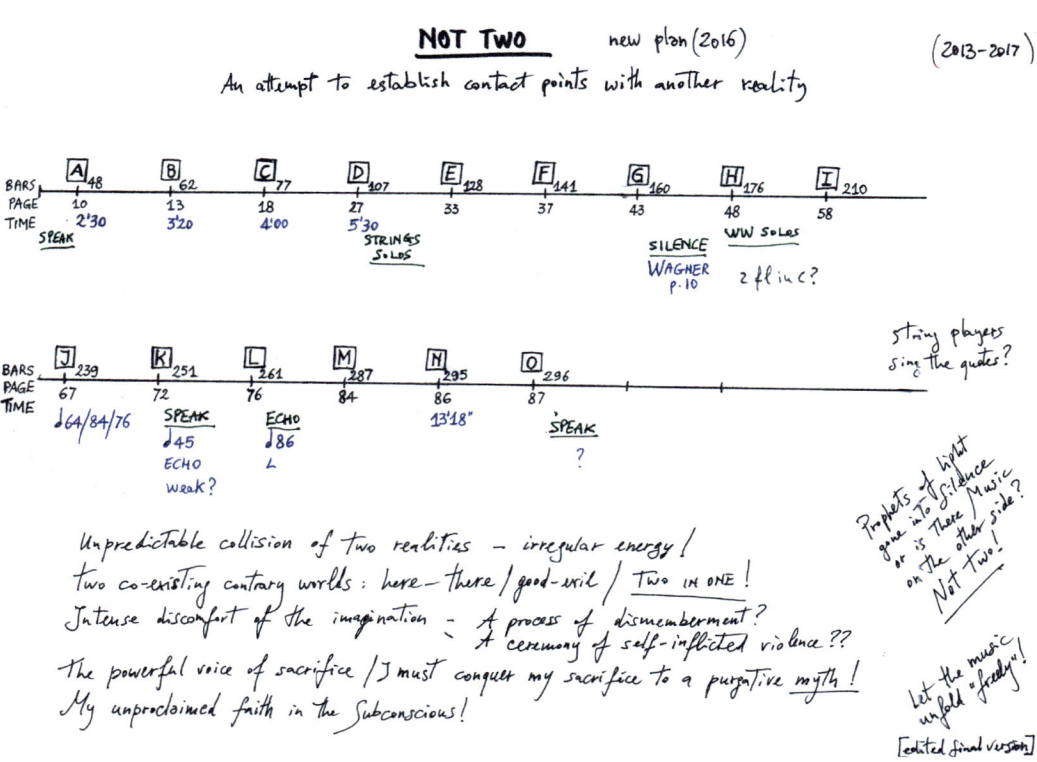

Fig. 5.26: *Not Two*, general plan.

147

DW. Does it come from a desire not to over-state (a finding of a 'middle way' that corresponds to some of my observations about Classical form)?

JP. Yes, indeed.

DW. Is this a matter of really wanting the music to 'speak for itself', without guiding the audience?

JP. Yes. I like inviting people to discover the music, rather than imposing listening directives on them.

DW. Considering Osho's statement _"The truth cannot be conveyed, but the thirst can be given. No teaching worth the name can give the key through words",_ do you intentionally shy away from being too direct, or one might say 'directive'?

JP. These words touch me and do reflect my intentions. I can indicate a street, but not the exact address…

DW. Your music requires significant commitment from the performers/performing organisations. Mounting a piece like the _Piano Concerto_ is not for the faint of heart, requiring as it does specialized tuning for many instruments, and a 16-voice chamber choir in addition to the orchestra. And in _Not Two_ you call on the musicians to also sing, and several wind players to play multiphonics. I am reminded of the saying attributed to Stephen Hawking; he was told that every equation you include in a book would halve the sales. Certainly, for orchestras, which tend to be very conservative institutions, even including quarter tones, let alone re-tuned pianos (two!) and harps (two!) would 'halve the sales', in terms of getting performances. What is your take on this situation? Are you ever tempted to 'water things down' in order to address this?

JP. I am fully aware of this burning problem and in many ways, I am still paying the price for it. I think there are many approaches to this question, each proposing a different personal stance. I should also mention that I have written a lot of music that is technically easier to play than the pieces we have discussed. The majority of my works are not so 'unreasonable' to perform, if I may use that word. I have often attended concerts of new music in Europe where the organising institution manages to schedule pieces with _very_ complex orchestration, so I often wonder why should they not include these less-demanding pieces in their programmes as well? Re-tuning a piano is easy to do and a safe practice for the instrument, if they employ a professional piano tuner (which they do anyway). Retuned harps can be heard in many works of new music. Microtonal music has become a standard in the world of contemporary music, at least in Europe. I still believe that where there is a will there is always a way. I strongly believe that artists should remain loyal to their inspiration and to the nature of their art. By the same token, they should be equally prepared to pay the price for it, if necessary.

A work like my _Piano Concerto_ can only exist for what it is, in the physical (acoustic) embodiment that it needs to have in order to be such. The phenomenological essence of _Not Two_ can only be manifested by the orchestration it needs to have in order for its true spirit to be brought to life. As soon as we begin to succumb to the conditioning of external forces such as the rules imposed by music festivals and institutions, we begin to depart from the authentic nature of art and to enter the world of compromise which will, soon or later, lead to the death of art. I believe music is a sublime experience that keeps us close to the pristine state of existence and that we should honour and defend this experience with undying integrity and zeal.

DW. Even though your music is nowhere near as difficult to play as some of the so-called 'new complexity' composers, it is challenging to perform. How do you find that performers react to the music in this regard? Does this become more of an issue with orchestral players?

JP. This discussion has focused only on a small part of my musical output, but I will reply in relation to the 'challenging' pieces in my compositional output. My experience with performers varies from country to country and from individual to individual. Generally speaking (and I need to stress the word 'generally'), we are facing a profound aesthetic division between Anglo-Saxon and continental European countries that is reflected in the taste and attitude of many performers. The approach of orchestral players, though, seems to be more or less the same everywhere I go, meaning rather conservative. I must say that only once in my life I have been confronted with an aggressive and disrespectful attitude towards my music by a clarinettist of a London-based ensemble who was unable to play a few bars of the piece. Another clarinettist who played the same piece in a Tokyo-based ensemble had no problems with it and played the clarinet part well. How much are the attitudes of performers influenced by their technical ability or musical interest, let alone passion for contemporary music? This is a question I would like to pose to all performers. That said, from Japan through to the USA, I have been working with many wonderful performers who have been totally committed to the music they play. These musicians have achieved astonishing results with their fervour and dedication.

DW. The music also requires significant commitment from listeners. Any music which relies more on texture and colour than 'hummable' melodies still (even 75 years after the death of Webern, and 85 years after the premiere of George Antheil's *Ballet Mécanique*) faces an uphill battle with many audience members. And you consistently 'push the envelope' with non-standard tunings, unexpected use of instruments, and frequently subtle forms. You could also sum up all aspects of the question this way: does the music have to be so difficult? How do you answer the often-posed question: 'for whom are you writing?' Are you writing for today's audience or the future? And, 'pace' Milton Babbitt, do you care if they listen? Finally, and in summation, what in your opinion is the composer's social (or moral) obligation to the audience and to the larger society? How can this (or these) obligation(s) be most successfully met?

JP. As I mentioned earlier, I do care if people listen, of course I do, and I am not particularly fond of what it sounds to me as a rather totalitarian statement; the Babbitt phrase, I mean. But I really don't want to speak for him, and, who knows, maybe he changed that position with age? I always like to talk to people after a performance or discuss music in social or educational contexts and I do understand this kind of predicament very well because I felt the same when I started off. My answers are still the same: education and the willingness to discover something new. Either people have these two prerequisites, or it simply won't work. Can I 'understand' and appreciate contemporary literature or painting? Up to a certain point: yes! After that point: no, because I feel I need to know more about the technical and aesthetic background in order to appreciate the idiosyncratic universe of a work of art. So, what do I do? I have only two options: if I am truly interested in discovering the New, I will do some reading about the developments of literature or painting in the past 100 years. If I can't really bother with all that, I'll leave it there and that's the end of the story. It is my choice, really. It is that simple! Of course, as an acoustic art that unfolds in time, we know that music demands more attention than the other arts. Listening is far more complex than seeing, and in a world dominated by a visual culture, listening to something we cannot hum is something that requires an effort of some sort, or a willingness to learn something different. I am sure that those people who love music will always make an effort to 'understand' and discover new territories of the musical art.

Those who go to the concerts only because they need to join a social event aimed at providing some sort of light entertainment, perhaps will never be interested in anything else.

Earlier on, I made clear as honestly as possible that I never know what to reply to questions like *'are you writing for today's audience or the future?'*. I honestly don't think in those terms, and I don't think I have to feel responsible for what people want or don't want to hear. I want my music to be heard of course and I am grateful to those who are willing to listen to it. Music is powerful enough and doesn't need me to speak for it. You know, there have been a few pop songs that have changed my life. A song is not as difficult to listen to as a piece of new 'classical' music of course, but the psychological substance of the 'enlightening' experience is the same. With regard to the composer's social or moral obligations towards the world (audience and larger society), I can only speak for myself, especially as we live at a time of huge cultural, social and political divisions where composers will come up each with a very different view on this matter. Sometimes, I have felt that the notes I write may reflect a condition of knowledge that could, perhaps, illuminate the life of other people, just like the music of some composers that has illuminated mine.

There was a time in Japan when the life purpose of an artist was to celebrate unity between mankind and nature. In order to do so, the artist had to live in close relationship with nature on a daily basis. I think what was meant by that is, not that an artist is speaking from a position of knowledge (although I suspect this can be possible), but that the artist's 'obligation' is to access a condition of Knowing which can be conveyed to, and shared with the world through art itself. I find this idea most revealing and it certainly resonates with the way I am trying to live my own life. The only thing I would add is that my notion of nature does not only include the tangible dimension of physical reality, but it also embraces the psychological and spiritual dimension of our existence; what we refer to as the 'inner life'. In this case, the act of celebrating unity between mankind and nature implies the awareness that we are not here by accident, and that each of us is on a path of self-realisation, a way leading to the restoration of our divine nature through the experience of love and pain, failure and success, happiness and tribulation. Sometimes, this journey may not be particularly nice, but it is *real*; it has not been traced by a pre-established destiny but lies entirely in our hands. In this context, the composer's 'obligation' is to remind us that we can claim our divinity by living on the threshold of doubt and certainty, light and dark, with courage and determination, and by sharing poetics of intuition, knowledge and evolution with the world.

CHAPTER SIX

INSTRUMENTAL MUSIC

IT'S ALL ABOUT THE FLUTE
Carin Levine

CL. Let's begin with *Inwards* (2005) for bass flute and electronics: in your compositions, you often speak of meditation. This piece is very pronounced in this character. I find the idea of breathing to be particularly important here. One could imagine that this piece is one large breathing movement. Could you please elaborate on the idea of breathing in *Inwards*?

JP. Your perception of one large movement corresponds exactly to the idea of the piece. I wanted a music Gestalt deriving from, and always referring to, the act of breathing. *Inwards* is entirely based on sounds that are inhaled and exhaled in alternation throughout the piece. This is because I wanted to create music that is constantly 'breathing'. *Inwards* was commissioned by the Landesmuseum Stuttgart for an event-exhibition called 'Erster Atem, letzter Klang' (first breath, last sound) that took place at the Old Castle of Stuttgart, in November 2004. The focus of the exhibition was the discovery of the first flute of history dated approximately 30,000 BC. The initial score of *Inwards* was for solo bass flute; that is, without electronic instruments. After the premiere, I decided to extend the instrumentation by adding electronics because I felt impelled to diffuse the breathing sounds on a larger and moving space defined by six loudspeakers located around the audience. I also wanted the *breathing* flute to move from one location to another according to 11 different motions taking place within the concert hall. The world premiere of this final version took place again in Stuttgart, at the Siegle Haus, on 19th February 2005. The performers were Antje Langkafel (bass flute) and myself at the electronics.

    In this final version, the breathing of the flautist through the instrument moves from one location to another according to 11 different routes distributed around the audience. The idea was to create a performance situation where the audience would find itself in the middle of a breathing creature, as it were, as if wanting to experience the rhythms of breathing from within the breathing body itself. I ask the flautist to play this music 'inwardly', I mean with a strongly centred and focused attitude as in Zazen or Yoga meditation, always emphasising the inhaling and exhaling of vocal and instrumental sounds. In many religious traditions of the world, breathing is referred to as a symbol of the physical interpretation of the spirit and the earliest expression of the divine on the mental plane. For example, the first volume of the Upanishad mentions that *"the sun is the outer self, the inner self is breath. Hence the motion of the inner self is inferred from the motion of the outer self."* We find a similar assertion in the Bible: *"And* (God) *breathed into his nostrils the breath of life; and man became a living soul"* (Genesis, ii 7). Breath and word are thus symbols of divine emanation. In Indian and Japanese mythology, even the essence of the Asuras (who are both deities and demons) is based on breathing. In Hindu, the word 'Asu' means breath and originally meant both 'the living' and 'the living God'. Although in the Rig-Veda and Brahmanas, this word gradually acquired a negative sense attached to fighting deities, or demons, the notion of breathing as a generator of life remains connected to the origin of any living creature. When I wrote *Inwards,* I was deeply immersed in symbolism of this kind.

CL. *Conditional Action*, written in 2016, is your most recent composition for flute. In this very virtuoso piece, you have used two flutes. Was it your intention to challenge a performer

to perhaps discover a new level of mental and musical consciousness through the difficulties of your composition?

JP. The proposition of a musical challenge reflects the desire to confront myself, the performer and the listener with deeper levels of consciousness. As a composer who doesn't detach music from real life, this confrontation with our inner self can also take place through a dialectic approach to musical form. When I speak of dialectics in my works, I refer to the articulation of what I call a transcendental argument, or debate, based on reflective assertions typified by a polyphonic discourse that is best articulated within a chamber music context. Typically, these transcendental arguments begin with a sound, a motif, a chord or a specific gesture I have carefully selected as a musical statement. Such assertions spring from intuition, perception, sometimes a concept or an emotion. *Conditional Action* is full of semantic references disclosed by recurring 'tremoli', intervals, motifs and rhythms that are comparable to imaginary claims about our existence on this planet. They begin with what I consider a conditional statement represented by a double multiphonics 'tremolo' in bar one which immediately disintegrates into single pitches scattered by the two flutes over a range of three octaves played at different paces. You can see the 'tremolo' in Fig. 6.1.

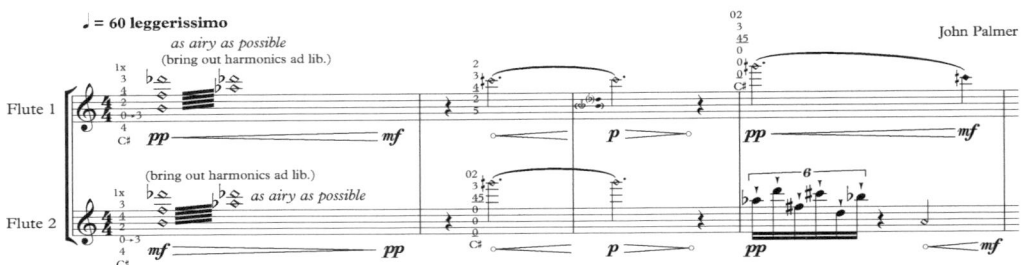

Fig. 6.1: *Conditional Action*, bb.1-4.

The single notes merge again when the multiphonics reunite from bar 22 to 25. A second 'conditional' action resumes in bar 26. Below you can see bars 22 to 27 (Fig. 6.2).

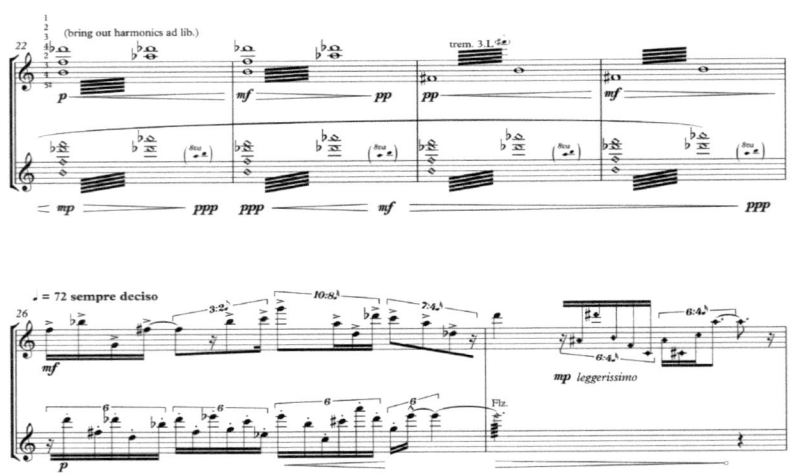

Fig. 6.2: *Conditional Action*, bb.22-27.

The above action leads to the next polyphonic 'tremoli' from bar 60 to 66 (Fig. 6.3). The third action begins in bar 67 (see Fig. below) and will lead to a conclusive statement of self-doubt.

Fig. 6.3 *Conditional Action,* bb. 60-68.

With this in mind, the difficulties of this composition may be compared to the difficulties of existence we may experience in daily life, and the unfolding of the musical assertions I mentioned earlier reflect the articulation of this experience while inviting the listener to search for deeper personal visions and intellectual horizons. Perhaps I should add that *Conditional Action* was inspired by Roy Bhaskar's book *Dialectic, The Pulse of Freedom*, where the philosopher argues about his theory of dialectics known as critical realism. While reading the book I have been thinking that if music resembles a dialectic search for the self, Bhaskar's book is one of the most musical books I have ever read: an enthralling quest for self-knowledge calling for uncompromising ethical, social and political awareness.

CL. In *Conditional Action*, I was also impressed by your compositional technique where the two flutes are so strongly intertwined that it often seems as if there is only one flautist performing. Was this your intention, or is this a result of my own listening experience?

JP. Yes, this was indeed my intention! In order to appreciate the music of *Conditional Action*, it is important to be aware of my flute trio *Hellawes*, written in 1991, for an imaginary meta-instrument that I called the 'Polyflute'. The idea of this meta-flute was born from a desire to write for the flute in a polyphonic manner. In order to achieve this goal, the meta-instrument I had in mind must consist of more flutes unfolding the same musical idea at the same time. That is to say that, in my mind, I am writing for one polyphonic instrument although I am using two or more flautists.

CL. In *Afterglow* (2006) for alto flute, piano and electronics, one is again confronted with the idea of breathing, but in a totally different manner. In this piece, the electronics have a major role, so that the listener has a definite feeling of listening to a trio. Could you explain in detail what role the electronics play in this piece?

JP. *Afterglow* is indeed a trio. In all my works, the electronics are always dealt with as a musical instrument and not as mere ornamentation to acoustic instruments. This piece was inspired by a very short poem about light and darkness that I wrote in 2006. My idea was to convey a sense of changing light emitted after the removal of a source of energy, whereas the light colours are explored through resonance and the source of energy is mainly represented by the piano and the flute sounds. Initially, the subtle colour changes resulted from resonance triggered by 13 gestures of the piano. The electronic instruments retain primary importance throughout the piece as they shape every single resonance in a different way. Each resonance follows a numerical scheme based on 13 gestures and 13 different durations corresponding to hidden numbers of bars. I say 'hidden' because the score is written in time notation, thus representing the succession of seconds. The initial gestures are based on the following palindromic form:

13-12-11-10-9-8-7-6-5-4-3-2-**1**-2-3-4-5-6-7-8-9-10-11-12-13.

During the process of composition, I extended the number of gestures to 17, each gesture triggering a resonance based on different durations ranging from six to 33 (hidden) bars. The electronics consist of reverberation, ring modulation, as well as delay and spectral transformations of the flute's material pre-recorded on a soundfile. The decay time of the reverberation is variable from six to 30 seconds. The ring modulation parameters are variable from 200 Hz to 1000 Hz. Especially at the beginning of the piece, the electronic part is made of very subtle spectral components of the flute to be heard at the border with silence. The role of the electronics is to shape space *through* sound and sound *in* space. In my mind, both sound and space are attributes of moving colours in time. The role of the alto flute remains crucial throughout the piece because it provides the timbral material to the electronics. The main sonic source consists of multiphonics and harmonics. On the other hand, the piano 'colours in' the timbral variations of the flute with short phrases stemming from the flute's motifs. The alto flute and the piano are thus interlocked by the electronics and projected onto dissimilar spaces delineated by the spectral content of the flute.

CL. In *Hellawes*, you incorporated the fascinating idea of your Polyflute on a larger scale. I very much like the expansion of this idea by including phonetic vocal sounds. In comparison to *Conditional Action,* I find the Polyflute in this piece even more sophisticated and complex. Could one consider this flute trio as being a part of a new process concerning the principle of the Polyflute? Is this piece a result of a continuous compositional process that began over 20 years ago? Is *Conditional Action* perhaps a reduction of the very complex processes found in *Hellawes*?

JP. Yes, the *Conditional Action* duo may be considered as a smaller-scale realisation of the Polyflute writing that I began with *Hellawes* in 1991. In this work the Polyflute consisted of the

C-flute, the alto flute and the bass flute. The idea of creating an imaginary polyphonic flute became clear to me in 1990 when I wrote a piece for flute quartet that, for some obscure reasons, was performed on a Swiss radio two years later without my knowledge. In the score of the *Flute Quartet I* (this was the title of the piece), you could see very clearly that the treatment of the polyphonic lines was strongly interlocked and the single parts so fused together that would create a very cohesive texture comparable, for example, to the astounding fabric of interwoven twigs, leaves, and feathers that characterises a bird's nest.

What is important to stress about the Polyflute is that composing for this instrument is not like writing for two or more separate flutes. Instead, I write for *one* polyphonic instrument executed by two or more flautists. This difference is very important. Approaching the compositional work with this mindset will produce a texture that is unique in its timbral and expressive qualities. Another integrative aspect of the Polyflute is the inclusion of vocal sounds as essential components of the sonic fabric of the music. These hybrid sonorities consist of the integration of vocal and instrumental sounds which can be heard very clearly in *Hellawes*. The Polyflute remains a lifetime project as I intend to explore in more detail the exceptional articulation and dynamic nuances, unparalleled expressivity and technical agility of this meta-instrument by using different numbers of flutes in different polyphonic and timbral settings. The extract below (Fig. 6.4) is taken from *Hellawes*, from bar 129 to bar 136, and should give you an idea of the kind of textural density I am talking about.

Fig. 6.4: *Hellawes*, bb. 129-136.

CL. *Still* (2000-2001) is another piece of yours that is influenced by Japanese elements. Is there any particular Japanese composer who plays a large part or has influenced this piece? Is there a particular haiku that you have used?

JP. I am not influenced by any Japanese composer at all. The music I write stems from my mind and my own perception of sound. The form of *Still* is constructed on a haiku consisting of 17 musical syllables (5+7+5). This results in 17 verses, or meta-syllables, which in the score are delineated by letters ranging from A to Q. These letters also indicate cues for the musicians. Similar to a fractal, each verse contains a smaller haiku that is built on 17 musical syllables. In the example below, you can see verse and section E which is the last verse, and 'fractal', of the first grouping of five sections or meta-syllables. This is also the point where the guitarist swaps the classical guitar with the 12-string guitar. The microtonal tuning of each of the 12 strings helps creating a sonic universe of more aethereal and elusive quality. As you can see in the example below, I use standard, light and half finger pressure on both the viola and guitar in order to reinforce the subtetly of the texture with unpredictable harmonic sounds (Fig. 6.5).

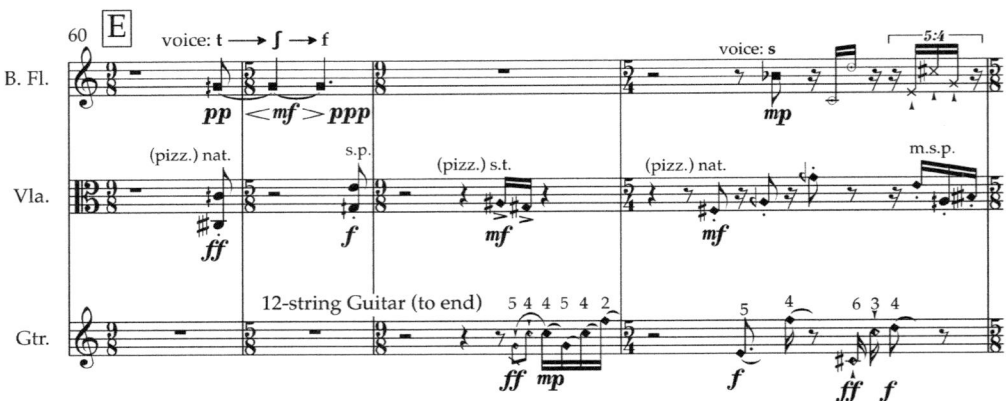

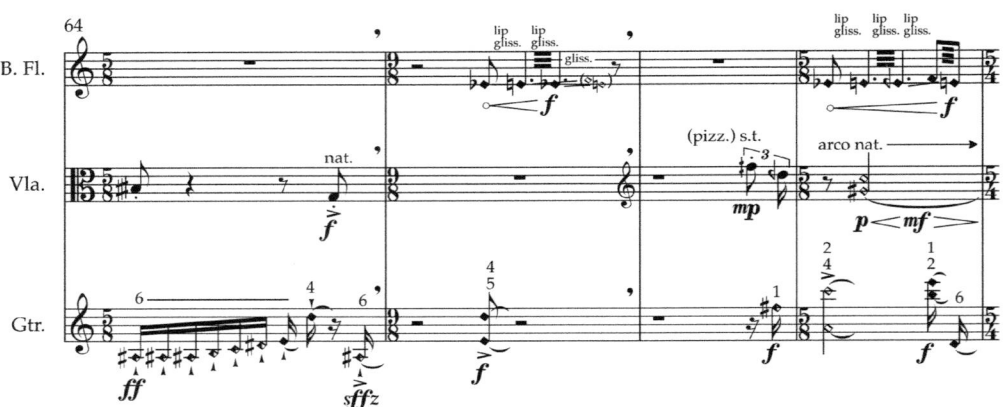

Fig. 6.5: *Still,* verse E.

CL. In *Still*, I feel the piece has been composed in an open form. Could you please explain the idea of form in music pertaining to this piece?

JP. The form of *Still* is very hermetic, I should say. By dividing the large haiku into smaller haikus, I created a fractal structure where an assigned musical material is revisited from different and smaller-scale perspectives. The overview of the large (outer) form can be grouped in five sections corresponding to A, B, C, D, E (bars 1-69), seven sections corresponding to F, G, H, I, J, K, L (bars 70-192) and again five sections, this time corresponding to M, N, O, P, Q (bars 193-332). In the smaller (inner) form, each of these 17 sections delineates a musical verse characterised by its distinct declamatory quality, much like in poetry. The 17 verses are grouped into two large sections (or verses) numbered 1 to 8 and 10 to 17, whereas verse 9 is the centre, the axis as it were, of the meta-haiku. The haiku form itself is broken by a short prologue of three bars which is defined by the number zero. The figure below shows an overview of the large form and the inner form. The pitch content played by each instrument is based on its original, reverse, inversion, and reverse-inversion form. Each of these forms is also related to a quarter-tone scale matrix allocated to an instrument of the trio.

Overview of the large (outer) form:

A B C D E (5) - bars 1-69

F G H I J K L (7) - bars 70-192

M N O P Q (5) - bars 193-332

Overview of the smaller (inner) form:

Verse	Section & Cue	no. of bars	bars	tempo	other indications
0.	-	3	(bb. 1-3)	4/4 crotchet=60	prologue
1.	**A**	19	(bb. 3-22)	4/4 crotchet=60	
2.	**B**	24	(bb. 23-46)		
3.	**C**	1	(b.47)		
4.	**D**	12	(bb.48-59)		
5.	**E**	10	(bb. 60-69)		
6.	**F**	9	(bb. 70-78)		
7.	**G**	18	(bb. 79-96)		
8.	**H**	14	(bb. 97-110)		
9.	**I**	16	(bb. 111-126)	[middle point]	
10.	**J**	18	(bb. 127-144)		
11.	**K**	18	(bb. 145-162)		
12.	**L**	30	(bb. 163-192)		
13.	**M**	20	(bb. 193-212)		
14.	**N**	11	(bb. 213-224)		
15.	**O**	24	(bb. 224-247)		
16.	**P**	36	(bb. 248-283)		
17.	**Q**	48 (46+2)	(bb.284-332)		includes epilogue (bb. 331-332)

Fig. 6.6: *Still,* outer and inner form.

157

CL. In 2010, you wrote *Transference* for solo flute with clarinet, violin, violoncello and piano. This piece is a strong contrast to the other flute pieces we have discussed thus far. I find the intense sound colours and general language of this piece very refreshing. Has *Transference* in some way been influenced by spectral music?

JP. In *Transference*, the flute is the leading instrument of the quintet and the piece is a sort of continuation of my quartet *Transitions*, written a few years earlier. This piece is based on dialectics, in that it is typified by polyphonic discourse, and there is no relation whatsoever to spectral music. In any case, I don't follow compositional definitions of this kind. When I compose, I abide by my own musical intuition, control of structure and sense of form. My compositional techniques are a result of a personal approach to music. It goes without saying that what the listener may hear or associate my music with, is something beyond my control.

CL. In 2013, you composed *Trans-solo 5,* for flute solo. As part of the large *Trans* cycle, the six *Trans-solos* include the flute as well as the other instruments of the chamber group, namely the piano, clarinet, violin, cello and viola. All these very short pieces require a high level of virtuosity. In particular, microtonality is very emphasised in this composition. How does the concept of microtonality play a role for you in this piece and in your music in general?

JP. If I listen to microtonality from a tempered tuning tradition, I would say that microtonality adds both colours and emotional quality to a musical discourse that remains essentially tempered. If I listen to microtonality from a neutral perspective, as a natural musical fact 'uncontaminated' by Western temperament, I perceive it as an open and 'pure' treatment of pitch that includes a richer, extended and refined, level of tone nuances and timbral shading. Writing for acoustic instruments may suggest both perspectives, more often the earlier though, as you can hear in the pieces of the *Trans* cycle for example, where the dialectic of the music springs from a tempered approach to tuning that is extended by quarter tones. I seldom use smaller microtonal intervals, by the way. When I work with electronic instruments, my approach to microtonality is more 'pure', meaning detached from equal temperament. This allows me to explore pitch configurations with a more adventurous and liberating attitude. These two approaches merge when I use acoustic and electronic instruments in the same piece. I should also add that sometimes I create precise matrixes or charts where microtonal pitches are set in a one-to-one relation to a word, a specific instrumental technique or any other structural component of the music. By contrast, some other times I use microtonally freely and out of my intuitive response to a pitch construct.

CL. Composing for the flute is a major challenge for composers these days. The flute has the luxury of a large repertoire beginning around 1950. You seem not only to draw on the modern flute techniques, but also call up the Eastern flute tradition. Which musical world (Eastern or Western) has had a larger influence on your music with flute?

JP. I have never thought in terms of 'Western' or 'Eastern' because I can be inspired by any music I hear, regardless of where it comes from. When I compose, my sonic imagination is related to perceptions, emotions, poetry, visual or intellectual references that are very personal, and I never think in terms of 'influences'. I write what I need to write in order to achieve a specific musical goal and idea that is in my mind. I have always listened to any kind of music without categorisations or hierarchies of any kind, and what I have written from the beginning of my musical journey follows a personal evolution that is consciously unrelated to specific music traditions. The flute is an instrument I loved immediately when I first heard Ian

Anderson's solos in the music of Jethro Tull back in the 1970s, as well as in a lot of European and Asian folk music I heard as a boy. In those days I would not be able to differentiate Turkish from Japanese, or South-American from African music for example, but I do know that every time I heard any kind of flute instrument, I was emotionally very taken by this unique mixture of sound and air that makes the flute sound one of the most sensual timbres I know of. The instrument's timbral expressivity and dynamic agility are equalled only by the saxophone, really. Listening to flautists like Steve Kuyala (also in jazz pieces) and Robert Dick in the early 1980s was an additional source of inspiration that opened the doors to an even richer world of sonorities that still remains very important to me.

CRAFTING SILENCE, BUILDING SOUND
INWARDS, AFTERGLOW, THREE HAIKUS
Gavin Stewart

GS. Your works for low flutes and electronics seem meditative in nature; both *Inwards* and *Afterglow* exist in a space that seems filled with static energy. How do you connect 'breathing' to 'doing' in these works, and is there a non-musical influence?

JP. First of all, I would like to say that there is no static energy as such. Any form of energy is associated with motion. Even the smallest mass contains a form of motion. Energy may have different degrees of motion, of course, and I guess what you are referring to is a low level of energy delineated by slow or subtle motion. In *Inwards*, regular inhaling and exhaling is the drive that defines the compositional process. In *Afterglow*, the breath reference is less obvious, yet the sounds of the alto flute, extended by the electronics and adorned by the piano, constitute the 'living' character of the piece. The connection between 'breathing' and 'doing' is the sound itself, because breathing *is* doing: for this reason, I see no difference between the two activities. The non-musical reference in both works is the act of breathing itself. The succession of inhaling and exhaling allows us to live. 'In-haling' is also closely associated with 'in-spiring'. The notion of 'inspiration', therefore, may be interpreted as inhaling 'something' that will trigger a creative process of some sort. Metaphorically, this suggests a stimulus to undertake creative action through mind *and* body. Also, in a meditation context breathing is used to calm the mind. From this perspective, breathing implies the primary manifestation of spiritual energy in the physical plane. Breathing epitomises the act of living throughout our physical existence. In poetic terms, I like to think that when I am inhaling, I am *listening*, and when I am exhaling, I am *celebrating*. Both physically and symbolically, the notion of breathing has remained a major source of inspiration in my musical work: from the flute to the trombone, from the accordion to the organ.

GS. The use of text is evident in each of three works considered in this dialogue: recited text in *Three Haikus* and spoken phonetics in *Inwards*. Interestingly, the only work that doesn't use the performer's voice is *Afterglow*, and that has a poem given in the programme note. What is the significance of this poem both to you as the composer and to the players, and how is it crafted into the composition?

JP. For the sake of clarity, I should mention that I also use traditional flute techniques that do not include phonetics in several works of mine. In the three pieces you have selected, *Afterglow* is the only one without phonetics. The reason for this is that I wanted gentle air-like alto flute sounds, especially 'tremoli', to create a basic sense of sonic translucence throughout the piece which I wanted to explore in spectral terms and in relation to subtle resonance taking place on the edge of silence. This idea is linked with the content of a poem I wrote which inspired me to write the music. I wanted to create a musical counterpart to the poem itself. The text displayed below reflects the original word arrangement; this should give an idea of the visual layout of words and the sparsity of verses I have used. The spacing is as important as the words themselves. Notice also the lack of punctuation:

declining lights
into darkness
oblivious

revealing universe
of tomorrow

At a poietic level, the significance of poems in my musical works is considerable since it provides the framework of the artistic content and the goal of the music as a reference to life experience. Players should pay much attention to any text I write that is related to the music; they should read it carefully and meditate on its meaning. They should allow the mental images resulting from the words to inspire their imagination before beginning to work on the piece. In the case of *Afterglow*, the images in my mind evoked by the poem are crafted into the music through the use of soft dynamics and subtle timbral changes perceived as sonic and metaphorical transitions taking place between light and darkness, one sound-colour and another. The changing timbre of the flute sounds, extended and refined by the electronics, should resemble a kind of impression we experience when observing the changing conditions of glow after the light source has disappeared. The most notable example being the rapidly changing colours following sunset, the glow of an incandescent matter after the source of heat has been detached, or any other kind of persisting luminescence following a generative spark of energy.

A subtle treatment of 'sonic afterglow' in the piece is the use of resonance as an expedient of glimmering and extended luminosity. As a result of 13 triggering gestures played by the alto flute and the piano, each resonance brings out a specific partial extracted from the notes played by the alto flute: I have called this technique 'harmonics resonance'. The compositional procedure is rather simple: each note played by the alto flute is scrutinised in its spectral content; I then select different harmonics of the flute sound and use them as individual components for a new sound that will be used as resonance played by the electronics. For example, right at the beginning of the piece, the alto flute begins with a D4 quarter-flat. I transposed this note an octave lower in order to obtain a clearly audible spectrum out of which I selected a C6 (transposed) partial as a specific 'harmonic resonance'. This first resonance takes place on the edge of silence from 0'13" to 0'40" and is followed by a second resonance beginning at 0'48" with the C6 partial and a newly added F#6 partial. This is how I create an afterglow of subtle resonances closely related to the source notes played by the alto flute.

As the title suggests, the music of *Afterglow* is based on the notion of light, and subtle forms of colour variations. The timbral shadings exploited by the harmonic resonances are also explored as musical space. As you know, the alto flute lacks the big resonance body of the piano, so one of the functions of the electronics is to 'rectify' this situation by providing the alto flute with an enhanced virtual space through digital reverberation. The piano resonance is in turn enhanced by amplification. In addition to reverberation, the phrases of each instrument are articulated by restrained ring-modulation and pitch transposition aimed at creating a stronger variety of timbral shading. All in all, the electronics provide an extended space through reverberation, and a richer timbral context provided by the harmonic resonances, the ring-modulation and pitch-shift. The thinner the harmonic resonance, the softer the loudness of the resonance will be. The softer the resonance, the stronger will be the perception of distance.

GS. Continuing on the textural enquiry: is there a source for the phonetics in *Inwards*? What is the performer trying to say? What philosophy governed the decision to never hear a tangible word?

JP. The source of the phonetics in *Inwards* is arbitrary, namely, the phonetics were chosen as vocal sounds of *musical* significance to be associated with the traditional sounds of the bass flute as an additional colour. The only philosophy behind the choice of phonemes is the 'philosophy' of sound itself. Therefore, there is no semantic discourse involved in this work. This was a decision that resulted from a desire to enhance the timbral qualities of the bass flute by adding additional breathy and vocal sounds. The breathy sounds are used in the range between C4 and D5 with a closed mouthpiece, while the phonemes are used on a larger range. The combination of vowels and pitches will produce a richer bass flute timbre. For example, the 'o' and 'i' [ee] vowels will merge very well with the traditional pitches of the instrument; the 'a' contributes to render a brighter timbre of the note that is being played; the 'u' is very effective in creating a darker timbre. In *Inwards* I used six consonants and nine vowels that I combined with alternating pitches being inhaled and exhaled. I also used gradual changes of vowels in order to create a timbral modulation on the same pitch.

GS. Can you talk about the process for composing *Inwards*?

JP. The music of *Inwards* was inspired by the act of breathing perceived as the origin of life. I explored breathing in conjunction with the motion of sound in space. There are two main compositional elements at stake in this piece: breathing and (moving) space. Breathing is based on the inhaling and exhaling of sounds resulting from the combination of traditional pitch and vocal sounds sung and spoken by the flautist. Additionally to what I have said in the previous answer, I should add the use of multiphonics, timbral fingering, singing coupled with 'glissando' notes, and vocal sounds spoken or sung directly into the mouthpiece without pitch production. These tone-production techniques are elicited by 62 gestures or phrases of different duration. Here the use of space as a compositional process is of paramount importance.

    <u>Space:</u> each of the 62 gestures triggers a different spatial attribute controlled by two reverberation units and projected via six loudspeakers. The first effects processor (originally a Lexicon PCM-60) has a demanding function in that it provides a large variety of changing spatial attributes and pitch processing comprised of 14 dissimilar types of reverberation types and decay time. Some of these 'programs' include a harmoniser and pitch-shift, this means that the audience will hear a chord or an interval out of a pitch played by the flautist. The second effects processor (originally an Alesis Q2 unit) consists of three alternating reverberation programs providing a stable sense of space throughout the piece based only on changing decay times of each reverb setting. For the technically-inclined reader, I would like to detail some motion-related components of *Inwards*, though it may be difficult for the layperson to follow.

    <u>Moving space:</u> I delineated 11 trajectories of the breathing sounds to be projected from six different loudspeakers located around the audience. I numbered the loudspeakers one to six (1-2 left and right at the front, 3-4 left and right in the middle, and 5-6 left and right at the back). Motion 1 is circular and clockwise: 1-2-4-6-5-3. Motion 2 is also circular, but anticlockwise: 1-3-5-6-4-2. Motion 3 comprises the trajectory 1-6-5-3/4, whereas the motion in 1-6-5 is fast, and from 5 to 3/4 is slow. Motion 4 consists of 2-5-6-3/4, whereas 2-5-6 is fast, and from 5 to 3/4 it is slow. Motion 5 comprises 1/2 to 5/6 (through 3/4) in parallel motion, fast and slow. Motion 6 goes from 5/6 to 1/2 (through 3/4) in parallel motion. The route of

motion 7 is 5-4-1-2-3-6. Motion 8 encompasses 6-3-2-1-4-5. Motion 9 involves 6-3-4-1-2, fast and with a slow ending on 1 & 2. Motion 10 begins from 5 and ends on 3 and 4 at the same time. Finally, motion 11 goes from 3/4 to 1/2. The two charts below should visualise this (Figs. 6.7 and 6.8).

loudspeakers

1	**2**
3	**4**
5	**6**

front (L+R)

middle (L+R)

back (L+R)

motion 1: **1-2-4-6-5-3** (circular clockwise)

motion 2: **1-3-5-6-4-2** (circular anticlockwise)

motion 3: **1-6-5-3/4** (1-6-5 fast; from 5 to 3/4 slow)

motion 4: **2-5-6-3/4** (2-5-6 fast; from 5 to 3/4 slow)

motion 5: **1/2 to 5/6** (through 3/4) in parallel motion; fast/slow

motion 6: **5/6 to 1/2** (through 3/4) in parallel motion

motion 7: **5-4-1-2-3-6**

motion 8: **6-3-2-1-4-5**

motion 9: **6-3-4-1-2**; fast (with slow end on 1 & 2)

motion 10: **5 – 3/4**

motion 11: **3/4 – 1/2**

Fig. 6.7: *Inwards*, list of motions 1.

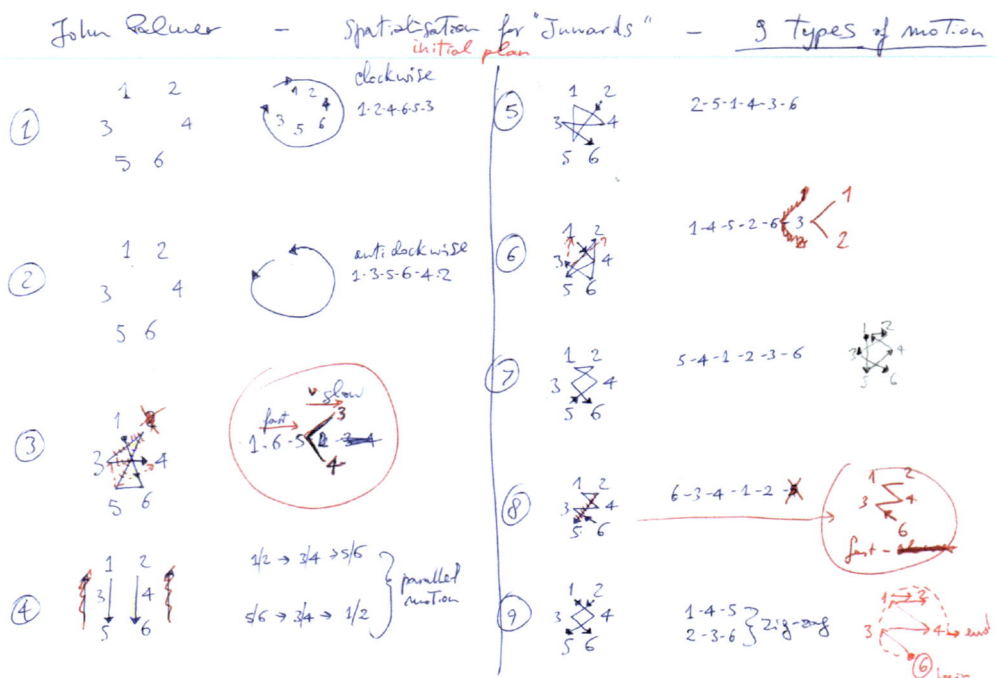

Fig. 6.8: *Inwards*, sketch for list of motions 2.

GS. There's a performance direction in *Inwards* that suggests you would accept a version without the specialised electronics. How does this fit with your concept for the piece, and what do you think is lost in the trade-off for an easier and readily accessible performance?

JP. Actually, the direction you are referring to is outdated and I should amend this in the score soon. The performance with the electronics was so convincing that, following the premiere, I decided to go for one final version of the piece that includes electronics. I am aware that this decision is making the performance of *Inwards* more difficult to stage, but the musical results are much more captivating than an acoustic version. I can no longer envisage a version without electronics.

GS. Both *Inwards* and *Afterglow* use pretty involved electronics but in vastly different ways. Is there a philosophy governing the manipulation of acoustic sound, as seen in *Inwards* beyond simply amplifying the flute?

JP. Oh yes. It's not only about the 'manipulation' of acoustic sounds, but also about the *creation* of new sounds and indeed new spaces. Each of these two pieces shows a different focus and usage of electronic instruments. In *Inwards*, the electronics are performed live and their main musical function is to provide an extension and mobility of space, including some minor enrichment of pitch and spectral content of the bass flute. Their musical function remains essentially related to the projection of the bass flute sounds in space.

In *Afterglow*, the electronic instruments are both live and fixed in the electronic studio. Their function is threefold: i) *timbral* (mainly through ring-modulation applied live to the alto flute; ii) more specifically, *spectral,* to fortify the spectral content of the alto flute by adding the harmonic resonances I mentioned earlier; iii) *spatial*, by providing varying degrees of 'harmonic resonance' throughout the piece to both instruments and in particular to the alto flute.

GS. Both *Inwards* and *Afterglow* exist in prescribed spaces that encompass the audience. Is there an underlying philosophy that governs your created spaces, and how do you go about the process of creating them?

JP. First of all, I should mention that a prescribed space that encompasses the audience occurs only in *Inwards* as the six loudspeakers are located in front (on the stage), in the middle and at the back of the hall, therefore surrounding the audience. I don't have a pre-established philosophy of space: any spatial decision I make is strictly related to the content of the music I am writing at a specific time in my life. Thus, the process of creating space varies from work to work. For example, in *Beyond the Bridge*, written in 1993 for cello and electronics, space is a major preoccupation of the piece. The idea of this composition was based on an imaginary world to be perceived beyond a stationary sense of space represented by the notion of a bridge. In order to achieve this, I needed to create three dissimilar spaces: one being the acoustic space triggered by the cellist who is performing in front of the audience; a second space being elicited by an 'alter-ego' cello pre-recorded and diffused from behind the audience with at least two loudspeakers located at the back of the concert hall; finally, a third space occupied by a second 'alter-ego' cello is projected by at least two other loudspeakers located outside the concert hall, thus creating a 'lontanissimo' effect. The combination of these three 'interacting' spaces (close, far and very far) constitutes the poetics of the music. I should add that the listening experience of these three spaces is also reinforced by a changing perception of time prompted by the recurrence of three motifs on each space and at different points in time.

GS. There are explicit references to Japanese music in *Inwards* with the use of Mura-iki, but also subtle hints towards Japanese musical aesthetics such as 'ma' and extra-timbral information. To what extent are you consciously aiming to engage with this musical lineage?

JP. I am not referencing Japanese music, nor am I trying to engage with this musical lineage. The Japanese tradition is perhaps the only culture in the world that has so clearly valued the experience *and* inclusion of silence in daily life as well as in music. This has evidently attracted me because it is already part of me and my musical aesthetics regardless of Japan. My musical world is not Japanese, but a reflection of who I am. I am often asked to talk about 'ma', and although I cannot describe myself as a specialist on this topic, I must confess that I sense some confusion in the West about the meaning, or the application, of 'ma' in music. Sometimes I come across musicians who think that the 'ma' is the inclusion of a rest between two notes, something that is created as a compositional element. Some other times I hear musicians saying that the 'ma' is something that takes place in the imagination of the performer who experiences a sense of 'emptiness' regardless of the number of rests written in a score. Some other people speak of 'ma' as the perception of a gap between the two notes of an interval that is not necessarily linked to a structural compositional element. This latter view suggests that the concept of 'ma' is less dependent on the existence of a 'horizontal' or temporal gap, but rather related to the perception of a vertical space.

In my opinion, to describe 'ma' as the silence between two notes or events is far too simplistic. How can we *listen* to something if we are unable to perceive it and experience it with full mind and body? Isaac Stern once described 'ma' as an 'emptiness full of possibilities, like a promise yet to be fulfilled'. Assertions of this kind may well sound inspiring and insightful, but to me, they are romanticised attempts of little musical significance. The truth is that we cannot transfer a perception of the world that is so essentially Asian to a Westerner without really experiencing, understanding and ultimately *feeling* the psychological nuances of a knowledge that is so rooted in traditional Japan. Clearly, the 'ma' is a crucial component of Japanese music that stems from an all-encompassing understanding of art, *and* a perception of life that is typical of countries of the Far East.

In Japanese visual art, 'ma' refers to a perception of an empty space that holds as much importance as the rest of the artwork. This perception of emptiness is so typical of Japanese sensitivity that in my view cannot be experienced by the Western mind unless one practises Zen or a similar form of meditation, or leads a lifestyle based on a similar Weltanschauung (a particular philosophy or view of life). One of the first things that we will read in a Zen book for English-speaking readers, for example, is that the Japanese word for 'emptiness' has not the same meaning in English: in other words, in Zen, the concept and the experience of emptiness is not the same notion of what we Westerners understand as 'emptiness'. There is a problem here that is essentially cultural, as the same assignment of meaning to a specific notion, transferred to another language, may change radically from one culture to another.

'Ma' is often translated into English as the concept of 'negative' space: but what does a negative space really mean to a Westerner? Is our perception of space the same as that of a Japanese person? Can we in the West really perceive 'ma' as a rest or a musical space that resembles an *active* form of silence? If yes, would this not require us to give silence a meaning? And what kind of meaning would it be? Critically, how could we really experience the 'ma' if we may be unable to spend one day in silence for example? And another question: would a musical 'ma' relate only to silence or may it include the perception of resonance? How do Japanese musicians perceive resonance? I am not saying that is impossible for a Westerner to experience the 'ma'; in fact, I think it is! What I am saying is that such a focused experience is so idiosyncratic of Japanese culture that cannot just be transferred to Western music as an idea detached from its cultural context or a mere 'feeling' about how I want to listen to a rest placed between two notes. I am just worried that 'ma' in the West is risking to be understood as a fashionable concept detached from a specific cultural experience and perception of life, and that there may be a tendency to intellectualise a perception that simply cannot be grasped unless we develop a set of practices, disciplines and behaviour that correspond to a *living* experience rather than a rational construct of the mind.

GS. You say that *Three Haikus* is for a 'poet/musician'. Is there a rationale behind the use of the musician beyond their instruments in your music?

JP. I am not sure I understand your question well. As I mentioned earlier, each piece I write holds its distinct identity since it mirrors a chapter of my life that has its own genesis and idiosyncratic rationale. *Three Haikus* has been written for an ideal artist who should be a poet and musician at the same time. The shakuhachi player is also the poet who is reciting the haikus while playing the shakuhachi. The poet who recites the haiku is also the musician who is playing the shakuhachi. I wanted the performer to be aware of this double function during the performance. The text of each haiku is fully integrated into the score, so the performance is actually unfolding on two simultaneous layers.

GS. Is there a new flute and electronics piece on the horizon? What kind of musical space would you want to create in a new work?

JP. I began writing a piece for flute 4 years ago. For some reason, the collaboration with the flautist did not continue and I decided to stop working on it because I have so many specific ideas in my mind that can only be realised by working closely with a flautist. The idea of the piece is essentially based on language, meaning that the music will result from a kind of speech articulated in a polyphonic manner. In this context, the flute will be used as the resonance body of the speech. The very experimental nature of this piece requires close collaboration with a flautist. However, I intend to pursue the writing for my imaginary polyphonic flute that I have called the Polyflute, a meta-instrument consisting of two or more flutes playing simultaneously. Following my *Flute Quartet 1* in 1990, I consciously wrote for the Polyflute in my flute trio *Hellawes* in 1991 and many years later in my flute duo *Conditional Action* in 2016.

GS. You have written works for shakuhachi and flute. Would you ever consider combining them in the same piece? And, if you did, would you seek to find common ground between them? How would you do that?

JP. I love this combination and I have already used it in my piece *Koan*, for solo shakuhachi and ensemble. An alto flute is part of the ensemble, and, as you may recall, there are several moments in the piece where the two instruments are interlocked in a parallel polyphonic line resembling an almost 'double-melismatic' manner. I mean that the shakuhachi and the alto flute are interlaced and crisscrossing each other in a virtuosic manner. I find this kind of texture to be of extraordinary beauty, both timbrally and polyphonically, and the timbral affinity of the two instruments reinforces the same 'entangled' cognition of polyphony I am exploiting with the Polyflute. This kind of texture definitely deserves more attention.

TROMBONE MUSIC: FROM *TRANSFIGURATION* TO AN ANTI-OPERA
Patrick Crossland

PC. Our first musical experience together was preparing for the premiere performance of your composition for trombone and electronics entitled *Transfiguration*. This powerful piece was inspired by our mutual friend, the inimitable Vinko Globokar. Can you discuss his influence on your work and how that translated into the inspiration for, and creation of, *Transfiguration*?

JP. I met Vinko for the first time in Lucerne in 1989 as I attended a week-long workshop in experimental composition and performance that he gave at the local Conservatoire where I participated as a pianist. Three years later, I attended a composition masterclass he gave in Dartington (England). On both occasions, we worked on specific topics, as you can imagine in a context of that kind. After Dartington, we kept in touch throughout the 1990s; I went to visit him in Berlin a couple of times and he visited me in London. I interviewed him and wrote an article on his music. We also discussed a new piece I would write for him. This was the time of the Balkan wars and, at some point, I proposed to write a piece for trombone and electronics dealing with this topic. When he came to London, we recorded all the extended techniques of his repertoire as a trombonist. These techniques plus other sounds I asked him to record provided the basis of the trombone material for *Transfiguration*. From an instrumental point of view, this piece was truly inspired by Globokar's virtuosity. We can hear Vinko's techniques, his idiosyncratic breathing and his voice throughout the electronic part of the piece. I can even smell his cigar when I listen to those recordings: seriously! Perhaps *Transfiguration* is the best case of a composition where the soloist's virtuosity perfectly matches the concept of the work and any other aspect of performance and narrative. Being that he has Balkan origins himself, his identity, both as a man and as a trombonist, was the perfect counterpart for the realisation of my idea.

I can't really say that Globokar's music has influenced my work because our idioms are very different, and in any case, I don't subscribe to a specific style in my output. What I mean is that I am not interested in composers who always use the same techniques and the same musical logic throughout their life. I like variety and change, development, variation and evolution. Having said that, Vinko is a composer I respect a lot, one who, in my opinion, has remained underrated in the new music scene. I am convinced a reason for this must be linked to his strong sense of integrity, humility and unwillingness to sell himself. This is a trait I have always admired in his personality.

PC. I find your notation system in *Transfiguration* fascinating and practical: your use of separate staves for playing while inhaling and playing while exhaling, and another for the manipulation of the mute. Can you describe how you developed this system which conveys a tremendous amount of information and yet is still decipherable in a performance environment?

JP. I like to make my music as practical as possible to perform. The discourse of the trombonist in *Transfiguration* is based on the following features: inhaling and exhaling (breathing), timbral variations (the use of the mute), speaking and singing into the trombone and the production of traditional tones. Inhaling and exhaling provide a sense of drama throughout the narrative of the piece, and, in order to make this as easy as possible to read and practise, I decided to use two staves dedicated exclusively to this feature. The same thing applies to the mute changing. There are several moments in the piece where the mute is clearly acting as a filter to the trombone sound. This continuous change of colour needed to be notated as meticulously as possible as you can see on page 6 of the score (Fig. 6.9). The integration and interaction of these three techniques are crucial to the narrative of the piece, also in relation to the electronic sounds.

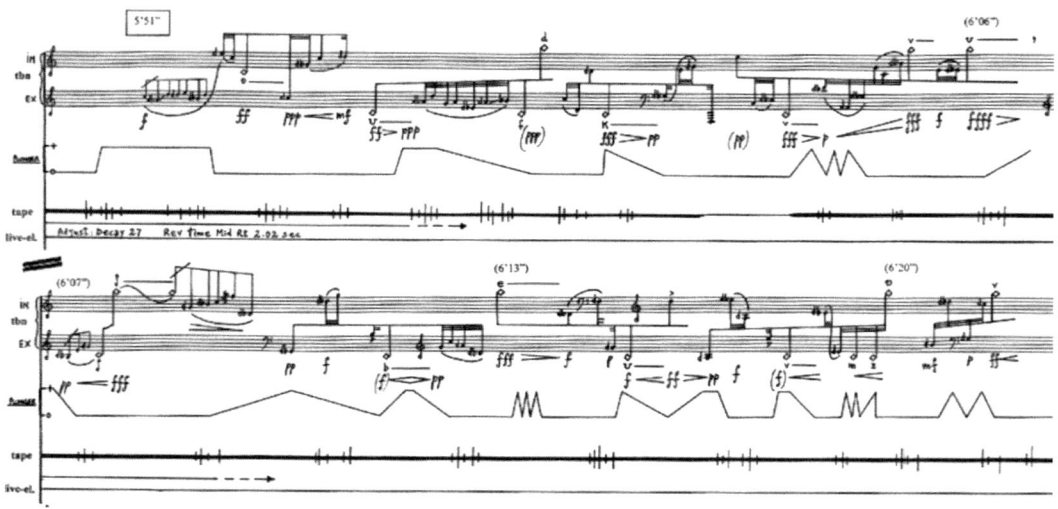

Fig. 6.9: *Transfiguration*, 5'51" to 6'20".

PC. You wrote *Transfiguration* as a clear statement of protest against any kind of war. Can you tell me more about the genesis of this piece and how you organised the structural level of the composition?

JP. Throughout the Balkan Wars, I had been questioning ongoing issues such as utopian images of a better world succumbing to the daunting reality of despotic and oppressive political regimes. I felt unable to reconcile my political and artistic purposes, knowing that personal grief and disbelief cannot change the blatant contradictions of such appalling circumstances. I conceived *Transfiguration* during the 1999 KlangArt Congress in Osnabrück, Germany. Suddenly, one afternoon, it became clear to me that I had to make a musical statement about the problem of war and the human tragedy that affected the countries of former Yugoslavia in the past decades, and that I had to write this piece for the virtuosity of Vinko Globokar. Ironically, I finished composing the electronics in May-June 2006 when Montenegro voted for its independence from Serbia, thus breaking the last political link that held together the old state of Yugoslavia.

The genesis of the piece is almost identical to the genesis of *Epitaph* (for cello and electronics) in that both pieces are born from strong grief about the death of people caused by some kind of distress. In the case of *Epitaph*, it was the suicide of a friend; in the case of *Transfiguration*, it was the death of thousands of innocent people as victims of war. In both cases, I felt a need to create a structure based on a visual symbol of hope, light and rebirth. An asymmetric star was the symbol I had used for *Epitaph*, and I decided to use it again for *Transfiguration*, just with another shape from which I would establish the inner and outer form of the piece. Symbolism is very important for the creation of my musical works.

I began by splitting the word 'Yugoslavia' into two parts (yugo/slavia) as a symbol of disintegration of the ideology that created it. The 10 letters of the word were split into four letters (yugo) and six letters (slavia). Then I included the number 86 corresponding to the full

167

note range of the trombone including quarter-tone steps, the number 13 (the positions on the trombone with the pedal notes, including quarter tones) and 12 (the partials for each position of the trombone slide). I used these numbers to create the pitch material and the large form of the piece, and arranged them in the shape of an asymmetric star made of 10 beams, each of a different length depending on the proportions resulting from the principal number 4, 6, 10, 12, 13 and 86. Figure 6.10 shows the correspondence between the numbers determining the length of a section and the beams (ray number) of the star.

ray no.	1	2	3	4	5	6	7	8	9	10
length	10	8.6 (86:10)	13	12	6.6 (86:13)	7.1 (86:12)	1.3 (13:10)	1.2 (12:10)	4	6

Fig. 6.10: *Transfiguration*, ray number and length correspondence.

The star below (Fig. 6.11) is but the matrix of the form of the piece in terms of total duration, number of sections, length of each section and pitch content. The vertical line represents the 12 partials of the trombone and the horizontal line represents chronological time. The length of each duration is related to the calculation above, for example, ray no. 1 (see line 1a – beginning – and 1b – end) corresponds to 10, and so forth.

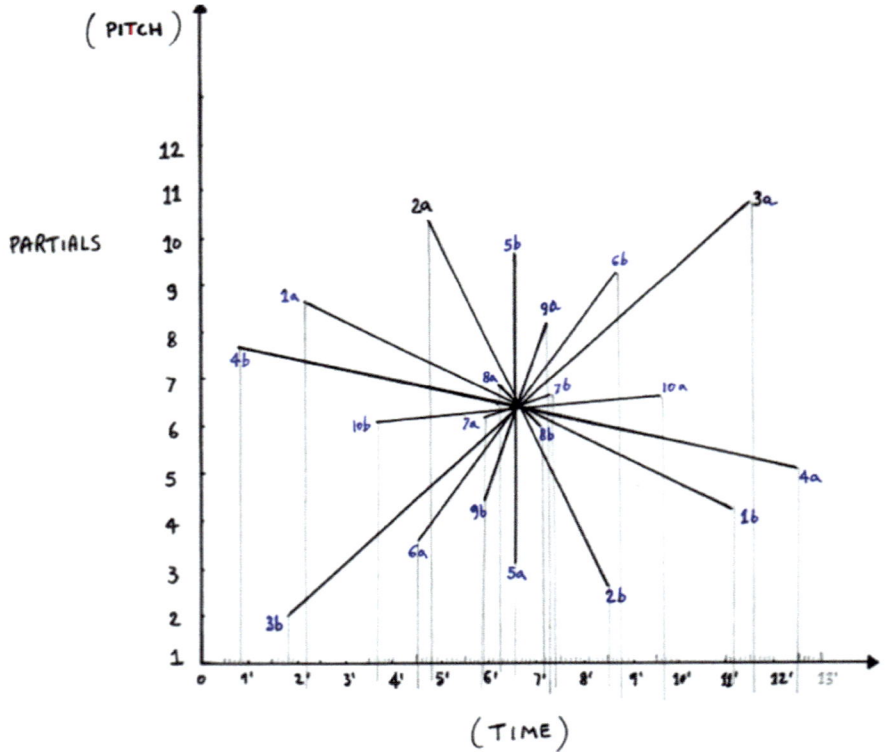

Fig. 6.11: *Transfiguration*, star matrix.

I mentioned the partials: Figure 6.12 shows a note on each of the 12 partials so that you can see on which note each line of the star begins. Figure 6.13 displays all the number of beams (to the left) and the corresponding pitch regions of the 10 beams. For example, pitch region 5 (beam 5) begins on F3/B2 and must end on C5/F♯4 or D5/G♯4.

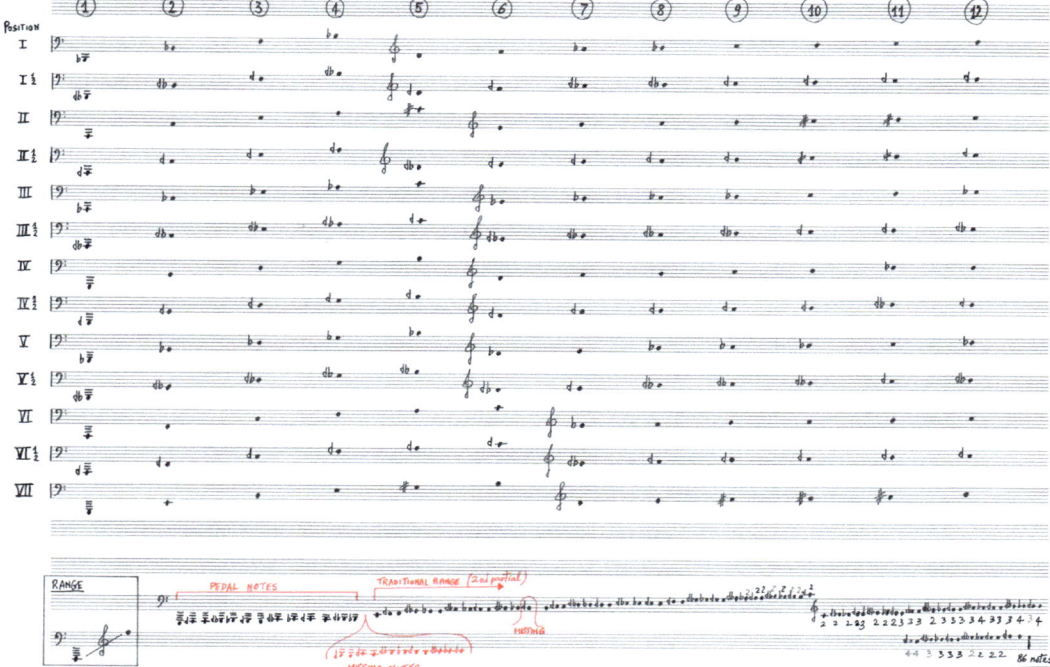

Fig. 6.12: *Transfiguration*, partials and positions.

In the lower diagram of Fig. 6.13, each pitch region is ordered chronologically from beginning to end of the piece. Down below, there is a numerical pattern which shows the quarter-tone interval paths that define the trajectory of the melodic lines of the trombone part.

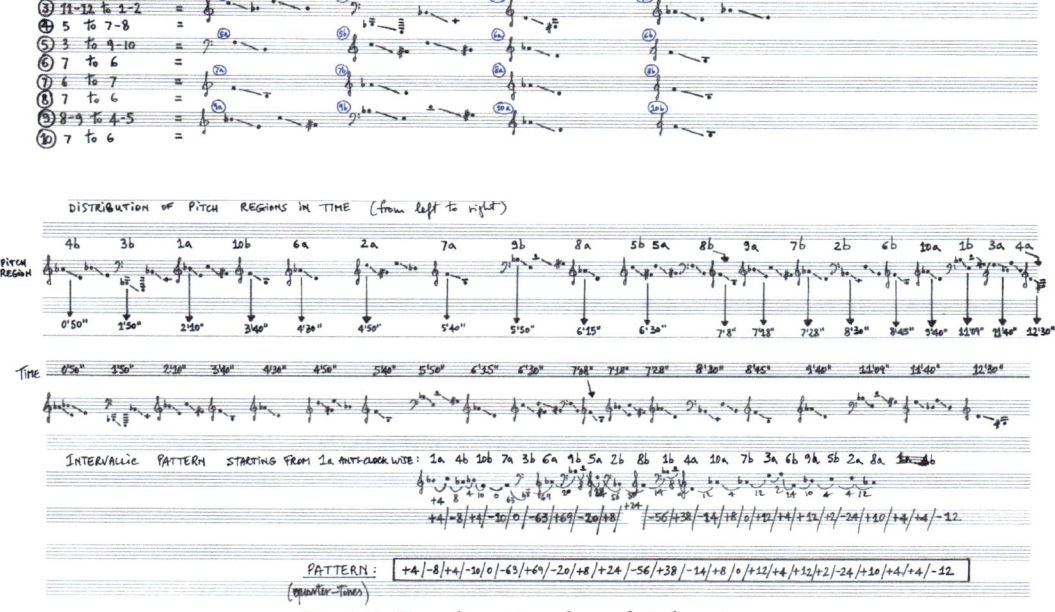

Fig. 6.13: *Transfiguration*, chart of pitch regions.

169

Finally, the following chart (Fig. 6.14) shows the first two pitch paths resulting from the above procedures. This is the linear unfolding of each beam of the star. Each line is delineated by the colour red. The first red rectangle comprises the final pitch unfolding the content of first beam of the star. The second one begins at 1'50" and so forth.

Fig. 6.14: *Transfiguration*, examples of pitch paths.

I also created a pitch-phonetic chart in order to establish a one-to-one correspondence between the pitch to be played or sung and the phonetic sound to be sung or spoken (see Fig. 6.15). This is equally important because an intervallic relation will also correspond to a phonetic relation between two vocal sounds.

Fig. 6.15: *Transfiguration*, pitch-phonetic chart.

An example of the realisation of the above material can be seen in Fig. 6.16 at 1'52" (line 3b) and 2'04" (line 1a). The unfolding of pitch may stop before the beginning of another intersection point in the star (considered as a chronological order of entries). In each case, a beam is unfolded both with notes and vocal sounds according to what I have explained above.

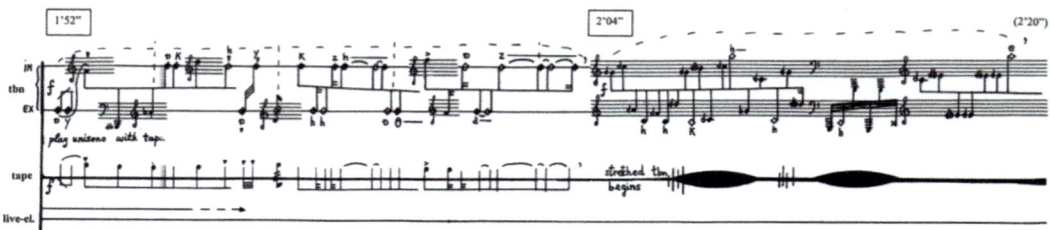

Fig. 6.16: *Transfiguration*, score extract from 1'52" to 2'20".

170

Perhaps one of the most dramatic moments occurs around the fourth minute of the piece where the stretched breathing of the trombonist returns as the background sound in the electronic part. This is juxtaposed by the trombonist with a combination of inhaling and exhaling pitches and vocal sounds visually reinforced by the lifting of the trombone in the air and a sudden crescendo of men's voices leading to the sound of marching troops at 4'30" (see Fig. 6.17).

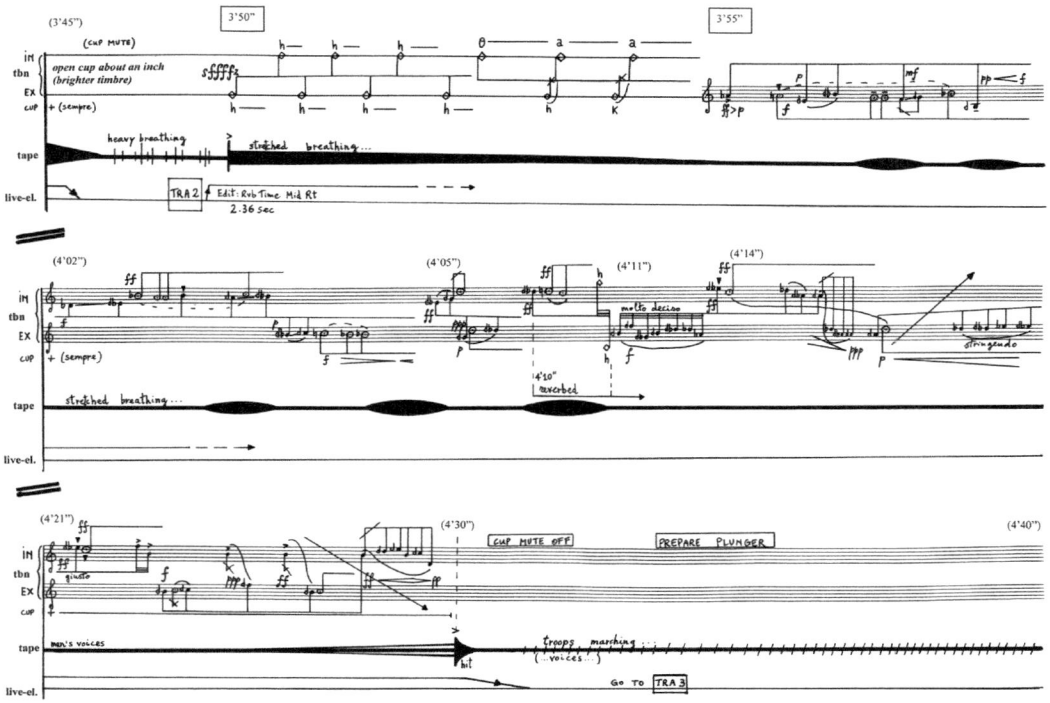

Fig. 6.17: *Transfiguration*, score extract from 3'45" to 4'40".

PC. Breath plays such a fundamental role in your trombone works, particularly *Transfiguration* and *Towards the Soul*, with the inhaling and exhaling playing as well as the instruction to breathe through the instrument without buzzing the lips. Other non-trombone works such as *Inwards*, *Transient* and the incredibly dynamic *Drang* (with its artificial breathing), focus on this essential act of survival. It's often said of great music and superior performances that the music 'breathes'. What are your thoughts on the significance of the Breath in your music?

JP. Breath is a recurrent theme in my music. Breathing is the most natural act and the most powerful symbol of life. Our physical life is made possible by breathing in and out for a finite period of time. Breathing can be experienced with careful awareness of exhalation and inhalation, and even by stopping the area of the body in which the breathing takes place. We can also control the length of each breath phase and the number of breaths. Inhaling and exhaling are two complementary motions that, together, provide the basis for physical existence. For me, music is a form of movement that includes mindful breathing. Understanding music as a form of breathing stimulates a new awareness of sound as an expedient for enhanced consciousness. Most of the time, we tend to breathe too superficially and with much tension. Breathing well is an art that goes hand in hand with the awareness of our spiritual centre. The pieces you have mentioned, with the addition of *Thereafter*, for organ and electronics, are based on the notion of breathing as a symbol of consciousness. In *Transfiguration*, the physical breathing of the trombonist is used as a dramatic force, a continuous flow of tension, anxiety and a distressed search that remains associated with the tragedy of war throughout the piece.

Towards the Soul, for trombone quartet, portrays a different music scenario. Based on the harmonic series of four fundamental notes (C, D, E and F♯), this quartet explores the interaction of inhaling and exhaling on the edge of silence. This 'quasi-silence' texture, as I call it, is almost imperceptible and in slow motion. It symbolises an inner journey to a deeper awareness of breathing as a living force between sound and silence. In order to stress this atmosphere of sacred 'inwardness', I use what you have named the 'shadow notes': almost imperceptible sounds produced by allowing the lips to vibrate as little as possible. The effective range you established for these micro-sounds goes from D3 to F4. However, all the pitches below and above this range should equally be played the same way and therefore as softly as possible. At the beginning of the piece, the bass trombone begins by exhaling the lowest C. The second gesture in bar four begins the same way but is reinforced by the second tenor trombone. The third gesture begins in bar seven and is triggered by *inhaling* the lowest C while the consequent exhaling motion is reinforced by the third tenor trombone on the second fundamental note D and prolonged by the second and first trombone on the fundamental notes E and F♯. From bar 11 the exhaling and inhaling sounds will follow one another in a swing of interwoven breathing echoes chasing each other until the end of the piece (Fig. 6.18).

PC. You have composed a number of duos and trios featuring instrumentalists and live and/or pre-recorded electronics. As a performer, I feel that playing with a 'machine' requires an approach that is quite different from making chamber music with other instrumentalists sharing the stage with me. How would you ideally like performers of these works to approach your music?

JP. First of all, by making a distinction between what you call a 'machine' and a musician. If you are playing the trombone and I am playing live electronics, you are not interplaying with a machine, but with another musician. I may be located in the middle of the audience (more frequently) or on stage (less frequently) but I am still another musician who is performing with you. It is a chamber music scenario where you are interacting with what I do with the electronics as I am interacting with what you are doing with the trombone. The awareness of a mutual interaction is imperative as we are effectively making music together and, at the same time, it's about two performers, not one.

The situation of an electronic part that has been fixed in the electronic studio and is played back during the concert is different. No matter how many subtle alterations I may be doing from the mixing console (and I usually do this), these are too little for the electronic part to be considered as a 'live' instrument (although the concept of 'live-electronics' seems to have changed somewhat lately). In this case, I would agree with you that you would be playing with fixed electronics that cannot be changed and will always sound the same regardless of where you are performing. Here, the comparison with a machine is more appropriate, although I find the term 'machine' unmusical rather reductive. However, there is a way to make this 'interaction' with fixed electronics both *lively* and *musical* and that is by exaggerating the dynamic contrasts, phrasing and articulation of the acoustic instrument. By doing so, the acoustic performer is triggering an impression of fluctuating dynamics in the electronics. In psychoacoustics, this is called an auditory illusion. The important thing to be aware of is that the listener will hear the electronics as if responding to the instrument. Accordingly, the more the acoustic performer differentiates the dynamic and agogic shape of a phrase, the louder or

Fig. 6.18: *Towards the Soul,* beginning.

softer, nearer or farther, the audience will perceive the electronic part. This stratagem can produce astounding sensations of an active interplay taking place between the acoustic and fixed electronic part. Generally speaking, I think the performer of an acoustic instrument must come to terms with an element of abstraction that makes this kind of interplay different to the traditional acoustic chamber music setting. When I perform at the piano with electronics, I know I am interacting with an invisible instrument that is providing me with unparalleled (and imaginary) sounds impossible to be achieved by acoustic instruments. I therefore must feel more responsible for the performance of the piano part since I represent the concreteness of the acoustic sound as opposed to the abstractness implied by the electronic sounds. The context of the performance is now calling forth a different kind of approach to interpretation because the 'real' (concréte) sonic nature of the acoustic instrument is enhanced by a 'surreal' musical dimension (the electronics). The resulting symbolism is impossible to obtain in a performance with acoustic instruments. If, for example, a trombone note is projected on a larger acoustic space provided by reverberation, or is repeated by a delay, what is happening is what I would call a 'transcendental' dialectic of music. The repetition or projection of the trombone sound onto an (electronically) extended acoustic space abstracts the trombone note from its original physical space and timbre in order to redefine it within a new imaginary space and possibly timbre. Thus, sound processing and projection become a formidable proposition of transcendental meaning where the very nature of the acoustic instrument is defined anew. The consequence of this status quo on the performance of the trombonist will be significant.

Firstly, because the trombonist will need a higher degree of imagination about the way to produce sounds on the instrument. Secondly, because by interacting with an invisible musician (the electronics), the trombonist needs to be *actively* responding to the electronics and able to model the trombone sound to the sonic transformations that are taking place through the electronics. Thirdly, the acoustic performer is challenged by a changing sense of space throughout the performance and must be able at all times to trigger such wider spaces or timbral transformations with an extended palette of technical devices such as articulation, loudness, agogics and general sound gestalt bearing in mind that such enhanced spaces are impossible to achieve without electronics. Fourthly, the acoustic musician must respond to the emotional effect of the electronic part on his mind and adjust his interpretation accordingly. You may remember those passages in *Transfiguration* where, at some point, in the tape part (the 'fixed' electronics), we hear the crying of people and some excerpts of Balkan folk songs. The significance of these highly emotional sounds in the narrative of the music and the effect on the mind of the trombonist will be of major importance to the interpretation of the trombone part.

Another interesting psychological situation arises when an instrumental note is extended through reverberation within a context defined by a succession of other, unprocessed, notes. Out of a melody made by several notes, the chosen one that is about to be electronically processed must contain a particular semantic potential in the mind of the composer. This specific note should stand out of the context in order to emphasise a sign of special relevance within the phrase. The trombonist must be able to understand this distinct sound-condition within a melodic contour and play the note accordingly. In such a case, the trombonist should be able to extrapolate the selected note and 're-invent' it on an extended space and timbral context. This selective process of 'pitch-abstraction' (as I call it) should ensure that a specific shaping of pitch density, loudness, timbre, control of duration, must clearly stand out within the dichotomy of the abstracted (processed) note and the other (unprocessed) notes. By highlighting specific sonic qualities and textural meaning perceived in a melodic configuration, the performer is effectively activating a deeper quality of musical introspection that is being enriched by the transformation of sound.

The psychological stimulus caused by the intervention of the electronic manipulation of sound will affect the performer's perception of the musical context and elicit a set of corresponding accents, dynamic gestalt, phrasing and articulation that will mould the electroacoustic texture of the music. In such a context, the instrumentalist's perception of intensity, duration and timbre is freed from the restrictions of the usual acoustic boundaries in order to be extended to wider, otherwise inaccessible, sonic contexts.

The instrumentalist's perception of the sonic stimulus provided by electronic instruments is corresponding to the perception of a reality related to the scientific description of the same phenomenon. For example, the nearest a scientific description can get to the reverberation phenomenon is by giving the measurements of its depth, time delay, spatialisation, and other acoustic factors. The nearest a percept can get to the experience caused by the reverberation is by portraying it through sensory attributes such as depth, loudness, warmth and tone-colour. According to these assumptions, the instrumentalist's interpretation will act as a primary cognitive activity which discerns spectral and spatial characteristics that are otherwise not recognizable in the traditional acoustic perception of pitch, timbre, space, duration and loudness. The impact of this awareness on the performance will usually produce a refined and sensitive interpretation of the instrumental part.

The electroacoustic environment provides an ideal domain to the performer for the representation of perceptual meta-constructs elicited by transformed trombone sounds that will now assume a textural significance of a higher order. This description implies that the same melodic configuration played in the electroacoustic context should produce a more introspective interpretation. The sonic representation provided by an electroacoustic texture can be truly revealing as the instrumentalist's mind is now compelled to re-evaluate the sound of the instrument within an enhanced context while having to shape the interpretation accordingly. The establishment of a certain melodic, harmonic and timbral structure reflects patterns of perceptual categories responding to sonic stimuli triggered by the abstracted world of the electronics. If the task of interpretation is to unfold a revelation of such patterns, then an instrumentalist must create musical representations that must transcend their abstracted sonic counterparts.

PC. As a performer of your own music, do you find the line between creation and interpretation sometimes blurry?

JP. Yes, especially when I improvise, and to a lesser degree when I perform from a score. This is because of a natural sense of 'appropriateness' that seems to accompany me when I create something new. The French call a world premiere a 'creation' and this is an interesting concept really, because it shows that music is music only when it is performed, therefore *heard*. When I perform a piano piece of mine, I find myself in the unique position to 'create' (in the French sense) what I have written down as a composer. This is a circumstance where the dividing line between composition and interpretation can be at times indistinct, at least in my mind. As a pianist, I must make an effort to combine analytical thought about the composition with a sense of evocativeness in my interpretation that should match the genesis of the notes I have written (the poietic level of creation). What I have sometimes found uncomfortable in the past is being constantly able to listen to the inner voice of the composer while interpreting the music in front of an audience. At times this may trigger a feeling of uneasiness as I am confronted with a double exposure as a composer and pianist, interpreting 'myself', as it were, rather than the music of someone else.

PC. One of my favourite relationships is that between performer and composer. I have been fortunate to have had a number of opportunities to work directly with composers and I cherish all of these experiences. I am humbled and delighted when I am able to provide

inspiration. How do you find working with performers during the composition process?

JP. I usually enjoy it, although this is very dependent on the kind of performer I am working with. I am always interested in exchanging experience and insights with other musicians, and I am aware that some of my best pieces were born in collaboration with great performers. I feel that a true musical relationship inevitably becomes a personal friendship, and that the creativity resulting from such a friendship can be a 'subversive' force in the music that is taking shape. Like any true friendship, the relationship with a performer is essentially creative and must be critical: it is like a mirror reflecting different aspects of my personality that are being exposed to the other person and vice versa. A fruitful collaboration cannot fully unfold if one of the two participants is suppressed or weakened by the other. Both roles become essential contributors to the process of music creation. When the understanding between the two musicians is strong, it will pulsate with an energy that cannot be stopped; it will benefit the quality of both composition and performance because when two musicians connect at a soul level, this connection will always be present in the music. In this sense, I believe the presence of the performer will always live in the music, and I think *Transfiguration* is a case in point.

PC. It cannot be denied that you have written an unusually large number of works featuring the trombone. What do you find most compelling about the instrument?

JP. I consider the trombone as one of the most expressive and malleable instruments of a Western orchestra. I love the warm, powerful but also elusive timbre of the instrument as well as the variety of timbral transformations that can be achieved by using different mutes. The wide pitch range and the use of the slide enabling the production of microtones and glissandi are additional features that I particularly appreciate. The trombone is also a perfect instrument for extended techniques among which I would like to mention the sing-and-play technique and speaking into the instrument. The resulting sounds are very effective and inspiring. I am also very fond of the shape of the instrument and its potential theatrical power.

PC. What do you find most challenging about writing for the trombone?

JP. This depends on the kind of music I have in mind. Amongst the many possibilities of the instrument, I probably find the most challenging the production of slurring ('legato' tonguing) as the slide needs to move between the notes, and 'pianissimo' sounds especially in the lowest and highest register of the instrument.

PC. *Prelude to a Dream* and *Prelude to a Prelude* are two parts of a trilogy for solo trombone. Is the third piece already composed or planned? Please describe your concept for the *Three Acts for a Dream*.

JP. The trilogy is an important component of the 'anti-opera' I have in mind. The material of the third piece, *Three Acts for a Dream*, was written down some years ago, and I will finalise it as soon as the two other pieces will be premiered. Each of these three pieces will denote a transition from one conceptual layer of the anti-opera to another. The transition will designate a change of perception in the search for an ideal world in the jungle of a digital era.

PC. Can you describe this 'Anti-Opera' for solo trombonist you are planning? What is the role of the interpreter in such a work?

JP. It is about the role of theatre and acting critique in the era of digital culture and human obsolescence. The entire opera will be 'narrated' by a trombonist, a kind of Prometheus figure who is the protagonist of a story taking place at the edge of madness and idealism. The performer finds himself questioning an interpretation of art in relation to his personal life and a rapidly changing society. It will be a theatrical work with very little scenery and filled with symbolic objects combined with movement and different forms of light and space. The idea of a hypothetical world of dreams will be supported by rituals, masks, stylised movement and an acting style resembling that of Antonin Artaud. The libretto is based on a selection of concepts about the human condition, portrayed by Günther Anders. The life of Antonin Artaud himself will be re-visited by the spectre of symbolism and surrealism as a fleeting historical phenomenon, and the critical world of an imaginary theatre will deal with the idea of a contemporary dream taking shape in different and even contrasting forms. The central topic will be the notion of Dream as a living condition: 'I dream therefore I am'. The main actor is the trombonist whose theatrical role is split into three interacting characters, each being the alter-ego of the other. The Artaud techniques of communication through visual poetry, movement, gesture and dance (instead of words) will be reassessed within an interpersonal story unfolding at the edge of the impossible and in relation to theatrical acting and music interpretation. I am also planning to keep the problem of music interpretation as a perception of life as the central allegory of the performance.

SURRENDER TO THE MUSIC: *OVER* AND *WITHOUT* FOR VIOLIN
Theodore Flindell

TF. When I started working on *Over,* I was reminded of my very first encounter with your music a couple of years earlier when I performed your quartet *Transitions*. I felt again as if I were being thrown into a vast sea of sound-shapes and almost violently dragged out of an even more gigantic ocean, or 'stream', comprised of an infinite force, a hurricane of music that had been and will always be there. Similarly, all the other pieces of yours that I have had the privilege to hear or play seem to have neither a tangible beginning nor an ending. To me, they are hinting at *another* music that seems to always be there, before and after the piece I am playing. Nevertheless, your music has a clear form. Do you believe in the existence of such an extra-dimensional stream? And is the act of connecting to this stream a kind of returning to a perennial dimension, and therefore an essential part of your work as a composer?

JP. Your insights are very inspiring! You are touching upon some very important aspects of artistic creativity and its ontological significance. Metaphysics is a realm that is not physical, yet it exists, and phenomenology has shown us that what we call 'consciousness' is consciousness of *something* that exists! Perhaps we shall never know what art actually is, but in my experience, it reflects an intuition of multi-dimensional levels of existence, not only emotionally, but much more intriguingly, in terms of sensing subtle perceptions of what we call 'time' and 'reality'.

When listening to music carefully, very often we may experience a sensation that time has stopped or that what we hear is bringing up memories, feelings and sensations that, although may seem familiar to us, are impossible to identify on a rational level and to locate in the labyrinth of place and time that resides in our mind. I experience music as an art that brings me closer to a sense of timelessness despite, or perhaps, because of the chronological flow of the sounds I am hearing. This is probably what you are defining as 'stream'. Personally, it is like being transported onto layers of perception that reside beyond the *known* reality of chronological time, as if dwelling in a surreal state where past, present, and perhaps future, seem to merge in a non-linear fashion. I suspect this may relate to what you define as 'extra-dimensional'.

Music makes the invisible audible. Perception *is* a reality. A possibly 'unvoiced' music that is lingering beyond time while encompassing any music that is being heard is a fascinating view that suggests more than a mere hypothesis. Music gives sound to something that we can neither touch nor see, but that is here somewhere near, constantly present in an intimate dimension. When we read about works of art being timeless, what is being conveyed to us is the idea that art has the power to elicit dimensions of our existence that are not restricted to a specific time, notion or place, and that is therefore indicating something of a perennial nature. Music is a gate to unknown areas of the mind and a reminder of the complex and sublime nature of our existence. Connecting to this stream consents us to 'breathe' in a timeless dimension, provided that we are willing to enter the unknown. This is both the rationale and motivation of my work as a composer.

TF. Speaking of the 'stream', it seems to me that a returning question in the field of contemporary composition is the problem of converting the undefinable quality I mentioned earlier into discernible form. There are only very few composers of the past and present who manage to resolve this problem convincingly. It seems to me that in many musical works of the traditional repertoire, this considerable substance is simply not there, or it gets lost in the music. This is not the case in your music. I have the impression that you are very much aware of this issue, and that you are dealing with it in a rather original way. It seems to me that, in your music, you are saving as much as possible of this energetic flow without compromising the content of the music by neither taking refuge in some serial system nor in chance operations, just to name the two most prominent techniques of the past 70 years. Would you agree with me? And how do you move along that thin blue line?

JP. I am touched by your words. Discernible form is the indispensable container in which the musical flux can flow as energy that runs freely and uncontrolled. The problem of form became very clear to me in the late 1980s when I was critically studying John Cage's indeterminacy as opposed to serial and similar techniques used by other composers. It is not by chance that the title of my PhD Thesis a few years later was *Formal Strategies in Composition*. My major preoccupation in those days was to investigate forms in composition that would be both defined and spontaneous, controlled and uncontrolled at the same time. In the early 1990s, I realised that anarchic music was too feeble and ineffective for what I had in mind. On the other hand, the rigidity of serial procedures would produce mechanical and often uninspiring music that was far away from what I was looking for. In the following years, I became gradually aware that music is the highest expression of consciousness and that the morphologies of sounds we choose stem from a labyrinth of experiences, desires, memories, sensations and feelings that are living in us and cannot be described by mathematical or chance procedures. If too strictly formalised, this labyrynth risks sounding dull and monotonous while making no justice to the power of the poetry inherent in those psychological conditions that reside in the mind. This 'poietic' and indeed potentially 'poetic' level is where everything begins, and I think it must remain a living reality, a reminder of the music we write. What John Cage didn't understand is that music is not sound and that sound itself is not music! As a creative manifestation springing from a 'hidden' knowledge of the composer, composition comprises the architecture and design of sounds that are syntactically, and perhaps 'grammatically', related to one another, similarly to language.

Throughout all these years, I have gradually come to the conclusion that the energetic flow of my music should reside in a cohesive and compact form that can fully integrate intuitive processes. I realise that my intuition always knows what I need to do; that my instinct is wiser than my logical mind since it is visionary and limitless; that a feeling may *know* much more than intellectual speculation. This doesn't mean that I am denying the power of logical thinking. On the contrary, this is a necessity that provides clarity of form to the musical texture, but in order for the music to be and remain alive, I need to integrate my intuitive intelligence in the process of composition. I feel naturally inclined to find discernible forms regardless of the procedures I use. To me, the word 'discernible' is a synonym for 'living'.

TF. *Over* is quite extraordinary in its technical demands: masses of extreme leaps must be played at very fast speed, conflicting with legato sequences of concentrated diversity of phrasing, articulation and clashing dynamics, to name only some of the challenges of the piece (see the first page of the score, Fig. 6.19). I remember very well the dress rehearsal on the eve of the first performance. It was the first time I played the piece in your presence. I was full of doubts and in fear of losing control during the performance. You insisted on reminding me to forget any kind of psychological restriction that was going through my mind, and encouraged me to surrender to the musical substance without worrying about the rest…

JP. I wanted you to *feel* the music and concentrate on the music as an indicator of consciousness, to concentrate on the emotionality of the music as the evolutive force intrinsic in the sounds you were producing. The music I write is essentially emotional and, as such, evolutive in the most *human* meaning of the word. Sounds, phrasing, articulation, form and meaning are strongly interconnected because they constitute complementary aspects of the same artistic-psychological reality. Each phrase of the music contains a desire to make a statement sublimated by an associated emotion. This passionate attitude is important to understand the substance of the music. I am aware that dealing with perception and sentiments is not fashionable these days, especially in the modernistic circles of new music. I am equally aware that the idea of biography in music may come across to some people as egotistical and self-referential, but this is not the way I see it. I think sentiments, emotions, dreams, desires, sensations and perceptions are what bring us together as a society made of people who are inexorably connected to one another and interact on all levels of human endeavour. Your experience is also mine; my experience is yours. We are the results of key choices we have made on the threshold of situations that we now may have forgotten, but we all share the same experience of joy and suffering, desires and difficulties, and the same sense of failure, success and hope. The music I write explores the meaning of these psychological circumstances that define the human condition. This is why it is so important to perform this music with full awareness of its emotional content and personal significance. Ultimately, consciousness is what allows us to evolve as individuals and artists. As musicians, we are particularly fortunate in that we are dealing with an extremely creative form of consciousness that we call music, and that we can share this art honestly and resolutely with our audiences.

TF. A striking aspect of *Over* is that virtuosity does not come across as a means to brilliant cleverness or as a demonstration of technical gloss, but as a powerful tool of authentic expressivity. And here is where the title of the piece comes into play. Could you tell me more about the role of virtuosity in this piece?

JP. In the context I have just described, the role of virtuosity epitomises the willingness to confront oneself with the complexity of life. I am alluding to an uncompromising quest for the meaning of fulfilment, happiness, pain and suffering, and a search for a transcendent resolution. Virtuosity represents the perfect symbol of dialectic confrontation with the question

Over

John Palmer

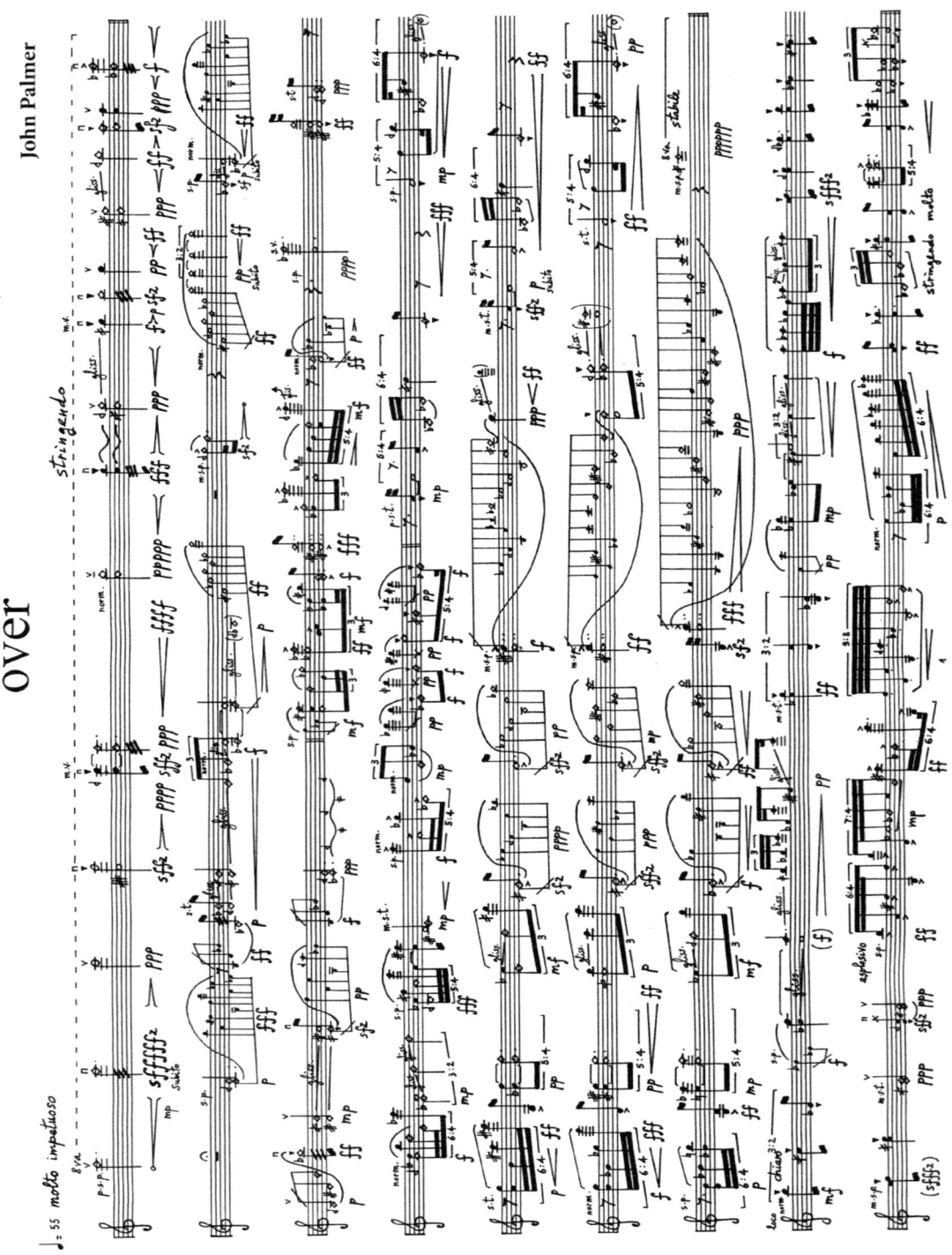

Fig. 6.19: *Over*, page 1.

180

of personal evolution. It exemplifies the willingness to comprehend life in all its manifestations, the impetus leading to personal and social progress, and the determination to challenge everything, including the impossible.

T.S. Eliot said, *"we had the experience, but missed the meaning"*. What is the importance of meaning in relation to the events that shape our lives? I personally would not want to live a life without meaning, and I am sure each of us, in one way or another, is looking for a meaning that can give a sense to what we are doing on this planet. As far as I am concerned, meaning provides a key to the way we experience the world. Virtuosity means 'to search', it signifies the willingness to debate and discover new paradigms of existence. In the programme note of *Over*, I simply referred to all the meanings of the word 'over' that I found in an English dictionary at that time. All the notions I found reflected what I was experiencing at that particular time in my life. It challenged a sense of personal failure and inability to evolve as a result of an intense experience of suffering. The programme note reads as follows:

"At the other side of. Beyond. Extending directly upwards from. Higher than a specified amount, rate, or norm. Above so as to cover or protect. Extending above (an area) from a vantage point. At a higher level or layer than. Higher in rank than. Higher in volume or pitch than. Expressing passage or trajectory across. Finished!"

This says it all. Virtuosity stands as a weapon, particularly against two social plagues of our times: superficiality and consumerism. Both are being boosted by a distorted use of interpersonal relations, communication, marketing policies and social media that endorse a disturbing notion of normality in our lives, obfuscating a sense of direction, especially in the young generations. Comfort and selfishness are becoming the mindset of the majority. Virtuosity signifies a courageous philosophical attitude against an increasing stabilisation of mediocrity as a latent lingua franca of contemporary society. More specifically, the virtuosity of *Over* wants to urge us to confront ourselves with our own shadows while endorsing dialogue and constructive reflection about the human condition. It epitomises an uncompromising call to defy the boundaries and limitations of those mental constructs that hinder our evolution and self-transformation.

TF. The piece appears like an insistent storm of sound hitting violently against a rock, an insistent and fierce knocking at a door, or even a desperate ploughing through a resistant layer of soil. Many passages also suggest a dialectical argument taking place within the same discourse, generating an enormous amount of tension. The violinist is faced with a most challenging task to bring to life a new kind of virtuosity that is essentially transcendental in the deepest meaning of the word. Would you call this a kind of drug-free form of 'breaking through to the other side'?

JP. Yes, you could say that. Technically speaking, the dramatic scenario of *Over* originates from the pitch material of my quartet *Transitions,* for clarinet, violin, cello and piano, which you know well. In order to emphasise a situation of restraint, I established a 4-part polyphonic material that I squeezed into one part to be executed by a soloist. Four main melodic lines are subdivided into 16 units and 'intersected' by four harmonic spaces. The violinist is facing what seems to be an impossible task. That is the allegory of what I have said earlier. It stands as the metaphor for creative consciousness at work, being brave, daring and heroic, and indicating a feasible path to self-knowledge through the adversities of life.

TF. *Without,* for solo violin, was written a year earlier. In a short foreword, you say that in this piece *"silence is explored as a dynamic force coming from and ending in sound"*. A lot

has been speculated about silence and its relation to sound; John Cage even wrote a notorious book named *Silence*. However, I found your statement quite stunning. As far as I can see, it suggests a reversal of the more common view on this complex issue.

JP. That's right. It is a similar situation of *Satori*, for solo harpsichord, where the perception of silence is elicited by the phrases of the solo instrument rather than the other way around. The dynamic force I am referring to is the experience of 'ma' as a fully integrative musical space.

TF. *Over* almost never comes to a state of stillness. The score is consistently referring to musical indications such as 'molto impetuoso', 'sempre avanti', 'molto drammatico', and so on. Only towards the very end of the piece you introduce some sustained sounds in rather soft dynamics with indications like 'calmo' or 'statico', like a foreboding of something new that is about to come.

JP. Exactly. This 'something new' evokes what you have described earlier as the 'stream'. A life story cannot be defined by a single experience. Each end of a piece insinuates the beginning of a new piece, much as in daily life where, for example, each form of death implies a new birth. The story of this moment is the precursor of the next story.

TF. In *Without*, it seems to me that the music is unfolding in this newly reached dimension, hinting at a secret link between these two pieces. Although written a year later, could *Over* be seen as the preliminary act to *Without*?

JP. Yes, for the very reason I have just mentioned. The two pieces are interlocked in a kind of Yin and Yang relationship. In fact, I conceived them almost at the same time. If *Over* is investigating the dark side of existence, the fullness of emotions intrinsic in the outburst of pain and despair, *Without* is concerned with the lightness prompted by the confrontation with emptiness as a result of contemplation. The music springs from a meditation on a Zen saying whose English translation reads like this:

> *Cherry blossoms are falling*
> *Beautiful like snowflakes*
> *The remaining rest do cling*
> *Without knowing their destiny.*

However, like the symbols of Yin and Yang, *Over* and *Without* are not complete opposites. In fact, each aspect has a little part of the other in it, like the crest and trough being the two complementary parts of a wave. Fullness is complementary to emptiness as motion is complementary to stasis. Fig. 9.2 (page 335) shows the beginning of *Without*.

TF. Though no electronics are used, the spatial effects in *Over* are astonishing, especially if you think that it is a single violin producing all those sounds. I have already mentioned the extremely loud, noisy and aggressive sections, as well as the 'pppppp' sounds at the end that seem to come from very far away. But what I haven't mentioned is that in between there is a sort of a middle area, a kind of intermediate realm (I am thinking of the striking German word 'Zwischenreich') being present throughout the music. This mysterious dimension is evoked by phrases that are played using semi-harmonic finger pressure on the strings. The use of this technique implies that the resulting pitches cannot be controlled by the violinist; they rather decide 'by themselves' in which direction they are going during a performance, adding an extra aleatory element to the music. You are using this kind of writing quite

frequently in all your pieces for string instruments; when did you discover this technique?

JP. I use this finger-pressure technique quite regularly when I write for string instruments as it adds several timbral subtleties to a single note and elicits an ambiguous perception of pitch, harmony and melody. I am particularly fond of it because, as you have suggested, it creates an indefinable dimension of sound that adds a mysterious aura to the traditional sound of the instrument. Also, it stimulates an illusion of space in the ear of the listeners by prompting, for example, a sudden sensation of distance to a phrase; a kind of 'lontano' or 'lontanissimo'[30] effect that renders the perception of space more diversified and interesting. As you know very well, all this can be controlled swiftly by the degree of intensity of finger pressure you put on the strings. It's an astonishing technique that enriches the timbre of a single pitch or a phrase by adding unpredictable harmonics, hence unexpected colours to the aural texture. I also use it with alternating finger pressure (harmonic/semi-harmonics/normal) in order to obtain a 'vibrato/tremolo'-like effect that characterises much of my music for strings. These are thrilling sounds that I particularly love. I must have discovered this technique some 30 years ago, I guess.

TF. As we've been discussing silence in music I now dare go even further and, rather than dwelling on the abstract meaning of silence, I'd like to refer to the practical meaning of silence as an experience of peace, calmness and composure; all qualities that play such an eminent role in Eastern spirituality. I know that Zen has been playing a serious role in your work for some time. In his *Integral Yoga of the Supramental*, the eminent Indian yogi Sri Aurobindo, with whom I feel a very strong kinship, describes calmness and peace not only as experiences of the mind, but also as realities of the physical dimension that are indispensable preconditions for the yogic path. For Aurobindo, the search for the true inner self excludes the superficial needs, worries and fears of the ego by which we are constantly detracted and obstructed. Would you agree with the notion that, especially in our time, it is crucial for music to be experienced not only as a mere acoustical phenomenon and intellectual activity, but also as an art that is deeply connected to the soul (I should say the spirit) and that this is a fundamental question for our future on this planet?

JP. Absolutely! Music allows us to enter deeper levels of inner transformation and spiritual evolution. As a vehicle to self-discovery, it can connect us with our deepest spiritual needs and take us through the 'dark night of the soul' in order to achieve enlightenment. Surely, the excursions of the intellect are necessary and exciting as they help to widen our mental horizons on many important issues of life, but they cannot replace the passionate quest for the immanent values of the soul. I also think that your question is essentially an ethical one. Earlier on, we talked about the importance of meaning: well, in ancient Greek the word 'Ethos' holds a meaning that is musical *and* moral at the same time. Isn't it interesting? This meaning hints at the formative power of music as the art that unifies thoughts, emotions *and* behaviour. In my view, this ethical tripartition is the essence of a meaningful existence.

TF. What I find particularly stunning in your music (and I am aware this is not easy to put in words) is that you seem to take the considerable risk of letting your pieces shimmer between form and formlessness. In my opinion, this remains a strong quality that characterises your music, rather than a cause for objection. In this sense, is this quality of form and non-form related to the 'stream' I mentioned earlier?

JP. I would think so, although it's not up to me to establish that, really. The magic of

---

[30] Lontano (it.) = far. Lontanissimo (it.) = very far.

composition consists of making the invisible audible. I believe that the invisible seeks to express itself through the act of composition, and I can only say that I compose in relation to a realm of images that are formless but need to take an audible form in order to be heard.

TF. There haven't been many composers in the last 70 years who have stood for a spiritual core of music; Karlheinz Stockhausen was one, Jonathan Harvey another. In your opinion, will the future of Western music depend on whether we will return to a new and more spiritual attitude towards music and art?

JP. Not necessarily, because the future of music will depend on the future of humanity in the first place. Music is a reflection of the human condition. If humanity will continue to foster an increasingly materialistic attitude at the expense of a spiritual outlook on life and art, the future of Western music will reflect this course of action whether we like it or not. If a spiritual awareness will surface (or re-surface?) in our society, the music of the future will reflect that accordingly. If I observe the forces that are shaping the current events of the world critically and objectively, I will have to admit that these very same forces may well shape the history of the future. I do want to see a society embracing ethical values that will continue to bring out the best in us as individuals and as a living collective. I don't see *one* uniform society, but many separate and diverse cultures, each with numerous and varied communities. Perhaps one of the absurdities we are experiencing at the moment is that global interests are clashing with local realities, that there is not *one* leading ethos, but a plurality of cultures living side by side in their ethnic and cultural diversity. Even the concept of 'Western culture' seems to be losing the identity that we grew accustomed to. Perhaps the question could be formulated differently: how could we keep a more ethical journey constantly fresh and more meaningful in our daily lives? Everything offers potential for spiritual enhancement and artistic discourse. My question is: how can each of us sustain and upgrade the spiritual values of this world with messianic zeal?

TF. Without wanting to deny the scientific achievements of recent centuries, do you think it is possible to embrace technological progress and, at the same time, recognize a world existing beyond the material? Is it possible to create a kind of music that can continue to lift our spirit, picking up a thread that somehow has gone lost in the course of the last century?

JP. Yes. I believe this has clearly happened and is still happening. You mentioned Stockhausen and Harvey earlier on, but there have also been Messiaen, Penderecky, Pärt and Taverner, not to mention many living composers who have nurtured and are still cultivating a spiritual dimension in their music. Why is this music not performed more often? I think the real problems are three. One is the intelligentsia that runs the ensembles and festivals of new music, opera houses and orchestras. Many of these people still adhere to a modernistic-materialistic aesthetic of music where very little space is given to music bearing a human reference. The second issue is the quality of many musical works that often leaves much to be desired, although this is a general problem that applies to all idioms and aesthetics of contemporary composers. A third concern is linked to the expectations attached to how 'spiritual' music is supposed to sound. For example, I find that some musical works by Gérald Grisey, Simon Emmerson, Roger Reynolds and other composers have a spiritual connotation, although many of these composers themselves may not be inclined to feel the same. This is a rather complex topic that deserves a larger platform for discussion. Back to your question, I think embracing technology with a metaphysical attitude to art is one of the most inspiring endeavours of our times, one that has produced some of the very best musical works of the past 70 years.

TF. Over the last two decades, electronics seem to dominate the new music scene. When I

listen to contemporary music, I often feel that the electronics are factually abusing acoustic instruments, as if being a means for alienation, deconstruction and, in the end, abolition. Do you envisage a fruitful coexistence of acoustic and electronic instruments? And how do you see the future of instrumental music, particularly for string instruments?

JP. I personally don't see the electronics dominating the new music scene. At least, this is not what I experience as a concertgoer. But I know exactly what you mean about an 'abusive' way to use electronics as stand-alone instruments or with acoustic instruments. In fact, what you are saying reminds me of my own feeling about electronics back in the 1980s, and I must agree with you on this point. However, I must also say that, meanwhile, I have heard several musical works where acoustic and electronic instruments coexist in the most astonishing and inspiring way. After all, it is not a matter of mere orchestration, but a question of how a composer touches upon archetypal motifs with the language and instruments of the present. I do think it is rare to find a composer able to work with electronics in a sensitive and imaginative way. Perhaps this is a result of electronic composition being taught as a mere catalogue of software programs manipulations. This attitude will certainly produce technically-minded composers who are disconnected from the poetry of imagination.

With regards to your last question, I am not worried about the future of instrumental music, nor about the future of string instruments. This is a major body of instruments that have shaped the history of music and I am sure will continue to do so in the future.

TIME AND SPACE IN *BEYOND THE BRIDGE*
Claudie Reduron

CR. When I listen to your music, I am impressed by three recurring elements in your output: time, space and colour. I would like to begin by discussing the use of time and space in *Beyond the Bridge*. The mesmerizing way you deal with time and space in this work inspired me to paint a picture I named *Listening to Beyond the Bridge*. What exactly motivated you to write this piece?

JP. In short: my preoccupation with time and space. I wanted to explore an imaginary journey projected onto different spaces and times which could be clearly discerned by the faculty of memory. In 1991, while I was writing *Omen* for orchestra and choir, it became clear to me that music, as indeed life, relies on an implacable flow of time. What occurred to me was an unexpected awareness of time being both an intangible continuum and a measurable form of transience. I observed that no matter how exact my notion of chronological time may be, I experience a sense of motion that is irregular, relative and non-linear. Suddenly, I was reminded of the concept of eternity discussed by Saint Augustine in his *Confessions*:

"… if nothing passes away, there is no past time, and if nothing arrives, there is no future time, and if nothing existed there would be no present time. Take the two tenses, past and future. How can they 'be' when the past is not now present, and the future is not yet present? Yet if the present were always present, it would not pass into the past: it would not be time but eternity." [31]

If the present were a static occurrence that would not move into the past, there would no longer be time as such, but stasis as a negation of time (Augustine's eternity). I noticed that the

---

[31] Saint Augustine (1991:231).

determining cause of what we call 'time' was the realisation of the very moment in which the present becomes past. In music, this would occur when we listen to a melody from beginning to end, or, in a longer context, to the gradual evolution taking place from one phrase to a second, third, fourth one, and so on. Robin Maconie describes music as *"an experience of transience"*[32] and explains that an indicative strategy of time perception is shaped by an action that causes a dying or recurring sound. Maconie argues that the decay of sound is *"a measure of the influence of time"* and *"the renewal of sound is a token of the persistence of life and measure of the passage of time."* [33] Accordingly, the awareness of a present that is constantly becoming past reinforced my perception of music as a fleeting experience of time where present and past are predictably interlocked. Neither the past, nor the future 'are', as the past is a reminiscence of the previous present (activated by memory) which I no longer hear; physically speaking, it no longer exists. On the other hand, the future transpires as a projection of the mind to a moment that has yet to come and that I can only imagine, but not hear. In this case, the expectation of a future event is induced by the nature of the sonic information I would receive.

CR. I guess the 'now' is central to this reasoning…

JP. Indeed. The awareness of the 'now' is one of the most fascinating psychological circumstances I still experience to this day. It entails a potential learning process about the way I relate to my inner world (emotions, thoughts, feelings and perceptions) and to external events as well. My awareness of the 'now' is connected to the duration of such perception. This cognizance conjures what I name 'glimpses of consciousness' (this is an experience I tried to capture in my piano pieces *Déjà-vu* and *Glimpse*, by the way) that is initially short, but whose immediate manifestation can be prolonged by memory on longer segments of linear time. By becoming 'memory', the transcendental significance of the 'now' evolves into an autonomous mental event whose subjective duration may elude the rational mind. Susan Pockett's research has shown that, within linear time, a duration of 'now' can vary from about 10 milliseconds to some seconds and in extreme cases even up to hours.[34] I also found illuminating Edmund Husserl's description of the 'now' as a process of appearance and transformation. He writes, *"As a new Now always appears, it transforms itself into a past, whilst at the same time the continuity of the past's course of the preceding points* [the preceding 'nows'] *shifts constantly down into the depth of the past."* [35]

The reversibility occurring in the transformation of the present into the past (I mean the re-conversion of the past into the present) is another topic that I decided to explore in *Beyond the Bridge* and this is the reason why this piece is constantly recalling a determined musical event (a phrase, a chord, a specific articulation, a sound and even an entire section) at different points in time throughout the composition. By the same token, the reminiscence of time past in music (the already heard) must be related to a present event that is evoking the past by repeating, varying or developing it further. What intrigued me even more was the question as to whether a present event may be perceived as the realisation of a past prediction of the future, that is the present experienced as the future of the past, and, at the same time, as the past of a future event.

Is chronological time a perception of a shrouded eternity? If so, what is linear time in the face of death? How many kinds of time reside in the human mind? And can music exist in a non-linear form of time? Perhaps this may sound strange to you, but more recently I have

---

[32] Maconie (1990:66-74).
[33] Ibid.
[34] Pockett, Susan (2003:55-68).
[35] Husserl (1928).

become accustomed to a dichotomy involving linear and psychological time, as I often experience that the natural subdivision of weeks, days and working hours doesn't necessarily match the 'inner clock' of my mind-body bio-system. The sense of time I experience does not seem to coincide with the usual convention based on a division of 24 hours a day and seven days a week. I seem to detect another activity of my psychological time that is not cyclic, but highly independent and unconstrained by the conventional understanding of time.

CR. In _Beyond the Bridge_, it seems to me that there are explicit musical elements such as motifs, melodies and even sounds that hold the piece together in each of the different spaces I hear. How important is memory in the relationship between the spatially and temporally displaced melodies?

JP. It is very important because the perceptual process I have explained relies on the faculty of memory. One of the things I found so interesting in Saint Augustine's writings is the way he depicts memory as a multidimensional ability capable of performing several functions simultaneously. For example, reconstructing the past and anticipating the future, which suggests the ability to travel in psychological (non-chronological) time. When I wrote _Beyond the Bridge_, I was thinking of three forms of mind-activity: linear, psychological and spiritual. In the context of these delineations, I implied a psychological connotation linked to the awareness of what is a form of 'subjective time' as a cognitive instinct of consciousness (in general terms) and spiritual awareness (in specific terms). To mention Saint Augustine's argument again, [36] I was concerned with three kinds of questions that can be exemplified like this: Does a thing exist? What is it? Of what kind is it? I converted Augustine's reasoning into musical terms so that (in my adaptation) I retained the images of the sounds of which music is made, knowing that these sounds are passing through linear time and that as soon as they pass, they will no longer exist as acoustic manifestation. The images that are signified by the sounds can be reached by the mind (that is, stored in the mind through the faculty of memory), and what at this time my memory will remember are not the sounds, but the things which those sounds signify. Yet, these images (the signified 'things') have been there before the sounds, otherwise, I wouldn't have been able to recognise them in the first place. They must have been somewhere stacked up in a remote corner of my mind, and only now they are brought to life by the memory of the sounds. These images (and meanings) have been there before I remembered them, otherwise, my memory would not find them. They have been there already. The question brought up by memory is: where have these images been all this time? How is it possible that as soon as they are elicited by sound, I recognise them and acknowledge their existence?

CR. How did you achieve this sense of cohesion which is so clearly audible in the form of _Beyond the Bridge_?

JP. The architecture of a musical work is very important to me. Structurally, I created a network of relationships based on five main 'Manifestations' as I called them at that time. These are: 'Principle', 'Distribution', 'Space', 'Time' and 'Method'. These 'Manifestations' unfold in three steps which I called: 'Outer Form' (the overall shape of the piece), 'Inner Form' (the shape of each section) and 'Design' (the specific textural decisions of rhythms, melody, harmony, metre and so on within a local context). The 'Manifestations' are hierarchic (to be read left to right in the chart below) and similar to fractals. On the top of the procedural hierarchy, I identified five basic principles of composition: Statement, Contrast, Repetition, Variation and Development. Together with three different locations of the sonic sources, these are the most important

---

[36] Saint Augustine (1991:188, paragraph x, 17).

elements of the architecture.

I also included 'Symmetry' and 'Asymmetry' as equivalent categories for the distribution of events and comprised two levels of basic space ('locational' and 'textural') along with the three forms of linear time I have explained earlier: past, present and future. Any combination of these 'Manifestations' would either be accepted or refused (Method). The inclusion of this atypical category called 'Method', allowed me to be able to make compositional decisions based on my instinct and perception of the musical events. The chart below (Fig. 6.20) shows an overview of the morphological principles and procedures I used for the piece. From this structural perspective, the music of *Beyond The Bridge* exploits a construction of superimposed, multi-dimensional form that emphasises three independent spatial and temporal layers by creating a recurrence of events (similar, developed, contrasted or repeated) distributed throughout the composition.

Steps	1	2	3
Manifestation	**Outer Form**	**Inner Form**	**Design**
Principle	Statement	Statement	Statement
	Contrast	Contrast	Contrast
	Repetition	Repetition	Repetition
	Variation	Variation	Variation
	Development	Development	Development
Distribution	Symmetry	Symmetry	Symmetry
	Asymmetry	Asymmetry	Asymmetry
	Morphological	Morphological	Syntactic
			melodic/harmonic
			rhythmic/durational
			timbral
			dynamic
Space		Locational:	Textural:
		a)　horizontal	a)　linear
		b)　vertical	c)　intervallic
Time	Past	Past	Past
	Present	Present	Present
	Future	Future	Future
Method	Acceptance	Acceptance	Acceptance
	Refusal	Refusal	Refusal

Fig. 6.20: *Beyond the Bridge*, chart of principles and procedures.

CR. In *Beyond the Bridge*, one can clearly hear a three-dimensional space outlined by the cello playing on stage, a second cello playing behind the audience through loudspeakers in the hall and a third cello playing outside the concert hall. How do these three spaces relate to time? I mean, how did you design the interaction of the three spaces and time in the

piece? Did you think in terms of vertical and horizontal extents, or chronological and relative time?

JP. I wanted to illustrate an imaginary journey symbolised by the cello and considered the form of *Beyond the Bridge* in terms of a time-space voyage in which single notes, melodies, chords and different kinds of articulation are projected on three different spaces and times. I reinforced any conceivable perception of time by assigning three different locations to the three instruments (the cellist performing live, and the other two 'ghost' cellists diffused by the loudspeakers from two different locations).

The journey begins from far away and unfolds on three interchanging spaces related to each other through a network of motifs based on three themes projected at different points in time: a single note, a rhythmic figure and a short motif. The interconnection between spatial and temporal layers is evoked by the repetition, variation and development of these musical themes throughout the piece.

The three thematic elements or 'themes' (not in the classical sense of the word though) can be seen below (Fig. 6.21). These are three simple musical features (called A, B and C) that define each section of the piece and generate the texture of the piece:

A = this is the note D5, the generating material of section A. The note D is also generating the pitch material of the entire piece which is extracted from the harmonic series of D2.

B = this is a rhythm consisting of two semiquavers notes followed by a semiquaver rest and another semiquaver note played at MM = 82. The speed of the tempo is an integral part of the thematic material.

C = this is a short motif consisting of four notes to be played at MM = 100. The 'sforzando' and the articulation, including the 'crescendo', are all integrative elements of this thematic material.

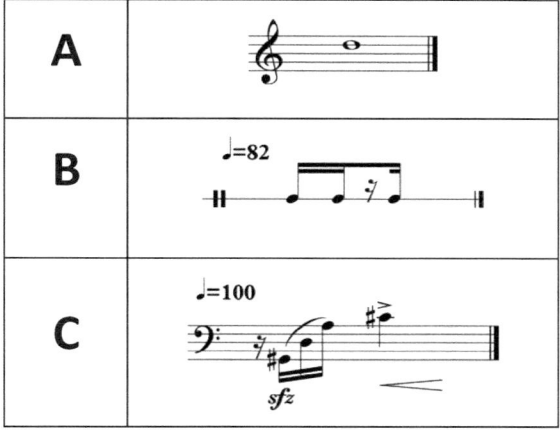

Fig. 6.21: *Beyond the Bridge,* thematic material.

The network of temporal actions is based on the traditional definitions of the three tenses: the present (the 'now'), the past (activated by memory) and the future (the anticipation of an event to come resulting from a projection of a sound onto space). I also differentiated the two aspects of time I mentioned earlier: absolute (the perception of chronological time) and relative (a perception of relative time depending on the intensity of the texture and the recollection of musical events taking place during the journey). The organisation of space is delineated by three locations of the sonic sources:

1. the location of the cellist playing on the stage of the concert hall;

2. the location of an invisible (or 'ghost') pre-recorded cello diffused by loudspeakers located behind the audience, in the concert hall;

3. the location of another invisible ('ghost') pre-recorded cello diffused by loudspeakers located outside the concert hall.

Locating the third sonic source outside the hall was a major spatial strategy that would enhance the sense of 'dislocated' time I was after.

In the chart above (Fig. 6.20), I included two forms of space, 'locational' and 'textural' as components of 'Inner Form' and 'Design'. They are musical elements fully integrated into the architecture of the piece: 'locational' space (the 'topographical' distribution of sections, single sonic events, location of sonic sources) and 'textural' space (the temporal distance between two or more sounds within the texture). 'Textural' space implies a more traditional perception of musical space:

Firstly, the perception of a linear (horizontal) space when listening to the unfolding of a melody, or between instrumental events grouped as sections in the locational space.

Secondly, the (vertical) perception of intervals in a chord, or in other vertical sonic events (this could also include the superimposition of sections, chords or other constructs). Thus, a chord would evoke a sense of 'vertical' space that is different to the sense of space evoked by a melody or a pedal point (the prolongation of a note) which would be perceived as 'horizontal' in linear time. This kind of spatial relation in composition has been articulated very clearly, amongst others, by Gyorgi Ligeti in the 1960s:

"*when listening to music, where the sonic process is primarily temporal, imaginary spatial relations come into being at different levels; above all at the associative level, where the pitch alteration evokes a vertical dimension of space, whilst the persistency of the same note evokes the horizontal spatial dimension. The alteration of dynamics and timbre, such as differences between open and muted sounds, produces an illusion of proximity and distance, and in general of spatial depth. Musical shapes and events are then imagined as if they would take place in an imaginary space, feigned by themselves*". [37]

With regard to the Inner Form, I built an asymmetric distribution of superimposed sections to be morphological correspondences related to the three sections A, B and C (each related to the thematic material A, B and C). In the Outer Form, I arranged them in such a way that they would evoke musical correspondences (temporal connections) heard from three different locations: the live cello on stage; the 'ghost' cello 1 located behind the audience (tape 1); and the second 'ghost' cello located outside the concert hall (tape 2). In the chart below (Fig. 6.22), you can see the general plan of the piece. The horizontal unfolding of the three sections **A**, **B** and **C** is assigned to each of the three locations of the sonic sources listed on the left side of the chart (live cello, ghost cello 1 and ghost cello 2). Section A opens and concludes the piece.

---

[37] Ligeti (1966:291).

Regarding the terminology, the abbreviations are: **St** = Statement; **Va** = Variation; **De** = Development; **Co** = Contrast; **Re** = Repetition.

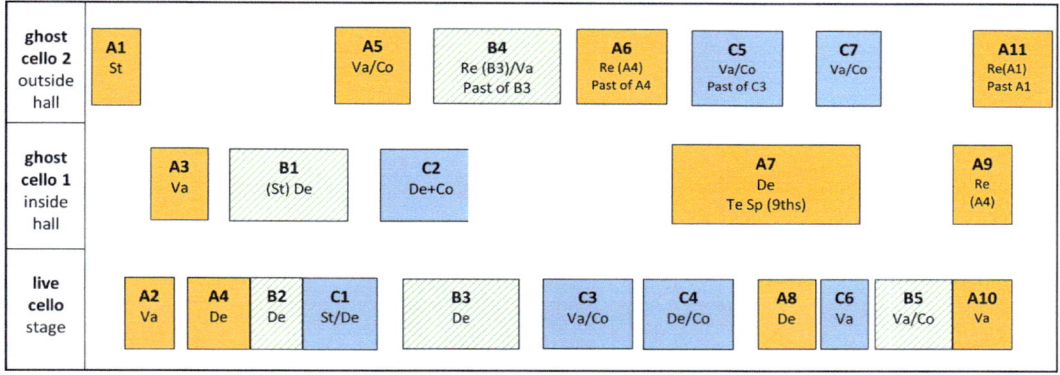

Fig. 6.22: *Beyond the Bridge,* general plan.

Let me read you the beginning of the piece from the chart.

The sequence of events begins with the ghost cello 2 (outside the hall) playing a very high D, namely D7. This is the **first** thematic material of the piece played as a statement **A1-St**.

The **second** event **A2-Va** occurs on stage, when the cellist takes over the same note and plays it beyond the (physical) bridge of the instrument with some subtle timbral and pitch variations. This gesture is also theatrical and metaphorical at the same time, as it visualises the audacity of the task implied in the search for a distant place situated beyond a symbolic bridge.

The **third** event **A3-Va** is another timbral variation on the same note played by the ghost cello 1 (from the loudspeakers behind the audience).

The **fourth** event **A4-De** is the first development of the note D played by the live cello on the harmonic series of the same note. In this section **A4**, I also applied the parameter of 'textural space' in order to create a wide intervallic range in the cello part from 1'20" to 2'20". The notes are played at an irregular pace and are sustained by electronic reverberation.

Further on, section **B1(St)-De** is commenced by the ghost cello 1 inside the hall and characterised by the pizzicato playing of the rhythmic statement **B** played at MM=82; here the ghost cello plays the Statement and Development in the same section.

You can also see a short superimposition with section **B2-De** (Development) played by the live cello while the ghost cello 1 (behind the audience) is continuing the Development of **B**. Next, the cello on stage begins section **C1St/De** by playing the third 'theme' **C** (the short 'sforzando' phrase at MM=100) and developing it immediately. The remaining unfolding of the sections is based on the shifting of the three sections around the three locations (stage, behind the audience and outside the hall).

The diagram below (Fig. 6.23) should give an idea of the instrumental setting I used in *Beyond the Bridge*. The protagonist of the journey (the cello located in the centre of the stage) is visualised by the photo of the instrument. Loudspeakers 1 and 2, left and right behind the cello, are used for amplification and live-processing of the cello. Loudspeakers 3 and 4 are located at the back of the hall (behind the audience) and play back the second cello ('ghost' cello 1) from within the hall. Loudspeakers 5 and 6 are located outside the concert hall and play back the sound of the third cello ('ghost' cello 2) from far away.

An example of the interaction of the three celli can be seen in the example below, from 5'20" to 6'00" (Fig. 6.24).

191

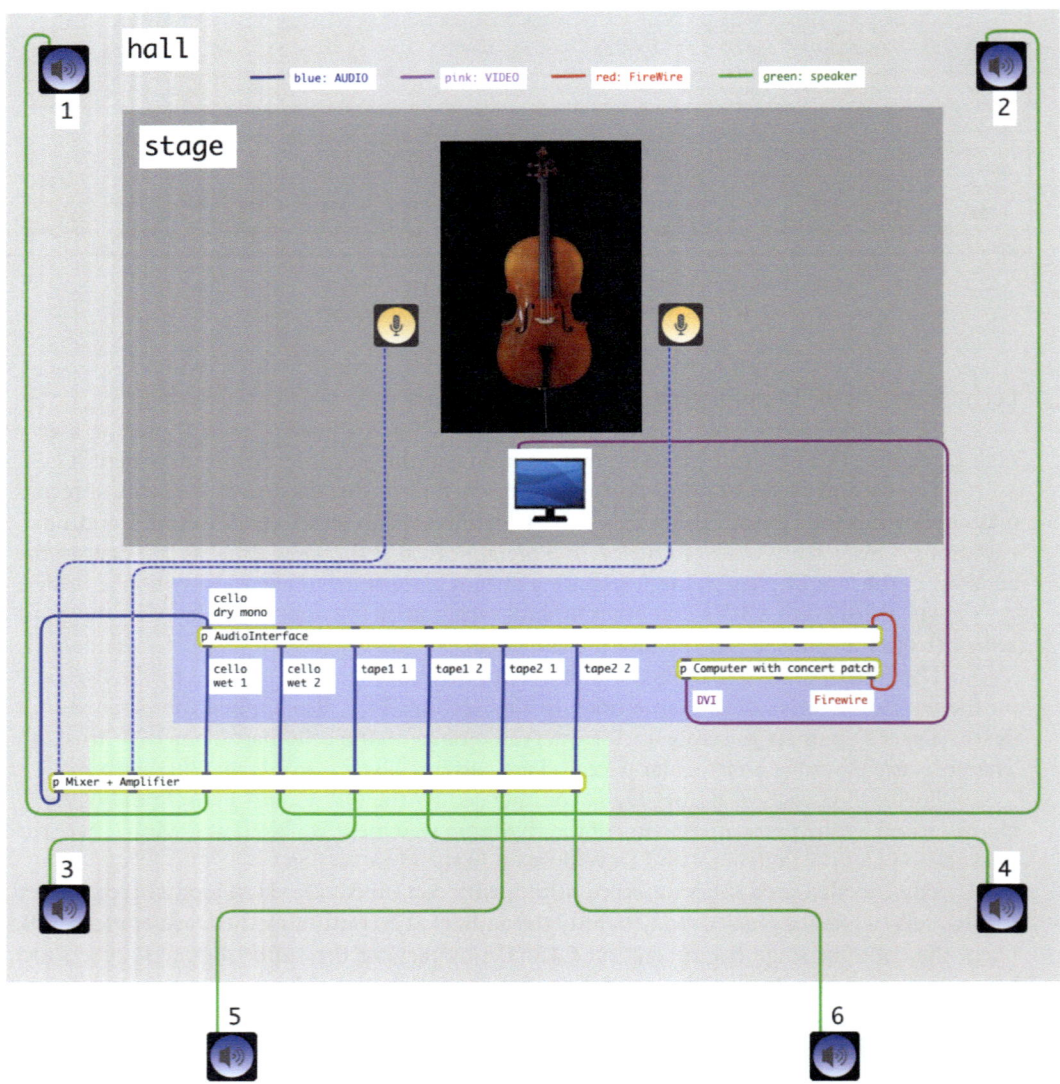

Fig. 6.23: *Beyond the Bridge,* diagram for spatial location.

Fig. 6.24: *Beyond the Bridge,* score excerpt (5'20"- 6'00").

CR. The American pianist David Dubal wrote, *"Sound is time that is space that is eternity".* **Do you think it is possible to relate this sentence to the music of** *Beyond the Bridge***?**

JP. The phrase certainly fits with my idea of the piece. Sound is a manifestation of time *in* time. In *Beyond the Bridge*, as in other works of mine, I projected segments of time from different locations and superimposed layers of space hoping to instigate a sense of 'meta-space' in the mind of the listener. My goal was to evoke a reminiscence of what timelessness could be within the conventional notions of past, present and future in a potential 'a-temporal' condition where the three dimensions may exist all at the same time by 'memorising' the past and the future without ontological hierarchy. But this idea should not be taken as a nihilistic argument the way that, for example, Jean-Paul Sartre would put it, by identifying temporality as an 'intra-structure' of the being in the 'mode of being' of being *for* itself.[38] To me, the present is not a 'limit of an infinite division' but a living field of perception and information that unifies everything material and spiritual beyond any type of mental construct.

CR. More generally, are you concerned with the ephemeral present or are you trying to question the eternal?

JP. As Emanuel Swedenborg said, *"What is infinite and eternal in itself cannot but look to what is infinite and eternal from itself in finite things."* [39] Thus, the union of the infinite (traditionally identified with the divine) and the finite suggests that mind and matter are one same energy and therefore indivisible. In this domain of 'oneness', there is no separation of past, present and future. Even the concept of 'now' may be non-local, thus timeless, and any temporal paradox, such as an effect preceding its cause, may be real, as all points in time may co-exist in an everlasting continuum residing beyond the laws of causality. I remain fully focused on questioning a meta-temporality of an immaterial (quantum?) domain that connects everything in nature beyond the 'before-after' paradigm. This takes into consideration that perhaps, as Carlo Rovelli has recently pointed out, [40] our concept of time comes not from knowledge, but from ignorance, and therefore it may be an illusion.

CR. Do you always have a mental representation of your work before you begin to compose?

JP. Most of the time. A composition may begin with a precise idea or with a vague notion of what I am embarking on; this can be a mental image, a sensation or a very definite musical 'object', such as a sound, a chord, a melody. If the initial substance seems to have enough potentiality to be converted into music, I decide to unfold it. (Sometimes I take up the challenge to undertake a composition even when this 'substance' has no apparent potentiality). It can be a few notes or a shaft of undefinable intuition that comes across my mind. I experience sensations that sway from side to side, so to speak: perceptions that drag me into a musical image that is waiting to be unfolded. For the sake of clarity, I should conclude that if the art of composition was restricted to defining a number of sonic components put together by different means according to an internal order of structural relations, I would no longer find myself in the position to differentiate an organized succession of sonic events from a work of art. As for Plotinus, who so emphatically stressed the significance of inventiveness in relation to creative vigour, there is one essential element without which music would be non-existent: the power of imagination.

---

[38] I am referring to Sartre's views on Temporality as exposed in his seminal essay *Being and Nothingness*.
[39] Swedenborg (1996:38).
[40] Rovelli (2018).

EPITAPH, ALMOST, SECOND STRING QUARTET
Neil Heyde

NH. Jonathan Harvey has described the cello (which, of course, he knew intimately) as having a hermaphroditic quality. Do you think of the cello (or other instruments) as having 'anthropomorphic character' in this kind of way?

JP. I agree with Jonathan's description, although I would use the word 'androgynous' rather than 'hermaphroditic'. Each musical instrument has a distinctive sonic personality and the cello's unique timbre, versatility, resonance body and extensive range offers a formidable source of colours, unparalleled subtlety and intensity of sound. Of all orchestral instruments, the cello is the only one that retains extraordinary lyrical potentials and a matchless timbral density in all registers and over a range of eight octaves; a unique quality that, for me, is 'alchemical'. In my mind, this exclusive attribute evokes a sense of union and sublimation of polarity that makes the cello the androgynous instrument par excellence.

The symbolism attached to an interchangeable gender-role is intrinsic in the timbral power of the instrument obtainable on both low and high registers, and suggests mirrors of darkness and lightness, shadow and distinctness, Animus and Anima. Let me offer an analogy: according to C.G. Jung, the Animus-Anima dichotomy is a compensation law of the Persona where what is lacking in the male nature arises in his feminine part which he called *Anima*. What is lacking in the female nature arises in her masculine part, the *Animus*. The vast range and sonority of the cello bring to my mind a similar situation. By transferring this 'compensation law' of the Persona to the cello, the inner feminine attitude in the male nature (Anima) is superbly exemplified by the high registers of the instrument, whose timbre is complemented by the large resonance prompted by the lowest strings. On the other hand, the inner masculine aspect of the feminine (Animus) is symbolised by the timbral richness of the low register being complemented by the vibrations of the higher strings and the inclusion of the high partials of a low pitch. The male cannot be such without Anima, and the female cannot be herself without Animus: the two 'compensated' genders are perfectly evoked by the timbral-registral characteristics of the instrument. The ambiguity inherent in the sonic identity of the cello is therefore defined not by addition, but by the blending of high-low range with low-high resonance, thus insinuating the balance of masculine and feminine energy: rational and emotional, firm and sensitive, dense and subtle. The analogy also reminds me of an insight by Aristotle about the nature of vocal and instrumental sounds. By describing the human voice as a sound produced by a creature with a soul (psyche), Aristotle implies that singing is the voice of the soul as it contains words, therefore meaning (semantics). If experiencing meaning through the human voice speaks directly to our consciousness, the lyricism of the cello (detached from semantics) recounts the subconscious, the subliminal self.

NH. When you look back over all of the cello repertoire you have written, do you sense an instrumental identity that surprises you? Or are these pieces, in certain respects, responses to particular contexts, players or performance situations? (Our collaboration, for example.)

JP. Both. What I have just said about the cello remains a central perception of the instrument in all the works I have written so far. Every time I choose the cello in my compositions, I know what I can count on: I am writing for an instrument with an enormous personality and versatility which always gives me a musical 'guarantee' in any piece I write. What I mean is that I can use the unique qualities of the cello in virtually any kind of texture (polyphonic, homophonic, timbral, pointillistic, and so on), and literally in all genres. A recent example can be heard in the two-sided textural function and theatrical role I assigned to the cello in the narrative of my chamber opera *Re di Donne*. Naturally, each musical work is born in a specific context, and each context will lead to different choices, uses and roles of an instrument. All the cellists I have worked with have their distinct personalities, and their contribution to a musical work is exclusive, thus incomparable to another. Similar to the notion of polysemy[41] in linguistics, the cello offers the best adaptability to all textural functions in a piece. Of course, it may be argued that this applies to all orchestral instruments, but I think the expressive and timbral ductility of the cello remains unsurpassed.

It goes without saying that within the instrumental and small chamber group category, a new work is usually very connected to the musicianship of a performer. Even though the idea, form, material of the piece may be already fixed in my mind, the new piece will respond to the personality and virtuosity of the cellist I am writing for. *Epitaph* is a case in point. Although the form and compositional procedures were set up to the minutest detail, the fact that I wrote the piece for you, not another cellist, played a major role in the unfolding of the music. Before I wrote *Epitaph*, I had been very impressed by specific qualities of your playing. These assets were very much in my mind during the process of composition, and your musical personality was constantly present in my inner ear during the compositional process. Had I written the piece for another cellist, I am sure the music would sound different. Perhaps not much different, but surely not exactly the same. In my experience, the extent of this difference varies from situation to situation and from interpreter to interpreter.

NH. 'Unstable' sounds, where the pitch element can vary wildly between iterations, are a vital part of your string writing. In many parts of *Epitaph*, for example, these have the feeling for me of being mediately expressive. What draws you towards using these kinds of sounds?

JP. Before I answer about 'unstable' sounds, I would like to mention how I perceive sound in the first place. Roger Scruton speaks of sounds as *"objects in their own right, bearers of properties and identifiable separately both from the things that emit them and the places where they are located."*[42] But if the cello sound *may* be perceived as separate from the instrument that produces it, in actuality, it cannot really be separated from it. The same applies to the acoustic space which permits the sound to exist. The reason why I mention this is that the 'sound object' being inevitably related to source and space, is a psychoacoustic phenomenon whose properties are in constant motion throughout the duration of the sonic event. The idea of sound as a fixed acoustic experience doesn't really exist, and one doesn't need to look at a spectral analysis of the sound to understand this, since it is possible to hear the timbral motion of a sound rather well by the 'naked' ear. The attack, sustain and decay phase have different and mutating sonic properties. What we call 'sound' is a combination of several micro-sounds (partials and residuals) changing in time. They are identifiable. The inner mobility of this acoustic mass makes each note sound like a progressing event rather than a fixed sonic experience.

My perception of sound is always focused on the inner life of a spectrum with its fluctuating morphology. When I work on a cello piece, I usually start by playing the cello myself and listening to the sounds I want by using different degrees of dynamics, articulation and phrasing while focusing on the inner mobility of pitch during my playing. By listening to the inner kinesis of a single note in relation to the fundamental of its harmonic series, I clearly hear that no sound is really stable. I begin to experiment with all the timbral possibilities that are available on that instrument by using different finger and bow pressure on the strings. This

---

[41] The same word having different meanings in a different context.
[42] Scruton (2009:20).

timbral instability is much accentuated by the bow pressure exerted on the string. There are four reasons why I do this:

1) sensual/timbral: I like the colours and sensuality evoked by such unpredictable sonorities. Their timbre can be strident and fugitive, discordant, screeching, fragile and powerful at the same time.

2) dramatic: I use sonic unpredictability as an element of additional expressivity in the musical discourse. Thus, timbral modifications serve as a reinforcement of emotional activity. The exploitation of the inherently unpredictable behaviour of a sound within a deterministic system allows me to emancipate randomness to an emotional element of significant intensity where each spectral change of the sound becomes a form of enhanced allusion to drama and pathos. Metaphorically, Benedetto Croce would define this as a circumstance of 'feeling as activity', the two poles of which, pleasure and pain, comfort and discomfort, constitute the drive of the discourse. Technically speaking, 'feeling' is a direct consequence of these changes of timbre.

3) structural: by using 'unstable' sounds, I am creating de facto a system within a system, that is a layer of unstable sounds within an intermittent layer of 'stable' sounds, for example, the fundamental note of the spectrum appearing and disappearing depending on bow and finger pressure.

4) acoustic/philosophical: randomness is emancipated to an important component of the music. The Greek philosopher Epicurus was the first Western thinker who argued that randomness, as the lack of patterns or correlations, is *objective*, and a part of the 'proper nature' of events. I see this description as being very much connected to the perception of sound I have explained earlier. One ongoing question in my work is how, when and to which extent nonlocality of unpredictable sound events can be integrated in a meaninful musical context.

In cello pieces like *Epitaph* and *Almost,* or my string quartets, I felt it necessary to go through each sound I produced on the instrument one by one and explore the calibration of every single movement of the finger on the string in combination with the bowing pressure. Of course, this would vary later on from cellist to cellist, and from instrument to instrument, but it was important for me to get a first-hand experience of sound production in order to better understand the implication of the technique in relation to the sonic result. I keep a vividly emotional approach to timbre in all my works since I am after a unity of intention about all aspects of sound production, from the acoustic and technical to the philosophical and cognitive. I work with *feeling* as a compositional activity (as in Croce's notion) and this is particularly the case for works with specific emotional, ethical or social content.

NH. What do you think about expressive or compositional 'control' in relation to these unstable sounds? Part-harmonics form a really important subcategory of these unstable sounds. From the player's perspective, the sense of contact with these is very interesting. One is much more aware of the sense of touch and the different inherent tensions in the cello's four strings. What kinds of expressive associations do these materials have for you?

JP. Earlier on, I mentioned the relationship between randomness and stability in terms of emotionality (expressivity) and structure (controlled form). Both aspects belong to the same phenomenological reality of a musical work. In my music, timbre is synonymous with dramatic power and is a major compositional element by default. My search for timbral gestalt depends on unpredictable deviations of pitch content (the unstable sounds) that enables me to generate more dramatic narrative. Specifically, the randomness I was referring to earlier on releases the sensation of independently-moving colours in my mind. The attractiveness of this technique consists of providing a highly-energised stream of varying colours resulting from unlimited micro-layers of vibrations. These abstract 'molecules' of sound elicit a sonic perplexity that can be perceived as both volatile and, paradoxically, steady. Also, timbral instability endows several layers of unpredictable 'micro-form', an aleatory flow of myriad sonorities that will change from performance to performance. This performance-related indeterminacy is another important aspect of the compositional concept of both pieces.

In terms of compositional 'control', I am creating a sense of tentative stability relying on unstable micro-sounds which provide an indefinable background of sound. There is indeed an obscure kind of background-foreground relationship implied in the technique. I should also mention that in such a context the identity of a single note is challenged from within, as it were, implying that the traditional perception of melodic lines is defied and perhaps even abolished. Symbolically, I like to think of timbral unpredictability as a critical challenge to personal advancement in that I am metaphorically searching for content through diversity, yet never locating a secure truth.

NH. You use bow overpressure very widely. For the player, this requires significant physical tension. Is this choreographic aspect important to you, or is the sonic dimension something 'in itself'?

JP. Music comes first, and it is the resulting sound I am primarily interested in. Obviously, the choreographic aspect is an additional and very important dramatic feature of a performance.

NH. Your 'mapping' of time and different kinds of 'presence' is fascinating. Did you have particular gestural 'starting points' for any of these pieces or is the 'mapping' a starting point from which the individual gestures coalesce during the process? Can you contextualise in this sense your work on *Epitaph*?

JP. The cello works you have scrutinized spring from an emotion, a distinct perception or an idea. *Epitaph* and *Almost* are linked to each other, having been both inspired by your virtuosity. These two pieces epitomise two opposite approaches to form and 'mapping'. While the structure and pitch content of *Epitaph* is organised to the minutest detail, *Almost* is based on a more intuitive unfolding of 13 fragments extracted from *Epitaph*, but played at a slower tempo. Having said that, the instrumental presence is equally strong in all my cello works as they truly are idiosyncratic cello pieces. The resulting music qualities would be 'un-transferable' to other instruments. In the case of *Epitaph*, symbolism and virtuosity are two keywords for understanding the way I approached this work. As a sign of emotional impetus, pain and rage, a certain kind of apparent virtuosity had to be the dominant musical feature of the piece. I knew that in order to achieve this musical result, I had to set significant restrictions in the cello part and push the virtuosity of the cellist to the limit.

To start with, I decided to channel the emotional intensity I was feeling at that time to a rigorous architectural design that would allow me to produce an impeccably well-defined course of action. The coalescence of the individual gestures of the cellist is therefore strongly rooted in the fixed structure of the piece. In the programme note of the piece I wrote that *"the loss of a close person is always a moment of inner silence and introspection as we are directly confronted with fundamental questions such as separation and the meaning of our existence on this planet."* The horror of losing a friend who took her life by jumping in front of a speeding train and the painful awareness of my impotence towards this tragedy urged me to express my feelings of anger, pain and social denunciation. I wanted the music to epitomise a constant release of uncompromising energy throughout ebb and flow.

The main question was how I could turn my feelings into meaningful and creative inspiration while allowing the onslaught of emotion to be translated to structural decisions such as the choice of pitch material and the construction of formal relationships. I decided to create a highly compressed form, including a fixed set of temporal relations on which I would articulate material based on symbolic relationships between emotion, numbers, sound and form. I knew that in order to write this piece adequately, I needed to play every single note myself and keep the highest degree of mental intensity during the decision-making process. An important concept I referred to was the coincidence of opposites (C.G. Jung's 'Coincidentia Oppositorum') demarcated by specific points of contact between the acoustic and electronic forces. Most of these conjunctions are rather subtle, but some of them can be clearly heard at least on four occasions: at 3'40-4'09 linearly (acoustic-electronic timbral transference), at 5'52, 6'28" and 8'00" with the superimposition of timbral sources.

As a symbolic tribute to my lost friend, I chose the number eight, a symbol of endless life, as the generative factor for the form of the piece. The number eight would also define the total duration of the piece. I divided the complete quarter-tone range of the cello into 107 positions and corresponding pitches, 65 on each string (on the fingerboard). By this early stage, I had already established the basic numbers of the piece: 8, 65 and 107. The next step was the determination of pitch. In order to do this, I recurred to another symbol: the star, as an image of light in the midst of darkness. The graphic representation below represents the star I created as the originator of the form. Each of the eight beams has a different length; each length is determined by proportional values deriving from the combination of 8, 65 and 107.

The vertical line on the left side represents a scale of 65 pitch values (the quarter tones position on each string). The horizontal line defines chronological time. Each of the eight beams indicates a specific duration resulting from the division or addition of the three main numbers 8, 65 and 107. The beginning of a beam (line) is marked with 'a', the end with 'b'. The direction of the beams in relation to the cardinal points was established by intuition (Fig. 6.25.)

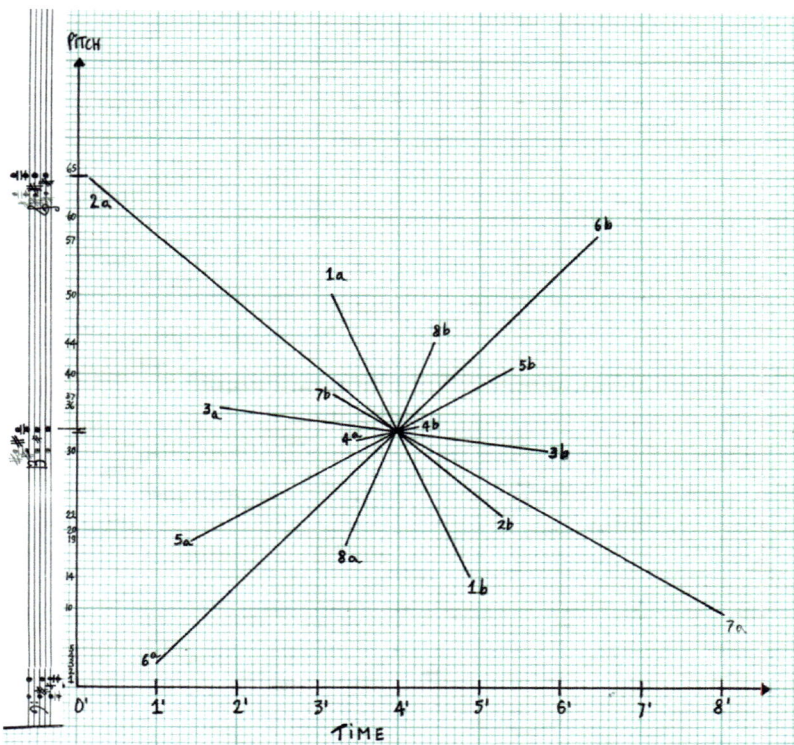

Fig. 6.25: *Epitaph*, star matrix.

199

The numerical proportions are represented below (Fig. 6.26).

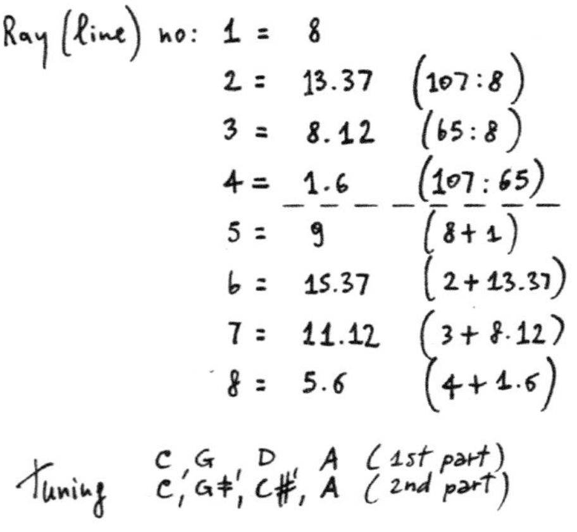

Ray (line) no:
1 = 8
2 = 13.37 (107 : 8)
3 = 8.12 (65 : 8)
4 = 1.6 (107 : 65) / (8 + 1)
5 = 9
6 = 15.37 (2 + 13.37)
7 = 11.12 (3 + 8.12)
8 = 5.6 (4 + 1.6)

Tuning   C, G, D, A (1st part)
c', G#', C#', A (2nd part)

Fig. 6.26: *Epitaph*, numerical proportions.

The chart below shows the quarter-tone positions on each string and the corresponding pitches (Fig. 6.27).

Fig. 6.27: *Epitaph*, quarter-tones positions.

The following chart is crucial as it shows the complete plan of the organisation of sound. The eight beams (lines) are now translated into pitch regions delineated by the length of the pitches and allocated at specific points in time. A central pitch region is recognisable in the middle of the chart corresponding to 4'00", the centre of the piece (Fig. 6.28).

The next charts (Figs. 6.29 and 6.30) show the subsequent step to the unfolding of pitch material. In Fig. 6.29 the pitch material is assigned to each string of the cello at a specific point in time defined by the beams. Each horizontal line, marked as I, II, III and IV (also the strings of the cello) is considered as a long melodic line over the entire duration of the piece whereas each note occurs at the indicated time and the space between two notes is filled by intervallic material resulting from the 'PATTERN' matrix (Fig. 6.30) where the numerical proportions result from the anti-clockwise unfolding of the pitches displayed in the star. There is an obvious resemblance to a background-middle ground-foreground structure that can be seen unfolding in the chart displayed in Fig. 6.31 where the first 'PITCH PATH 1' derives from I, the fixed pitches are assigned at specific points in time and the intervallic patterns stem from the 'PATTERN'. Three other similar pitch paths are unfolded in the same fashion (for the second, third and fourth string of the cello). Each horizontal line represents both a string and a single

200

spine of the structure, i.e. the background. A 4-part polyphony is therefore assigned to the four strings of the instrument: each string is associated with a polyphonic part.

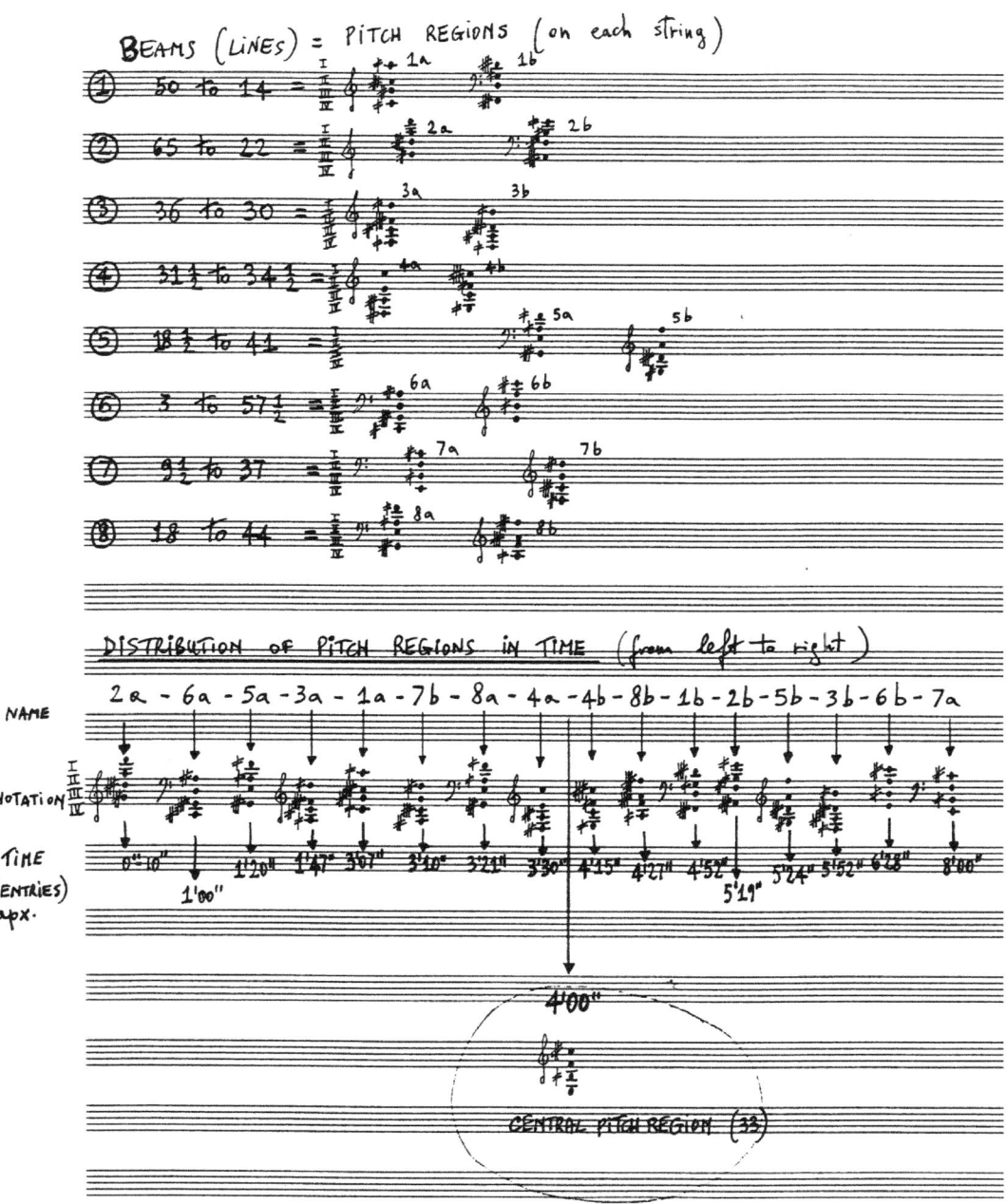

Fig. 6.28: *Epitaph*, beams and pitch regions.

Fig. 6.29: *Epitaph*, distribution of pitch material in time.

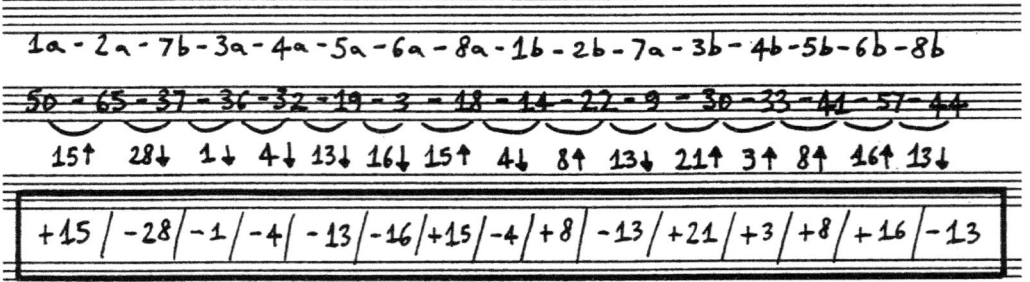

Fig. 6.30: *Epitaph*, intervallic pattern in quarter tones and 'PATTERN' matrix.

Fig. 6.31: *Epitaph*, pitch path 1.

In the chart below, the four 'pitch paths' are superimposed. They constitute the middle ground of the form. You can see at which point in the piece, within the initial four minutes, melodic 'polyphonic' lines are supposed to begin (Fig. 6.32).

202

Fig. 6.32: *Epitaph*, example of superimposed pitch paths.

The first page of the score (Fig. 6.33) provides an example of the unfolding of the first beam from 0'00" to 0'99" and an idea of the finger and bow pressure techniques I discussed earlier. I haven't mentioned the relationship between cello and electronics as this topic would deserve much more space in this conversation.

NH. Do you think of your work (not the 'pieces', but your work as a whole) as 'virtuosic' in any sense?

JP. This is a particularly insightful question, especially because you write 'in any sense'. I have spoken about my thoughts on virtuosity in my works in other conversations, but your question goes beyond the surface of established canons of music understanding. Since I like words, meaning and etymology, my immediate reaction takes me straight to the meaning of the Italian word 'virtuoso' meaning 'virtuous', and its closest synonyms such as 'worthy', 'honourable' and 'upright'. The common understanding of a musician of extraordinary technical skills is visibly superseded by the authentic meaning of the word which provides a far more interesting notion of 'virtue' including intellectual and ethical values. If I look back at the history of Western music, I have always found it culturally irritating and decadent to notice how strongly Johann Mattheson's treatise of 1720 *Der brauchbare Virtuoso* contributed to establishing a meaning of the word that is solely linked to dazzling dexterity on the instrument coupled with a sense of glamour in a performer's career. I am indeed referring to Mattheson's notion of 'virtuosi pattrici' (practical virtuosi). By contrast, Wagner's 1840's article *The Virtuoso and the Artist*, in all its sarcasm, is truly enlightening for his time and certainly more artistically encouraging as it aims at restoring the true nature of the virtuoso: *"The real dignity of the virtuoso rests, therefore, solely on the dignity he is able to preserve for creative art: if he trifles and toys with this, he casts his own honour away. To be sure, it is of little import to him, should he not have sensed that dignity at all."*[43]

---

[43] Osborne (1973:139-140).

'In any sense', you are asking me if I feel that my compositional work is reflecting intellectual and artistic qualities such as virtue, worth, honour, and perhaps even dignity? If that is the case, my answer is simple: I am trying! Perhaps it is beauty that will remain in the end…

Fig. 6.33: *Epitaph*, beginning.

NH. In the *Second String Quartet (Dream)*, the managing of individual and corporate gestures in the ensemble is sometimes very sharply differentiated, sometimes 'quasi unison' and in other places almost fully corporate. What do you think about the correlation between the activity of the players in chamber music like this? (Is the handling in this piece conceptually specific?)

JP. In order to understand the gestural gestalt of the *Second String Quartet,* I have to explain briefly how the music was born. Similar to *Koan,* for shakuhachi and ensemble, this quartet was written out of an irresistible impetus triggered by a letter of Franz Kafka to his friend Milena Jesenka in which he describes a dream of his:

"Yesterday I dreamt of you. I no longer know what happened, I only know that we continuously turned into each other, I was you, you were I. Eventually, you caught fire, I remember that we tried to extinguish the fire with a cloth and took an old jacket with which we tried to put out the flames. Yet, the transformations started again and went so far that you were no longer there, but I was the one who was burning and, at the same time, I was also trying to extinguish the fire [...]. At the end, you were rescued and fell into my arms [...]. But still, the uncertainty of the transformations increased, perhaps it was I, who fell in somebody else's arms."

While reading Kafka's words, I was so struck by these images that I began to 'hear' the sound of string instruments in my mind. It was a very vivid sensation, and I remember a strong sense of urgency that made me decide to write a string quartet immediately. I rushed to my desk and sketched out the details about the form. I wanted to keep any pre-determined strategy to a minimum and envisage a form based on asymmetric proportions. The original German text of Kafka's letter was my starting point: I divided the text into distinct phrases or paragraphs that would be used as autonomous units for the structure of the quartet and established six sections: A1, A2, B1, A3, B2, A4 (see Fig. 6.34). The three red lines delineate a large division of the whole into three sections. I also underlined words carrying a particular significance in the narrative of the dream and whose images triggered precise musical ideas that I had to use in the quartet:

schlug ('I hit') in B1;
anders ('different');
geisterhaft ('ghostly') and *ins Dunkel gezeignet* ('shown in the dark') in B2.

These four notions serve as additional generating factors to the texture in sections B1 and B2. Thus, the Kafka text was to set the form of the quartet. It is, of course, impossible to describe exactly what is happening during the process of imagination: how a mental image can relate to artistic creation in general and to a musical gesture in particular. This is a topic that has always fascinated me, and I am inclined to agree with both Aristotle and Hume that, essentially, the purpose of imagination is to *re-create*, that is to give mental shape to an original idea that is already existing per se. The magnitude of passion in my creative imagination resonates with Mary Warnock's explanation that *"...a lively image is intrinsically more likely to be associated with a passion than a faint image. The more lively and detailed the picture in the mind, the more intense the feeling",*[44] to which I should add that 'the more intense the feeling, the more concrete the sounds I choose'.

I am clearly not a specialist in this area of studies, but I am sure that a complex set of categories must be at stake, including challenging paradigms resulting from research in quantum physics and neurology. There is scientific evidence that by tuning into the endless

---

[44] Warnock (1978:38).

possibilities of the quantum field through a process of brain frequency coherence (where brain waves are in unison with one another), the massive expansion of our energetic field results in enhanced awareness, perception, intuition, imagery and extra-sensorial activity. Many records show that in high states of concentration, an electron extends itself to the immaterial energy of the quantum field and that at that moment an unlimited amount of quantum possibilities turn into creative and material possibilities.[45] Whatever the source may be, the imaginary world creates artistic creation in acoustic form. If epitomes elicited by a verbal description trigger sonic equivalents, this may explain why, when reading Kafka's letter, I could connect immediately to the timbre of specific instruments (the strings) and specific musical gestures, as well as getting a clear idea of the music I felt impelled to give voice to.

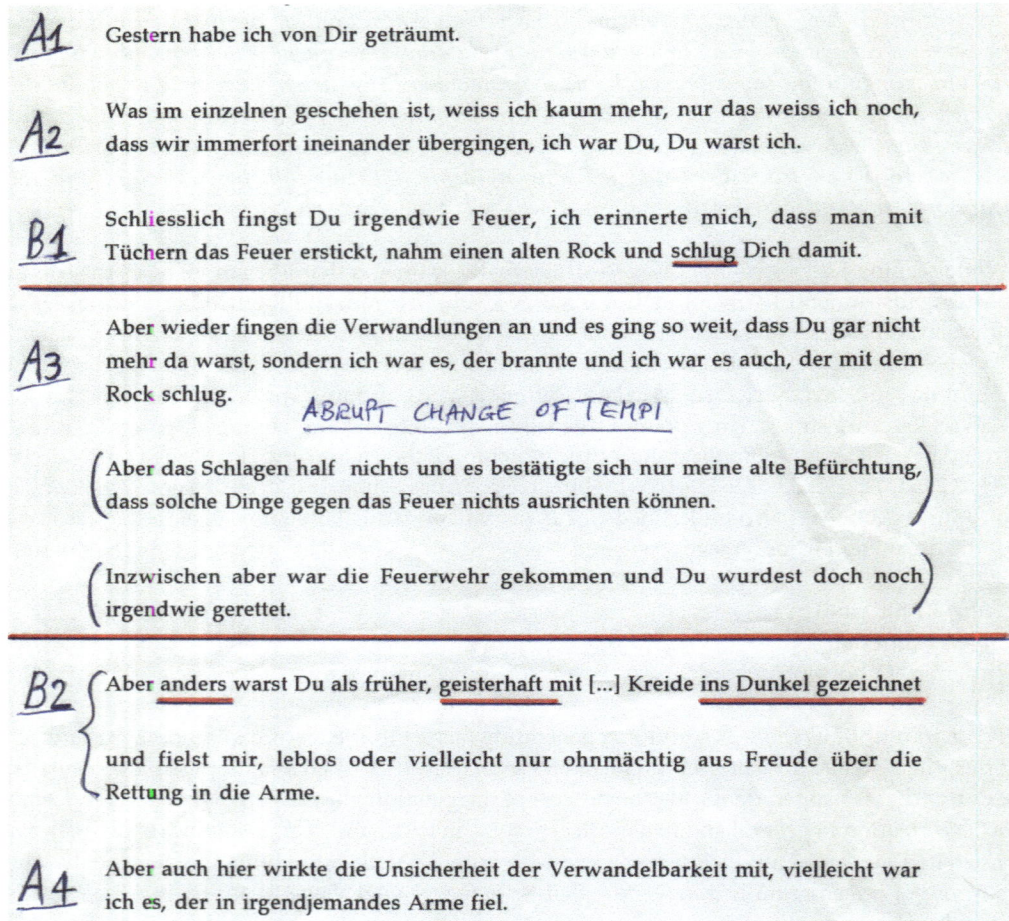

Fig. 6.34: *Second String Quartet*, Kafka's text.

Back to the form of the piece, I transferred the 'I-you' dichotomy of the dream into a 1:2 proportion based on the adjacent notes C♯ and D. The next step was to establish six sections and their duration. My mind already knew what I needed to do, so much so that I could hear

---

[45] One example can be found in the brain scanning tests conducted by Dr. Joe Dispenza (2017:67).

the music unfolding in my imagination while sketching out the form. The narrative of the music was based on the sonic images triggered by Kafka's letter and the evolution of the music reflects the chronological description of the dream. The momentum was so compelling that I completed the piece within two weeks. The following chart shows the basic outline of form and the most relevant ideas I felt important enough to be mentioned in correspondence with the sections of the piece (Fig. 6.35).

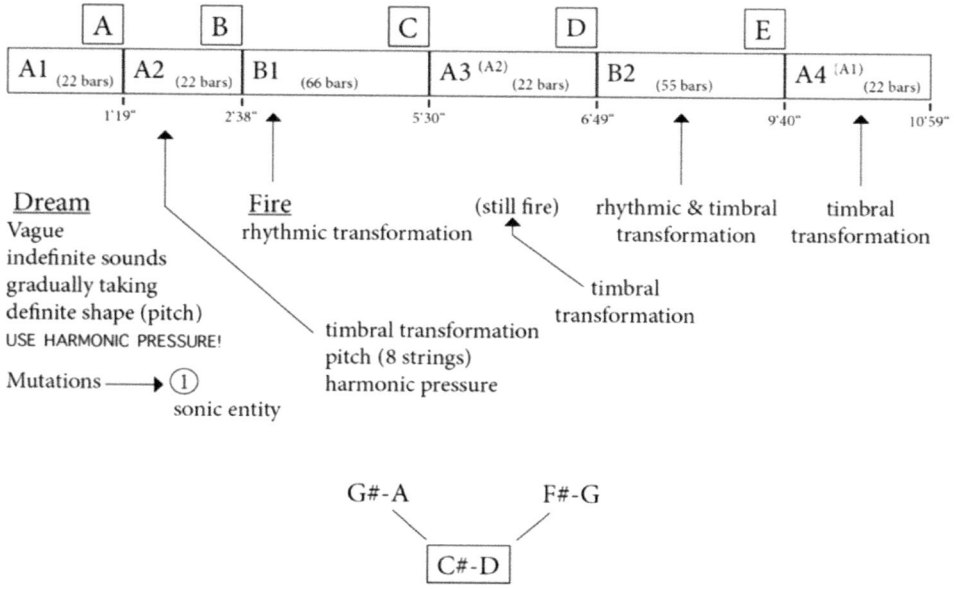

Fig. 6.35: *Second String Quartet*, outline of form.

The handling in this piece is conceptually specific. The quasi-unison you mention signals the 'you-I' polarity: two entities becoming one and alternating their roles. The two interlocked violins are reinforced by the viola and cello mainly in a communal range based on the violin's register that will be exploited by all four instruments throughout the piece. In the *Second String Quartet*, the four instruments remain interlocked in this continuous dilemma. Heterophony, mirroring motifs, alternating rhythms, waving unisons and dynamic promiscuity remain a constant tenet until the end of the piece. The four instruments are an expansion of the two (Fig. 6.36).

The reason why I have shed some light on these compositional details is related to your question about the correlation between the activity of the players in chamber music of this kind. The answer is that I have no general answer, because each piece I write has a different genesis, and therefore a definite identity and narrative. The connection between the activity of the players is always related to two main factors. Firstly, it is related to a mysterious 'taste' in the mind of the composer that is intrinsic to the idea of the piece, much like in Plato's view that all forms reside essentially in a non-physical world of which the physical manifestations are just replications. In a Schenkerian sense, I would identify this dimension as the 'ontological background'. Secondly, the performative logic of the interplay consists of the gestalt of the physicality of sound: the concord of technique and style (including a coherent shape of gestures), articulation, phrasing, dynamic calibration, ornamentation, pace and tempo coordination, polyphonic transparency, values of interdependence and, more importantly, unity of intent. By referring again to Schenkerian terminology, I would call this sonic manifestation the 'acoustic foreground'.

Fig. 6.36: *Second String Quartet*, beginning.

NH. All of these pieces seem to me to be searching for some kind of transcendence. If you recognise this observation, is it something that you conceptualise directly, or is it a matter of establishing a field of activity that might allow this to emerge? In other words, is it essentially a compositional or performative dimension in your work?

JP. For me, composing is taking refuge in the power of reflection. This artistic work, being so solitary, gives me the opportunity to face myself with the basic questions of life such as: What are we here for? What is our role in a civilised society?

I keep spending my life searching for some kind of transcendence in every possible activity I undertake, and I integrate this awareness into my musical work. Consequently, many titles provide a clear reference to this preoccupation. The same awareness prompts me to ascertain fields of activity that should hopefully allow this to transpire. For these reasons, the compositional and performative dimensions in my work are strictly interconnected. The search for transcendence comes with a set of questions that encourage me to continue on this path. The answers are written in the eternity that awaits me.

CHAPTER SEVEN

ACCORDION AND PIANO

A DISCUSSION ON *DRANG*, FOR ACCORDION
Sergej Tchirkov

ST. In 1999 you composed *Hinayana* for oboe and *Satori* for harpsichord: both works have been inspired by and reflect upon Buddhist philosophy. A key vision that shaped these two compositions was an intention to practise *"a deeper insight into the truth of reality"*, as you have written in the programme note to *Satori*. The same year you started to work on *Drang*, your first and, so far, only accordion piece. What kind of 'insights into the truth of reality' were you trying to discover when you first approached the accordion and embraced its tradition? What aesthetical approach did you choose and how did the instrumental aspect inform your choice?

JP. There is no direct connection between *Drang* and the other works you mention, and the words *"insight into the truth of reality"* were related to *Satori* and the concept of non-duality in Zen. *Hinayana* is linked to Tibetan Buddhism. *Drang* is a very different piece and has no reference to Buddhism whatsoever. An imaginary link to Eastern philosophies could be cautiously suggested in connection with the physicality of breathing as a symbol of earthly life. Indeed, at the end of the 1990s, I was exploring breathing as a musical force. I learned to play the accordion at the age of eight or nine, I think. I was self-taught. I was already playing the piano and the organ, and it was relatively easy for me to play the instrument as an amateur. I investigated the logic of the buttons on the left side and I was soon in the position to play songs using both hands. I perceived the accordion as a portable piano and enjoyed playing it outdoors. My repertoire consisted mainly of folk and pop songs, including the French chansons. This period lasted two or three years. The tradition I embraced, if I may use that word, was mainly that of French, Argentinian, Italian and some Balkan folk music. My approach to the instrument was very much down-to-earth, I must say. When I wrote *Drang*, many years later, I related to the accordion not in connection to its cultural roots (folk music), but as an instrument like any other, considered in its own prominence and technical idiosyncrasies. What attracts me to the accordion is its uniqueness, being a twofold keyboard instrument able to create varying dynamics and different timbres and, at the same time, being depending upon air production. A 'breathing' and portable version of an organ, if you like. From a technical point of view, I focused on two main aspects of the instruments: air production and timbre.

ST. The title and the nature of the music clearly refer to the extremes of emotion, theatrical perspective, dramatic dynamic changes and other qualities that were typical of the German Sturm und Drang movement in the 18th century. While working on *Drang*, have you been thinking of or influenced by any specific Sturm und Drang oeuvres and their historical connotations? To what extent has the cultural context contributed to the language of *Drang* and your choice of material?

JP. I think any musical work is related to a cultural or historical tradition in one way or another. The idea of the piece was to write a strongly emotional piece. Every time I think of 'Sturm und Drang', I am inevitably reminded of the emotional reaction expressed by poets and musicians against the constraints of rationalism of the Enlightenment in the 18th century, but the piece has its own life and there is no direct relation to the historical movement apart from the meaning of the German word 'Drang': emotional urge, drive, impulse. These are notions of a more universal extent. By the same token, there is no connection between the historical context of the 18th century and the choice of the material I have used for this piece. I was interested in giving voice to the challenging, the daring, the visionary. *Drang* is an appeal to the world to bring out the Promethean that is latent in each of us.

ST. In the programme note to *Drang* you stress the importance of the virtuoso aspect of the work. What does virtuosity mean for you? Is it a set of extraordinary instrumental skills? Or is it an agency that is rooted in the structure of the composition and reveals itself at the moment of the performance?

JP. When I speak about virtuosity, I am not referring to a set of extraordinary instrumental skills. It's not about playing loud and fast! That kind of virtuosity does not interest me. On the contrary, it leaves me cold. I find it shallow, pretentious, superficial and at times even ridiculous. My understanding of virtuosity is about a philosophical and emotional quality linked with the Promethean. It is implied, rather than rooted, in the structure of the composition, although it is a quality that is not structural per se. It reflects a compulsion, an irresistible urge to act in a certain way. It is pure dialectics unfolding in a confrontational discourse. In a world full of apathy, selfishness and disconnection from our humanity, any obstacle that comes across our life is an opportunity to advance our dignity as human and divine beings. Virtuosity epitomises the courage needed to face the obstacle, the challenge to the impossible, the drive that will conquer adversity, the necessity of wanting to be better human beings, the bridge taking us onto lasting triumph, and the impulse leading to the acquisition of self-knowledge through the dark night of the soul: the need to make God 'dangerous' again!

ST. While performing your music I have always been fascinated by the ability to create real-time 'gaps' between my interpretative gestures (what I wanted to do) and my physical gestures (what I actually do). How important is for you the real-time nature of music, the uniqueness of a performance? Which role does the precarity of performance play in the structure of your compositions?

JP. Any music performed on stage is a real-time experience. A score is not the music, but a set of graphic instructions: music is what we hear acoustically. Imagining sounds in my mind while I am composing or studying a score is only an approximation, an idea about the music. If a score may be compared to a visual representation of the source, a performance is about the message being channelled, that is, communicated to a listener. Each performance is unique, unequalled and of paramount importance. I don't think the precarity of performance, as you put it, can play a role in the structure of a composition, and I am not sure if 'precarity' is the word I would personally use. I prefer to think of a performance in terms of 'uniqueness' and perhaps 'plausibility' of the communication. The performer must read the artistic meaning of the information in order to communicate it to the audience. The 'gaps' between your interpretative and physical gestures you are referring to when performing *Drang* sheds light on the predicament of virtuosity I vehemently advocate, namely a syllogism of constraint and resistance, structure and emotion, demand and emancipation. The forms and procedures I use vary enormously from work to work as I don't have a fixed pre-established modus operandi. My experience as a performer helps me predict gestures and interpretative decisions that will be taken by the performer, while the instructions of the score must exist as a congruent manifestation of the musical idea. The clearer the information in the score, the more varied and subtle the interpretation.

ST. Like in most works of this period, the score of *Drang* is very complex. Your writing is very detailed and precise. You also encourage the performer to make individual choices and to take spontaneous decisions. Indications such as 'sempre esaggerato', 'avanti' and 'molto rubato' sometimes prevail over the rhythmical precision and metronome marks. Is this way of writing an attempt to exaggerate the gestural nature of music and facilitate the production of 'presence' in the work?

JP. Yes. Exaggeration is very important because it strengthens contrast, and the performer must use as much contrast as possible in order to emphasise the dramatic character of the music, the suffocating search for something elusive and essential through passion, anxiety, desire and anguish. The indications you mean refer to a level of information that, hierarchically speaking, stands above the metronome indications and the notes. *Drang* is also a very physical piece and the accordionist must ensure to keep the tension of the physical gestures as high as possible throughout the piece.

ST. Talking about notation, do you experience any kind of limitation to your artistic idea resulting from our Western tradition? If yes, could you describe your effort to overcome this and the development of your approach to notation over the years?

JP. I take that your question refers to the notation for acoustic instrumental sounds. I need to specify this because when writing for electronic sounds, the problem of notation presents gargantuan proportions. Generally speaking, no notation is all-encompassing. I am not an expert on non-Western notations, but from what I have seen, I can say that if notation is about providing a visual image of a sound-event, Western notation remains the most comprehensive type of notation for acoustic instruments. To be specific, I am referring to mensural notation. Having said that, as a performer and improviser myself, I can say that mensural notation is far from ideal in terms of visualising musical ideas that use complex combinations of rhythm and metre. Many pieces of mine that were born out of improvisations have been impossible to transcribe exactly by means of mensural notation. I have often resolved this problem by using time-space notation especially in pieces where an acoustic instrument is playing with electronics. This type of notation helps to visualise the information in a more organic way than mensural notation, because by referring to the unfolding of chronological time the performer is invited to focus on the fluid psychological relationship between the information written on paper and the gestural aspects of the performance. As a performer, I have mostly found this situation much more liberating than the strict precision of mensural notation. The information-imagination-performance (eyes-mind-sound) interface can alter enormously depending on what kind of notation is being used.

There was a point in my life where I explored the use of complex notation in contemporary music. I remember discussing this issue with cellist Neil Heyde during one of our recording sessions in Hatfield and in conjunction with Brian Ferneyhough's *Time and Motion Study II* which we performed at Conway Hall in London in 1999. The discussion was about whether the complexity of such a notation justifies the musical result, and whether improvisation, or space-time notation, may provide a better and more liberating musical result of the same musical idea. As you know, opinions on this topic differ. My experience as a pianist has shown me not only that mensural notation can be limited and limiting for the performance of complex music, but also *musically* unsatisfactory. The question remains as to 'how effectively can I notate what I want?' As a performer, I remain highly sceptical of unnecessarily complex notation. The effect it has on me is one of reduction, rather than celebration, of the musical idea. This condition of reduction contradicts the syllogism of constraint and resistance I mentioned earlier. It tends to discourage me instead of triggering the desire to interpret. I feel like being reduced to a machine that at its best will produce an approximation of the written information. Musically unjustified complex notation won't give me any space for interpretation. In such a tyrannical setting, there is no space for artistic sensitivity to give voice to music. This is obviously a personal consideration that has no judgmental value about the artistic integrity of composers who adopt a similar approach to notation. But let me tell you something else. I once decided to conduct an experiment: I listened very attentively (and several times) to a very complex solo piece by a composer whose name I won't mention, *without* looking at the score. I wrote down the tempo and the metre I perceived according to the listening experience. Then I wrote down the notes I heard one by one and the number of bars I took under scrutiny. Subsequently, I read the score on my Sibelius notation program and played the music from the new score with the simplified notation. Finally, I recorded it, listened to it and compared the result with two other recordings by different musicians played from the original score. The outcome was intriguing: the score with the simplified notation was much easier to read, and the subsequent interpretation produced a much better musical result. The interpretation was perceived as sonically clearer and much more precise than the two interpretations based on the original score. The new score had put me in a much better, and easier, psychological and technical position to interpret the piece in a truly musical manner.

A crucial factor that seems to be too often neglected by some composers is the precision of the performance resulting from overly-complex notation and its perception by our cognitive faculties. I wish more attention would be addressed to this important issue. Experience teaches me that the easier the notation, the more precise and clearer is the musical result. If you listen attentively to pieces using complex notation, you will unmistakably hear that the music sounds unfocused and blurred, and, in all cases, inexact when compared to the score. If this is a deliberate choice aimed at creating a flow of chaotic energy of an indistinctive music quality (whose effect I can understand in philosophical terms), I can assure you that we can achieve much better results by using improvisation, time-space notation or a simplified, indeed 'rational', notation. Also, by using a more reasonable notation, I'll have the performers on my side, which is an important psychological aspect for the musical quality of the performance.

At that time, I was performing pieces like *Etudes Astrales* and *Music of Changes* by John Cage, and many other piano works written in time-space notation. As a performer, I still find this kind of notation a more intelligible vehicle for attaining acoustic clarity and enhanced expressivity. In any case, the re-notation experiment confirmed my performer instinct about the use of irrational (irresponsible?) and excessively complex mensural notation. What I can say for sure is that since I use a lesser degree of notational complexity, the music I write can always be played exactly and clearly.

Drang is a challenging piece, but, as you know, can be played well and with full emotional intensity. I always choose notation depending on the nature of the piece I have in mind. Dogmatic and monolithic approaches to compositional procedure do not interest me. When I write music for acoustic instruments, I don't experience limitations to my artistic ideas because the first question I ask myself is: what kind of notation is the most accurate for the music I have in mind? The notation I choose is always appropriate to the nature of the music I want to write. Grace notes, to mention but an expedient I use, can be a very useful device for creating complex textures that are 'musical' to perform while, at the same time, keeping the rhythmic notation intelligible enough to endorse the dramatic power of the music.

ST. The music that you write is always very personal and genuine. Have you ever worked on a piece in close collaboration with a performer already at the stage of pre-composition? How do you see the ethics of composer-performer collaboration?

JP. I have tried to involve a performer in the pre-composition phase very few times in my life, especially in the early days, and the majority of times I have noticed a polite lack of interest in wanting to know the background of the music. The impression I was given was that many performers want to receive the score, study it, play the piece and that's it! This attitude has inevitably provoked a sense of self-protection that I have acquired in order to survive negative situations of this kind.

On the other hand, I have experienced the most inspiring encounters with those performers who have shown genuine interest in any information that will eventually lead to the writing of the score, and these moments have been extremely gratifying to me. These are musicians who will play your music with body, heart and soul, and you will feel it in their performance. I truly love collaborating with performers who are committed to the music. When working with one performer, it is easier and faster to access a deep level of communication. I believe the composer-performer alchemy is a mutually beneficial and inspiring experience, because the new work will be born *also* in relation to the input of the performer, thus putting the composer in the position to exploit more in depth the practical aspects of the performance.

There is another level that I should mention. I always say that any professional relationship is first of all a human relationship, and this applies particularly to our musical world, that is the world of artists. Any musical friendship is a personal friendship. It is hard for me to separate the two. And friendship is a creative and powerful energy. I have seen the most touching friendships being born out of a musical circumstance. Music can unite people; it can offer a sense of belonging, intimacy and identification; and it can unveil the basic ethics of sharing the most essential values of our existence in the most creative and beautiful way.

ST. Do you see substantial development potential in alternative modes of communication between composer and performer (oral tradition, text instructions and video-scores, for example)?

JP. In my experience, oral communication informed by acoustic experience, or rather the other way around, remains the most effective way to exchange musical information. I have seen, and used myself for my teaching, three-dimensional scrolling scores at the Ina GRM in Paris and found them very interesting. I don't know if this kind of research has been continued, but it is certainly very inspiring. I am sure there is big potential in modern technology that deserves to be exploited diligently for artistic and educational purposes. I think that any form of sound representation can be extremely useful for the cognition of musical structure.

ST. You have worked with electronics a lot. How has your experience with electroacoustic composition informed your approach to acoustic sounds? What have you learned about sound?

JP. The benefits of working with electronics are immense! The perception of acoustic sounds becomes much more refined. I have learnt to hear all sorts of acoustic sounds in their spectral characteristics. For example, by playing a low note on a piano, I am able to naturally hear the first partials of the harmonic series of that pitch, thus hearing that note in a (almost) spectral way. In psychoacoustics, we say that we hear what we know, and this is really true. I can hear combination-tones on a violin almost immediately, I can detect the harmonics when a hornist plays a single note on his instrument. I have learnt to hear sounds on the edge of silence, the changing harmonics of a tam-tam or a church bell, and so on. The electronic studio work is undoubtedly one of the most powerful ear-opener experiences for a contemporary composer.

ST. Do you feel divergences between your extra-musical ideas (your work at a poietic level)

and the score? Do you want performers to know them, or would you prefer them to relate to the score as the only source of information about the work?

JP. The poietic level is of primary importance in the music I write. This is where everything begins, and I usually invest a great deal of time in it. The more I know about the universals of a musical work, the better I can appreciate the music. Jean-Jacques Nattiez has provided us with such a superb account of the relation between the 'poietic' level, the immanent structure of the work (the 'neutral' level) and the 'esthesic' process that to refute the interconnection of this tripartition would be ludicrous. And I don't mean this only in a philosophical context. The score is the sign of an originating impulse, whatever that may be: if I performed a piano piece by another composer, any information provided about the genesis of the piece will inevitably help me understand the music in relation to its raison d'être and put me in a much better position to interpret the music according to its inherent specificities. I am not saying that without knowing where the music comes from, we cannot perform or appreciate it: this would be too reductive towards the intrinsic power of music. What I am saying is that any scrutiny of the poietic level of a musical work will provide a significant benefit to the performance.

By the way, I find the idea that a composer's job is *only* to write music rather restrictive and dull. Of course, my main preoccupation as a composer is to write music, but this doesn't mean that composers shouldn't discuss it. One of the reasons why we are experiencing a growing gap between classical music and the majority of people is ignorance. So many music-lovers simply do not know how to listen and any information about the extra-musical level of a composition can be such a benefit to the listener. Composers who are willing to get out of their comfort zone and share their experience about their music with the world can certainly help to create a more attentive and vibrant musical culture. The discussion doesn't need to be highly intellectual. Answers to questions such as 'why do I choose a specific sound rather than another?', 'why this chord instead of another?', 'why is this phrase occurring at this particular point in the composition and not earlier?' may be revealing. Look at pop musicians! In all their naïveté and lack of knowledge, they manage to convey their music emotionally (not technically!) often in a disarming and effective way. They are not afraid to talk about those feelings which instigate them to write a song. And people do relate to that. Clarity can be very powerful.

"JUST THROW YOURSELF INTO THE FIRE!"
ON THE NOTION OF MUSICAL VIRTUOSITY IN JOHN PALMER'S *DRANG*
Sergej Tchirkov

[*"Just throw yourself into the fire!"* These were the words of John Palmer just a few seconds before this author went to the stage to perform *Drang* for the first time in 2000.]

The phenomenon of virtuosity in performance has long been neglected by traditional musicology with its focus upon the text as a work of art, but over recent decades it has become an important topic of academic studies and artistic processes. In 1999, John Palmer composed a work for accordion to which he explicitly attributes a virtuoso-like character.[46] However, the problematic term itself demands examination to elaborate a framework for its use both regarding the specific composition of Palmer and concerning the relevance of virtuosity in contemporary academic, artistic and social discourse. A key vision of this essay will be to

---

[46] Programme note to *Drang*.

problematise the notion of virtuosity as a transcending dialectical force that determines the relationship between the performers' embodied knowledge of their instrument and the composer's musical ideas, as represented through a written score. To do this, I will examine musical virtuosity as an artistic phenomenon that affects the 'production of meaning' in the work *Drang*,[47] for accordion solo.

My close artistic engagement with the piece and my exchange with the composer, which has lasted over twenty years so far and resulted in the conversation published in this book, fostered my interest in further explorations of composers' attitudes towards the notion of virtuosity. Besides these topics, I will also question the historical and symbolic aspects that virtuosity may evoke in the context of an overly complex and technically demanding work. I will also analyse how virtuosity is realised in sonic events and performing gestures, and how it interacts with the structure of the composition. Before approaching the main topic of this writing, I first will analyse the main instrumental aspects of the accordion that contributed to shaping John Palmer's approach to the composition. An examination will be undertaken on how these aspects are represented in the score. This will be done from the performer's perspective; some brief references to the recent history of accordion performance will be needed at this stage in order to deeper understand the context of creation. I will proceed with a short discussion about the title of the work, its emotional meaning, the historic connotations it may evoke and how it informs the performer's strategies.

With the knowledge gained on the instrument, the score and the title, as well as on the composer's verbal instructions, I will approach the issue of virtuosity. Here, I will try to provide perspectives on the genesis and development of instrumental virtuosity and relate the findings with the structural, timbral and gestural aspects of Palmer's work. The philosophical aspect of virtuosity will be questioned both from the composer's perspective (a large citation from the interview with John Palmer will be used) and with regard to the presumed potentiality of virtuosity to act as an independent dialectical force that constitutes the performer's narrative and creates the musical meaning of the performance.

Drang was written in 1999, around the turn of the millennium. In the interview, the composer stated that from a technical point of view, he focused on two main aspects: air production and timbre of the accordion.[48] Whereas timbre is a sound quality that is unique for every musical instrument, the ability to produce air noise is a particular characteristic of the accordion. Indeed, the air sounds of the accordion resemble human breathing, but, at the same time, they never sound *"as natural as the breathing of a wind player or singer since the bellows motion is mechanical"*.[49] By the time *Drang* was written, this effect had already been well known and widely used by composers like Salvatore Sciarrino in *Vagabonde Blu* (1998), or Dieter Schnebel in *Medusa* (1993), or else by Sofia Gubaidulina who composed the legendary *De Profundis* in 1978. The latter made use of the sounds produced by pressing the air button of the accordion to create a dramatic effect of devastation and solitude. The air sounds in *De Profundis* resemble a survivor's human breath after a devastating mass of clusters, followed by pitch-bending tones that resemble moaning. *Medusa* by Schnebel has a programme that explains the use of nearly all the extended techniques in the piece: the air sounds picture the wings of Perseus's winged horse when Perseus travels to find the cave of Medusa.[50]

Salvatore Sciarrino approaches the air sounds from a different perspective: he seeks to find a 'quintessence of accordion'[51] with all the actions that it may imply: pressing keys, moving

---

[47] The German word *Drang* means strong impulse, urge, drive, strong desire, stress. See also my discussion on the title below.

[48] A Discussion on *Drang*, for Accordion, p. 211.

[49] Buchmann (2010:94).

[50] Dieter Schnebel, *Medusa* for accordion (Schott Music, 1993).

[51] Wilson (1999).

bellows and producing the air that resembles *"the breathing of the machine"*.[52] An important aspect of Sciarrino's approach to this technique is that, unlike Schnebel or Gubaidulina, he does not use air production to create an effect. The air noises in *Vagabonde Blu* are considered an aspect of the instrument's specificity. As Peter Niklas Wilson notes, *"this is not an effect, but a very different, anthropological conception of musical language"*.[53] Still, in Sciarrino's work, the physical actions of the performer are intentionally excluded from the performance, the accordionist is required to remain immobile on the stage to let the audience focus on the instrument and the actions that come from within the accordion. Paraphrasing Lydia Goehr, we can speak here in terms of a perfect performance of *"instrumental music"*.[54]

The instrumental specificity gave impulses to John Palmer's composition too, although his approach is different from that of Sciarrino. The air sounds in *Drang* are not meant to resemble natural, calm breathing, nor do they refer to machine-like breathing. The control of airflow, air sounds, and, in a broader perspective, the bellows goes beyond producing or enhancing the dramatic effects which are doubtless present in the composition. The bellow/air/breathing technique in *Drang* requires visible, audible and very gestural actions from the performer. These actions are implied by the notation. A look at the score shows the use of the air button on the grace notes (Fig. 7.1), the inevitable leaps between the air sound and the following chord (Fig. 7.2), the dynamics exaggerations and meticulously written remarks (Figs. 7.1 and 7.2): particularly challenging and unstable techniques that encourage the performers to overcome the difficulties, using all their physical and mental concentration.

Fig. 7.1: *Drang*, use of the air button.

Fig. 7.2: *Drang*, example of leaps between the air sound and a following chord.

---

[52] Ibid.
[53] Ibid.
[54] Goehr (1996:1-22).

The production of the air sounds in *Drang* is deliberately put in such a challenging context that the performer is explicitly required *"to keep the tension of the physical gestures as high as possible throughout the piece"*.[55] The idea behind the air sounds is always instrument-specific, but in contrast to Sciarrino, Palmer makes it clear that it is not the accordion that can breathe; it is the performer who makes or even forces it to breathe, to suffocate, to inhale, to exhale and to exclaim. Paraphrasing Goehr again, this situation can be seen as a 'perfect musical performance' *"on the instrument"*.[56]

The use of air sounds in *Drang* implies the performers' awareness of their relationship with the instrument. But besides the air sounds, there are some other technical aspects that require this awareness. Here again, I will refer to the score, which is replete with extreme dynamic indications as well as verbal interventions combined with a highly complex texture. The dynamics in *Drang* vary from very quiet sounds to extremely loud. As with the air sounds, Palmer often uses rapid changes from very powerful sound flows to very quiet, almost inaudible tones. More than that, the dynamic signs may often indicate either a concrete performing gesture, aimed at a 'perfect performance of music' (a specific sound production technique, as in Fig. 7.3) or an interpretative gesture aimed at 'the perfect musical performance' and a gesture that guides the performer's interpretative strategy of a phrase, passage or motive (Fig. 7.5).

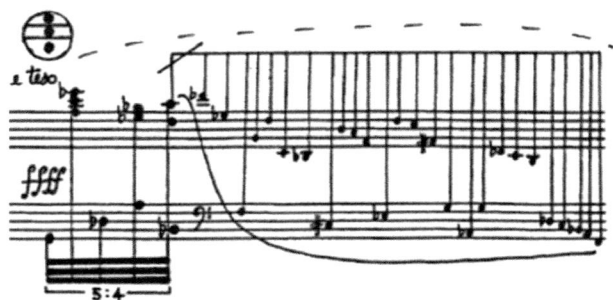

Fig. 7.3: *Drang*, specific sound production technique.

Fig. 7.4: *Drang*, specific sound production technique (2).

---

[55] A Discussion on *Drang*, for Accordion, p. 211.
[56] Goehr (1996).

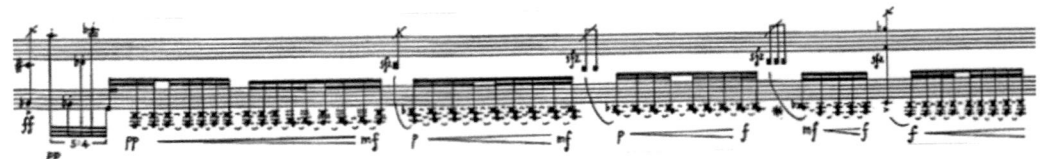

Fig. 7.5: *Drang*, example of gestures.

Fig. 7.3 reveals yet another important role of the dynamics, namely its power to affect timbre. As quoted above, Palmer was particularly attracted by the ability of the accordion to create varying timbres. In addition to three manuals, the accordion offers a variety of register stops that activate different reed ranks and change the colour of the sound. The selection and the colour of the registers depend on the model of the instrument as well as the quality of the reed ranks and vary from instrument to instrument. Still, the score of *Drang* contains precise indications of register switches, including some reed combinations which are not commonly used. Fig. 7.3 above shows a relatively rare combination of reed blocks used under special dynamic conditions: given the extreme loud dynamics, 'fortissimo' mark, most performers would automatically switch a 'tutti' (4'+8'+8'+16') register, which is the most common choice for loud and very loud chord progressions. However, Palmer deliberately suggests a combination of reeds that include an 8' in 'cassotto' (a box inside the accordion that serves as a particle filter) and excludes the 8' outside of 'cassotto'. Thus, the high air pressure will affect three and not four reed blocks, which most likely would result in a pitch-bending effect of the reed inside 'cassotto'. As the chords are short and the texture is dense, the pitch oscillations will hardly be perceived as such, but the overall perception will result in a distorted sound. Fig. 7.4 above shows yet another fragment where the combination of registration, dynamics, and articulation leads to timbre transformation. The chord sounds an octave higher, and it is to be performed on a +4 register only. This register activates the smallest and thinnest reeds, which most likely would not have enough time to begin vibrating on the given pitches, but as the air pressure is high, they will produce a distorted, approximately-pitched sound.

The need to expand on the technical details shown in these examples provides insights on how consciously John Palmer approaches the acoustic and technical characteristics of the instrument. To a large extent, the attention to the slightest timbral change results from the composer's experience of working with electronics which Palmer describes as *"one of the most powerful ear-opener experiences for a contemporary composer."*[57] The choice of timbres and registers suggested by the composer is therefore as important as the notes themselves, and the eventual approximation of registration by the performer would result in the loss of emotional intensity, which is essential in the piece. The same can be said about dynamics. Failing to observe subtle differences in 'crescendi' from 'pianissimo' to 'mezzo forte', from 'piano' to 'mezzo forte' and from 'mezzo forte' to 'forte' (as in Fig. 7.4) would result in the loss of the inner logic of the music and again, the loss of emotional intensity. And yet, another implement, which according to the score clearly urges the performers to exaggerate the physicality of their approach to the instrument, is the complex nature of the texture in terms of pitch structure and metric organisation. Here a brief explanation of some curves of the recent history of the accordion is needed.

The rapid development of the accordion in Europe since the late 1970s led to an increased interest by composers of the late 1980s and 1990s.[58] This fostered the development of performance practice. But the latter rarely crossed with the rise of the style represented by those British composers who were engaged with writing very complex scores and who *"pushed the*

---

[57] Palmer, A Discussion on *Drang*, for Accordion, p.211.
[58] Buchmann, (2010:14).

prescriptive capacity of traditional staff notation to its limits".[59] Apart from Michael Finnissy's *Stomp* (1981), the accordion was completely ignored by so-called New Complexity composers until the early 2000s. Obviously, by the time *Drang* was written, there have been some very challenging and technically demanding works by Luciano Berio, Edison Denisov, Nikolaus A. Huber and Mauricio Kagel to name a few, but the majority of the most advanced accordionists were not accustomed to read complex mensural notation. For these reasons, the score of *Drang* with its strict but clear rhythmic and metric organisation may seem fairly complex to many accordionists.

The precision with which Palmer approaches the air production, dynamics indications, timbre and registration marks suggests that the actual notes and passages meticulously written out in the score are meant to be accurately performed, though at the beginning this may seem an impossible task. To make it possible, the performer must find an approach that would guide the technical process, prioritising information provided by the score and *internalising* it.[60] The score provides a clue to finding such an approach; in the performance notes the composer pwrites: *"rubato techniques are essential for the performance of this work and the performer is encouraged to emphasise – and exaggerate – much of the phrasing and articulations"*. The strictness of the rhythmic configurations and the metronome marks becomes contingent on yet another level of information that prevails over the notes: the verbal indications. These play an essential role in the work: they guide technical realisation, help to create a relational field between all the information that is contained in the score, and yet, they condition the way of communicating a musical idea to the listener although the audience is not supposed to know any of these indications.

The remarks have a dialectical nature: they refer both to the internal work and homework of the performer, as well as to the act of performance. The three most frequent remarks that illustrate this ('esaggerato', 'drammatico' and 'sempre avanti')[61] indicate the dramatic flow of the music and encourage the performer to exaggerate and emphasise much of the phrasing and articulation. But how much of the phrasing and articulation can be exaggerated? Normally, the question would be asked by the performer while practising. Still, what happens to the performance when nearly all the details and gestures are exaggerated in real time? Specifically, what would happen to the performers' notion of the internalised score and the narrative that they want to communicate through a 'perfect musical performance'? Part of the control over the performance will be lost and the performance will become eventualised. This transition from the music's 'object-status' to its 'event-status'[62] does not mean that the performer's control will be completely lost; an 'operative' control function will be taken by other performative agents. The latter depend on the degree of the performer's 'mutual engagement' with the instrument but also on the force that relieves the performer from a responsibility to control every aspect of the performance, and that unleashes the emotional intensity that shall take over the command of exaggerated gestures, actions and responses. The moment when the performer's strategies are being transformed into a one-time-experience is a triumph of virtuosity: *"Virtuosity brings into sharp focus the relationship between music's object-status and its event-status [...] It draws the performer right into the heart of the work, foregrounding presentational strategies that are hard to illuminate through the familiar, pedigreed methods of music analysis"*.[63]

So far, the discussion has only been based on the information provided by the score, and on the instrumental aspects. This short overview of the composer's approach to technical

---

[59] Fox (2001).
[60] Rink (2018:97-98).
[61] All the remarks are listed at the end of this essay.
[62] Sampson (2003:2).
[63] Ibid.

characteristics of the accordion shows that the gestural perspective of the performance is already implied by the notation method. The information contained in the score requires the performer to be aware of the body-instrument relationship, and such an awareness is the necessary condition of the playability of the nuances indicated in the score. It has been discussed how the proper realisation of all the notated elements contributes to the 'production of presence':[64] how air production and bellows control dynamics and timbre indications as well as verbal instructions, how they create tension and encourage the performers to consciously make use of their physicality in the performance. The notion of virtuosity, seen as an agency which eventualises the music, has been briefly introduced. The knowledge on these specific aspects shall contribute to a better understanding of a more general context in which the content of *Drang* unfolds.

Certain aspects of this general context can only be examined on a poietic level of the composer's work.[65] The term 'poietic' is understood here as *"the determination of the conditions that make possible, and that underpin the creation of an artist's work"*.[66] Specifically, I shall examine the title of the work which, in the case of *Drang*, evokes both historical and emotional associations, raises questions and leaves space for interpretation. In the programme note, the composer writes: *"This music is to be played with much Sturm und Drang character; impetuous, yearning, passionate, gestural, directional and always virtuoso-like"*. We can see a clear reference to the movement of the late 18th century that *"exalted nature, feeling, and human individualism and sought to overthrow then Enlightenment cult of Rationalism"*.[67] Although certain references to the socio-cultural phenomenon of the past can be found in John Palmer's work, neither the choice of material nor the structure of the work draws from the historic style. Perhaps this is one of the reasons why this work is entitled *Drang* and not *Sturm und Drang*, as if wanting to avoid the temptation to fall into a historically loaded perspective. The title *Drang* has multiple meanings and can be interpreted in many ways. Below, I am listing three basic notions which are the most pertinent to the composer-performer interaction:

1. The composer's impulses are clearly set at the level of the pre-compositional work. Besides the choice of material, this includes the decisions of prioritisation of procedures, gestures and modes of communication to the performer.
2. The stability of the notation and the instability of the real-time realisations *put pressure* on the performer to oscillate between structure and emotion, interpretative gesture and physical action. As strong and profound as an emotion can be, it remains a human phenomenon rather than an instrumental one. Therefore, it requires performers to disconnect themselves from the instrument at a certain point of preparatory work in order to reflect on the emotions and strategies of expression.
3. The *urge* to explore the tensions, potentialities of transformation, the variety of possibilities and/or to challenge mental concentration and physical control.

Certainly, from the performer's perspective, the same can be applied to nearly every composed, score-based piece of music. Many performance narratives may imply the interaction of all of these and many more notions. But being derived from the title (and giving titles is a prerogative and responsibility of a composer) these notions reveal a specific composer's attitude that

---

[64] Gumbrecht (2004).

[65] I agree with some other researchers who argue that the work of a performer can also be considered as poietic, and who criticize Nattiez semiology as being *"still dependent on the view of composers as 'true creators' and works as 'ideal objects': stable and fixed artworks that should make up the primary object of study for musicology"*. See also Frisk (2006).

[66] Nattiez (1990:12).

[67] Encyclopedia Britannica. https://www.britannica.com/event/Sturm-und-Drang.

determines 'the conditions that make possible [...] the creation of an artist's work'. In *Drang*, the title and the programme note explicitly state *"a syllogism of constraint and resistance, structure and emotion, demand and emancipation."*[68] If the agency of a composer involves the construction of a musical work,[69] then, based on the above-mentioned meanings of the word *Drang*, it can be said that, with this title, Palmer not only seeks to describe his conception of musical meaning based on an 'ideal object' that he has in mind, but anticipates the performer's gestures, specific performing behaviour and the development of the performer's narrative. Hence, the title *Drang* creates a relational field for a composer-performer interaction already on the poietic level.

Seen as an impulse, urge, drive or pressure, the title *Drang* implies a strong emotional environment that places the passionate aspect above all the others in the projection of a musical idea. In *Drang*, an emotion (*"a complex experience of consciousness, bodily sensation, and behaviour that reflects the personal significance of a thing, an event, or a state of affairs"*)[70] is understood as a driving force behind the music and *in* the music.[71] The emotion of the composer as 'a complex experience' is embodied in the score, the title and the programme note. This understanding interacts with the experience of the performer and creates a new shared experience that manifests itself in the performance. The emotional state of the performance depends on many factors that include interpretation, practising, problem-solving methods, verification, and more, but it is the performer's own virtuosity that drives the degree of the emotional intensity in the real-time, onstage performing experience.

The composer emphasises the virtuoso character of the work. The programme note of the piece explicitly encourages the performer to play 'always virtuoso-like'. This is a very courageous composer's message, as the late 20th century has almost completely banned the notion of virtuosity in contemporary music from professional discussions. Instead of referring to a performance or a work as 'virtuoso', musicians prefer to talk in terms of extended techniques, difficulty, density, complexity, precision and plausibility of performance. One reason for this is that virtuosity is a very ambivalent notion and a difficult topic for academic research. Widely referred to in colloquial speech as a set of excellent skills and demonstration of superior technique in performance, the terms 'virtuosity' and 'virtuoso' do not have, so far, any stable academic definition. The Oxford bibliographies entry says about virtuosity and virtuoso that *"the precise meaning of the terms varies widely, although they generally encompass extraordinary skill, technical ability, and an element of display".*[72] It can be said, though, that virtuosity has been questioned from ethical, aesthetical and formal perspectives.[73] The development of interdisciplinarity and performance studies has contributed to increased interest in the topic, while the increase of practice-based and artistic research has opened new perspectives that hopefully will shed more light on the artistic aspect of this phenomenon.

Another reason why virtuosity has been almost excluded from contemporary music discourse is the heavy connection of this concept with the Romantic tradition and the romanticised image of a performer. The notion still evokes too many negative connotations, as has been evidenced throughout the history of music from the late 19th century onwards. Many

---

[68] A Discussion on *Drang* for Accordion, p. 211.

[69] Östersjö (2008:50).

[70] Solomon (1998).

[71] The scope of this study cannot address the issues of a psychological approach to music and emotion. See, for example, John A. Sloboda and Patrik N. Juslin *Music and Emotion* where the authors argue that the *"psychological approach to music and emotion [...] seeks an explanation of how and why we experience emotional reactions to music, and how and why we experience music as expressive of emotion"*. Juslin and Sloboda (2010:71).

[72] VanderHamm, David (see Bibliography).

[73] Jankélévitch (1979).

19th century composers like Beethoven, Schumann or Wagner spoke against the superficiality of performance at the expense of the meaning of music and defended 'true virtuosity' as a vehicle to transport a musical thought and its meaning.[74] John Palmer agrees with the classics:

"When I speak about virtuosity, I am not referring to a set of extraordinary instrumental skills. It's not about playing loud and fast! That kind of 'virtuosity' does not interest me. On the contrary, it leaves me cold. I find it shallow, pretentious, superficial and at times even ridiculous. My understanding of virtuosity is about a philosophical and emotional quality linked with the Promethean".[75]

This essay will return to the philosophical meaning that Palmer puts into the notion of virtuosity. But first, it is advantageous to draw a historical parallel that may shed light on the transcendence of virtuosity in the work's structure. Again, the assumptions are made on the information provided by the title and the programme note. The composer writes that the music is to be played *"with much Sturm und Drang character"*.[76] The only reference to the historical movement is the word 'character', a notion that does not imply any stylistic, structural or aesthetic connotation. Palmer explicitly confirms that, *"there is no direct relation to the historical movement apart from the meaning of the word: emotional urge, drive, impulse"*.[77] Still, the discussion on the origins of virtuosity can hardly avoid the historiographical perspective, as the roots of virtuosity in Western music go the musical culture of the 'Sturm und Drang' period. The genesis of keyboard virtuosity[78] in the 19th century, as described by Carl Dahlhaus, can be found in the evolution of free fantasy style that emerged at the end of the 18th century.[79] Represented primarily through characteristic and non-thematic passages of often improvised figurations ('Spielfiguren'[80]), the category of virtuosity introduced a new paradigm that emphasises the instrumental aspect in the production of musical meaning. This is the point where a clear analogy with *Drang* can be discovered; we have already seen how an instrument's nature reveals itself in the production of meaning in Palmer's work.

Another musical example that illustrates this historical analogy is the extensive use of the grace notes in *Drang*. As was the case with the air sounds, the composer intentionally places the grace notes in such contexts in which they would be exceedingly difficult to perform. Often combined with even rhythmical patterns (Fig. 7.6), air sounds (Fig. 7.7) and extreme dynamics (Fig. 7.8), they trigger the same gestural approach to the performance as do the other aspects that have been discussed in previous sections. The grace notes represent a kind of quasi-improvised, non-thematic instrumental material that contributes to the creation of an effect of the instantivity without hindering the dramatic flow of music.

---

[74] Schumann (1854).

[75] A Discussion on *Drang* for Accordion, p.211.

[76] Ibid.

[77] Ibid.

[78] The characteristics of violin virtuosity can be seen already in the 17th century.

[79] Dahlhaus (1980:110-117).

[80] *"Eine Möglichkeit, das Instrumentale in der musikalischen Textur zu analysieren, bieten die sogennanten Spielfiguren: Spielfigur wird hier eine Tonfigur gennant, die nach instrumentalen Kriterien entstanden zu sein scheint. Diese Charakterisierung ähnelt formal der eines Motivs, das auch in Beziehung zu einer bestimmten Art musikalisches Denkens und den damit verbundenen, geschichtlich veränderlichen äusseren Charakteristika definiert wird".* Mäkilä (1989).

Fig. 7.6: *Drang*, example of grace notes (1).

Fig. 7.7: *Drang*, example of grace notes (2).

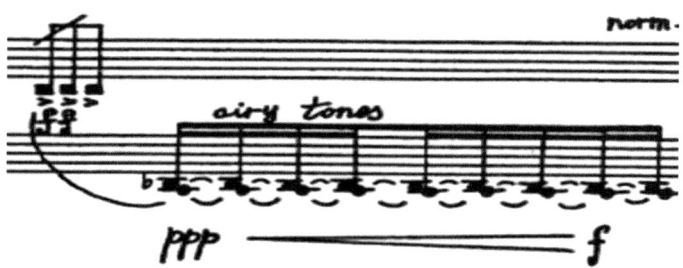

Fig. 7.8: *Drang*, example of grace notes (3).

The degree of instantivity of the performer's decisions that is responsible for the spontaneity of the performance is one of the most pertinent characteristics of virtuosity. But neither in historical perspective nor in contemporary music, can the performance virtuosity be limited to mere note figurations and their flawless execution. There must be another constitutive characteristic that empowers virtuosity as a 'Vehikel grosser Form'[81] (a vehicle to a larger form) and Dahlhaus sees it in the rhapsodic-expressive style of 'Sturm und Drang'. There would be little relevance in trying to apply an entire historiographical argumentation to Palmer's work, but the findings of Dahlhaus are important, not least because they have generated new questions. One of these questions is the relational field between virtuosity and instrumental timbre. As suggested by Helga de la Motte-Haber and Heinz von Loesch, virtuosity has drastically increased the role of timbre, the colourfulness of a musical process had become the purpose and not a tool of representation.[82]

Von Loesch goes one step further and states that neither timbre nor sound can be

[81] Dahlhaus (1980:110-111).
[82] De la Motte-Haber (2004:176).

considered separately as the central function of virtuosity, because it is impossible to sever a sound from its timbre. He suggests that the discourse about sound functions of virtuosity inevitably leads to structural aspects, as 20th century music was marked by increased attention to the integrity of sonic aspects that could be relevant to the structure of a composition.[83] It is then a sound with its unique timbral characteristics and not merely a thematic progression of tones that have been in the focus of virtuosity, at least in the 20th century. In other words, the development of virtuosity contributed to the awareness that what once was used to be a secondary facet of the music has become foregrounded. Concerning *Drang*, this confirms the assumption that it is not just the complex texture and technically demanding figurations that require a 'virtuoso-like' performance, but more importantly, it is the timbre, the sound and air production and the emphasis on the integrity of interaction between these. This integrity is a 'challenge to the impossible'; it is impossible to emphasise all the details and the interplay between them in a performance, but it is possible to *imagine* such a performance. Therefore, the emphasis on the integrity of interaction can be considered the characteristic that, from a historical perspective, enables virtuosity as a 'Vehikel grosser Form'. Hence, it is justified to argue that virtuosity is not only implied by the structure of *Drang*; it actually constitutes a part of the work's structure. This thesis indirectly echoes the legitimation of virtuosity by Theodor Adorno, who argues that *"the works of art that are deliberately conceived as a tour de force are semblance because they must purport in essence to be what they, in essence, cannot be"*.[84] Considering the distinction that Adorno makes between 'work' and 'performance', it is interesting to note that he sees in virtuosity 'the paradoxical essence of art' that *"should not confine itself to the reproduction of a work but should, rather, fully enter the facture [Faktur]"*.[85]

There is yet another piece of evidence that shows that virtuosity acts both structurally and performatively. The examples of air production, timbre transformation, complex texture and dynamics reveal the moment-bound nature of most of the performer's gestures. The object-status of music, represented by the score, implies its event-status as represented by the performance. The spontaneity of expression is thus considered as a score-based element; an aspect that is anticipated at the poietic level of the composer's work. We have just seen how virtuosity enables spontaneity of the performance in real time. Therefore, it is virtuosity that structures all the interrelated aspects contained by the score. All things considered, it is important to note that being a part of the work's structure, virtuosity remains a force that is not structural by nature, as echoed by the composer himself.[86] Therefore, it is not a postulate of this essay to attempt to structure virtuosity as such.

I have just tried to substantiate the notion of virtuosity in *Drang* in the context of historical connections with the 'Sturm und Drang' epoch. Drawing on recent studies on virtuosity, the transcendental nature of virtuosity has been explained as a force that reveals itself both on 'poietic' and 'aesthesic' levels. This attempt, however, would not be fully relevant to the topic of the research if not backed by the philosophical and emotional meaning that the composer puts into the notion of virtuosity:

"It reflects a compulsion, an irresistible urge to act in a certain way. It is pure dialectics unfolding in a confrontational discourse. In a world full of apathy, selfishness and disconnection from our humanity, any obstacle that comes across our life is an opportunity to advance our dignity as human and divine beings. Virtuosity epitomizes the courage needed to face the obstacle, the challenge to the impossible, the drive that will conquest adversity, the necessity of wanting to be

---

[83] Von Loesch (2004:14).
[84] Adorno (2002:106).
[85] Adorno (2002:279).
[86] A Discussion on *Drang* for Accordion, p.211.

better human beings, the bridge taking us onto lasting triumph, the impulse leading to the acquisition of self-knowledge through the dark night of the soul: the need to make God 'dangerous' again!"[87]

As poetic as John Palmer's own words on virtuosity might sound, they do precisely describe the actual musical meaning of the work and encourage the performer to think and act according to the musical narrative. More than that, everything that Palmer talks about in the cited passage is actually represented in the score! To match the emotional intensity of the composer's words with the verbal instructions of the score, here is a list of all the remarks written in the order in which they occur in the score:

'calmo, molto espressivo e drammatico, più mosso, rubato, all'improvviso, più mosso, sempre espressivo e drammatico, all'improvviso nervoso, calmo, quasi liberamente, esaggerato e sforzato, nervoso, incisivo e ben chiaro, molto rubato ma sempre avanti, avanti!, molto mosso, leggerissimo, sempre mosso e preciso, leggero, chiarissimo, piu lento, calmo, appassionatissimo (Sturm und Drang!), con slancio, rubato, con molto slancio leggerissimo, meno mosso, calmo, agitato, calmo, avanti, esaggerato, con slancio, calmo, calmo ma sempre vivace, sempre rubato, enfatico, martellato, pesante, leggero, fuggitivo, esaggerato, avanti, sempre avanti, drammatico, agitatissimo, violento, sempre impulsivo, preciso, riflessivo, con slancio, scuro pensoso, preciso, molto teso, più stringendo, sempre più stringendo, molto drammatico e teso, avanti, sempre teso, con tutta la forza, sempre teso ed esaggerato, come respiro irregolare e drammatico, più stringendo, sempre di più al fine'.[88]

This sequence of Italian words gives us a clear idea of the dramatic nature of the musical thought in *Drang* and communicates to us the composer's meaning of the word 'Drang'. These remarks sound no less dramatic than the composer's description of virtuosity. 'The challenge to the impossible' is the notion of Promethean; based on the definition, it may be understood as a reference to the creativity and willingness to risk in order to find new ways of creativity.[89] A parallel may also be drawn with the Adornian 'possibility of impossible', a notion that he attributed to virtuosity, as we have seen. But whereas Adorno focuses on the aesthetic and ethical dimension of virtuosity, Palmer associates 'challenge' with physical actions that are meant to be executed according to the symbolic representation provided by the score. These actions, to a large extent, determine the musical narrative of the performance in the way John Rink speaks about it: the performer follows the indications of the score and enacts a *"plot archetype, by shaping the unfolding tale on the spur of the moment"*.[90] In this sense, narrativity is seen as a poietic function of the performer and is based on *"the score-sound continuum"*[91] that includes the 'internalisation' of the score by the performer in a process that involves both rehearsals and performance. The continuous process *"entails both multi-level awareness—that is, multiple processing—and some sort of control over the flow of events"*.[92]

In *Drang*, virtuosity exaggerates the challenge of 'some sort of control', the process implied in the structure of the composition. The spontaneity of the interpretation, informed both by the 'instrumentality' surpassing the limits of the instrument and the emotional intensity of the performance, will transcend the accordionist's awareness of the performance creating a sense of courage that is needed not only to face an obstacle, but to *overcome* it as in

---

[87] A Discussion on *Drang* for Accordion, p. 211.
[88] Verbal instructions in the score of *Drang*.
[89] Cambridge English Dictionary, https://dictionary.cambridge.org/dictionary/english/promethean.
[90] Rink (2018:95).
[91] Rink (2018: 97).
[92] Rink (2018:99-100).

a real life situation where there is no way back to a previous existing condition. The performer's control over the flow of events becomes nearly discerned from the archetypes that were worked out at the process of score 'internalisation' and operates as to create the *"instantial variety with regard to some underlying framework."*[93] The awareness of this 'instantial variety' is essential and, as has just been shown, it depends on the performers' embodied knowledge of their instrument: the performance virtuosity. The embodiment plays an important role in this process, as the 'instantial variety' depends not only on the intellectual strategies (interpretative gestures) but also on the physical gestures that control the musical flow in its transition to the 'event-status'. Nicholas Cook argues that *"scores choreograph the performing body, but there is a gulf between symbol and body that is bridged by a combination of deeply internalized tacit knowledge on the one hand, and on the other the constant small decisions that are made in the real time of performance and monitored through aural feedback".*[94]

As we have seen, these 'small decisions' play an essential role in *Drang* and, among other factors, they are based on the way the performer approaches the instrument and the intensity of the performer's engagement with it. The tacit knowledge of the instrument is sensed through and with the body. It is an embodied knowledge that a performance transforms into explicit knowledge; at least it will be perceived as such from a listener's perspective. The manifestation of this embodied knowledge through the performance challenges every single symbol of the score and every 'plot archetype' of the performer, but it equally challenges the physical stamina of the performer. Virtuosity creates the situation in which every musical phenomenon points beyond itself by virtue of the associations and expectations it arouses, and by virtue of that from which it distances itself. This transcendence of the single musical elements is what is usually meant by the term 'content'.[95] Thus content emerges out of the performer's narrative. *"It [virtuosity] marks out a relational field in which text, instrument, performer and audience are all indispensable to defining significance".*[96]

On the contrary, a performance where a fast-stable-and-loud aspect is emphasised without justification cannot, in fact, be judged in terms of virtuosity, as the transformation from tacit to explicit knowledge does not happen during the performance; in such a case, it is the technical aspect of the performance that would prevail over the narrativity. The transformation of knowledge must be done at the stage of preparation, and the results of this process need to be as clear as possible. The machine-line mechanical realisation of the score will not leave space to the spontaneity of 'small decisions'. In the best-case scenario, a content would be created devoid of spontaneity in the performer's narrative, albeit reflecting the original musical idea of the composer. In the worst case, the performance would be limited to the mechanical reproduction of the sounds, lacking emotional or substantial musical meaning.

The musical idea of *Drang* provides a demonstrative legitimation of virtuosity as an agency that nurtures the collaborative aspect of creativity in the realisation of the musical content of the composition. The work of John Palmer is a representative example of how virtuosity interacts between humans, represented by the poietic meaning of the composer, the poietic and aesthesic function of the performer and the non-human agents of artistic processes as represented by the instrument and the score. It reveals the tension between the score, the performer and the instrument that arises from *"the novelty and the complexity of musical thought, and that imposes changes in the relationship with the instrument."*[97]

The specificity of *Drang* is that the conditions that allow the performer's narrative to emerge are conceived by the composer at the stage of the pre-compositional work. The

---

93 Rink (2018:95).
94 Cook (2018:117).
95 Adorno (1991:278).
96 Sampson (2003:2).
97 Osmond-Smith (1985:90-91).

unspoken impulses that guide the performer's gestures cannot be notated using mensural notation, but their development, enabled by the performer's virtuosity, is foreseen by the composer. The emphasis that John Palmer puts on the virtuoso aspect can be defined as an 'organic virtuosity', which Milton Babbitt describes as a virtuosity *"that must take into account the compositional materials of the work and the total sound ensemble. The elements of virtuosity are never separable from compositional considerations and are therefore never to be achieved as isolated instrumental accomplishments."* [98]

I hope this essay may have offered a step forward in the discussion of virtuosity approached from dissimilar, yet interrelated, perspectives. It could be anticipated that the combined use of artistic and scientific methods may reveal the importance of virtuosity from the listener's perspective, as well as sheding new light on the mechanics of the interaction between performers and their instruments in different performance environments. In 2020, Cat Hope and Louise Devenish published a manifesto on the new virtuosity.[99] This is evidence that the notion of virtuosity is still relevant in contemporary artistic discourse.

Regardless of the problematic contexts that the notion of virtuosity may evoke, it has always been considered an artistic occurrence par excellence, and, for this reason, its fully creative potential remains to be duly explored. For example, one could pursue this argument in the context of current research focusing on collaborative and co-creative aspects of music. Thanks to the methodology provided by empirical musicology and artistic research, many old notions are now being reassessed and defined anew. However, even by disregarding further research and the questions that have been directly or indirectly triggered by this writing, John Palmer's *Drang* remains an outstanding example of how compositional, philosophical and emotional practice can foster new and enriching perspectives on the old notion of virtuosity.

JOHN PALMER: COMPOSER, PERFORMER, IMPROVISER
Agnese Toniutti

AT. Your approach to music manifests itself through multiple points of view: composition, interpretation, improvisation. I would like to take advantage of this peculiarity of your career and look more deeply into some relationships between these experiences. What is the background to this multiplicity? Did these skills all begin at the same time or have they followed an order of development and investigation, starting from a specific exploration and then evolving to other interests?

JP. Regarding my background, I should say that my first contact with music occurred through improvisation. By the age of four or five, I could invent simple tunes on the piano and play back the songs I heard on the radio. Composition and interpretation came later. In my teens, these three approaches to music were interacting in a most natural way: whether I was playing Chopin on the piano, playing progressive rock as a keyboard player, or writing songs. Composition went already hand-in-hand with performance. There was no clear-cut connection between these activities, and improvising was an important part of composing. The two activities were two facets of music-making. My early compositions in the seventies were born from improvisations and were partly written out and partly improvised, much like in jazz. The background was a result of a variety of genres I listened to as a child. After playing a nocturne by Chopin or a minuet by Bach or Mozart, for example, I wanted to compose and play my own

---

[98] Babbitt (2011:222).
[99] Hope and Devenish (2020).

nocturne and minuet straight away. When I heard a song on the radio, I wanted to write my own song immediately; the same applied to the jazz pieces I would come across. This was the joy I felt by making music. There was no distinction between composing, improvising and interpreting.

This pleasure was triggered by a strong curiosity to understand particularly the harmonic fabric of songs and instrumental pieces. Classical, jazz, pop, rock and folk triggered in me the same desire to find out how music composition works in terms of melodic, harmonic, rhythmic fabric and form; but above all, harmony was my favourite thing. I can truly say that I learned classical harmony by listening to songs and recreating them on the piano by trial and error. Though I didn't know the technical names, by the age of 12, I already knew all the harmonic combinations of tonal classical music. For example, I perceived the effect of a deceptive cadence for the first time by playing the first three chords of *Let It Be* by the Beatles, in 1969. I still remember reconstructing the harmony of that song at the organ and becoming aware of the V-VI progression on the second and third chord as a form of cheating my expectation of an ordinary V-I progression falling on the word *'Mother Mary'*. A revelation of this kind would be a pure delight to me, and it was at that time that I began to love the psychology of tonal harmony.

Another strong memory I have is my reaction to Neapolitan Sixth and Secondary Dominant chords that I would hear in certain songs of the 1950s and 1960s. I also remember very vividly the bliss I experienced when I heard the fourth chord of the song *Thunderball* in the James Bond film in 1965 for the first time. I remember getting goosebumps. It was a root-position Neapolitan chord that injected so much dramatic thrill into the melody of the song. This is just to say that curiosity, listening, composition and improvisation occurred and evolved at the same time in my life. When I resumed classical music studies at the age of 19, my perception of composition, improvisation and interpretation entered a deeper level of discovery. I also began to perform music by living composers which fascinated me both as a pianist and composer. I studied piano pieces by J.S. Bach, the classic and romantic composers in a critical way. At the same time, I began to play and analyse piano music by Claude Debussy and Bill Evans, Beethoven, Schönberg, Webern and Henry Cowell. There was no historical chronology in my classical training. This new impact on classical music covered a wide range of literature from the late Renaissance to contemporary music. By playing music by other composers, interpretation became a major concern, and this surely refined my own piano playing. In 1987, I was performing pieces of mine, jazz standards and music by Frescobaldi Byrd, Haubenstock-Ramati, Cowell, Stockhausen, Cage and other 20th century composers.

AT. First of all, and beyond any formal definition, what does composition mean in your life? What is the pleasure of writing music? Why compose?

JP. To me, composing is an attempt to claim my own divinity. It's about reclaiming the Self in me. When I write music, I experience my own higher Self in action. It feels like a stone thrown into a lake where the effect of its impact ripples on and on. It expands my awareness of life and myself. Writing music is much more than a pleasure. Music expresses my poetics of growth as a man. It reflects a search for something invisible that wants to become audible. When I compose, I feel like getting closer to eternity: my mind dives into a flow of time that leads me into an abstract, non-linear perception of time where past, present and future seem to merge. I perceive this as a revelation of my true Self, untouched by the tyranny of chronological time: unspoiled and authentic. I compose because I want to plunge into my shadows, desires, and most intimate intuitions; I want to feel yearning and bliss, the struggles and hopes of the human race. Music leads me to experience uncharted territories of the mind, an abyss that is both dangerous and sublime, unpredictable and uncertain; a mirror of myself that can be entered only with a fearless attitude. W.B. Yeats once said, *"Man needs reckless courage to descend into the abyss of himself."* Art for me is a gateway to this abyss. Descending into the abyss means to discover the meaning of my existence, and this is why music, and more specifically composing music, is for me a powerful exploration of the subconscious: a cathartic experience.

AT. At the same time, why improvise? What does it awaken in you? What does it give you in terms of existential needs?

JP. To be very honest, I have never really related to the word 'improvisation'. It still sounds strange to me today. I suspect this notion derives from an intellectual/academic insolence of wanting to separate what has been written down on paper from what has not, to be specific: what is to be taken seriously, and what not. I have grown tired of this compartmentalisation! When I sit at the piano and begin to play, I never think that I am now going to improvise: I just play! What I play flows from myself free from any planning or pre-established route. The notes I play show me the way to go. It is a most natural activity that stems from a desire to listen to this very moment, listen to what my inner voice has to reveal at this precise point in time. During the unfolding of this uncharted journey, I experience myself through the mirror of sound; I enter doors leading to unknown places in my mind where I can experience altered shades of consciousness. This is probably one reason why I 'improvise'. Diving into the music of the moment is like entering unknown areas of the soul where I can touch and unearth unpredicted aspects of myself. By entering this inner space without a pre-established intention or sense of direction, I reunite with my Self in the most immediate way. This is why, to me, music is the strongest manifestation of awareness. When I play, freed from any fixed idea, I am subconsciously searching for unity with my inner voice.

AT. The piano is your 'native' instrument. How does the physicality of style-specific piano playing affect your improvisations? For example, a pianist specialised in Baroque repertoire develops a technique that is quite different from the technique required by the Romantic or impressionistic repertoire. In this sense, has your pianistic background affected your improvisational choices? If yes, how?

JP. When I started to play the piano, I first improvised in the pop and jazz idioms and my piano technique was minimal. I began to interpret classical pieces later on, from the age of 20 onwards. The standard classical piano training was a massive gain for me, and the various techniques I learnt helped improve my sensitivity for sound production enormously. From D. Scarlatti and J.S. Bach through to W.A. Mozart, I learnt how to produce the clarity and lightness of touch that typifies the Baroque and Classical repertoires. Studying the harpsichord as a second instrument enhanced the lightness of my touch even further. From Beethoven to Scriabin, I learnt how to achieve 'bigger' sounds and pronounce the importance of harmonic progressions. From Debussy and Ravel, I learnt how to use the piano as a colouristic instrument. From Henry Cowell to John Cage, I learnt to use the piano as a source of new and more daring sounds. All these experiences improved my understanding of the instrument. The acquisition of historically-informed touches and articulations contributed to my improvisational skills, not only in terms of technique, but also as compositional vehicles that would allow me to create a larger palette of sounds instantaneously. For example, controlling a gradual or sudden transition from one texture to another: this is a feature that occurs often in my piano playing. A light touch would inspire me in playing 'staccato' passages monophonically or polyphonically, or I would make a more confident use of dynamic nuances in order to create stronger contrasts in my playing. I think the piano collection *Musica*

Reservata exemplifies this variety of touch, phrasing, articulation and stylistic textures rather clearly.

AT. When you improvise, is there only one behavioural process at stake, or several? I mean this in terms of the unfolding of the music, how you establish the succession of the phrases, choose the chords, and so on.

JP. There may be different processes at stake, and each one may involve a different methodology. But to be very frank with you, when I 'improvise' I don't think in terms of process, at least not consciously: I just open myself to the unpredictable. A phrase follows another because I allow it to be so: I let it flow. The use of harmonic patterns, for instance, goes hand-in-hand with the evolution of the music. I usually don't plan it. Of course, this evolution will include a process of some kind, but this is both irregular and variable because it relies solely on the immediate perception of what I am playing at a specific point in time. A process is also a result of my response to *what* I am playing and can potentially lead anywhere. It is up to my intuition to trace a path that makes sense and follow a route without knowing where it will lead me. On the other hand, it is also true that I *can* plan the direction of my journey in advance, or during the playing, if I wanted to. What I mean is that I can equally pre-establish points of departure and arrival and determine what types of textures I want to play at specific moments during the unfolding of the music. This practice can be very useful, but not necessary. It is certainly more defined and may produce a clearer structure and a more perceivable form. When I let go of any pre-conceived idea and dive into the music, everything becomes more hazardous and I have to swim with the tide, as it were. Actually, I think any experienced improviser will integrate both approaches in the most natural way.

AT. What intellectual, auditory, kinesthetic faculties does improvisation involve?

JP. If by 'intellect', you mean the faculty to think in an intelligent way, the intellect plays an important role in keeping what I am playing within an intelligible form, one that can be perceived as cohesive. In this sense, the intellect is important. The auditory faculties are of paramount significance: I have to be listening very carefully to what I am playing in order to react to it in the most musical way. Without a highly-focused form of listening, whatever I play may easily fall apart. The reactive mechanism is of fundamental importance because every nerve, muscle and joint of the body is responding to what I am hearing and playing, reacting to my intuition and preparing for the next decision. Everything is happening within split seconds and the body has to be very responsive to anything that is taking place during the performance, whether it is an interval, a chord, a rest, a melody. It is like an inner orchestra where feelings, thoughts, muscular movements and neural connections are interacting with the sound that is being played and, at the same time, making the next decision. Quite an extraordinary circumstance if you think…

AT. How is improvisation related to your emotions?

JP. Very much. Without the emotional charge, what I play would sound flat and lifeless. My music is essentially emotional, whether it is notated or not.

AT. During a performance or a listening experience, I sometimes experience what I call a state of 'presence' that paradoxically suggests a state of 'absence'. In this unique moment, my listening is highly focused: I can silence any thought that may come across my mind and

enter a deeper responsiveness to the music. Does this happen to you while you are improvising?

JP. If by a state of 'presence' you mean a deep level of awareness, well yes, that happens to me all the time because I am fully concentrated on what I am playing. When I play the piano, I don't think of anything else: I am immersed in the music. The notion of being linked to an experience of absence fully resonates with me. If my focus is so present, my ego must be absent. This apparent contradiction implies that presence and absence are but two sides of the same reality. This is the union of opposites, the *Coincidentia Oppositorum* that C.G. Jung describes as a necessity for complementarity and mental balance. It is also the concept of non-duality in Zen meditation. The full awareness of the present moment unconditioned by external events can take place only if all the other activities of the mind are absent. In order for this consciousness of listening to take place, a kind of 'universal void' must be accessed uncompromisingly. In this sense, the practice of improvisation may be compared to a game of absence/presence, appearing/disappearing, emptiness/fullness where the improviser is converting something essentially undefinable into a sonic reality.

AT. Do you have any kind of routine or ritual during the preparation of your improvisation sessions?

JP. The only things I need before I begin to play the piano are a clean and silent environment, and a silent heart. I need an empty mind; I need to feel centred and in peace with myself.

AT. What is your definition of 'composing'? Is it a creative process clearly distinct from improvising, or do you find analogies between the two?

JP. The difference is essentially delineated by the restriction of time. When we improvise, we are composing instantly and what we play cannot be changed anymore. When we compose, we have time to plan the music we have in mind: we take time to define a form and a set of relationships between textural components like metre, pitch and so on. A combination of the two occurs when I define in advance the routes of my improvisation either in my mind or in writing, or when I write down and revise an improvisation.

AT. In your catalogue of piano works I notice seven titles that are defined as 'improvised composition/composed improvisation'. How is this ambiguity articulated? What do you mean exactly?

JP. The difference is subtle and includes a hint of irony, but it is also related to what I have just said. What I want to convey is that an improvisation is an instant form of composition and that a composition may be the result of an improvisation. If you listen to musicians who only improvise, you may often get the feeling of weakness of form about what they are playing, or perhaps a deliberate desire to plunge into chaos, where the anarchy of sound-events establishes the rationale of the music. The problem with aleatory music is that since everything is left to chance, it is impossible to establish relationships between the sonic events. Our cognitive faculties cannot relate to this kind of music because our brain functions in terms of integration and segregation of the information that is being heard. But integration and segregation cannot take place in the brain if relationships of pitch, timbre, duration and form are missing in the music. I personally think, hear and play as a traditional composer in that my notions of 'improvised composition' and 'composed improvisation' are implying a form of the music that is intelligible, and therefore possible for the listener to relate to. When I write *Composed*

Improvisation, I imply a piece whose form was delineated in my mind before playing the piano. I have an a-priori idea of what I am going to do and the composer in me is guiding the pianist. When I write *Improvised Composition*, I am putting a slight emphasis on the pianist who is leading the game.

AT. Some of the pieces of 'improvised composition/composed improvisation' have an audio recording, and others do not. Is there a score in both cases that can make it possible for other performers to perform? Are there other pieces in your catalogue that have a connection with the improvisational process?

JP. The inclusion of audio recording on my website is a dilemma I haven't resolved yet. I find the internet has raised serious questions about intellectual property and copyright issues and this is too big a subject to be discussed here. You ask about a score: most of my 'improvisations' were born without a written score. Each time I play them again, they will obviously sound different, but the composer in me remembers in most cases the main components of the piece. In order to make these pieces available to other pianists, I have written out the score of what I played in the first place and fixed the piece on paper, as it were. The scores of *Musica Reservata, Manhattan, Athena* and *Shambhala*, amongst others, are the result of this practice. This kind of transcription can be extremely tedious and time-consuming. Think of the music of *Musica Reservata* and *Manhattan* as a case in point.

I have also produced scores that supply only the basic information of the piece, similar to a jazz score where the pianist has to improvise on the given harmonic material. The risk with this practice is that you never know what the pianist is going to play, and to me, this remains a major problem with many classical pianists who do not have a culture of improvisation: they are used to interpreting what has been written in a score instead of *creating* music from a set of given information. There are other cases where a score doesn't make much sense and I prefer to leave the audio recording as an aural document of the music. If a score is available, I likely will have invested some time in writing down and 'editing' the music. There are other cases where I am planning to produce a score transcription with the help of a software program. I am told this reproduction can be very accurate for simple piano pieces, and I am planning to try it out soon with a piece called *Remembering*. I should also add that most of my 'improvisations' are not known to the public. I have many recordings that are still in my archives and remain unreleased to this date. There are pieces that are not even listed in my catalogue because I am too critical about making them public at this stage.

AT. As a performer myself, I know that bringing the composer's musical idea to life is a process of great complexity. When you transcribe an improvisation, how do you choose a specific set of indications that will convey your musical idea to the performer as effectively as possible?

JP. I choose the indications according to the nature of the music I have played. I record the music, or I keep playing it again and again, knowing that there will always be differences each time I play it. The indications can be very exact or looser, depending on the music genre. If the texture is pointillistic, for example, I would make sure that the indications are as accurate as possible. If the music is closer to jazz, I would use fewer indications, but expect the performer to know how to inject that jazz 'feel' (syncopations, agogic accents, inflexions, grace notes, mannerisms) into the music. If the character is of a meditative nature, my indications will be focused on resonance, time and colour.

In pieces like *Musica Reservata, Manhattan, Athena, Eulogy* and *Shambhala*, we are dealing with improvised compositions that I felt to be convincing enough to deserve to be performed as accurately as possible by other pianists. To you, the question of whether the music was initially improvised may not be relevant. For them, it is now a piano piece like many others. When I decide to write down my improvisations as exactly as possible, I am thinking as a composer. This means that the information I am fixing on paper is focussed on the textural relationships of the music as meticulously as possible: how harmonies, melodies, rhythms and any kind of structural proportions including phrasing and articulation relate to each other in my improvisation and whether I can possibly improve them during the process of transcription. (I can reconstruct all this by listening to a recording or/and playing the piece again on the piano). The representation of the music in the score may sometimes be more accurate than what I have played in the first place because I have had that extra time-factor that has allowed me to listen to the music while transcribing it. I will do some editing, improving details here and there: it is now the composer in me who is listening to the music from an objective and critical position. The same happens if I played the 'same' improvisation (which in any case won't ever be the same!) a second time.

You can get an idea of what I am saying if you compare the first recording of *To the Night (1)* and *To the Night (2)* from *Musica Reservata* to the first score, and more importantly, if we compare the first score to the final score. The differences can be significant. Again, to the pianists who want to perform the piece, what I am discussing now may not be of relevance. They will study the score and perform the music with the same dedication they will study and play any piano piece. I remember that in the first score of the *Musica Reservata* pieces, I often notated only the theme of each piece while leaving the development to the pianist. But when I heard other pianists playing from it, the results were so unacceptable to my ears that I decided to write out the score myself as precisely as possible.

If I include aleatory moments in the score, I am establishing a different relationship between composer and interpreter. This relationship must take into account all the risks that may result from the pianists' understanding of the music and their performance skills. An extreme case is when a score consists only of few verbal, or graphic, indications. In this case, it is the performers who are totally responsible for the music. Their performance may be excellent or very poor, but the title of the piece and the name of the composer will remain the same. In my experience, this is a very problematic situation. In the 1990s, I performed John Cage's, Haubenstock-Ramati's and Karlheinz Stockhausen's indeterminate pieces and, at some point, I decided to stop performing these works because I realised that the music I was playing was actually mine, not theirs. And this didn't feel right to me. I felt cheated because I was effectively playing a Palmer piece, not Cage's or Stockhausen's. I was the author of the music I was playing, but the composer's name on the concert programme was another one. When I realised this, I felt a lack of respect towards my musicianship, as if the composer was taking advantage of my pianistic and compositional skills while getting all the benefit from the musical result. By the same token, I stopped creating scores of this kind after the *Now* series of the 1990s for cello and piano. In fact, I am planning to re-write the scores of these pieces in the near future.

AT. I have personally worked with you and appreciated our musical exchange very much. Do you enjoy working with performers? How helpful is your own performance experience when dealing with them? Do you think that performers who are trained to improvise can more easily connect with your music?

JP. I *love* collaborating with performers who are willing to share the magic of music with curiosity, respect and enthusiasm! I don't appreciate working with egotistical performers. My own experience as a performer and improviser is a big asset when I work with performers because it gives me a first-hand understanding of what they are doing. This enables us to work faster and find the most musical solution to the interpretation of the piece. And yes, if performers can improvise, this is a bonus that can only facilitate their understanding of this kind of music. However, I am not sure if a musician *can* be trained in improvisation, but that's another matter! I have worked with pianists who played my 'improvised compositions' pieces without having experience or interest in improvisation. As I said earlier, for these kinds of performers it doesn't really matter if the music was originally improvised or not. They will simply relate to the (finished) score the same way they relate to any other score of classical music.

AT. I am intrigued by the genesis of your piano piece *Athena*: in the programme note you write that you wrote the piece *"perhaps in a state of trance"*, and that it resurfaced to your (auditory?) consciousness several years later, without the help of any notation. I have the impression that some of the themes we talked about above can be condensed here. Is that so?

JP. In the 1980s, I experienced recurrent dreams where the Greek goddess Athena would speak to me. In those days I was living in Switzerland and going through a very difficult time in my life; I was swallowed by the intensity of a deep personal and artistic crisis and was on the verge of giving up music altogether. In these dreams, Athena would whisper to me words of comfort and support. I experienced similar situations during the daytime when I would go into a kind of trance, or perhaps, daydream; I would experience an intense sensation that Athena was with me. Somewhere, in some obscure corners of my mind, I sensed (not 'heard') a gentle and very subtle kind of music wanting to come out of myself. Unlike in the case of *Spirits*, where the music was heard in my dreams, in *Athena* I decided what notes to write and how and where to write them according to a sort of spell I was feeling like being under. By 'spell', I mean a circumstance of enchantment where you experience yourself transported into another, undefinable dimension. The music I played was very vivid at that time, but then it suddenly vanished from my consciousness, as if being swept away from my memory altogether. Then, in 2013, the memory of this music resurfaced in my mind during a recording session and without any conscious relation to what I was doing or playing at the time. I promptly decided to record it and notate it as accurately as I could. I cannot explain further what exactly happened to me, how and why it happened. The only thing I know is that it happened the way I have described it. Carl Gustav Jung speaks of the artist translating archetypal motifs into artistic form. If we look at music from this perspective, any musical work reflects an expression of the subconscious, may it be personal or collective. The subconscious is always present in our life.

FROM THE PIANO TO THE SCORE AND BACK:
TO THE NIGHT (1) AND *TO THE NIGHT (2)* FROM *MUSICA RESERVATA*
Agnese Toniutti

The aim of this essay is to examine some aspects of the relationship between composition, improvisation and performance in John Palmer's work *Musica Reservata* for solo piano. This is a collection of twelve piano pieces *"composed mostly during the night"* from December 1988 to May 1989 as the composer states in the programme note of the score. The awareness of the particular genesis of two of these pieces, *To the Night (1)* and *To the Night (2)*, will help any pianist interested in Palmer's piano music to shed light on the connection between performance-related issues, composition and notation. As a classically trained pianist, I have experienced the paradox of musical ideas and notation on several occasions. Although a score remains the most reliable vehicle for the transmission of the compositional thought to the performer, it is often inadequate and incomplete as a set of instructions related to the musical idea of a work. A score can be compared to a traditionally codified time-machine that allows us to get in touch with the masterpieces of the past. It is an invaluable object resembling an X-ray of the musical idea, a pale image of imaginary sounds of great importance that can present singular levels of inaccuracy in the conveyance of a musical concept. Yet, it is possible to reach a compromise between an imaginary and a physical reality lying between the inspiration of the composer and the effectiveness of a medium whose function is to put an interpreter in the position to achieve a performance. Any paradoxical situation is a potential for a solution, and it is often in the gap of information that the seeds of inspiration can eventually emerge.

In the past century, the exploration of this grey area has prompted many performers and composers to create a considerable number of graphic scores, including aleatory performances and happenings. With reference to both traditional and unconventional musical writings, a useful preparation for a performance is the collection of any available information that will help delineate a context in which an interpreter can have ample scope for informed decision making. In the classical repertoire, the help of historical musicology and performance practice remains a reliable reference upon which a set of performance-related attitudes can be duly based. This kind of information, although not specified in a score, will often be orally transmitted from a teacher directly to a student. In the case of a living composer, the situation is different. Besides deciphering the idiomatic language of the composer, a performer can have direct access to the original source of information. The fact that a musical work may have little or no performing tradition at all can turn out to be an advantage for the interpreters, because it will put them in a decision-making position where freedom and responsibility can become the major assets for a first-hand, 'historically-correct' realisation of the performance.

I believe it is always a good idea to begin a study of this kind by examining the background of a composer first. In the case of John Palmer, this will turn out to be crucial. Palmer's lifetime experience as an improvising pianist in virtually all musical genres is a major factor to be considered when approaching some of his piano works.[100] An initial look at the score of *Musica Reservata* will give the same impression one gets from any traditional piano score. But it is the programme note that should put the reader on the alert:

"*Musica Reservata* is a collection of 12 short pieces for solo piano composed from December 1988 to May 1989, mostly during the night. It may also be performed by two pianists on two pianos by playing two different pieces or indeed the same piece simultaneously. In my performances of Musica Reservata I have often included improvisation as an integral part of each piece, after or during the exposition. However, such a practice is not compulsory. Each piece of Musica Reservata may also be performed alone, as an autonomous, self-contained piece.
The title refers to the notion of Musica Reservata mentioned by Adrian Petit Coclico, a pupil of Josquin des Prez, who coined the word in the preface to his book Compendium musices (Nuremberg, 1552). Although there is no consensus on the meaning of the term, we know that it must have referred to music that made use of chromaticism and voice leading as devices for stressing emotions in motets and madrigals of the 16th century. Musica reservata also referred to music performed in small circles such as the aristocratic courts of that time, implying a sense of intimacy and inwardness.
Musica reservata may also be played on the harpsichord.*"

Very often, for John Palmer, 'intimacy and inwardness' means simply sitting at the piano and

---

[100] This does not hold true for all piano works. See *John Palmer: Composer, Performer, Improviser*, p. 229.

improvising, or even imagine of doing so.[101] The music of *Musica Reservata* springs from a compositional process that is a sort of 'keeping track' of some intimate moments in order to be able to return to them again and again; this is done by the means of improvisation or by using memory as a form of 'inner dialogue' with the music itself as explained later. The genesis of *To the Night (1)* and *To the Night (2)* is a case in point that will help us understand how an emblematic compositional process of this kind takes place.

These two short pieces were written on the same night, 30th April 1989. They constitute the core of the entire collection and indeed, define the musical character of *Musica Reservata*.[102] Although the original manuscripts are no longer available, luckily for us, the photocopies of the original hand-written scores have survived to this day. As it happens, they had been used by the composer for an arrangement for two pianos he made at the end of 1989 for a performance that took place at the Conservatoire of Lucerne, in Switzerland.[103] It would be useful for the reader to know that the original titles of these two pieces were *First Night-Thought* and *Second Night-Thought* whereas the ordinal number 'first' was shortened by the composer using the German abbreviation form '1.' (meaning '1st') and '2.' (meaning '2nd'). In the photocopy of the original manuscript, therefore, you will read the titles *1. Night Thought* and *2. Night Thought*. In order to avoid possible confusion arising from the similarities of these titles, throughout this article I will consistently use the final titles of *To the Night (1)* and *To the Night (2)*. The arrangement of the piano-duo version of 1989 has made it possible for the composer to keep the original scores of these two short pieces all these years, and this has turned out to be very helpful for my analysis.

What follows is a comparative overview of both pieces by discussing some of the most noticeable similarities and dissimilarities that can be found when looking at the original and the published score. Below you can see the original and final scores of both pieces, one following the other. Figs. 7.9 and 7.10 refer to *To the Night (1)*. We should not forget that both photocopies of the original manuscript were used for the piano duo performance mentioned earlier. The red squares were made by the composer explicitly to indicate the most important material to be used by each pianist for this performance.

By looking at the two scores, you will notice a number of changes and refinements that have been undertaken in the texture of the final version. These improvements mainly address the notation of rhythms, metric changes (as in bars 11 and 19 of the new score), melodic lines and articulation. Although the essence of the pitch content remains the same, the final score shows a more elegant execution of harmonic prolongation reinforced by syncopation and a more condensed execution of the simple polyphony. An example of this can be seen in the three final bars of both scores. Compare the end of the final score with the end of the original score and you will notice the importance of rhythmic compression in relation to the wider sense of space achieved by exaggerating the rhythm-duration paradigm. Refer to the notation of the final motif in bars 20-22 and compare it to the final two bars of the original score.

---

[101] Conversation with John Palmer, May 2021: the composer told me that *some* of the pieces in *Musica Reservata* were 'improvised in the mind' while walking at the lake of Lucerne and notated later when he was back home.

[102] Conversation with John Palmer, May 2021.

[103] The date of the performance was 11th December 1989, and the second pianist was Peter Färber.

Fig. 7.9: *Musica Reservata,* original score of *To the Night (1).*

239

7. to the night (1)

30.4.1989

Fig. 7.10: *Musica Reservata,* final score of *To the Night (1).*

The sense of time is another major difference that can be noticed clearly. Compare, for example, the semibreve chord in bar 4 in the final score with bar four of the original score where the same chord (A minor, without D3) loses its importance as it is integrated into the crochet motion, setting the pace for the unfolding of the melody. By comparing both scores, one can see that the final score contains small diminutions of pitch material in order to emphasise space and resonance. The advent of compression-expansion logic evidently gives an enhanced form of breathing space that is missing in the first score. In bar nine of the old score, the E5 is repeated five times. Bar 11 in the new score shows the same E5 but played three times within a metric change of 3/4; this is paradoxically more directional in its resolution to E minor with an unresolved fourth suspension (the low A) in its second inversion. A renewed sense of tranquillity here is highlighted by tiny signs of contrast, rather than similarity, that bring out subtle but decisive changes of perception of the harmonic fabric of the thin polyphony. Indeed, polyphonic writing is more elaborated. Notice, for example, how the G3-G4 octave on the second beat of the third bar in the first score becomes a ninth (G3-A4) in the final score. A similar change occurs in bar five in both scores where the B2-B4 octave on the third beat of the old score becomes a tenth (G4-B5) in the new score, thus reinforcing the root of the tonal centre on G (this is also the reduction of the rhythmic motion in the old score).

The same refinement is evident when comparing the second beat of bar 10, the A3-A4 octave, with the second beat of bar 13 in the new score, where the A3 is now a C4 resulting in a more elegant voice-leading resolving on the 'fermata' on the third beat. The D3-G4 dyad on the third beat becomes a G major triad (second inversion) with the addition of B3 on the fourth beat, confirming the G major feel that is hanging in the air. The more meditative character depicted by the final score is accomplished by similarly changing small but important details. This can be seen in the repetition of the tritone F4-B4 in bars 15 and 16 of the old score disappearing in bar 19 of the new score, thus creating a sense of tranquillity that seems to be of less concern in the first version of the music. By looking at the detailed phrasing, tempo, pedal and articulation marking, it is clear that the composer must have felt compelled to specify as many details as possible that would give any other pianist a closer idea of the music he had in mind. Compared to the final version, the first score comes across as a set of very basic instructions (including only pitch) that relies entirely on the performer's knowledge of the composer's idiom and aesthetics.

A similar transformation can be noticed by comparing the two versions of *To the Night (2)* (Figs. 7.11 and 7.12) and investigating the details that show the more 'tactile' nature of the new score. Sometimes, an interval change may suffice to render a melodic flow more elastic and a harmonic texture more intriguing. The piece fluctuates between the Aeolian mode (in A) and the lesser-used Dorian mode (in D). Like in the previous piece, the writing of both polyphonic parts is very thin and airy so as to express a kind of contemplative serenity that can only be experienced during the night. The gentle diatonicism of the two parts is suddenly contrasted by an unexpected minor second occurring in bar seven of both versions, in the Ab3-G4 and the end of the triplet, prolonged by the fermata, as if wanting to confirm its importance. In the first beat of the same bar, the A3-E3 falling fourth played 'portato' in the first score is changed into an A3-D3 falling fifth in the new score, of which the D3 functions as a false leading note to the E3 on the second beat. In fact, the D3-E3 in the new score is nothing more than the same D3-E3 interval in the fourth bar but compressed. Further, the D3 is now reinforcing the appearance of the short C major feel on the second beat (E3-G4-C5) leading to the chromatic clash at the end of the triplet. Similarly, in the following bar, the Eb3 that occurred twice in the old score is avoided in the new score by introducing a D3 instead. The harmonic implications of this alteration are very relevant as they emphasise the G major chord (D3-G3-B2), creating a solid harmonic ground that was missing in the first score (as compared to the perfect fourth E4-A4 in the treble clef).

In bar 15 of the original score, G3 is played three times, and in the new score, only once. This reduction is a major device for the expansion of the original harmonic field, from G-A-D-E to G-A-B-D-E, and for widening the pitch range by adding A2 (rather than A3!) in the bass clef, a more sophisticated bass line. But this is not only a matter of register expansion per se, as the A2-E3 fifth at the end of the bar turns out to be the exact mirror of the G4-D5 fifth that is being held in the treble clef.

Another change of melodic motion can be detected in bar 17 where the simultaneous E3-E4 octave on the last beat in the old score is changed into a delayed D3-E4 major ninth in the new version, reinforcing the unexpected chromaticism introduced by the appearance of Ab4 and Ab2. Similar to the previous example, this introduction is not casual and should not be considered as a one-dimensional form of adjusting an octave into a ninth. In fact, there is much more to it. The G4-Ab4 minor second that was introduced linearly on the first two beats is effectively mirrored twice: by the G3-Ab2 (the fourth and fifth note in the bass clef), and transposed onto the Db5-D3 minor ninth on the third and fourth beat. By keeping the polyphonic lines thin and flowing, the composer creates a stronger harmonic cohesion within the same bar, so that the D-E-F-G-Ab harmonic block is strengthened and counter-balanced by the Ab-B-C-Db-D-E block.

The importance of this newly-created harmonic tension is twofold, as it connects perfectly to the more elegant and stretched ending of the piece. Indeed, it is the end of the piece that epitomises the composer's incessant search for richer harmonic content articulated by simple but effective intervallic changes. This is irrevocably confirmed by the 'allargando' motion reinforced by the resonance (triggered by the sustain pedal) in order to achieve a half cadence kind of suspension. It is interesting to notice that the enigmatic chord E-D-G-G#-A-C-F[104] is a fusion of the two preceding harmonic blocks and projects the transparency of the subtle polyphony onto a wider final space.

The composer's preoccupation with providing additional textural information, such as 'fermatas', 'tempo' and 'rubato' indications, compression and expansion of melodic and harmonic content in both pieces, is but a reflection of his own interpretation of these pieces. As he confirmed to me in one of our discussions, in the original score the information provided was reduced to a minimum. In both pieces, spatial expansion, achieved by the introduction of 'fermatas', the extension of note values and additional bars, stands as an important feature that allows the music to 'breathe' better and enjoy the perception of the subtle chromaticism introduced at several points in the scores. Other examples of this feature can be seen in bars 4, 10 and 12 of *To the Night (1)*. Anticipation and syncopation are also employed effectively in bars 15, 16, 17 and 20 of the same piece, and in bars four, five and 13 of *To the Night (2)*. Overall, the polyphonic setting of the final version remains simple, resembling a Two or Three-Part Invention by J.S. Bach with few harmonic blocks. The spirit is very similar if not the same.

As for the performative aspects of the piece, one could be surprised when listening to the first recording of both pieces played by the composer at the piano and the harpsichord, and to the recording of the performance of the piano-duo version in 1989. First of all, the solo piano recording doesn't include *"improvisation as an integral part of each piece, after or during the exposition"*,[105] at least not as I would have imagined. There was neither melodic variation nor harmonic development in these interpretations. Palmer played all the notes as written in the score without adding any ornamentation or improvisation on the chordal sequences. On the other hand, the interpretation was extremely expressive, emotionally dense and rich in agogics, phrasing, articulation details, rhythmic variations and tempo changes: all of which made a lot of musical sense. As you can imagine, none of these details were written in the initial score.

---

[104] More specifically, E2, D4, G4, G#4, A4, C5, F5.
[105] Programme note of *Musica Reservata*.

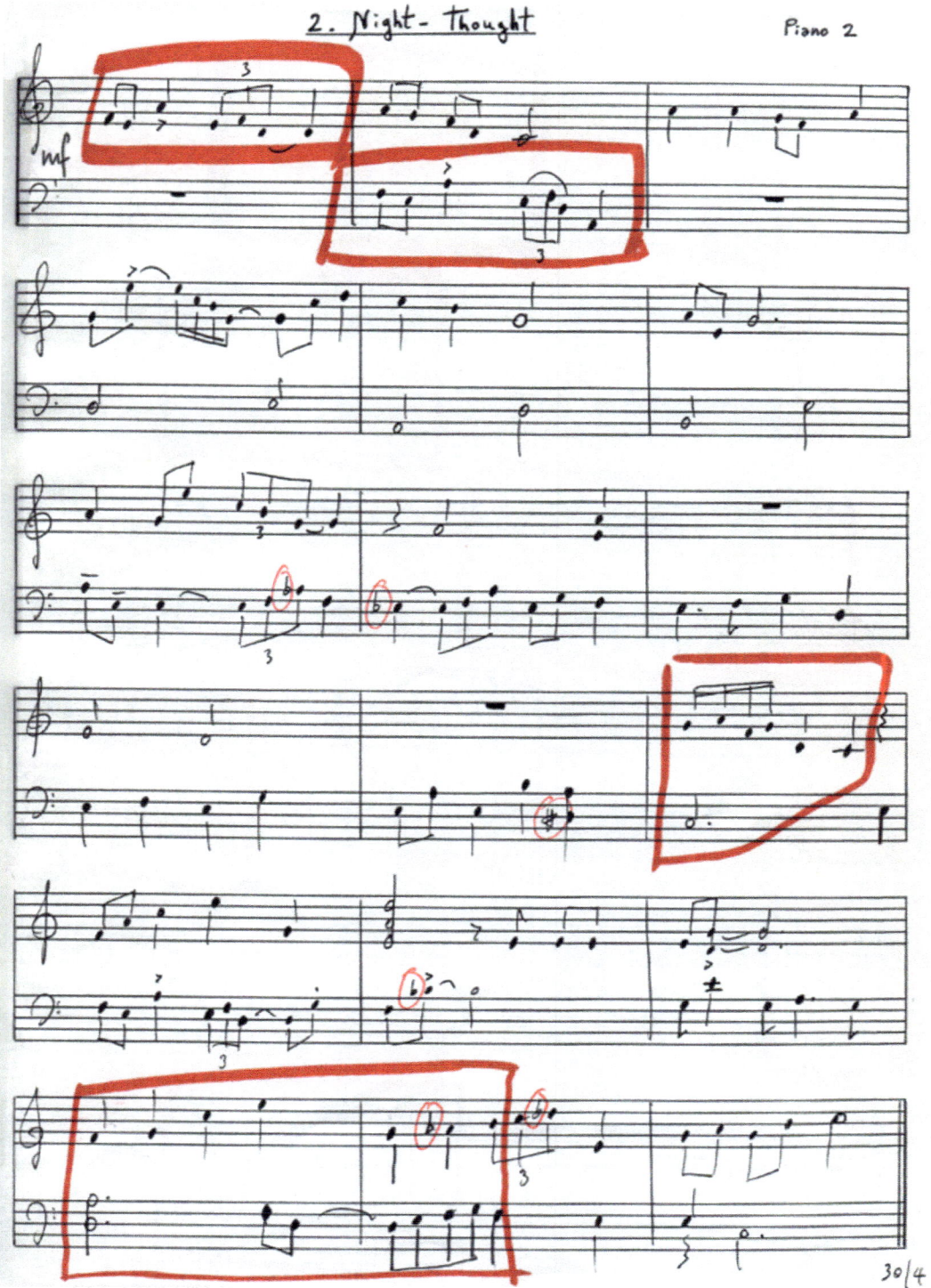

Fig. 7.11: *Musica Reservata,* original score of *To the Night (2).*

8. to the night (2)

30.4.1989

Fig. 7.12: *Musica Reservata,* final score of *To the Night (2).*

As a pianist myself, I would usually hesitate in taking so much liberty for my own interpretations. The next figures show the transcriptions I made of these two piano recordings (see Figs. 7.13 and 7.14). Due to the agogics used by the composer, it wasn't an easy task. Nevertheless, I hope they will be of use to other pianists. The readers will easily be able to compare my transcriptions with the two scores of each piece. This challenging task emphasised that mensural notation doesn't offer the means to describe the shaping of timbre in relation to phrasing and articulation, a fundamental feature in piano playing; this makes an exact transcription of piano pieces of such a refined nature impossible to achieve.

It is crucial to mention that the composer's recording of *To the Night (1)* shows regular tempo changes that never sound abrupt or unmusical. In fact, each tempo change is justified by the agogic gestalt that links two contiguous phrases. The result is the impression of a natural flow of melodic lines enriched by brief 'ritenuti' (such as in bars five, six and seven), additional rhythmic syncopations (such as in bar 10) and tuplets (bars 11 and 15). Similarly, the recording of *To the Night (2)* includes smooth metric changes, 'accelerandi' and 'rallentandi'.

Apropos of interpretation, it is also telling to hear that in the two harpsichord recordings of the composer seemed to endorse a much freer approach to the (original) score. He used ornamentation, such as a mordent played on the last E5 in bar nine. He added passing notes on the left hand in bars six, seven, eight and 17, and went further by taking the liberty to repeat some bars. Moreover, he prolonged bar 11 five times, including rhythmic variations on each repetition; he repeated bar 15 twice and expanded bar 18 with 'arpeggi 'on seventh chords. It would seem that this interpretation on the harpsichord was an experiment about articulation rather than a development of the written material.

Fig. 7.13: *Musica Reservata,* Toniutti's transcription of the first piano recording of *To the Night (1).*

Fig. 7.14: *Musica Reservata,* Toniutti's transcription of the first piano recording of *To the Night (2).*

Palmer planned the performance of the piano-duo version by adding an ad-hoc form, including an improvised introduction, two solo guided improvisations and an exposition. In the figure below, the reader will see that the composer defines the total duration of the performance (approximately 7'30") and divides it into four sections (Fig. 7.15). Notice that the first pianist (Piano 1) is performing *To the Night (1),* while the second pianist (Piano 2) is playing *To the Night (2).*

The first section is 2'30" long and consists of an introduction played by the first pianist. The arrow shows the initial material of the introduction (on the right side of the sketch). The two diatonic chords are built on F3-C4-D4 (in the left hand) and B4-E5-B5 (in the right hand). The word 'sequences' (marked in red) and the falling lines (straight and whirly) indicate that the first pianist begins the performance by transposing the initial chord downwards first. The introduction is soon followed by a joint exposition of the thematic material of both pieces played by both pianists.

The second section (Solo 1) includes the solo of the second pianist. The third section (Solo 2) corresponds to the improvisation of the first pianist. As at the beginning of the performance, the triangle (triangolo) signals the opening of the final section (Reprise) that is played by both pianists simultaneously.

1.2. NIGHT - THOUGHT
(Arrangement for two Pianos)

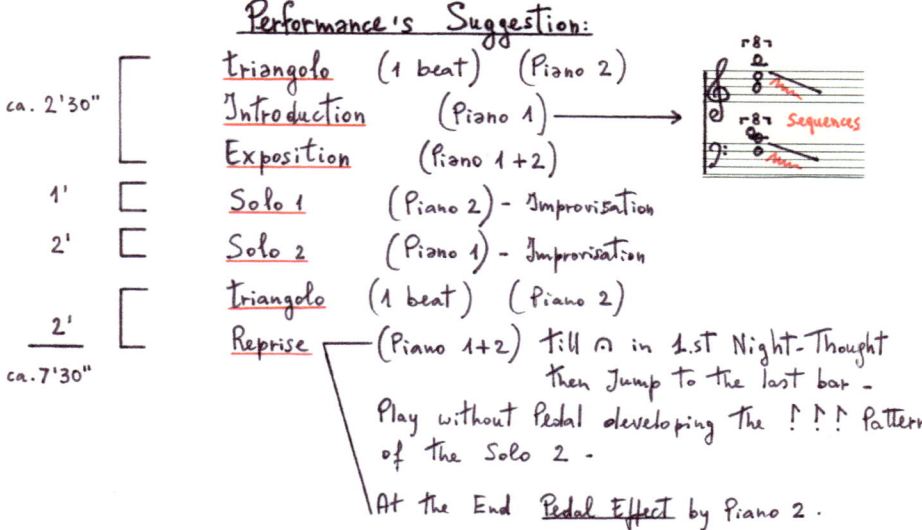

Performance's Suggestion:

ca. 2'30"	triangolo (1 beat) (Piano 2)
	Introduction (Piano 1)
	Exposition (Piano 1+2)
1'	Solo 1 (Piano 2) - Improvisation
2'	Solo 2 (Piano 1) - Improvisation
2'	triangolo (1 beat) (Piano 2)
ca. 7'30"	Reprise — (Piano 1+2) till ⌒ in 1st Night-Thought then Jump to the last bar -

Play without Pedal developing the ♪ ♪ ♪ Pattern of the Solo 2 -

At the End Pedal Effect by Piano 2.

first performance in Lucerne - Switzerland
December, 13th, 1989

Fig. 7.15: *Musica Reservata,* performance plan of the piano duo version of *To the Night (1)* and *To the Night (2)*, as performed in Lucerne in 1989.

There is a recording of this performance in the archives of the composer which would be helpful to those who are interested in exploring in more detail the textural relationships of two simultaneous performances that are explored in this kind of dual improvisation. In the recording of the piano duo version, a clear jazz feel can be heard in the composer's interpretation of *To the Night (1)* (Piano 1) while the second pianist, who plays *To the Night 2,* comes across as being somewhat restrained in his playing and more preoccupied to respond to the composer playing than taking more initiative.

As we have seen in Figures 7.9 and 7.11, the fragments circled by the red colour denote areas of particular harmonic and melodic significance to the composer. By emphasising these selected segments, both pianists would converge through their performance on the essential material of both pieces. Personally, the listening experience of these recordings made me realise how both my classical background and the conventional appearance of these scores had misguided me about the nature of this music. To me, *"playing two different pieces or indeed the same piece simultaneously"* would mean performing the piece from beginning to end, after setting a tempo to relate to. Also, I understood the word 'simultaneously' in terms of having to begin the pieces at the same time with the second pianist while leaving the rest of the performance to flow on by itself, that is, implying no interaction with the other pianist to take place during the performance. The idea of improvisation I had in mind was related to a variation of a melodic line or an interpolation of melodic and harmonic nature. Listening to the recording of the performance gave me a better sense of what the composer was after in the performance instructions.

It goes without saying that the original scores of both pieces retain the best possible representation of the meaning of this music, but that doesn't mean that they are set in stone. As a result of being a pianist-improviser, one could assume that in Palmer's mind, there is no separation between composition, performance and improvisation, and for him, music of this nature cannot be depending on notational issues. In the specific context of a piano-duo version, it is the interplay between the two musicians that will set the logic of the performance, and the content of the score will need to remain flexible to this necessity. Both pianists must attune to each other: 'tempo', phrasing and articulation will need to be shaped in relation to an interactive form of spontaneous performance. From this perspective, a conventional score can suddenly open up unexpected possibilities of interpretation. If, for example, an interpreter will need a faster tempo for a given phrase, a rhythmic compression for another phrase, or to reduce the number of bars in order to better interact with what the other pianist is playing, then the performance must be sufficiently elastic to accommodate all these needs. In a scenario of this kind, the information contained in a conventional score will never suffice as the performance will inevitably include a large number of spontaneous interventions that exceed the traditional thinking imposed by classical norms and predictable styles. The same considerations will apply to solo performances.

As the composer has stated, in an idiom standing between baroque and jazz, the score of *Musica Reservata* has been used as a kind of 'canovaccio'[106] as in a plot of the Commedia dell'Arte, or the notation of a jazz standard: basically, as an outline for a performance, and self-explanatory plan for a pianist who must know how to approach it. In the solo recordings, each piece is clearly recognizable, and the improvisation remains always musically driven as if Palmer is giving himself the time to listen carefully to what he is playing and respond to it in the most natural way. Each of these recordings offers just one possibility of interpretation out of many others. As the composer stated in a recent interview, each interpretation of his is bound to be unique and unrepeatable, and this remains intrinsic in the nature of the music. At this stage, we could ask ourselves, why then bother writing a more detailed score? Within a jazz context, this question would be surely legitimate. Palmer himself gives us the answer. Having been confronted with the problem faced by other pianists who tried to play from the original scores, the composer became soon aware that he had to produce a kind of 'final written image' of the music, that is a score that would include as many details as possible.

Being a classical pianist himself, Palmer was conscious of the problem of conveying the idea of a freer and more imaginative way to interpret a piano piece of this kind to classically trained pianists. However, he was equally aware that jazz musicians tend to exaggerate personal

---

[106] In English: a tea towel or a canvas.

contributions to what is written in a score and often get carried away by stylistic (jazz) clichés that may damage the nature and intimacy of this music. The problem is twofold: classical pianists are not trained in improvised performance and one of their main obsessions is to respect the score as the ultimate will of the composer. In addition, classical pianists are usually allowed personal contributions within a limited range of interpretative options set by the idiom or style of the music. If it's true that this may suffice to differentiate one interpretation from another, it is equally true that it will exclude liberties such as changing metres or rhythmic indications during a performance. In the end, for Palmer, it was clear that he had to reach a compromise where he would write down a 'final' version of the *Musica Reservata* cycle while mentioning with a slight sense of trepidation, that improvisation is allowed but not needed.[107] What is also important to mention is that not all the pieces of *Musica Reservata* have a similar genesis: as far as I have been able to examine, some pieces went through a complex elaboration of the first written version, while others are almost identical. Apart from the original scores of *To the Night (1)* and *To the Night (2)*, no other original score seems to have survived to this day, which makes it impossible to discuss this important aspect of performance and composition in relation to the remaining pieces of the cycle.

Another aspect worthy to be mentioned is that I have been able to listen to original recordings of other pieces of the collection played by the composer in 1989 and to compare them with the final (printed) score. In the case of *First Path*, the refinement of the revision is very striking: in the old recording, one can hear a very basic pointillistic music made of single notes played 'staccato' and using wide intervallic leaps. In the final score of this piece, I am confronted with a much denser texture that is more cohesive in terms of rhythmic structure, pitch density and sense of direction. By contrast, in *Untitled* there are few differences between the old recording and the new score in terms of melodic and harmonic content. Palmer has also confirmed to me that when he composed *Musica Reservata*, he thought of the complete music as a cycle, a kind of concept album, and that architectural concerns about the general structure of the collection made him opt for minor or major re-elaborations of the original pieces, always keeping the large form of the cycle in mind. Finally, according to him, all the pieces were born in the same spirit and share the same approach to composition.

Considering all the points I have made, it seems clear that a multi-faceted musical background and expertise in jazz and improvised performance will be a large advantage to any pianist who will want to tackle the *Musica Reservata* pieces in a 'proper' way. Conversely, it is equally true that a pianist doesn't need to be an experienced jazz pianist in order to play this music. I realise these statements may sound contradictory, but in my view, they are not. Surely, any knowledge of, and experience in, jazz and baroque idioms and techniques will be an asset to any classical pianist. On that note, I would like to offer the following suggestions.

Firstly, I can recommend contacting the composer in order to listen to the recordings of his interpretations and performances of these pieces. This can be beneficial and enlightening to any pianist, and I should add that Palmer is helpful in sharing material or information that may enhance the understanding of his music. I would also recommend listening to some piano jazz playing (especially Keith Jarrett and Bill Evans) and baroque keyboard music, whose idioms linger in many of the *Musica Reservata* pieces, particularly *To the Night (1)* and *To the Night (2)*. Incidentally, this was the same advice Palmer gave me in 2014 when I performed six pieces of the collection for the first time.

Secondly, my suggestion would be to 'learn' the scores as well as possible in order to retain a clear image of the music in the mind and indeed in the fingers. Following that, it would

---

[107] Another little change that may justify this process could be the omitted indication ♩=52-60 'molto rubato' in *To the Night (1)* in the draft for the published score, which was changed into a metronome indication of ♩=58 'calmo' in the final version.

be extremely beneficial to the pianist to begin experimenting with one musical element at a time: rhythm, tempo, articulation, phrasing and so on, changing from subtle to more evident variations of the written text and critically comparing what one is playing with what is written in the score.

Lastly, I would produce as many different experiences of the same piece as possible, each time adding a different degree of freedom and a different expressive quality to the playing: the more varied the modifications, the larger my palette of interpretative possibilities. I am confident that, by doing so, each performance of *Musica Reservata* will offer diverse insights about the music and a more critical understanding of what pianists must be able to do when confronted with more liberated decision-making processes in piano playing. Both epiphanies will gratify the art of interpretation and illuminate the world of intimacy and inwardness where *Musica Reservata* resides.

FROM *DÉJÀ VU* TO *ANAGRAMS*
Késia Decote

KD. Some of your piano music reflects so much of a transcendental quality. Can you tell me more about the creative process that reflects the mystical in your music?

JP. This is a very personal matter and the last thing I would want is to come across as a guru to the readers. I often feel that the more one speaks about such topics, the higher the risk is to cause misunderstandings of all sorts. I can fill up pages with beautiful words, but what would the point be? Words like 'spiritual' and 'mystical' have become so overused and even abused nowadays that I prefer to let the music speak for itself without additional verbal explanation. I am just a person who is trying to live as honestly and ethically as possible, in connection with the universe and the world I live in. I don't have general rules about my creative process. Anthony Storr once said that *"To be oneself, to realise one's own personality to its fullest extent, is to develop from childhood to maturity"*.[108] I find this apparently unpretentious statement very illuminating. Hence, I could say that I am trying to achieve personal maturity through my daily work and the wonderful art that is music.

KD. Although there are different views about the phenomenon of 'déjà vu', one fact is unquestionable: it is a perceptual experience, one that relates to memory and awareness. In the music of *Déjà vu*, we see a contrast of strict and free elements. How are the aspects of perception, awareness and memory explored in the musical material of this piece?

JP. First of all, I should mention that I have experienced the déjà vu phenomenon several times in my life, hence when I wrote this music, I related to a first-hand experience rather than a concept or a theory. The music of *Déjà vu* unfolds on two parallel layers representing the present and the past (the memory of the past, to be exact). In order to create an immediate vicinity of sound (the present) I constructed a texture based on a quasi-serial technique based on the number eight, which included eight pitches and eight durational values. These are unfolded by eight rules and eight exceptions in a strict and consistent way throughout the piece, with no exception whatsoever. (I think this is the only piece I have written where I have used a strict pitch organisation from beginning to end). This texture should emphasise the flow of chronological time implied in the perception of the present. Due to the rigorous organisation

---

[108] Storr, Anthony (1966:26).

of pitch and durational values, the resulting texture sounds gaunt and pointillistic. The unfolding of this layer establishes the duration and the form of the piece, and it is based on a palindromic structure related to bar numbers. For example, bar 1 corresponds to bar 80, bar 2 to bar 79, bar 3 to bar 78 and so forth until the axes 40/41 and 41/40.

The second layer (the memory of the past) consists of undetermined (free) pitch material and gestures that are prolonged by resonance. The notes are projected onto a wider space by using both the sustain and sostenuto pedals. The resonance of this second layer creates a sense of space that hints at the déjà vu phenomenon of remembering something of the past, especially from a very distant past. In the score, these gestures are circumscribed by rectangles and supported by the prompt use of the two pedals (see Fig. 7.16). By disturbing the flow of the linearity of the strict layer, these free gestures dissolve the sequential precision of the present by introducing an abstract, non-chronological, temporal dimension (the past) reinforced by the additional use of rubato and the use of rests ad libitum.

Fig. 7.16: *Déjà vu*, beginning.

251

KD. In *Glimpse,* **we have such a simple starting point followed by four notes on the name C-A-G-E opening up to a rich listening experience with generous resonance and a great sense of freedom. Can you tell me how this relates to the glimpse of consciousness brought to you by the work and thought of John Cage?**

JP. The initial gesture that triggers *Glimpse* bears a resemblance to a short moment of enlightenment, a glimpse of perception that is sometimes possible to experience during meditation or thereafter. The notes that follow are always the same, C-A-G-E, played in different registers and in changing succession, with an emphasis on the note A. In the lower register of the piano, the A elicits a tonal centre based on the A minor chord (A, C, E) being expanded by the minor seventh G (a minor seventh chord). The chromaticism intrinsic in the initial gesture (the symbolic breakthrough) prolonged by the sostenuto pedal, is outshined by the recurrent diatonicism of the four notes as a sort of displaced chant that underlines the final tribute to the composer's life.

Although by 1992 I had moved away from Cage's ideas about music, as I wrote earlier, I felt like saying a heartfelt 'thank you' to a person who had been so inspiring to me in the late 1980s. At a time when my studies of Buddhism were focused on (mainly) Hindu and Tibetan thought, it was Cage who accelerated my involvement with Zen. I find the notion of 'glimpse' to be pertinent to our discussion because Zen emphasises an approach to Buddhism that is different to the Tibetan or Indian. Tibetan Buddhism derives from various Buddhist beliefs that are appropriate to the characteristics of Himalayan cultures and religions. These are complex and have 'decorative' belief systems based on elaborate rituals for example. Tibetan Buddhism is more of a religion in the way we understand this word in the West. For instance, they have many divine beings (the Bodhisattvas) that are the counterpart of Christian saints. Like in Christianity, they are visualised and prayed to as individual deities. Buddhism in Tibet merged with the Himalayan religions that had a shamanic nature and also included the worship of nature spirits and ancestors. On the other hand, Zen Buddhism is much more minimalist than Tibetan Buddhism due to the influence of Taoist philosophy that came to Japan from China. Zazen (Zen meditation) has a strong focus on breathing and emptying the mind. It doesn't worship deities and it remains very concentrated on the mind. In a way, it is more essential and 'dry' than Himalayan Buddhism. From a Western perspective, I suppose that Zen is more 'philosophical' than Tibetan Buddhism because one is focused on emptiness and the attentiveness of the mind. Zen is sharp and somehow more severe. The 'glimpse' I am referring to in the title is a reminder of the latter approach which Cage tried to convey to the West by stressing the importance of silence and advocating a new focus on sound detached from any psychological perspective.

KD. *Shambhala* **is inspired by the concept of 'place'. What were your thoughts about building** *"an imaginary place of peace and happiness"* **through music? What is your experience in building a place to be, through listening?**

JP. The story of *Shambhala* goes back to a long time ago when I lived in Florence in the 1970s. It is one of those pieces that I composed at the piano by improvising on the instrument in a state of meditation. The piano has always been a vehicle for contemplation to me. Jiddu Krishnamurti once said that meditation means not only to ponder over but also to 'measure'. As a form of meditation, I can say that I have always found music to be a form of measurement with myself and the world. *Shambhala* is one of those pieces where the experience of 'measurement' (which is also 'exploration') is at its most effective. The place in question is an imaginary pure land that in Tibetan Buddhism is named 'Shambhala'. Although there are literary references describing Shambhala as a physical place in central Asia, the myth refers to an imaginary place of peace and happiness dwelt by enlightened people. It is a powerful symbol. Music has the power to indicate imaginary places that have a life of their own, beyond the physical domain. These places are everywhere and nowhere, yet they are always here for us to be entered through sound, for example. The deeper I listen, the better I can enter such dimensions. When I began to play *Shambhala* on the piano, I didn't 'think', but just listened to the sounds I was playing. The first three notes I played were D, C, A using the sustain pedal in order to create a vast resonance. Other notes followed as a contour to these three notes that remain the hidden theme of the piece. The more I listened, the more the music would continue to evolve. I didn't think; I *felt*. I continued to respond to the sounds and keep listening. I don't think it was a matter of deliberately wanting to build a place, but rather an experience of deep listening, keep playing the piano intuitively and let the music evolve by itself.

KD. *Shambhala* **explores both the traditional piano playing on the keys, and the extended techniques of plucking and scratching the strings. What are the thoughts behind the relationships that happen between the sounds from these two aspects of piano playing techniques?**

JP. It's about the awareness that I can extend the palette of colours on the instrument by plucking or scraping on the strings. These techniques simply produce different timbres that complement the traditional piano sounds. In the case of *Shambhala*, it is the sustain pedal used throughout the piece that is crucial, as it generates a large space for these notes and colours to merge. The slow pace of the piece makes it possible to perceive both layers as integrative, rather than contrasting. In fact, the pianist, by alternating traditional piano sounds on the keyboard and those played on the strings, is playing two instruments simultaneously. In this sense, the piece was conceived as a duo for two instruments played by the same musician.

KD. What aspects of the myth of Athena do you find more intriguing? Which of these aspects are present in your piano piece *Athena,* **and how did your creative process unfold to depict them in music?**

JP. The myth of Athena is a very complex one and it would take an entire book to deal with the symbolism attached to it comprehensively. Usually, the goddess Athena (the Roman Minerva) is associated with wisdom, warfare, arts and handicraft. In the pantheon of ancient religions, the myth of Athena is certainly one of the most complex and captivating. The aspect I find intriguing is the symbol of wisdom, the principle of the 'buddhi' that includes a kind of intuition descending from the 'Supreme', meaning the highest form of intelligence. To that, I would add the aspect of the creative arts. I found it interesting that in Greek societies Athena would always dwell in the centre of a city as a reminder of moral order, knowledge, creativity and artistic life. She was the bringer of wisdom from Hera, wife of Zeus. The Roman emperor Julian, the last non-Christian emperor and philosopher, wrote of Athena: *"Unto men Athena gives good things, namely wisdom, understanding, and the creative arts; and she dwells in their citadels, I suppose, as being the founder of civil government through communication, of her own wisdom".*[109]

The aspects present in this piano piece are that of wisdom, knowledge and a concealed form of devotion. The creative process was intuitive and unfolded from improvising at the piano, similar to the genesis of *Shambhala*. During the mid-1980s, I experienced many dreams about music, artistic creativity, C.G. Jung and Athena herself. While I was going through a difficult time, it was also a time of great discoveries such as the I Ching, the philosophy of Taoism, the psychology of Jung, the I Ching, Hinduism and Buddhism. Athena appeared in my

---

[109] Emperor Julian (2012:243).

dreams at least on one occasion, in May 1986. The dream was so vivid that I went to the piano immediately and began to play...

KD. You wrote *Athena* perhaps in a state of trance. How was the experience of the journey from an acquired knowledge about the myth of Athena, then engaging with it deeply, to a nearly non-conscious way until pouring it into music?

JP. As I mentioned in the programme note of the piece, Athena's image has been persistent in my dreams, especially in the second half of the 1980s when I lived in Switzerland. Only when I returned to England in 1990 in Elstree, Hertfordshire, did I write down the score, I think, in a state of quasi-trance, or perhaps trance; I cannot tell exactly. This was another period of my life strongly characterised by intense dreaming, and it was the time when I dreamt the music of *Spirits* over a period of two weeks. (I scored the music of *Spirits* for a synthesizer using a voice-like sound that resembled the sounds I had heard in the dreams.) For some inexplicable reason, the 1990 score of *Athena* disappeared soon thereafter, and the music was forgotten, as if having been erased from my mind at once. It was only several years later, in 2013 that the music reappeared in my consciousness. This experience prompted me to re-write the score and record the music in the same year. This recording is now kept in my audio archives, and the reconstructed score has been published by Composers Edition. What I should mention is that I began to play the music of *Athena* at the piano following a specific dream I dreamt of in May 1986 while living near Zürich. The music I played was instantaneous, as if triggered by another force residing beyond me or within me. What I wrote in the first score of 1990 was the result of these piano sessions. The music was not an outcome of an acquired (rational) knowledge about the myth of Athena, as you have suggested. On the contrary, it sprang from my memory of the dream. I sat at the piano and played intuitively, without any kind of rational thinking; the music would flow freely as I recalled the dream.

KD. Can you tell me more about the dream?

The following informal account is what I wrote down in my diary in May 1986:

"Last night I dreamt I had an appointment with my music teacher at 9:00 pm. I realised it was already 8:45 pm and I was still far away from the meeting place, in fact, I was with some relatives in a house that was situated 8 miles away from my teacher's house. I remember the distance exactly. It was wintertime, I had no car and outside it was cold and dark. I began to feel extremely nervous since I knew I was going to be late for the lesson. I wanted to call the teacher and tell him about the delay, but I had no telephone in the house and there was no telephone in the area either. Despite an increasing sense of panic, I decided to leave the house and go to the lesson anyway. I began to walk as fast as I could, and, at some point, I tried to ride a bike I had found down the road, but the bike broke down after a few metres and I had to continue on foot. By this time, I began to feel desperate and started to run, still hoping I would arrive at the teacher's house in time. The road was dark and unknown to me, and I actually knew that it was impossible to get there in time, nevertheless, I continued to run through the darkness of the night. I then began to sweat a great deal and I realised that the sweating was also the many tears that were going down my face. Although I was still far from the meeting point, I kept running and running. Suddenly, I discovered some wonderful Greek ruins in a town which seemed familiar to me. I could clearly see what was left of gigantic palaces and majestic walls. I also noticed that the walls were still intact! I could not understand how such a beautiful ancient architecture was still to be found in a dirty and ugly modern town. Then I saw two criminals standing between the ruins, and I saw them coming towards me with bad intentions. I started running fast and for a while managed to

leave them behind me. But as I turned my head backwards again, I saw the two men were still after me. I rapidly decided to hide by lifting up my body, as if flying, and remaining suspended in the air. At some point, I realised I had managed to reach up to the top of the Greek walls and keep my body suspended by holding my elbows between two of the walls. I felt in great distress and lost, feeling that the criminals would still get me. As I looked up in the air in front of me, I saw a big face made of stone that seemed familiar to me and I realised it was the face of Athena. I was puzzled by this apparition and felt very unsure. Then the goddess looked at me. I could feel she was loving and kind to me, although she retained a noble and somewhat detached expression. I suddenly felt safe. Then she looked at me and said, "you should not go". I felt unsure. She continued with a caring tone, "you'll never get there! Stop running and let things go their own way. Wait now, be patient and eventually you will overcome". As she spoke to me, I noticed her words filling me with peace and some kind of unknown love. I felt this love strongly. I wanted to stay there, yet an uncontrollable surge took over my body. I jumped down the walls and started running away. After a few metres, however, I was exhausted. As I suspected, I missed the appointment and found myself alone, anxious and still in the middle of the night. Yet I knew that from this moment on Athena would remain with me."

(Gossau, 26th May 1986)

KD. In these two pieces, you allow lots of freedom to the performer, especially in the approach to tempo and rhythm. What does this freer relationship mean to you in terms of music and life?

JP. Due to the nature of both pieces, it was necessary to leave tempo and rhythm gestalt to the performer. It is important for me that the pianist should enter a similar state of mind, let alone a meditative attitude and allow the sounds to dictate the shaping of 'tempi' and rhythmic proportions.

In *Shambhala*, the indications 'lentamente, senza tempo, calmissimo' provide enough information to the pianist to enter a space of intimacy that should reflect a sonic universe unfolding in the continuous resonance of each sound produced by the piano (see the beginning of the piece in Fig. 7.17). The pianist should respond to the persistent sound-resonance (action-reaction) connection permitted by the sustain pedal. The pedal indication 'Ped. al fine' has to be carried out literally: in order to allow the gestures and timbres to merge into one another, the pedal must be kept down from beginning to end.

In *Athena*, the only given indications are 'Adagio, sempre rubatissimo' (see the beginning of the piece in Fig. 7.18). The short phrases should be 'whispered' very softly, as they refer to the voice of Athena who whispered to me in the dream with a gentle and consoling tone. An evocative sense of dreaming and imagining should be recreated by the performer very sensitively. The sustain pedal is marked with the indication 'Ped. sempre'. Now, although the two indications are very similar, in my mind at that time the indication 'Ped. al fine' would indicate that minor pedal changes are permitted. After all, the piece *Athena* is about a voice speaking softly which implies an element of communication that is absent in *Shambhala*. Thus, the indication 'Ped. sempre' should allow short and subtle pedal changes between the phrases.

While the music of *Shambhala* is essentially contemplative, the music of *Athena* is expressive, albeit within a 'supernatural' halo created by the resonance. The meaning of this 'freer relationship' as you put it, may differ from context to context. You specify *"in terms of music and life"*. What comes first to my mind is certainly a sense of ethical responsibility inherent in the way we perform a musical work or behave in daily life. To me, music and life are not separate.

shambhala

John Palmer

lentamente, senza tempo, calmissimo

Fig. 7.17: *Shambhala,* beginning.

Athena

John Palmer

Fig. 7.18: *Athena,* beginning.

KD. *Anagrams* displays a very rational method of permutations of musical phrases differently from other pieces like *Athena,* which you wrote in nearly a state of trance. Do you see this more as a rational composition method as opposed to intuition, or just another strategy to access thoughts and ideas that are deep within?

257

JP. *Anagrams* and *Athena* are very different pieces. In *Anagrams*, (see the beginning of the piece in Fig. 7.19 below) only the pitches are pre-determined, while the shaping of all the other musical components is intuitive. The methodology of the two pieces is very different, but I believe that is because of the extreme nature of *Athena* rather than the rational nature of *Anagrams*. The latter is much more chromatic and complex music for sure, but both approaches access the realm of the subconscious in two different ways.

Anagrams

John Palmer

Fig. 7.19: *Anagrams,* beginning.

KD. The music that you write often contains codes and cryptic messages. *Anagrams* gives me a sense of mystery, and even a shift of perception when you ask the pianist to play certain passages reversely. Can you tell me the role of the mysterious in your music, and your thoughts about the sharing of it with performers of your music and audiences?

JP. I can relate to what you are saying about *Anagrams* because it has the same effect on me. My perception seems to shift at different places during the piece and, like you, more so when I ask the pianist to play certain passages reversely. It's as if perceiving a quasi-cyclic substance that is interconnecting the musical phrases whereas, at the same time, the phrases themselves keep changing: an entity that sounds 'known' and 'unknown'. There is something in the way we seem to respond to the pitch and rhythmic arrangements in this piece that evokes a sense of the cryptic. *Anagrams* is built on a pitch configuration that I converted, through a process of (synaesthetic) perceptive equivalence, from a phrase of the Egyptian *Book of the Dead*. The resulting musical phrase is permuted in different fashions, just like an anagram that evolves in more anagrams. As in numerology, the notes I write often contain codes and hidden messages that are brought to acoustic life by sound.

Having mentioned this, if I were to speak about the 'mysterious' in my music, it wouldn't be mysterious anymore! I can only say that I have always been naturally attracted by meaning in general; more specifically by symbols, codes, anagrams and riddles which I often use in my music. The role of the mysterious in music is the same role of the mysterious in life, but sometimes I wonder if there are mysteries at all? Sages and mystics of all ages have long maintained that there is a field of cosmic interconnectedness at the roots of our physical reality. Today, these ancient ideas and theories have found confirmation in quantum physics. Research on the 'quantum field' has shown that what lies at the foundation of space itself consists of a tiny area of energy waves from which all things are born. These energy waves range from dreams, thoughts, mental images, and what we call consciousness, to atoms and galaxies, stars and planets, living organisms and even physical objects. The human mind has no boundaries and any musical discourse that is constructed around a sense of self-awareness may sound 'mysterious' because it is the strategy of the psyche (the soul) to express and manifest itself in domains that are endless, unfathomable, and that convey a sense of what we often call the 'magical'. Perhaps the fatal world 'mystery' is nothing more than a comprehensive explication of the enduring memory of the universe that connects events, happenings, thoughts and human behaviour. If it speaks to us, it is because it speaks about universal truths that are in each of us through the 'mysterious' language of the subconscious. This is one reason why I consider instrumental music to be the most enigmatic art of all. Perhaps this is the true mystery of music.

KD. *A-mors* is such a personal piece relating to love, and really transpires so much intimacy. Yet, it presents a very deliberated structure, drawing from the Latin word 'amors' and grounding the structure on the number 8 (the infinite). Can you tell us about this creative process that combines the expression of feelings and exploration of semantics into musical structure?

JP. There are a variety of ways in which I approach the creative process, for example, by using systems of unfolding pitch and forms. Sometimes I use one-to-one procedures between pitch and word for example. Other times, I allow words and verses of poems to establish the form of the music. On other occasions, I work intuitively on selected texts, allowing my imagination to be unrestrained from any kind of architectural structure. Another technique is meditating on a text. The case of *A-mors* is unique because I was asked to write a simple and short piano piece about the topic of love, and I decided to write a piece based on a love song I wrote in 2012 (I have been writing songs since 1973). There was a reference I had read at that time about the

Latin word 'amors' (love) to be interpreted as 'a-mors' (with the alpha privative). Thus, the word 'a-mors' would literally mean 'non-death'. In other words, love is the absence of death. Armed with this new insight, I revisited my song *Being with you* and used its simple melodic lines as the basis for the piano piece. The original song was written in C major and has a really simple melodic structure, harmony and form. I constructed the piano piece on four short sections, each based on eight gestures. The number eight, as a symbol of the infinite, is a philosophical and structural reference I have used a couple of times in my works. The pitch field I use in the piano piece is based on fragments taken from *Being with you* in C major, at times transposed in A major. I transposed the song for this occasion in order to create a more interesting and ambiguous sense of tonality. The technique I used may be loosely defined as a 'fractal passacaglia', a method that may be worth exploring further in the future. Basically, it's about creating subsets of fragments of a given passacaglia line. The idea is really simple, and it seems that it worked well in *A-mors*. The choice of fragments and subsets I employed in the piece was based on pure intuition. The creative process that combines the expression of feelings and exploration of semantics into musical structure depends on the approach to the composition. I usually tend to combine intuition and a solid sense of form, symmetric or asymmetric. In the case of *A-mors*, the exploration of semantics is reduced to a very minimum. I selected only four fragments from the song including the theme and used them bitonally by superimposing C major and A major. Due to the restrictions I imposed on myself, *A-mors* is one of the most minimalistic pieces I have ever written.

KD. How is the experience of hearing such an intimate piece in such public contexts, being played by different performers, to varied audiences?

JP. It is a touching experience. It feels like sharing and celebrating an aspect of the beauty and importance of love with the audience in a very unpretentious way.

KD. We have seen your music relating to mythology, spirituality, perception, awareness, semantics. In *Eulogy* we see a focus on the properties of sound itself, your only 'spectral' piano piece. The creative process of exploring a spectral thought in a composition for piano is fascinating. Can you tell me something about it?

JP. A eulogy is a speech or a text written in praise of a person who has died or retired. In December 2012 a dear friend of mine, the composer Jonathan Harvey (who had also been my teacher), passed away and I decided to write a simple piece dedicated to his memory. Thinking of Harvey's predilection for timbre, I wanted to use a spectral reference in a piece for solo piano, which is a kind of contradiction of course, mainly due to the tempered tuning and, to a lesser extent, the percussive sound production of the instrument. Nevertheless, I decided to tackle the 'impossibility' of the task and wrote a piano piece entirely based on the tempered harmonic series of a single note, where the unfolding of its 'spectral' content would be shaped by short melodic lines stemming only from the partials of the overtones series. I knew I had to abandon pure spectral techniques and come up with a compromise of some sort.

The form consists of three sections, each comprising 21 bars. The next decision was to leave the unfolding of the tempered harmonic series entirely to my intuition. The sonic content of *Eulogy* may be described as a variation on a single note, ambiguously a C2-C3 fundamental, which is never played by the pianist. This 'enigmatic' C is a soundless symbol of unity from which all the other notes of the piece unfold and its real fundamental remains obscure until the end of the piece despite a hint of C3 supplied by a motif in bars 7-8 that appears again as the conclusive gesture of the piece (see Fig. 7.20).

Fig. 7.20: *Eulogy,* motif in bars 7-8.

The notion of the note C representing unity as a self-contained universe is viewed from different angles, namely short harmonic and melodic fragments based on its harmonic series, and their scattering throughout the keyboard of the piano. The unfolding of the harmonic series is asymmetrical and unpredictable. A selection of segments of the harmonic series in C is also transposed according to a hidden system of register changes that injects constant harmonic motion to the texture. Being a eulogy, the musical discourse is characterised by rising melodic lines as a declamatory sign of praise to the life of the late friend. In its basic simplicity, the disjointed unfolding of the C tempered harmonic series conjures up changing chords and motifs occurring in dissimilar combinations within a range of six octaves. Throughout the piece, a sense of the note C is hanging in the air although it is never played in its fundamental nature. This imaginary pedal note is hidden behind the musical surface, as it were. Yet, it is always present as it is called to life by the unfolding of its overtone series. The attentive listener should be able to perceive the audible layer of the melodic and harmonic unfolding of the overtone series (the foreground) persistently relating to, and calling forth, the inaudible low C note (the hidden background). In such a case, a melody may be perceived as the temporal unfolding of harmony, and harmony itself as the unfolding of timbre in time. It is a slow interaction of stasis and motion that I compare to a process of consciousness evolving through space.

KD. I would love to hear about your relationship with the piano itself, since you are a fine pianist yourself. How is your personal relationship with the sonic universe of the piano, and what role does it play on your approach to composition and music in general?

JP. Well, the piano is my instrument. I virtually grew up with it and I am told I was already banging on it at the age of two although I began my first formal piano lessons at the age of six. The relationship with the piano is a family relationship, really. When I was a teenager I also trained as a piano-tuner, which gave me a more complete knowledge of the instrument. The sonic universe of the piano is unique, and it has inspired me throughout my life. I entered the world of classical music because of my piano playing; that was my private reality before I began to take piano lessons. When I went into jazz later on, it was because of the jazz pianists I listened to. The same thing applies to the encounter with atonality and modern music: the piano was always the vehicle that led me into these different idioms and musical styles. It goes without saying that I love the timbre of the piano and am very fussy about it as I had the privilege to work with pianos since early childhood and throughout my life. I also worked as a piano technician in several piano shops in the late 1970s, and I would be able to recognise the timbre of a Steinway, Bösendörfer, Yamaha, Blüthner, Gotrian-Steinweg or Kawai immediately.

The piano has been my reference instrument for years, albeit not without difficulties when it came to understanding instruments like woodwinds, strings or the voice, for example, but that's another matter. I still remember in 1989 hearing the Swiss composer Thüring Bräm saying *"I love and hate the piano!"*, a statement that struck me at the time. I understood what he meant a few years later when I realised that the experience gained at the piano became a sort of limitation to my listening skills due to the fixed semitone-based keyboard and the impossibility to change the timbre once the key is hit. Pianists tend to listen to music that way, which is rather one-sided of course. To some extent, I resolved this problem, at least partially, by training further and playing other instruments, *and* by using different piano tunings for my *Piano Concerto*. But the practice of detuning a piano is still not taken seriously by the music community and industry, and I believe it should be time for that to change now. We need microtonal pianos: they are easy to make and not difficult to tune. If I summarised the most crucial benefit the piano has had on my musicianship, I must mention harmony. My love-affair with harmony is something that has been made possible by the piano and many hours spent on improvising. I am passionate about it and 'possessed' by it. To me, harmony remains the fundamental component of music discourse. When I hear a melodic line, for example, I hear it as the unfolding of harmony in time. When I hear an unaccompanied melody, I naturally harmonise it in my mind in real time, and if I hear the same melody repeating, I will harmonise it differently. I think it is a sort of obsession!

THE BORDERLINE BETWEEN SOUND AND SILENCE
Ricardo Descalzo

RD. It seems to me that in your most recent music for piano, you have a tendency to put aside virtuosity. I wonder if this is true and what are your thoughts and feelings about this issue. Do you think you could ever imagine a virtuoso piano piece from your actual mindset? Are you still attracted to virtuosity? If so, is it in a different way as it was in the past?

JP. My actual mindset remains open to any compositional idiom and technique. I have never put aside virtuosity in my musical work, and my musical language is not fixed to a specific idiom or technique. The music I write evolves continually and is not attached to a specific vernacular. More importantly, it springs from the heart as well as the mind. When I compose, I use the appropriate language for the music I have in mind at that moment in time. I abhor monolithic idioms and dislike dogmatic approaches to composition. Therefore, my music doesn't follow ideologies. I am well aware that there are many composers who stick to a specific idiom and technique throughout their lifetime, but that kind of thinking and composing is not for me. There is a widespread opinion in the academic world that endorses the idea that a composer must pursue a sense of idiomatic homogeneity in his oeuvre. This is interpreted as a sign of artistic and intellectual consistency. I disagree with that: to assume that the work of a composer must reflect a uniform language is, in my view, restrictive and arid. Firstly, because it limits the potential of the composer's creativity by submitting oneself to a form of aesthetic ideology that may turn to be fatal to artistic freedom and invention. Secondly, because it doesn't take into account the diversity of events and circumstances that shape our existence on a daily basis and the effect that these circumstances have on the artistic output, thus denying the most natural fact of life which is change and evolution. Artistic creativity is a *living* force, not a static doctrine, and should respond to varying psychological and intellectual conditions without the dictates of pre-established restrictions.

Today, the notion of virtuosity is debatable, but I take it that you are referring to the traditional understanding of this term as conveyed by the classical tradition of the West, so I will reply according to this view. I have used virtuosity as a dialectic force consistently throughout the years and I would still do so today if I had to. (I have also written at length about my idea of virtuosity in other conversations in this book). If by 'virtuosic' you mean a piece that is technically difficult and fast to play in order to show how pompous and quick a performer can play, I can tell you that I have always found this kind of music uninteresting to perform and boring to listen to. By the same token, I find this kind of virtuoso music artistically, intellectually and psychologically speaking, shallow and banal. The use of virtuosity I use in my works is connected with dialectics, that is a setting of confrontation, dialogue and debate that defines much of the classical chamber music repertoire. Within a dialectic discourse, virtuosity can be a formidable way to articulate a sense of dramatic drift and interlocution that can only be achieved by a texture that is daring and 'demanding'. (I am thinking of my pieces *Epitaph, Verso l'Alto, Koan* and the entire *Trans* cycle for example). In such a context, virtuosity is not a showcase of finger dexterity and imposing gloss, but an exceptional expedient for emotional attributes aiming at stirring the depth and intensity of the musical discourse. The decision of whether or not I need to use virtuosity is always linked to the nature of the music I write. I have no fixed rules about this, and my piano repertoire presents clear evidence of the variety of idioms and textures that I have used over the past 40 years.

RD. What are your thoughts about using space as a musical entity or as a 'container of sound' and how does resonance relate to this? I imagine many of your piano pieces in deep hollow spaces, but this may be different for you...

JP. The notion of space is often an elusive and relative concept of something that is 'empty' and must contain sound. The traditional notion of a three-dimensional physical space has been superseded in modern physics by a four-dimensional continuum called space-time, meaning that space and time are complementary. In several works of mine, the space-time paradigm is a most vigorous constituent of the music; this applies particularly to my music for solo piano or for small chamber works including the piano (a very important instrument in this context due to its resonant body). I perceive resonance, time and space as three interrelated and complementary aspects of the same sonic and psychological reality. My perception of space retains psychoacoustic attributes that are almost impossible to describe verbally, as they depict a form of imaginary existence that is autonomous from that of sound and yet is related to it.

A musical space is not a tangible reality. If it were a sonic 'body', it would itself have to be in a place, and if space had no presence, sound would paradoxically have to be in a non-space, which means that it would not exist. In order to experience space, therefore, I must perceive time as a measurable entity elicited by resonance or silence. Since resonance must contain sound, the perception of space is linked to an immediate boundary of sound, insofar as sound is attached to this border. Therefore, resonance and space are connected to sound and time, from which they are distinguished in the same way that the boundary of a sound is distinguished from the sound itself. There are many instances in my piano music and much of my electroacoustic works where the search for a differentiation of 'boundary' should be audible to any attentive listener. To me, a musical space is not a synonym of emptiness, since the perception of space implies the inadmissibility of the void and the existence of 'natural' sonic places to which sound is drawn. Some of my musical works illustrate a succession of almost kaleidoscopic psychoacoustic situations resulting from multiple combinations of resonance combined with a 'corresponding' manipulation of timbral and spatial attributes. *Woanders*, for piano and electronics, is a case in point. In such cases, the relationship between space and time can be perceived as a totality of interrelated micro-textural events based on subtle transformations of one or two musical elements during the duration of a resonance. In *Three Imaginary Dialogues*, for 4-hands piano, a more restricted, but no less effective, mobility of resonance may be perceived as the result of superimposing layers of sound prompted by 'phased' harmonic relationships taking place over a range of seven octaves. Such an articulation of resonance in space and time brings up an awareness of memory to my mind.

In pieces like *Waka, Athena, Shambhala, Eulogy, Déjà-vu, Transparence, Present Otherness, In the Temple* and *I Am*, to mention a few, I have attempted to recreate a condition of 'living' memory as a response to the perception of the magical and elusive. The relationship between space and resonance reminds me of the notion of gravitational waves that was predicted by Albert Einstein about a century ago. Einstein's notion at that time suggested that space is a matter-energy reality excluding a physical void, naturally bowed, to which only a geometry of bowed surfaces could be applied. Could an aural image of equivalent 'curved' resonances apply to our perception of musical space? Could gravitational resonance waves supply further acoustic indicators of the 'inner motion' of space I am referring to?

In terms of empirical cognition, the complex nature of the relationship between a musical space and I, the listener, suggests that there is no absolute truth about the way we perceive space-time and resonance. Furthermore, a notion of a 'container of sound' would be too restrictive to me because it would imply that space is a fixed entity, an immovable reality imposed on our auditory system. Is the perception of 'resonance-*in*-space' the same as the perception of 'resonance-*of*-space'? And how far can my perception of resonance be detached by the sound that generated it? One could equally deny the existence of space as an independent reality residing outside of sound, being detached from sound as it were, especially as 'pre-existing' sound. Yet, if space did not exist as an independent physical reality, how could a resonance fluctuate in our mind? The existence of 'something' beyond the sound itself that falls under the activity of our senses is not fully detectable by the mind. It would not result from what we hear, but from a logical deduction about what we do not hear, or rather from the relationship between what we hear and what we do not hear. Since our perception may not be able to establish the existence of an acoustic limit to space, we could assume that there is something beyond the psychoacoustic experience of space. Does the existence of this limit to the audible universe, even if removed from the reach of our cognition, suggest that we can hear by intuition? Would the perception of a musical space, therefore be predictable? Do sound, resonance and space really coincide as cognitive realities? The questions are endless! My experience of musical space remains eclipsed by that sense of the magical I mentioned earlier that I seem to experience again and again when I listen to 'space-resonance'. Perhaps some verses of the Roman poet and philosopher Lucretius can better express what I have so far tried to explain:

> *"The living force of his soul gained the day:*
> *on he passed far beyond the flaming walls of the world*
> *and traversed throughout in mind and spirit the immeasurable universe".*[110]

RD. Much of your piano music is full of near-to-silence experiences. Even, some of your titles refer to it. How far do you think you can travel towards silence and how important is it for you? Where does this search come from?

JP. I call this dimension the 'quasi-silence'. It is a kind of ritualistic exploration of the border between the known (sound) and the unknown (silence). The distance to the realm of silence can be very far and very near at the same time: this depends on how we want to listen to it. As I keep telling myself: it is not the destination that is important, but the journey. Listening to the

---

[110] *"Ergo vivida vis animi pervicit et extra processit longe flammantia moenia mundi atque omne immensum peragravit mente animoque"* (Lucretius, Book I:72–74).

'quasi-silence' implies a number of important reflections. The most obvious allusion is the contemplation of the events that have prompted a resonance. These events are melodic phrases, sonic gestures of any kind, single sounds, rhythmic patterns and so forth. The borderline between sound and silence conjures up a moment of reflection where I ask myself, 'what happened to the musical events I have just heard?' This question often brings to mind the theory of parallel universes (and lives), about which I wonder what may have happened to other universes, sounds, or lives of mine, that I may or may have not chosen or heard.

My perception of 'quasi-silence' calls forth a multi-dimensional experience of something (a metaphysical entity) that is outside of me and, at the same time, inside of me. This 'something' evokes a series of parallel images in my mind that seem to be timeless. Travelling towards silence is like facing space against nothingness, feeling however that where there is silence, there is being. This moment is very important to me. A near-to-silence listening condition reminds me of a near-to-death experience. There is a strong similarity between the two. Where is this 'borderline' perception taking me to? Am I experiencing one 'linear' occurrence or a combination of 'perpendicular' intuitions? What I do know is that unless I learn to inhabit silence, the uproar and distraction of society will deceive me into a false recognition of who I am; as I also know that when I learn to face the 'quasi-silence' with full concentration, something begins to happen.

I will go further and mention another sensation I experience in relation to the 'quasi-silence' and the notion of parallel universes: what if my parallel lives (those I may have never consciously chosen) were all here with me now at the border of silence? Could this experience reveal an aspect of the secret of death? Could all these 'lives' be elicited by a fluctuating resonance one step away from silence? This threshold may divide one form (life, reality) from another, one sound from another, a detail from the whole, but beyond this perceived limit affixed to the border of silence, I clearly sense the existence of another dimension. Beyond a border, there is always something else: another form of existence that is there to be explored. Any boundary to silence seems to always imply the thought of something beyond *what* is included by the boundary, that which cannot but be a more distant or closer space to infinity, perhaps restricted by its own boundary. If I didn't want to hypothesise any spatial limit to silence, I should acknowledge nothingness as a limit, a perception of the void that is not even silence, but non-existence.

My lifetime quest comes from an innate desire to understand who I am, where I come from and where I am going to. Although it is an individual journey, this process also implies a relation to others and the world we live in. I want to remember who I am by remembering the past (my origin) and (I know this may sound absurd) the future. Silence is the best friend of the soul because in silence, we remember who we are. In the quasi-silence dimension, I find myself suspended on a thin line between past and future, near and far, on the threshold of a psychological dimension stimulated by resonance, micro-sounds and time. This is one of the most challenging and powerful experiences of music. It is a synonym for true reflection, and a potential for self-transformation as a human being. In the quasi-silence dimension, I know I am touching a part of myself that is sacred. If silence is the greatest victim of contemporary society, listening to the quasi-silence is the most generous form of experiencing music because when I listen on the edge of silence, I open up my mind to reflections *of* sounds that have been played (words that have been spoken), thus allowing fantasy, imagination, intuition, awareness and the universe of my subconscious to have free play and foster a condition of mystical unity with myself and the universe; the ultimate understanding of who I am.

RD. In much of your music, meditation and the sacred seem to be of utmost importance. Does meditation affect your process of composition? What relation do you see in regard to those kinds of inner experiences and your sound world?

JP. Meditation means to think over, but also to breathe deeper and measure oneself with one's inner world, including one's shadows. Writing music is a similar experience in that I 'measure' myself within a universe that is living within me and around me. Some of my piano pieces are born out of meditating on a specific topic. More often, though, I meditate while I am playing the piano. In such moments, I allow myself to enter the awareness through which I experience myself and the universe by breathing consciously and creating a sense of mental emptiness that allows me to unplug from my daily occupations and feel the 'now'. By so doing, I am aware that the information that is filtered out by the conscious mind passes onto the subconscious and vice versa. This experience includes perceptions, images, impulses, feelings, emotions and intuitions. In such a context, sound is a perennial activator of a cosmic memory that prompts me to plunge into a mysterious world. The pieces I write under such a circumstance have no pre-determined structure, and they are born spontaneously from a specific moment in time that is unrepeatable. In such cases, I respond to sound in the most intuitive way. Heaven on earth isn't a place to visit, but a living condition.

RD. In your use of electronics with acoustic instruments, is there a specific non-musical idea that may inspire you to use this combination?

JP. Each piece is different, and it is impossible for me to provide a general answer because the approach to the instruments I use in a composition is always different and very much depending on the idea I am pursuing in my mind. In any case, electronics are very important to me. They are complete instruments: abstract and sensual, metaphysical and imaginary, dreamy and factually 'concrète' in the most Schaefferian sense of the word. Moreover, electronics are the perfect instruments for the enhancement of focused listening. When I enter the dimension of an electroacoustic sound or space, I inevitably begin to hear better, to play better, and even to *feel* better. The art of how to listen to sound and music remains a primary circumstance for composition and performance.

RD. How important is or has been spectral music and spectral techniques in your music? How is it related to the above-mentioned spirituality in your music?

JP. I don't follow specific schools or styles designated by the academic world and, consequently, I don't see my musical output fitting into any of the most common descriptions of 'modern' or 'post-modern' music. The music I write is free from stylistic categorisations and compositional dogmas. I only know two kinds of music: good music and bad music. I often work with the spectrum of a single note, or more notes, without ever thinking that I am writing 'spectral' music. Nor do I blow my own trumpet announcing to the world that I am writing spectral music as some composers do. I can certainly tell you that I love to explore the (spectral) universe of a single sound. Symbolically speaking, the spectrum of a sound is the mirror of the spirit of life.

RD. Can dreams or trance experiences turn into a musical work?

JP. Yes. I have experienced this many times.

RD. Have you ever dreamt of a musical image and tried to transcribe it afterwards?

JP. Yes. *Spirits*, for synthesizer, is music that I dreamt of over a period of two weeks; day and night. It resembles what I would define as a mystical experience. *Shambhala* and *Athena* and some other pieces were born out of a trance or quasi-trance experience. Very often I dream melodies, chords, or timbres which I include in my pieces. I also dream well-known melodies.

RD. I am most interested in having your overview of your evolution in writing for piano over the years. What are the most important changes you have passed through and how has your 'path to knowledge' evolved over the different periods?

JP. Being my instrument, I think the piano offers the closest evidence of my personal journey and process of 'individuation'[111] through music. I have an archive comprising several recordings of performances and rehearsals including improvisations I have played in the past 35 years, although I have to admit that I have often thrown away scores and recordings of the past which I felt did no longer reflect my current sense of identity. In retrospect, that may have been a mistake. Who knows? How can the end result of a musical work be evaluated by the same person who created it? We may sometimes speculate much about music, and discussions on music may come across as entertaining and even enlightening at times, but in the end, it is always the music (whatever the genre and idiom) that will speak for itself. My evolution in writing for piano over the years reflects my evolution as a human being, and I mean this in the most natural way. The piano repertoire surely shows different and contrasting aspects of my personalities (notice the plural form of 'personalities', as each of us has many personalities rather than only one). Like the personalities, these pieces are all connected to each other and I have never planned an evolution of my life, nor my piano pieces, systematically. From a pianistic and compositional point of view, the most important changes I have experienced are the transition from aleatory to fully notated pieces, especially at the beginning of my compositional output in the 1980s, from polyphonic to gestural and more resonance-based textures and vice versa, and from the use of the full chromatic scale to more restricted scales and vice versa. All of these transitions are recurrent as they depend on the nature of the music I need to write.

My 'path to knowledge' evolves continually and will end (in the material form) the day in which my spirit will leave the body. One thing I can say is that writing music feels like entering a dimension of endless time. What would a 'path to knowledge' be without time? To honour the dignity of this path means to celebrate life and the eternity of our human values with art. Sometimes, the music I write is passionate and even on the edge of despair when referring to the world I see around me. Other times, it is focused on my search for the spirit in its most genuine and uncontaminated way. In the latter case, I experience time as a form of concealed eternity, as the only real and ultimate companion that will finally take me through the journey to a different world. But in both cases, the trajectory includes passion and contemplation, the sensual and the spiritual as two sides of the same coin resembling the search for ethical integrity. During the process of composition, I often feel as if I were on the edge of dying, about to enter another dimension that can only be hinted at by sound. I am saying this because it is well known that when a person is close to death, the veil between the physical and invisible world is very thin. It is a mysterious boundary that is also experienced in moments of great suffering or sickness. This is how, today, I would describe the experience of composition as a mirror of my path to knowledge.

RD. I am very interested in simple forms that work perfectly and run away from very complex music that has no meaning for me. But it may not be always like that. How do you deal with simplicity and complexity in music?

---

[111] As intended by C.G. Jung.

JP. My first thought is that I may, perhaps, have a natural inclination towards simplicity. But then, I ask myself, what is simplicity? And what is complexity? By superimposing layers of simple melodies or rhythms, we will obtain a complex texture: will the resulting music be perceived as simple or complex? Where would the 'morality' of this music reside exactly? Meaning is another big topic. I wonder what is the meaning of 'meaning'? C.K. Odgen and I.A. Richards[112] have tried to answer this question by examining the relations of thoughts and language and dividing language into symbolic and emotive functions. A science of symbolism may reveal how all forms of intellectual, emotional and social life are influenced by our changing attitudes to the use of words. We assign meaning to sound configurations the same way we do to words and phrases. But is a language like another language? I don't think so. Let me give you an example: to me, the French verb 'oublier' (translated into English as 'to forget') is not the same as the English 'forget', the German 'vergessen', the Italian 'dimenticare' or the Spanish 'olvidar'. Each of these words will be translated by all the dictionaries as 'to forget' but they have each a very different nuance, colour and quality of 'forgetting', something that is unique to their language. I can't imagine Schönberg's *Pierrot Lunaire* having been written in the idiom of Mozart and Brahms. Do tonal[113] idioms signify something other than themselves?

My truth is that I don't think in terms of idioms and techniques. For instance, I never think, 'Oh yes, now I am going to write a simple piano piece' or, 'I am now writing a complex ensemble piece'. And the same applies to the idiom I use in my musical works, regardless of how we want to call it: atonal, tonal, modal, microtonal, and so forth. When I compose, I plunge into a perception, an idea, a vision, an emotion. This is the first and most important preoccupation for me. It is this 'poietical' dimension that generates the methodology, the procedures, the idiom and the style of the music. Each of my works is a unique artefact that reflects an exclusive universe where I never plan the idiom first. Pieces like *Epitaph*, *Koan* or *Transfiguration*, for example, sound the way they must sound (in this case: passionate, intense, impulsive, anxious and, at times, ruthlessly fierce) according to what I am trying to convey. It is the content I choose that defines the means by which the music must take shape. Works like *Waka* or *Athena*, which have a completely different genesis than the works I mentioned earlier, needed a much more reduced and 'simple' texture in order to articulate what they are supposed to convey. From a cognitive perspective I find simplicity can be a much more complex psychoacoustic reality than complexity because when dealing with less information, our mind (neurologically speaking) is more challenged by integrating and segregating all the sonic data presented in a minimal scenario where the plainness of the material will require the most focused listening. Psychoacoustics show that this will not be possible when listening to a complex texture.

RD. I am curious to know your thoughts on musical notation and especially the allowance of a certain amount of freedom to the performer, as in the case of *Glimpse* and *Shambala*. How do you relate to spatial notation and how do you choose between this and traditional notation?

JP. I tend to be very pragmatic in these matters. As a pianist who has performed all his early piano pieces himself, I have been faced with the problem of how to notate what I had in mind since the beginning of my composing. Again, it has always been the musical context and the practicality of how to notate the sound I had in mind that made me choose the most appropriate musical notation. *After Silence (1)*, *Glimpse* and *Shambhala* must be based on a slow flow determined by the pianist, hence the space-time notation I have used in these scores. *Glimpse* was written as a tribute to the life of John Cage and as such should be played with an

---

[112] C.K. Odgen and I. A. Richards (1923).
[113] In the general meaning of the word; *not* in the sense of Western functional tonality.

appropriate attitude. The music is based on the resonance triggered by the initial gesture and the recurrent C-A-G-E motif to be played 'largo, molto calmo'. This information is needed in order to give the pianist the quality of the music I was after. Each of these C-A-G-E motifs, scattered throughout the registers of the piano, is followed by a resonance corresponding to a specific duration written in seconds. Space-time notation allows all the motifs to be played freely within the 'largo, molto calmo' indication, including the resonances notated in segments of seconds. When I wrote this piece, I saw this notation to be the most appropriate for the idea I had in mind. Surely, I could re-write the score in mensural notation, but I would still prefer to keep the visual sense of temporal 'elasticity' provided by space notation. The same applies to *After Silence (1)*.

The first score of *Manhattan* (1989) was written in space-time notation as well. I performed this piece many times in the 1990s and I always felt at ease with the visual fluidity provided by this kind of notation. Yet, two years ago I re-wrote the score in mensural notation. Why did I do that? Because I know that the majority of classical pianists have significant problems performing the kind of rhythmic texture I employ in this piece from a score written in space-time notation.

Shambhala is a meditation on the idea of a pure world as depicted in Tibetan Buddhism. It is a piece that needed to be notated the way I did, with no time-signature or tempo marking, with the only musical indication being 'lentamente, senza tempo, calmissimo'. The latter should say it all: the pianists should enter this space of timelessness, as in a meditation, in order to determine the (slow) pace of the music according to their perception of an imaginary paradise on earth. It was important for me to encourage the performers to enter the most appropriate state of meditation in order to play the music with the right character.

Many of my early piano and chamber music pieces were often notated in space-time notation but I subsequently revised the score by using mensural notation wherever it would make sense. *Musica Reservata* is the most representative example of this change of notation as all the original pieces of this cycle were improvisations written in space notation. Eventually, I re-wrote the score in mensural notation in order to make sure that any pianist would be able to obtain a clear understanding of the performance of the 12 pieces. Another issue related to the choice of space-time notation is the instrumentalist's interaction with the electronics. Most, if not all my works using acoustic and electronic instruments, use time-space notation and have been conceived with a certain freedom about the way the instrumentalist would interact with the electronics. I have never used click-tracks, for example, as I think they are a form of prison for the instrumentalists that will ultimately damage the quality of performance. Even in those rare moments where a performer has to play in unison with the electronics, I prefer the instrumentalist to learn the relevant passage by heart, rather than be restricted by the mensural writing of the same passage. I have tried all these possibilities myself at the piano and have come to the conclusion that the less restricted the notation is, the more precise and musical the interplay with the electronics will be.

MORE QUESTIONS ON *MUSICA RESERVATA*
Jeffrey Holmes

JH. Regarding your piano work *Musica Reservata*, what is your relationship to the title 'Nocturne(s)'? Is it a programmatic reference, such as used by Debussy, with actual musical gestures that illustrate the programmatic ideas? Or is the title more of a formal or textural designation, such as used by Chopin to indicate a (usually) ternary work that is an imitation of a Bellini-style opera aria, featuring a repeated chordal accompaniment with a highly

ornamented melody? Or do you have your own interpretation and use of the term 'Nocturne' in a musical context?

JP. The first idea that comes to my mind when I hear the term 'nocturne' is its literal meaning 'nocturnal'. By this definition, I associate anything that is related to the night, in this case, a musical composition. The night has always been very important in my life because of the atmosphere of silence, solitude and intimacy that comes with it. Silence and darkness are strong instigators of reflection, study and meditation. Having grown up bilingually and lived some of my youth in Italy, I got accustomed to the noun 'notte' (night) and its adjective 'notturno' (nocturnal, of the night). These are words that belong to daily language, so in my mind, the idea of a 'nocturne' is immediately related to anything that happens in the night time, not particularly to a musical genre. The musical form used by John Field, Frederik Chopin and many others were not much of a concern to me. It is the idea of the night represented by music that fascinated me. As a child, Chopin's *Nocturnes* were certainly the pieces I enjoyed most playing at the piano. Obviously, there is a strong programmatic and formalistic element attached to a musical Nocturne, and Field's and Chopin's works have created a stylised form of this genre in the piano repertoire. Although Chopin's nocturnes are richer and more daring that Field's pieces, I still feel that Field's nocturnes deserve more recognition in the academic and concert establishment.

It's interesting that you mentioned Debussy. Actually, I don't consider his *Three Nocturnes* for orchestra as nocturnes. To me, they lack all the ingredients of a 'night-piece' I mentioned earlier: intimacy, reflection, contemplation, quietness. The first of the orchestral pieces, *Nuages*, is more of a colourful surrogate of *La Mer*; the second nocturne *Fêtes* is too extroverted and rhythm-gripped for a nocturnal piece; and the strongly descriptive character of the third piece *Sirènes* is more of an impressionistic music-painting than an intimate night piece. It is said that Debussy chose this title, *Nocturnes*, not as a reference to the piano tradition by the same name, but as a tribute to the paintings of the American painter James A.M. Whistler, whose decision to entitle his night-related pictures *Nocturnes* was influenced by his patron Frederik Leyland, an English shipowner who loved Chopin's nocturnes. But while Whistler's paintings retain all the characteristics of a nocturne in the visual realm, Debussy's orchestral pieces don't.

JH. The title of *Musica Reservata* appears to reference a specific style and period of vocal music. One of the characteristics of this style is extensive ornamentation. Your work *Musica Reservata* is often very simple in terms of texture and figuration, and for long stretches, seemingly devoid of decoration and ornamentation. Other than resembling choral music in the appearance of the notation and the chordal figurations, how does this music fit under the designation of *Musica Reservata*?

JP. The first answer is historical: the title refers to the notion of 'Musica Reservata' mentioned by Adrian Petit Coclico, a Netherlandish composer of the Renaissance and pupil of Josquin des Prez who coined the word in the preface to his book *Compendium Musices* published in Nuremberg, in 1552. Although there is no consensus on the meaning of the term, the term referred to music that made use of chromaticism and voice leading as devices for stressing emotions in motets and madrigals of the 16th century. The notion of 'Musica Reservata' also referred to music performed in small circles such as the aristocratic courts of that time, implying a sense of intimacy and inwardness, typical of the night time, which is one of the aspects I explore in my piano cycle. The other aspect to be mentioned is, again, language. 'Musica Reservata' is the Latin for the corresponding Italian of 'musica riservata' (almost identical). In English it means music that is 'reserved', 'confidential' or even 'secret'). If I read or hear 'musica reservata', coming from the Italian language, I perceive this concept as a living, contemporary notion, rather than a historical expression of an old musical genre. Moreover, I love the sound and the colour of the words. Back to the historical meaning, the emphasis on the musical expression of the meaning of a vocal text through a conscious use of rhythm and chromaticism was also described by the Dutch humanist Samuel Quickenberg around 1560 in his comments on Orlande de Lassus's *Penitential Psalms*. Quickenberg exalts the expressive force of 'the individual affections' illustrated by Lassus's psalms and states that *'this genre of music they call musica reservata.'*[114] The term was clearly presented in terms of musical 'affect' (emotional impact) especially in relation to words. In his treatise *Astrologiae iudiciarie isagogica* (printed in Cologne in 1559) Jean Taisnier mentions 'musica reservata' as *'genus chromaticum'*, a highly chromatic idiom of the time. And Nicola Vicentino in his treatise *L'antica musica ridotta alla moderna prattica* (printed in 1555) writes:

"they understand that (as ancient writers show) chromatic and enharmonic music was reserved appropriately for another purpose than was diatonic music: the latter was sung at public festivals in communal places for the benefit of coarse ears, whereas the former was used to praise great personages and heroes for the benefit of refined ears amid the private diversions of lords and princes." [115]

In 1611 Reimundo Ballestra mentions that 'musica reservata' was a performance by soloists, as opposed to vocal groups.[116] Although there is still no consensus on the term, and perhaps there will never be, in many other historical references the notion 'reservata' indicates 'expressiveness' achieved by chromaticism including enharmonic modulation as expedients of emotional qualities depicted as 'reserved' (confidential, secret, private) as contrasting to the diatonicism of the 16th century. As for my title choice, it was a combination of historical evidence, the elegance of the name and the implication of a 'confidential' and 'private' character of a music written in the intimacy of the night that caught my imagination. In fact, it was the music that came first, not the title. I remember looking for a title that would bring up the intimate atmosphere of the meditative pieces while I was writing them in the night time. Also, I should mention the poem I wrote in the same period during one of my night walks along the lake of Lucerne on 13th December 1988. This poem is important because it really is the unsung text of the music that conveys the state of mind from which all the pieces were born.

from tranquillity reflecting
mirrors of space
for invisible nights

silver
from black
blending

while listening
through the barely audible

---

[114] Printed in Vol. xxvi of the new Lassus Edition, 1995.
[115] Vicentino (1996:33).
[116] More on the subject can be found in *The New Grove Dictionary of Music and Musicians* (2001:475).

JH. *Musica Reservata* employs improvisation in various ways. Yet even the composed music clearly avoids any regularity of pulse or phrasing. Thus, distinctions between composed music and performer-generated improvisation are vague. What criteria and/or goals compel you to choose specific notation or to invite improvisation?

JP. Each musical work I write has a different story and illustrates a unique musical context. I don't have one general rule about improvisation that I apply to all my works. It is important to mention that I wrote these pieces for myself as night reflections of a highly personal and private (reserved) character. As a pianist, I have improvised all my life, and this is still my most immediate relationship with the piano. As for *Musica Reservata*, when I played these pieces at the piano for the first time, the last thing I had in mind was the idea of other pianists playing them. Each piece was a very private contemplation, a meditation at the border of a prayer, if you like. Although in the score they are listed as number six and seven of the cycle, the two pieces *To the night (1)* and *To the night (2)* are the pieces I wrote first. Both were born as improvisations which I later fixed on a score. As I mentioned in the score, all the pieces of the *Musica Reservata* cycle could be slightly varied with ornamentation and some stylistically appropriate and sensitively executed improvisation. This would indeed reflect the original idea of the pieces, as well the historical notion of 'musica reservata'. As discussed further in the book (especially in the article by Agnese Toniutti), all these pieces were born as improvisations. It was only when other pianists began to play the pieces I had loosely notated in the form of a score, that I realised I had to write down as much as possible in order to avoid misunderstandings about the nature and the interpretation of the music. This was a necessity that came later, especially due to the fact that the majority of classically-trained pianists cannot improvise. Therefore, I ended up writing down the improvisations in such a way that any pianist can play these pieces *without* having to improvise. What we can see in the score today are the twelve chosen and refined versions of what I played. All this to say that when I 'wrote' (perhaps I should say, 'played') the pieces of *Musica Reservata*, I was deeply focused on these very private and, to some extent, 'mystical' moments. My mindset at that time was not at all addressed at choosing or rationalising criteria and goals for future musical performances or intellectualising specific notations for improvisation.

JH. *Musica Reservata*'s tenth piece, *Incidental*, appears to be a departure from the other 11 pieces in terms of tempo, gesture, texture, and overall pacing of musical activity. What unites this piece with the others? In what ways is this piece similar to the others as being titled a 'Nocturne'? In what ways does it fit under the referential title of *Musica Reservata*?

JP. No one of these pieces is titled a 'nocturne'. I avoided that word deliberately since I did not want to elicit associations with the nocturne tradition of the Romantic period. They are all night-pieces in the sense I have discussed earlier. Indeed, *Incidental* is different to the others, but I cannot give you a rational answer for that, the nature of the pieces being what it is. It is the cryptic (and irrational) language of the soul that 'justified' the music of *Incidental* to manifest itself in such a context. My inner (reserved!) voice knew well that *Incidental* belonged to the cycle.

CHAPTER EIGHT

ELECTROACOUSTIC MUSIC

LUMINOUS IMAGINATION:
THEREAFTER, TRANSPARENCE AND *WOANDERS*
Anne LeBaron

AL. Indeed, these three works create a lovely triptych full of similarities and are also embodying differences, with the larger ensemble piece occupying the centre of the triptych, and with the chronological order of their creation represented from earliest to latest (2013, 2014, and 2016). *Thereafter* (organ and electronics), *Transparence* (viola, ensemble, and electronics), and *Woanders* (electronics and piano) all share a similar approach in the handling of the acoustic instruments and their interactions with fixed and live electronics. A dialectic of opposition is established, coloured by ambiguity and evolving into unity. Was this an intentionally realised formal technique or did it emerge unbidden as you composed each piece?

JP. It was intentional for each of the three pieces. Timbral ambiguity, opposition and unity are major preoccupations in much of my music. However, these works are not connected to each other, at least on a conscious level.

AL. The use of space characterises each of these pieces in distinctive ways and relates to the expansion of the sound palette achieved in your electronics. Could you comment on the degree to which the enhancement and augmentation (or compression, if applicable) of the space is critical to *Transparence*?

JP. First of all, I would like to mention that my perception of space as a musical feature elicits varying forms of what I call 'nonlocal cognition'. The universe in which we live is not static, and I am incessantly searching for musical spaces of a mobile and transcending quality. Gaston Bachelard has written one of the most insightful descriptions of space as a manifestation of an 'immensity' that resides in each of us. He speaks of an 'Intimate Immensity' and argues that the relationship of immensity, memory, imagination and meditation is based on facets of a limitless space that is living in an individual. He writes that this immensity *"originates in a body of impressions which, in reality, have little connection with geographical information. We do not have to be long in the woods to experience the always rather anxious impression of 'going deeper and deeper' into a limitless world."*[117]

To me, the experience of space represents one of the finest and most subtle forms of 'perceptual poetry' where motion in space (or a 'moving space') is synonymous with a quest for timelessness and the ultimate experience of freedom. Motion implies flexibility and progress, and is always proportional to the willingness to explore unknown dimensions of perception. The mobility of space in my music implies the attributes of expansion and diversification, the degrees of which vary from work to work according to the nature of the music.

The importance of space in *Transparence* is connected to the notion of reminiscence, timbral transfiguration followed by dissolution, and locality of sound. The physical space,

---

[117] Bachelard (1994:185).

maintained by the ensemble on stage, is opposed to a non-physical space delineated by pre-recorded excerpts from *Transitions* (quartet), *Transference* (quintet), and the *Trans*-solos pieces, re-proposed by an invisible ensemble. The sounds of this 'ghost'-ensemble are projected onto larger spaces through reverberation and played back in quadraphonic spatialisation from at least four loudspeakers located around the audience. This dichotomy of space is characterised by *what* the ensemble is playing on stage in relation to *what, where* and *how* the ghost-ensemble is playing from these other spaces perceived through the loudspeakers. The pre-recorded and processed fragments suggest not only a dislocation of space but also a dislocation of time because the extracts re-proposed by the ghost-ensemble are inserted at different points in the score thus evoking an additional sense of temporality of events within the piece. Also, in the quadraphonic playback of the ghost-ensemble, the spatialisation of the fragments is distributed around the audience in a circular motion.

The next aspect to be considered is the relational perception of space in conjunction with the recollection of previous events played by the ensemble on stage. I have called these specific moments 'space/memory' locations where the division of the two ensembles (the 'real' one performing on stage and the invisible one that I call 'ghost-ensemble') is well-defined and ambiguous at the same time. When I wrote *Transparence*, I was concerned about the question of how a hypothetical sense of memory might sound like. Therefore, I tried to evoke a distinct 'memory-sound' quality by using timbral modifications based on ring-modulation and filter, and by diffusing the sonic sources of the ghost ensemble using varying degrees of reverberation and delay assigned to four independent locations in the concert hall (the quadraphonic setting). It is important to stress that all these modifications may elicit a sense of memory only *in relation* to what the physical ensemble is playing on stage.

There are five instances in the piece where these 'space/memory' moments hold a particular significance. The first one is elicited by the viola and its ghost-counterpart in the electronics part (bars 94-101). The second one is again a 'duet' taking place between the visible and invisible viola (bars 102-108) based on single notes and double-stops played on each instrument. The evocation of a larger acoustic space is emphasised by the decay time of the reverberation to the real viola being 5 seconds long and contrasting with the much longer decay time of the dramatically altered viola sounds in the electronic part. The third moment (bars 111-113) follows immediately and is more subtle than the previous one since the clarinet 'tremoli' in the electronics are now masked by the 'tremoli' played by the bass clarinet on stage contoured by the other instruments. The fourth moment (bars 163-170) is characterised by the instruments of the real ensemble improvising on the clarinet 'tremoli' of the electronic part; similar to the previous moment, their sound is heard at the edge of masking the 'ghost-tremoli'. The next 'space/memory' moment (bars 182-184) is more obvious as it elicits a window for a very short yet distant sonic space generated by a fleeting rhythmic gesture of the piano.

AL. Can you explain more about how you used live electronics in *Transparence?*

JP. In my musical world the use of electronics, especially live electronics, reflects a perception of nonlocality that occurs in varying degrees. Titles like *Nowhere, Afterglow, Beyond the Bridge,* and *After Silence (1)*, to mention a few, suggest a concern for imaginary spaces as *"expansion of infinite things"*[118] to quote Bachelard again. Different spaces suggest sensations in constant movement, intimate metaphors of spatial poetry (similar to what Bachelard would refer to as "poetic spatiality") characterised by fluctuating perceptions of width, depth, distance, spaciousness (i.e. surrounding effect and 'feeling' of space) and prompted by modification of pre-delay, attack, size and decay time of reverberation. Similar to the interpretation of a piano

---

[118] Bachelard (1994:202).

or orchestral piece that will vary from concert hall to concert hall, I adjust the live electronics to the space of the concert hall where I am performing. I perceive any spatial modification I make of an instrumental sound as a search for a nonlocal reality (the electronically-extended space) in relation to a local one (the acoustic space of the concert hall), a sensation of being ambiguously *here* and *somewhere else* at the same time, a perception of parallel spaces sounding simultaneously. As I love to play with words, I want to give you an idea of the kind of ambiguity I am referring to: the word 'nowhere' can be read as 'now-here'; a title like *After Silence* can be read as both a temporal condition following a silence or an allusion to a search for silence. Live manipulations of space make me *feel* music beyond the static attributes of a confined acoustic location while influencing my perception of loudness and timbre.

In *Transparence*, an important function of the live electronics is to connect, and blend, the (acoustic) sounds being performed on stage with the pre-recorded and processed sounds of the ghost-ensemble played from the soundfile (the electronic part). This connection creates spatial and timbral ambiguity throughout the performance of the piece. The same acoustic and aesthetic considerations apply to the projection of the phrases played by the viola onto wider acoustic spaces, where a specific purpose is to create a sense of 'sonic aura' through subtle alterations of timbre in space around the phrases of the viola. Some other times, this sonic aura is achieved by juxtaposing the melodic line played by the viola extended by reverberation with the same line played by the ghost-viola. A note I wrote in one of my sketches reveals a timbre-specific preoccupation: *"a passage to the invisible / a world gradually becoming transparent"*. The allusion refers to instrumental sounds that must lose their pitch identity in order to become 'something else', namely a transparent quality of timbre resulting from the process of pitch disintegration leading to quasi-silence.

AL. In relation to the use of space in general: you employ resonance in so many diverse ways, and it plays an important role in these compositions. How would you articulate the connection of resonance to the importance of space in these pieces?

JP. A resonance is the quintessence of a spatial dimension: the two are inextricably linked to one another. I have written several works where resonance is one of the major attributes of the musical discourse: in *Thereafter, Transparence* and *Woanders*, as in other works, there is an intense focus on resonance as an 'after-image', that is a sonic bridge existing between pitch and the realm of silence. I can dedicate an enormous amount of time to modify the timbral and spatial attributes of a resonance, at times by superimposing several resonances in order to create a baffling perception of space, as I did in *Woanders* and *Nowhere*. Resonance is also a reflection of pitch, and I do mean 'reflection' in both its acoustic and philosophical meaning. The relationship between pitch and resonance is similar to the relationship between the visible and the invisible: this is imagery that is emphasised, for example, in the second movement of *Thereafter* by the timbral transfiguration of the four Isis chords. Pitch is the 'originator', the principal energy and the 'rational' (the Yang principle). By contrast, resonance opens up the door to imagination, intuition, and perception of pitch (the Yin principle).

You may remember Barry Truax's definition of 'listening-in-search' as the *"focus on one sound to the exclusion of others"*.[119] To me, a resonance is the most intimate region of this 'listening-in-search' mode because the attractiveness of sound is best represented by the aural image resulting from the resonating chord or phrase circulating and dispersing in time and space. Resonance represents the 'breathing' moment of a sonic event. In *Transparence*, the resonance evolving from the phrases played by the ensemble suggests what I would call a moment of 'dialectic interrogation' of the music debate taking place on stage. Resonance is now

---

[119] Truax (2001:22).

elevated to larger spatial dimensions evoked by the sound of the ghost-ensemble. In such cases, the search for enhanced space may be compared to a need to reformulate the spatial attributes of sound as a reminder of the simultaneousness of space and time as cohesive manifestations of pitch perceived on distant dimensions.

AL. Each of these compositions expresses dream-like qualities; while listening, I found myself journeying to worlds not of this earth. In dreams, we often travel to other places, often unrecognizable. Do your compositions ever emerge from dreams, and do you ever enter trance-like states when composing?

JP. *Spirits*, for synthesizer, is music I dreamt, rather than composed. This dreaming experience was so strong that I felt impelled to write down the music immediately. I remember that when I was dreaming this music, I found myself suspended in the air. The sounds I heard resembled voices singing short motives recurring over a very long span. I hesitated to make this music public for about three years as I felt unsure about the reaction of the audience. Two years later, I felt it was time to break the silence, get over my hesitation and take responsibility for my musical life regardless of what people may think of it. In February 1993, I performed *Spirits* for the first time at the BMIC[120] in London. It was clear to me that this music had been channelled by my subconscious. Apart from that experience, I very often dream music. More specifically, I dream of chords and short melodies. Other times, I dream of sounds of captivating beauty. On a few occasions, I have used the melodies I dreamt of in my compositions. Dreaming is a very important area of interest and research in my life. I have read a lot about it and attended specific courses on the subject. I have also learnt how to remain conscious while dreaming. This is called 'lucid dreaming'. It is indeed a very interesting experience because while I am sleeping I am aware that I am dreaming, and I am able to recognize my thoughts and emotions during the dream. This is not easy to do, but when it works, I can assure you that it is a mind-altering experience.

In the Talmud, it is written that a dream that is not interpreted is like a letter that has never been opened, and I agree with this view very much. I treat my dreams with urgency and determination, being aware that dreaming is a sense just like sight, smell, touch, taste, hearing, and, as such, it is a vehicle to access a condition of knowing. Dreams take us to other regions of space and time where it is possible to experience re-enchanted dimensions of life and the awareness of deeper states of responsibility. As the physicist Amit Goswami states, *"Dreaming is a conscious experience, though different from that of the waking state".*[121]

Trance-like states during composition are very frequent, indeed. Works like *Present Otherness, In the Temple, After Silence (1), Athena* and *Shambhala*, for instance, have been written is such states. I am not really qualified as to whether I can describe these circumstances as pure trance experiences, but I can certainly tell you that they have been very strong trance-like events, at the very least. These are magical moments that are impossible to verbalise. *Thereafter* and *Woanders* were also born from such experiences.

AL. Do you consider silence to serve a formal function, or do you think of silence as more of a dramatic contrast to sound?

JP. Silence is not an abstract category. What I mean is that I don't *think* of silence, but I *experience* it with my senses. Perhaps this is something I have acquired through the experience of meditation, reflection and contemplation. Although I don't intend to romanticise this

---

[120] British Music Information Centre.
[121] Goswami (1993:106).

perception of silence, the sensuality I am referring to goes hand in hand with the way I listen to music, and I cannot detach the significance of silence from the importance of listening. Sometimes, I even wonder whether I may be able to perceive 'gestures' of silence? Generally speaking, I notice a tendency to associate stillness with a contemplative condition similar to a state of trance. Although this aspect is undeniable, the perception of silence is more complex than that. In the European music tradition, silence has been regarded as the background against which sound is perceived. Japanese music has reversed such polarities and treated silence as an experience to be perceived against the background of sound, which I find immensely revealing and more appropriate to my aesthetics of music. I can experience silence against the background of sound by using a very focused listening attitude that I like to compare to what Louis Pasteur called 'the prepared mind'.[122]

In the past 20 years, I have learnt that the art of listening to silence is very multidimensional, and that it is music that indicates the way I am supposed to perceive silence. When I listen to a single sound or a melody, I know my ear is developing codecs that are encoding and decoding a sound data signal. It is a stratagem of the brain that is telling me how to 'interpret' the acoustic signal. When listening to silence, these codecs are also connected to my expectation and psychological anticipation of silence as a result of the preceding sonic event: for instance, a dense gesture including many notes played loudly will induce a perception of silence that is very different to a situation where a rest is placed immediately after a delicate gesture containing a few notes and played softly. If a dramatic gesture will prompt a dramatic sensation of silence, a soft gesture will generate the opposite impression. In other words, I can attune my expectation of silence to the way I perceive the contiguous sounds within the given (chronological) flow of time. Also, my sensation of silence will change dramatically if I mentally enter the dimension of non-linear time. This applies also to the process of composition, but I suspect it is impossible to verbalise it adequately. As with any other component of the music texture, silence serves an important function in the form of a musical work. I call this structural aspect an 'integrative silence' in which a rest, for example, stands as the 'negative' counterpart of a sound. If sound is Yang, silence would be Yin.

AL. I have another question related to ambiguity, in this case, the elusive border between sound and silence. Your 'border' silences (at the beginning of *Thereafter,* for instance, or during the long closing section of *Transparence*) are infused with subtle energies. Is the 'border' between silence and sound more useful to you than silence itself (if there is such a thing)?

JP. Your 'border silence' definition corresponds to what I call 'quasi-silence'. We are trying to depict a musical region characterised either by resonance or fragments of subtle sounds living at the border of silence and illuminating a tenuous realm between stillness and sound. At the beginning of *Thereafter,* the quasi-silence is evoked by controlling the pressurized air produced by the wind system of the organ as a simulation of breathing, while in the closing section of *Transparence* it is the fusion of filtered instrumental sounds blending with air and wind sounds that leads to the concluding silence of the piece.

I wouldn't say that quasi-silence is more 'useful' than silence, simply because these two conditions, although being similar, remain different. But they do merge, blur and 'interact' by underlining a concealed meaning that connects two or more sounds. This can be heard very

---

[122] During a lecture on microbiology he gave at the University of Lille, I think, in 1854, he said that *"in the fields of observation chance favours only the prepared mind."* What he meant by that was that a scientist must know as much as possible about his subject in order to be prepared to recognize the significance of chance observation with an open and attentive mind; in other words, that knowledge is based on the attention to the world. This description applies perfectly to the way we should listen to music.

clearly in the music of Anton Webern, for example, where dying resonances bring up varying degrees of tension between the instrumental sounds depending on the timbre, loudness and register of each note. Much too often I experience a musical culture where a rest is considered as a marginal phenomenon, a transitory deflection of sound that is deliberately obscuring silence. I experience the opposite: each rest I write is a constitutive element of the music fully embedded in the musical discourse, and opens up a 'memory-space' pervaded by the absence of an active sound and by the concealed presence of what is no longer being heard. It is a space where the memory of sound becomes suddenly alive as if wanting to re-interpret the music from a distant perspective. A resonance can sharpen a high level of concentration putting me in the position to absorb the preceding event (a melody, a chord, and so on) anew in its full distinctiveness and within a dissimilar acoustic space. By the same token, a constant prolongation of sound can evoke a periphery of sound that may enable me to perceive the preceding sonic event in its concealed quality.

AL. In *Thereafter,* a voice is heard clearly towards the end of the piece, vocalising 'a', 'e', 't' which is likely related to the Egyptian symbolism that you refer to in the programme note. Could you elaborate on why you chose the texts that appear in this work?

JP. I didn't use a traditional text, but fragments of words taken from the reading of a sacred text in a temple that I had recorded years earlier. I wanted to emphasise the sacred symbolism of the living universe perceived in ancient Egypt, where all things are permeated by energetic forces that contain a soul. These short vocal sounds are stressing the importance of sensuality as a divine vehicle in these ancient traditions. Our senses are bridges to physical areas and psychological realms that we call 'soul'. In this context, being 'sensual' means to experience the dignity of our soul. Distorted religious traditions in the West have led us to believe that the divine resides outside of us, but if we can feel our body living in our soul and the soul being connected to the universe, we can experience the divine because the divine is living in us; in other words, we *are* divine. This is the most essential teaching of Buddha, really. Perhaps this is also what Saint Augustine meant when he wrote of God, *"You are more intimate to me than I am to myself"*. Similarly, Heraclitus said that everything is eternal, changing and becoming, and called the unity that contains all opposing forces the 'logos' within us.

AL. The synergy between the electronics and the piano in *Woanders* seems visceral. When you first thought of parallel worlds, did you have a musical vision immediately, or did you live with this idea over time, with the music gradually emerging as a result?

JP. I did have a musical vision immediately. The notion of parallel worlds continues to inspire me on many levels. The German noun 'woanders' means 'elsewhere', and by choosing this title I was fully aware of my task from the very beginning of the compositional process.

AL. Could you explain what you mean by a poly-harmonic series in *Woanders*?

JP. The idea of parallel universes in *Woanders* is exploited in terms of interaction between the near and the far, here and there. I decided not to use the traditional situation where the real piano (on stage) is triggering the invisible (parallel) pianos heard on the loudspeakers. I was interested in creating a situation where all these multiple pianos are chasing each other without a hierarchic principle. The pianist playing on stage represents only one of these several realities and has to decide how to deal with the invisible pianos by anticipating events, responding to them, or reinforcing them through simultaneous action. This is achieved by following a set of synchronised cues with the other pianos, and by trying to 'alter' the phrases of the invisible pianos through different degrees of articulation and dynamics. The electronic part consists of three pre-recorded and processed pianos paradoxically representing the future, the past and the past remote. These pseudo-parallel dimensions are reinforced by the piano part, being played on stage, which represents the present.

The idea of parallel realities inspired me up to the point that I decided to challenge the traditional idea of using one harmonic series (the one 'obvious' reality) and create a larger 'meta-harmonic' series based on each note of the chromatic scale instead (a wider all-encompassing reality). In the figure below you can see the new (hybrid and artificial) poly-harmonic series based on the chromatic scale of the note C. Each tempered interval of the new overtone series is based on its own fundamental note. For example, the first note, the lowest C2, is the fundamental of the harmonic series based on C2; the second note, C#3 is the octave of the harmonic series based on C#2; the third note, A3, is the fifth of the harmonic series based on D2, and so forth (Fig. 8.1).

Fig. 8.1: *Woanders*, poly-harmonic series.

The pitch material of all the pianos (live and pre-recorded) stem from the above poly-harmonic series unfolded in a zig-zag motion beginning from the C5-E5 axis and expanding in both directions (see Fig. 8.2 below).

Fig. 8.2: *Woanders*, axis of the poly-harmonic series.

Although they derive from the same pitch field of the acoustic piano, the sounds of the ghost pianos have been re-tuned, stretched, transposed and filtered. In this manner, I created a more ambiguous sense of tonal similarity characterised by timbral diversity (the parallel worlds).

AL. Your music conjures dream worlds, colours, shapes, movement. Your electronics, especially, signify a spectrum of feelings and perceptions, from menacing to comforting. They also reflect a wide range of colours, from buttery to a gentle harshness. I would imagine everyone responds in different ways; one person's perception of a sound that evokes danger may be another person's balm. Do you have 'stories' in mind or even a general feeling that you wish to convey when composing, or do you focus exclusively on technique?

JP. All the techniques I employ in my musical works stem from perceptions, emotions and what I call 'images of the mind' which I feel impelled to articulate through sound. Technique is only a method for achieving constructional tasks that enable me to create the form of a musical work. Art is not a display of techniques, but, as Kandisky would say, *"a power that has a purpose and must serve the development and refinement of the human soul".*[123]

AL. *Thereafter* and *Woanders* both begin with a compelling sense of space that is realised in utterly different ways. The general form of each work seems to be similar: beginning with non-pitched sounds, barely perceptible (in the case of the organ), with gradually increasing activity towards the centre of each piece, which then winds down, recalling the gentle beginning. Were you aware of these formal similarities, especially when composing the later *Woanders*? Do similar trajectories inform other works of yours that are for small forces plus electronics?

JP. No, at that time I wasn't aware of what you describe, and I certainly didn't have the time to reflect on this, but the similarities you are mentioning do not surprise me at all, because music expresses 'e-motional' values, that is values in (e)motion. These 'moving' values (or images) are always 'here-and-there' simultaneously, they are present today, as they have been yesterday and will be tomorrow. Being both in the individual and collective unconscious, they will inevitably appear in similar forms in different musical works while being in constant development and transformation throughout a lifetime.

AL. Ambiguities abound in *Transparence,* often a result of the interactions between the acoustic instruments and the electronics. This quality of illusion, quite magical, begins to take hold early in the composition, with the brief passages of an 'afterglow' where the electronics echo and elongate the acoustic instrument. Eventually, the sounds dissolve into one another (electronic and acoustic). The technique for accomplishing this effect is masterful. To what extent do you need to coach the musicians on their improvised interactions with the electronics?

JP. I have grown very cautious about the inclusion of improvisation in my music due to repeated frustration I have experienced throughout the years with many classical instrumentalists who are unable to improvise even within a well-defined musical context. For this reason, aleatory moments in my music tend to be kept to a minimum and are restrained by a given pitch material and metric or temporal framework. I wrote *Transparence* for the musicians of the Modern Art Ensemble in Berlin whom I have worked together with over a time span of 20 years. I was lucky enough to write for excellent musicians I knew well, each of them having formidable technical and improvisatory skills. This knowledge encouraged me to include some improvisations in the piece without a shade of hesitation. When I know the musicians for whom I am writing well, a few verbal instructions will be enough to convey the musical idea I have in mind.

Apart from the 'Senza Misura – Calmissimo' of the viola beginning in bar 239 (where the violist interplays with the ghost-viola in the electronic part by interspersing dyads and single notes), there are two moments in *Transparence* where the instrumentalists are asked to improvise. The first moment occurs in the middle of the piece, from bar 165 to 171. Here, the double 'tremolo' of the viola in bar 163 triggers the 'tremoli' of the ghost-clarinet in the electronics for about 22 seconds. All instrumentalists are asked to 'colour in' and interact with the sounds coming from the electronics with sparse sounds played at a dynamic ranging from

---

[123] Kandisky (1994:210).

'pianississimo' to 'mezzo forte'. The bass clarinet is asked to take over the 'tremolo' from the ghost-clarinet of the electronics in order to create a point of contact between the visible and invisible ensemble. The interventions of the solo viola are processed with ring modulation and transposition of 150 cents. A semitone corresponds to 100 cents, so a +150 cents pitch-shift corresponds to a pitch three quarter tones higher than what the viola is playing. This improvisation is characterised by sparse sounds to blend with the sounds of the electronics.

The second and final improvisation is built up gradually from bar 314 to the end when the process of the final pitch dissolution is already taking place. Here in order to keep a homogeneous flow of sparse pitch distribution, I assigned improvisatory interventions only to the flute, the bass clarinet and the piano. The indications are self-explanatory: *"sparsely play airy and 'transparent' sounds using extended techniques and interacting <u>sensitively</u> with the electronics al fine."* Meanwhile, the musicians had obtained a good idea of the kind of 'transparent' sounds I was referring to by listening to the processed instrumental sounds I use in the electronic part. In such a case, the flautist, clarinettist and pianist have to 'colour in' the sounds they hear in the electronics. In *Transparence*, I resolved the question of coaching the instrumentalists on their improvised interactions with the electronics by playing them the sounds that occur in the electronic part. By so doing, the musicians were provided with a precise indication of the sound quality I was after.

TIMBRAL AND SPATIAL AMBIGUITIES IN THE MESMERISING MUSIC OF JOHN PALMER
Anne LeBaron

Gaston Bachelard writes of poetic reverie as a phenomenology of the soul, stressing that when consciousness is associated with the soul, it is less intentional, more relaxed, than consciousness associated with the mind. Indeed, he goes on to declare that *"soul and mind are indispensable…for following the evolution of poetic images from the original state of reverie to that of execution."*[124]

Experiencing the music of John Palmer, studded with such poetic evolutions, confers aural images on a listener that resonate with ambiguities. In this essay, I will concentrate on how timbral and spatial ambiguities characterise three compositions by Palmer: two for soloist and electronics (*Thereafter* and *Woanders),* and *Transparence*, for solo viola, ensemble and electronics. I'll also examine other types of ambiguities that relate to spatial multidimensionality, such as space/memory, after-images, relationships between pitch and resonance, resonance as the breathing moment of a sonic event, memory-space, images of the mind, sonic auras, and the border(s) of silence. To illustrate my points, five examples will be provided.

If the phrase 'what you see is what you get' were altered to 'what you hear is what you get', we would have a description of forthright, earnest, direct musical language. Think of music composed by Paul Hindemith, Aaron Copland, John Williams and even Philip Glass. A subversion of this phrase, 'what you *think* you hear is not what you get', might begin to describe the music of John Palmer. In fact, this phrase could apply to works of any number of composers, most of whom are still active: *Piano Phase* by Steve Reich, *I am Sitting in a Room* by Alvin Lucier, *Partiels* by Gerard Grisey, *Nymphea* by Kaija Saariaho, *Aura* by Anna Thorvaldsdottir, *A Fluttering of Wings* by Morton Subotnick, to name a few out of hundreds of possibilities. In John Palmer's music, carefully plotted ambiguities enliven and charm, drawing a listener into

---

[124] Bachelard (1964:xvii).

his beguiling aural universe of enigmas. These sonic ambiguities can also take on a structural role, functioning to formally frame sections of selected compositions.

Thereafter (organ and electronics)

The beginning of *Thereafter* implies gusty winds that fuse into rushing waters and whooshes of traffic, all coated in a bestial sheen. Not until the whistle-high and rumble-low sustained tones enter, do shadowy shapes begin to move through one another like beings drifting through an underworld. With a sudden ringing gesture, these mystery-laden figures are swept aside, only to soon return with a more solid definition. Metallic sounds are softened by the ghosts of voices. Actual voices appear momentarily, as though humanity has been summarily banished from this world yet refuses to leave completely. The intrusion of a pulse introduces the organ in a virtuosic display, upsetting the dystopian soundscape. The pulsing gesture, returning in dialogue with the organ, takes its place as one of several layers of motion that eventually subside into a transparent timbre, where a solo voice articulates fragments from a sacred Egyptian text. (I will delve into specifics in a brief analysis to follow.)

When I listen to *and* watch an online performance of *Thereafter*, the visual dimension heightens the sense of mystery already present in the aural experience. The initial view is of a trinity of performers (an assistant sits on either side of the organist, while the performer stretches his arms out to form a kind of cross) is riveting with its layers of symbology.[125] As the player opens and closes the air vents on either side of the organ, a seamless illusion unfolds, propelled by the reinforced and filtered air sounds of the electronics, forming a 'shadow organ.' The alluring vocal 'ahs' soon emerge into the foreground. Notably, theirs is the first timbre identifiable as something other than the organ itself and its shadow. When they reappear towards the end of the piece to project three intoned vowels, the effect is one of a metaphysical journey that returns to a semblance of where it started, although the memory of where it started has now been changed for the listener, coloured by the fantastical sonorities surfacing throughout this relatively short composition.

How does the composer achieve the timbral ambiguities that define *Thereafter*? In his introductory notes, he instructs the organist to avoid tempered tuning as much as possible by not opening the stops fully.[126] The partially open stops result in microtonal, airy sounds: blurred, abstract sonorities. For the first eighty seconds, he avoids tempered tuning, allowing him to exploit ambiguities among silence, organ air sounds that are panned in all directions, and reinforced and filtered air recordings. A breathing, cavernous entity emerges, giving way to a new timbral ambiguity grounded in the note C3. The subtle expansion of the timbre begins with the low electronic resonance of C3, prolonging the organ sound in time, and with the introduction of two subsequent spectral variations of C3, extending the spatial aspect of the timbre with an aethereal upwards registral expansion (Fig. 8.3).

The breathy sounds and the transformed C3 form the first two parts of section I, *Ausar (…and breathed)*, representative of the male principle, the breath of life, and the number 3.[127] The third part of section I combines clusters played on the organ keyboard and its pedals with the nearly invisible electronic sonorities of a reversed bell and a subterranean rumbling. Beating sonorities in the organ and electronics ensue. There are no boundaries, only a blend of sounds growing in volume; think of an audible tumbleweed picking up speed.

---

[125] Palmer writes in the programme note to his score: "*Thereafter* was inspired by the sacred trinity of ancient Egypt consisting of *Ausar, Auset* and *Heru*, and the related symbolism of Egypt's mystical triangle as described by Plutarch in volume V of his work *Moralia*."

[126] There are also passages where the composer gives explicit instructions for the manipulation of the stops.

[127] The first tones played by the organ, C3, occur three times on page 2 of the score.

Voilà! With a sudden bright cascade of bells, we are propelled into section II, *Auset,* the female principle, symbolised by the number 4.[128] The technique of sculpting with ambiguity that was observed in Fig. 8.3, with the electronics 'smudging' the organ chord, reappears at the beginning of *Auset.*

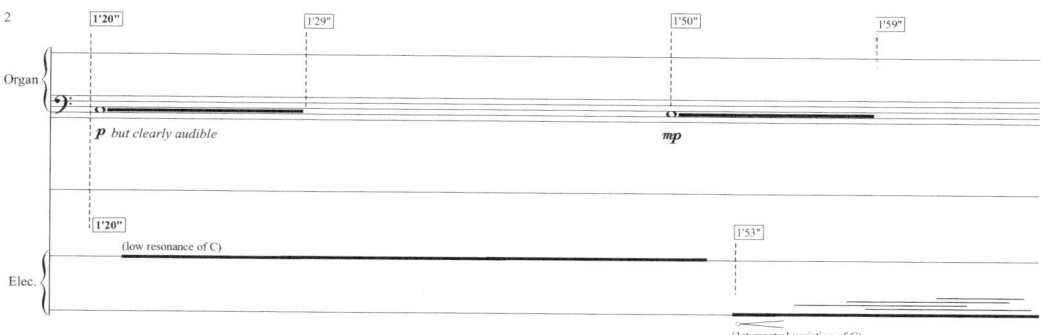

Fig. 8.3: *Thereafter,* page 2, first system.

This time, however, the organ timbre itself shifts subtly with the manipulation of specific organ stops (Fig. 8.4). The most striking moment in this four-part section, an elusive utterance of voices, stands out because there is *no* tonal ambiguity; the pure sound image of voices contributes a fleeting layer of mystery and humanity. Vocal sounds are also mixed into the electronics where they lose their distinctive identity while functioning as components of the sound objects that comingle with the organ's pitch-specific chords and clusters.

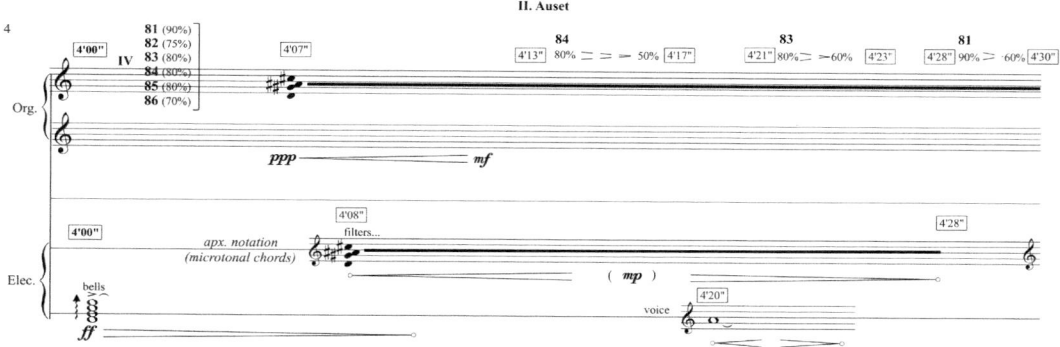

Fig. 8.4: *Thereafter,* page 4, first system.

In section III, *Heru,* male and female join in a 'perfected result,' symbolised by the number five.[129] As this section begins, the force of two layers of pulsating energy, supported by a relentless C1 played by the organ pedal and embellished by the gathering momentum of cluster chords, hurls the listener into the epicentre: a ferocious unleashing of the organ. One feels that

---

[128] Observe the four-note chords in Fig. 8.4: the 'Isis' chords. These are articulated four times on page 4 with subtle colour transformations, shared evenly between the organ and its 'ghost'.

[129] The initial organ chord of this section consists of seven pitches, the unification of 3 + 4.

the organ, restrained to sustained tones and chords in sections I and II, is finally given free rein to become maximally expressive: a true arrival, with the former verticalities recast into linear eruptions.[130] The perpetual motion of this virtuosic cadenza-like display eventually becomes fractured by vertical sonorities, while the electronics assume the role of ghost organ with great panache and assertiveness. The symbolism of this third section, a uniting of male and female principles, is brilliantly rendered by the sole synchronisation of the organ and the 'other' organ. As the first interruption of the driving perpetual motion, this fusion materialises as a kind of mega-organ. (Fig. 8.5) The intensity of section III, riddled with entangled ambiguities shooting between the electronic echoing of the organ and the organ itself, dissipates with a haunting close. A voice, reminiscent of those former elusive vocals, appears briefly. Here, the voice intones 'a,' 'e' and 't'.[131] We are led back into the original breathy space and ultimately return to silence.

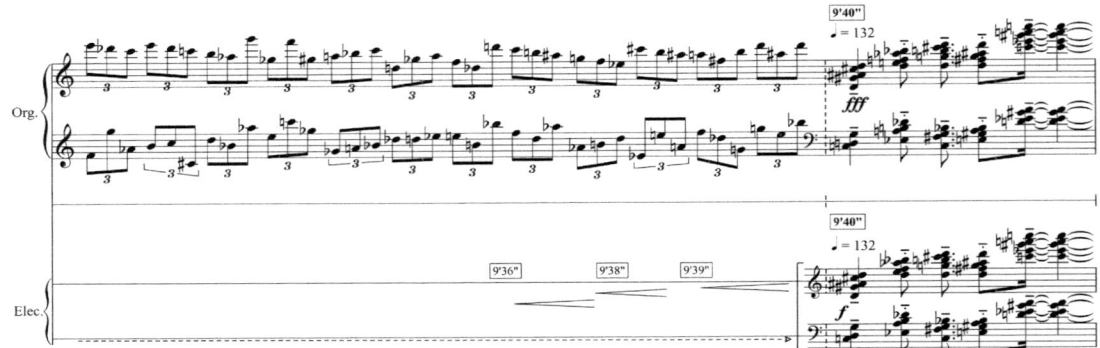

Fig. 8.5: *Thereafter*, page 12, second system.

Transparence (solo viola, ensemble and electronics)

Transparence, for viola and ensemble (flute, bass clarinet, violin, cello, piano, pre-recorded and live processed electronics) is concerned with reminiscence, timbral transformation followed by dissolution and the locality of sound. In this work, Palmer grapples with creating the sound of a hypothetical sense of memory. First, he sets up the dichotomy of a physical space on stage, occupied by the performers, in contrast to the non-physical space of the 'ghost ensemble' (comprised of pre-recorded, processed excerpts from other, related, compositions of the *Trans*-cycle). The 'ghost' sounds are spatialised around the venue, resulting in a dislocation of space and time. Another facet of these perceptual manipulations, of how space is perceived by the listener along with the recollection of previous events performed by the onstage players, is crystallised in several 'space/memory' locations throughout the piece. In other words, as Palmer articulates, *"the division of the two ensembles (the "real" one performing on stage and the invisible*

---

[130] The pitches on page nine and following derive from and expand the chord at the top of page five, which itself is a transposition and inversion of the Isis chords from section II.

[131] John Palmer explains, *"These are fragments of words taken from the reading of a sacred text in a temple that I had recorded years earlier."* Refer to the interview I conducted with the composer on page 273 for a deeper discussion.

one, *the ghost-ensemble) is well-defined and ambiguous at the same time.*"[132] How might one imagine a sound incorporating these opposing properties? Only upon hearing the recording of this piece was it possible for me to understand that such a sonority, one that the composer describes as a *"passage to the invisible"*, or a *"sonic aura"*, can indeed be achieved.

Palmer points out five significant 'space/memory' moments, three of which are in proximity to one another (bb. 94-113). These are heralded by an earlier instance of resonant timbral ambiguity (bb. 53-56),[133] preparing the listener for many such events throughout the piece. The next easily perceptible 'moment', a transparent passage where viola dyads and their resonances are artificially lengthened by reversing the viola sound, serves to enlarge the auditory space. A similar moment, albeit shorter in duration, arrives at bar 135, where the piano resonance is elongated. Following one of the many flurries of intense activity, the entire ensemble is prolonged with a reverberant moment of space/memory at bar 144, abruptly cut off by the resurgence of the ensemble at bar 145 (Fig. 8.6).

Fig. 8.6: *Transparence*, bb. 144-145.

Following a variety of subsequent transformative exchanges between the live ensemble and the pre-recorded and live electronics, an utterly different 'space/memory' moment appears. The

---

[132] Palmer attempts to evoke this 'memory-sound' by timbrally modifying, extending and dislocating the sonic sources of the ghost ensemble. The techniques he employs are described in my interview with the composer on page 273.

[133] A flurry of activity in the piano elides with a microtonal chord in the violin and cello. The viola's 'tremolo' merges with the 'ghost' viola of the electronics, reversed and then time-stretched.

players improvise with the electronics (bb. 165-171),[134] sculpting a radical moment of timbral ambiguity not only between the ensemble and the clarinet 'tremolo' in the electronics but among the individual players. The role of the bass clarinet differs, however. Taking over the 'tremolo' from the ghost clarinet, it forms a point of contact between the live ensemble and the ghost ensemble, while also heightening the ambiguities inherent in the overall texture.

About two-thirds of the way through the piece, following a lengthy dense outpouring by the ensemble, the viola performs an 81 second cadenza marked 'mystical,' interacting with the electronics while maintaining a transparent sound world (bar 214). This quietly alluring cadenza is perfectly situated, formally balancing the weight of what came before. Later, the most potent 'sound/memory' of the piece, formed by vaporous echoes of the ensemble, is set into motion by the piano at bar 277. As *Transparence* draws to a close over the next 50 bars or so, the textures thin out and become increasingly airy and pointillistic.

Transparence embeds its own memory-shadow in the mind's ear. After hearing the recorded performance, I was struck by the directness of the formal architecture. The ghost ensemble events that are quiet, and therefore more readily perceived, function throughout as respites from the powerfully intense ensemble writing. These respites alternate with the contrasting active and demanding sections. The overall impression of *Transparence* is therefore one of the dialogues within and beyond the live ensemble, with a special focus on timbral transformation in the more serene sections.

Woanders (piano and electronics)

Prior to my discussion of *Woanders*, it's worth paying attention to whether Palmer uses timbral transformations structurally, and if so, how. The American composer, theorist, and author Fred Lerdahl briefly explores hierarchies of timbre in his 2020 book, *Composition and Cognition*.[135] Spurred on by asserting a lack of understanding by spectral composers on how to organise timbre,[136] he attempted to construct timbral hierarchies during a stint at IRCAM in the mid-1980s. Lerdahl's explanations of why this effort proved to be problematic are generally insightful. He goes on to make a statement that, on the surface, seems convincing enough: *"The more central timbre is to an aesthetic, the greater is its burden in providing perceptual order."*[137] However, when considering how central timbre is to John Palmer's aesthetic and compositional practice, as I've emphasised in this essay, Lerdahl's pronouncement gave me pause. Although an analysis of timbre as a structural element in Palmer's music is beyond the scope of my essay, clearly Palmer's attraction to timbral *ambiguities* and how they behave in multiple contexts offers a productive line of enquiry. In Palmer's music, timbres are actually sacrificial objects to be diluted, dissolved, and resurrected. Whether he employs timbral ambiguities in structural or other ways that are not simply associative may not even matter, because they are so centrally embedded in his compositional aesthetic.

Resonance, functioning as a sonic bridge between pitch and quasi-silence, features prominently in *Thereafter, Transparence,* and *Woanders*. In *Woanders*, Palmer superimposes layers of resonance, thereby modifying its timbral and spatial characteristics, leading to a perplexing sense of space. Perhaps this technique is reflective of the title, which translates to 'elsewhere.' The notion of parallel worlds, central to *Woanders*, likewise implies the idea of 'elsewhere.' There is no hierarchic principle at work in this piece. Indeed, it is composed for

---

[134] Palmer illuminates how he prepared the performers for this passage and others where improvisation is called for: he had them listen to the processed sounds so that they would understand the transparent quality he desired from each instrument (see my interview with the composer).

[135] Lerdahl (2020:95–97).

[136] The accepted view at that time was that timbre was thought to be associative, not hierarchical.

[137] Ibid, 97.

electronics (in their various roles and representations) and piano, not for 'piano and electronics' (a description that tends to place emphasis on the piano). Three pre-recorded pianos, altered electronically, represent the future, the past, and the past-remote, while the piano on stage signifies the present. The resultant parallel dimensions are thus equally weighted.

In *Woanders*, an unusual degree of autonomy is granted to the player. Free to interact with the invisible pianos at various points in the score, the performer may anticipate them, respond to them, or play synchronised cues with them. In this latter option, the player 'triggers' the ghost pianos while attempting to alter their sounds by applying different degrees of articulation and dynamics to the onstage piano. Despite the multi-dimensional complexities arising from the layers of ghost pianos combined with the acoustic piano, *Woanders* is readily comprehensible due to an ingenious artificially created poly-harmonic series based on a chromatic scale.[138] The intervallic content of the scale, the manner in which it unfolds by expanding horizontally in both directions beginning with the C5–E5 axis, and the repetitions of chosen intervals impart a resilient identity to the composition. For instance, the first pitches heard, a linear ascending C5–E5, span a major third. This simple outline repeats, with rhythmic variants, for seven bars (bb. 13-20), before the pitch field begins to expand incrementally (Fig. 8.7). The origins of a striking sonority evoked by a rising C♯5–E5 in one of the invisible pianos (bar 88) can be traced to this hybrid scale.

The pitches played by the piano and emanating from the ghost pianos are like beacons, surrounded by a fog of resonance. Studded throughout with metallic, percussive, and vocal utterances that embellish the invisible pianos, *Woanders* moves into quasi-silence as it approaches the end, with pitched noise bands (sounding like exhalations of breath) based on C and E ascending a major third. The entrancing sonorities that lead up to the breath sounds recall the haunting ending of *Thereafter*.

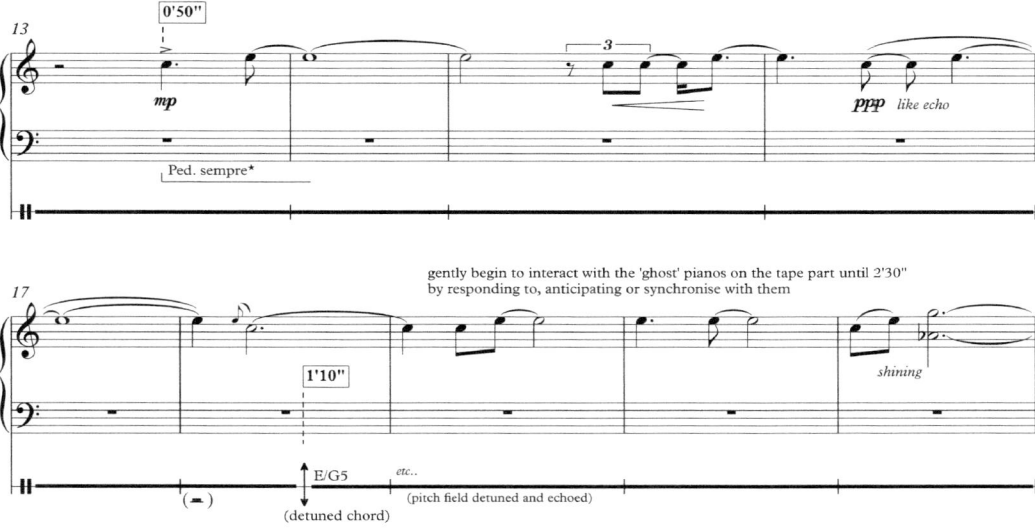

Fig. 8.7: *Woanders*, bb. 13-21.

---

[138] The construction of this scale, and its implementation, are illustrated in my interview with the composer, Luminous Imagination, on page 278.

The three works by John Palmer discussed in this essay (*Thereafter*, for organ and electronics; *Transparence*, for viola, ensemble, and electronics; and *Woanders,* for electronics and piano) share similar approaches. Ambiguities abound, often a byproduct of interactions between the acoustic instruments and the 'ghost' instruments. Dialectics of oppositions are established, coloured by timbral ambiguities and evolving into unities. Palmer's compositions are laced with perceptual poetry. In his own words: *"The experience of space represents one of the finest and more subtle forms of 'perceptual poetry' where motion in space (or a 'moving space') is synonym to a quest for the infinite, the timeless, and the ultimate experience of freedom."*[139] I find John Palmer to be an exceptionally perceptive composer informed by art, philosophy and the realm of the spiritual. The works discussed in this essay reveal these sensitivities and philosophical explorations in extraordinary and exacting ways. His aesthetic sensibilities reflect a lifetime of observation and contemplation, illuminating many aspects of his music, such as striking juxtapositions of compositional precision and performer agency. Forging a logic of contradictions by means of timbral and spatial ambiguities, he welcomes the listener into enchanting multi-dimensional worlds of translucent sonic imagery that remain potent long after the music comes to a close.

I AM, MÉMOIRES, PRESENT OTHERNESS, "...AS IT FLIES...", TRANSIENT, PHONAI
Andrew Lewis

I Am

AL. This is a general question about your music really, but *I Am* seems a good place to raise it. It has to do with the concept of transcendence, or 'the ineffable' as you write elsewhere. Transcendence is a good word, as it implies going beyond something to towards whatever is 'ineffable'. (You write a bit about this in the programme note of course: sensual/spiritual, physical/metaphysical…). It seems to me that there is an inherent tension in pursuing transcendence in fixed-medium music because the materiality of the sonic sources is very strong. With note-based music, there are more intangible elements (the role of performers in realising and interpreting, the implied pitches and rhythms in the spaces 'between the notes' and so forth) but in acousmatic music, every sonic detail must be decided, realised and then fixed forever. That's a long question, but really, it's about materiality versus transcendence (or better, transcending the material) and how you approach navigating this from a creative point of view. (As I say, this question could equally be applied to other pieces, and not just acousmatic ones. It might be helpful to refer to some other pieces too, by way of illustration and amplification.)

JP. Your words instantly brought to my mind the excellent article *The Relation of Language to Materials* where Simon Emmerson discusses some important aspects of abstract and abstracted syntax in the electroacoustic domain.[140] As you suggest, your question can be applied to all my pieces, including the acoustic ones, and it is indeed a huge question that would deserve a much bigger context for discussion. For practical reasons, I will confine my points to some aspects of my composing with a special reference to the acousmatic repertoire. First of all, I would like to clarify what the notion of transcendence means to me and why it is important in my work. I

---

[139] My interview with John Palmer on page 273.
[140] Emmerson (1986).

understand the term 'transcendence' as an activity of rising above something in order to reach a greater condition of whatever nature. It is the transformation of something into something else of a higher order, consequently of a higher significance. The reference to the Latin word 'trans' says it clearly: it means 'across', 'beyond', 'on the other side of'. The existence of this 'something' located beyond the physical level is achieved via a crossing, that is a transformation of one condition into another. The word 'trans-formation' itself indicates that something has been 'formed' anew through a process of change. Transformation, therefore, implies a process. This point is crucial because by familiarising myself with a transformational process, I come to terms with the fact that the 'transcended' is not only the final sonic result per se, but also what is happening during the process of transformation; the 'abstraction process' of the sound, to refer to Emmerson's terminology. In a piece like Harvey's *Mortuos Plango Vivos Voco*, for example, the appeal we experience is not related to the original sounds of the boy and the bell or to the targeted sounds, but to what happens in between: namely, the change occurring when the two sound objects transform themselves into something else. Transformation is a process of gradual abstraction. Transcendence includes meaning and symbolism.

By employing a process of transformation from one sound to another in my works, what I am proposing is an experience of gradual transcendence that is to be perceived in the sonic changes that are taking place. When, on the other hand, I propose 'finished' abstracted sounds (sounds that have been already transformed, but this transformation is not heard in the piece) the perception of transcendence is direct, so to speak. The new sonic image appears to the ear suddenly, thus calling for a quicker shift of perception in the listener's mind. With this in mind, when I speak of a 'transcendental' experience what I mean is that my awareness is being enhanced (trans-formed) by the relationship between my perception and the process of transformation that takes place between two sounds. Transcendence and transformation are related. If in a musical work the transformation process is gradual, my experience of the 'transcendental' is being guided by the sonic change that is taking place. If the transformation is direct, the experience of transcendence is immediate, therefore I must mentally react faster in order to 'be with it' and relate the implied allegory to the original sound.

There is another association that comes naturally when I compose with sound: in their most physical property, sound objects (and I am deliberately using the Schaefferian notion) relate to the conscious as much as their transformed (abstracted) sounds suggest the subconscious. My perception of transcendence, as the realm of the subconscious, resides on the psychological attributes of elusiveness, indistinctness and ambiguity, and this is the reason why abstracted sounds are so significant in my musical world. If I was asked to define the subconscious, I would refer to Jung's notion of an 'a priori conditioning factor of consciousness and its content' that allows primordial images (the archetypes) to be elicited by sound. In a larger context, sonic transcendence is comparable to two important transformational processes: firstly, the alteration of the physicality of people, events and places occurring in dreams; secondly the notion of reincarnation. What I mean by 'reincarnation' is an occurrence of re-creation, thus sonic re-embodiment. In the first case, if I dream of an event that happened in my life, the singularity of this event will be different in the dream: I will 'see' things that I didn't see in the physical event. (In musical terms, I will 'hear' things that I didn't hear in the original sound). When I wake up, I may wonder about the difference between these two realities, perhaps compare the evidence of each manifestation and 'read' the altered state of mind resulting from a newly acquired knowledge. In the second case, the notion of rebirth as a transformational process is indicative of a new state of 'consciousness' intrinsic in the presence of something new in relation to a previous state of existence. The parallelism with abstracted sounds is evident: alteration of timbre and rebirth of an old sound in a new one. The notion of 'progress' entails the concepts of sophistication, innovation and expansion.

Present Otherness is a case in point for both gradual and sudden sound transformations within a context of continuous renewal of the original sound object (the trumpet phrases played by Markus Stockhausen) which allude to what I have just said. *I Am* is a more complex situation because in this piece I am also using words, and that implies a new level of insights regarding semantics, or lack of semantics, verbal objects as pure sound objects, and language (Japanese, English and German) that is 'abstracted' and, at the same time, 'abstract' (Japanese to the non-Japanese listener, for instance), de-contextualized, re-contextualised (Japanese) and electronically transformed (English and German). In my experience, the acousmatic context remains the perfect genre for transcendence because the materiality of the sound objects can be transformed endlessly, something which is impossible to achieve with acoustic instruments. This is perhaps the reason why I don't experience any 'inherent tension' in pursuing transcendence in this genre. On the contrary, I can transcend the 'strong' materiality with even 'stronger' means of transformation. And that is exactly where the fascination of sonic and perceptual transcendence takes place.

Transferring this rationale to a pitch-based electroacoustic discourse opens up a wider range of topics of which the first one that comes to my mind is: how can I transcend pitch allegory? Three answers arise off the top of my head: by transforming its timbre (acoustically and electronically); by altering the spatial relations of the sounds (mainly electronically and to a lesser extent acoustically); a third riposte is more complex because it implies a pitch-transcending-pitch condition depending on techniques related to the idiom of the composer (Arvo Pärt, Steve Reich and Tristan Murail would each do it very differently). Since my own pitch-based idiom includes 'codes' concealed in the choice of melodic and harmonic configurations, in order to transcend a melody or a chord, for example, I would work on 'altered' intervallic configurations to produce 'transcended' melodies or chords. With the addition of electronics, I would merge such pitch alterations with augmentations of spectral content and/or spatial attributes.

AL. An impossible question really, but in your programme note of *I Am*, you speak of 'searching'. Is this your own actual searching, or some imagined protagonist's (or perhaps, the listener's)?

JP. It is my personal searching which is proposed as a condition of searching that is 'transferable' to anybody; much like in poetry, where poets verbalise their perception and experience of life. *I Am* deals with a search for spiritual transcendence and self-realisation. It illustrates a double journey taking place simultaneously: one journey is physical and represented by Japanese sounds; the other one is spiritual, and explores an existential question about human nature: who am I?

AL. Either way, what do you feel is the role of composing and listening in this search?

JP. For me, composing and listening go together. In *I Am*, I created an imaginary journey using mainly sonic references of Japanese life and less evident ones consisting of a collection of short poems called *I Am* that I wrote mainly while visiting Japan in 2001. The extracts of the poems are transformed in such a way that they can be barely heard. My music is autobiographical, and I don't have any problem making this public. Writing music for me is like writing poetry: both reflect my search for self-realisation. The great thing about acousmatic composition is that we can listen to sounds while we are composing. This 'immediacy' allows us to fix our images in sound in a most precise way. The role of composing in my personal search is to give voice to those sensations, illuminations, emotions and images I come across on my earthly journey. The texts I have used for the realisation of *I Am* are the short poems I mentioned above (in English, with few short extracts translated into German), extracts from Buddhist writings recited in Japanese and English, descriptions of Buddhist temples in Kyoto (spoken in Japanese) and casual Japanese conversations. The remaining sounds have been collected mainly in Japan and can be divided into two categories: sounds with a ritualistic reference (e.g. temple bells and chanting) and 'secular' sounds taken from everyday life, including Japanese traditional instruments (sho, shamisen, shakuhachi and koto) and nature (seashore, rain, birds). The sounds are proposed in their original form and transformed electronically. As I hinted earlier, the transformation of the physical nature of a sound evokes changing perceptions of the spiritual dimension of existence. It resembles a personal journey where the sensual and the spiritual, the physical and the metaphysical go hand in hand. The journey itself symbolises a search for the spiritual that is a challenge to the rational mind and complacent states of mind. In this light, I see no separation between the yearning for eternity and the chasm of desolation, or between the desire of love and the feeling of loss. Both dimensions are facets of an all-encompassing reality.

AL. Do they pose questions, suggest solutions, move the search forward, suggest directions, encourage the searching process, and so on? This question might apply to *I Am* but equally to other pieces, both as a listener and as a composer. (For example, a composer might see successive works as stages in a search or a journey, and a listener might interpret them as such.)

JP. Yes. All of this. They surely pose questions in the first place. Hopefully, they may encourage a similar searching process in the listeners, but I wouldn't dream to impose this on anyone. They do suggest directions by using certain symbols that are 'attached' to the sounds I use, or by creating wider sonic scenarios that offer a meaning that can be discernible. The elusive is a major question in art. Regarding *I Am*, I actually created three versions of the piece before I submitted it to Deutschland Radio (the commissioner) for the broadcast premiere. One version is what is now the official version of the piece (without the spoken English and German texts). The second version included such spoken texts. A third version was a compromise between the two versions. I remember sending these versions to a selected group of friends including composers, performers and non-musicians, asking which version they would prefer and why. The resulting feedback was really interesting and to some extent even enlightening: an excellent topic for a debate on acousmatic art, the meaning of sound and the elusive in music.

Generally, I can say that my approach to composition is very personal and that I don't follow a specific methodology or school of thought. What I write is linked to my perception of life and experience of the world. Earlier on, I mentioned poetry because that is another important aspect of my life, and I occasionally paint, too. I experience art as a mirror of the human condition and personal experience. I perceive my life as a journey, and I consider art as a manifestation of a personal journey; as Robin Maconie once said, "*a musical composition is a proposition about the way the world is perceived* ".[141] Surely, all the works I have written are interconnected because each of them represents a stage of this journey. I think all the works of a composer define and redefine themselves in time. They are all related to each other as single pieces of a puzzle, each of them being a component of the big picture. Yet, they redefine themselves in time and in relation to the evolution of the composer's individual voice. They also redefine themselves in conjunction with the reception of the audience as an indicator of a specific Zeitgeist. I think that, as single works of art, they are both inclusive and exclusive, and a new piece will shed light on an old piece and vice versa. Artistic output is a living force.

---

[141] Maconie (1990:176).

AL. Hard to resist this question, but the parallels with Karlheinz Stockhausen's experience of travelling to Japan are hard to ignore. For example, the timescale of this piece, and *In the Temple*, are completely different to some of your other works. Stockhausen referred directly to a new concept of time as one of the things he acquired from his time in Japan (the contrast between the very slow and the very fast, in contrast to the middle-ground time-spectrum of European music). Were you conscious of this parallel when visiting Japan, and (regardless of whether you were) do you think you experienced something similar?

JP. I was aware of Stockhausen's journey to Japan, but there are no parallels with that. If at all, there was a more personal connection to John Cage's travel. John's encounter with Japan and the consequences of Zen philosophy on his creative work had been a major inspiration for me, but the long timescale of *I Am* and *In the Temple* (52') is due to the fact that both works were commissioned by Deutschland Radio in Berlin and the duration of the commission was set at 52 minutes. I am aware of Stockhausen's reference to time and I studied and performed his music back in the 1980s and 1990s. I think that what he said about the new perception of time he acquired in Japan is an experience that many other artists have shared. But during my stay in the country, I didn't think of Stockhausen at all. Whereas, I did feel the connection with Cage, a composer who had been closer to my musical, philosophical and personal world in those days (we were also friends). But much more importantly, I immersed myself in traditional Japanese culture. I was already studying Zen by that time, and, for example, I spent some time in a Zen monastery sharing the monastic life of the monks and deepening some important concepts of Japanese Buddhism. I also studied Japanese poetry and visited the Kyoto area rather intensively. This experience expanded my knowledge of Zen philosophy and traditional Japanese art: music, poetry and theatre in particular. And, of course, the subsequent perception of time was a major learning experience for me. For example, I deepened the Japanese concept of 'ma', not only a specific perception of silence taking place between two words or musical sounds but as a distinctive awareness of time as well. On top of that, time has always been a foremost interest in my perception of life, literary writings, and a major preoccupation in my musical work since my composition *Beyond the Bridge*, for cello and electronics (1993). Unlike a Western notion of time as a reconstruction of the past and anticipation of the future, as Saint Augustine would put it, the Zen experience of time is completely different and focused on the 'now'. Studying, practising and experiencing time from this perspective initiates an immense shift in the way we Westerners tend to act, perceive and live our daily lives. Although I had been studying Zen before I went to Japan, being in the country and experiencing this culture first-hand changed much of the way I think and live.

AL. Arising from the time question, some of your pieces strike me as sympathetic to, or resonating with, the inheritance of Elektronische Musik (Stockhausen et al). Perhaps this is because some of the (to my ears) constructed/systematised interventions in the material (see some of the comments about gesture and cutting, below). In contrast, the longer time-base of *I Am* suggests something more 'French' (Bayle, Parmegiani, and especially some of the 'Cinéma pour l'oreille' school such as Calon or Chion). Rather than 'composed structures' the emphasis is much more on the presence of the sound and the essence of the 'now'. I would be interested to know some of the reasons for this. The Japanese influence and spiritual dimensions, certainly, but perhaps others too? For example, if the piece was commissioned for broadcast, and if you were asked to write for an extended duration, these prosaic considerations are bound to play their part too? I wonder also if you are especially motivated as a composer to explore a different approach or perhaps, for you, it is not different at all, but only seems that way to the listener. For example, perhaps you are working in exactly the same way in this piece as in some others, but just with much longer durations?

JP. I have great admiration for the French composers you have mentioned, and I consider works like Parmegiani's *De Natura Sonorum* and Bayle's *Erosphère* enthralling sonic odysseys of unparalleled sophistication. In *I Am* there is indeed an emphasis on the presence of the sound and the essence of the 'now'. Undeniably, prosaic considerations did play their part too. As I mentioned earlier, Deutschland Radio gave me a precise duration for the composition that I had to adhere to. My approach to each piece is different in any case. First of all, it depends on the idea I have in mind. As the idea begins to unfold, the piece begins to take its course. Sounds are equally important to me. Very often it is the sound that supplies me with the idea, so to speak. Ultimately, the idea and the sound merge, unfolding together. When I compose, I never think of the music of other composers, nor do I refer to traditions or national styles: I write what I have to write, and I keep my focus on that. Perhaps one of my characteristics as a composer is that I don't seem to belong to any tradition in particular; this may have given me given a sense of freedom in my composing. In any case, the focus on the essence of the 'now' is intrinsic to the music (and poems) of *I Am*.

As I mentioned earlier, the piece is directly connected to Zen philosophy and the renewed impact this had on my life following my visit to Japan in 2001. Since the music I write is very personal, it reflects the experiences of my life in a very natural and, I hope, authentic way. Poetry is another topic that is very important to mention at this stage. *I Am* is also the title of a collection of 17 short meditations I wrote in Japan and soon thereafter, in the same year. These shorts texts are an inspirational source for the music; they define the nature of the composition, its form, duration, the content and most titles of the movements. Most of the sonic gestures of the piece are derived from the recitation of the texts which I recorded (with my voice) and processed to such an extent that the words are no longer recognisable. In fact, I can say that *I Am* (the acousmatic work) is the sonic introspection of *I Am* (the collection of texts). The succinct nature of these meditations bears resemblance to the immediacy of the haiku form, but their rhythmic structure remains asymmetrical. The imagery is similar, endorsed by few words, and contains no syntax or punctuation. They can be defined as glimpses or snapshots of thoughts, feelings and perceptions.

Most important is also the use of space as an integrative part of the text which is a clear impact of the notion of 'ma', in its visual form, on my literary writing: a space between words perceived as the 'negative' counterpart of words. In this context, the term 'negative' is to be understood as 'absence of', in this case, the absence of words. More specifically, the non-appearance of words (the empty space on paper) is an integrative part of the text. Therefore, in order to read the words, the speaker must be able to 'read' the spaces between the words as an essential part of the content.

In the music, as in the texts, space and time are interlocked in the perception of the 'now': they are the two complementary aspects of empirical existence. Here below I want to show you two of the texts of *I Am*. The first (on the left) and the fifth (on the right). It is important to notice the alignment, the space between the lines, the asymmetric form of each verse and the grouping of words in space. From text five, the extract *fragments of perception* gives the title to the fourth movement of the piece, and the fragment *mirrors uncertain* is the title of the fifth movement (see Fig. 8.8 below).

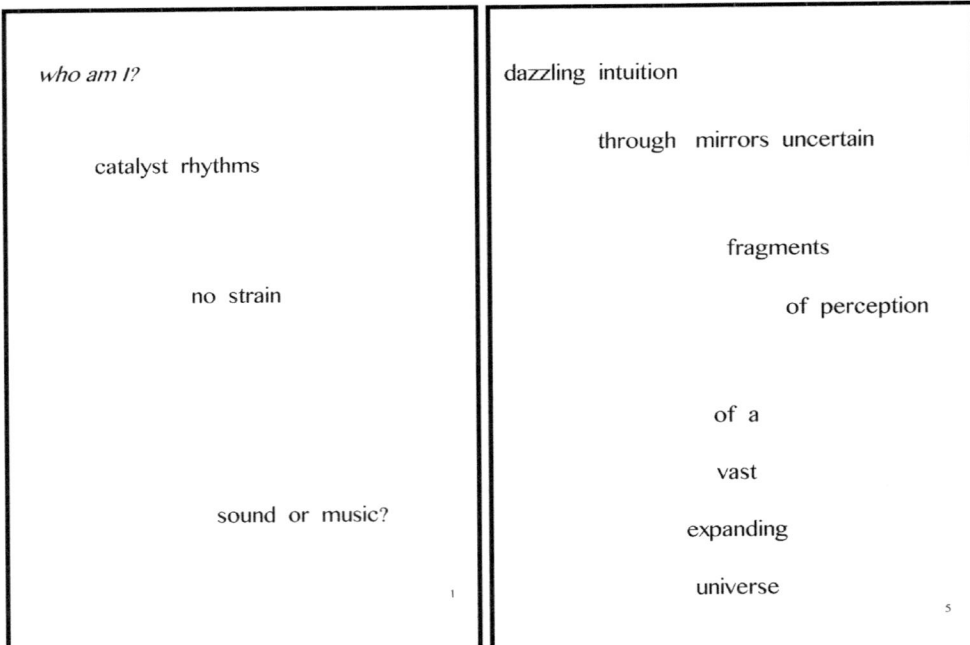

who am I?	dazzling intuition
catalyst rhythms	through mirrors uncertain
	fragments
no strain	of perception
	of a
	vast
sound or music?	expanding
1	universe 5

Fig. 8.8: *I Am*, text 1 and 5 from the *I Am* poems.

Mémoires

AL. In *Mémoires*, you have used samples from Luc Ferrari, a composer who made extensive use of 'anecdotal' sounds and (famously) created works in which the representation of everyday reality is almost all there is. On the other hand, the piece appears quite 'abstract' for the most part, with the referential sounds appearing fleeting, as 'windows' or 'episodes'. How did you approach using these sounds, and integrating them musically with the more abstract structures?

JP. I wrote *Mémoires* in the summer of 2011 and dedicated it to the memory of Luc Ferrari. All the sounds used in this work belong to the Luc Ferrari sound archives in Paris and have been kindly offered by the PRESQUE RIEN Association for which this piece has been written. No other sound sources have been used for the realisation of this work. Brunhild Ferrari invited me to participate in the first edition of the PRESQUE RIEN Composition Prize. The only condition of the competition was the use of samples taken exclusively from the Luc Ferrari archives. These are sounds that Luc collected throughout his life. I was given a selection of 30 or 40 samples that were sent to me prior to the competition and decided to take up the challenge and write a piece for the competition. In the end, *Mémoires* turned out to be the First Prize winner. Brunhild Ferrari's idea of using her husband's samples for different works intrigued me. How far can specific connotations attached to concrète sounds alter their meaning in dissimilar contexts and in the hands of different composers? To be very honest, when I listened to the samples for the first time, I didn't have a clue about what I was going to write, but I decided to take time and allow the samples to speak to me, as it were. So, I began to listen carefully to the imaginary world of each sample and allowed these soundscapes to inspire me and create new sonic scenarios that

294

I would shape from scratch. The 15 selected samples (each of different duration, scenery and timbral quality) prompted me to write a piece that would resemble the narrative of a life story. Below you can see the duration of each sample I used for the piece (Fig. 8.9).

008 – église-orgue-marteau (3 excerpts of 10" each)
009 – boîte à musique (19")
010 – feux d'artifices (0" - 36")
012 – téléphérique (0" - 0'46")
014 – eau (0'- 30")
019 – dans la maison (28")
020 – enfants campagne stratford (2 excerpts of 20" each)
021 – oiseaux (0" - 43")
025 – duels (0'- 35")
026 – sons percussifs resonants (0"- 25")
029 – Shakespeare voix (complete)
032 – cloches et carillon (first fragment: 40"; second fragment: 40")
045 – horloge (0"- 10")
047 – Spiel-Kunsthalle 1 (23" - 50")
048 – Spiel-Kunsthalle 2 (1'51" – 2'38")

Fig. 8.9: *Mémoires*, list of samples selected from the Luc Ferrari Archives.

Mémoires consists of 15 sections (14 plus a Coda) and each of them occurs as a window, or indeed an 'episode', as you suggest, to the story (Fig. 8.10). The piece is divided into two parts: the first seven sections present thematic expositions of the original recordings with some variation. They are mirrored in a palindrome by the following seven sections where the sonic material is developed. A coda (section 15) ends the work.

Section	musical content	form	beginning at	duration
1	music box/hammer	original (thematic)	0"	1'07"
2	music box	spectral variation	1'07"	0'56"
3	children	original (thematic)	2'03"	0'57"
4	fire, steps, bells	original (thematic)	3'00"	0'45"
5	telepherique/duel/perc.	original (thematic)	3'45"	0'38"
6	countrys./Shakesp. voice	original (thematic)	4'23"	1'46"
7	clock/water/Spiel 1 & 2	original (thematic)	6'10"	0'46"
8	music box	developed timbrally	6'56"	0'46"
9	tutti	rhythmic variation	7'42"	1'31"
10	children	variation (stretch & timbre)	9'13"	0'38"
11	bells	variation (spectral)	9'52"	0'45"
12	music box	variation (superimposition)	10'37"	0'58"
13	thematic fragments	variation (rhythmic)	11'35"	0'55"
14	cadenza (perc/Spiel)	cadenza (rhythmic)	12'31"	1'04"
15	bells (mantra for Luc)	variation (drone, rhythmic)	13'35"	2'44"

total duration: 16'20"

Fig. 8.10: *Mémoires*, original list of events and sections.

The approach to these chunks of sound was very intuitive; I let my imagination dictate the degree of sonic abstraction I wanted to achieve. The first half of the piece (0'01" to 6'59") comprises sections One to Seven and all the expositions of the samples including some variations. The second half of the piece (7'00'-16'20) from Section Eight to the end, is highlighted by 'Development' (as I called it) which includes the transformation of all the concrète sounds exposed in the first part. Each hammer stroke marks the beginning of a new scene. Concrète and abstract sounds are also integrated into the exposition of the hammer and the music box. This is audible at the very beginning when the thematic sounds are followed or contoured by their transformation. Here, the spatially displaced hammer strokes are followed by the music box statement (memory) and in the last 20 seconds of the section, both sonic objects are timbrally altered as if announcing the spectral transformations of both sounds taking place in Section Two.

AL. In this piece, and to some extent in *Present Otherness*, you have original material that is quite strongly gestural (that is, certain kinds of physical processes and energy trajectories are clearly audible). Often, you then cut completely across these innate trajectories and edit the sounds together in a way that is very audibly 'composed'. In doing so, of course, you create other gesturalities and trajectories, ones that arise as a result of the energy structures you have artificially imposed (artificially in the best possible sense, of course!). The result is still highly gestural and arguably much more so than the original, but also unconnected, to a certain extent, to those of the original material. It creates rather an arresting impression and a distinct musical character. Could you say something about this 'interventionist' process, about your approach to gesture, and also whether this is something that you pursue in other pieces? (Presumably, it is much more difficult to do this with live instruments because of the native gesturalities which are rather persistent and hard to change.)

JP. I agree with you that it is much more difficult to do this with acoustic instruments for the very reason you mention. The 'interventionist' process is related to the 'abstracting' process. When I chose the Ferrari samples, I made sure I would select a variety of sounds each with a different timbre *and* gesture which would, later on in the piece, facilitate the concrete-abstract connection in the mind of the listener. The 'artificial' energy structures would remain gestural and to some extent timbral, as they are connected to their sonic sources. A case in point is the fencing sounds appearing for the first time in Section Five. 'Concrète' gestures generated 'artificial' gestures and in the second part of the piece (for instance from 7'42" to 9'15") the superimposition of sonic events and radical transformations of short segments of sound accelerate, I think, the impression of drama in the music. I tend to hear these moments as 'cadenzas', in the classical sense of the world, and I have used this kind of complex texture in some of my early pieces for acoustic instruments with electronics such as *Renge-Kyo* (for piano and electronics), *Vision* (for harpsichord and electronics) and *Transfiguration* (for trombone and electronics), just to mention a few. Within the acoustic instrument-electronics dichotomy, I believe it is easier to perceive the 'cadenza-like' function of such passages. I mentioned the word 'drama' in its Greek meaning of 'action', and in such textures, this kind of gesturality is the synonym of 'action' as an element of musical drama.

AL. This piece has distinct kinds of musical material which, on the face of it, would normally be associated with completely separate musical genres: (a) chords and note structures, (b) sound objects (or at least, unidentifiable non-'note' sounds), (c) anecdotal/referential sounds. What led you to bring these together (perhaps it is a feature found in much of your music), and what appeals to you about doing this?

296

JP. As I said earlier, I was given a catalogue of samples to choose from, and the 15 samples I selected needed to be as different as possible in terms of timbre, gesture and mental association. What led me to bring these sounds together is an innate sense of 'variety-within-unity' that characterises my view of musical form and aesthetic discourse. It is indeed a feature that can be found in other pieces I have written. As a classical musician (pianist and composer of acoustic music), I have a strong predilection for pitch. To that, I can add that I love timbre and space, so when I hear a note, for example, I hear it not only in terms of high or low frequency, but also as colour and distance. The same thing applies to timbre: a spectrum is not only a timbral universe of immense beauty but also an astonishing area of harmonic relationships taking place between the sounds of the partials.

Present Otherness

AL. As with *Mémoires*, this is a piece that uses material from another composer (and the title of the piece is explicit about this, referring both to Harvey's original title and the idea of another being somehow present). Could you say a little about the challenges and possibilities of working like this? For example, is it necessary to 'erase' the other presence in the material, before you can create your own; or do you somehow embrace the other's musical presence and work with what the other brings to the material? There is also the presence of Markus Stockhausen, of course, and the same questions might apply to his presence (or absence).

JP. I find it interesting to read about the link between *Mémoires* and *Present Otherness*. To be honest with you, I have never thought of that but, on second thought, I can understand where your question comes from. Well, the two projects were completely different. *Mémoires* is a piece I wrote for a competition that I would have not entered had Brunhild Ferrari not asked me to do so. The genesis of *Present Otherness* was very different. Harvey had just written a piece for trumpet and electronics for Markus Stockhausen and came up with the idea to invite other composers to use the recordings of the trumpet's phrases for an acousmatic work, and to release a kind of concept album. The title of Jonathan's piece was *Other Presences* and it was to be the first piece of the CD.[142] Like for *Mémoires*, the only condition for the new piece was to use only specific recordings, in this case the samples of the trumpet. I accepted the challenge, knowing that I would not keep a resemblance to Harvey's work.

I was aware that other composers had been invited to do the same, of course, and I loved the title of Harvey's piece, *Other Presences*, because of its elusiveness which reflects an aesthetic of sound that I share with Jonathan's music. Of course, embracing the project meant also embracing the presence/absence of Markus Stockhausen and his trumpet recordings. Looking back at the project, I think that it worked very well, and all composers managed to write something original, or at least compelling, out of the given material. I think the main point by composing in such a scenario remains how to articulate your own, hopefully original, discourse. My previous experience in using material from another composer was confined to the piece *Between* (2000) for harpsichord and violin, based on a fragment by J.S. Bach's *The Art of Fugue*, commissioned by the Bach Centenary of Bremen and Radio Bremen for violinist Matthias Cordes. Interestingly enough, at the beginning of this year, I was commissioned to write a piece for piano, vibraphone and flute by the Zwischen Zeiten Symposium in Dresden, inspired, again, by J.S. Bach (a composer I love), and the condition was to use an extract from the *Goldberg Variations*.[143]

---

[142] The CD was released on the Sargasso label in 2008.
[143] The title of this piece is *Aria a 3* (2021).

What I should add is that, apart from *Mémoires*, where I needed to keep the original sounds for the narrative of the new piece, the way I work in such cases can be so radical that I tend to abolish any direct aural reference to the original piece. From a given material I can generate new intervals and timbres paradoxically based on a single note. The latter was the case for *Present Otherness* as I decided to dismantle the trumpet phrases and manipulate the spectral characteristics of the chosen notes in order to reconstruct an entirely new sonic scenario based on spectral transformation. Thus the selected phrases of the trumpet turned into a spectral piece. I began to work by choosing and analysing the spectral content of ten pitches extracted from some phrases of the recording. The original succession of these notes was Ab4, Gb5, C4, Bb4, C#5, Eb4, D4, E4, F4, A4, and this was to become the main material for the new piece. The figure below shows these notes also in terms of basic major and minor chords connections. These chords can be heard as background harmony in several passages of the piece (Fig. 8.11).

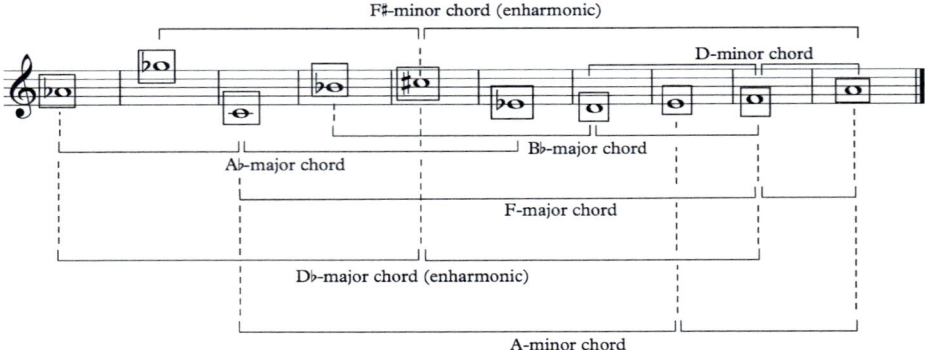

Fig. 8.11: *Present Otherness*, pitch and timbral material.

The next step consisted of isolating and extracting the partials of each spectrum and re-ordering them in order to create hybrid sounds that I would at times merge with only two trumpet phrases of the recording, modified and transposed to extreme ranges. An example of such extreme transpositions can be heard at the beginning of the piece with the low sound. Analysis, re-synthesis, cross-synthesis and the use of extreme ranges became the technical keywords of the new piece. The example below shows one of these hybrid spectra (spectrum 11) consisting (from bottom to top) of the second partials of C4, E4, F4, Gb5, Ab4, A4, C#5 (Fig. 8.12).

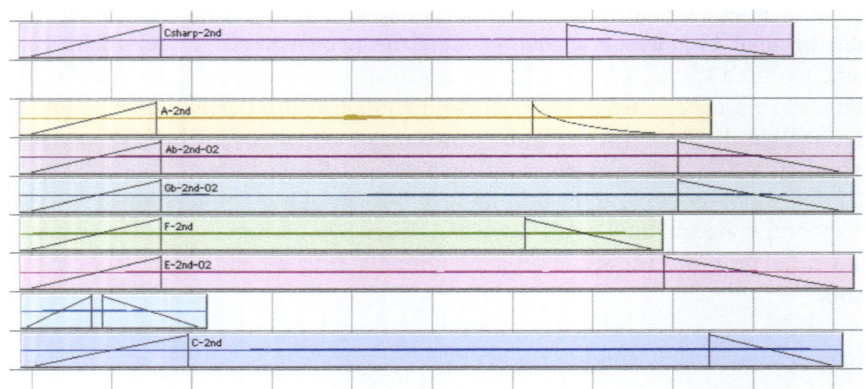

Fig. 8.12: *Present Otherness*, example of superimposition of partials (spectrum 11).

298

On other hybrid spectra I would be more daring and use the 'presence' of *different* partials from the 10 original notes and change them within the same continuum in order to create more ambiguous colours. All in all, the timbral ambiguity of *Present Otherness* relies on the presence *and* absence of the partials of 10 trumpet sounds. From a psychological perspective, I wanted to investigate the dichotomy of a 'present' perception of reality (a full awareness of 'now') and a more subtle perception of the elusive (something else). An 'otherness' experienced as 'present' in a phenomenological sense: not alien, but a discernible suggestion of the unknown. Hence, the here-there, near-far, loud-soft, action-stasis and fast-slow dichotomies set a scenario for the surreal to become real and vice versa. As the inner fabric of sound, I perceive a spectrum as a symbol of unity and consciousness. In this sense, spectral transformations offer a theatre of ever-changing perceptions of the inner world. *Present Otherness* questions two things: the presence of an invisible reality that is both challenging and disturbing, and the duality of 'near' and 'far', 'here' and 'there' as a dialectic of an integrative awareness of the Self. The diagram below shows how I sketched out my thoughts on this issue (Fig. 8.13).

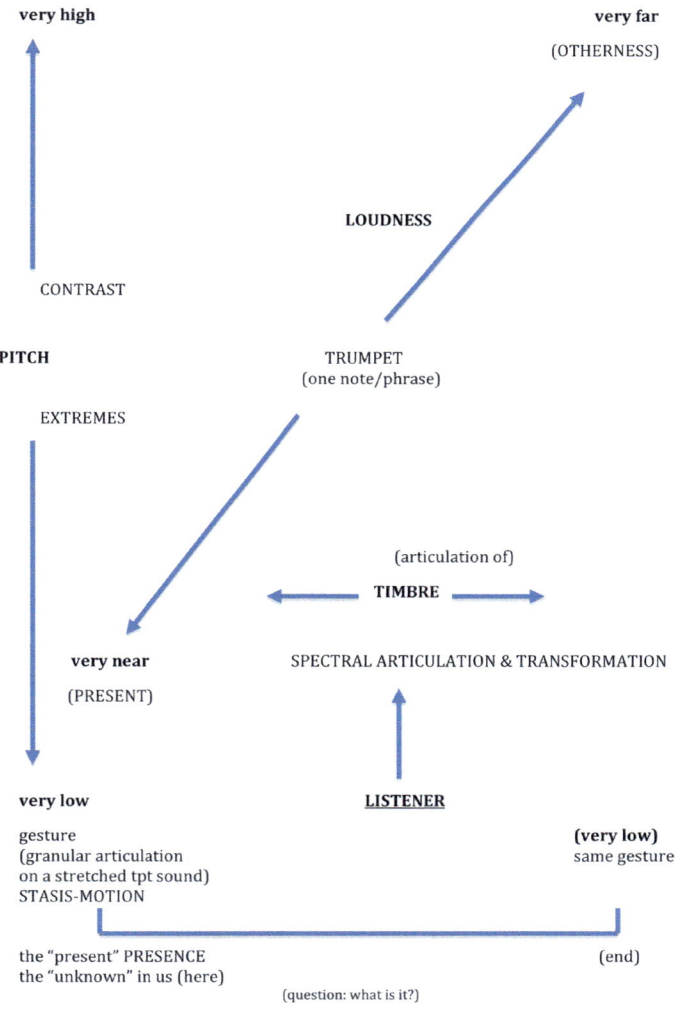

Fig. 8.13: *Present Otherness*, diagram of dualities.

AL. Following on from this, how would you compare the process here to that of *Mémoires*? **I have in mind the fact that you knew Harvey, but did you also know Ferrari? So, there is this additional layer of presence: your impression of Harvey as a person (and Ferrari?). Do you think this made a difference to the process, and even to the music? (Of course, the original materials are very different too, so perhaps it's a difficult comparison to make.)**

JP. I knew both personally. I met Luc Ferrari and his wife Brunhild in London in the 1990s and we decided to keep in touch. I went to visit Luc and in Montreuil, Paris, several times. We became friends. I interviewed him, studied and wrote about his music. The acousmatic piece *"...as it flies..."* was dedicated to him and Brunhild. I met Jonathan Harvey in Dartington in 1992 and we connected on a human, philosophical and artistic level immediately. I studied privately with him from 1992 to 1995 and we became very close friends. Jonathan and I were kindred spirits. We could speak about anything and we shared the same views about music, art, culture and the spirit. Jonathan soon became like family to me, and our human connection remained very strong until he passed away. It's hard for me to say whether knowing these two men made a difference to the process of composing the music. I have never thought that way, but I think your point is an interesting one, since, as Rudolf Arnheim said, *"art is a reflection of life"*. I suspect that somewhere in the subconscious these presences may have played a role, but it's difficult or impossible to define up to which point this may have been the case. *Mémoires* and *Present Otherness* are very different pieces anyway. Certainly, *Present Otherness* means more to me personally. There is more of a philosophical stance in it, more intellectual and musical depth I would say, and the imagery linked to spectral transformations, gestural and spatial motion remains constantly pronounced throughout the piece.

AL. In technical terms, this piece (again, like *Mémoires*) **is constructed very much linearly and monodically: one sound at a time. That is not to say that there is no polyphony, but that the polyphony arises as a result of rapid juxtapositions rather than actual simultaneity (somewhat in the manner of some Bach solo violin music). Is this a musical choice (what you want to hear) or a methodological choice (how you prefer to work) or both? Or does it perhaps arise for other reasons?**

JP. For both reasons. Idea, sound and method always go together when I compose. I am very attentive about object, procedure and form at the same time, and remain well aware of this tripartition throughout the creative process. Certainly, polyphony arises as a result of rapid juxtapositions, but also as a result of slow juxtapositions, as, for example, between 6'09" and 6'44" on the long pedal as a sustained gesture. Here, as in other cases, a delayed polyphony is evolving at slow pace, being based on superimposed stretched partials that are merging and always changing in time. Many of those 'one-sounds-at-time' are actually a myriad of micro-sounds (the partials of these new spectra). This is a layer of simultaneity that is present most of the time in the piece as the example of hybrid spectrum 11 (Fig. 8.12) has shown.

AL. The macro-structure of this piece also seems to reflect the micro-structure, with distinct blocks of different characters juxtaposed. I'd be interested to know how the structure has arisen (top-down or bottom-up) and whether working with pre-existing material resulted in a different approach to other pieces. For example, one might imagine that starting with source material leads to a bottom-up process, from material to form. Yet, this piece seems quite architectural in form, as if planned and designed at a more abstract level. (There actually appears to be some golden section structuring, especially the main division between the active and passive parts of the piece, though perhaps this is coincidental.)

JP. The structure has arisen in both ways: top-down and bottom-up. I also designed the form of the piece rather meticulously by fixing the superimpositions of partials and the basic shapes of the gestures including cross-synthesis transitions. Working with pre-existing material did not result in a different approach to other pieces in the use of spectral techniques. Ultimately, sonic sources are not decisive factors for method and technique, at least in my approach to composition. Since all the notes derived from a trumpet, the hybrid spectra I created are actually based on trumpet partials that imply a stronger focus on micro-harmonic motion. Your reference to a golden section is interesting, however, I have not included this consciously in the piece. I have experienced situations in other works of mine where a golden section or similar relationships have been heard and proved to be there by other people. I have found this claim fascinating in terms of the implicit power of the subconscious during the process of composition. Perhaps a detailed analysis of this piece may give evidence of the same...

AL. It seems that the original material is more fragmented and modulated in the earlier part of the piece, then later there is a sense of 'revealing' the original, or at least something designed to sound more like note-based trumpet music than sound-based music.

JP. Yes, as approximately from the third minute onwards. The 'revelation' was important in order to include a reference to a 'conscious reality' (the trumpet sounds) in the piece. The whole point of *Present Otherness* is to sink in, that is to learn, face and understand the 'other' in order to learn more about 'oneself'. This 'otherness' that may seem so different and far from where I stand, can actually be an integrative part of myself. 'Revelation' was the necessary ingredient to insert at some point in the piece in order to stress the temporality of the discourse. Since a musical discourse is always a reference to existence revisited through the experience of sound, my investigation of temporal formation needed to ensure a level of internal balance between an abstract spectral formation evolving in slow motion and more intelligible patterns of pitch structures advancing at faster rates of inner motion with more composite rhythmic constructs.

"...as it flies..."

AL. I'd like to ask about meaning and utterance in this piece, as well as sound as material. To what extent are you motivated by/interested in (a) the meaning of words (for example, most of the audible words are backwards, obscuring their meaning), (b) the forms of utterance (the energy of certain kinds of vocal delivery) and (c) the sounds themselves in a more abstract sense (noise, pitch, texture, etc.).

JP. I was interested in and motivated by all the things you mention. Obviously, the degree of attention varies from work to work. The question of meaning is of primary importance in all kinds of music and a debate on the topic becomes a question about the nature of art. When working with words, we are dealing with 'objects' (I prefer the word 'events') that are both sonic and semantic. Following an intense period of research, I came across contrasting opinions and different techniques on the subject. When I wrote *"...as it flies..."* I came to the conclusion that it is ultimately my reality that counts, since I can be 'I' only by confronting myself with other views of life. These other 'opinions' can only reinforce my opinion about what I want to do: 'I think *and* do, therefore I am'.

The use of a poem as text layer in acousmatic music can be problematic. I can 'transfigure' words significantly but it would be a shame to lose them altogether, as they can highlight form and provide imaginative focus. Thinking from the perspective of Western art (from the Ars Nova to today) words could merge with sound on a sophisticated and ambiguous level. Electronic instruments provide us with unprecedented means that help us to create refined and enigmatic textures by allowing words and vocal sounds to be disconnected, half-heard and allusive, rather than semantically obvious. From this perspective, rather than being stated, concepts and meanings are indeed stronger if mediated by symbolism, and I think *"...as it flies..."* is a case in point. As you suggest, most of the audible words in this piece are played backwards, obscuring their meaning, thus suggesting a dimension indicating a reality that exists beyond words. I do this because I am interested in the mystery of the ineffable, and I believe abstraction and transformation are the best way to achieve such results.

The only sonic material I used in *"...as it flies..."* are the words of a poem by the English poet, painter and visionary William Blake (1757-1827) entitled *Eternity*. The first thing I did was to ask a female Welsh friend of mine to record the whole poem by using different declamatory inflexions and a selection of single words of the poem emphasising a particular syllable or accent. The poem reads as follows:

> *He who binds to himself a joy*
> *does the wingéd life destroy*
> *But he who kisses the joy as it flies*
> *lives in Eternity's sunrise*

I explored the semantics of the poem in three ways: firstly, in its entirety, where each line of the poem is taken both as a recitation module and syntactic-rhythmic unit; secondly, as single words considered as sound objects per se; thirdly, by examining individual micro-formations such as phonemes, vowels and consonants, including the breathing of the speaker. Some of the consonants, vowels, phonemes and words units were used most frequently according to their timbral property; for example, I extracted the now-concealed meaning of 'flies' and 'as it flies' from the consonants 'f' and 's'. I also used segments of breathing (short and long inhaling and exhaling sounds) that we recorded in the same studio session, as I wanted the sensuality of breath to be present in the piece as well.

The figure below (Fig. 8.14) shows how I divided the text into three categories. On the left, I made a list of single-most used words. In the centre, I planned a gigantic superimposition of all the words of the poem which I transformed by transposition and time-prolongation. On the right side, I listed couplings of words to be superimposed and cross-synthesised.

By setting this initial framework, I would stress the energy of hybrid kinds of vocal delivery that contains elements of similarity and dissimilarity. By superimposing sound objects such as words, the newly-established meta-word becomes one and two sonic realities at the same time, thus instigating a gestural and semantic morphology exceeding a single dimension. It is the blurred distinction of the new consonant/vowel 'super-formation' that is perceived as one timbral and meta-semantic identity. Words couplings like 'but/does' will reinforce the dental (d/t) property of 'but/does' prolonged by the 's' of 'does'. The compound word 'kisses/flies' will inevitably stress and stretch the common consonant 's' as well as bringing out the percussive 'k/f' clash followed by the ambiguous 'l' sound which I would later prolong with time-stretching.

A 'broken language stream' defines unexpected 'timbre streams' whose phonemic identities exceed the traditional repertoire of timbre and semantic objects. The 'continuity, discontinuity and periodic' description of language strings defined by Luciano Berio in 1958 in relation to his piece *Omaggio a Joyce*[144] may be revisited from within superimposed formations of vocal utterance. These can be aurally conflicting of course as our auditory mechanism will struggle to identify the super-formation 'eternity's/sunrise' for example, due to the fierce phoneme clash on the first two syllables.

---

[144] Berio's classification as stated in his programme note to *Omaggio a Joyce* (1958) for voice and tape.

single words most used	All words superimposed as one phonetic event	Words coupling (also reversed) superimposed and cross-synthesized
He	He	
who	who	
joy	binds	but / does
life	to	himself / destroy
kisses	himself	kisses / flies
as it flies	a	eternity's / sunrise
lives	joy	life / binds
eternity	does	as / it
sunrise	the	winged / lives
	winged	in / a
	life	he /joy
	destroy	who / lives
	but	to / the
	he	
	who	
	kisses	
	the	
	joy	
	as	
	it	
	flies	
	lives	
	in	
	eternity's	
	sunrise	

Fig. 8.14: "...*as it flies*...", categorisation of Blake's text.

I used the complete recitation of the poem only at the very end of the piece as a background layer to the music, processed in such a way that the words are almost imperceptible. Another restriction I imposed on myself was a strict selection of six processing techniques to be used in the piece: time-scale modification (time prolongation used also as a rhythmic device), transposition, filter, cross-synthesis, freeze, and reverberation. The sketches below (Fig. 8.15) indicate how I planned to emphasise the energy of the broken words and the abstraction of larger chunks pushing the vocal sounds to the border with noise and pitch, and often resolving in long resonances. Time-scale modifications would be used not only as prolongation but also as a device for rhythmic gestalt; the preoccupation of timbre would be highlighted by filtering, cross-synthesis, superimposed text (in chunks or single words) and transposition. Also, by splitting the Blake's poem into irregular segments, the resulting fragmentation of language would be gradually recomposed and transformed into another language. Utterance (no matter how concealed) was very important to me as a dialectic device within a timbre-based discourse, and I delineated three categories of psychological qualities: 'ambiguous/hybrid', 'sensual', and 'transcendental'. Timbral ambiguity would result from superimposition, trimming, cross-synthesis, prolongation (time-stretch) and filtering. An idea of sensuality would be emphasised by the shaping of new sonic gestures deriving from the original sounds, whilst a sense of transcendence would be elicited by playing words in reverse form, reinforced by glissandi and spatial mobility.

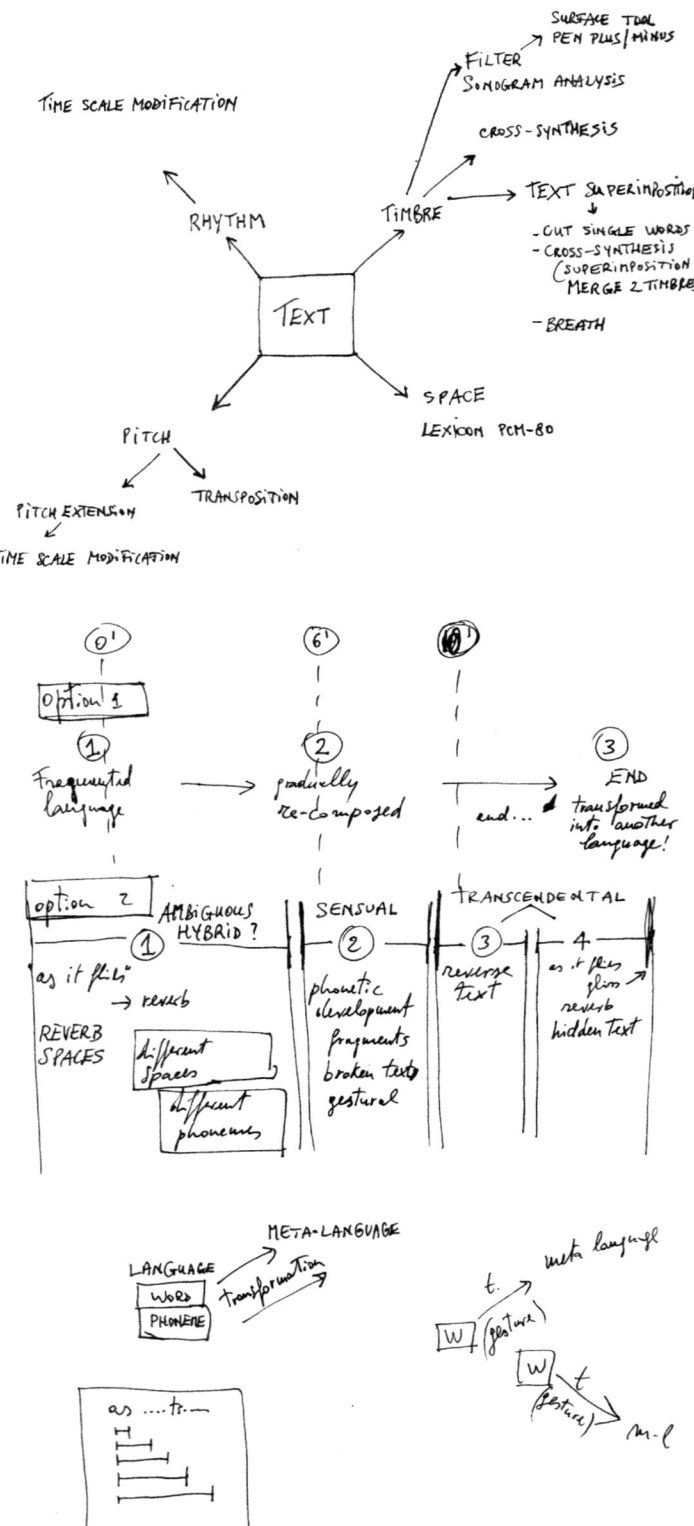

Fig. 8.15: "…*as it flies*…", sketches 1 and 2.

I also created ambiguous pedal points by superimposing different durations of stretched words or words couplings, reversing and superimposing them at different points in time, as the sketch below illustrates (see Fig. 8.16).

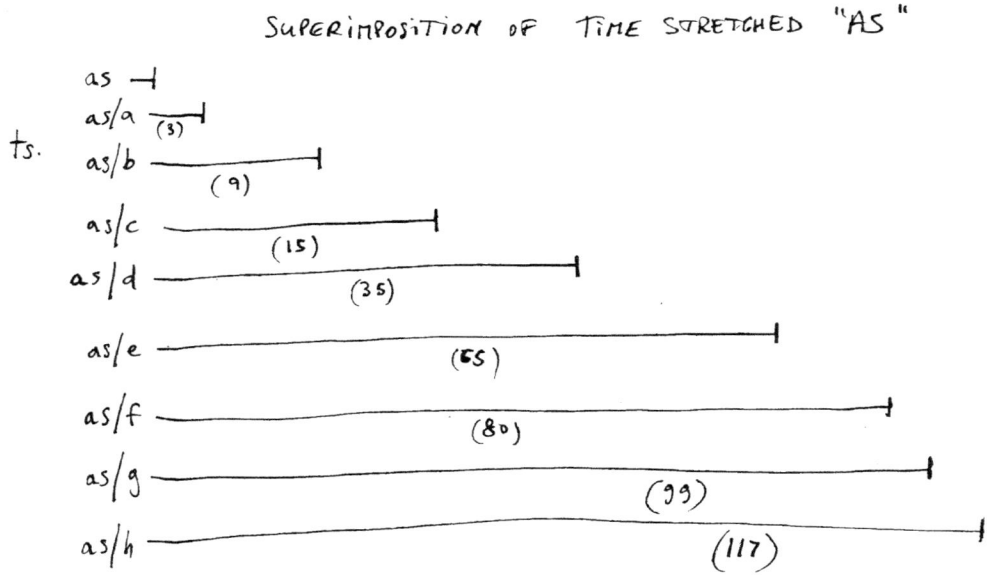

Fig. 8.16: "...*as it flies*...", superimposition plan for stretched words.

AL. I was not able to listen in 8-channels, but the spatial element seems highly mobile. I imagine different 'voices' coming from different directions, like a multiplicity of one into many. Even in stereo, this seems clear. How did you conceive the spatial elements in the piece: intuitively or consciously structured? Pre-planned or in-the-moment? or ... ?

JP. Intuitively: simply by using my imagination. At that time, I did not have an 8-channel system and had to rely solely on my inner sense of motion of sound in space. It was only when I reached the Engine 27 venue in New York City for the world premiere, that I was given the 8-channel system of the venue with an assistant at disposal one day before the concert, and was able to transfer and establish all the spatial movements I had in mind on the eight channel system just a few hours before the concert. Space is very important to me, especially when I work with the acousmatic medium. Yet, none of my stereo electroacoustic pieces is really 'fixed'. What I mean is that I do set the basic panning motions and create a sense of illusory space by manipulating loudness in the studio, but when I perform the piece, I instinctively add spatial motions of sound from the mixing console in relation to the acoustic characteristics of the performance space, especially in the front-back direction. This live modification of space allows me to achieve a sense of quadraphony within a stereo system. Like a conductor who will have to adapt certain dynamic and agogic nuances of the orchestral piece to the specific acoustics of a concert hall, the same thing applies to the acousmatic performance: I fix the cardinal motions of sound in the stereophonic or quadraphonic system, but during the performance, I complement it with additional (often subtle) motions in order to make the music sound more ductile and 'breathing'.

AL. I have to ask you about the golden section here because the biggest signpost of a change of direction in the piece (the silence with three-times-repeated Doppler-like sound) is exactly on cue. (Perhaps it's not structurally important, but it interests me!)

JP. I am not aware of this, but again I wouldn't be surprised if the golden section, or elements of it, were to be found in this piece as well.

Transient

AL. This piece works very well as an acousmatic piece, but I wonder how you feel about this unintended life? It certainly raises a few questions. For example, preparing a piano is not an exact science, because different timbres and pitches can be produced no matter how precisely one specifies and executes the preparation. Different pianos will respond differently, for example. So 'live', one might get different sounds, but acousmatically they are fixed and perhaps leads the listener to make connections between the piano and voice that are not necessarily intentional. Is that a problem? A delight?

JP. That's a point I have been thinking a lot about, as you can imagine. The first time I was 'forced' to face this dilemma was in 1994 when my piece *Beyond the Bridge* (for cello and electronics) was awarded a prize at the Bourges International Electroacoustic Composition Competition and, much to my surprise, on the night of the concert, the piece was diffused as an acousmatic piece. I felt angry, cheated, and very disappointed about the Bourges organisation. Interestingly enough, it was in the last Bourges Competition in 2009 (Section II: Trivium) that *Transient* was awarded a Special Mention and probably perceived as an acousmatic piece. The same thing happened in the same year in Japan at the JSEM/MSJ Electroacoustic Festival 2009, Nagoya City University, where the piece was highly acclaimed as an acousmatic work.

Although it remains a trio, both receptions made me think very much about the relationship of the composer and the audience to the same musical work. What do we do when a piece seems to be successful in another genre and, perhaps, even to a different kind of audience? As you have suggested, the acousmatic scenario will prompt different connections between piano, voice and electronics, and the listener may hear the fixed acoustic parts as being more integrated with the other sounds. This connection would be reinforced by the absence of performers on stage, making the listening experience more abstract and, perhaps, eliciting a more integrative perception of all the sounds of the composition. I suspect the 'success' of the acousmatic version may be a result of the substantial processing that is taking place in the voice and piano parts. Had the voice and piano not been processed to such an extent, an acousmatic version may have not worked. This acoustic-electronic ambiguity distinguishes both the piano and voice part and may be the reason why the acousmatic version seems to work well. The sonic blur works perfectly without interpreters on stage. I subsequently capitulated to the reality I was faced with and created three versions of the piece: a trio (its original version), a duo (for soprano and electronics, where the piano part is included in the fixed electronics) and the acousmatic piece. From a practical point of view, it became important that the music should reach as many people as possible; the three versions I made out of the same piece allowed me to accomplish this without having envisaged it in the first place. In my heart, however, *Transient* remains a trio for soprano, prepared piano and electronics. The genesis of the piece is this, and remains so.

What you say about piano preparation is very relevant, and it is equally applicable to any (live) interpretation of the vocal and piano part on stage. Perhaps I am too much of an instrumentalist myself to feel that hearing the 'dry' recording of a piano and a singer from a loudspeaker doesn't really make sense. As a composer, too, having precise aesthetics of electroacoustic composition, I cannot justify the mere duplication of an acoustic instrument in the electronic part, unless I am using a loudspeaker as a musical device for spatial displacement or a similar compositional feature. Therefore, *Transient* works much better out of the unpredictability of interpretation: in its original format.

AL. The soprano part is constructed with clear pitches (as well as whispers), while the prepared piano and electronics have much more sonically complex and morphologically fluid sounds. How do you go about integrating these in this piece, and presumably many other pieces?

JP. In terms of timbre, I usually integrate them by using the sounds of the instrument as the sonic source for electronic transformation. This is how I create timbral fusion and indeed a sense of 'integrity' that characterises the piece. In terms of form, I construct precise networks of pitch-timbre, pitch-word and often pitch-time associations. These 'relational systems' (as I call them) allow me to establish interconnections between the textural components I use in the construction of the piece. The systems differ from work to work, although the basic idea remains the same: to create an all-encompassing unity.

     In the case of *Transient*, it is imperative to mention that, again, a text is behind the music. In 1988, I wrote a short poem for a friend who passed away that year. This poem (bearing the same title of the musical work) generates the 'outer' form of the music (the large framework) as well as the 'inner' form of temporal divisions and interrelations between single elements such as pitch, timbre, word, dynamics and so forth. The text of the poem is sung, spoken, whispered and 'breathed'. Breathing is another important vocal source that I have pictured as a metaphor for life. The unfolding of the music is based on a system where a word, a phrase or a concept of the poem is associated with a specific pitch and duration. I began by meditating on the text and establish a correspondence of pitch (according to the meaning of each word or concept) and its colour (as I am synaesthetic). In *Transient*, the relation between word (meaning) and pitch establish a musical syntax consisting of phrases articulated in six sections, each corresponding to a verse of the text. Initially written in 1988, I revised the text in 2008.

transient

as from now
I have passed the night

transient breath
of whispered existence

after-breath
on past delusion inscribed

I have come to fly
over the sacred waters

time nameless again
in the timeless land

for now I remember
the original name

Below you can see the initial layout of the system I mentioned (Fig. 8.17). Words and concepts are correlated with certain pitches in relation to verse number and its duration. The general duration of the piece derives from the number eight, as a symbol of the infinite, being divided by the number of notes in each verse. Therefore, the number 480 (480 seconds corresponding to eight minutes) is divided by 26 (the number of times the notes appear in the relational chart below), resulting in 480:26 = 18.4 seconds for each note. Verse One contains four notes and generates 73.8 seconds (as a result of 18.4 x 4) which is equivalent to 1'13.8", and so on.

WORDS	**PITCH**	**VERSE**	**DURATION in "**	**DURATION in '**
as from now	A	**verse 1**	73.8"	1'13.8"
I have passed	E / B-flat			
(the night)	B			
transient	B-flat	**verse 2**	73.8"	1'13.8"
breath	F			
of whispered	E-flat			
existence	C-sharp			
after-breath	F	**verse 3**	73.8"	1'13.8"
on past delusion	B-flat / B			
inscribed	D			
I have come	E	**verse 4**	55.2"	0'55.2"
to fly over	C			
the sacred waters	F-sharp			
time	G	**verse 5**	128.8"	2'08.8"
nameless	E / E-flat			
again	A			
in the timeless	G / E-flat			
land	G-sharp			
for now	A	**verse 6**	73.8"	1'13.8"
I remember	E			
the original name	C-sharp / E			
				total duration
				7'98.86" (8'00")

Fig. 8.17: *Transient*, compositional procedure layout.

You will notice that a word or a concept is always associated with the same pitch. For example, the words 'breath' and 'after-breath' correspond to the note F; the note A is associated with the temporal adverbs (or concepts) 'as from now', 'again' and 'now' and so forth. Similar to a foreign language, the word-pitch 'dictionary' will produce the musical phrases below. Once the vocabulary is learnt, a listener could understand the cryptic (unspoken) message by only hearing the motifs of the verses grouped in the figure below. The figure below shows the six musical verses corresponding to the six verses of the poem (Fig. 8.18).

Fig. 8.18: *Transient*, verses and pitch fields.

The chart below (Fig. 8.19) shows a summary of the complete set of correspondences between verse number, phrases and motifs in relation to time.

verse	phrase	motif	time
1	as from now I have passed the night	A, E, B-flat, B	0'00"- 1'13"
2	transient breath of whispered existence	B-flat, F, E-flat, C-sharp	1'13"- 2'26"
3	afterbreath on past delusion inscribed	F, B-flat, B, D	2'26"- 3'39"
4	I have come to fly over the sacred waters	E, C, F-sharp	3'39"- 4'34"
5	time nameless again in the timeless land	G, E, E-flat, A, G, E-flat, G-sharp	4'34"- 6'43"
6	for now I remember the original name	A, E, C-sharp, E	6'43"- 8'00"

Fig. 8.19: *Transient*, chart of verses, phrases and motifs.

I mentioned synaesthesia. In my case, I don't only experience colour-word associations but also other references including colour- timbre. The case of the prepared piano is an interesting one because the timbres of the preparation were selected according to my synaesthetic perception of the words which implied another (perhaps more cryptic) layer of relationships between the sounds of the prepared piano, the motifs, the words and the electronically transformed sounds.

AL. Golden section: again, in this piece, there is a sustained quiet moment at the golden section. Coincidence?

JP. I don't believe in coincidence.

Phonai

AL. In *Phonai*, comparisons/contrasts with other famous works combining children's voices and electronic sounds are hard to avoid, and perhaps better embraced (*Gesang der Jünglinge* and *Mortuos Plango, Vivos Voco* in particular). The sound world is obviously a long way from both and very original, but the concept of integrating/opposing/juxtaposing these two different kinds of sonic material (recognisable/abstract) is common to them all, as are some of the issues that flow from this. Was this in your mind when composing, and if so, how did you approach it? Were you inclined to focus on the ways in which this piece is not like those (both in terms of sound-world and approach), or work with the reality of the existence of these other works in some way (developing, alluding to, opposing and so on)? What I mean here is something akin to the problem of writing for string quartet. How does one approach it when the repertoire is already so full of gigantic, influential masterpieces?

JP. I can understand the reason why you are asking such a question, but perhaps you will be surprised to hear that there is no connection between *Phonai* and the two pieces you mention and that the genesis, context and preoccupation that led me to write this piece are completely different. When I returned to live in England in 1990, I decided to study electroacoustic music, an area of composition that I didn't have the opportunity to deepen in the previous decade. The motivation and genesis of *Phonai* are originally linked with the synthesizer, rather than the human voice, and in order to explain this, I must go back to the beginning of the piece. In the same year, I decided to complement my piano performances with a synthesizer and, wherever possible, with a harpsichord. I had played the synthesizer back in the 1970s in some progressive rock groups but then abandoned the instrument when I went back to my classical training as a pianist in the 1980s. What I had in mind in 1990 was to use a synthesizer not the way it is used in pop music, but as a pure electronic instrument: a *real* synthesizer that would allow me to perform sound synthesis combined with acoustic sounds live. My goal was to give the synthesizer a status as an electronic instrument that could be used for 'synthesis performance' on stage. As a performing pianist, the 'live factor' was very important in those days. In London, 1990, I began to look around for a synthesizer that would put me in the position to use synthesis techniques and finally bought myself a Yamaha SY-77. In the following months, I explored the synthesis possibilities that the instrument offered me using the six-operator AFM (Advanced Frequency Modulation) synthesis with 45 algorithms and 16 waveforms, and FM synthesis combined with sampled sounds (in AWM2) that could be mixed with the AFM sounds. I was particularly interested in the Time Variant Filters which would allow me to create new synthesis techniques combining AFM, AWM2 (Advanced Wave Memory 2) for sample-based synthesis, and the combination of these two methods called Realtime Convolution and Modulation (RCM) synthesis. Parallel to this preoccupation, I was looking for compositional procedures that would allow me to merge determinate and indeterminate procedures. I wanted to find a convincing way to blend the approach to indeterminacy that I had learned from John Cage's work with a determinate and strict organisation of musical material.

Towards the end of 1992, I wrote a piece for the Yamaha SY-77 called *Electrophony 1*. The number '1' implied that this piece was meant to be the first in a series of works that would exploit the potential of the synthesizer as an electronic instrument that would perform 'classic' electronic music in my concerts. When I wrote this piece, I already knew Stockhausen's and Harvey's works but my mind was focused on the synthesizer and my concerts as a pianist-composer. The piece was based on a principle of expansion and contraction of register, embracing a range of ten octaves and including both the temperate tuning system and microtonality (quarter tones).

Electrophony 1 was the first piece I wrote for synthesizer as a 'live-electronic-studio' capable of standing as an autonomous instrument in the New Music concert scene. My hope was to bring out the potential of electroacoustic music through a 'concertante' instrument being no less inferior to any other traditional acoustic instrument. Little did I know of the ruthless commercial policies of the pop music industry which didn't consent to my pursual of artistic objectives. I soon realised that the manufacturers of synthesizers were not at all concerned about synthesis as an open platform for artistic creativity. The abandonment of this project was a result of the frustration I felt about the established commercial attitude of music instruments companies, perhaps with the exception of Moog synthesizers (although I am not entirely sure about this, either). In the following four years, I performed this initial version of the piece by doing basic synthesis and other sound manipulations during my concerts. I would be able to edit the synthesis 'programs' of the instrument while playing on the keyboard, which was exactly what I wanted. My hope was to combine the pianist in me (by playing the keyboard) with the composer (by doing sound transformations on stage). In terms of architectural procedures, I integrated determinate and indeterminate correspondence between form and sound. The chart below gives you an idea of the general preoccupations in those days (Fig. 8.20).

Electrophony 1 – (1992/93)
(a model of expansion and reduction of register)

compositional procedures:

DETERMINATE	INDETERMINATE
(discipline)	(freedom)
volume	pitch
time (rhythm – some rests)	time (rests)
register	timbre

Fig. 8.20: *Phonai,* compositional procedures (1992/1993).

The chart below shows detailed planning of the parameters. You can see the importance of number five in the choice of degrees of loudness, approximate metre, durational values and rhythm. The 10 (5 x 2) register patterns are of utmost importance as they allow the distinction of 10 independent routes, while the vertical boxes with the numbers 1 to 5 show the degree to which I move the data entry slider up and down in order to change register swiftly (Fig. 8.21).

<u>5 PARAMETERS</u>

1) <u>VOLUME</u> : 5 DEGREES : pp - p - mf - f - ff

2) <u>TIME</u> : 5 DEGREES : VERY SLOW - SLOW - MODERATE - FAST - VERY FAST

 10 (5x2) DURATIONS AND RHYTHMS : [20' DURATION]

 { 5 DURATIONS : ♩ ♩. ♪ ♪. ♪

 { 5 RHYTHMS : ♫♫♫ ♫♫♫♫ ♫♫♫♫♫ ♫♫♫♫♫♫ ♫♫♫♫♫♫♫ 128 RHYTHMIC PATTERNS
    (10.6)

3) <u>REGISTER</u> : 128 NOTES = 10 OCTAVES . THE WHOLE RANGE IS SHARED IN 5 SECTIONS:

 VERY LOW - LOW - MIDDLE - HIGH - VERY HIGH (include improvisatory)

 <u>CHANGES OF REGISTER</u> : THEY FOLLOW THE 5 ASSIGNED DEGREES OF TIME :

 VERY SLOW - SLOW - MODERATE - FAST - VERY FAST

4) <u>PITCH</u> : 128 NOTES = 10 OCTAVES . { MICROTONALITY : ¼ TONE TUNING

 { EQUAL TEMPERAMENT

 PITCH BEND : 0-12 UPWARDS ONLY

 (128 NOTES UNDER CONTROL OF SLIDER)

5) <u>TIMBRE</u> : 2 DIFFERENT TIMBRES : 1) AFM ELEMENT (RANGE : C3 to G8)

 2) AWM ELEMENT (RANGE : C-2 to B2)

 THE AFM ELEMENT (C3 to G8) HAS 2 TIMBRAL VARIATIONS :

 1) A METALLIC, HARSH TIMBRE CAUSED BY A FIRM FINGER ATTACK

 2) A MELLOW, SOFT TIMBRE CAUSED BY A GENTLE FINGER ATTACK

<u>REGISTER PATTERNS</u>

	1	2	3	4	5	6	7	8	9	10
↑	5	4	1	3	2	2	5	3	4	4
	4	5	3	4	4	1	1	2	2	3
	3	2	5	1	5	4	3	5	1	2
	2	3	4	5	1	5	2	1	3	1
↓	1	1	2	2	3	3	4	4	5	5

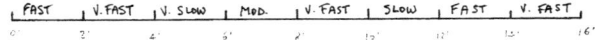

FAST	V. FAST	V. SLOW	MOD.	V. FAST	SLOW	FAST	V. FAST
0'	2'	4'	6'	8'	10'	12'	13' 16'

Fig. 8.21: *Phonai,* original plan of parameters.

311

The next figure show how I implemented parameters such as panning, microtonal tuning, portamento, modulation and reverberation (Fig. 8.22).

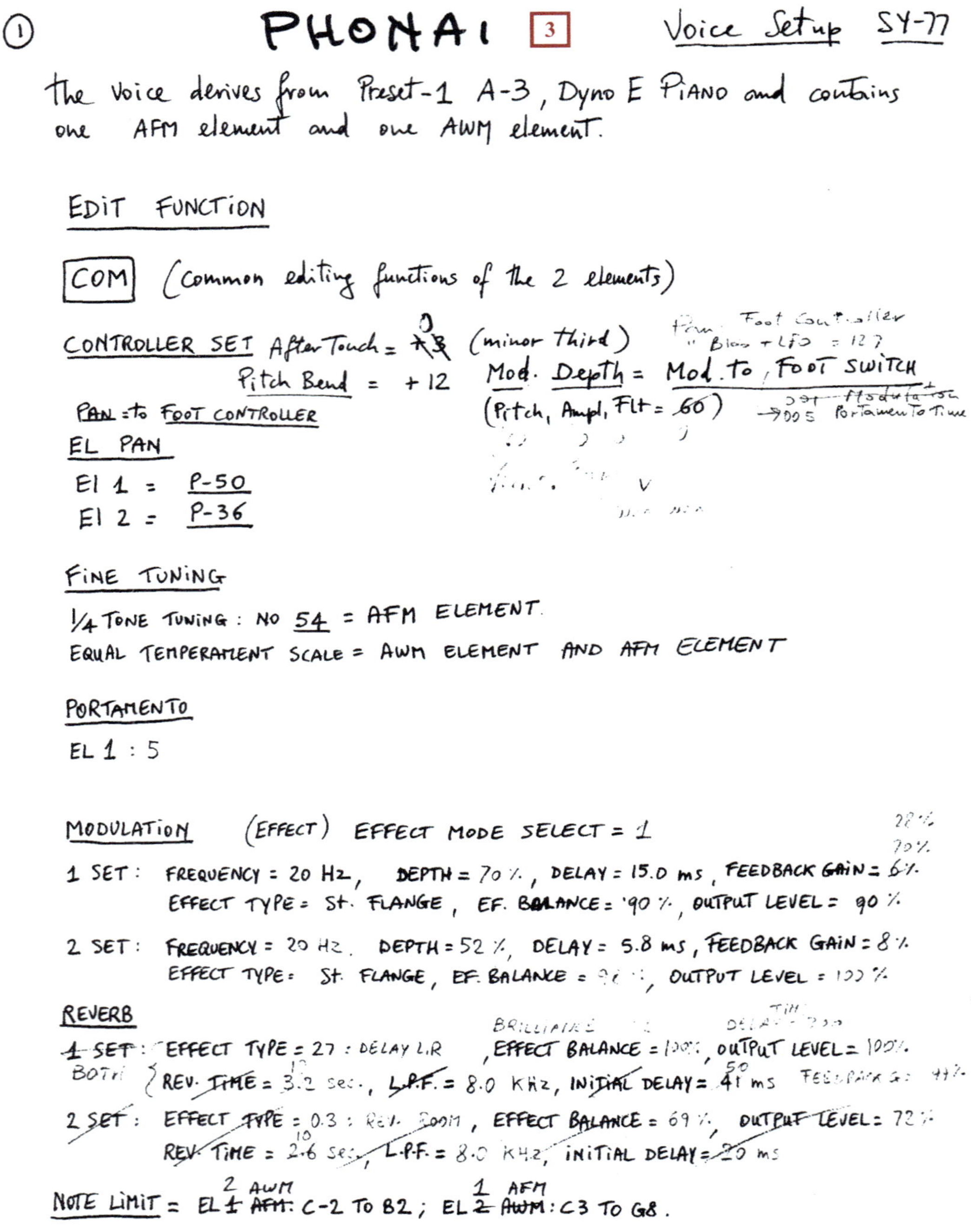

① **PHONAI** [3]   Voice Setup SY-77

The voice derives from Preset-1 A-3, Dyno E Piano and contains one AFM element and one AWM element.

EDIT FUNCTION

[COM] (Common editing functions of the 2 elements)

CONTROLLER SET After Touch = ♪♩ (minor third)   Pan. Foot Controller
                Pitch Bend = +12   Mod. Depth = Mod. To Foot Switch
PAN = to FOOT CONTROLLER   (Pitch, Ampl, Flt = 60)   Portamento Time

EL PAN
   El 1 = P-50
   El 2 = P-36

FINE TUNING

¼ TONE TUNING : NO 54 = AFM ELEMENT.
EQUAL TEMPERAMENT SCALE = AWM ELEMENT AND AFM ELEMENT

PORTAMENTO

EL 1 : 5

MODULATION   (EFFECT) EFFECT MODE SELECT = 1

1 SET : FREQUENCY = 20 Hz,   DEPTH = 70 %, DELAY = 15.0 ms, FEEDBACK GAIN = 6 %.
         EFFECT TYPE = St. FLANGE, EF. BALANCE = 90 %, OUTPUT LEVEL = 90 %.

2 SET : FREQUENCY = 20 Hz, DEPTH = 52 %, DELAY = 5.8 ms, FEEDBACK GAIN = 8 %.
         EFFECT TYPE = St. FLANGE, EF. BALANCE = 96 %, OUTPUT LEVEL = 100 %.

REVERB
1 SET : EFFECT TYPE = 27 : DELAY L.R   , EFFECT BALANCE = 100 %, OUTPUT LEVEL = 100 %.
BOTH { REV. TIME = 3.2 sec., L.P.F. = 8.0 KHz, INITIAL DELAY = 41 ms
2 SET : EFFECT TYPE = 0.3 : REV. ROOM, EFFECT BALANCE = 69 %, OUTPUT LEVEL = 72 %.
        REV. TIME = 2.6 sec., L.P.F. = 8.0 KHz, INITIAL DELAY = 20 ms

                    2 AWM   1 AFM
NOTE LIMIT = EL 1 AFM: C-2 TO B2; EL 2 AWM: C3 TO G8.

Fig. 8.22: *Phonai*, original implementation of parameters.

312

Pages one and two of the original score will give you an idea of the notation I used for the performance of the piece. Obviously, the written notes do not correspond to the notes we hear as these are determined by the register I chose (the red boxed numbers operated by the data entry slider). On page one (Fig. 8.23), the tempo indication is FAST, the notes sound in the lowest region of the complete range and the note-shift value is -64, which corresponds to the lowest octave of a piano keyboard. The panning controlled from a dedicated pedal is notated with straight lines going up and down. The third phrase presents a big shift of register, namely from the lowest region (1) to the middle region of the complete range (3). The fourth line of page one shows the first gradual change of register, from region 1 (the lowest) to region 2 (the second-lowest region). The gradual change of register is indicated by the arrows. This plays a crucial factor in the music, and what is notated as a repeated B4, for example, is effectively a continuously change of pitch that I controlled with the data entry slide operated by the left hand. Page two (Fig. 8.24) shows prolonged panning (with no sustain pedal) and an extreme and much faster change of register. The full range of the total register is used on nearly each and every single phrase played on the keyboard (Figs. 8.23, 8.24, 8.25, 8.26).

Fig. 8.23: *Phonai,* page one of original score.

313

Fig. 8.24: *Phonai,* page two of original score.

Four years later, I decided to add a contrasting layer of sonic events in order to strengthen the narrative of the piece and create a more diverse music scenario. I was in search of an extra element of vitality that would liven up the composition. The additional sounds would need to be clearly contrasting with the synthesizer sounds and written for fixed media, as I was too busy playing the synthesizer live. So, I decided to add a 'concrète' counterpart (a 'tape part', as we used to call it in those days) to the synthesizer by using some voice recordings I had made of my children Grace and Iris, at that time being 5 and 3 years old. This is the decision that marked the birth of *Fhonai,* the new title of the now extended piece for synthesizer and tape. In Greek, 'phonai' means 'voices': the reference to the children's voices is clear. The first two pages of the final score should give a clear idea of the new setting, especially of the interplay I created between the synthesizer and the children's voices (see Figs. 8.25 and 8.26). In terms of narrative and performance activity, the addition of this new layer created, in my opinion, a much more interesting, lively, and (why not?) entertaining piece which was also more fun to perform.

I performed this new version for synthesizer and tape in several concerts in Europe and, at some point, I realised that, out of practical concerns, the piece could well be played as an acousmatic piece. Similar to *Transient*, there are two performance options for *Phonai*: the original version for synthesizer and tape (soundfile) and the acousmatic version. The concern about acousmatic vs. performing instruments is the same I have discussed earlier about *Transient*. Wherever possible in such dilemmas, I keep preferring the stage, as musical theatre, to be filled by performers. Whether acousmatic or not, there remains two superimposed layers: the original synthesizer composition (which can still be performed on a Yamaha SY-77 or SY-99 synthesizer) and the acousmatic composition of 1997 that includes the children's voices. The synthesizer layer is based on a principle of expansion and contraction of register, embracing a range of ten octaves and including both the temperate tuning system (semitones) and microtonality (quarter tones). When I added the layer with the children's voices, I wasn't thinking of the Stockhausen and Harvey pieces at all, not only because of my instrumental preoccupation of that time (my obsession with the synthesizer) but also because of the light and lively character of my children's vocal utterances which are in stark contrast with the solemnity of the two works you mentioned. Although I can see why you are pointing out these two works, for me, there is no discernible link between *Phonai* and them.

Your point about the approach to a repertoire that is already full of outstanding and influential masterpieces is a very important one. However, I don't think a composer shouldn't feel intimidated by it. My own policy is to always listen to the inner voice and follow the power of inspiration and individual artistic creativity. Any masterpiece can be seen as a challenge and an opportunity to dare expand the repertoire as originally as possible. This is exactly what Harvey did with *Mortuos Plango, Vivos Voco*. Had he felt intimidated by the reputation of *Gesang der Jünglinge*, he would have never written his masterpiece.

AL. There is quite a bit of humour in this piece (from the very beginning). It's not something one encounters much in 'serious' new music. Do you have any thoughts about (a) the appropriateness of humour in this context (I suppose, its aesthetic function really, if it has any) and (b) the compositional difficulties of working with humour alongside other kinds of emotional or spiritual 'colours'?

JP. Humour and lightness are an important part of life and the music I write reflects my life. What is serious music anyway? I find some pop songs or jazz pieces to be very serious indeed. Humour belongs to life: why should it be excluded from our artistic creativity? For me, art suggests a holistic process that includes the entirety of mind, emotions, spirit and body. The meaning of existence cannot be found from breaking things down into parts but rather from the awareness of the whole. Hence, I see no conflict, whether aesthetically or compositionally, working with humour alongside other aspects of life such as intellectual, emotional or spiritual values. Lightness is not superficiality. Lightness is refreshing.

Phonai

John Palmer

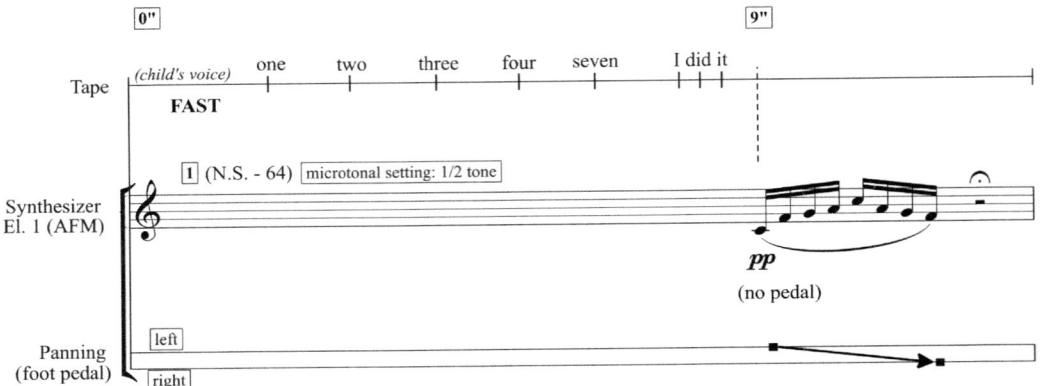

[Note Shift: set slider of Element 2 (AWM) at 3 (N.S.= 0) before the beginning of the performance]

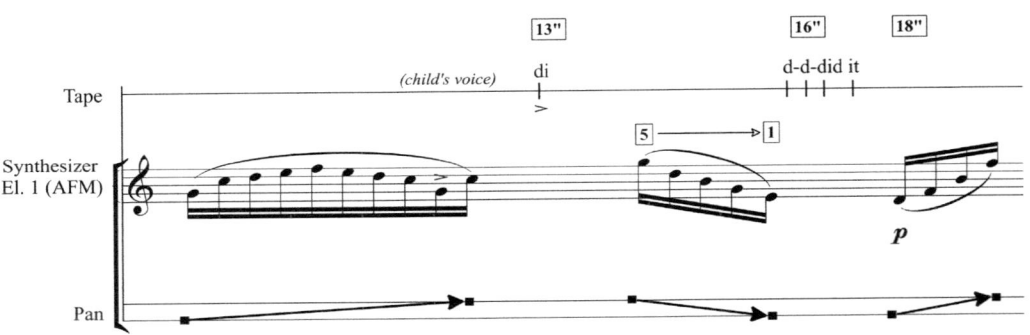

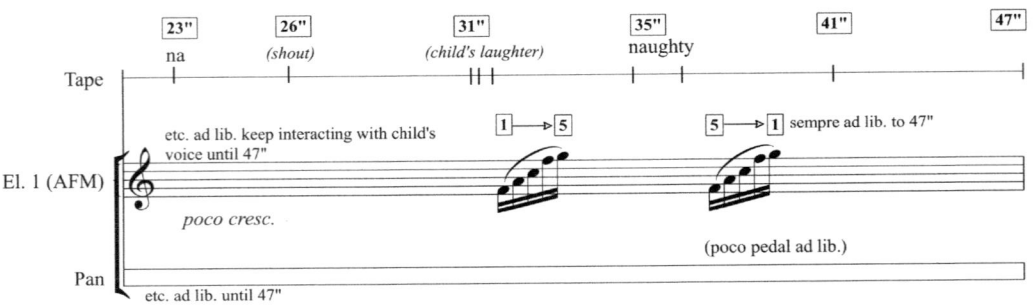

Fig. 8.25: *Phonai,* page one of revised and final score.

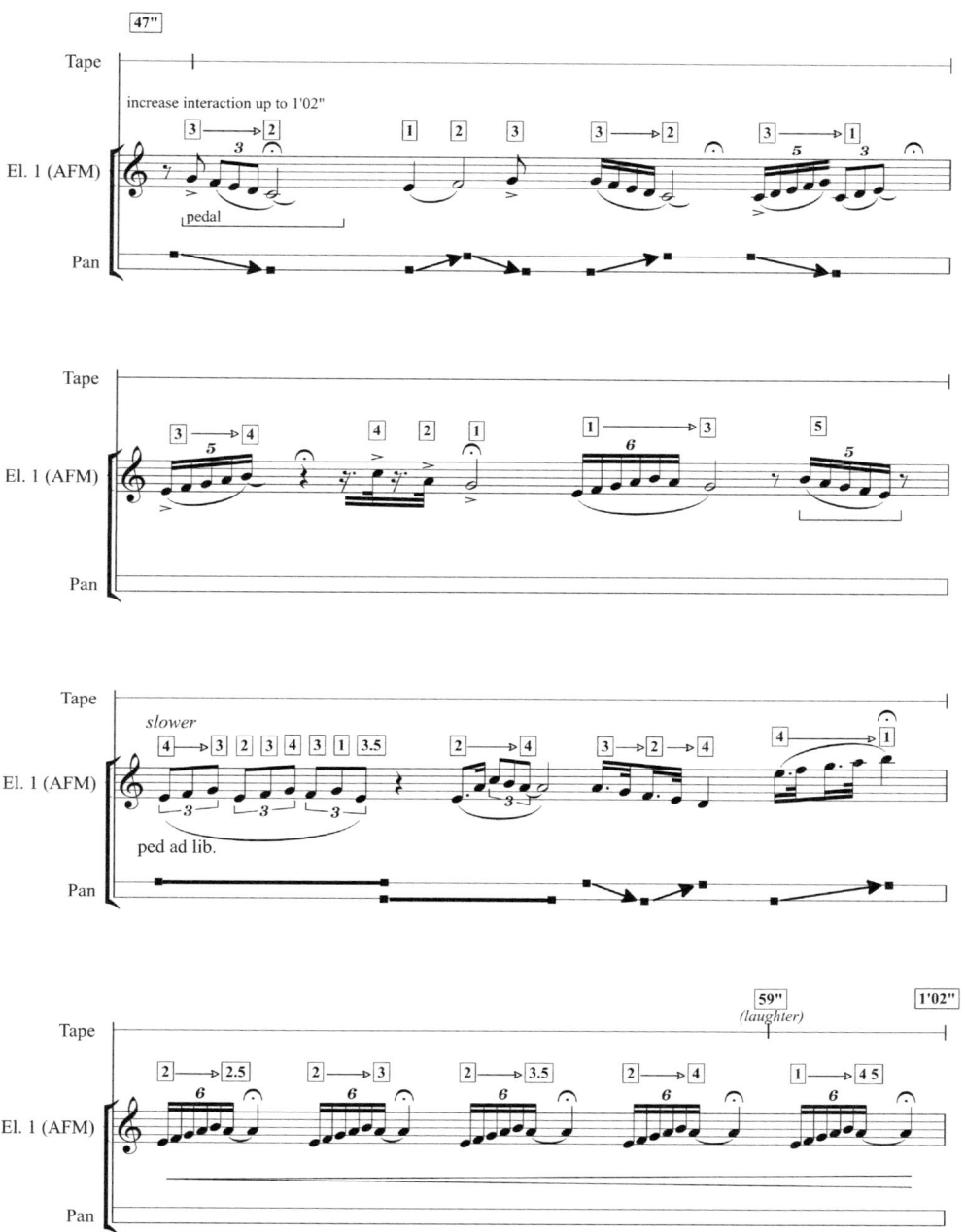

Fig. 8.26: *Phonai,* page two of revised and final score.

IN THE TEMPLE
Christina Meissner

CM. First of all, I would like to say that as soon as I began to listen to In the Temple, *I surrendered myself to the profundity of the sounds I was listening to. I then decided to talk about this piece because it really got under my skin. Perhaps this work resonates with me because, as a cellist, I am searching for the same musical path. It is a journey that fascinates me in all its sensual and sonic power; a journey on the edge of nothingness, as if I were seeking stability while walking on a fine line. I am under the impression that this unique work may play a special role in your compositional output. What makes this work so special compared to your other compositions?

JP. You are right about the uniqueness of *In the Temple* in my output. This was the first conscious attempt to discern music composition in relation to forms of energy rather than sonic constructs per se. The criteria I used for the selection and transformation of the sound objects have been based solely on my perception and intuition of the energy of each sound I worked with.

CM. What happens in the planning of such an extensive acousmatic composition as *In the Temple*?

JP. *In the Temple* was a big project that took me 18 months to complete. In order to understand its genesis, I should tell you about the background of the story. To start with, I should mention that since childhood I have been fascinated by temples of all civilisations. My first physical contact with a temple must have been in Rome when I was seven years old. I also remember the Greek temples of ancient Akragas and Selinus amongst other minor ones in Sicily, the Parthenon in Athens and other temples in Greece and elsewhere which have regularly made a strong impression on me. Each time I enter a temple I seem to be taken into an invisible world that is calling me to enter something mysterious and inexplicable. Like ruins, ancient temples are not empty. Moreover, the sacred and the secret are two expressions of the same reality. Later on, I experienced similar situations in different places in Europe, particularly in Gothic cathedrals especially in England. I am particularly referring to Salisbury, Winchester, Canterbury and York. I have always been attracted by the sacred in all its manifestations and by ancient buildings dedicated to the worship of the divine in whatever form and religious context. To experience a functioning subterranean temple, however, is a unique experience that is impossible to express verbally. This extraordinary event occurred in the Spring of 2003 as I entered an underground temple at the feet of the Italian Alps in the Federation of Damanhur, near the town of Ivrea. As I plunged into the cave of the temple, I descended a secret underworld of thousand colours, a maze of halls and corridors rich in all sorts of ornamentation and striking lighting effects such as luminous spheres and reflections of beams of light on enigmatic paintings and sculptures carved into the rock. Intense perfumes would emphasise a truly multi-sensorial experience of astonishing beauty. I soon found myself in an underground location merging spiritual and scientific knowledge, architectural mathematics, colours and light, and walking an allegorical pathway to a lost sacred heritage. The concept and form of *In the Temple* is connected to the architectural structure of the temple itself: seven halls and one labyrinth with interlinking corridors. Each space of the temple, so I was told, is built according to precise mathematical, acoustic and spiritual laws. Like in many spiritual traditions of the world, architecture is a medium between the spiritual and the material, similar to the great tradition of the stunning Gothic cathedrals of France and England. I divided the project into five phases:

Phase One was dedicated to the measurement of the acoustic characteristics of each hall of the temple and began on 14th April 2006. Below you can see the data collected by the Sound Level Meter I used. You can see the data of the Sound Level Percentiles triggered by three sonic sources: a drum, a pianola and a saxophone. This gives you an idea of the kind of measurement I undertook for each hall of the temple. The example below refers to the Hall of Column and was made on 14th April 2006. I recorded the acoustics of the halls including the corridors of the temple. Out of all these measurements, from a musical point of view the most interesting data was the average value of the reverberation in each room. This average value can be seen at the bottom of the chart.

Reverberation times were taken on a scale of either 50Hz-315Hz or 800Hz-8kHz. I do not know exactly which one of the two scales I referred to because the precise Hertz range display was not been written down on the day of the measurement. However, the setting of the instrument has not been changed during recordings. This means that all the data I took remain proportional throughout the recording of the temple (see Fig. 8.27).

Temple of Mankind - acoustic measurements - 14th April 2006

1. Hall of Column

Sound level percentiles				Frequency		A- network		
	room	pianola	drum				pianola	
Leq:	44.7	66.7	73.1	1.3-oct	1 Min	L 0.1%:		
F Max:	47.6	79.8	88.5	5.0 kHz		L 1.0%:		87.1
F Min:	38.9	38.4	38.1	6.3 kHz		L 5.0%:	76.1	78.5
Le:	54.3	76.3	84.1	8.0 kHz		L10.0%:	67.6	68.5
Peak:	59.1	91.2	106.0	10.0 kHz		L50.0%:	40.7	40.2
I Leq:	75.8	74.6	83.7	12.5 kHz		L90.0%:	39.3	38.9
F Tmx5:				16.0 kHz		L95.0%:	39.3	38.6
F SPL:				20.0 kHz		L99.0%:	38.8	38.8
				A-netw.				
				C-netw.				

50 Hz ⟵——————⟶ 315 Hz
800 Hz ⟵——————⟶ 8 kHz

REVERB (drum): **3.42 – 3.13 – 3.36 – 3.42 – 3.76 – 3.34 – 3.26 – 3.15 – 2.70**

(average: 3.28)

Fig. 8.27: *In the Temple,* example of acoustic measurements.

Phase Two began on 6th September 2006. Back to the temple, I recorded extracts from ancient sacred texts spoken in each room of the temple. **Phase Three** began in October 2006. This is the time when I analysed all collected data and began to work on the form of the piece in terms of sections (movements), vocal and instrumental sounds and the musical features to be employed on each movement. **Phase Four** started on 15th December 2006. Here I began to transform the selected sounds electronically on IRCAM's Audiosculpt and Metasynth, while adding other subtle sonic sources. **Phase Five** began on 29th January 2007 and was dedicated to the organisation of movements, the finalisation of form and the selection of the final sounds to be used for the composition. The figure below shows a list of superimposed low frequencies combinations I used for the sixth movement. They relate to gong, voice and breath sounds. This is rather technical of course, but since you asked about what happens in the run-up to such an extensive acousmatic composition, I wanted to give you an idea of the kind of background technicalities that led to the composition of the piece.

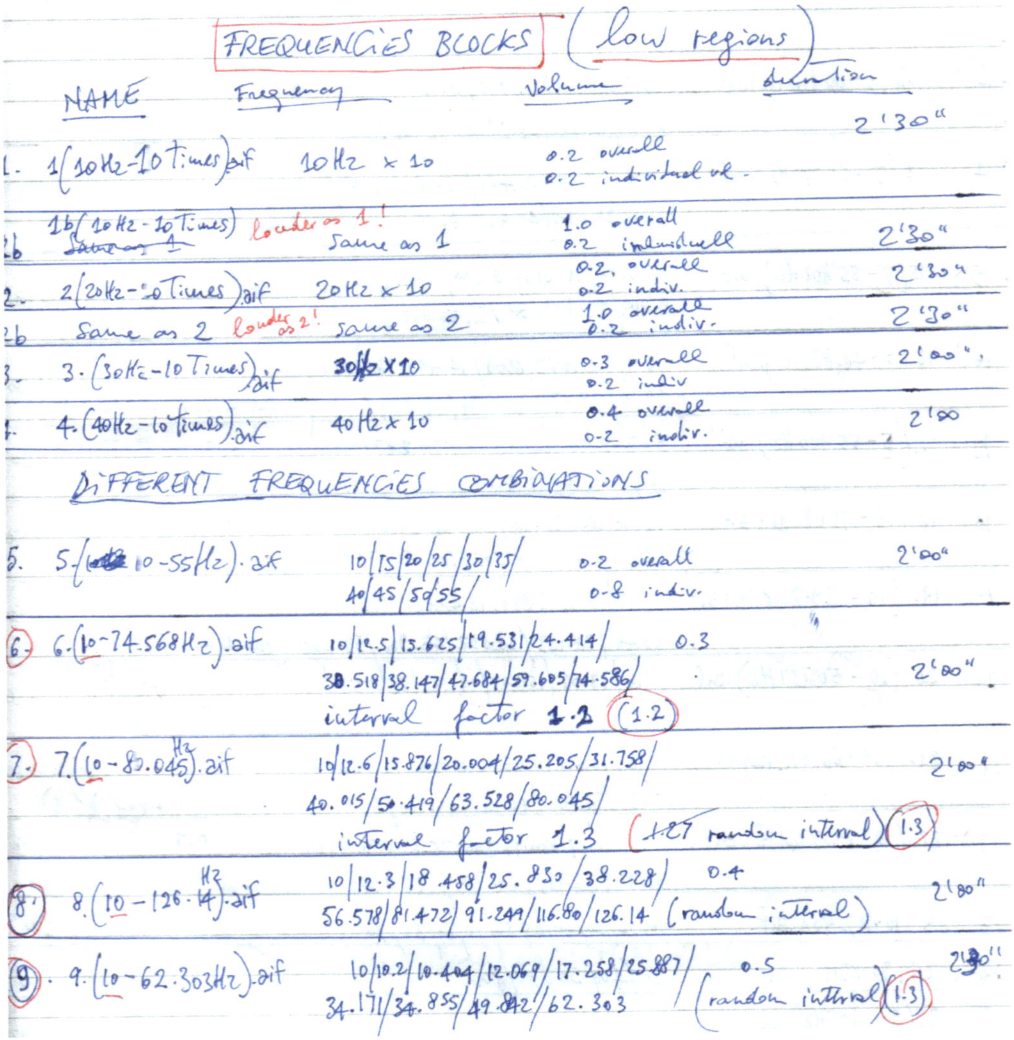

Fig. 8.28: *In the Temple,* example of frequencies blocks.

The form of *In the Temple* is thus structured in eight movements linked by sonic episodes associated with the corridors of the temple. As each hall retains its specific musical characteristic and symbolism, the resonance of each movement is related to the acoustic characteristics of each space according to the research I conducted on the premises of the temple.

CM. Is it a psychological, sensual, metaphysical experience that you try to trace musically?

JP. Yes. The **first movement** is about the beginning of an imaginary journey. The walking in the woods and the discovery of a cave entrance can be clearly imagined by the sonic narrative I sculpted in this opening section. It is a very Dantesque image I had in mind, hence the reference to the beginning of Dante Alighieri's *La Divina Commedia* I mention in the programme note of the piece: *"Nel mezzo del cammin di nostra vita mi ritrovai per una selva oscura ché la diritta via era smarrita."* [145] Once the stones are removed, an imaginary person enters the cave. This is the beginning of the **second movement** (the Lower Hall of Earth) where some distant voices are heard as a prelude to the **third movement** (the Higher Hall of Earth) where the idea of humanity perceived throughout the ages is symbolised by superimposed voices and the first spoken ritual of the piece. The **fourth movement** (the Hall of Metals) articulates the fight with the enemy and a symbolic Game of Life. Here fragments of rituals are heard together with metal sounds. The **fifth movement** (the Labyrinth) comprises of 29 deities. Each divinity is portrayed by a specific sound-event that represents the predominant essence of the deity. The sonic depiction of such symbolic qualities was by far the most difficult task I experienced in the whole composition. The **sixth movement** (the Blue Temple) is about meditation taking place on the edge of sensorial perception. The **seventh movement** (the Hall of Water) is about the symbolism of water and the female principle characterised by fragmented rituals. The **eighth movement** (the Hall of Spheres) symbolises the access to the Synchronic Lines of the earth and is focused on alchemy as a means for spiritual transformation. It is the central nervous system of the piece. The **ninth movement** (Hall of Mirrors) is about the sense of dreaming as a form of spiritual transcendence.

Each movement is related to a hall of the temple representing a specific element (earth, fire, ether, water, air), principle (male, female, unity and dream), a numerical proportion, a specific colour, note, timbre, image, gesture and motion. I interpreted this rich symbolism as a doorway leading to deepest realms of the soul. Metaphorically, going through each hall requires that I leave the same predictable connections to old behaviour, thoughts and experiences in order to step into the unknown: it is a journey of purification implying the death of my old self and the beginning of a new identity. The symbolism of entering the temple is comparable to the notion of entering 'the dark night of the soul' which depicts a journey leading to the discovery of a new unfamiliar self. It is about a personal transformation that remains rooted in the spiritual and the sensual; both realms perceived as two manifestations of the same reality.

CM. Did the place of this temple you visited play any role in your composition?

JP. Very much so. I mentioned the synchronic lines earlier on. The temple is located on a crossing point of four synchronic lines, thus providing a unique source of psychic energy. As a little child, I remember reacting differently to specific places, and throughout the years I have become increasingly perceptive to the 'Ortgeist', that is the 'spirit of a place' that is active in any location of the earth. I believe that anybody who is mentally open to it can feel the energy of a place, especially in areas situated on ley or synchronic lines. Allow me to explain: a place is not only a geographical surface, but a source of energy coming from within the earth. The shape of a landscape that marks any place results from its natural morphology in which natural

---

[145] *"Midway life's journey I was made aware / That I had strayed into a dark forest / And the right path appeared not anywhere."*. Dante Alighieri, *The Divine Comedy*, beginning of *Inferno*.

manifestations such as hills, plains, winds, rivers, lakes and rocks have each a natural energy level that contributes to the geo-dynamic and psychic quality of the location. Our ancient predecessors knew this well and built their houses, temples and roads in relation to this 'Ortgeist'. Many cartographers and archaeologists, especially in Great Britain, are aware of this tradition, particularly since the work of Alfred Watkins in the early 1920s. But the science of mapping roads and building important temples and places of worship is as old as humanity. The location of East Grinstead, Sussex (England), is one of the many examples that I could mention. It is well-known to the locals that cognitive clarity in East Grinstead is enhanced by the ley lines at the intersection of the High Weald sandstone ridges with their quartz crystalline structure. It is no wonder that several spiritual, meditation and religious centres are located in such a small town. Modern civilisation has almost managed to destroy this natural relationship with the earth. The result can be seen in the annihilation of natural landscapes justified by the increase of population and industrial expansion. Back to your question, yes, the music of *In the Temple* is *also* a result of my awareness of the temple's location.

CM. Metaphorically speaking, what kind of notes are the first to appear on paper?

JP. In the case of *In the Temple*, music composition was not conceived in the traditional way, but as a process of dealing with mystical and magical symbols as a source of energy. Each sound I chose and transformed was the result of a long process of conscious intuition and meditation about a perceived level of energy intrinsic in the sounds and symbols I dealt with. This is an approach similar to the method used in physics (for example, the calculations about the consumption and transformation of energy), as well as in alchemy. Composing music this way means that I am dealing with sound as a form of energy that I can perceive and respond to creatively. This approach will sound elusive to a conventional musician, but it is truly factual, although opposite to the traditional approach to 'classical' composition. In retrospect, I can say that *In the Temple* was my first large-scale endeavour to write a piece of 'alchemical' music.

CM. How did you incorporate the acoustic qualities of the rooms of the temple into your composition?

JP. I incorporated the acoustic qualities out of the measurements I made, of which I have shown you some results from the Hall of Column. Essentially, I used the average reverberation level of each acoustic space. This means that each movement has its own spatial quality including a specific degree of reverberation. However, I had to alter such qualities in conjunction with the narrative of events unfolding in the music. This means that, eventually, the initial reverberation settings have been adjusted to the development of the music narrative. An extreme example of this spatial modification can be heard in the Hall of Mirror with the use of superimposed choirs each projected onto much wider spaces, as a description of the experience of dreaming that is supposed to take place in that hall. From an alchemical perspective, the natural acoustic qualities of the rooms can be transformed into different fields of spatial and sonic energy corresponding to the amount of conscious attention of the composer.

We shouldn't forget that in order to be heard, a space needs a sound. This is a very important concept also in what I call 'magical composition', where the perception of the composer is an additional form of energy responding to the energy of space and sound. It is the perception of sound and space that gives sound and space an energetic value. My intuition, the intensity of my imagination and the activity of all my senses produce energy by performing their function. In a broader sense, the energy that I produce as an individual is usually used for my own physical survival, but in this approach to composition, my artistic goal is to accrue this energy in relation to the sound and space I am dealing with. Ultimately, it is about transforming potential energy into music. I can do this through meditation or a highly focused concentration of the mind on what I am listening to. I can also exploit other mental sources that permit me to access stored energy and transform it into audible form. In both cases, I am functioning as a filter. I realise that the notion of 'energy' may sound too abstract and non-credible to many musicians, but this is exactly the approach I used when I composed *In the Temple*, and one that I am gradually refining in smaller-scale works.

CM. What meaning does the title *In the Temple* have for you?

JP. As I have hinted at earlier, the 'temple' is actually the inner self. I believe that our physical body lives in a temple that is traditionally known as 'soul', or 'spirit'.

CM. The first time I listened to this work, I heard steps that led me into the music: someone is moving slowly; at some point, he stops and moves into the next event. This uneven rhythm of walking and stopping suggests to me that something very spontaneous, solitary, inquisitive, even reverential is happening in the narrative of the piece. Also, the steps seem like inviting me to become the walking person. This awareness prompts an astonishing sense of intimacy and an inevitable perception of both intense and tender experiences of life. However, these never seem to have anything threatening about them. One feels alone, and yet guided.

JP. I can understand very well what you are saying because your description corresponds to my personal experience. The walking person is each of us who is keen to embark on a journey of self-discovery. But unlike Dante's *Divine Comedy*, where the poet is accompanied by the spiritual guides of Virgil (throughout hell and purgatory) and Beatrice (throughout heaven), in *In the Temple*, there is no guide, as it is a journey that we must undertake alone. Although I resist the notion of a universal truth that must be pertinent to all human beings, I cannot deny that there is one truth that does apply to everyone, namely that, at some point, our physical body must die and that each of us is essentially alone, especially in the face of death. However, solitude is not desolation, even when this appears to be so, and by facing the abyss of bleakness with the bravery of mindfulness, we can turn loneliness into an experience of fulfilment and belonging. I believe this is an endless task but the only enduring value that can unite me with my inner self. In a context of this kind, contemplation and solitude can be powerful means of self-knowledge.

CM. Your words seem to come from the heart, and what you are saying makes sense to me. It is a long journey though, isn't it? I'm aware that my thoughts determine the way I perceive my life circumstances, and that the inner journey is an ever-unfolding search for the centre. Ultimately, it is something that concerns each of us, whether we're conscious of it or not. The symbolism of the steps linking the different rooms of the temple is so effective! Only later on I found out that each time they occur, the steps indicate a new room of the temple which symbolically corresponds to a new stage of awareness. Consequently, when the steps enter a new hall, they introduce a new kind of sensorial experience. Do you associate these rooms with specific topics? Can you tell me more about this aspect of the composition?

JP. Each movement reflects the symbolism of each room which I have revisited and reinterpreted with the approach I mentioned earlier. The **first movement** (*Beginning*) marks the beginning of the journey and the discovery of a cave.

In the **second movement** (*Lower Hall of the Earth*), I reflect on the notion of life as represented in the landscape paintings on the walls. Life is depicted in terms of age as temporal continuity seen from an imaginary ancient sky. It is therefore linked to the notion of time. I used the recording of the recorder, as a symbol of earth, made in the same room. The sound of the recorder is split and transformed into different sounds merging with voices. This is the first impression of the surreal space of the spirit. The associated picture is 'nature'.

The **third movement** *(Higher Hall of the Earth)* is linked to the Higher Hall which is dedicated to the earth and the masculine power of generation. The notion of time is equally important here. Distant voices mixed with unearthly sounds based on cello and gongs are heard singing an ancient melody based on the notes C, Eb, F, G, A, C. Fragments of spoken rituals are heard in the background. The colours associated with the second and third movements are red and green. The associated picture is 'mankind'.

The **fourth movement** *(Hall of Metals)* corresponds to the Hall of Metals. Based on the elements of ether and fire and the principle of action and opposition, I explored sonic bodies in motion, often in a spiral motion. Most of the sounds are based on a Tibetan bowl and Indian discs. The main colours are gold and silver. I shaped most sound events on numerical proportions based on the number eight. The sonic energy occurs in a spiral motion, clockwise, from the ceiling; anticlockwise from the floor.

The **fifth movement** *(Labyrinth)* corresponds to the labyrinth of the temple and comprises the images of 29 deities, each of them being interpreted as containers of specific energy. The principle is unity and the colour yellow; the symbol is the divine force. You can hear 29 sonic events following one another. Each sound unit corresponds to my perception of the divinities. These are (in chronological order): Aphrodite, Ra, Osiris, Brahma, Persephone, Buddha, Ades, Enlil, Poseidon, Anubi, Brigit, Christ, Balder, Mitra, Sin, Gea, Marduk, Ganesh, Jahve, Horus, Pan, Thot, Bran, Cybel, Bastet, Astarte, Athena, Allah and Amaterasu.

The **sixth movement** *(Blue Temple),* corresponds to the Blue Hall (which is a temple inside the temple) and the association with the female principle, the notion of birth and concealed meditation. The colour is blue, and the music should resemble a circular effect of reflection depending on where the listener stands. This movement relies on the lowest frequencies of the entire work. The frequencies cross the edge of the inaudible and although they cannot be perceived by the human ear, they are there to contribute to the overall sensation of sound. I deliberately challenged the listener to hear the quasi-silence and beyond. This is the most inwards-going moment of the composition.

The **seventh movement** *(Hall of Water)* corresponds to the Hall of Water. A ritual in an ancient sacred language is clearly heard here for the first time. The music of this movement is linked to the previous one as they both symbolise the feminine. The element of this movement is water and the colours are blue and silver. The sounds derive from tubular bells.

The **eighth movement** *(Hall of Spheres)* corresponds to the Hall of the Spheres which is also the hall of alchemy. In terms of energetic power, this is the 'neural' centre of the composition symbolising the access to the synchronic lines I mentioned earlier. The principle is the masculine. The colours are gold, red and brown. The main sound is a whistle as the symbolic access code to the synchronic lines. The whistle is the sonic element of alchemy.

The **ninth movement** *(Hall of Mirrors)* concludes the work and corresponds to the Hall of Mirrors. The element is air and the principle is the sense of dreaming. The colours are indigo and gold. The notion of mirrors is used for sound reflection and multiplication. The long-sustained gestures are based on the multiplication of tam-tam, string, saxophone, bowl sounds and voices.

CM. With this work, you lead the listener into a very touching and profound experience, a sort of archaic form of meditation about the nature of being. One experiences the fullness of solitude: the human being (the self) that is now ready for new discoveries…

JP. This was the idea. I did mention solitude earlier on and the importance of feeling one with oneself and the cosmos. Solitude is a source of reflection and healing that is often confused with the idea of loneliness and therefore perceived as something negative to stay away from. But the two concepts are different. 'Al-one' actually means 'all-one', namely 'one' with the 'all' (the whole). When we are One-with-the-All, we are never really lonely. And, as Thomas Edison said, *"The best thinking has been done in solitude. The worst has been done in turmoil."*

CM. In the movement of the Blue Hall, there is a wonderful sense of peace and focus, as if pointing out the essential nature of our existence. Everything could fall silent here, but then the music continues…

JP. This sensation may be a result of the energy associated with the female principle of the Blue Hall which I connected to the sixth movement, and the notion of birth I mentioned earlier on. Composing this movement was one of the most challenging and enthralling experiences of my life because I worked on the edge of the audible by using the lowest frequencies I could, including those that we cannot hear.

I selected 141 frequencies and analysed each of them individually, also those which were inaudible to my ears. Although we don't physically hear such frequencies, the brain will actually sense them, and this can be a mind-blowing experience: disturbing to some people, perhaps inspiring to others. There are several psychoacoustic phenomena that take place on the border of the inaudible. For example, very often a low degree of intensity causes a perception of a lower note (I mean, a note that sounds lower than its frequency). Another feature is delay, meaning that the ear will need a few seconds in order to perceive the lowest audible sounds. There is also the beating phenomenon that occurs when two different frequency oscillations are superimposed and consequently produce a third periodic vibration resulting from the difference between the two frequencies. Imagine what would happen by superimposing more of such similar frequencies. All these subtle phenomena contribute to a quasi-silence texture of baffling psychological quality. As a matter of fact, I initially wanted to write this movement only using such inaudible frequencies but had to abandon the idea due to the fact that the commission from Deutschland Radio was made for a piece to be broadcast, and there is no way a radio-based audience would manage to hear such frequencies through a traditional radio or a podcast. In the end, I had to settle for a compromise where I would make it possible for a radio audience to hear something.

Although in this movement one can always hear a sound, there are many moments where I superimpose inaudible sounds with sounds on the edge of the audible. This combination creates a sense of mystery and inwardness that can either fascinate or frighten the listeners, depending on their expectation and willingness to be challenged by the unfamiliar. I know that many people find this listening experience very disturbing. As for me, this is one of the areas of psychoacoustics I like most, as I love to be challenged by what I don't know. I must also say that meditating on the colour blue helped me to embrace the low sounds as a gateway to an elusive, perhaps mystical dimension.

CM. One artist creates works of art from nails, the other from objects made of felt or grease. How would you describe your 'Erkennungsmaterial' (material of recognition)? With that, I also mean: what attracts you? What do you question repeatedly? What emerges permanently in your life and thus defines you?

JP. To answer these questions appropriately it would take me at least 20 pages! Certainly, artistic suicide would occur if I limited myself to embrace only one perspective or remain content with the answers and descriptions offered by someone else instead of exploring the same question myself. I believe there are doors to be continuously opened, spaces to be constantly discovered, questions to be asked anew. I am attracted by mystery and beauty, critical questioning and the joy of discovery. I simply question anything that I feel needs to be questioned. Ultimately, I would like the music I write to speak for me since everything that is written is governed by its own rules, and as F.W.J. Schelling once said, *"if we know the product of intuition, then we know the intuition itself. We therefore need only deduce the product in order to deduce the intuition".*[146]

CM. Are you always composing or are there phases in your life when you take a break? Does the development of new ideas need some space now and then?

JP. The concepts of time and space are relative, and I don't want to lose my curiosity for sustained novelty. In addition to my willingness to learn from the past, I keep sensing a profound need to live in the 'now' and be projected onto the future. Ideas come and go on a daily (and nightly!) basis. I compose almost each day of my life. Beneath my activities lies a seed of desire to discover who I am. No matter how many others have asked the same question before me, I feel this is what I am here for. It is therefore essential to keep alive in me the desire to search, doubt and question, as there is more art in honest doubt than in deceitful certainty.

CM. Do you work on several pieces in your mind at the same time during the embryonic phase of creation?

JP. Sometimes. One of the perpetual wonders in life is that there is always room for another idea, another opinion, another interpretation, and each of them has the right to fill a place in our artistic universe. Neurogenesis has confirmed that the brain continues to grow throughout a lifetime. The nature of perception remains a mystery to me, and the music I write reflects a desire to explore an aesthetic experience of sublimation of the senses, an adventure that transcends the rational and the verbal; a journey from the finite to the infinite which reminds me of a phrase attributed to Albert Einstein: *"the more I study physics, the more I'm drawn to metaphysics".*

---

[146] Schelling (1964:362).

CHAPTER NINE

EASTERN INSPIRATIONS

EASTERN IMPACT
Ikuko Inoguchi

II. *November Steps* **for shakuhachi, biwa, and orchestra by Toru Takemitsu is perhaps the most known piece written for Japanese instruments. Did this work or any other work written for Japanese instruments inspire you?**

JP. Not much, to be honest. In fact, I remember being disappointed when I heard it. To my ears, the orchestral works by Takemitsu (at least those I have heard) sound more Western than Eastern. They also retain a strong French influence. I can hear Debussy resonating in them. I found the two in cadenzas in *November Steps* interesting, but not more than that. The rest wasn't very appealing to me. The same consideration applies to *Autumn*, also for biwa, shakuhachi and orchestra. Having said that, perhaps it is time I should listen to these works again after so many years. In any case, I found clearer signs of Japanese sensitivity in Takemitsu's chamber music.

II. You visited Japan in 2003. Was this trip work-related? What was your itinerary? Any notable experiences?

JP. It was 2001 actually and in conjunction with the World Music Days Festival where my piece *Koan* had been scheduled as the climax of the festival, being the last piece in the last concert. This was a great and unexpected joy for me. I decided to take advantage of this event in order to spend some weeks in the Kyoto area, and during this time I also entered a Zen monastery for a short time in order to deepen Zen Buddhism and practise Zazen within a clear set of monastic rules. The Japan trip is still the most revealing journey I have ever undertaken in my life. I remember communication with the locals was cut to the minimum due to the language barrier, but it has certainly been the strongest travelling and cultural experience in my life.

There is something I have to say at this stage. Since I am used to getting a lot of questions about Japan and the influence of Zen in my music, I have the impression that many people love to conceptualise about this, as if implying that it is because of Japan that I write what I write. If my impression is correct, this would be extremely reductive. It is not much a country per se, but what we already have within ourselves that makes us feel an attraction for a culture, a country or even a person. Japan could be any other country or entity, really. For example, take the student-teacher relationship. When we choose a friend, a teacher or a mentor, it is because we see qualities in this person that are already within us. In other words, this person mirrors values and desires that are already in us. The same applies to a country or a culture. To be specific, I am not particularly interested in modern westernised Japan. The sensitivity to nature, art and philosophy that is already in me is partly reflected by those values that characterise traditional Japan. I think this is a very important point that needs to be clarified. It is not Zen that made me compose certain musical works, but my own search for those values that I see reflected *also* by Zen culture. Notice that I have emphasised the word 'also'.

II. Your acousmatic work *I Am* is largely based on samples of sounds collected in Japan. Did your stay in Japan influence your approach to sound and the way you listen to sound?

JP. No. It was my work in the electronic studio that refined my listening skills. However, my stay in Japan reinforced my growing perception of a specific, more subtle, relationship between sound and silence.

II. You describe *I Am* as a spiritual journey. How did your experience in Japan influence your understanding of spirituality?

JP. My experience in Japan clarified several things I was working on at that time of my life. Being there gave me the possibility to plunge into literature, rituals and events that opened deeper perspectives of how to look at nature, life and the spirit. One of the reasons why I find Zen literature fascinating is that it is full of psychological challenges to the Western mind. We can see this also in traditional Japanese poetry. The two are sisters. Zen spirituality differs profoundly from other Buddhist traditions of Asia in that there is a stronger emphasis on the concepts of emptiness and non-duality. The latter implies that spiritual emancipation can take place beyond the dualistic way we look at things. The Zen notions of no-mind, the subconscious and emptiness, for example, are supported by the idea of Formlessness, meaning that we live in a physical state of form but are, or can be, detached from it. I have to add that Zen is particularly tough on artists as they tend to attach emotions to their art. (This is a point that can help us understand better John Cage's attitude towards sound.) In Zen, if artists become too idealistic, they will end up in a dead-end because there is a philosophical gap between an ideal and the intention of an artist to reach the ideal. In that sense, Zen is the opposite of any idealistic tradition of the West, including Christianity. My own approach to Zen remains somewhat controversial to this day because I deliberately embrace both attitudes. The reason for that is that both attitudes reveal ethical values I treasure. In Japan, I also discovered the Mumon-Kan, a collection of 48 koans written in the 13th century. Koans are powerful challenges to the mind, both philosophically and psychologically. Initially, our dualistic mind will go crazy, but with perseverance, we can see that the way we perceive life begins to change. *I Am* represents a journey into the subconscious. If you read the poems on which the piece is based and then listen to the music, it should be possible to discern this personal journey as something that we in the West would call a 'search for the self'. *I Am* is an attempt to portray that everything changes, that easy is not different from difficult, that bad is good and good is bad, and that ultimately everything is in the mind.

II. Both *Renge-Kyo* and *I am* finish with the sound of sea waves. Is your use of natural sound associated with your understanding of spirituality?

JP. This is an interesting question because it was in Japan that I became fully aware of the link between spirit and nature. I had already known this in conjunction with the life of Francis of Assisi, a man I have always admired, but in Japan, it made a click in my mind. I observed it in many levels of everyday life of Japanese society, at least in the Kyoto area; I admired it in temples, gardens, cemeteries and Ikebana exhibitions; I read it in the haikus of Basho and in many other poets, I heard it in Japanese traditional songs. In many spiritual traditions, water is the symbol of the sacred meaning of life, the symbol of purification, healing and even protection. Jesus Christ was baptised with water. The waters of the river Ganges are still considered to be sacred in India. The Nile was sacred to the Egyptians. Masaru Emoto's research on water has stunned thousands of people in recent years. So yes, in both *Renge-Kyo* and *I am*, the water sounds are a symbol of the search for inner purification.

II. What is your interpretation of the Japanese concept of 'ma'? How did you learn about it? Did your understanding of 'ma' change after your trip to Japan?

JP. Since I was a young boy, I have always had a natural predilection for silence. When I am silent, I am more likely to remember my nature and the reality of life. In silence, I have the chance to reflect more on my life. Silence promotes the perception of my inner centre, the intimate space of the mind, and sharpens the awareness of thinking and breathing. It is like opening a door to my inner self and, if so wished, including the presence of the others. Silence is also a symbolic condition of a mind that is living in the present. A mind that is aware, attentive but not alerted, solicited but not agitated, ready but not impulsive, reactive but not tormented.

I came across the notion of 'ma' when I was living in London in the 1990s as I began to research shakuhachi and Japanese music. I remember that it resonated with me immediately. This was the time when I began to listen to traditional Japanese music. In England, I also discovered the work of Frank Denyer, which I found equally inspiring. Attending many concerts of traditional Japanese music when I was in Japan provided me with a first-hand experience of Japanese sensitivity that I have never forgotten.

Rather than trying to understand 'ma', it is more important to me to *perceive* it, to *feel* it, knowing that this perception will inevitably change with time, age and experience. I don't think that 'ma' can be reduced to a pre-established or static notion. I see it rather as a 'flexible' reflection of how a physical or musical space may be sensed by the beholder or listener. When 'ma' is described as a 'negative' space, I think we should not interpret the word 'negative' as something that is bad or reductive, but perceive it as a living space of silence in music: a mental space where emptiness is as important as a filled space, and silence as important as sound. It is Absence perceived as an essential counterpart of Presence. I remain a strong advocate for a culture of silence in the West.

II. You have composed three pieces for shakuhachi. The second work, *Three Haikus*, and the third work *Silent/Listen 1* display a significant stylistic change from the first work *Koan*. Do you think your approach to the Japanese instrument has changed over the years? Did you have different aims or goals in mind for these works?

JP. I certainly had different aims in each of these works you mention; hence the diversity of idioms you are referring to. However, I should say that I don't think in terms of an approach to Japanese instruments. An instrument is an instrument. I own a koto, for example; this beautiful instrument is just another musical instrument. Of course, it is a Japanese instrument, but it is primarily a *musical* instrument that has been manufactured in Japan. I think your question is valid for any instrument, and yes, my approach to a musical instrument changes with me and my personal growth. Each instrument has a geographical origin. The modern guitar, as we know it, was brought to Spain by the Moors in the 8th century; does it mean that by composing for guitar today I am writing Arabian or Spanish music? What I mean is that an instrument that is initially linked to a specific culture over time becomes part of a world heritage. Therefore, I think that the differentiation between Western and Eastern instruments will, at some point, disappear. It is part of cultural integration and evolution.

II. By combining Western and Japanese traditions, what would you like to communicate to your audience?

JP. I would like to contribute to cross-cultural understanding by keeping different traditions alive in mutually enriching dialogue.

JAPANESE REFERENCES IN THE MUSIC OF JOHN PALMER
Ikuko Inoguchi

As John Palmer stated in a recent interview with this author, *"Japan is an important country for me"*;[147] Japan and Japanese culture (e.g. music and philosophy) have been providing him with a source of inspiration for over 25 years. From the earliest work, *Renge-Kyo,* for piano and electronics (1993) to the latest *Yahari* for guitar (2017), he has consistently produced works with a Japanese reference in every decade. Within these works, it is possible to locate four main areas of Japanese culture in which he sought new ideas: Buddhism (including Zen), traditional Japanese music, Japanese literature and language, and a close relationship between nature and life. This can be seen in the titles and programme notes to his music, instrumentation, performance style, and formal and rhythmic structure. In his music, these four areas often serve as a combined interest within a single piece of composition. For instance, *Koan,* for shakuhachi and ensemble (1999), exhibits his interest in Buddhism, in particular, with Zen, as shown in the title, as well as with traditional Japanese music in the use of the shakuhachi. The structure of the work also relates to that of the Japanese haiku, a short poetic form. Since the shakuhachi is an instrument that is made of a natural material, the work may also be considered to reflect the Japanese special connection to nature. His exploration of Japanese culture is an extension of his interests in the interrelation between music, art, literature, religion, philosophy and aesthetics; his music also embodies this interrelation. Accompanied by the composer's biographical information, tracing the trajectory of his interest in Japanese culture and its impact on his compositional practice, this essay discusses the Japanese references that are displayed in his music.

The aforementioned *Renge-Kyo* is the first work in which a Japanese reference is used in the oeuvre of Palmer. 'Renge' is the Japanese word for lotus, while the word 'kyo' has several meanings, depending on context and kanji characters applied to it. In the work, the word 'kyo' carries a double meaning: 経 as sutra (a Buddhist scripture) and 響 as resonance. The former clearly indicates his interest in Buddhism. According to the composer, he was introduced to Tibetan and Indian Buddhism in the early 1980s. His reading of these branches of Buddhism encouraged him to explore Japanese Buddhism, including Zen, and to practise Zazen meditation. His study of the music and writings of John Cage, many of which draw upon concepts and philosophies that Cage learned from Daisetz Suzuki's lectures on Buddhism at Columbia University in the early 1950s, also provided additional resources. This assisted Palmer in reconfiguring the idea of sound and the way of listening: he states that Cage's interest in Japanese aesthetics showed him a more attentive way to listen to music, especially to sound itself, and he found that Cage's ideas of sound and silence were 'Zen-like'.[148]

Renge-Kyo is centred on the principle of causality and the idea of the simultaneous cause and effect.[149] Buddhism, for instance 'Kegon', teaches a view that all things, e.g. events in the

---

[147] Palmer's biographical information and comments are based on the interview with the composer in February 2021.

[148] Through the use of chance operations, Cage aimed to liberate sound from Western art music tradition and personal taste, and his well-known *4'33"* (1952) manifests his view of silence as the duration that is filled with sounds that are unintentionally made.

[149] See the programme note of the work: *"I wrote Renge-Kyo having been inspired by the principle of causality. I was intrigued by the interaction of cause and effect taking place from the most tenuous occurrences in daily life to large-scale events that may shape the history of the world. In Japanese Buddhism Renge (the lotus flower) symbolises the simultaneousness of Cause and Effect (the flower and the seed pod) and the ability of self-purification (the blossoms in the muddy swamps). Kyo means Sutra (teaching) and Sound as vibration; it represents the continuity of all things. I associated the Cause with the piano and the Effect with the electronics. Throughout the piece the two instruments are interrelated in an asymmetric*

past, present, and future, are related and influence one another. This means that cause and effect are not considered two separate entities but are interrelated. In this work, Palmer associates the idea of cause with the piano and effect with the electronics. In the opening, the piano part and the electronic part (tape and live electronics) consists of different materials; however, from around 3'00" onwards, both parts play phrases consisting of the same pitch. For instance, at 3'00" both parts play G♭ at the same time, and at 3'33" both parts play a phrase containing the same pitches but with a slight rhythmic variation. At 6'47", both parts play identical phrases in a synchronised manner. At 3'10" where the tape part plays back the recorded sounds of the piano for the first time in the work, the pianist is instructed to look up to the ceiling with an expression of surprise; a nod to Cage who integrated theatrical elements into musical performance. The music also contains bell resonance, corresponding to the meaning of 'kyo' as resonance, as well as possibly alluding to the sound of a Buddhist temple bell.

Another major work that explores concepts of Buddhism is the previously introduced *Koan*, for shakuhachi and ensemble. The koan is a research question or riddle given from a Zen master to students so as to help them experience spiritual awakening while challenging students' worldview based on their knowledge and everyday experience. The work *Koan* aims to portray the learner's psychological turmoil and evolution to reach the state of enlightenment, referenced later in this paper. *Satori* for harpsichord (1999), *Without,* for solo violin (2006) and *Silent/listen 1* (2014) for two shakuhachis also display connection to Japanese Buddhism. The Japanese word 'satori' refers to the spiritual awakening or enlightenment that Buddha experienced in his lifetime and that anybody who practises Buddhism may attain. These works will be discussed later in conjunction with the inspiration provided by traditional Japanese music and/or literature. *From the Lake* was inspired by part of the *Buddhacarita* (Acts of the Buddha), an epic poem describing the life of Buddha, written by Aśvaghosa in Sanskrit. The title *Nowhere to hide* was taken from *Wúménguān* (The Gateless Gate), a collection of forty-eight koans, compiled by the Chinese Zen monk Wumen Huikai.[150]

The second area of Palmer's interest in Japanese culture is the most obvious: music. The first work reflecting this is *Koan*. Before composing the work, he came across an article entitled *The Potential of the Shakuhachi in Contemporary Music* written by the Japanese shakuhachi player Yoshikazu Iwamoto in 1993. The article, accompanied by a tape recording, demonstrates various techniques of shakuhachi playing, extending from techniques derived from the Honkyoku tradition (e.g. 'muraiki' [uneven breath], trills, 'vibrato' and 'komi-buki' [breath pulsation, cultivated by players of the Nezasa School]) to those of contemporary music (e.g. multiphonics and fingerings to play quarter tones).[151] *Koan* explores both traditional and new shakuhachi playing techniques, and the sonority and effect of these which are also imitated by Western orchestral instruments.[152]

The form consists of 17 sections, a reference to the structure of the Japanese haiku (which will be discussed later), indicated by rehearsal letters from A to Q. Sections A and B start calmly with the tonal centre D, established by a pedal note first played by the piano and

---

alternation of actions and reactions taking place on two superimposed and at times altered layers of time."

[150] Despite their popularity in Japan, these sources are not of Japanese origin. For the purpose of this article, further discussion will not be included.

[151] Iwamoto (1993:13–39).

[152] In *Koan*, traditional Japanese techniques are expected to be applied where the performance indication *alla maniera orientale* is indicated. This is contrasted with the instruction *alla maniera virtuosa occidentale*, which directs the shakuhachi player to detach themselves from the Japanese tradition as much as possible. The composer's use of the words 'oriental' and 'occidental' is not intended to be viewed as the dualistic image between the two whose political connotation has been problematised by Edward Said's *Orientalism* and in post-colonial discourse.

later by the cello. This tonal centre is restated with long sustained notes first by woodwind instruments in section A and also by the shakuhachi in section B. The work is written for the standard D shakuhachi, so the note D is the fundamental note. From section C onwards, after one bar of the shakuhachi's sustained note D with the 'muraiki' technique, the tonal centre D disappears (although it temporarily returns in section D). Instead, the music shifts to an atonal language with a dense polyphonic texture and rhythmically complex passages. In section E, the work briefly employs canonic writing: the motif played by the shakuhachi is imitated by the flute and vice versa. The work also explores the aspects of 'bravura', exploiting the extreme contrast between the registers and dynamics of each instrument. The intensity of the music and the virtuosity that it demands from the performers could be seen as an allusion to the psychological confusion or turbulence that the work aims to communicate. At the beginning of section O, the ensemble section (i.e. the piano and the percussion parts) suddenly drops out after a long 'diminuendo' as if the learner's mind quiets down, and the shakuhachi re-enters. The first note of this re-entry (B♭) is the same note as the first note of the shakuhachi's first entry. The tonal centre D returns in this section and is heard as a pedal note played by the piano. In section P, the shakuhachi also plays a sustained note D, doubled by the flute. The work ends with the melodic interval of a minor third, D and F played by the shakuhachi. This consonant ending suggests that the learner attains spiritual harmony. Palmer's interest in traditional Japanese music also alerted his attention to the concept of 'ma'. In an interview with Christian Morris in 2014, the composer talks about this:

"Since the late 1980s, traditional Japanese music, in particular, has been a constant source of inspiration to me. I'd like to refer to the Japanese concept of 'ma', this amazing energy we call silence but that may also be experienced as the very origin of a sound. (I think I first realised the power of silence when I practised meditation in a Japanese monastery in 2001.)" [153]

The Japanese word 'ma' literally means 'in-between' and is often translated as 'silence' or 'empty space'; it is not a passive but an active entity. Although 'ma' is often discussed in artistic contexts (paintings, architecture, music, and dance), it is considered to prevail in Japanese daily life (e.g. verbal and nonverbal communication). In a daily conversation, an expression such as 'ma ga warui' ('ma' [timing] is bad) is often heard. Thus, 'ma' is an essential factor underlying a sense of timing in Japanese aesthetics. In traditional Japanese music, the word 'ma' refers to beats, rhythm, time between two notes, and timing. A beat in nōgaku and kinsei hōgaku (music from the Edo period, such as shamisen music) is understood as a point established by the action of hitting an instrument. 'Omote-ma' (front) and 'ura-ma' (back) means the first and second beat, respectively, while 'ō-ma' and 'shō-ma' indicate how fast or slow a beat should be felt in performance.[154] When the word 'ma' is used by itself, it refers to the length between two points.[155] During 'ma', the sound may be continuous or broken off, but the performer must maintain concentration to keep tension and momentum.[156] 'Ma' also refers to timing. It is important to note that 'ma' is the duration that cannot be mathematically and scientifically defined, nor intellectually planned. In the words of Nō actor Hisao Kanze, good timing of 'ma' happens incidentally and 'naturally'.[157] This performance practice closely relates to the Japanese view of time as unmeasurable and an aesthetic of highly valuing concentration on the 'now', influenced both by Buddhism and Zen.

---

[153] Morris, Christian, *John Palmer Interview* in *Composition Today* (see bibliography).
[154] Satoaki (1983:140).
[155] Ibid.
[156] Ibid. (145).
[157] Takemitsu (2000:196).

In *Satori,* for harpsichord (1999), and *Without,* for solo violin (2006), Palmer aims to capture the essence of 'ma' and highlight the aural and visual aspects of it. The work *Satori* employs long, sustained notes (e.g. semibreves, dotted minims, minims and tied notes) with occasional notes with smaller values (e.g. quavers and semiquavers). Because of the nature of the instrument, sustained notes quickly decay after the initial attack. Although aurally the sound disappears, in notation and the performer's mind the sound continues to ring. This paradox resonates with the concept of 'ma' in the way that the duration between two sound events within which the sound may continue or break off. The work is marked 'tempo rubato' and contains a number of 'fermatas'. This appears to conform to the performance practice of 'ma' whose duration is mathematically or scientifically indefinable. *Without* explores also the visual aspect of 'ma'. Compared to *Satori,* the instrumental interventions in *Without* are more varied, sharper and richer in rhythmic content and dynamic contrast. These differences can be seen in extracts from the first pages of both works as reproduced below (see Figs. 9.1 and 9.2). The performative nature of 'ma' is reinforced by physical gestures *"resembling some acting elements of Noh theatre that the violinist must integrate as an integrative part of the performance"*.[158] This can be read in the performance instructions:

"At the end of each phrase the performer should stop moving, both arms remaining motionless in the same position where they stopped moving. Such a frozen posture should be retained consistently every time a rest occurs. Body movement is resumed one second before the next phrase begins. Non-action and body gestures are intended to emphasise a visual experience of 'ma', rather than music theatre."[159]

The concept of 'ma' serves as a stylistic reference in the composer's other works such as *Still* (2001), *Three Haikus* (2014) and *Silent/Listen 1* (2014).

The third area of Palmer's interest is Japanese literature, in particular, the haiku and tanka, or waka.[160] These literary forms provide him with metric, rhythmic, formal structures and programmatic inspiration, as well as sonic material. As touched upon earlier, *Koan* has 17 sections, coinciding with the total number of syllables contained in the haiku. The casual students of poetry will know that the Japanese haiku is a short poetic form, consisting of three parts with a 5-7-5 division. Just as the haiku number 17 provided the composer with a structural reference also for *Still,* the tanka numbers are integrated into the rhythmic organisation of *Waka* for percussion and ensemble. The Japanese tanka is a poetic form longer than the haiku, having a 5-7-5-7-7 division. In *Waka,* these numbers appear in changing metres (5/4, 4/4, 3/4, 5/4, 4/4, 3/4, 4/4, 3/4) as well as the division of a beat (e.g. quintuplets and septuplets).

The aforementioned *Without* relates to a Zen saying, *chiru sakura / nokoru sakura mo / chiru sakura*, displaying the haiku structure. This Zen saying, known as 'Zengo', is included in

---

[158] As expressed by the composer in a personal correspondence with the author.

[159] Extract from the programme note of *Without*.

[160] The Japanese word 'waka' is a generic term for Japanese poetic forms, such as the 'chōka' (long poem), 'tanka' (short poem) and 'sedōka', vis-à-vis Chinese poems ('kanshi'). These types of waka are contained in the oldest collection of Japanese waka poems *Manyōshū* from the Nara Period as well as in *Kokinwakashū* from the Heian Period. Later, both 'chōka' and 'sedoka' became obsolete, and' tanka' became the main form of 'waka'. Because of this historical development, in modern Japanese language, the words 'waka' and classical 'tanka' (not the contemporary 'tanka') can be used interchangeably. In Palmer's work *Waka,* the Japanese word 'waka' is used by the composer as the synonym of 'tanka', both displaying a 5-7-5-7-7 structure. For detailed discussions of the history, types and structures of Japanese classical poems, see Haku Itō, *Manyōshū no Kōzō to Seiritsu Jō* (Tokyo: Hanawa-shobō, 1974) and Noriyuki Kojima and Eizō Arai, eds., *Kokinwakashū: Shin Nihon Koten Bungaku Taikei* (Tokyo: Iwanami-shoten, 1989).

Eiwataiyaku: Zengo Senshū (1994), a selection of Zen sayings compiled by Chosuke Imoto, who provides a direct translation into English from the original text: *Cherry blossom petals are falling / Beautiful like snowflakes / The remaining rest do cling / Without knowing their destiny.* The number of syllables and letters of the English translation, instead of the 5-7-5 structure of the original in Japanese, are used by the composer as the underlying principle of bars and metric grouping as well as pitch density (Fig. 9.3).[161]

Fig. 9.1: *Satori*, bb. 1-20.

---

[161] Imoto (1994). The composer bought the book in the Zen monastery where he stayed. The original Zengo is believed to have been the last haiku by the Zen monk and poet Ryōan, composed just before his death (known as 'jisei no ku').

Fig. 9.2: *Without*, bb. 1-20.

syllables	2	2	2	1	2
	cherry	blossom	petals	are	falling
no. of letters:	**6**	**7**	**6**	**3**	**7**

syllables:	3	1	3		
	Beautiful	like	snowflakes.		
no. of letters	**9**	**4**	**10**		

syllables:	1	3	2	1	2
	The	remaining	rest	do	cling
no. of letters:	**3**	**9**	**4**	**2**	**5**

syllables:	2	2	1	3	
	Without	knowing	their	destiny.	
no. of letters:	**7**	**7**	**5**	**7**	

Fig. 9.3: Zen poem's analysis by the composer.

Similarly, *Three Haikus* was, as the title suggests, inspired by three Japanese haikus: *hasu no ha no / tsuyu to kieyuku / wagami kana* (like dewdrops on a lotus leaf I vanish); *mune suzushi / kie o matsugo no / mizu no awa /* (the foam on the last water has dissolved, my mind is clear); *harai arai / kokoro no tsuki no / kagami kana /* (I cleansed the mirror of my heart, now it reflects the moon).[162] These haikus are recited by the shakuhachi player as part of the music: each syllable (or the consonant and vowel of a syllable) is spoken, whispered or sung with a wide range of dynamics between or in tandem with the shakuhachi sounds. For that reason, the performer plays also the role of a poet. Moreover, Japanese texts are used in the acousmatic work *I Am* as sonic and semantic material.

The fourth area of Japanese culture that Palmer has assimilated into his compositional practice is a close relationship with nature.[163] Japanese arts and literature exemplify the closeness between nature and Japanese people's life: in paintings and music, as well as literature, natural objects or scenery are often chosen as a subject matter.[164] For instance, the haiku must have a seasonal word called 'kigo' within its condensed form, and there are a number of pieces in the shakuhachi Honkyoku repertoire in which the sound of the instrument is meant to imitate the cry or movements of an animal (e.g. 'Shika no Tōne' and 'Tsuru no Sugomori'). The aforementioned *I Am* uses collected samples of natural sounds, such as rain and bird's cry, as well as the Japanese well-kwon song *Sakura*. Both works *Renge-Kyo* and *I Am* finish with the

---

[162] These are the original haikus and translations as seen in the programme note of *Three Haikus*.

[163] Although the composer was aware that a close connection between nature and spirit also exists in European culture (e.g. Francis of Assisi), his visit to Japan presented him with more examples of an inseparable relationship between nature and life.

[164] For a detailed discussion of the relationship between nature and traditional Japanese music, see Eishi Kikkawa, *The Musical Sense of the Japanese* in *Contemporary Music Review* Vol. 1, Part 2 (1987:85–94).

sounds of ocean waves, which the composer uses as 'a symbol of the search for inner purification'.[165]

As seen above, the four areas of Japanese culture (Buddhism, music, literature, and an intimate relationship between nature and life) have both individually and collectively given Palmer the opportunities to explore new ideas for programmatic themes, structural and rhythmic framework, the relationship between sound and silence, and a performance style. The reader of this book may be able to locate other aspects of Japanese culture in the works discussed in this essay as well as in other works. One hopes that Japanese aesthetics may continue to inspire his future.

ZEN, JAPAN AND THE SHAKUHACHI
Masataka Matsuo

MM. Which came first, your interest in Japan or your encounter with Zen? Also, how did these encounters happen?

JP. Zen came first. The interest in Zen Buddhism was a natural evolution of my search for a philosophical dimension that would fulfil my life. My long-time interest in meditation and the spiritual was rooted in Christian mysticism. At the age of 19, I came across Hinduism and a year later, Tibetan Buddhism and Taoism. These Eastern approaches to spiritual practice opened a new way to look at meditation and the transcendental. As I continued to read and study Buddhism in my early twenties, I came across Zen and other Eastern forms of philosophy through the work of Swiss psychologist Carl Gustav Jung and the writings of both Daisetz Teitaro Suzuki and Shunryu Suzuki. When I came across the work of John Cage in 1986, I rediscovered Zen from a different view, one that was related to aesthetics and music. This new perspective enriched my previous knowledge on the subject considerably. Cage's thoughts made a big impact on my music thinking of the late 1980s and early 1990s. In those days, I found his work to be an impeccable combination of philosophy, art and personal lifestyle informed by Zen culture. I continued to study Zen on my own and practise it with some Buddhist groups I joined in Switzerland and England.

MM. What did your encounter with Zen bring to you?

JP. There are so many important aspects of Zen that it is difficult to unify them with one answer. In the Western world, we tend to separate meditation from everyday life. This division does not fit the idea and purpose of Zen because in Zen's philosophy the mind, the body and the perception of the world go together. Zen has taught me to live in the moment and focus my attention fully on the situation I am experiencing right now. Even if I found myself in the middle of a stressful or painful conversation, for example, I can listen actively to another person and focus on that very moment in time while letting go of any other thought that tries to enter my mind. Zen has brought more peace and silence in my life and fostered a non-chronological perception of time. This enhanced perception of life helps me to listen more carefully to myself and what I experience around me. During artistic creation, it enhances my ability to focus on sound or a specific type of silence occurring between two sounds. The awareness of time in

---

[165] This was expressed by the composer in an interview in February 2021. In Christianity, water also symbolises a source of life, and this gives, for example, a religious context to *Les Jeux d'eaux à la Villa d'Este* from *Années de pèlerinage, troisième année* by Franz Liszt.

general and in music in particular, which has always been very important to me, has become sharper and more refined. Last but not least, Zen has taught me to go beyond the dualism of being and non-being, the dualism of rational thinking, and the Buddhist notion of emptiness.

MM. What kind of things have you come to pay attention to in Japanese culture and Japanese traditional instruments?

JP. Japan is an enormous source of fine features of all sorts. I think the care of, and focus on, detail is perhaps the most striking feature of Japanese culture. The art of calligraphy, the flower arrangement called Ikebana, a traditional tea ceremony or a Gagaku performance are a case in point. Another important aspect that comes to mind is the connection with nature. Japanese literature, painting and the arts, in general, have always had a strong relation to nature and the seasons, each of which is linked to different traditions. I am struck by the number of artists who have dedicated themselves to study landscapes and transcend them into a subject of contemplation that conveys peace and a sense of wonder. Japanese gardens are another manifestation of this intimate relationship with nature. They are conceived as miniatures reproducing nature according to the principles of Shinto philosophy and later on Buddhism. Gardens are also linked to legends about their creation, and many legends depict them as a re-creation of places inhabited by gods. Therefore, a Japanese garden is considered a sacred space. The rich symbolism attached to gardens was something that struck me when I visited Japan in 2001. Every single detail of a Japanese garden has a highly abstracted meaning and many of these symbols are connected to nature, such as the notion of the eight perfect islands, the lakes and the Mount Horai, which symbolise the idea of a flawless world. Meditating in these gardens means entering this meta-world of symbols and images. I find that the simplicity of these gardens is often very challenging to the Western mind: many of them consist only of rock and white sand, indicating a micro-cosmos dominated by the sea, a symbol of purification and inner cleansing.

Another unique aspect of Japan is its philosophical and religious tradition represented by temples. I am often struck by the stark contrast between the discretion and simplicity of the temples' inner forms and space, and the spectacular architecture of the outer form. Even the location of Buddhist temples seems to reflect a philosophy of unity strongly linked with the landscape, as they are often located in unthinkable places, hidden among the foliage of trees in the forests, or surrounded by lakes. Like Shinto philosophy, Japanese Buddhism is very rooted in nature. I see another unique characteristic of the Japanese perception of art in the slowness of action that characterises Nō theatre coupled with the use of masks that intentionally hide facial expressions. The actors' codified gestures interact with the sparsity of sound provided by the musical instruments as another baffling indication of time as a philosophical unity that encompasses all the senses. Japanese traditional instruments, too, seem to be a result of this all-embracing view of life. One can hear that each Japanese instrument belongs to a performance aesthetic that is linked to a specific musical genre. The simplest sound of a biwa, shamisen, sho or taiko contains a sonic intensity and symbolic power that coexist in perfect harmony with the music.

MM. It seems that you are interested in Japanese short poetry literature, haiku and tanka (or waka). How do you perceive these literary forms and how do you transform their structural characteristics and poetical charm into music?

JP. I love Japanese literature for all the reasons I have mentioned earlier, and I am particularly fond of short poetic forms, particularly in Japanese, but also those of ancient Egypt and Greece. I think it is a kind of focused imagery that I find most powerful as a result of brevity and simplicity. Brevity implies discipline and focus, attention and awareness. Paradoxically, brevity also encourages a sense of drama (action) by raising questions in the mind of the reader that may or may not be answered by further reading. Haikus and wakas also elicit rhythm not only as a succession of accents, but also as a compressed form of metre. T.S. Eliot would speak of the *feeling* for syllable and rhythm as *"penetrating far below the conscious levels of thought."*[166] A compressed form of this kind is a crystallisation of the 'rhythm of experience' that can be only perceived in the silence surrounding the poet or the reader. The more restricted the number of syllables and verses, the more focused the imagery deriving from the words will be.

I have used the haiku and tanka (waka) forms in a dozen of my works. My application of these forms tends to be precise: for example, I use the 5-7-5 syllabic structure of the haiku form for establishing the number of sections, bars, metres and (musical) verses. In this fashion, I create a scaffolding of proportions that covers the most important components of a piece. Sometimes I also create fractal-like structures where the same proportions are applied within one section of the work or a single phrase. In *Waka*, I constructed the large form by creating an outer (large) form of five sections, each based on the numerical proportion of 5-7-5-7-7 whereas each section is subdivided by the same proportion of verses (Fig. 9.4).

outer: 5	7	5	7	7
inner: 5 - 7 - 5 - 7 - 7 (x5)	5 - 7 - 5 - 7 - 7 + (5 - 7) (x7)	5 - 7 - 5 - 7 - 7 (x5)	5 - 7 - 5 - 7 - 7 + (5 - 7) (x7)	5 - 7 - 5 - 7 - 7 + (5 - 7) (x7)
5 - 7 - 5 - 7 - 7	5 - 7 - 5 - 7 - 7 + (5 - 7)	5 - 7 - 5 - 7 - 7	5 - 7 - 5 - 7 - 7 + (5 - 7)	5 - 7 - 5 - 7 - 7 + (5 - 7)
5 - 7 - 5 - 7 - 7	5 - 7 - 5 - 7 - 7 + (5 - 7)	5 - 7 - 5 - 7 - 7	5 - 7 - 5 - 7 - 7 + (5 - 7)	5 - 7 - 5 - 7 - 7 + (5 - 7)
5 - 7 - 5 - 7 - 7	5 - 7 - 5 - 7 - 7 + (5 - 7)	5 - 7 - 5 - 7 - 7	5 - 7 - 5 - 7 - 7 + (5 - 7)	5 - 7 - 5 - 7 - 7 + (5 - 7)
5 - 7 - 5 - 7 - 7	5 - 7 - 5 - 7 - 7 + (5 - 7)	5 - 7 - 5 - 7 - 7	5 - 7 - 5 - 7 - 7 + (5 - 7)	5 - 7 - 5 - 7 - 7 + (5 - 7)
	5 - 7 - 5 - 7 - 7 + (5 - 7)		5 - 7 - 5 - 7 - 7 + (5 - 7)	5 - 7 - 5 - 7 - 7 + (5 - 7)
	5 - 7 - 5 - 7 - 7 + (5 - 7)		5 - 7 - 5 - 7 - 7 + (5 - 7)	5 - 7 - 5 - 7 - 7 + (5 - 7)

Fig. 9.4: *Waka*, outer and inner form.

Secondly, I assigned a cardinal pitch to each section and a corresponding number of bars, as you can see in the chart below (Fig. 9.5).

cue	A	B	C	D	E
waka	5	7	5	7	7
pitch	G	B	C	E	**Fsharp** (main motif)
bar	1	41	118	158	235
instr.	marimba radiating	marimba radiating	marimba radiating	marimba radiating	marimba radiating

Fig. 9.5: *Waka*, assignment of pitch and bars.

The chart below shows the unfolding of the outer and inner form of *Waka*. Each of the five sections (named A, B, C, D, E) is delineated by a set of five or seven units corresponding to a number (A1, A2, etc.). The bar numbers are to be seen at the beginning of each section and the arrows show the correspondence of the pitch content between two sections (Fig. 9.6).

---

[166] Eliot (1933:119).

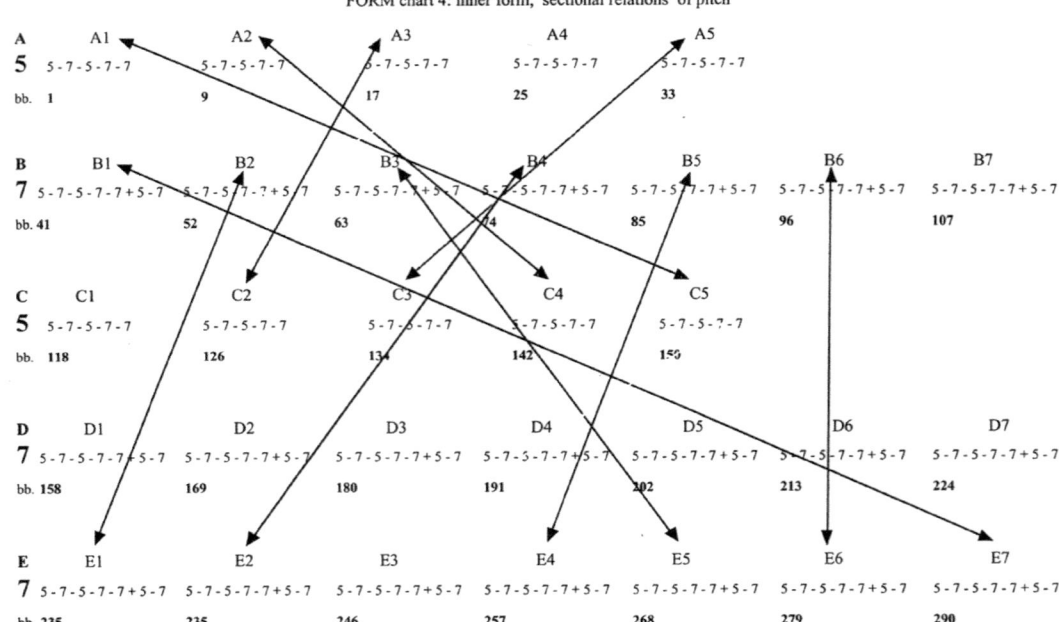

FORM chart 4: inner form, sectional relations of pitch

A A1   A2   A3   A4   A5
5 5-7-5-7-7   5-7-5-7-7   5-7-5-7-7   5-7-5-7-7   5-7-5-7-7
bb. 1   9   17   25   33

B B1   B2   B3   B4   B5   B6   B7
7 5-7-5-7-7+5-7   5-7-5-7-7+5-7 5-7-5-7-7+5-7 5-7-5-7-7+5-7 5-7-5-7-7+5-7 5-7-5-7-7+5-7 5-7-5-7-7+5-7
bb. 41   52   63   74   85   96   107

C C1   C2   C3   C4   C5
5 5-7-5-7-7   5-7-5-7-7   5-7-5-7-7   5-7-5-7-7   5-7-5-7-7
bb. 118   126   134   142   150

D D1   D2   D3   D4   D5   D6   D7
7 5-7-5-7-7+5-7   5-7-5-7-7+5-7 5-7-5-7-7+5-7 5-7-5-7-7+5-7 5-7-5-7-7+5-7 5-7-5-7-7+5-7 5-7-5-7-7+5-7
bb. 158   169   180   191   202   213   224

E E1   E2   E3   E4   E5   E6   E7
7 5-7-5-7-7+5-7   5-7-5-7-7+5-7 5-7-5-7-7+5-7 5-7-5-7-7+5-7 5-7-5-7-7+5-7 5-7-5-7-7+5-7 5-7-5-7-7+5-7
bb. 235   235   246   257   268   279   290

[19 original pitch sections (5 of 5, 14 of 7). D remains independent]

Fig. 9.6: *Waka*, form unfolding procedure.

Other times, I have used the structure of a specific haiku (or a similar short poem) for the structure of the musical work I intend to compose. I used this technique for *Three Haikus* (for solo shakuhachi), *From the Lake* (for oboe and piano), *Without* (solo violin) and *Nowhere to hide* (solo viola).

MM. *Three Haikus* is a short and concise work, similar to Japanese haiku, while *Waka* is a long and profound work. I am interested in the difference in your approach between these two works. I would be grateful if you could explain it.

JP. These two pieces are similar of course, but also very different. The music of *Three Haikus* was inspired by haikus written by three Japanese poets on the verge of death.

The **first** haiku was written by Senryu in 1827. The text of the poem reads like this: *hasu no ha no / tsuyu to kieyuku / wagami kana.* The meaning in English is: *like dewdrops on a lotus leaf I vanish.*

The **second** haiku was written by Mitoku in 1669: *mune suzushi / kie o matsugo no / mizu no awa.* The meaning in English is: *the foam on the last water has dissolved / my mind is clear.*

The **third** haiku was written by Renseki in 1789: *harai arai / kokoro no tsuki no / kagami kana.* The meaning in English is: *I cleansed the mirror of my heart / now it reflects the moon.*

I wrote the piece for a shakuhachi player who has to be both musician and poet. The performer plays the shakuhachi and, at the same time, declaims the words of the poems. Both words and instrumental sounds belong to the same artistic expression and must remain interlocked throughout the piece. The haiku texts need to be fully integrated into the musical phrases in order to achieve a declamatory balance between words (spoken, whispered and sung) and shakuhachi sounds. Thereby, the text becomes an essential component of the shakuhachi's

340

phrases. The performance should resemble a final meditation on life and death. Like I have shown earlier with the charts of *Waka*, in *Three Haikus* the structure of the haiku establishes the form of the piece. In the score of the first haiku, you can see the integration of shakuhachi and voice sounds. The spoken text is notated in the lower stave. The Japanese text is spoken and occasionally sung inside the shakuhachi, as you can see in Fig. 9.7.

With *Three Haikus*, I wanted to explore the ephemeral: a circumstance that lasts a short time. The recurrent reference to death is the common denominator of the three poems and the focus of the music remains on the sacredness of life experienced in its fleeting essence. The rhetoric of both text and music remains somewhat gaunt throughout the piece. The texts speak clearly: the focus remains on the 'now' and there is no assurance for a future of any sort. The only pledge is the transition from life to death that is about to take place.

The approach to *Waka* stems from an attempt to find a meaningful correlation between musical and literary declamatory forms. As I have shown earlier, I used the 5-7-5-7-7 verse structure as a pitch, metric and rhythmic pulse for the work. My intention was to find a form of musical poetry that can be perceived as such by any listener. The main question at the time was whether musical phrases can equal or even surpass the evocative imagery supplied by verbal description. In other words, how far can a melodic line or agglomeration of acoustic elements instigate the same or very similar imagery?

Unlike *Three Haikus,* the metres of *Waka* are included in the framework of numerical proportions. This will render a cohesive form for a piece like *Waka* that is about 20 minutes long; you can see this in Fig. 9.8. The following chart (Fig. 9.9) shows the 19 pitch fields that I used to define each section of the same piece. Each pitch-field is defined by the 'classical' forms: original (O) or Prime, inversion (I), reverse (R) and reverse inversion (RI) and subsequent transpositions. As a result of this detailed and comprehensive organisation of form, the texture of *Waka,* that is its verse structure, remains accurate throughout the piece.

MM. I presume that the shakuhachi must be important to you. If so, I would like to know in what sense this instrument is so special to you? As a Western composer, what do you find so charming about it?

JP. When I heard Yoshikazu Iwamoto playing the shakuhachi examples in Volume Eight of *Contemporary Music Review*, I immediately fell in love with the sound of the instrument. There is a unique quality in the timbre of the shakuhachi that is earthly and heavenly, sensual and spiritual at the same time. I think this is due to the combination of three interrelated factors: the material of the instrument being a simple piece of bamboo plant with a unique timbre that is different to a typical 'wood' sound; secondly, the strong presence of breathing as a major audible component of timbre; thirdly, the specific techniques that are employed for the production of sound.

The shakuhachi timbre is a perfect embodiment of the sound of nature (the timbre of its material) and life (the audible breathing involved in the sound production). Furthermore, the instrument offers a wide range of timbral subtlety and pitch production that can be controlled in a number of very effective ways by the player. Obviously, the sound of the instrument is so linked with Zen culture that it is impossible to neglect the psychological associations attached to Buddhist meditation and perception of nature. And I think it's not a coincidence that the shakuhachi, and not another Japanese flute like the shinobue, the ryuteki, the komabue or the kagurabue, retains such a strong connection with Zen meditation and spiritual attainment. The secularisation of the shakuhachi that followed from the new schools of Tozan-ryū, Ueda-ryū and Chikuhō-ryū (at the beginning of the 20th century) is evidence of the remarkable quality and adaptability that characterises the instrument.

three haikus

Fig. 9.7: *Three Haikus*, beginning.

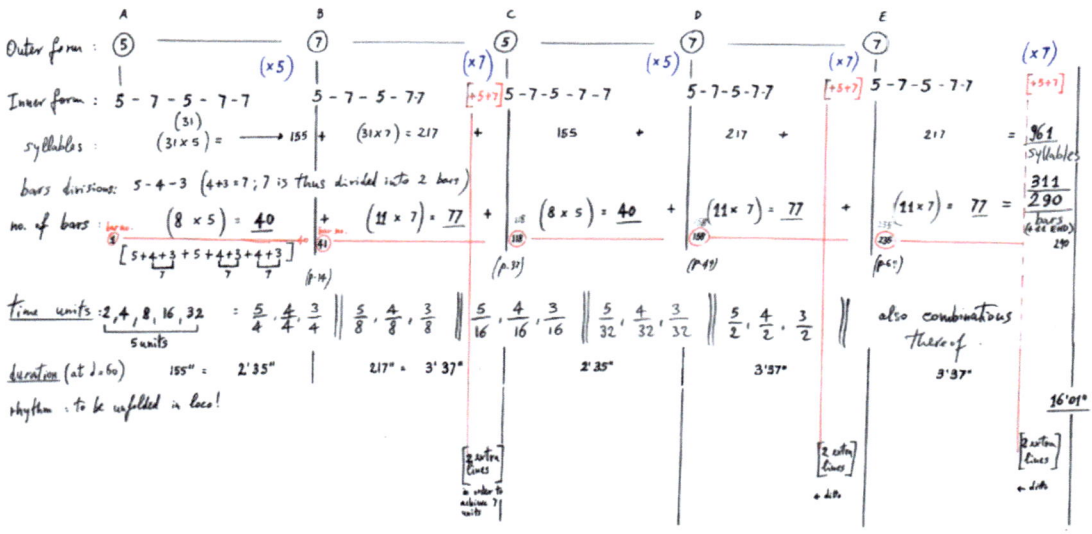

Fig. 9.8: *Waka*, general plan.

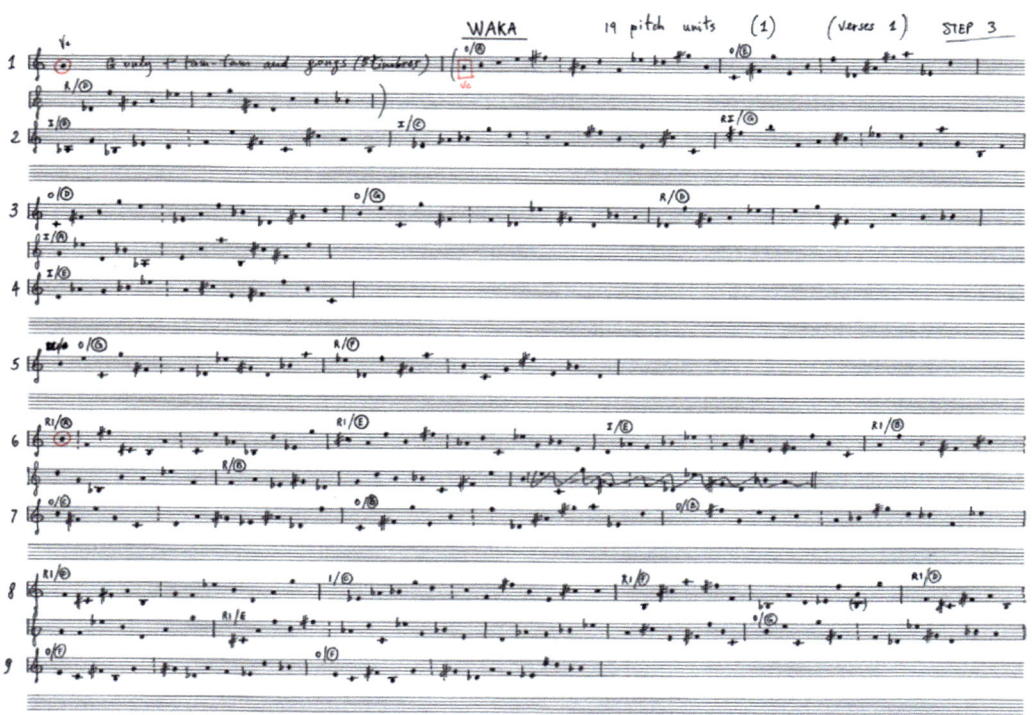

Fig. 9.9: *Waka*, pitch fields.

MM. Do you feel that there is some approximation between the various playing styles that have been handed down in the world of the shakuhachi and the Western European contemporary music vocabulary that has developed rapidly since World War II?

JP. Yes. From my Western perspective, I would rather speak of similarity though. For instance, the Mura-iki technique (breathing into the shakuhachi with great power), and the various vibrati techniques like yoko-yuri (the lateral, basic vibrato), tate'-yuri (vertical vibrato), take'-joge'-yuri (up-and-down vibrato), take'-yuri, komi-buki and others, are what we would call 'extended techniques'. What I found amazing is that these techniques have been created many centuries ago. Also, the shakuhachi's versatility makes it possible to transfer virtually all Western extended techniques for wind instruments to the instrument (for example, multiphonics) obtaining powerful musical results.

MM. Back to *Three Haikus*, the appearance of the score resembles a suite made by small pieces that utilise extended techniques, but when played by a player who has trained in the traditional shakuhachi playing method, one could think that the performance will have a strong 'taste' similar to Honkyoku. What do you think of this opinion?

JP. This would be acceptable to me as long as the music is executed according to the indications given in the score. I must accept the fact that *Three Haikus* is somehow rooted in Honkyoku. But from my perspective, *Three Haikus* is not a Honkyoku piece, just as Pierre Boulez's *Second Sonata* is not a Romantic piano piece, although it is rooted in it. The main question is whether our understanding of tradition includes evolution or remains associated only with the past, and thus not evolving. Should tradition involve progress? I personally think so because tradition is a living force and an enduring expression of artistic creativity. Honkyoku is a very pure tradition, which I love, yet the performance of *Three Haikus* will require an 'extended' and a wider attitude towards the instrument, both from a technical and aesthetic point of view. I am aware that many traditional shakuhachi players will find it challenging to inject new sounds or extra-musical elements reinforcing a sense of passion or drama in the music. Conservative musicians will not be interested in playing works of this kind, but this applies also to Western classical music: I know many excellent classical musicians who are only interested in playing classical and romantic works. I think this remains a personal choice. One of the recurrent topics raised by shakuhachi players around the world is whether the shakuhachi should be only used for traditional Japanese music. I am aware that many shakuhachi players (Japanese and non-Japanese!) would never play a piece like *Three Haikus* or *Koan*, because their approach to the instrument remains strictly linked to the Japanese tradition of the past. On the other hand, there are many shakuhachi players out there who are performing contemporary music with great devotion and passion.

MM. In *Koan*, I think that both the contrast and fusion of the shakuhachi with the wind instruments of the ensemble is rather an attractive feature of the music. How far are you aware of this aspect of the piece?

JP. I am well aware of it, and while writing the piece I dealt with the shakuhachi not only as a 'solo' instrument but also as a member of the woodwind section of the ensemble. This was very deliberate, and I think it is clearly audible; for instance in the duets for shakuhachi and alto flute, shakuhachi-clarinet and shakuhachi-oboe. These and other similar passages are rather important in terms of creating a timbral unity in relation to the psychological connotations attached to the notion of koan. The contrast and fusion of the shakuhachi with the wind instruments of the ensemble is also a symbol of the inclusion of dissimilar aspects of the same reality in the allegorical discourse. From an instrumental perspective, I wanted to create an integration of the shakuhachi with the woodwinds of the West focused on both diverging polyphonic writing and timbral blend.

MM. As the executive chairperson of the festival, it was a great honour and an impressive experience for me to be present at the performance of *Koan* which we scheduled as the final piece of the last concert of the ISCM World Music Days 2001 in Yokohama. I still feel proud that we managed to 'close the curtain' of the International Music Festival with the performance of *Koan*. Please tell me your memories and impressions of that time.

JP. One of the things that impressed me most was the impeccable organisation of the event and the efficiency of everyone involved in it. I also remember being struck by the quality of all the Japanese pieces scheduled in the festival. You have so many excellent composers in Japan who certainly deserve more recognition in the West and I often regret not being able to hear more music from your country. Another thing I remember well was the impressive musicianship and commitment of all the performers of the festival, including the ComeT Ensemble of Tokyo, Kunitaka Kokaji who conducted *Koan* with the shakuhachi virtuoso Teruhisa Fukuda, another exceptional musician. Throughout the period of the festival, one could clearly see and hear the highest level of professionalism and dedication.

The ISCM World Music Days 2001 have been a very enriching experience, and I still remember feeling honoured and grateful to have had *Koan* performed as the highlight of the festival. Today, exactly twenty years later, I want to say thank you again for that wonderful festival and memorable experience.

CHAPTER TEN

MUSIC THEATRE

PALMER THE UTOPIAN
Aanaya Shanaya

AS. John, as you know, I left the music scene 16 years ago because I could no longer identify myself with the attitudes and values of the classical music establishment. I particularly refer to the contemporary music concert scene and all that comes with it. To make a long story short, I felt crushed between the invasive superficiality of the North American direction, the dry over-intellectualism of Europe and the struggle of Asian composers to retain an individual identity amid tradition and evolution. I guess my Indian background plays a role in the way I perceive these three musical attitudes, especially having been based in Australia and New Zealand for so many years; two countries that hold a Western identity, but nevertheless are floating between these approaches to music and culture. I know I am generalising and that there are exceptions to be found in each tradition and place you go, but I had to leave the concert scene after 23 years of dissatisfaction that brought me to a bitter conclusion: contemporary art has disconnected itself from the soul. My story is as simple as that. So why have I accepted your invitation, the readers may ask themselves? The reason is simple, perhaps naïve: you are the only living composer I know whose music still speaks to my heart, soul and mind. I still remember the premiere of your *Utopia* in Berne in 1990 and the discussion with you and Annette Meriweather on that cold and foggy evening in Huddersfield in November 1996. These, and other exchanges we have had throughout the years, are memories I treasure to this day.

JP. I realise how difficult it must be for you to re-connect with a reality you have so clearly scrapped from your life. I can only say that I feel honoured and grateful to you for having made an exception for me.

AS. You also know why I left secular life and decided to spend the rest of my life in an Ashram here in India. I am mentioning this because I want the readers to understand where I am coming from when discussing music and culture. For those who don't know what an Ashram is, I can say that it is a place comparable to a Buddhist or Christian monastery that is open to anyone, regardless of beliefs, ages and faith, who want to live a life free from material and emotional distractions and based on spiritual values in a non-sectarian environment. Life here is about self-awareness, reflection, meditation and a healthy lifestyle close to nature. But this doesn't stop me from being who I am, and as you know well, I am a slightly unconventional person, and I talk frankly in any kind of discussion I am involved.

JP. Please do so and thank you for your explanation. I think it is important to mention your current perspective on life as well.

AS. Before I focus on your work *Utopia*, let me begin with a preliminary statement: I have always found your music boldly utopian! Most of your mythological references imply, directly or indirectly, places of the mind, *worlds elsewhere* to which you seem to refer to without losing grip of the world here and now, in you and around you. There is always a tinge of realistic idealism about the things you do and the propositions you allude to in your music.

JP. What you say reminds me of my enduring fascination with Atlantis, a subject I read all I could about by the age of 15. What has kept striking me in all these years is that most accounts of forgotten or imaginary places don't come across as representations of daydreaming or entertaining fantasies, but as descriptions of countries and places as realistic models of social coexistence based on common morality, justice and ethical values. According to Plato, the mythical state of Atlantis epitomised a highly advanced civilisation based on moral and spiritual beliefs. Thomas More's *Utopia* modernised Plato's classical description of the perfect republic primarily by its social realism and pragmatic politics. Francis Bacon's *The New Atlantis* depicts a mythical island called Bensalem where the high ethical standards of its inhabitants cohere with scientific research about nature and its effect on the organisation of an enlightened society. The same considerations apply to Tommaso Campanella's *City of the Sun* and Jean-Jacques Rousseau's *On The Social Contract*.

Whether it's about a fictional place (a forgotten land or a temple), an object-symbol like the Holy Grail or the story of a human or superhuman being involved in an unusual event, myths are allegories of human behaviour. They invite us to reflect on events, emotions and situations that any individual or civilisation keeps coming across over and over again. References to arcadian societies symbolise ideals of the best imaginable socio-political condition (usually, the idea of a self-governed society) that have often been idealised as impossible conditions of socio-political progress. To many people, the words 'utopia' and 'myth' have become synonyms of a fantastic world or situation that is impossible to achieve, but this is misleading. A utopia is a myth as much as myth is utopia, but it is always up to each of us to understand what utopias are really about and learn from what myths have to tell us. The authority of myths consists of the fact that a story is not told in order to prove itself but to represent or signify itself. Very often in history, we have experienced moments where a nation has been on the verge of reaching a utopia. I am thinking of India in 1949 for example, or some of the 19th century utopian communities in the USA such as Brook Farm, Oneida and The Shakers. Utopias signify dreams that we can make come true. The Greek word 'mythos' means not only 'tale', but also 'true narrative', and 'myo' means 'teach'. A myth is about teaching something that is true. There is indeed a recurrent subject in my music that is utopian and mythical, and I am glad you have spotted this important feature of my work. Works like *Asgard, Thereafter, In the Temple, Hellawes, Shambhala* and *I, Medusa* show clear reference to a utopian or mythical condition. In other pieces like *There, Transparence, Somewhere, Legend, Vision, Hieroglyphs, Poem for the Absurd,* the allusion is concealed, more formalistic, at times even cryptic; but it is there.

AS. Let's talk more specifically about your work *Utopia*, for mezzo-soprano, wind quartet and electronics. This really is a piece of music theatre as it involves a great deal of theatrical actions that are as important as the music. I know you have written many texts and poems throughout your life and that in the past, you have not been very keen to make public this regular aspect of your creativity, although many of your musical works stem from texts or poems of yours that you often include in the score as a programme note to the piece.

In *Utopia*, each of the five instrumentalists has a text to be sung or spoken. A peculiarity of the text of the singer is that it is written in two languages: English and a second, cryptic language whose origin is not specified. These texts can be found in the score. What the listeners don't know is that in 1989 you wrote another text called *Reflections on Utopia*. As I was going through my personal correspondence, I came across this text which you personally handed to me after the Swiss tour of 1990. I remember the explanations you gave me at the time and you telling me how private this text was meant to be. After so many years,

and following your recent revision of the piece, would you now be prepared to disclose the text? I realise I may be putting you in an uncomfortable situation, but this is me, and I know you will understand the spirit behind this request. I personally think that the text provides further insights that may help the listener to better appreciate the content of the piece, but I leave it with you to decide…

JP. I see you haven't changed much despite all these years spent in the Ashram! (I do mean this with affection, of course). I have been thinking at length about your question and… alright then, here it is:

Reflections on Utopia

suicidal forces of blind existence
the abyss within
how foreign can pessimism be to a pseudo-Christian society?
thought divorced from action
not yet the worst possible world
rising zealotry glorified
booming consumerism
the new century

o v e r b u r d e n e d

by which new ambiguity at the end station of civil coexistence?
this trembling me lost in narcotised indifference
can outbursts of grief transform a dream into physical reality?
re-inventing the Pristine!

How foreign may pessimism be to a pseudo-Christian culture?
How far will instinctive outbursts of grief oppose human degradation and political speculation?

Thought divorced from action in an overburdened world
Consumerism over the primal sacredness of life
Indifference: the fatal death!

blunders of suicidal forces
crushes of blind existence
they preach redemption by will
indifference prevails everywhere

I see those dead eyes
preys to false creeds
the undemanding optimism of
I hear their words through my sorrow
stemming from grief

No debating responsibility
No acting regeneration
Distrust!

Yet my heart is still beating
and with it a loud dissent
despite of
or because of
the abyss we carry within
unspoken!

If fear generates pessimism
pessimism necessitates a state
and the state will demand a religion
before the final deluge

but my heart is still beating
and with it a silent dissent
despite of
perhaps because of
the abyss we carry within
for a different
much different
and more meaningful
vision.

(late summer 1989)

AS. Thank you, John. I confess that I didn't expect you would have done it, but I am grateful you did. I won't comment on the text itself, as I prefer words to make their impact on the readers without an additional commentary or discussion.

JP. You've made it again! In the end, it may be I who has to thank you. We shall see…

AS. Let's move on. In the programme note of *Utopia* you write:

"Based on the experience of the past and projected onto the future, the idea of a utopian society affirms a present that can be written anew at any time and by any kind of people of different cultures, languages and attitudes. In this story, four characters (the woodwind quartet) are trying to establish a dialogue based on a common language and within a diverse society. Their counterpart is another individual (the singer) who is after the idea of an ideal world; her search doesn't seem to attract the attention of the group, nor are her attempts to synthesise the diversity of the four characters. How far can a quest for a unifying and transcendental goal establish a common ground for conjoint creativity?"

I know you have revised *Utopia* recently. Do you wish to add anything to the programme note and the previous text that may help the reader to better contextualise what this work is about?

JP. *Utopia* was commissioned by Ensemble Tetraphonia of Basle, Switzerland, in 1989. The initial version was premiered by Ensemble Tetraphonia and Heidrun Schulz at the Zähringer Theater in Berne on 10th March 1990. The 2020 revision was commissioned by the Musica Nova Festival Reutlingen, Germany, for the 50th anniversary of the festival and includes the addition of electronics. At the end of 1989, I was asked to write a work that would be loosely connected with the celebration of the 700th anniversary of the Swiss Confederation to take place in 1991 and explore the combination of a wind quartet with a female voice. While honouring the commission, I decided to rise above the political idiosyncrasies of the Swiss Union and deal with the idea of a utopian society in universal terms. I envisaged a form of music theatre that would emphasise the idea I had in mind within a context of dispute and conflict determined by contrasting expressions of human behaviour.

AS. How does the allegory of each character relate to theatrical settings and actions?

JP. There are three main positions of the musicians on stage and two off-stage positions. All musicians are standing throughout the piece and have to move from one position to another. To start with, I decided to associate the role of the female singer with the idea of a 'utopian' world and assigned her the leading role of the piece. The singer personifies the notion of utopia. She herself *is* Utopia, not as an idyllic or romanticised appearance, but as an *Idea* in search for understanding and recognition of the world, which is represented by the four instrumentalists. The realism of this search implies the necessity of having to go through dark tunnels of doubt, resistance and rejection. The singer is the character who walks on stage more than anyone else. On the other hand, each of the four instrumentalists represents a different character with distinct psychological attributes. The flute represents denial and negation. The flautist shows a constant unwillingness to accept that something unpleasant might be true. The bassoon symbolises boredom. The bassoonist should convey an annoyed and bored attitude, at times also rude. The clarinetist epitomises laziness. The character is easy-going and superficial, at times sharp and funny. The oboe personifies egocentrism. This character is essentially selfish, pseudo-intellectual and snobbish. Each of these characters illustrates a different form of rejection of the singer's vision. The narrative is focused on the challenging encounters of these five individuals. The singer is somewhat detached from the group although she is constantly looking for points of contact with each of the instrumentalists throughout the duration of the piece. The four characters ignore her throughout the piece. At times she must experience frustration and despair when seeing the instrumentalists not responding to her dream.

The piece begins with the singer wandering around the stage, looking for the source of worldly and otherworldly sounds that are heard from the loudspeakers. As she approaches the instrumentalists a series of theatrical movements involving all musicians begin to take shape on stage. Throughout the piece, the singer will continue to communicate passionately with each instrumentalist of the group. The movements and dialogues that take place on stage keep changing until the end of the piece where the group splits into three parts and the singer remains alone in front of the audience.

AS. As a woman myself, don't you think you have overestimated the idea of womanhood?

JP. Funny you said that! When we finished the Swiss tour in 1990, Heidrun Schulz, who sang the mezzo-soprano part, told me, *"John, ich glaube du hast die Frau überschätzt!"* which translated literally means, *"John, I think you have overestimated womanhood!"*

What can I say? I remember I was somewhat shocked and even upset to hear that. Ever since, I have thought of this statement many times in my life as I tend to be very self-critical about what I write. Do I idealise something or someone by assigning to this object or person a specific role for a dramatic play or musical work? I can hear someone arguing that it is about the association of an idea (utopia) with a gender (woman), but my goodness me, we only have two genders and the choice at my disposal is rather restricted, isn't it?

AS. I take your point. I guess the question may be interpreted in terms of a romanticised idea of women which may come across as old-fashioned and patronising nowadays.

JP. It may, yes, but who is saying it is so? In any case, the piece is about the question of a utopian world, not gender issues.

AS. Let me ask you another question about the instrumental techniques. This is one of the very few chamber pieces where you have used a wide range of extended techniques for all instruments. Do these have a particular sonic, morphological or theatrical significance in the dramaturgy of the piece?

JP. Yes, they do, as they are meant to highlight specific aspects of human behaviour sonically. They accentuate such aspects by including non-referential instrumental sounds to the instrumental parts. All sonic events are incorporated components of musical and theatrical dramaturgy and are supposed to emphasise an enhanced degree of dialectics and psychological communication between the characters. The morphological aspect was particularly important in the first version of the piece that was superseded by the revised version. The reason for this is that I wanted to create a kind of music texture that would sound as cohesive as possible and would integrate traditional pitch and non-traditional sounds at the same hierarchical level. In the original plan, these extended sounds were fully included in a one-to-one matrix, meaning that each sound was assigned to a specific pitch, loudness, articulation and duration, similar to a serial procedure, but not really the same and made in a more personalised system. The morphological importance of these extended techniques still applies to the new version of the piece, but in a less strict manner and unrestrained from a fixed procedure.

The sounds are: airy sounds and key percussion divided into three instrumental ranges (low, middle and high), tongue-ram, 'glissando' (rather traditional, actually), sing-and-play simultaneously, speak vowels and consonants just before producing a sound (for the instrumentalists), speak without producing instrumental sounds, playing intervals by overblowing, the use of quarter tones, multiphonics and timbral changes produced by different fingering.

AS. By comparing the new score to the old one, I can see a significant reduction in extended techniques, especially in the vocal part. Why is that?

JP. You know, when you are young there is a tendency to get lost in an idea and adopt techniques that you feel you must adopt in order for the music to sound as original as possible. With age and experience, you realise that the musical result is by far more important than using an array of techniques that may not necessarily reach the musical result you wanted. The revision took place 30 years later, and I am glad I used a much more 'relaxed' musical attitude towards the organisation of form and morphology of all sonic events. The extended techniques included in the new version are undoubtedly much more musically meaningful than in the original version. The ones I used in the vocal part of the revised version were reduced to humming, random repetition of words, breathy sounds, 'Sprechgesang', gradual timbral changes on one vowel, inhaling and exhaling breathing sounds.

AS. Towards the end of *Utopia*, there are two rather dramatic scenes. One of them occurs as the climax of a debate reached in the centre of the stage. Here the frantic instrumental texture on which the singer sings *"in order to find light"* is suddenly replaced by an extremely reduced texture based on an A-minor chord while the musicians walk slowly in a processional manner and in different directions. The singer sings the question *"over*

nowhere" three times, while the increasing rhythmic superimposition in the procession leads to a standstill where each musician stands as petrified and the singer returns to her original position in the middle of the stage singing *"no dream is dream not being dreamed"*. The second scene occurs at the very end of the piece where the oboist, clarinettist and bassoonist disappear behind the stage and create a spatial 'allontanandosi' effect by walking as far as possible behind the stage. While they walk away, not being seen by the audience, they now repeat a second processional pattern based on the repetition of a C-minor chord as if symbolising a sense of defeat or final detachment from the world. This strongly evocative moment is reinforced by the singer sitting in a meditation posture, facing the audience and whispering words in a mysterious language, *"loudly and slowly but rhythmically, like a Tibetan mantra chanted al fine"*, as you write in the score. This is compelling imagery indeed, and one is not sure if what we are witnessing is the final sentence of human desolation or a prelude to a vision that may materialise later. Of the many images that come to my mind, I seem to hear those words by Rabindranath Tagore, *"I wanted to sink in, to learn and understand the 'them' as I learned more about the 'me'."*

JP. I am glad you mentioned some elements of the (music) texture such as the processions in A and C minor and the repetition of rhythmic patterns, as these play a major role in the portrayal of the drama that is taking place on stage. Music texture is too often underrated in the perception of stage works! Paradoxically, the Utopia I have tried to depict is not the glossy and ecstatic idea of an easier world, but an 'I-You-Us' paradigm that is perennially revisited in a deictic kind of reasoning. Communication depends on fluctuating psycho-temporal conditions whose raison d'être subsists at any point of social interaction and therefore can change the relationships between people at any point in time. We may come closer together; someone else may become prominent at the expense of another; or your life companion may unexpectedly leave you. Utopias set fundamental questions about the burning problem of relationships. A human connection can be suddenly reversed not out of coincidence, but as a result of basic misunderstandings that may have been lying there, between people, and yet remain buried and unexamined amidst the indifference of modern society. Understanding the 'them' as I learn more about the 'me', as well as understanding the 'me' as I learn about the 'them', are Utopia's final considerations of the social drama she has been faced with. However, the unspoken question is: where does she go from there?

AS. Has she not, perhaps, discriminated too far?

JP. This may be debatable, of course. Is success achieved by getting the end result?

AS. Not necessarily. Often it is about progressing every day at a continuous pace.

JP. Exactly.

AS. Acknowledgement may be a wonderful thing, but it should not affect my sense of identity.

JP. No. My conscience should not depend on external sources.

AS. Exactly!

JP. Utopia's unspoken question still remains: where does she go from there?

AS. Let me offer an answer with a verse by Rabindranath Tagore from his work *Gitanjali* :

When I go from hence let this be my parting word,
that what I have seen is unsurpassable.

I have tasted of the hidden honey of this lotus
that expands on the ocean of light, and thus am I blessed -
let this be my parting word.

In this playhouse of infinite forms I have had my play
and here have I caught sight of him that is formless.

My whole body and my limbs have thrilled with his touch
who is beyond touch;
and if the end comes here, let it come -
let this be my parting word.

JP. I know these touching verses and you know how much I love Tagore, but I suspect Utopia's unspoken answer may encompass other reflections of a more psycho-social nature unless of course, we consider society as a multiplication of singularities, in which case the poem would be appropriate. How can inner transformation unfold? Utopia considers the space of narrative as a complete whole that must be examined within the context of multiplicities. Unity and agreement have a nature, too. An idea may be perceived as a complex entity comprising of cooperating views and deeds, or as an irrelevant behaviour within the 'I-You-Us' paradigm I have referred to.

AS. Could a possible solution be evoked by the semantics of the fractional discourse that encompasses a collateral domain of partly-concealed texts as in the example below, in bars 204-205, where the theatrical cross-talking fortifies what potentially is a more complex matter of signified structure?

Fig. 10.1: *Utopia*, bb. 204-205.

JP. One plausible solution, yes, but only one, because it is impossible to bypass the temporal aspect of parallel narratives. I would insist on multiple narratives (not necessarily discourse) converging in one cumulative meta-discourse which I hinted at earlier. Whatever the connection between one layer (or let's call it a sub-narrative) and another may be, the statements made by the five characters are emphasised by the presence of texts that have autonomous existence and no reliant consequence on the general communication. Each text conceals a plurality of messages (the diversity of vocal and sonic utterances sustains this) and consequently contains semantic patterns whose substance resides and, more importantly, changes in time. There is also an element of misery…

AS. Are you implying that temporal patterns unfold on a multiplicity of interacting layers within a superstructure?

JP. Yes. The narrative, with its several components, unfolds in time, but the semantic arrangement of utterances, comprising several meanings and portrayed by sound and word, pitch and noise, is manifold and beyond temporal structures. The question is how to identify interacting principles of transformation from word to word, phrase to phrase, word to sound, sound to sound, sound to noise, noise to noise. But I may be going too far now. Actually, the point I wanted to make was this: within every failure lies an opportunity for success. 'I-You-Us' relationships evolve in many dissimilar ways; but the narration and refraction of all the events in the piece point to a whole that cannot be achieved unless a fundamental change takes place in the mind of each individual of a society. Within the same world, I can make a difference if I am perceived for the things I am doing as a result of who I am. This level of communication comes first. It is more basic than the other but more truthful. And to mention Tagore again, *"It is truth, therefore poetry"*, a phrase I love and that I have recently turned into: *"It is poetry, therefore truth."*

AS. There is a strong sense of existentialism in this final scene, which is comparable to some works of the Theatre of the Absurd tradition, particularly Samuel Beckett, although the subtle psychological introspection sustained by the musical texture adds an emotional layer that, on the whole, reminds me of Luigi Pirandello's *The Rules of the Game*.

JP. You have hit the nail on the head. I find *The Rules of the Game* a very insightful exploration of the human mind, no less than *Six Characters in Search of an Author* and *One, No One and One Hundred Thousand*. As an antipode to Pirandello, in Beckett is reductionism, the form of introvert psychology relying on the absence of knowledge, which renders the discrimination of scopes and constraints a different, but no less interesting form of examination of human nature. *Waiting for Godot, Happy Days, Endgame* and *The Unnamable* come to my mind as I am speaking to you. Perhaps the coexistence of existential concerns justified by four opposed forms of behaviour may be closer to *Endgame*'s portrayal of bare existential meaning: *"Infinite emptiness will be all around you…"*

AS. Does love play any part in all this, or is it unthinkable in such a context?

JP. We have reached a point in history where everything that needed to be said on the subject of love has been said. I have nothing to add to it.

AS. Is love not an energy of the mind, rather than a feeling?

JP. Yes, I think so.

AS. Why could a search for arcadian ideals not be complemented by love?

JP. What I see determines who I am and how I relate to life. Imagine 'absence' as a transformed invisible 'presence' of something that you think might have vanished, but that has now come back to you in a different form. Perhaps utopia is nowhere else but in each of us, concealed in the many and pronounced in the few?

AS. Sometimes, I think we are dwelling in a timeless space of inexplicable abundance where separation can become union within a few seconds, and emptiness can immediately turn into fulfilment. Sometimes I look back at what the world calls 'art' and wonder why so much art needs to be negative in order to address the problem of the transcendental…

JP. There are questions that may never be answered perhaps because they are rooted in the convolution of crossing cultural streams that have reached unprecedented levels of complexity. Other questions may only be answered by strict analysis, or, by contrast, in silence, at the end of a long day or during a glimpse of an intuition that we may have sensed in its fugitive presence. I vouch for both, although I am more inclined towards the latter. Real beauty is a light that comes from the soul.

AS. o v e r b u r d e n e d
by which new ambiguity at the end station of civil coexistence?
this trembling me lost in narcotised indifference
can outbursts of grief transform a dream into physical reality?

JP. *re-inventing the Pristine!*

AS. …*my heart is still beating*

JP. *despite* of
perhaps *because* of

AS. *the abyss we carry within…*

JP. Perhaps it is beauty that will remain in the end…

EXIT INTERVIEW

FINAL REVELATIONS
Sunny Knable

SK. It has been a pleasure getting to know your life's work through this book project. As a composer, performer and teacher, I can relate to many aspects of your personal and musical thought processes. Not only have I learned a lot about John Palmer, the man and John Palmer, the composer, I've also been awakened to the breadth of your knowledge of all sorts of topics, from the worlds of language, art, theatre, international influences and extra-musical topics, to the inner-quest for a spiritual life. This book is a good reminder to young composers that a life in composition is not just about pushing notes around on a page. You demonstrate through example what it is to be a whole musician. English speakers might call you a 'Renaissance man' but the French would say that you are *un véritable homme-orchestre*, as in a man who plays the whole orchestra. This is an apt title.

In the course of editing these articles and interviews, I found myself nodding in agreement with your pronouncements about today's popular culture, smiling at many of your touching, poetic statements about your life as a composer, searching through musical examples to see how you construct and organise your work, looking up specialised terminology, and finally, taking note of a few questions of my own. I wonder if you might oblige me (in the most succinct way possible) with a few answers in this final interview.

SK. How did this project come about?

JP. In the past years, I have noticed an increased interest in my music. When the COVID crisis began and concert life was brought to a standstill, I asked a couple of musicians I had worked with in the past if they were interested to ask questions that I would reply to in a video interview. I must confess to you that I didn't expect their response to be so warm and enthusiastic. Encouraged by such a passionate reaction, I decided to ask other musicians if they would do the same, so the circle got bigger and bigger until it became clear to me that all these contributions could be put together in a book. This is how everything began. A few weeks later, I was amazed to notice that the range of the contributors covered four Continents including Australia, Japan and India, Russia, Europe, and North and South America. I felt very honoured by so much interest and zeal.

SK. How did it change from the original intent to the current form?

JP. As I may have hinted in the first answer, when more contributors accepted to participate in the project, the number of topics increased to the point where I understood that the best way to discuss and honour all the questions was to reply in writing. A reduced video version may still happen in the future. Meanwhile, I had grown fonder of the written discussion because this gave me more time to reflect on the questions I received over the past eight months. Taking more time to think about the questions was my way to honour the participation of so many wonderful musicians and friends.

SK. Were you limited or aided by the COVID-19 period we've been living through?

JP. I was aided by it because all the musicians I contacted are very busy professionals and under normal circumstances, they may have not had the time to participate. I was aware of this situation when I contacted them. I am sure the standstill of concert life has facilitated the project.

SK. How has the process been for you, given that you've been juggling many responsibilities of being a professor concurrently?

JP. In the past eight months, I have focused on two jobs at the same time: the full-time academic position with all that comes with it, and the coordination of this project. Additionally, I was commissioned a small piece at the end of December 2020 which I had to finish by mid-February 2021. All in all, I have been working seven days (and nights) a week and taking very few short breaks. On the physical level, the process has been truly exhausting, but, as in many similar activities, enthusiasm and passion always provide food to the mind and an enormous power that transcends the physical limitations of the body.

SK. As for the content of this book, a number of thoughts occurred to me while reading. One of them I jotted down has to do with a recurring theme about how others perceive you. Every artist I know can relate to the struggle to define oneself. Is there a person whose opinion you trust enough to give you that kind of insight? Perhaps a family member or friend?

JP. While I was going through my personal archives some weeks ago, I found a statement written by my sister Pia where she is referring to me as a young boy. Perhaps her opinion of me might be insightful in the context you have delineated. Here it is: *"My earliest memories of my brother are that when he came home from school he was very busy studying, especially music on the piano. Sometimes I had the impression that he would retreat into silence as if to seek answers that the world around him could not give him. He spent a lot of time alone, silent, detached and far from the others."*

SK. This is a loaded and perhaps cliché question akin to, "if Beethoven were not deaf, could he have written the Ninth Symphony?", but in this case, we have the gift of being able to ask the composer himself. I'm fascinated by the subject of synaesthesia. If it's not too personal to ask, is there an aspect of being synaesthetic that is integral to your work as a composer? As in, if you were not synaesthetic, do you think you'd compose music in the same way or with a similar result?

JP. I had to think very carefully about this question as I didn't want to give you a quick and cheap answer. I have made an effort to recollect many personal and artistic situations related to my experience of synaesthesia. My (very honest) answer to the first question is: yes, being synaesthetic is an inevitable component of my work as a composer. But this doesn't mean that I think about it in a particular way before or during the process of composition. It is something that flows naturally in me like, for example, when I look at a picture, when I read a number or when I read or hear a word. It is a 'meta-sensation' (to be more precise: a neurological condition of crossing sensations) encompassing several sensations occurring at the same time which I experience when I see, hear, smell, eat, read or think of something.

The (equally candid) answer to your second question is: if I were not synaesthetic, I am sure I would compose in a different way because I would perceive certain combinations of sounds another way. Consequently, the music I compose would not be the same. Franz Schubert once said that the note F♯ for him had a green colour. In the 1960s or 1970s, some laboratories in the USA (I cannot remember where exactly) conducted research on the chlorophyll process in plants. Well, you may be surprised to hear that the chlorophyll process oscillates at the equivalent frequency of the note F♯ (F♯4, if I remember well). The first question that came to my mind back in the 1980s was: is there a physical correspondence between light and sound? According to several studies I have read, the answer is: yes. But a more important question is another: can such equivalences be perceived the same way by all (synaesthetic) people? Many self-professed synaesthetic musicians I have been talking to in the past 30 years have come up with different answers of the like: "C major sounds blue" or "C major sounds yellow". My consistent impression is that many of these statements sound superficial to me and make me wonder how seriously these musicians take synaesthesia. In my case, I can say that I have been observing myself quite attentively in the past three decades in order to test my own synaesthetic experience as seriously as possible. As far as I know, the scientific community hasn't been able to provide a general answer to this important question. Having said that, I must confess I am not updated on the subject, and I should really catch up with the current research on this fascinating subject.

SK. Your answers to the interviews in this book range from being highly intellectual to extremely personal. I share your feeling that divulging something as personal as a dream which inspired a composition can make us as artists feel vulnerable or even embarrassed. Where is that line for you between the personal and the public? In this internet age, do you think it's better to guard some personal aspects of your work for yourself? You mention musical codes a few times throughout this book, for example, but never reveal them to us.

JP. When I was asked those questions, I asked myself the same question you are asking me now: how personal should my answer be? I know of several colleagues who have been misunderstood throughout their lives by statements they have made during one interview. At times they have also paid a big price for one single misunderstanding. Regardless of the internet, this remains a 'dangerous' area because, in the West, music discussion has been reduced to analytical and intellectual arguments. All the composers I have heard talking about music would not go so far about personal issues. For example, they would not speak about what they experience *and feel* during the process of composition: this is still a taboo area. But feelings, sensations, emotions, life experience, personal events are *major ingredients* of our behaviour: this includes not only everything we think and do but also the way we perceive the world and relate to one other. Why separate the intellect from the emotional, the physical from the metaphysical, the psychological from the philosophical, the professional from the personal? Ah, René Descartes, is it really you who managed to sanctify such-nonsense? Well, if that is the case, I would urge everybody to read Antonio Damasio's book *Descartes' Error: Emotion, Reason, and the Human Brain.*

Back to your point, if someone asks me about dreaming, I have two choices: either I don't answer at all or I want to answer as honestly as possible, risking being misunderstood or ridiculed by other readers. I was aware of this dilemma and decided to be honest and take full responsibility for it. Throughout these conversations, I have chosen to remain as authentic as possible because I have grown sick and tired of this 'unreachable-genius' composer image that is so rooted in European academic and public domains. If I were a different John Palmer, my music would surely sound different. Our professional activities are a mirror of who we are, whether we like it or not. I want to be myself: why should I give a different image of something that is not me?

You asked why I have never revealed my musical codes to the reader. I can understand the reasoning behind this question, although I have given some clues. But if I revealed such codes to the readers, the cyphers would no longer be secret. In that case, why did I decide to keep them secret in the first place? There must be a reason for it. I cannot, and should not take away the readers' or listeners' right to plunge into the unknown and discover *by themselves* uncharted realms of the imagination and the enthralling revelations of symbols. This discovery should remain highly personal. I can indicate a path, but each person must walk the path alone. I cannot do this for them. To *know* the path is not to *walk* the path. What is the meaning of mystery? What is the significance of the mystical? Have you ever noticed that both words, 'mystery' and 'mystical', have the same root ('myst') in common?

SK. Any artist can relate to the idea of being misrepresented. About halfway through this book, I had a sense that you felt misrepresented or misinterpreted by the labels of Zen practices, spirituality and Japanese influences, which have a way of reducing you and your work. What are the keywords that you would use to describe your own output? Is there a way to include those labels mentioned above and have them not be misused or misconstrued?

JP. You are right; I did have that feeling, but it is not the first time that it happens to me. I often feel that we all, as a society, have a tendency to pigeonhole the activities of other people. Although I can understand the need to contextualise an artistic output, on the other hand, I feel an inclination (perhaps a subconscious one) to blur an individual's work with that of other artists. I tried to explain this when I was asked about influences, a word that epitomises this attitude. It seems to me that we don't understand how shrinking the notion of influence can be. This is one reason why I have always been allergic to labels of all sorts. Epigones apart (and these will be easy to hear), we are all unique musicians, don't you think so?

You ask what are the keywords that I would use to describe my own output. Is it not music that describes itself? It's true I have been doing this all the time throughout the book, but this is a necessity resulting from a verbal conversation. Ideally, I would like to remain silent and let the music speak to those who are willing to listen. By accepting the self-imposed limitation of a discussion, however, I hope I have provided the readers with some indications of my views about art in general and music in particular. Let me summarise once more: to me, writing music is like writing a poem or painting a picture. I give voice to something that I feel is important enough (for me) to be declared as a 'public statement': this is what we call the musical work. Each note I write reflects a small portion of my life. More notes together become a phrase; more phrases become a musical work. More works together will be my final testimony. When I compose, I take refuge in the realm of reflection about the human condition while going through a potential process of self-knowledge.

SK. What would you like to be remembered for outside of the musical world?

JP. As a good friend and an honest man who has always tried his best and loved to the best of his capabilities.

SK. Is there one piece or a group of pieces you would point to as representing the whole of you? I'm thinking of how history has a tendency of picking pieces that represent the composer, but composers don't get a say in the matter. I've found that the more popular a piece of mine is, the less personal it was for me. This is why I ask, to give you a chance to point us in the correct direction.

JP. My heart, mind and soul are in every piece I write, and any selection of works will be inevitably painful for me. Nevertheless, I would answer that the following pieces resonate with me in a particular way: the orchestral works *Not Two, Hypothetical Questions, Piano Concerto,*

There, Double Concerto; the ensemble works *You, Legend, Transparence, Koan, Waka*; *First String Quartet, Second String Quartet*; the chamber works *Between, Transient, Theorem*; *Vision* (for harpsichord and electronics); *Thereafter* (for organ and electronics); *Woanders* and *After Silence (1)* (for piano and electronics); *Musica Reservata, Anagrams, Shambhala, Athena, Hieroglyphs* (for solo piano); *Over* (for violin); *Three Haikus* (for shakuhachi). *Transfiguration* (for trombone and electronics); *Utopia* (music theatre); *I am, In the Temple, Present Otherness* (acousmatic)…

SK. What haven't you explored in musical composition? Is that the inevitable next step?

JP. I have explored everything I wanted to explore so far, but I have at least three 'ready-to-go' opera projects I would like to bring to completion. And I still dream to create sounds that have not been heard yet.

SK. You mention that Cage had an early impact on you but only up to a certain point. I like the way you put him in a historical and personal context: that his revered status in the field of new music was inflated beyond what his music offered. In the classroom, we talk about his ideas but not all that often his music. Are there other figures like Cage who were inflated beyond their musical offerings? Or perhaps a better question: who, in your opinion, has been overvalued?

JP. Yes, there are other figures who have been inflated beyond their musical offerings in the past 250 years. Specifically, in the 20th century, I am thinking of the post-war generation who used to meet regularly at Darmstadt: the advocates of modernism. I am not saying they were all bad composers; I believe some of them have been alright and others quite good, but not as great as the history of music books and the academic music community keep portraying them! In my opinion, they were very lucky young composers who lived at a time where the desire to rebuild a new society in Europe joined forces with the economic boom of the 1950s and 1960s, allowing any musical experiment to be taken seriously by the music intelligentsia including state institutions, music publishers and festivals of new music. They were a bunch of composers, many of them of a mediocre level, who had a huge promotional network behind them that commissioned new works and performed their music everywhere. Many of these musical works are poorly written or have little artistic significance, yet they have become 'Classics of Modernism' as they say in Germany. Another group of composers that have been inflated beyond their musical offerings are the so-called minimalists.

History seems to repeat itself as the same applies to Baroque, Classical and Romantic composers. In Europe, we keep hearing the same works again and again: always the same pieces consecrated by Academia and the classical music industry. Many works by these 'great' composers are not good at all, but no one dares to dispute them perhaps for fear to clash with the status quo of the concert and academic establishment. W.A. Mozart is the most striking example that comes to my mind, but I could mention many other names, and the list would be very long!

SK. And those who have been overlooked?

JP. Josquin Des Prez, John Dowland, William Byrd, Orlande de Lassus, Claudio Monteverdi, Giovanni Gabrieli, Alessandro Grandi, Heinrich Schütz, François Couperin, Georg Philipp Telemann, Franz Xaver Richter, Christian Cannabich, Carl Philipp Emanuel Bach, Alexander Scriabin, Josef Matthias Hauer, Arnold Schönberg, Alois Hába, the later Stravinsky, Bernd Alois Zimmermann, Roberto Gerhard.

SK. When I read your thoughts on each composition, I can surmise that each piece is a personal journey for you, but each of us operates in the world of connections: friendships, mentors, students, colleagues, performers, audience members, critics, proponents, associations, and perhaps, even competitors. Do you still have people you emulate? Look up to? Feel competition with? Or is all of this outside of what really propels you as an artist?

JP. Most of this is outside of what propels my work. I certainly don't emulate anybody or feel competition with anybody: why should I? There are composers whose music speaks to me in a very direct way and I think I have discussed this in various conversations in this book.

SK. Do you feel that, at a certain point, each composer must leave their influences, teachers or heroes behind?

JP. Composers shouldn't follow heroes or teachers, but their own inner voice. This is what I tell everybody, including my students.

SK. Every musician I know is more than one aspect of being a musician. This 'juggling-routine' is not only natural, it is necessary in that we frequently need to support ourselves doing something other than our primary focus. It is for that reason that I have trouble introducing myself to people. Should I lead with 'composer', 'performer', 'professor', 'writer', 'artist', or just, 'musician'? In your case, where do you put the 'musicologist' in that list of the many things which comprise you?

JP. I believe this confusion arises especially in countries where pop music dominates the scene, namely the English-speaking world. In Continental Europe, there is a rigid distinction between all these activities which I equally find detrimental and suffocating. In the UK and the USA, for instance, if you take up a guitar and sing a song, you will be perceived as a composer, which is ridiculous of course! Boundaries seem to have been broken by the advent of digital technology. I feel like an artist firstly, but if I said this publicly, I know the majority of people would not understand me. Music is indeed art. More specifically, I am a musician, of course. Yet I know this still won't satisfy an audience, so I will say that I am a composer. When I perform, I am a performer. I am also a musicologist because I research and write on music. As a professor, I am also an academic. All these facets are parts of who I am. I think the order of these definitions depends on the priority they have in our lives.

I perceive you as a composer, performer and musicologist. The fact that you also teach may not be relevant for an artistic profile. I know people like us who have two or three CVs depending on whom they are approaching. For a website, I would not hesitate to write what I do. The problem with the word 'artist' is that the majority of people won't understand what we mean exactly. The problem with the noun 'musician' is that we will be most probably perceived as pop musicians and this (with all respect and love for popular music) may devalue the kind of work we do. I don't particularly like the word 'educator'. I read it a lot in American websites and to me, it comes across as something a bit pompous. If it's about teaching, I would prefer the word 'teacher'. Or I could be more academically specific and write that I am a Professor, a Lecturer or whatever my academic position is. However, I think all these things are not that important, really. The most important thing is to *never* forget who we are. Self-knowledge is an open-ended adventure.

SK. Does being a musicologist inform your compositional life in more than a general sense?

JP. Yes, because all perspectives of music are connected to each other. For example, pitch-class set theory and psychoacoustics have been tremendous tools that have helped me understand much better what I do in my works and have made me aware of so many important details intrinsic in the art of composition.

SK. Are there times you wish that you could live on commissions alone, locking yourself in your room with a piano for 8 hours a day? Or do you do better in the world, mingling, sharing ideas and working with others?

JP. I had that wish years ago. My life has been a very solitary path due to basic necessities I had to face in my youth, such as rebuilding my existence from zero when I was 18, having to take up several jobs in order to survive, getting married and bringing up three children. When you are very young, lacking the support of your family is something that marks your life. From a professional point of view, I am aware I have lost 10 years of my career by having had to deal with basic existential problems, so I have never really had much time to socialise and make contacts. Mingling has always been very difficult, and the recurring change of countries has been a real challenge when it came to building up an entourage of like-minded people around me. Yet, I don't regret anything of what I went through in my life, because that is what has made me who I am today. Whenever I can, I do enjoy sharing ideas and working with others very much, and these moments have been some of the most gratifying times in my life.

SK. What words would you like the reader to linger on as they close this book?

JP. I certainly want to thank all those who have taken the time to go through this book and given me the opportunity to reach them (I hope) in some way or another. Ultimately, I wish the topics discussed in this book may have helped other musicians, and indeed non-musicians, to appreciate further this wonderful art that is composition, and to recognise that music is not only an organisation of sound but a much deeper and mysterious revelation of the psyche: images of the mind.

BIBLIOGRAPHY

Adorno, Theodor, *Aesthetic Theory*, reprint. Continuum (London, New York), 2002.

Adorno, Theodor, *Fragment über Musik und Sprache* (1956) in Paddison, Max, *The Language-Character of Music: Some Motifs in Adorno* in *Journal of the Royal Musical Association*, Vol. 116, 2. 1991.

Bachelard, Gaston, *The Poetic of Space*. Beacon Press, Boston, 1994.

Babbitt, Milton, *Three Essays on Schönberg* in Peles, Stephen et al, eds, *The Collected Essays of Milton Babbitt*. Princeton University Press, 2011.

Babbitt, Milton, *Who Cares if You Listen?* in *High Fidelity Magazine*, vol. 8, no. 2, 1958.

Bhaskar, Roy, *Dialectic, The Pulse of Freedom*. Verso, London, 1993.

Buchmann, Bettina, *The Techniques of Accordion Playing*. Bärenreiter Verlag, 2010.

Cage, John, *Silence: Lectures and Writings*. Middletown, Conn. Wesleyan University Press, 1961.

Cone, Edward T. *The Composer's Voice*. University of California Press, 1974.

Cook, Nicholas, *Music as Creative Practice*. Oxford University Press, New York, 2018.

Dahlhaus, Carl, *Virtuosität und Interpretation* in *Die Musik des 19. Jahrhunderts, Neues Handbuch der Musikwissenschaft 6*. Laaber, 1980.

De la Motte-Haber, Helga, *Schwierigkeit und Virtuosität* in *Musikalische Virtuosität*, eds, Heinz von Loesch, Ulrich Mahlert and Peter Rummenhöller. Schott Music International, Mainz, 2004.

Dispenza, Joe. *Becoming Supernatural*. Hay House UK, 2017.

Eliot, Thomas S., *On Poetry and Poets*. Faber and Faber, London, 1969.

Eliot, Thomas S., *The Use of Poetry and the Use of Criticism*. Faber and Faber, London, 1933.

Emmerson, Simon, *The Relation of Language to Materials,* in Emmerson, Simon (ed.) *The Language of Electroacoustic Music*. Macmillan Press, 1986.

Emperor Julian, *Oration to the Sovereign Sun* in *The Works of Emperor Julian*. Forgotten Books, 2012.

Fox, Christopher, *New Complexity* in *Grove Music Online, Oxford Music Online*. OUP, 2001.

Frisk, Henrik & Östersjö, Stefan, *Negotiating Musical Work*. Paper, EMS Conference, Beijing, 2006.

Gamō, Satoaki, *Nihon Ongaku no Ma* in *Ma no Kenkyū*. Hiroshi Minami (ed.). Tokyo: Kōdan-sha, 1983.

Goehr, Lydia, *The Perfect Performance of Music and the Perfect Musical Performance*. New Formations 27, 1996.

Goswami, Amit, *The Self-Aware Universe*. Tarcher Putnam, 1993.

Gumbrecht, Hans U., *Production of Presence: What Meaning Cannot Convey*. Stanford University Press, 2004.

Harvey, Jonathan, *Music and Inspiration*. Faber and Faber, London, 1999.

Heidegger, Martin, *Being and Time*. State University of New York Press (SUNY), Albany, NY, 2010.

Hope, Cat and Devenish, Louise, *The New Virtuosity: A Manifesto for Contemporary Sonic Practice* in ADSR Zine, Issue 11, 2020.

Husserl, Edmund, *Vorlesungen zur Phaenomenologie des inneren Bewusstseins* edited by Martin Heidegger (special edition from: *Jahrbuch fuer Philosophie und phaenomenologische Forschung,* Vol. IX, Freiburg i. Br.). Halle, 1928. (Reference translated by the composer).

Imoto, Chosuke. *Eiwa Taiyaku: Zengo Senshū (Zoku Zen no Kakehashi)*. Shimonosaki, 1994.

Iwamoto, Yoshikazu, *The Potential of the Shakuhachi in Contemporary Music* in *Contemporary Music Review,* Vol. 8, Part 2. Harwood Academic Publishers, 1993.

Jung, C.G., *The Spirit in Man, Art, and Literature*. Ark Paperbacks, 1984 (1966).

Juslin Patrik and Sloboda John, eds, *Handbook of Music and Emotion: Theory, Research, Applications*. Oxford University Press, 2010.

Jankélévitch, Vladimir, *Liszt et la Rhapsodie. Essai sur la virtuosité*. Plon, Paris, 1979.

Kandisky, Wassily, *Complete Writings on Art*. Da Capo Press, 1994.

Kikkawa, Eishi, *The Musical Sense of the Japanese* in *Contemporary Music Review*, Vol. 1, Part 2. Harwood Academic Publishers, 1987.

Laban, Rudolph, *The Mastery of Movement*. Macdonald and Evans London, 1960.

Lee, Hermione, *Virginia Woolf*. Vintage, 1999.

Lerdahl, Fred, *Composition and Cognition*. University of California Press, 2020.

Ligeti, György, *Metamorphoses of Musical Form* in *Neues Forum* No.148/149. Vienna, 1966.

Lucretius, *On the Nature of Things,* Book I, translated by H. A. J. Munro. H. A. Johnstone, 2013.

McGilchrist, Iain. *The Master and his Emissary: The Divided Brain and the Making of the Western World.* Yale University Press, Newhaven and London, 2009.

Maconie, Robin. *The Concept of Music.* Clarendon Press Oxford University Press, 1990.

Mäkilä, Tomi, *Virtuosität und Werkcharakter. Eine analytische und theoretische Untersuchung zur Virtuosität in den Klavierkonzerten der Hochromantik.* Katzbichler, Munich, Salzburg, 1989.

Meyer, Leonard, *Emotion and Meaning in Music.* The University of Chicago Press, 1956.

Metzer, David, *Musical Modernism at the Turn of the Twenty-First Century.* Cambridge University Press, 2009.

Morris, Christian, *John Palmer Interview* in *Composition Today* - www.compositiontoday.com/interviews

Nattiez, Jean-Jacques, *Music and Discourse - Toward a Semiology of Music.* Princeton University Press, 1990.

Nono, Luigi, *The Historical Reality and Music Today* in *The Score.* London, July, 1959.

Odgen, C.K. and Richards, I. A., *The Meaning of Meaning.* Ark Paperbacks, London, 1923.

Osborne, Charles, *Richard Wagner Stories and Essays.* Peter Owen Limited, 1973.

Osmond-Smith, David, *Luciano Berio: Two Interviews with Rossana Dalmonte and Bálint András Varga.* Marion Boyars (ed.), New York, London, 1985.

Östersjö, Stefan, *SHUT UP 'N' PLAY! Negotiating the Musical Work.* PhD Thesis, Lund University, 2008.

Palmer, John, *Conversations.* Vision Edition, 2013.

Pockett, Susan, *How long is "now"? Phenomenology and the specious present. Phenomenology and the Cognitive Sciences.* 2. 55-68. 10.1023/A:1022960122740, 2003.

Rink, John, *The Work of the Performer* in *Virtual Works - Actual Things: Essays in Musical Ontology (Orpheus Institute Series).* Paulo de Assis (ed.). Leuven University Press, 2018.

Rosen, Charles. Temerson, Catherine. *The Joy of Playing, the Joy of Thinking: Conversations about Art and Performance.* Harvard University Press, Cambridge, Mass. & London, 2020.

Rovelli, Carlo, *The Order of Time.* Penguin Books, 2018.

Said, Edward. *Orientalism.* Pantheon Books, New York, 1978.

Saint Augustine, *Confessions.* Translated by Henry Chadwick. Oxford University Press, 1991.

Sampson, Jim, *Virtuosity and the Musical Work: The Transcendental Studies of Liszt.* Cambridge University Press, 2003.

Sartre, Jean-Paul, *Being and Nothingness.* Routledge, London and New York, 2003.

Schelling, F.W.J. (1800), *Deduction of the Art Product in General*, section VI of *System of Transcendental Idealism* in *Philosophies of Art and Beauty.* A. Hofstadter and R. Kuhns (eds.), The University of Chicago Press, 1964.

Schumann, Robert, *Gesammelte Schriften über Musik und Musiker*, Vol. 2. Leipzig, 1854.

Scruton, Roger, *The Aesthetics of Music.* Oxford University Press, 1999.

Scruton Roger, *Understanding Music.* Continuum, London New York, 2009.

Shimada, Yumi, *Sakura, Sakura - a study of its development and popularisation into a school song.* Ongakukyōikugaku 32, no. 2, 2002.

Snelling, John. *The Buddhist Handbook.* Rider, 1987.

Solomon, Robert, *Emotion* in *Encyclopedia Britannica* (1998), www.britannica.com/science/emotion.

Storr, Anthony: *The Integrity of the Personality.* Penguin Books, 1966.

Suzuki D.T., *An Introduction to Zen Buddhism.* Rider, 1969.

Swedenborg, Emanuel, *Divine Providence.* The Swedenborg Foundation, West Chester, 1996.

Takemitsu, Toru, *Oto, Kotoba, Ningen* in *Tōru Takemitsu Chosakushū*, vol. 4. Tokyo, Shinchō-sha, 2000.

The New Grove Dictionary of Music and Musicians, (Ed. Stanley Sadie). Vol. 17, p. 475. 2001.

Truax, Barry: *Acoustic communication.* Ablex Publishing, 2001.

VanderHamm, David, *Virtuosity/Virtuoso*, in *Oxford Bibliographies Online.* https://www.oxfordbibliographies.com/view/document/obo-9780199757824/

Vicentino, Nicola, *Ancient Music Adapted to Modern Practice.* Yale University Press. 1996.

von Loesch, Heinz, *Virtuosität als Gegenstand der Musikwissenschaft*, in *Musikalische Virtuosität.* Heinz von Loesch, Ulrich M. and Rummenhöller Peter (eds.). Schott Music International, Mainz, 2004.

Warnock, Mary. *Imagination.* University of California Press, 1978.

Wilson, Peter N., *The breath of the machine in search of the quintessence of the accordeon.* Liner notes to *Push Pull.* Teodoro Anzellotti, CD Hat [now] ART 131, 1999.

Wittgenstein, Ludwig, *Tractatus Logico-Philosophicus.* Routledge & Kegan Paul, London, 1961.

Yeats, William B., *A Dialogue of Self and Soul* in *The Collected Poems of W. B. Yeats.* Wordsworth, 1994.

INDEX

CHRONOLOGICAL LIST OF WORKS BY JOHN PALMER

(this list does not include songs)

1.	*Missing Rhymes* (piano) - 12'	1984 (rev. 2012)
2.	*Children Pieces* (piano) – 12'	1985
3.	*Hieroglyphs* (piano) – 9'	1985-1986 (rev. 2012)
4.	*Poem for the Absurd* (piano) - 12'20"	1986
5.	*First String Quartet* – 20'	1986
6.	*Three Preludes* (piano) – 6'	1987
7.	*Alpha* (piano) - 7'	1987
8.	*Song for You* (piano) - 9'	1987
9.	*Stream* (piano) - 5'	1988
10.	*Sketches (1)* (piano) - 4'20"	1988-1989
11.	*Musica Reservata* (piano) - 52'	1988-1989
12.	*Asgard* (ensemble, 2 speakers, electronics) - 21'10"	1987-1988
13.	*Transient* (sop, pno, electronics / acousmatic) - 8'	1988 (rev. 2008)
14.	*Déjà-vu* (piano) - 8'	1988
15.	*Three Cadenzas on Mozart* (piano) - 6'	1988 (rev. 2008)
16.	*Double Games* (4-hands piano) - 12'	1989
17.	*Manhattan* (piano) - 5'20"	1989
18.	*Sounding the Day* (24 hours - shorter duration allowed)	1988-1990
19.	*Utopia* (music theatre–mezzosoprano, fl, ob, cl, bs, elect.) - 21'	1990 (rev. 2020)
20.	*Spirits* (synthesizer) - 18'20"	1990
21.	*Athena* (piano) – 6'	1990
22.	*Shambhala* (piano) - 13'	1990
23.	*There* (string orchestra) - 5'	1990-1991
24.	*Hellawes* (C-fl, alto fl, bass fl) - 11'00"	1991
25.	*This World* (2 soprani, percussion) - 8'	1991
26.	*Omen* (orchestra and choir) - 9'	1991
27.	*No us* (SATB choir) - 4'	1991
28.	*What else* (SATB choir) - 3'	1991
29.	*Where to* (SATB choir) - 5'	1991
30.	*Hypothetical Questions* (orchestra) – 20'	1991 (rev. 2011)
31.	*Piano Concerto* (piano, choir and orchestra) - 23'	1992 (rev. 2001)
32.	*Concertino* (orchestra) - 9'	1992
33.	*You* (trombone and ensemble) - 18'10"	1992 (rev. 2009)
34.	*He* (8 voices or 16 voices - SATB) - 6'20"	1992
35.	*Glimpse* (piano) - 2'14"	1992
36.	*Phonai* (synthesizer & electronics / acousmatic) - 11'10"	1992 (rev. 1997)
37.	*Nowhere* (cl, pno, electronics) - 14'	1993

38.	*Reflections* (tpt, pno, electronics) - 23'30"	1993
39.	*Beyond the Bridge* (cello & electronics) - 13'	1993
40.	*Renge-kyo* (piano & electronics) - 11'30"	1993
41.	*Vision* (harpsichord & electronics) - 11'	1994
42.	*Legend* (harp & ensemble) - 18'10"	1994 (rev. 2008)
43.	*Theorem* (vl, vc, pno) - 12'40"	1995
44.	*Second String Quartet* - 20'	1996
45.	*Waka* (percussion & ensemble) - 29'10"	1996
46.	*Epitaph* (cello & electronics) - 10'05"	1997
47.	*Now (1)* (cello & electronics) - 8'	1997
48.	*Encounter* (hpsch, perc, electronics) - 19'20"	1998
49.	*Mosaic* (harpsichord) - 14'	1998
50.	*Now (2)* (cello, piano, electronics) - 10'	1998
51.	*Koan* (shakuhachi & ensemble) - 21'	1999
52.	*Hinayana* (oboe) - 13'10"	1999
53.	*Drang* (accordion) - 10'	1999
54.	*Satori* (harpsichord) - 8'10"	1999
55.	*Between* (violin & harpsichord) - 12'05"	2000
56.	*Transitions* (vl, cl, vc, pno) - 30'	2000
57.	*"...as it flies..."* (acousmatic) - 13'20"	2001
58.	*Still* (bass flute, viola, guitar) - 13'	2001
59.	*I am* (acousmatic) - 52'	2003
60.	*Now (3)* (2 celli & electronics) - 10'	2003
61.	*Inwards* (bass flute & electronics) - 15'	2004
62.	*Without* (violin) - 10'	2004
63.	*Transfiguration* (trombone & electronics) - 17'	2005-2006
64.	*Over* (violin) - 10'	2005
65.	*Almost* (cello) - 10'	2005
66.	*After Silence (1)* (piano & electronics) - 15'	2005
67.	*From the Lake* (oboe & piano) - 15'	2005
68.	*Afterglow* (alto fl, pno, electronics) – 13'	2006
69.	*En Avant* (piano) – 5'	2006
70.	*In the Temple* (acousmatic) - 52'	2007
71.	*Fado* (4-hands piano) - 9'	2007
72.	*Present Otherness* (acousmatic) - 11'	2008
73.	*Blurring Definitions* (ensemble) - 11'	2008 (rev. 2016)
74.	*Hypothesis* (percussion) - 7'	2008 (rev. 2017)
75.	*Antithesis* (vl, vla, vc) - 5'	2008 (rev. 2021)
76.	*Trans-solo 1* (piano) - 3'	2010
77.	*Trans-solo 2* (clarinet) - 3'	2010

118.	*Woanders* (piano & electronics) – 10'	2016
119.	*Yahari* (guitar) – 6'	2017
120.	*Not Two* (orchestra) – 20'	2017
121.	*Vajra* (harpsichord) – 10'	2018
122.	*Somewhere* (cello) – 5'	2018
123.	*Re di Donne* (chamber opera) – 60'	2019
124.	*I, Medusa* (mezzosoprano, db, electronics) – 13'	2019
125.	*Aria a 3* (alto fl, vibra, pno) – 4'35"	2021

For further information and a complete works list by genre visit: www.johnpalmer.org

The vast majority of John Palmer's scores are published by Composers Edition
https://composersedition.com/johnpalmer/

Other scores of an educational nature are published by Bellmann Musik
https://bellmannmusik.com/Service/Komponisten/O-bis-Z/Palmer-John/

CONTRIBUTORS

Paul Alan Barker is a British composer and Professor of Music Theatre at the Royal Central School of Speech and Drama in London. He is an award-winning composer of operas, theatre and concert music, performed and recorded internationally and at major festivals; an author of books and chapters on music, theatre and performance; a pianist and conductor, especially of his own music, and a stage director. *El Gallo* (2009) and *QIQI* (2020) were respectively an opera for actors and a symphonic work for theatre company and orchestra, commissioned by Teatro de Ciertos Habitantes in Mexico. He has also composed for such as clarinettist Joan Lluna, Brodsky Quartet, violinist Tasmin Little, soprano Sarah Leonard and the London Festival Orchestra. There are several CDs of his operas and vocal music.

Daniel Biro is a French composer, keyboard player, producer, improviser, songwriter and label director. At the age of 12 he got his first analogue synthesizer and has since been hooked on all things electronic. After moving to London in 1985 he founded the ground-breaking experimental music label Sargasso and has since collaborated with theatre and contemporary dance companies, film and TV productions (BBC, Channel 4, The History Channel, Arte), as well as numerous recording projects. He has released many albums as a solo artist or with his jazz/rock/experimental bands Mysteries of the Revolution and Echo Engine. Recent work includes an ambient song project with Colin Bass (from progressive rock band Camel), and monthly online solo keyboard improvised 'Synthrospections' concerts.

Eva Böcker is a German cellist and has been a member of Ensemble Modern since 1994. She was a pupil at the Purcell School and the Royal College of Music Junior Department in London, before studying with Boris Pergamenschikow in Cologne and Johannes Goritzki in Düsseldorf. She has been an active chamber musician throughout her career, and has participated regularly in international chamber music festivals such as *Open Chamber Music* in Prussia Cove. Over the past thirty years she has worked together with many composers and has performed at leading international festivals for contemporary music. In 2011 her Solo-CD *Spoken Tones* appeared on Ensemble ModernMedia. From 2014 to 2020 Eva Böcker taught the cello at the Académie Supérieure de Musique in Strasbourg. She currently teaches at the Hochschule in Frankfurt.

Anna Cepollaro is an Italian music critic working for *La Repubblica* newspaper, and host and correspondent of the Italian RadioTre national broadcasting company. Additionally, Cepollaro works for Il *Manifesto-Alias* and various national newspapers. She has overseen the review of several shows including Cimarosa's *Desperate Husband*, directed by Paolo Rossi at the Teatro San Carlo in Naples and *Roman de Fauvel* by Gervais du Bus at the Olympic Theatre in Rome with David Riondino and la Reverdie. She is the press officer of the Teatro Lirico Sperimentale di Spoleto amongst other artists and festivals. Cepollaro has been teaching Communication Techniques in several Italian conservatoires. She also runs the post-graduate Master in Management and Communication of Cultural Enterprises at the Conservatory of Naples.

Patrick Crossland is an American trombonist and has worked closely with several prominent composers. Solo performances include the Walker Art Center's *Festival Dancing In Your Head*, the Darmstadt Course for New Music, where he was awarded a Solo Performance Prize, and the *Utopia Jetzt!* Festival (Germany) where he performed his acclaimed *V for Grock* multimedia recital. In 2009 he premiered his *Krieg dem Krieg* project featuring thematic works for trombone and electronics. In addition to his activities as a soloist and chamber musician, he is an avid improviser, working with a wide range of musicians, dancers, and actors. He is a member of the Composers Slide Quartet, Ensemble Laboratorium, and Zinc & Copper Works. He teaches trombone and other music courses at the University of Maryland Baltimore County.

Késia Decoté is a Brazilian pianist specialised in contemporary music. Her debut solo album *Para a frente* (Nonclassical) features piano and toy piano works dedicated to her by emerging UK-based composers. She has also released an album of improvisations with cellist Bruno Guastalla. Decoté's latest CD, *Isolation*, presents a collection of piano miniatures written by composer Charlotte Botterill reflecting on her experience of the lockdown due to the pandemic crisis in 2020. She holds a PhD in Arts & Music and

MA from Oxford Brookes University, MMus and BA in Piano from Universidade Federal do Rio de Janeiro. Her interests focuses in exploring innovative ways to present piano music, looking for creating unique and deeply immersive artistic experiences for her audience.

Ricardo Descalzo is a Spanish pianist, teacher of contemporary music and multiple awards winner, having obtained the first prize in more than fifteen national and international piano competitions. Descalzo has has performed around the world and given masterclasses in contemporary music for pianists and composers worldwide. He is currently working on an audiovisual project recorded at the Alicante Provincial Council's ADDA Auditorium, *Piano Today*, which is becoming a reference for anyone interested in the piano repertoire of recent years. He has been a teacher of contemporary piano at Musikene, Centro Superior de Música del País Vasco for 17 years and is now teaching at Esmar, Escuela Superior de Música de Alto Performance in Valencia.

Theodor Flindell is an American-German violinist. He studied with Thomas Brandis and Axel Gerhard at the Berlin University of the Arts and with Shmuel Askenasi in the USA. He was a scholarship holder of the German National Academic Foundation, and the DAAD. In 1999/2000 he was a member of the Frankfurt Museumsorchester (Frankfurt Opera) and played in numerous other orchestras and chamber music ensembles. He is a member of Modern Art Ensemble and the Kammerensemble Neue Musik in Berlin.

Neil Heyde is an Australian cellist and Professor at the Royal Academy of Music in London. He has been cellist of the Kreutzer Quartet since the mid 1990s. As a soloist and chamber musician, Neil Heyde has appeared throughout Europe, and in China, the USA and Australia, broadcasting for the BBC, WDR, ORF, Radio France, RAI, NRK, DR, Netherlands Radio and many other networks. His discography extends to more than 40 recordings, mostly with the quartet but also including film and solo work, expanding the repertoire for both cello and quartet through exploratory collaborations and by advocating music from outside the mainstream. A performance film and documentary exploring Brian Ferneyhough's *Time and Motion Study II* for solo cello and electronics by Colin Still is freely available on iTunesU.

Egbert Hiller is a German musicologist and music journalist. He has been active as a jazz and theatre musician for many years, studied musicology, theatre, film and television studies as well as art history in Cologne. His PhD dissertation *Rapture, Dream and Death - On the Relationship between Text and Atonality in the Vocal Works of Arnold Schönberg, Alban Berg and Anton Webern* was published in 2002 by the Viennese publisher Lafite. His focus is on contemporary music, Romanticism, early Modernism, cultural politics and cross-epochal issues. He produces features, portraits of composers and works for Deutschlandfunk, Deutschlandradio Kultur, WDR, SWR and BR. His activities include CD projects for *Musik in Deutschland*, lectures, moderations, academic publications, programme notes and CD booklets.

Jeffrey Holmes is an American composer of post-spectral, teleological music incorporating elements of mysticism and lyrical expression. His creative inspiration is rooted in primitive myths, transcendent legends, and dramatic elemental landscapes in their primal and violent natural states. Commissions and performances have come from some of the most renowned orchestras and ensembles in the world. His music is published by Composers Edition, recorded on MicroFest Records, Centaur Records, Ablaze Records and Sono Luminus, and has been described as *Music of raw power and vision...a particularly impressive combination of technical prowess and deep expression* (Fanfare Magazine), *Captivating...haunting and slightly disorienting* (Los Angeles Times).

Ikuko Inoguchi is Japanese pianist, performer-scholar, and musicologist. After completing her education in Japan, she was awarded a Master of Music from UCLA, a DMA in Piano Performance from the University of Colorado, Boulder, and a PhD from City, University of London. She is particularly interested in researching and performing repertoire including cross-cultural influences. Her scholarly work involves historiography, philosophical and musicological investigations of musical time, aesthetics of rhythm, and practice-based research. Research interests include the music of the 20th- and 21st-centuries, the music of Japanese composers, concepts of time and temporality, exoticism, and *Japonisme*. She is currently a Visiting Research Fellow at City, University of London.

Carin Levine is an American Flautist and one of the most renowned flautists today. She has won numerous awards, the Kranichstein Musikpreis for the Interpretation of Contemporary Music and recently the Life Achievement Award from the German Composers Society. Her continuous collaboration with composers, established and upcoming, have led to more than 1000 premiers. Teaching activities include masterclasses, worldwide. Levine is editor of the series *Contemporary Music for the Flute*. Her books on the subject of contemporary flute techniques *The Techniques of Flute Playing* Volume 1 and 2 are published by Bärenreiter. Carin Levine's concert seasons include appearances at the major international music festivals. She is also Artistic director of the Youth New Music Ensemble, Lower Saxony, Germany.

Andrew Lewis is an award-winning composer and an internationally recognised figure in the field of acousmatic composition. His recent work includes music for orchestras and ensembles, but retains a strong interest in the materiality of sound and the use of technology. He is especially interested in spatial sound, in the relationship between 'real-world' and 'abstract' sounds, and in the phenomena of aural perception as part of the creative process. His music has been commissioned and performed by prominent artists worldwide. He is Professor of Composition at Bangor University in Wales. Numerous recordings include two collections, *Miroirs obscurs*, and *Au-dèla*, as well as *Schattenklavier*. His music is published by Composers Edition and Ymx média, Montréal (electrocd.com).

Suzanne Josek is a Swiss musicologist, art educator, author, accredited yoga teacher and mother of three children. Her PhD thesis *Music and Spirituality in the Work of Composer Jonathan Harvey* was published by Schott Verlag in 2016. Her activities as a researcher, teacher (seminars, lectures, workshops) and her work as an art mediator are concerned with interdisciplinarity as a search for what is common in art, science and spirituality and in relation to her own experience and practice. Suzanne Josek is the creator of Radio Yoga FM and the Museum in the Body (www.kolumba.de).

Johannes Klumpp is a German conductor and Artistic Director of the Heidelberg Symphony Orchestra with whom he is recording the complete Haydn symphonies. Since 2013 he has been the Chief Conductor and Artistic Director of the Folkwang Chamber Orchestra in Essen, focussing on the symphonic works by Wolfgang Amadeus Mozart. He has created innovative programme formats for the ExtraKlang series at the Zeche Zollverein World Heritage Site and cooperated with renowned personalities such as the actress Martina Gedeck, the composer and pianist Hauschka and publicist Roger Willemsen. He has conducted renowned orchestras in Germany and worldwide and since 2013 has been Artistic Director of the Summer Music Academy Hundisburg Castle in Saxony-Anhalt.

Anne LeBaron is an American composer and Professor of Composition and Experimental Sound Practices Program at CalArts, California. Her compositions have been performed worldwide. As a Fulbright Scholar, she studied with György Ligeti and Mauricio Kagel. She is recipient of prestigious international awards and grants. Her seven operas celebrate legendary female figures and the most recent opera, *LSD: Huxley's Last Trip*, includes microtonal instruments built by Harry Partch. As a writer, she has published several essays including her keynote address *Sonic Ventures in Post-Truth Surrealism*, published in the Australian Journal *Sound Scripts*, Vol. 6. Her frequently cited essay, *Reflections of Surrealism in Postmodern Musics*, is published in the book *Postmodern Music/Postmodern Thought*.

Charlotte Leport is a British poet, writer and translator. She has been invited to read her poetry at diverse cultural gatherings from Brazil (ArtesVertentes) to Basle (Mizmorim). She hosts and facilitates events which honour and foster creativity, fellowship and culture, and founded the cultural series Music at the Abbey with her late husband, the poet Dylan Hayden. She has featured in the films of Isabelle Wuilmart and Bernard Chouraqui and translated the works of Maia Brami and others. While all the arts are important to her, she believes that music is the state to which all arts aspire and would with Verlaine say *"de la musique avant toute chose"*.

Masataka Matsuo is a Japanese composer. He received his MA degree from Tokyo University of Art. His works have been performed by various music groups and musicians all over the world including the Tokyo Philharmonic Orchestra, Lisbon Gulbenkian Orchestra, Badische Staatkapelle Karlsruhe, Hong

Kong philharmonic, Tambuco. His music has been awarded with many international prizes. He was a jury member for the Besancon International Competition in 1998 and a guest conductor for the Donetsk Contemporary Music Art Festival 2013. He was the Executive Chairperson of ISCM World Music Days 2001 in Yokohama. His recent works have been premiered in New York, Lisbon and elsewhere in the world.

Christina Meissner is a German cellist specialised in contemporary music, a founding member of the Ensemble Klangwerkstatt Weimar and a passionate advocate for new music. Her performances offer a compelling celebration of life where music is the ultimate voice of primary existential values. She has worked closely with Isang Yun, Toshio Hosokawa, Georg Katzer, Isabel Mundry, Helmut Lachenmann, Rebecca Saunders, René Mense and Georg Crumb, Adriana Hölszky, Peter Eötvös, Salvatore Sciarrino and Klaus Huber. Meissner's solo career is also documented on several CDs with recordings of works ranging from the Middle-Ages to the 21st Century. She teaches cello at the University of Music of Weimar.

Vittorio Parisi is an Italian conductor. Since 1995 he is Artistic Director and Principal Conductor of dédalo ensemble in Brescia and since 1997 he teaches Conducting at the Milan Conservatoire. Following his debut at Petruzzelli Opera House in Bari, in 1979, he has conducted the most important Italian symphonic and chamber orchestras and many Opera House orchestras both for operas and symphonic concerts. Parisi has conducted extensively worldwide and premiered many works of the most significant composers of the 20th Century. He has collaborated with Luciano Berio and John Cage. In the 1980s he was First Conductor of the Angelicum Theatre Orchestra in Milano, and from 2003 to 2005 Artistic Director and Principal Conductor of I Solisti Aquilani.

Claudie Reduron is a French writer and painter. Her paintings and drawings have been in several French cities including The Medici Fountain at the Paris Art Exhibition. She also gave a lecture about drawing and computers at the Festival des Arts Electroniques. Reduron turned her attention to abstract painting, notably at the Avignon Festival, where she exhibited *La Citadelle*. She also participated in the *In Situ* exhibition in Occitania. Her play *Sauvons la terre* was performed at Théâtre Carat in 2018. In March 2021 she published the novel *La clairvoyance des tilleuls*. More recently, she has published three short stories for the collection *A mots couverts*: *Composer avec la vie*, *Il est 5 heures*, *Paris s'éveille* and *Le temps suspendu*.

Klaus Schöpp is a German flautist, interpreter of contemporary music, improvising musician, composer and teacher. He studied classical music in Saarbrücken and Berlin with Roswitha Staege and Karlheinz Zoeller. He was a flautist in the Konzerthausorchester Berlin, played with several orchestras and ensembles and is a member of the *14 Berlin Flautists* ensemble. As the Director of the Modern Art Ensemble, he has initiated and organized many concerts and events since 1994.

Aanaya Shanaya is an Indian-Australian former singer of classical and contemporary music. After 30 years of international concerts activities that have taken her to four continents, she decided to leave the music scene in 2009. Since 2010 she lives in an ashram in India.

Gavin Stewart is a British flautist, composer and researcher. He sits on the council of the British Flute Society and has appeared as a guest artist in several international festivals and conventions including a residency with the International Contemporary Ensemble. He plays with Birmingham Contemporary Music Group as part of their NEXT programme and performs regularly with London based groups such as The Thinking Minds Project, PRISM ensemble and epoch ensemble. He is currently completing his PhD at Royal Holloway, University of London, where he is researching the Kingma system flute through the transcription of traditional Japanese Honkyoku.

Nick Storring is a Canadian composer/musician and writer. He is a Winner of the Canadian Music Centre's Toronto Emerging Composer Award, and electroacoustic competition Jeux De Temps. Storring's varied and idiosyncratic musical output spans from chamber compositions to meticulously constructed recordings consisting solely of his own overdubbed instrumental performances. He has collaborated with leading interpreters and international organizations within contemporary music. His discography features releases with Orange Milk Records, Mappa, Entr'acte, and Notice

Recordings. Storring is also a National Magazine Award-nominated writer whose work has been published in the Wire, Musicworks (where he is a contributing editor), Exclaim! and elsewhere. His liner notes accompany several notable recordings.

Sergej Tchirkov is a Russian accordionist. He has been awarded prizes at many international competitions in Europe and has received a scholarship from the European Centre of Arts Hellerau in 2004-2005. His interest for new music has led him to collaborations with many composers: so far he has premiered over 250 works. Both as a soloist and a member of an orchestra he has performed at various new music festivals in Europe and is a regular guest musician of many major ensembles in Europe. Tchirkov has been a guest lecturer at several universities in Europe. His thesis on John Palmer's *Drang* has been recommended as an education tool for higher schools of music. He is Lecturer at the Moscow Tchaikovsky Conservatory, deputy artistic director of the Studio for New Music Ensemble and Research Fellow at the University of Bergen.

Agnese Toniutti is an Italian pianist and independent researcher specialized in contemporary and 20th Century music. Her work investigates the complementary role of composition and improvisation in musical creativity, both as an author and interpreter. The work of Giacinto Scelsi, John Cage, Giancarlo Cardini, as well as the one of the artistic movements of the Seventies are some of her favourites on stage and in research. Her recent projects include the release of Subtle Matters (Neuma Records, 2021), a recording where she explores and re-interpretes the "timbre-piano" invented by Lucia Dlugoszewski and the verbal scores by Philip Corner. As a soloist and chamber music pianist she has performed in several venues and international festivals in Italy, Europe and USA.

Daniel Weymouth is an American composer and Professor of Composition at Stony Brook University, where he serves as Chair, Graduate Program Director and Director of a centre for Digital Arts. His compositions have been called "power-colour music." The power component (certainly a love of kinesis) may come from decades spent as a keyboard player of jazz, C&W, rock, disco, R&B and funk. The colour component has resulted in a life-long fascination with electronics, including working two years in Paris at IRCAM and Iannis Xenakis' CEMAMu. Concert music commissions have come from national and international ensembles and several musicians; recordings are on SEAMUS, Bridge, and New World Records.

Peter Wiegold is a British composer and conductor. His compositions have been commissioned by major British and international ensembles. Since 2011, he has been the director of Club Inégales, London, featuring guests from across world cultures, performing worldwide and releasing four CDs through NMC recordings. Much of his work is about exploring the dynamic between score and improvisation, and more recently between genres and between cultures. The latter leading to the creation of The Third Orchestra, featuring musicians from across world traditions. As a conductor, he has directed contemporary programmes with the most renowned British ensembles. From 2003 to 2018, he was a Research Professor at Brunel University, London.

THE EDITOR

Sunny Knable is an American multi-faceted composer with numerous awards to his credit, including three Best Composition Awards from the Festival of New American Music and the ANALOG ARTS Iron Composers Award. Knable's music has been described as "great!" (TheWholeNote), "genius" (Anchorage Press), "entertaining" (Audiophile Audition), "witty, romantic and lilting" (TheaterScene.net), offering up "sparks of colour and inventiveness" (Sacramento Bee), and possessing a "wealth of thematic invention" (feastofmusic.com). His works are widely performed. In 2019, The Perspective Collective commissioned him to write the one-act opera *The Pride of Pripyat*. In 2017, his chamber opera *Beethoven in Love* was performed at the National Opera Center and in 2016, his Symphony No. 2 *The Great Expanse* was premiered by Leo Eylar the California Youth Symphony, which had commissioned the work. Since its premiere in 2012, *The Magic Fish*, an opera for young audiences by The Brothers Knable, has been performed across the United States. Dr. Knable serves as Music Director of The Church-in-the-Gardens, composer for The Garden Players, a theatrical group for children and as an Adjunct Assistant Professor at Queens College and LaGuardia Community College. He holds a PhD in Music Composition from Stony Brook University, a Master of Arts degree in Composition from Queens College (CUNY) and a Bachelor of Music degree in Composition, Piano Performance and Jazz Studies from CSU Sacramento. Other professional credits include his debut album *American Variations* on Centaur Records and an album with bassoonist Scott Pool and pianist Natsuki Fukasawa, *Song of the Redwood Tree*, on MSR Classics. His bassoon works, *Song of the Redwood-Tree* and *The Busking Bassoonist* are published by TrevCo-Varner Music. All other works are published by *Trouvère Music Publishing*. He continues to reside in Forest Hills, New York, while fulfilling commissions from around the country.